INTERPERSONAL
COMMUNICATION
Readings in Theory and Research

INTERPERSONAL COMMUNICATION
Readings in Theory and Research

Mark V. Redmond

Iowa State University

Harcourt Brace College Publishers

Fort Worth • Philadelphia • San Diego • New York • Orlando • Austin • San Antonio
Toronto • Montreal • London • Sydney • Tokyo

Publisher	TED BUCHHOLZ
Senior Acquisitions Editor	CAROL C. WADA
Developmental Editor	CATHLYNN RICHARD
Project Editors	BARBARA MORELAND, JULIET GEORGE
Production Manager	KATHY FERGUSON
Art Director	PEGGY YOUNG

ISBN 0-15-501245-2

Library of Congress Catalog Card Number: 94-79544

Address for Editorial Correspondence:
Harcourt Brace College Publishers
301 Commerce Street, Suite 3700
Fort Worth, TX 76102

Address for Orders:
Harcourt Brace & Company
6277 Sea Harbor Drive
Orlando, FL 32887-6777
1-800-782-4479, or 1-800-433-0001 (in Florida).

Printed in the United States of America

4 5 6 7 8 9 0 1 2 3 039 9 8 7 6 5 4 3 2 1

The book is dedicated to my wife, Peggy, and to my children, Beth, Nicholas, and Eric, who continue to teach me about the wonders of interpersonal communication. This book is also dedicated to the many students who have provided invaluable feedback concerning earlier versions of this book and from whom future readers hopefully will benefit.

PREFACE

Interpersonal Communication: Readings in Theory and Research was born from the frustration I experienced in trying to identify an appropriate upper-level textbook. Introductory courses are designed to provide an overview of basic concepts and practice in skill development, whereas upper-level courses should provide an appreciation and understanding of the theory and research of interpersonal communication. Interpersonal communication textbooks tend to be written either for the elementary course or for specialized graduate courses. After experimenting with textbooks for years, I finally concluded that the answer was to search the literature and create a specific reading packet for the course. The belief that the current selection of readings might be of value to other instructors and the desire to reduce the cost of the reading collection led to this publication.

Several of the features in the book result from using these materials in an upper-level interpersonal communication course. My initial reading packet included four or five articles that dealt with definitions, theory overviews, and introductions to methodology. However, these readings were disjointed and the coverage was incomplete. For this book I have written two introductory chapters to provide a framework for the readings. Chapter 1 offers a fairly comprehensive review of some commonly held definitions of interpersonal communication. It also provides a taxonomy of conceptual approaches to the same subject. The coverage in the chapter is not exhaustive, but most of the significant areas are reviewed. Approaches are organized from general meta-theories to specific interpersonal communication theories and on to the less well-defined conceptual studies.

Because about half the readings in this book are research reports, the first half of Chapter 2 reviews the major research approaches and designs, with an emphasis on quantitative methods. That emphasis is a reflection of the nature of the majority of existing research. The second half of Chapter 2 provides a conceptual description of some of the statistical procedures students will encounter in reading the research articles.

After the initial two chapters (Unit 1), the readings are organized according to themes. Unit 2 is a sampling of articles dealing with four of the specific conceptual approaches to interpersonal communication discussed in Chapter 1. The remaining units and readings are organized loosely according to a framework beginning with attraction and initiation of relationships and concluding with relational disengagement.

Another major feature of this book designed to increase comprehension is the unit overview. Although each unit represents a collection of related readings, there is some variation in the level of detail included in the overviews. In some cases, statistical procedures are elaborated so students can make better sense of a given reading; in others a given construct or concept is discussed in detail, either because the article presumes prior knowledge or doesn't provide a clear explanation. Necessarily, some of my opinions are reflected in the overviews.

Several things are intentionally omitted from the overviews in order to provide potential pedagogical applications. One assignment that has proven valuable for my students is to write abstracts of each article. In doing so, they are challenged to identify the major elements and to thus develop an analytical perspective. Another possibility for students is synthesis of readings. With synthesis papers, which I sometimes use in place of examinations, students are required to combine and relate a specified set of articles.

At the end of each overview are questions to consider for each reading. These are designed to give students a focal point from which to read each article. Small group discussions may also prove useful in helping students understand and evaluate the material.

This book is also the product of much valuable feedback: from students who have been exposed to various versions; from colleagues, Drs. Changsheng

Xi and Frances Spisak, who have indulged me by teaching from the reading packet; and from the editors at Harcourt Brace, especially Cathlynn Richard who has continued to support me even when I became discouraged. Reviewers whose input has been instrumental in guiding the development of this textbook include Alton Barbour, University of Denver; Steven Beebe, Southwest Texas State University; William K. Rawlins, Purdue University; Beverly Robinson, Wright State University; and Shawn Spana, San Jose State University. Finally, acknowledgment must be made of the authors of the various articles included in the textbook. Without their efforts there would be no book.

This textbook differs considerably from most others to which students have been exposed. Other books provide the analysis and synthesis of theory and research; here, that responsibility rests with the students. The instructor's role in the process is to provide them with the necessary background tools, occasional elaboration and clarification of difficult and confusing material, and a great deal of encouragement. In the end, students will revel in their success at discovering and understanding the substantive body of work associated with their chosen discipline.

TABLE OF CONTENTS

INTERPERSONAL COMMUNICATION
Readings in Theory and Research

UNIT I

Interpersonal Communication:
Establishing the Foundations

The two readings that make up this section were specifically written as introductory chapters for this text. The purpose of the two chapters is to create a foundation for understanding the various selections included in the text. Each of these first two chapters represents material that is often the subject of entire courses, and, as such, both contain a large amount of information. The intention here is not to provide a substitute for coursework but rather to introduce issues and concepts that will create a common ground for the study of interpersonal communication. Additionally, the two chapters should provide an elementary understanding of the theory and research methods associated with interpersonal communication. Though neither is intended to be a complete treatment of its respective subject matter, the assortment of issues included should create an appreciation for the breadth of interpersonal communication theory and research. This text represents a modest attempt to include major and significant approaches.

The first chapter is composed of two parts: a review of components that are often included in various definitions of interpersonal communication, and a review of various conceptual and theoretical frameworks that have been applied to interpersonal communication. No universally accepted definition of interpersonal communication exists, though there are a number of similarities and commonly held elements in the definitions in use. The chapter includes nine of these elements. You already might

be familiar with many of the elements, and if so, the discussion should provide a quick review. Each element is briefly explained, and in some instances the debate over the validity of the element is also presented. You should gain a sense of the evolution of some elements that has resulted from an increased understanding of the nature of interpersonal communication. As you read through these elements, you might consider which constitute the way you have been taught or currently think is the correct definition of interpersonal communication.

The second section of the chapter deals with several of the ways interpersonal communication has been conceptually and theoretically approached. Only a few highlights of each approach as they apply to interpersonal communication are included in the discussion. The nine conceptual approaches reviewed are grouped into four categories.

The distinction among these four levels is essentially based upon the degree of completeness and specific applicability to interpersonal communication. There is strong overlap among the four categories and the distinctions are muddy. Metatheories represent theoretic models that can be applied to any activity. For instance, one metatheoretic approach is called "laws." Under this approach scholars attempt to identify laws that exist between and among a number of variables. In the physical sciences, we have the laws of gravity that explain the relationship between two or more masses. Using the laws approach, interpersonal communication

Theoretical and Conceptual Approaches to Interpersonal Communication

1. METATHEORIES: Laws, systems, and rules.
2. SOCIAL SCIENCE THEORIES APPLIED TO INTERPERSONAL COMMUNICATION: Pragmatics, symbolic interactionism, and social exchange theory.
3. INTERPERSONAL COMMUNICATION THEORIES: Constructivism, uncertainty reduction, and coordinated management of meaning.
4. CONCEPTUAL FRAMEWORKS APPLIED TO INTERPERSONAL COMMUNICATION: Competence/skills and relational development.

scholars attempt to find laws that apply to how we interact with others. Two other metatheoretic approaches discussed in Chapter 1 are "systems" and "rules."

The second set of conceptual approaches was generally developed to explain a broad spectrum of human social behavior but has been applied subsequently to interpersonal communication. These approaches include pragmatics, symbolic interactionism, and social exchange theory.

The third set represents theories developed about interpersonal communication. Many of the concepts and much of the support for those approaches are derived from a variety of disciplines and theories. The three approaches reviewed in the first chapter are constructivism, uncertainty reduction, and coordinated management of meaning.

The final conceptual approaches reviewed in the first chapter have not been developed as general theories, but instead represent a way of conceptualizing interpersonal communication. These conceptualizations affect the nature of the theory discussions and resulting research. The two approaches are interpersonal communication competence/skills and relationship development. Neither approach is represented by a defined body of overriding principles but rather by studies within each approach that focus on some aspect of interpersonal communication from that conceptual perspective.

The first chapter is intended to provide a stronger appreciation and understanding of the theory reflected in the readings. The second is intended to provide a fundamental understanding of

the research process to help you better comprehend the research-oriented articles. Some readers already will have an understanding of research methods and statistics. In that case, the second chapter will be simply a quick review. Others will have had little exposure to the manner in which a research study is conducted, and the second chapter should give enough information on research methods to increase your ability to comprehend the research articles. Research articles typically include the following:

1. A presentation of a theoretical explanation of concepts and their relationships.
2. A method or design for collecting data that will be used to assess that relationship.
3. A results section, which includes a statistical analysis of the data.
4. A summary of the findings, review of the study's limitations, and a discussion of implications of the findings.

The second chapter discusses the criteria by which to judge the first part of the research process, the legitimacy of a proposed theoretical explanation. Six criteria are discussed: validity, predictability, precision, consistency, scope, and utility. Next, the two general approaches to collecting data are discussed: qualitative and quantitative. The number of qualitative studies in interpersonal communication is considerably smaller than the number of quantitative studies; however, there seems to be a growing number of qualitative studies as that methodology becomes more developed. This text does not include studies that typically would be considered qualitative in nature, therefore the second chapter is geared more toward helping understand quantitative research.

Research involves the identification and description of some concepts or variables. The relationship between and among variables serves both as the basis for theory building and for research. The second chapter discusses independent variables that effect some change in a dependent variable. The relationship between those variables is posited in a hypothesis or research question. In designing a project to test that relationship a number of factors might contaminate the validity of any claim that is made about that relationship. These sources of invalidity are briefly reviewed in the second chapter. Try to watch for the potential effect of any of those sources of invalidity as you read the research articles. A number of standard research techniques or designs have been developed to control for these, and some of these designs also are reviewed.

The last part of the second chapter includes a Statistical Primer. For many students, statistics are intimidating. The section is meant to provide some demystification of statistics so that you can understand the statistical process by which researchers reach conclusions. The chapter presents the statistics most common to the studies included in this text. The emphasis is not on the numerical manipulations conducted on the data, but rather on the principles underlying each statistical method.

The statistical procedures discussed in the chapter that allow for the comparison of two or more groups include analysis of variance (ANOVA), F-test, and t-test. Some statistics have been designed to test for rates of change between and among variables. These include correlation, factor analysis, and regression analysis. When you read this section of the chapter do not get bogged down with concern for the mathematics involved, but concentrate on what is being done with the data. You can then use that understanding to appreciate better the research articles and answer such questions as: How have the data been manipulated and what relationships are being examined among the variables?

As you read the first two chapters keep in mind that they are intended to provide you with a framework to understand better the wide variety of readings included in this text. You might find it helpful to return to these two chapters from time to time as you read the other articles, since they function as reference sections for the rest of the book.

1

Interpersonal Communication: Definitions and Conceptual Approaches

M. V. REDMOND

DEFINITIONS AND COMPONENTS OF INTERPERSONAL COMMUNICATION

What is interpersonal communication? By the time you finish reading this text, you may have a better idea than you do now, but probably you still will not be able to answer definitively. There is no one universally accepted definition of interpersonal communication. Each existing definition tends to reflect a particular theoretical approach to the concept, and as theories change, so do the definitions. You probably have learned one definition already if you have had an introductory interpersonal communication course. Each text tends to present its own definition. Here are a few samples:

Interaction involving two or three people in close physical proximity, in which all parties have the opportunity to send and receive verbal and nonverbal messages. (Watson & Barker, 1990, p. 371)

Communication in which the parties consider one another as unique individuals rather than as objects. It is characterized by minimal use of stereotyped labels; unique, idiosyncratic social rules; and a high degree of information exchange. (Adler & Towne, 1993, p. 426)

Face-to-face communication in which each person influences what is being said by the other person. (Mader & Mader, 1993, p. 7)

The transactional process of creating meaning. (Verderber & Verderber, 1992, p. 7)

The process of transaction between people from which meaning is mutually derived. (Pearson & Spitzberg, 1990, p. 7)

Communication between two persons who have a relationship. (DeVito, 1993, p. 7)

Communication is interpersonal when the people involved are contacting each other as persons. (Stewart & Logan, 1993, p. 4)

A transactional process of exchanging messages and negotiating meaning to convey information and to establish and maintain relationships. (Wilson, Hantz, & Hanna, 1992, p. 6)

Each of the definitions tends to be slightly different from the rest, generally reflecting a theme the author follows throughout his or her book. Some definitions focus more on relationships as the key element of interpersonal communication, some focus on the transactional nature of interpersonal communication, and others emphasize creating shared meaning.

Ultimately the reader is left in a quandary as to the real definition of interpersonal communication. In one of his interpersonal texts, DeVito (1989) provides three definitions of interpersonal communication, acknowledging three distinct theoretical perspectives that affect the way the term might be defined. Many of the articles and texts on interpersonal communication never do define the term, perhaps because of the inadequacy of any one term to capture the essence of this phenomenon. So, why try?

There are legitimate reasons for defining terms. First, it is important for you to know the meaning of the term. Too many times we, as students, are simply expected to memorize a definition so that we can successfully respond to a multiple-choice question. But memorization does not ensure understanding. You need to understand what is meant by interpersonal communication, to understand the boundaries and components of interpersonal communication. It is probably more important to *understand* the term than to have a definition memorized. When you understand the term, you can construct the definition.

Second, defining terms is critical to effective communication. When an author uses the term "interpersonal communication," do you know what the author means? You could look up the definition in a dictionary, but is that how the author has conceptualized the term? The author might not use the term the way it is defined in a dictionary, but that does not mean the author has the wrong meaning. One way to reduce your confusion and frustration in understanding the articles in this book is to realize that the way interpersonal communication is defined and used is not the same from article to article. As you read the articles try to appreciate the definitional perspective of the authors.

Despite the wide variety of definitions associated with interpersonal communication there are a few prominent components that consistently appear in the definitions. There are also some unique elements that have generated significant theory and research. The following is a brief review and discussion of some of the major components and their application to interpersonal communication.

Situational Early attempts to define interpersonal communication generally identified the situation, described the elements of the situation and equated this to interpersonal communication. Such definitions usually included a statement such as "two people in face-to-face interaction." The number of individuals involved is usually no longer an element of the functional or relational definitions. We know that, at a minimum, interpersonal communication requires two individuals. Are interactions among three, four, or five people interpersonal? One definition gave a range from two to about twenty (Brooks & Emmert, 1976). Determining the upper limit is difficult. To contend with this issue some authors have chosen to focus only on dyadic interactions (interactions between two) (DeVito, 1990; Wilmot, 1975).

The problem with situational definitions is there are many exceptions to the rule—and the exclusion

of those exceptions appears arbitrary and capricious. For example, the inclusion of the notion of face-to-face interaction means that conversations over the telephone would not be considered interpersonal communication. The use of "process" or "transaction" to define interpersonal communication instead of "face to face" still allows the immediate interactive emphasis, which face to face implies, to be maintained. Certainly there is a distinction being made between written correspondence between two friends and the face-to-face transaction that occurs in interpersonal communication. It is important to recognize the difference between the type of interaction that occurs in person, and interaction over the telephone. This difference suggests conceptualizing interpersonal communication in terms of degree rather than the mutually exclusive classification of an interaction as being either interpersonal communication or not interpersonal communication.

Process/Interaction Process is used to describe interpersonal communication as a dynamic, changing, ongoing phenomenon. While that may seem obvious, interpersonal communication had been treated as a static phenomenon. Even today research tends to use static assessments, which is like taking a series of still photographs of an interaction and then treating the photographs as a representation of the interaction. What occurs between the time each photo is taken is lost information. This conceptualization tends to classify all interpersonal communication as being the same and having the same properties each time it occurs.

Related to this static conceptualization was the idea that interpersonal communication is interactive—that is, a series of actions and reactions. This perspective has been abandoned in favor of a transactional perspective. The transactional perspective recognizes that all the members of an interpersonal communication interaction are affecting each other simultaneously, not alternately.

Definitions that refer to interpersonal communication as transactional or process are emphasizing the dynamic, interdependency of interpersonal interactants. Process means there is mutuality of effect by the participants, the effects are occurring simultaneously, and the effects are irreversible, nonrepeatable, and cumulative.

Symbolic/Verbal/Nonverbal Interpersonal communication is defined sometimes in terms of the units or messages from which information about one's communication partner is garnered. These units or "signs" can be symbolic or symptomatic, and verbal or nonverbal. "Signs" are those things which are used as a referent or to represent something else. Those signs used in human communication fall into two categories: symbols and symptoms. Symbols have been defined as "a learned stimulus having a contextually flexible, arbitrary, and abstract meaning" (Dance & Larson, 1972, p. 10). Symptoms, by contrast, are stimuli to which a fixed meaning is attributed regardless of the context. A natural relationship exists between a symptom and the thing it represents. Thus a cough is a symptom of that which it represents, a cold. Both verbal and nonverbal messages can be, according to their common use, either symbols or symptoms. Motley (1990a) argues that whenever an individual intentionally selects or manipulates stimuli, then those stimuli are symbolic. I might cough as a physiological reaction to a scratchy throat without intentionally doing so, thus producing a nonsymbolic stimulus for anyone hearing my cough (a symptom); or I might cough intentionally to gain someone's attention, in which case the cough is being employed symbolically. The situation can be defined as interpersonal communication when symbols have been used between two or more people, or defined as non-interpersonal communication if it is dependent upon nonsymbolic stimuli.

The specification of the message as verbal or nonverbal is not a distinction between symbolic or nonsymbolic, since there are symbolic nonverbal stimuli. The inclusion of verbal and nonverbal messages as part of the definition of interpersonal communication is to emphasize that interpersonal communication can occur even though no words might be spoken. Two individuals who smile, or wave, or make some obscene gesture toward each other are using symbolic nonverbal messages to communicate interpersonally. Thus several channels are available for interpersonally communicating—air for sound waves, light for visual cues, even touch and smell.

Impersonal Versus Interpersonal Miller and Sunnafrank (1982) make the case for thinking about communication occurring along a continuum, with one pole being impersonal communication and the other interpersonal communication. They argue that where any given interaction lies along this continuum depends upon the kind of information the participants are using in relating to one another. Miller and Sunnafrank identify three kinds of information that individuals might use in interacting with others and for predicting the impact of messages. Those three kinds of information are cultural, sociological, and psychological. Cultural information is general information about language, dominant values, and so forth that can be attributed to someone from a given culture. At this level little is known specifically about the other person with whom we are interacting. Relating to someone simply on the basis of cultural information represents impersonal communication. Sociological information is information based upon another's membership groups—roles, jobs, organizations. By association, these groups provide additional information beyond the cultural information to allow for additional predictions about possible reactions of a specific other. Still, sociological information is fairly general, and when an individual is operating from sociological information the communication is still fairly impersonal. Psychological information is specific information about the unique other with whom we are interacting. Psychological information represents the information that distinguishes individuals from their culture and social groups. When we base our predictions of another's responses on psychological information we are communicating interpersonally.

Some definitions of interpersonal communication reflect the impersonal–interpersonal continuum presented by Miller and Sunnafrank by emphasizing participant development of unique relational rules and the treatment of each other as unique people. In essence, the more we recognize an individual as an individual, the more interpersonal is our communication.

As in the discussion of the situational approach to defining interpersonal communication, a continuum with degrees of interpersonalness might prove beneficial. Under Miller and Sunnafrank's approach there would be times when we react to close friends on the basis of cultural or sociological information and thus this interaction would be classified as impersonal, regardless of the relationship. As we gain more information about the other people with whom we interact, the interactions increase in their degree of interpersonalness.

Information and Message Exchange The term "exchange" is used almost interchangeably with "interaction" and has the same definitional limitations. Some definitions have defined interpersonal communication as an exchange of thoughts or feelings. The image that comes to mind is a process of exchanging or handing notes back and forth between two people. This conceptualization places an emphasis on the messages, and the accompanying research focuses on evaluating the nature and content of those messages.

The focus on messages is generally on the information conveyed. Research on self-disclosure presents a good example of the evolution from this perspective to a functional or transactional one. Initially, self-disclosure research focused on the nature of the information that was exchanged, and rules were generated about how individuals handled that information. One such rule is that of reciprocation: If A tells personal information to B, then B will reciprocate and tell similar information to A. Such a rule focuses on the nature of information exchange between two people. The relational approach to self-disclosure focuses on how sharing information affects the relationship.

Acting on information is a critical element of interpersonal communication. Dance and Larson

(1972) defined communication as acting upon information. By extension, interpersonal communication must be acting upon information within an interpersonal context. Theories, such as uncertainty reduction (to be discussed later), focus on the drive we have in interpersonal interactions to gain information about another. Information gives individuals power: the power to explain and predict another's behavior and ultimately to extend influence or control in an attempt to satisfy our needs.

Influence If you ask the person next to you at dinner to pass the salt and the person continues eating without passing the salt, has communication occurred? How can you tell? You might be inclined to say communication did not occur because the action you sought (passing the salt) did not happen. There was no apparent change in the other's behavior. However, that person might just be ignoring you, in which case you have influenced him or her but you cannot observe the effect as readily. One of the best ways we know communication has occurred is the observation of some change.

The terms "communication," "human communication," and "interpersonal communication" are not synonymous. Communication is the most global term, but it is not an exclusively human activity. There is a hierarchy among these terms. Human communication is one type of communication and interpersonal communication is one type of human communication.

One common characteristic of communication, human communication, and interpersonal communication is that they involve change as the predominant characteristic, change that occurs because of acting upon information (Dance & Larson, 1972). In human communication we tend to think more in terms of influence exerted symbolically by one person on another (the linear perspective), or influence by two or more people upon one another through symbols (the transactional perspective). The term "influence" has both an active and passive connotation. Influence might mean an intentional attempt to gain something from or change another—the active connotation. Influence might also mean simply having an impact or affect on another—the passive connotation.

One distinguishing characteristic sometimes included in definitions of interpersonal communication is that interpersonal communication involves mutual influence. All the parties involved in the interaction are influencing one another. This means that communication situations of unidirectional influence would not be interpersonal communication. For example, you are walking along and you see a female friend with whom you had a big fight the night before. You would prefer to avoid her so you quickly start walking in a different direction before she sees you. Communication occurred because you were influenced by what you saw. However, interpersonal communication did not occur because she was not influenced by you. If you had continued walking in her direction and she saw you, what would have happened? You might have exchanged greetings, or chosen to say nothing, but either way both of you probably were affected internally; certain thoughts or feelings were evoked about the fight and each other—feelings that would not have occurred if communication had not occurred.

One problem with conceptualizing interpersonal communication as mutual influence is that rarely is the degree of influence equal. A student sitting in a class listening to an instructor does have an influence on the instructor (particularly if the student starts snoring), but it is not the same amount of influence that the instructor would presumably have on the student. After all, the instructor is doing all the talking. So the question arises: How much mutual influence has to be present for a communication situation to be classified as interpersonal?

Intentionality In the previous examples neither the student nor your female friend can be said to have intentionally attempted to influence (though maybe the student was only pretending to snore in order intentionally to convey boredom to the instructor). The treatment of influence as an active process implies an intent on the part of an individual to act upon some goal that involves communicating with the other person.

Motley (1990a) contends that individuals go through a process starting with a goal, deciding whether to act upon that goal, and finally encoding and transmitting a message to accomplish the goal. Bavelas (1990) contends that such a process takes considerably more time than actually passes during a given interaction. Underlying the question of intentionality as related to interpersonal communication is whether we communicate with others for a reason. I contend that all interpersonal communication is need driven; we seek to fulfill some need and therefore the communication is intentional. If a stranger walking by me in the hallway says "Hi," why do I reply? What need is satisfied? There are actually several needs that might be fulfilled even in such a simple encounter. Perhaps I have a need to confirm my self-image of being a friendly person, and I behaviorally define friendly as someone who replies to strangers. Maybe the other might appear attractive to me as someone who can potentially satisfy my needs for social relationships, and I want to indicate an openness to initiating a relationship.

While interpersonal interactions might be need based, does this necessarily mean the communication is intentional? Both Motley and Bavelas seem to accept intentionality as a characteristic that differentiates interpersonal communication from non-interpersonal communication. This non-interpersonal communication is what was discussed before as a linear communication situation—independently acting upon information. Thus some scholars focus on interpersonal communication in which both participants intend to interact, though some of the information attended to or perceived might not have been intentionally transmitted by the participants. The ability to choose not to interact is one reason Motley (1990b) concluded that one cannot *not* communicate in interactive situations. Once an individual is in the interaction, the subsequent actions must be considered intentional, including attempts not to communicate.

Creating Meaning Interpersonal communication is sometimes defined as those situations in which the participants in an interaction work together to achieve some shared understanding of their messages. Under this definition, interpersonal communication represents the product of the interaction. The creation of meaning as a transactive process means the interpersonal participants are involved in the mutual definition of the symbols they use. This component emphasizes understanding as the primary objective of interpersonal communication. Participants send messages and monitor the degree to which the other understands that message. When the message is not understood the participants work to clarify the meaning. For example, if I ask you to hand me the book on my desk and you hand me a pad of paper, there is an apparent failure to create shared meaning. I might then say, "No, not the pad of paper, the red book next to the phone." At that time you hand me the book I was asking for. We have created shared meaning. It became necessary for me to elaborate and be more specific as a result of your action.

Pearce (1976) defines interpersonal communication as "the coordinated management of meaning" and emphasizes the enactment and management of "episodes" as the major component of interpersonal interactions. He sees interpersonal communication as the sequential enactment of episodes in which the meanings of messages are managed by the individual to achieve understanding, while coordinating this process with others through compromise, accommodation, and adaptation (p. 33).

The creation and coordination of meaning is an appealing approach to interpersonal communication because it reflects the interdependence of the participants in the development of understanding. Reaching understanding is not seen as an independent linear process. But the use of creating meaning as the primary defining element of interpersonal communication does have its limitations. Is not the intent of public speakers to create meaning with their audience? Adding "transaction" as a qualifying element to creating meaning does help focus more on the interpersonal context, but other questions remain regarding the issue of shared understanding. Is all interpersonal communication

dependent upon understanding? Can you influence another without understanding? In intimate relationships, has not understanding already been established, and so the interactions serve more to maintain the relationship? Most interpersonal communication probably occurs without recognition of whether understanding was achieved or not. We tend to be fairly egocentric in creating messages—we send messages that have meaning for us without specific adaptation to the other. Since we generally communicate with those who are similar to us, we do not have to adapt our messages, and so, egocentric communication can be effective in achieving our interpersonal goals.

Relationship Some definitions have focused on the developmental or relational value of interpersonal communication. These approaches tend to emphasize a functional value of the communication as it pertains to the initiation, maintenance, and termination of relationships. These definitions tend to limit what is called interpersonal communication to that communication that specifically serves to influence human relationships. Acceptance of this conceptualization raises two significant questions. First, is there any communication between two or three individuals that does not have an influence on the relationship? Second, what is the type of communication that occurs between two people that is not interpersonal? Underlying these questions is the notion that relationships vary in their level of intimacy, and therefore some variation must also be expected in the associated communication. A continuum moving from impersonal to interpersonal relationships is probably the most accurate way to conceptualize these interactions. This would mean that the actual relational function of communication will vary with the nature of the relationships. Communication models of relational development often identify changes that occur in the communication that correspond to specific relationship stages (Baxter & Bullis, 1986; Knapp & Vangelisti, 1992).

A fairly common perspective on messages in interpersonal interactions is that messages consist of two dimensions: content and relational (Watzlawick, Beavin, & Jackson, 1967). The content dimension of a message is the explicit information conveyed in the message itself. The relational dimension of the message is information conveyed about the nature of the relationship between the two interactants, often through nonverbal channels. If you raise your hand and ask a question during class, you have communicated your acceptance of the student-teacher relationship as defined in U.S. culture. There are times when the content of the message is a direct statement about the relationship; for example, "I feel trapped in our relationship." The content of that statement is about the relationship. The degree of explicitness communicated about the relationship obviously varies from message to message. The relational approach to interpersonal communication often focuses on the nature of such variations.

Almost any of the above elements can be combined to form a legitimate definition of interpersonal communication. Each time a restriction is placed upon how the concept is defined, the phenomenon to which the concept is applied simply becomes more narrowed and restricted. We can choose to claim that interpersonal communication requires intentionality. Such a restricting stipulation means that we are distinguishing between two types of communication that might occur between people: intentional (which we are labeling interpersonal communication) and unintentional. Thus, the interpersonal communication theory and hypotheses we generate would be about only intentional communication among people. This line of reasoning is then extended to each stipulation in the definition. The definitions advanced by others run the gamut from very general, nonrestrictive definitions, such as the transactional process of creating meaning (Verderber & Verderber, 1992), to detailed, specific definitions: it involves at least two people, involves feedback, need not be face to face, need not be intentional, produces some effect, need not involve words, is affected by context, and is affected by noise (Weaver, 1990, p. 17). The definition is often a reflection of the theory on which the definition is based. Moving from definition to

---

Summary of Definitional Components of Interpersonal Communication

SITUATIONAL Interpersonal communication is defined by the qualities that make up an "interpersonal" situation, such as the number of participants or being face to face.

PROCESS/INTERACTION Interpersonal communication is dynamic, ongoing over time, changing, transactional, cumulative, and involves mutual and simultaneous effect by the participants.

SYMBOLIC/VERBAL/NONVERBAL Some definitions include a specification about the nature of the interpersonal messages. Verbal refers to words and nonverbal to all other interpersonal cues. Symbols are stimuli that are arbitrarily assigned meaning and reflect intentionality.

IMPERSONAL VERSUS INTERPERSONAL Interactions range from being impersonal, when we use only cultural or sociological information about another person, to being interpersonal, when we use person-specific psychological information.

INFORMATION AND MESSAGE EXCHANGE Interpersonal communication is defined in terms of how interpersonal information and messages are conveyed between individuals.

INFLUENCE Interpersonal communication is conceptualized in terms of individuals mutually affecting some change in their partners.

INTENTIONALITY The fulfillment of interpersonal goals necessitates intentional interpersonal communication.

CREATING MEANING Interpersonal communication is seen as the product of individuals involved in creating a shared understanding.

RELATIONSHIP Interpersonal communication is defined in terms of serving the function to develop, maintain, and terminate relationships.

theory involves attempting to answer many of the questions raised in the discussion above. Theories can be thought of as elaborate sets of definitions of concepts that include the nature of the relationships among those concepts.

MAJOR THEORETICAL APPROACHES TO INTERPERSONAL COMMUNICATION

While a definition tries to provide a concise description of a single concept, a theory attempts to provide as nearly complete a picture of a phenomenon as possible, including many concepts and their definitions. More importantly, theory presents the relationships among a set of concepts or variables. A theory provides description, explanation, and prediction. A theory of interpersonal communication should identify the set of variables that make up the phenomenon of interpersonal communication and the manner in which those variables influence one another. A theory of interpersonal communication should be able to predict what will happen when two strangers begin interacting, how their relationship will progress, the nature and effects of conflict on their communication, the role of nonverbal communication in each partner's attempt to gain compliance from the other, the effect of how they think about the relationship upon the way they communicate with the other, and so forth.

Obviously, much is expected from a theory, and that might be why, as with the definition of interpersonal communication, no single universally accepted theory exists. The articles in this text can be thought of as contributing to the eventual development of a grand theory. The theories reviewed in this chapter have something to offer in describing, explaining, and predicting interpersonal communication. At times, both the theories and the articles might seem to be dealing with totally unrelated concepts, but what is occurring is similar to the wise blind men when they examined an elephant.

One felt the trunk and described the elephant as snakelike, while another felt its side and described the elephant as like a wall. Neither was wrong, only incomplete. Similarly, interpersonal communication is like an elephant, with scholars examining various parts and reaching seemingly unrelated conclusions. Perhaps one of you will discover what the "elephant" of interpersonal communication really looks like.

This discussion is not meant to be an exhaustive review of the various theoretical approaches developed for interpersonal communication, but rather a look at those approaches that continue to have a strong impact on the nature and direction of interpersonal research and scholarship. Some of the approaches were not developed as specific treatments of interpersonal communication but rather as attempts to understand and explain interpersonal relationships from the social-psychological perspective. In the initial study of interpersonal communication, communication scholars applied concepts and theories from a variety of fields, and they continue to do so. However, efforts have been made recently to develop theories more grounded in the communication discipline. You should be able to identify the influence of the theoretical approaches presented here in the articles included in this text. The approaches themselves overlap and share similarities. The following reviews are intended to provide an introduction and overview to help you understand relevant contemporary research. You also should notice a strong relationship between some of the issues already discussed and the approaches presented below since those definitions are often derived from or reflect a particular theoretic approach. The definitional components were presented in a progressively parallel manner to the conceptual approaches.

The approaches reviewed in this chapter progress from the most global type of theory to theories specifically developed about interpersonal communication to conceptual perspectives on interpersonal communication. The approaches are presented in four categories:

1. Metatheories
2. Social science theories applied to interpersonal communication
3. Interpersonal communication theories
4. Conceptual frameworks applied to interpersonal communication

Metatheories have broad application to a variety of phenomena. They have been applied to the physical sciences, the social sciences, and specifically to interpersonal communication. Increasing in their focus are theories that have been developed specifically to deal with human behavior. Theories have been developed to explain social behavior and interaction. Communication scholars subsequently have applied those theories to interpersonal communication, and these are reviewed in the second set of approaches. The third set of approaches has been influenced by previous social behavior theories, but the approaches are not simply the application of those theories to interpersonal communication. Instead, these theories utilize previous theory to develop a theory unique to the phenomenon of interpersonal communication. The final set of approaches is less defined by a set of principles and axioms than the first three. The last set represents more of a perspective applied by scholars when considering interpersonal communication.

METATHEORETICAL APPROACHES TO INTERPERSONAL COMMUNICATION: LAWS, SYSTEMS, AND RULES

COVERING LAWS

The covering laws approach (classical model or logical positivism), which originated in the physical sciences, essentially seeks to find observable or deduced regularities in nature. The covering laws approach illustrates well the three objectives of any theory: explanation, prediction, and control. Knowing that X causes Y (the general covering law formula) provides an explanation for why Y occurred, allows prediction of when Y will occur, and allows for the control of Y's occurrence (to the degree that X can be manipulated). A considerable amount of communication research falls within the covering laws approach in that the research seeks to find overriding principles to explain human communication. The application of this approach to communication research has been criticized because of its weakness in explaining individual communication behavior and its tendency to oversimplify communication to variable analysis (Infante, Rancer, & Womack, 1990).

SYSTEMS

Systems theory advocates the treatment of phenomenon as global and inclusive. A system is made up of many interdependent elements, each affecting others. The system cannot be understood by simply examining the relationships of pairs of elements—the focus is on the whole, not the parts. Systems theory has been most successfully applied to the study of organizational communication, because in that context the interdependence of organizational components easily can be seen as systemic. The systems approach has been applied to interpersonal communication in only limited ways, most notably in examining family communication. Open systems are defined as those being affected by additional elements outside the defined system. Families are open systems; elements external to the family have an impact on the family. One problem with the systems approach is determining the boundaries of a system. For instance, as a member of a family, when you go home you carry with you the impact of your college experiences. Those college experiences are affected by the university. The university is an open system and is affected by the multitude of disciplines that constitute the university. Each system can be seen being affected by other systems to the point that it becomes impossible to find any system boundary. Besides this inherent criticism of systems theory, there is also a concern for the ineffectiveness of this approach to predict or explain. Systems theory is primarily a descriptive approach.

RULES

Rules theory falls somewhat between the covering laws and systems theories and has been specifically applied to interpersonal communication in the form of two theories: coordinated management of meaning and constructivism. The specific application of rules theory to communication has been mainly through the efforts of Cushman and his colleagues, and Pearce and his colleagues. Cushman, Valentinsen, and Dietrich claimed, "A rule exists when—and only when—two (or more) people do the same thing under certain conditions because both expect each other to behave in a certain way, and each is aware of the other's expectation" (1982, p. 95). According to rules theory, when a person's effort to achieve a goal requires the cooperation of another, communication becomes a necessary element to goal attainment, and thus coordination and rules are required. Rules can be defined by the society in which the interaction takes place or by the individuals in a given relationship. Though rules might exist, individuals are still free to choose whether to follow the rule. This freedom of choice is a central element of rules theory as compared to covering laws.

Cushman and Whiting developed two communication rules propositions:

(1) that the interchange of information involves a transaction among symbol-using participants with the understandings which result from being guided and governed by communication rules;
(2) that communication rules form general and specific patterns which provide the basis for a scientific explanation and prediction of communication behavior. . . . (1972, p. 227)

Among the dimensions associated with the accuracy of understanding of communication rules are (a) level of understanding, (b) rule range, (c) rule specificity, and (d) rule homogeneity (Cushman & Whiting, 1972). The level of understanding is the degree to which mutual understanding or coordination is necessary and varies depending upon the content and procedure. Rule range "refers to the number of different contexts or circumstances in which the same action is applicable" (p. 233). Rule specificity is the number of possible actions that are acceptable in response to a given situation. Homogeneity of a rule represents the degree to which a given rule is understood by members of a system—breadth of awareness or sharing of a given rule. In applying the two functions of rules identified by Cushman and Whiting, Pearce (1973) specifically saw the governing and guiding of what rewards and costs individuals inflicted upon each other as a fundamental dimension of interpersonal relationships development. Pearce (1973) also claimed a hierarchical ordering because of some rules taking precedence over others. Rules theory, as applied to human communication, is descriptions not of norms or laws but of how individuals process information (Pearce & Cronen, 1980). Rules are not entities that exist, endure, or have power. Rules are only a useful way of describing how individuals process information (Pearce & Cronen, 1980).

It is this individual processing of information that makes the role of the self a central element of rules theory. In the specific application of rules theory to interpersonal relationships, Cushman, Valentinsen, and Dietrich (1982) present the self as the cybernetic control system for human behavior, and thus central to the development and deployment of rules. Interpersonal relationships are examined in terms of confirmation of self-concept. In order to provide such confirmation of another, the necessary rules for how to communicate such support must be known. Cushman et al. (1982) developed a rule theory approach to explaining attraction and the development of relationships, which included such rules as "the greater the reciprocated perceived self-concept support, the greater the likelihood of a friend relationship" (p. 108).

SOCIAL SCIENCE THEORIES APPLIED TO INTERPERSONAL COMMUNICATION

PRAGMATISM

Several approaches share the principles identified as pragmatism, in particular phenomenology and systems theory. Common to all of these approaches is the belief that interactions should be examined in toto, as a whole. It is only by examining all of both the elements and their interactions that understanding can be attained. Pragmatics and phenomenology focus primarily on behavior and emphasize prediction over explanation. One underlying assumption is that behavior reflects what occurs within an individual. An individual is viewed as an element of a system in which all that really needs to be known—indeed, the claim is that all we can know—is the input and output of the system. The term "black box" is often used to refer to the internal or psychological makeup of an individual. Some scholars believe we cannot actually know what constitutes the black box. In essence, we can never really know how individuals think or cognitively process information. Watzlawick et al. observed that it is not necessary to know what goes on in the black box to be able to study its function within the larger system of which it is a part. How the black box functions can be deduced by knowing what went into the black box (input) and what comes out of the black box as behaviors (output). Thus, if I know you started with certain amounts of flour, water, yeast, sugar, and salt, and ended with a white fluffy loaf of bread, I would know that you must have kneaded the ingredients, let the mixture stand for some period of time, and then baked it. If, however, you had the same ingredients, but the output was a solid, hard, roll-like item, I would know you did not let the mixture stand and baked it immediately after mixing, which prevented yeast from producing gasses to make the dough rise. In like manner, pragmatists make conclusions about human communication.

Ruesch and Bateson (1951) presented a model of human communication that distinguished four levels: intrapersonal, interpersonal, group, and cultural. Each of these four was seen as building upon one another, and all were further divided into four segments: evaluating, sending, channeling, and receiving. Ruesch and Bateson's model incorporated elements identified in the mathematical model of communication developed by Shannon and

Weaver, which included sender, receiver, channel, and message. Ruesch and Bateson integrated elements of systems, networks, perception, information, context, and codification into the discussion of their model. (See Figure 1.1.)

Interestingly, much of the early development of these approaches was motivated by individuals examining dysfunctional human behavior. In studying people with various psychiatric problems (for instance, Gregory Bateson wrote extensively on schizophrenia), the role of interpersonal communication began to emerge as a significant factor (Ruesch & Bateson, 1951; Watzlawick, Beavin, & Jackson, 1967). The principles of pragmatics derived from such observations by Ruesch and Bateson that a psychiatrist "explores the examinee's communication system at the interpersonal level and makes inferences as the events take place at the intrapersonal level" (p. 276).

Watzlawick, Beavin, and Jackson in *Pragmatics of Human Communication* (1967) developed several

FIGURE 1.1

The levels of communication

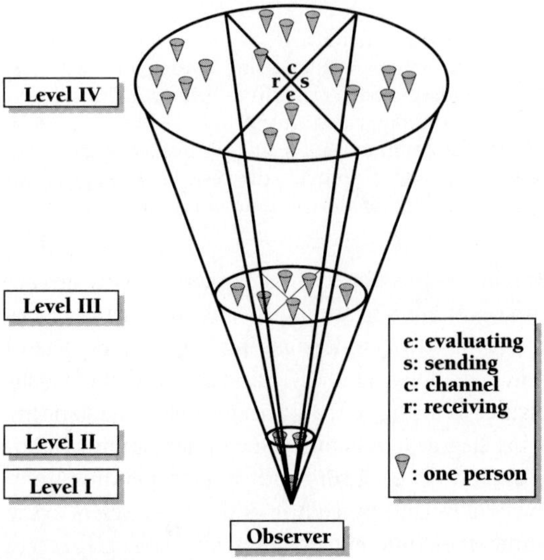

e: evaluating
s: sending
c: channel
r: receiving

▽: one person

(Ruesch & Bateson, 1951, p. 275)

principles of pragmatics that continue to influence communication research and theory (Bavelas, 1990; Beach, 1990; Motley, 1990a; Motley, 1990b). One major axiom posited by Watzlawick, Beavin, and Jackson is the impossibility of not communicating, or "one cannot not communicate." Watzlawick et al. essentially present behavior and communication as synonymous. They claim that one cannot *not* behave. This axiom implies that all nonverbal behavior is communication, communication does not have to be intentional or conscious, each communicational unit is a message, and a series of message exchanges is an interaction. In his challenge to this axiom, Motley (1990a, 1990b) questions the claim that one cannot *not* communicate because communication is intentional, symbolic, involves encoding, is interactive, or has fidelity (variation in quality). What seems to be underlying the controversy is the need to distinguish between communication and interpersonal communication. Communication might best be conceptualized as any acting on information (Dance & Larson, 1972). Thus, any perception of another person's behavior that affects some change in the perceiver would be communication (regardless of whether the other has intended the behavior to be seen or not). However, interpersonal communication can be conceptualized as an intentional and simultaneous mutual response to information between two or more individuals. With these distinctions between communication and interpersonal communication, Watzlawick's et al. axiom can be seen to be true of communication, but not true of interpersonal communication.

Additional principles developed by Watzlawick, Beavin, and Jackson associated with the pragmatic approach include:

- Every communication has a content and relationship aspect such that the latter classifies the former and is therefore a metacommunication (p. 54)
- The nature of a relationship is contingent upon the punctuation of the communicational sequences between the communicants (p. 59)

- Human communication is both digital and analogic (most nonverbal communication being digital and most verbal communication being analogic) (p. 66)
- All communicational interchanges are either symmetrical or complementary, depending on whether they are based on equality or difference (p. 70)

SYMBOLIC INTERACTIONISM

A variety of individuals have contributed to the development of symbolic interactionism, but the person most commonly associated with this approach is George Herbert Mead. Extensive notes on Mead's lectures on social psychology at the University of Chicago were compiled by former students into the text *Mind, Self and Society* (1934), which serves as an elaboration of his ideas on the role symbols have in the development of individuals and human interaction. Blumer (1969) coined the term "symbolic interaction" to describe the process identified by Mead. Mead was interested in the relationship between society and self—how society influenced the development of self and vice versa. Mead focused on the role symbols played in these relationships. He identified two types of actions that affect use: conversation of gestures and significant symbols. Gestures were defined by Mead as "that part of the social act which serves as a stimulus to other forms involved in the same social act" (p. 42). In essence, gestures represent behaviors by others that we perceive and respond to. That response is noninterpretive—we respond without interpreting the meaning of the act. A ball is thrown at our face, and we duck—a gesture and a response to the gesture. When we ask ourselves why someone threw a ball at us we move into significant symbols—adding interpretation as part of the response to the gesture. Gestures become "significant" when we attach interpretations to them. We are born into societies in which we are exposed to gestures and learn to act toward them as significant symbols. Further, development of our mind and self, and of what Mead called our "me" and "I," "arises through communication by a conversation of gestures in a social process or context of experience—not communication through mind" (p. 50). For Mead, we begin with an internalization of the society and experiences around us, and we are continually influenced by that. We eventually learn to perceive ourselves and affect ourselves through our own gestures and significant symbols.

Blumer (1969) identified three premises on which symbolic interactionism rests. The first premise is that we act toward the things around us, including others, on the basis of the meanings those things have for us. Thus, our actions toward a thing reflect the meanings we have for it. In the old television series *Get Smart,* secret agent Maxwell Smart used to take off his shoe and talk into its sole. Your first reaction might be that this is a rather strange man. After all, talking to the bottom of your shoe is not normal behavior. For Maxwell Smart his action is perfectly sane and is dictated by the meaning the shoe had for him. Hidden in the sole of the shoe was a telephone. Once you know about the phone, your interpretation of the way Smart acted is altered by the attribution of this new knowledge. The premise is reflected in the communication adage that meaning is in people, not in things.

The second premise is that the symbolic meanings arise from social interaction with others—in essence, we learn or are taught these meanings as a result of interacting with others. This premise strongly reflects Mead's notions of how society affects the development of self and meaning. This premise is meant as a direct challenge to those who claim meaning is intrinsic in a thing. Under this premise, meanings are a social product formed as a result of social interactions. If your father loved having mustard on his sandwiches and your mother reacted to mustard as one of the foulest things around, you might learn to attribute the same meaning to mustard as your mother. Thus, when someone offers you mustard for a sandwich, you act as if it is poison. In this manner our social interactions serve as the basis for gaining meaning for the things around us. You might wonder, though, why you would not be equally influenced by your father's love for mustard. That can be answered by the next premise.

The third premise is that the meanings go through an interpretive process applied by the individual. While your reaction to mustard might be dictated by differences in how outspoken or vehement each parent was in expressing like or dislike for mustard, it also might be attributed to the process of interpretation. Our reactions are not based solely upon one experience, such as your mother's reaction, but are the product of a wide variety of experiences and observations. Those experiences are combined in the attributing of meaning to what you perceive. According to Blumer, you go through two steps. First, you engage in a process of intrapersonal communication about the thing and its meaning; second, you select, check, suspend, regroup, and transform the meaning in light of the situation.

Manis and Meltzer (1978) identified seven basic propositions underlying symbolic interactionism that offer further elaboration of those presented by Blumer:

1. Distinctively human behavior and interaction are carried on through the medium of symbols and their meanings.
2. The individual becomes humanized through interaction with other persons.
3. Human society is most usefully conceived as consisting of people in interaction.
4. Human beings are active in shaping their own behavior.
5. Consciousness, or thinking, involves interaction with oneself.
6. Human beings construct their behavior in the course of its execution.
7. An understanding of human conduct requires study of the actor's covert behavior. (pp. 6–9)

SOCIAL EXCHANGE THEORY/SOCIAL PENETRATION THEORY

A large amount of research has been generated and a number of theories proposed using the social exchange approach. Several variations have been developed that are often labeled social exchange theory; primary among these is the work of George Homans (1961). Homans referred to his subject matter as "social behavior," which is understood to be face-to-face contact in which both parties reward the other directly and immediately. This conceptualization of social behavior is essentially what we now label interpersonal communication. Roloff (1981) presented a definition of interpersonal communication based upon the elements of social exchange theory as "a symbolic process by which two people, bound together in a relationship, provide each other with resources or negotiate the exchange of resources" (p. 30). Social exchange theory represents the application of an economic model to social interaction. Homans's intention was to develop a theory to explain human social behavior. Concepts such as cost, reward, and profit were incorporated in Homans's theory to explain decision making and social behavior.

Social exchange theory can be approached from two perspectives. The first explains the behavior or decisions of an individual in regard to others on the basis of costs and rewards, and the second explains interactions in terms of two people "exchanging" goods or services of equal value. (Your roommate gives you help doing homework and you give your roommate help cleaning the apartment.) In the simplest sense, the first approach says that humans are motivated by profit and act in ways to increase rewards and minimize costs. Thus we are attracted to relationships in which the positive outcomes exceed the costs incurred in that relationship (this is the underlying premise of social penetration theory). We keep friends who *reward* us with self-confirmation, make us feel valued and important, and satisfy our social needs even though it might *cost* us time, effort, personal freedom, or control. Foa and Foa (1980), in expanding on the outcome aspect of social exchange theory, developed a resource theory that identified six classifications of resources: love, status, information, money, goods, and services. These resources were further classified on two continuums: concreteness versus symbolism, and particularism versus universalism. (See

Figure 1.2.) In this model the six resources are classified according to how tangible or redeemable the resource is and how specific the resource is to the given relationship between two particular people. Love is regarded as falling halfway between tangible (concrete) and intangible (symbolic), probably because there are certain expectations about what you can get for loving someone. Love is highly specific to a relationship (particularism), in contrast to money, which is the least specific to a relationship, and thus is easily exchanged between strangers.

The specificity in identifying resources serves as one of the bases for the second manner in which social exchange theory is applied to human interaction. The second approach looks at given interactions as exchanges and states that when a person gives something to another, that person expects something of equal value in return. Violation of that expectation leads to conflict, distress, or termination of the relationship. Homans wrote of fair exchanges and distributive justice, in which individuals expect equal compensation for something they have given. These principles underlie what subsequently has been labeled equity and reciprocity. While equity theory has generated a significant amount of research, it also has been criticized for its limitations (Leventhal, 1980). When imbalances in costs and rewards within a given exchange occur, the prediction is that the individuals will engage in bargaining as a means to create equity and equality. Bargaining

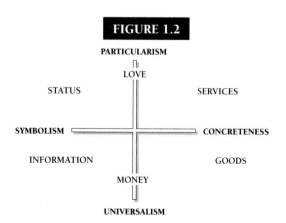

FIGURE 1.2

represents the most direct manifestation of social exchange theory in interpersonal communication. Besides being applied to explaining conflict and bargaining, social exchange theory has been utilized as a theory to explain relational development.

Social exchange principles have been applied to the whole continuum of relational development from initiation/attraction to termination. Altman and Taylor (1973) used social exchange principles in the development of their social penetration theory. According to their theory, individuals continually assess past and present interactions and make predictions about future interactions. When a pair of individuals makes positive future extrapolations, social penetration theory predicts that the pair will move successively to more intimate relational levels. As this process of repeated mutual positive assessments takes place, the pair will increase both the depth and breadth of information shared. As perceived costs exceed rewards, Altman and Taylor hypothesized a deterioration or "depenetration" process, which was essentially a reversal of the developmental or "penetration" process. More contemporary views of relational dissolution have challenged this conceptualization with the claim that dissolution is not just the reversal of relational development but involves a different process. (See the readings on dissolution in this text.)

INTERPERSONAL COMMUNICATION THEORIES

CONSTRUCTIVISM

The constructivist approach to human communication, and more specifically to interpersonal communication, was spawned by the work of George Kelly in his theory of personality, which posited the existence of "constructs" and was influenced by symbolic interactionism. In Kelly's (1955, 1963) original conceptualization, constructs are templates or transparent patterns that individuals create and attempt to fit over the reality of the world. Constructs represent a way of "construing the world." Kelly's theory focused strongly on the use of con-

structs for prediction and anticipation of events. According to Kelly, constructs allow humans to make sense of the chaos around them, to create order and structure. The Role Category Questionnaire (RCQ) was developed by Crockett (1965) as a means of assessing the sophistication or complexity of an individual's construct system, or what has been labeled "cognitive complexity." Respondents write out descriptions of various people, usually peers. The recorded impressions are typically scored according to differentiation among the peers, abstractness of the constructs used to describe the peers, and the degree of impression organization (Burleson & Waltman, 1988). This instrument has been one of the main tools used by constructivists in examining the role of constructs in human communication.

Among the many principles of constructs advocated by Kelly (1963) are the following:

- Constructs differ from individual to individual.
- Constructs might be highly developed on one issue or aspect but not necessarily as developed on another in any given individual.
- Constructs change and evolve as a result of experience; constructs have limited ranges of applicability.
- Constructs vary in permeability (how malleable or modifiable).

In communication, personal constructs are developed to fit the individuals with whom we interact. Constructs help stabilize our cognitions about messages, other people, ourselves, and communication contexts. Constructs enable us to modify and adapt our communication with another because of the ability to predict the other person's behaviors and reactions. Constructivist research has found consistent relationships between the adaptation of messages or person-centeredness of a message and the level of complexity of construct systems (O'Keefe & Delia, 1982).

An underlying principle of constructivism is that those with more developed interpersonal construct systems will exhibit more sophisticated and advanced communicative functioning (Burleson &

Waltman, 1988), or, put more simply, will be more effective interpersonal communicators. Cognitive complexity is seen as relating to a variety of processes associated with social cognition and social perception. Thus,

persons with relatively complex systems of interpersonal constructs should be better able than their less complex counterparts to form more organized and integrated impressions of others, recognize relevant dispositional and affective features of others, integrate potentially inconsistent information about others, represent and understand the cognitive, affective and motivational features of others' perspectives, and so forth. (Burleson & Waltman, 1988, p. 4)

O'Keefe and Delia (1982) examined the relationship between the complexity of interpersonal construct systems and messages. They argue that increases in construct differentiation and abstraction lead to more complex interpersonal objectives and obstacles to be overcome, which in turn lead to more complex messages to address multiple tasks. Those with complex construct systems thus face more complex communication tasks, which then lead to the expansion of the repertoire of strategies (O'Keefe & Delia, 1982).

While constructivism might appear to be predominantly concerned with the psychological or intrapersonal aspects of interpersonal communication participants, O'Keefe and Delia (1985) present this theory as being both social and psychological. The social aspect of constructivism rests on both the fact that construct systems are the product of socialization of an individual within a given culture, and that communication involves a coordination of perception, interpretation, and construct systems. O'Keefe and Delia (1985) define communication from a constructivist's perspective as people attempting to coordinate their behavior through an application of shared interpretive schemes. These interpretations might be correct or incorrect, creating understanding or misunderstanding. Further, they write, "It is the organization of interpretation and behavior around the attribution of the intent to communicate that sustains communication" (p. 65). Meaning is created by the application of inter-personal constructs and interpretive schemes with intersubjective meaning being dependent upon a momentary and partially shared interpretation (O'Keefe & Delia, 1985).

COORDINATED MANAGEMENT OF MEANING

The coordinated management of meaning represents an application of rules theory and systems theory to the interpersonal context (Pearce & Cronen, 1980). Two individuals, representing intrapersonal rules systems, become intermeshed in an interpersonal encounter requiring coordinated management. Pearce and Cronen claim the phrase "coordinated management of meaning" focuses attention both on individuals as processors of information (as discussed in rules theory) and on the interpersonal rules systems as the center of action.

As a preliminary to understanding this theory, Pearce (1976a) develops the concept of "episodes" as the units into which communication interactions are punctuated. Episodes are identified as those human situations in which some internal structure is evident and that structure is imposed by the actors. Episodes "appear as patterned sequences of reciprocal speech acts" (Cronen, Pearce, & Harris, 1982, p. 72). According to Pearce (1976a), meaning is episodic; therefore to understand meaning we must understand episodes. Episodes are particularly appealing because it is the actors, not the observers, who determine what is or is not an episode, and thus determine the meaning. Pearce identifies three referents for episodes:

Episodes₁ consist of patterns of meaning and behaviors which are culturally sanctioned and which exist independently of any particular individual or dyad.

Episodes₂ consist of patterns of meanings and behaviors in the minds of individuals. . . . These are private symbols which express an individuals' understanding of the forms of social interaction in which they are participating or in which they want to participate.

Episodes₃ consist of the communicators' interpretation of the actual sequence of messages which they jointly produced. (1976a, pp. 21–22)

Pearce (1976a) identifies three structural elements of episodes that affect meaning: hierarchy, clustering of rules, and degree of specificity. Meaning is seen as falling within a hierarchy of at least six levels: (1) content, which is the cognitive process of attributing meaning to verbal and nonverbal communication; (2) speech acts, which are acts performed by one person toward another; (3) episodes; (4) relationships, which is how the participants define their relationship (later relabeled "master contract," Pearce & Cronen, 1991); (5) life scripts, which are patterns of episodes that create communication expectations; and (6) cultural patterns (originally labeled "archetypes") (Pearce & Cronen, 1980).

We individually manage the meanings we attribute to what we perceive and make decisions about the application of rules. Interpersonal communication involves the management of meaning by both parties involved. In the coorientation of meaning between two people engaged in interpersonal communication, people predict the degree of agreement or disagreement about what episode is being enacted. Those predictions are subject to confirmation or disconfirmation in the subsequent interaction. Thus four possible combinations of agreement–disagreement and confirmation–disconfirmation are possible: a prediction of agreement, which is confirmed; a prediction of agreement, which is disconfirmed as accurate; a prediction of disagreement, which is confirmed as accurate; and a prediction of disagreement, which is disconfirmed. Management of meaning is especially needed when there is disconfirmation of the expectation. Individuals must reevaluate the meanings and their expectations. The need for management is also critical in enigmatic episodes—those episodes where the rules do not provide an adequate guide for action (Pearce, 1976a). Enigmatic episodes can be either equivocal or ambiguous. **Equivocal enigmatic episodes** are those for which the interpretation can be in two or more ways or which produce contradictions. **Ambiguous enigmatic episodes** are those for which the rules do not provide sufficient specificity or are incomplete.

Pearce (1976a) defines coordination as the establishment of a "contract" between individuals to enact a particular episode. An individual might propose enacting an episode$_2$ that can either be accepted or rejected. Once an episode$_2$ has been agreed to, then consensual rules exist and coordination has been attained and an episode$_3$ has been reached. Pearce identifies three strategies for coordination: casting, mirroring, and negotiation (1976a). Casting is seeking individuals to match to a desired episode$_2$. The development of a relationship is dependent upon one person accepting without modification the other's episode$_2$. Mirroring involves an individual willing to accept another person's episode$_2$. Negotiation involves both parties presenting their episodes$_2$ and reaching some mutually accepted episode$_3$.

UNCERTAINTY REDUCTION

Berger and Calabrese (1975) initially proposed uncertainty reduction theory as a way of approaching, analyzing, and understanding initial interpersonal interactions. They developed a set of axioms and theorems based upon the premise that when two strangers meet there is a large degree of uncertainty about each other and the interaction is driven by the participants' desire to reduce uncertainty about the other. Since that time, the theory has been applied to more than just the initiation of a relationship, and the original axioms and theorems have been modified (Berger, 1987; Berger & Bradac, 1982). Drawing from a theory that dealt with the nature of information and how information is conveyed and processed (information theory), uncertainty is conceptualized as a function of the number of alternatives present in a given situation and likelihood associated with those alternatives occurring (Berger, 1987).

Uncertainty reduction theory is based on the following premise: People are motivated to seek out information that will reduce uncertainty because reducing uncertainty increases their ability to predict accurately and ultimately control their environment. In applying this premise to initial interactions, Berger and Calabrese (1975) predicted that when interacting with strangers the resulting behaviors were essentially information-gaining strategies aimed at reducing uncertainty about the other. A corollary of the above premise was that the more individuals communicated and the more information obtained, the less uncertainty resulted. Berger (1987) revised this corollary in recognition of the fact that communication sometimes can actually increase uncertainty, intentionally or unintentionally. However, Berger points out that without communication, uncertainty will remain. Reduction of communication impairs the ability to predict and explain, thus limiting our ability to achieve our goals.

Two kinds of uncertainty have been identified: cognitive uncertainty or uncertainty about the attitudes and beliefs; and behavioral uncertainty, which is the uncertainty associated with anticipated behaviors. Uncertainty can also be considered not only in terms of how others think or act, but also about ourselves. Berger and Bradac (1982) apply the three traditional classifications of knowledge to the type of information used to reduce uncertainty: descriptive, predictive, and explanatory. Each type of knowledge probably is associated with varying relational goals. For example:

> Explanatory knowledge is extremely powerful since it may enable us to modify more efficiently another person's behavior or attitudes; that is, knowing why a person believes or behaves in the way he or she does gives us more possible ways in which to influence that person than if we can only predict what they will do. (Berger & Bradac, 1982, p. 9)

Three conditions have been hypothesized that might actually prompt our attempts to reduce uncertainty in interpersonal interactions (Berger, 1979; Berger & Bradac, 1982):

1. when our expectations about the other person have been violated,
2. when we know or anticipate we will be interacting with the person again,
3. when we are concerned about the impact or control the other person might have on us, particularly in controlling rewards and costs.

Specific strategies that individuals might employ to reduce uncertainty have been identified (Berger & Bradac, 1982). The strategies can be passive and observational in nature; active, involving some effort on the observer's part to gain information indirectly; or interactive, in which information is gained through direct interaction with the other. (A chapter from Berger and Bradac's book is included in the readings in this text and provides further elaboration on the above points.)

The knowledge necessary to reduce uncertainty and to facilitate effective interpersonal communication does not have to depend solely on the other. A certain amount of information about another can be garnered from the contexts in which the other is observed. Stereotypes, cultural generalizations, social norms, scripts, role schemas—all provide a base of information from which people can draw for reducing uncertainty in their interactions with others. It is for these reasons that an initial interaction between two strangers is fairly predictable.

CONCEPTUAL APPROACHES TO INTERPERSONAL COMMUNICATION

INTERPERSONAL COMMUNICATION COMPETENCE/SKILLS

Interpersonal communication competence (ICC) can be approached from two perspectives. The first represents the formal identification, theorizing, and research of the concept of "interpersonal communication competence"; the second is the broad set of studies attempting to identify the competencies or skills an individual should possess in order to be an effective or competent interpersonal communicator.

The phenomenon being examined as "interpersonal communication competence" is variously labeled as communication competence, interpersonal competence, social competence, and relational competence. The conceptualization of interpersonal communication competence continues to evolve, but there are some predominant elements that can be discussed.

One of the most accepted attributes of ICC is the underlying judgment of the appropriateness of a given behavior in a given situation. Larson, Back-lund, Redmond, and Barbour (1978) defined communication competence as "the ability to demonstrate knowledge of the communicative behavior socially appropriate in a given situation" (p 21). Underlying appropriateness is the possession of a knowledge of the social rules and norms that apply to a given interaction at the most general level of a given society down to the specific rules established within a given relationship.

In somewhat of a contrast to appropriateness, effectiveness or goal attainment also has been included in the conceptualization of ICC. The degree to which individuals accomplish their goals is considered the mark of communication competence (Parks, 1985). In this conceptualization a balance must be reached among all the goals an individual might have; an individual does not want to accomplish one goal at the expense of another goal, such as making a request from another, which might jeopardize the overall relationship.

Interpersonal communication competence as a set of skills casts a broad net that captures many interpersonal communication studies that examine traits or skills. These are usually skills people possess that lead to more effective or competent interpersonal relationships. Interpersonal competencies or skills are often the focus of introductory interpersonal communication texts and courses. These texts and courses begin with the premise that individuals can improve their interpersonal competence by enhancing their interpersonal skills, and then set about advocating and teaching various skills. A few samples from introductory interpersonal communication texts illustrates this philosophy:

In fact, communication skills are rather like athletic ability. Even the most inept of us can learn to be more effective with training and practice. (Adler, Rosenfeld, & Towne, 1992, p. 20)

One of the major goals of this text and this course is to spell out the nature of communication competence and to increase your own communication competence. By increasing your competence, you will have a greater number of performance options available to you. (DeVito, 1989, p. 6)

We view interpersonal communication as a set of behaviors that can be systematically examined, learned, and taught (p. 29). . . . This text is designed to assist people in becoming more competent in their interpersonal communication skills. (Pearson & Spitzberg, 1990, p. 32)

These texts typically present a variety of skills that might be utilized in the development of more competent interpersonal communication. The identification of what skills are important to competence is still subject to debate. These texts then proceed to elaborate on various interpersonal skills and to present ways in which those skills can be improved. For instance, Adler, Rosenfeld, and Towne (1992) identified the following as important to communication competence: a large repertoire of skills, adaptability, ability to perform skillfully, involvement, empathy/perspective taking, cognitive complexity, and self-monitoring. In one of the first attempts by a communication scholar to examine the skills comprising communication competence, Wiemann (1975) identified five skills: interaction management, empathy, affiliation/support, behavioral flexibility, and social relaxation. Many studies have been done on various skills that can be considered components of interpersonal communication competence, but those studies are not directly concerned with the issue of communication competence. A few studies have focused on skills within the communication competence context, for example, communicative adaptability (Duran, 1983) and empathy (Redmond, 1985).

The problem with defining ICC by some set of skills is in assessing the degree to which individuals must possess each of the various skills to be considered competent. Most of us are probably strong in some skills and weak in others. The strong skills might be sufficient to allow us to function competently in interpersonal relationships despite our possessing weak skills. Skill-based interpersonal communication research tends to examine the impact of a single trait or skill on an interpersonal interaction rather than to examine the impact of a full set of skills.

Spitzberg and Cupach (1984) indicted the trait or skills approaches to interpersonal communication competence, charging that those approaches ignored the importance of context on a person's ability to display appropriate or effective behavior. Several assumptions underlie their conceptualization of "relational competence." They believe relational competence is the function of both appropriateness of the behavior to a given situation and the effectiveness of that behavior. Competence is contextual in that what may be appropriate and effective in one situation might not be in another. Competence is seen as a matter of degree rather than a dichotomy of competent/incompetent. Competence is seen as composed of "molecular" (specific) behaviors and a "molar" (general) impression. Communication competence is functional—that is, it moves an individual to the accomplishment of goals. Competence is seen as relational and therefore interdependent between two or more participants. Competence occurs only in respect to the context of given relationships. In essence, one cannot be interpersonally communicatively competent all by oneself—competence is always within the context of an interaction with another. Finally, Spitzberg and Cupach see competence as an impression of a person, rather than a state or quality intrinsic in that person. By conceptualizing communication competence as the perception of another, the key to competence becomes impression management. This means that the emphasis is on knowing how the other person will perceive certain behaviors and then engaging in behaviors that create the impression in the other that you wish.

Spitzberg and Cupach draw upon cognitive, behavioral, and contextual approaches in developing a relational model of competence. Under this model, to be perceived as communicatively competent a person needs to (a) be motivated to communicate; (b) possess the knowledge about how to communicate; (c) be skilled in communicating; and (d) be sensitive to the context (pp. 117–150). An additional element of their model is the role that outcomes play in determining perceived competence. The judgment of competence depends upon the perception of how effectively individuals achieve their outcomes in a manner appropriate to

the relationships (Spitzberg & Cupach, 1984). By reviewing various skill inventories of communication competence, Spitzberg and Cupach developed a set of four potential skill areas that might contribute to communication competence: interaction management, social relaxation, expressiveness, altercentricism (other orientation). An extensive list of verbal and nonverbal behaviors were identified that contribute to each of these four categories.

RELATIONSHIP DEVELOPMENT

The final theoretic approach actually is based on a theme that runs across several of the approaches already discussed. Rules theory, uncertainty reduction theory, and social exchange theories have all been applied in the examination of relational development, especially the initiation of relationships. The primary emphasis of the relationship development approach is the study of interpersonal communication as it relates to the life of a relationship from initiation to termination. Included within this focus is both the effect that communication has on relationship development and how relationship development affects the communication. Relationally oriented interpersonal communication theory and research has included an examination into the nature of relational development, as well as the communication qualities, which vary across relationship type.

Scholars in social psychology and other disciplines have provided the initial models of relational development. Communication scholars drew from these models in developing interpersonal communication-oriented phase theories. The number and descriptions of the stages involved in relational development has varied. Berger and Calabrese (1975) identified only three: an entry phase, a personal phase, and an exit phase. Their interest rested primarily in the application of uncertainty reduction to the entry phase. DeVito (1989) presented a five-phase model: contact, involvement, intimacy, deterioration, and dissolution. In DeVito's model he also has exiting from the relationship available in any of the five stages. Wood's (1982) model places a strong emphasis on the nature of the communication by which each stage is identified:

1. A pre-relational stage of individuality
2. Invitational communication (auditioning)
3. Explorational communication
4. Intensifying communication
5. Revising communication
6. Bonding communication
7. Navigating communication
8. Differentiating communication
9. Disintegrating communication
10. Stagnating communication
11. Terminating communication
12. Individuals

Knapp (1984) separated his ten stages into two categories: coming together and coming apart. The five stages of coming together include initiating, experimenting, intensifying, integrating, and bonding. The five stages of coming apart include differentiating, circumscribing, stagnating, avoiding, and terminating. (A complete description of these stages can be found in the article by Knapp and Vangelisti included in this text.) Knapp advocates a number of principles concerning movement from one stage to another: movement is systematic and sequential; movement may be forward and backward; movement may occur within the stages; movement is to a new place; and the rate of movement varies (pp. 50–54).

Despite the call for basic descriptive research into any model of stage development (Delia, 1980; Wood, 1982), little substantive research into overall phase theories has been developed, though significant research has been done on individual phases, such as initiation and termination.

Altman and Taylor (1973) in their social penetration theory (discussed earlier under social exchange theory) included both the stages of relational development as well as the dimensions of communication they thought varied from relationship to relationship. They focused on the move toward intimacy in their classification of the relational stages: orientation, exploratory affective exchange, and stable exchange. For each of these stages certain differences were identified among nonverbal, environmental, and verbal behaviors. In more general terms, these can be classified as dimensions of interpersonal communication. Those eight dimensions are:

1. Richness—breadth of interaction
2. Uniqueness of interaction
3. Efficiency of exchange
4. Substitutability and equivalency
5. Synchronization and pacing
6. Permeability and openness
7. Voluntariness and spontaneity of exchange
8. Evaluation (p. 129)

In examining how these eight dimensions actually relate to differing relationships, Knapp, Ellis, and Williams (1980) had respondents indicate to what degree items relating to the eight dimensions applied to relationships classified as "lover," "best friend," "friend," "pal," "colleague," and "acquaintance." Their analysis yielded three dimensions instead of eight, which they labeled "personalized communication," "synchronized communication," and "difficult communication." Personalized communication was by far the most significant factor. Personalized communication included accessibility, openness, and self-disclosure. Synchronized communication referred to conversations characterized as "smooth-flowing, effortless, spontaneous, informal, and well coordinated" (p. 277). Difficult communication involved awkwardness of interaction and does not necessarily mean inaccurate communication.

Control, intimacy, and trust have been identified as three significant dimensions of interpersonal relationships (Millar & Rogers, 1976; Rogers & Millar, 1988). Rogers and Farce (1975) developed a method for conducting analysis of relational communication to examine specifically the control dimension as it relates to communication in their development of a system for coding messages, control, and transaction. Burgoon and Hale (1987) identified eight dimensions of relational message themes associated with interpersonal relationships,

---

Summary of Conceptual Approaches to Interpersonal Communication

COVERING LAWS   Covering laws are general principles of interaction that dictate the behavior of individuals.
SYSTEMS   A systems perspective attempts to include all elements in understanding an interaction because the elements are interactive.
RULE-GOVERNED   Under the rules perspective, we make sense of our interactions with others according to how those interactions fit within rules. Interaction rules vary in how much mutual understanding and coordination is needed by the rule.
PRAGMATISM   Behavior (therefore communication) reflects internal processes of individuals. Each communication with others includes content and relational messages. We cannot prevent others from attaching meaning to our actions.
SYMBOLIC INTERACTIONISM   We interact with others according to symbols. Symbols are learned and are culture specific. We attach meaning to symbols, and those meanings are the product of our social interactions. Our thinking (including self-concept) is the product of the symbols we have learned.
SOCIAL EXCHANGE THEORY/SOCIAL PENETRATION   Each of our interactions represents an exchange involving costs and rewards. We look for relationships that provide the best ratio of rewards to costs. We move to greater intimacy (social penetration) as long as the rewards actually or potentially increase relative to costs.
CONSTRUCTIVISM   Constructs are patterns of thinking. We develop sets of constructs to explain others and ourselves. Individuals vary in the complexity of their construct systems and therefore their development of complex communication strategies.
UNCERTAINTY REDUCTION   We possess varying degrees of uncertainty about what to expect in the behavior and attitudes of those around us. Those we know better we have less uncertainty about. We are driven to reduce uncertainty and thus increase the predictability and control of the world around us, specifically social relationships. Communication plays an integral part in helping to gain information and reduce uncertainty.
COORDINATED MANAGEMENT OF MEANING   We have certain expectations about what to expect on the basis of what episode we believe is being enacted. When that expectation is violated we attempt to manage the interaction with another by establishing a contract with another about what episode to follow. In this way we coordinate the meaning each of us places on the interaction.
INTERPERSONAL COMMUNICATION COMPETENCE/SKILLS   This approach emphasizes identification of the interpersonal communication skills necessary to be effective, particularly in relationships. Interpersonal communication competence may also involve the degree of appropriateness demonstrated in a given social situation.
RELATIONSHIP DEVELOPMENT   Interpersonal relationships are believed to progress from one identifiable stage to another as the relationship moves toward intimacy. Each stage possesses unique communication qualities.

---

including immediacy/affection (intimacy I), similarity/depth (intimacy II), receptivity/trust (intimacy III), composure, formality, dominance, equality, and task orientation.

CONCLUSION

This review of definitional components and theoretic approaches to interpersonal communication is by no means complete. It is intended to provide an appreciation for the complexity and inconclusiveness of the current study of interpersonal communication. Each of the theoretic approaches has some merit in helping us to understand and explain interpersonal communication. Some approaches have proven to be more productive than others, but many more approaches will be developed that will provide better explanation and prediction of interpersonal communication. The quest continues.

Having a strong understanding of these theoretic approaches will prove beneficial to your comprehension of the readings in the rest of this text. The readings have been essentially set up in a relational development framework because this seemed to be the most logical manner in which the variety of articles could be organized. However, this does not mean that the articles themselves all represent only a relationship development perspective. Each reading can be linked to one or more of the theoretical frameworks. In this way you can evaluate the manner in which a given piece of research or scholarship advances or extends each of the theories. By understanding these theories you will have built yourself an observation tower from which you can survey the landscape of research and theory and still have a solid central location on which to stand.

BIBLIOGRAPHY

Adler, R. B., Rosenfeld, L. B., & Towne, N. (1992). *Interplay: The process of interpersonal communication* (5th ed.). Fort Worth, TX: Harcourt Brace.

Adler, R. B., & Towne, N. (1993). *Looking out/looking in* (7th ed.). Fort Worth, TX: Harcourt Brace.

Altman, I., & Taylor, D. A. (1973). *Social penetration: The development of interpersonal relationships.* New York: Holt, Rinehart & Winston.

Baxter, L. A., & Bullis, C. (1986). Turning points in developing romantic relationships. *Human Communication Research, 12,* 469–493.

Beach, W. A. (1990). On (not) observing behavior interactionally. *Western Journal of Speech Communication, 54,* 603–612.

Berger, C. R. (1987). Communicating under uncertainty. In M. E. Roloff & G. R. Miller (Eds.). *Interpersonal processes: New directions in communication research* (pp. 39–62). Beverly Hills, CA: Sage.

Berger, C. R. (1979). Beyond initial interaction: Uncertainty, understanding, and the development of interpersonal relationships. In H. Giles & R. N. St. Clair (Eds.), *Language and Social Psychology* (pp. 122–144). Oxford: Basil Blackwell.

Berger, C. R., & Bradac, J. J. (1982). *Language and social knowledge: Uncertainty in interpersonal relations.* Baltimore: Edward Arnold.

Berger, C. R., & Calabrese, R. J. (1975). Some explorations in initial interaction and beyond: Toward a developmental theory of interpersonal communication. *Human Communication Research, 1,* 99–112.

Blumer, H. (1969). *Symbolic interactionism: Perspective and method.* Englewood Cliffs, NJ: Prentice-Hall.

Brooks, W. D., & Emmert, P. (1976). *Interpersonal communication.* Dubuque, IA: W. C. Brown.

Burgoon, J. K., & Hale, J. L. (1987). Validation and measurement of the fundamental themes of relational communication. *Communication Monographs, 54,* 19–41.

Burleson, B. R. & Waltman, M. S. (1988). Cognitive complexity: Using the Role Category Questionnaire Measure. In C. H. Tardy, (Ed.), *A handbook for the study of human communication: Methods and instruments for observing, measuring, and assessing communication processes* (pp. 1–35). Norwood, NJ: Ablex.

Crockett, W. H. (1965). Cognitive complexity and impression formation. In B. A. Maher (Ed.), *Progress in experimental psychology,* Vol. 2 (pp. 47–90). New York: Academic Press.

Cronen, V. E., Pearce, W. B., & Harris, L. M. (1982). The coordinated management of meaning: A theory of communication. In F. E. X. Dance (Ed.), *Human communication theory* (pp. 61–89). New York: Harper & Row.

Cushman, D. P., Valentinsen, B., & Dietrich, D. (1982). A rules theory of interpersonal communication. In F. E. X. Dance (Ed.), *Human communication theory* (pp. 90–119). New York: Harper & Row.

Cushman, D. P., & Whiting, G. (1972). An approach to communication theory: Toward consensus on rules. *Journal of Communication, 22,* 217–238.

Dance, F. E. X., & Larson, C. E. (1972). *Speech communication: Concepts and behavior.* New York: Holt, Rinehart & Winston.

Delia, J. G. (1980). Some tentative thoughts concerning the study of interpersonal relationships and their development. *The Western Journal of Speech Communication, 44,* 97–103.

DeVito, J. A. (1989). *The interpersonal communication book* (5th ed.). New York: Harper & Row.

DeVito, J. A. (1990). *Messages: Building interpersonal communication skills.* New York: Harper & Row.

DeVito, J. A. (1993). *Messages: Building interpersonal communication skills* (2nd ed.). New York: HarperCollins.

Duran, R. L. (1983). Communicative adaptability: A measure of social communicative competence. *Communication Quarterly, 31,* 320–326.

Foa, E. B., & Foa, U. G. (1980). Resource theory: Interpersonal behavior as exchange. In K. J. Gergen, M. S. Greenberg, & R. H. Willis (Eds.), *Social exchange: Advances in theory and research* (pp. 77–94). New York: Plenum Press.

Homans, G. C. (1961). *Social behavior: Its elementary forms.* New York: Harcourt Brace.

Infante, D. A., Rancer, A. S., & Womack, D. F. (1990). *Building communication theory.* Prospect Heights, IL: Waveland Press.

Kelly, G. A. (1963). *A theory of personality.* New York: Norton (originally published in 1955).

Knapp, M. L. (1984). *Interpersonal communication and human relationships.* Newton, MA: Allyn & Bacon.

Knapp, M. L., & Vangelisti, A. L. (1992). *Interpersonal communication and human relationships* (2nd ed.). Boston: Allyn & Bacon.

Larson, C., Backlund, P., Redmond, M., & Barbour, A. (1978). *Assessing functional communication.* Urbana, IL: ERIC.

Leventhal, G. S. (1980). What should be done with equity theory? In K. J. Gergen, M. S. Greenberg, & R. H. Willis (Eds.), *Social exchange: Advances in theory and research* (pp. 27–55). New York: Plenum Press.

Mader, T. F., & Mader, D. C. (1993). *Understanding one another: Communicating interpersonally.* Dubuque, IA: W. C. Brown.

Manis, J. G., & Meltzer, G. N. (1978). *Symbolic interaction: A reader in social psychology* (3rd ed.). Boston: Allyn & Bacon.

Meade, G. H. (1934). *Mind, self and society.* Chicago: University of Chicago Press.

Millar, F. E., & Rogers, L. E. (1976). A relational approach to interpersonal communication. In G. R. Miller (Ed.), *Explorations in interpersonal communication* (pp. 87–104). Beverly Hills, CA: Sage.

Miller, G. R., & Sunnafrank, M. J. (1982). All is for one but one is not for all: A conceptual perspective of interpersonal communication. In F. E. X. Dance (Ed.), *Human communication theory* (pp. 220–242). New York: Harper & Row.

Motley, M. T. (1990a). On whether one can(not) not communicate: An examination via traditional communication postulates. *Western Journal of Speech Communication, 54,* 1–20.

Motley, M. T. (1990b). Communication interaction: A reply to Beach and Bavelas. *Western Journal of Speech Communication, 54,* 613–623.

O'Keefe, B. J., & Delia, J. G. (1982). Impression formation and message production. In C. R. Berger & M. E. Roloff (Eds.), *Social cognition and communication* (pp. 33–72). Beverly Hills, CA: Sage.

O'Keefe, B. J., & Delia, J. G. (1985). Psychological and interactional dimensions of communicative development. In H. Giles & R. N. St. Clair (Eds.), *Recent advances in language communication and social psychology* (pp. 41–85). London: Lawrence Erlbaum.

Parks, M. R. (1985). Interpersonal communication and the quest for personal competence. In M. L. Knapp & G. R. Miller (Eds.), *Handbook of interpersonal communication* (pp. 171–201). Beverly Hills, CA: Sage.

Pearce, W. B. (1973). Consensual rules in interpersonal communication: A reply to Cushman and Whiting. *Journal of Communication, 23,* 160–168.

Pearce, W. B. (1976a). The coordinated management of meaning: A rules-based theory of interpersonal communication. In G. R. Miller (Ed.), *Explorations in interpersonal communication* (pp. 17–35). Beverly Hills, CA: Sage.

Pearce, W. B. (1976b). *An overview of communication and interpersonal relationships.* Chicago: Science Research Associates.

Pearce, W. B., & Cronen, V. E. (1980). *Communication, action, and meaning: The creation of social realities.* New York: Praeger.

Pearce, W. B., & Cronen, V. (1991). Coordinated management of meaning. In E. Griffin (Ed.), *A first look at communication theory* (pp. 38–47). New York: McGraw-Hill.

Redmond, M. V. (1985). The relationship between perceived communication competence and perceived empathy. *Communication Monographs, 52,* 377–382.

Rogers, L. E., & Farce, R. V. (1975). Analysis of relational communication in dyads: New measurement procedures.

Rogers, L. E., & Millar, F. E. (1988). Relational communication. In S. Duck (Ed.), *Handbook of personal relationships* (pp. 289–305). New York: John Wiley & Sons.

Roloff, M. E. (1981). *Interpersonal communication: The social exchange approach.* Beverly Hills, CA: Sage.

Ruesch, J., & Bateson, G. (1951). *Communication: The social matrix of psychiatry.* New York: Norton.

Spitzberg, B. H., & Cupach, W. R. (1984). *Interpersonal communication competence.* Beverly Hills, CA: Sage.

Stewart, J., & Logan, C. (1993). *Together: Communicating interpersonally* (4th ed.). New York: McGraw-Hill.

Verderber, R. F., & Verderber, K. S. (1992). *Inter-Act: Using interpersonal communication skills* (6th ed.). Belmont, CA: Wadsworth.

Watson, K. W., & Barker, L. L. (1990). *Interpersonal and relational communication.* Scottsdale, AZ: Gorsuch Scarisbrick.

Watzlawick, P., Beavin, J. H., & Jackson, D. D. (1967). *Pragmatics of human communication: A study of interactional patterns, pathologies, and paradoxes.* New York: Norton.

Weaver II, R. L. (1990). *Understanding interpersonal communication* (5th ed.). Glenview, IL: Scott, Foresman.

Wiemann, J. M. (1975). Explication and test of a model of communicative competence. *Human Communication Research, 3,* 195–213.

Wilmot, W. W. (1975). *Dyadic communication: A transactional perspective.* Reading, MA: Addison-Wesley.

Wilson, G. L., Hantz, A. M., & Hanna, M. S. (1992). *Interpersonal growth through communication* (3rd ed.). Dubuque, IA: W. C. Brown.

Wood, J. T. (1982). Communication and relational culture: Bases for the study of human relationships. *Communication Quarterly, 30,* 75–83.

2

Understanding Interpersonal Communication Research

M. V. REDMOND

In order to make sense of a number of the articles included in this text it will be helpful to have an understanding of the rudimentary elements of theory, research, and statistics. You will be presented with many claims made by the authors of the articles in this text—claims they argue are valid and accurate reflections of interpersonal communication. However, the claims forwarded in these articles should be read from a critical perspective. One way to look at these articles is from a consumer's point of view. From that perspective each article can be thought of as a potential product for you to purchase. The authors (including this one) are salespeople attempting to sell you something; you are a buyer of ideas and claims. Following this approach, you need to follow the adage of "Caveat emptor"—Let the buyer beware. You can beware only if you possess enough understanding of theory building and research methods to recognize the limitations of the claims. This chapter is to help you reach such an understanding by explaining some of the relevant concepts, terms, and common limitations. It will be a review for those who have had course work in statistics and research methods.

By necessity, this chapter will touch on only a few of the basic elements involved in research design, but enough elements will be covered to increase your comprehension and appreciation of the readings. Some of the articles include extensive and complex statistical analyses; these readings are included because they represent some significant aspect of interpersonal communication, not because of their statistical sophistication. The focus in read-

ing the articles should be on the conceptual and theoretical discussion. The critical objective is to understand the discussion, the research design, and the manner in which the authors reach their conclusions, which in turn should lead to a better understanding of interpersonal communication.

THE RHETORIC OF SCHOLARSHIP

From the reader-as-consumer perspective the authors are trying to sell you something, trying to persuade you of the truth of their claims, trying to prove they have a better approach than others, trying to convince you that they have arrived at a valid explanation or description of some phenomenon. Should you buy what they have to sell? There are certain principles that have been established that represent "good" science; that is, a standardized way of conducting research or of developing theory, which, when followed precisely, represents a valid study with acceptable claims. However, some of these principles are not always adhered to, some are stretched beyond their limits, and some are misrepresented or distorted.

Two general types of articles make up this set of readings: those advancing a particular theoretic perspective through logic and argument (sometimes in the form of a review of previous research), and those advancing a particular theoretic perspective supported by conducting a specific research study. The first type typically incorporates the results of previous studies as evidence to support its claims. (Readings in this category include chapters

3, 4, 5, 6, 10, 14, 16, 17, 18, 22, 24, 25, and 26.) The second type is usually narrower in scope and depends more upon the logic of experimental design to prove the validity of its claims. (Readings in this category include 7, 8, 9, 11, 12, 13, 15, 19–21, and 23.) Regardless of the type, the authors are attempting to use various rhetorical tools to convince you to accept their claims. Among the tools utilized are logic (inductive and deductive reasoning) and the use of supporting materials or evidence. As a reader you need to determine how well the authors have made their case. Are there flaws in their logic? Is the evidence relevant to the claim being made? Is their research study an adequate test of their theory? Was the study conducted in an unbiased manner? Can you have confidence in the significance of their results? These and other questions should be in the back of your mind as you read each article.

Smith (1988) presented six criteria to apply in determining the legitimacy of a theoretical explanation. First, *validity* represents the degree of consistency between the proposed explanation and observed facts. Second, the proposed explanation should consistently and with regularity provide *predictability* of effects. Third, *precision* is the degree to which the theory, concepts, and relationships are clearly defined. Fourth, the elements comprising the theory need to have *consistency* among themselves. Fifth, the explanation or theory needs to be broad in *scope* to have the greatest value (the more generalizable, the more valuable). And sixth, to what degree does the theory or explanation have *utility* or value in increasing our practical understanding? Explanation and prediction are the goals of theory and research. Interpersonal communication theory and research seek to explain what occurs within an interpersonal interaction and to allow us to predict what will occur in interpersonal interactions under a given set of defined circumstances. Underlying these goals rests the belief that there exist sets of common recurring patterns associated with human behavior that can be identified through observation, theory, and testing. The stronger the theory, the more it explains and predicts. Narrower investigations might provide only explanation or prediction of a specific interpersonal communication situation and thus have limited *scope*.

We know that people find other people attractive, and on the basis of this attraction form interpersonal relationships. We know that such attraction is based upon similarities, complementarity of needs, and so on. We can explain fairly well the process of attraction, yet we cannot predict if any two given people will necessarily form a relationship. (There are, however, computerized dating services based upon the claim that such predictions can be made.) On the other hand, when two strangers (in U.S. culture) approach each other from opposite directions on a sidewalk, invariably they will look down or away from one another when they get within six to eight feet of each other. We can predict this behavior the majority of the time (it is not absolute), but we do not know why it happens; we lack sufficient explanation.

Qualitative and Quantitative Methods

Two significant approaches to the proof by observation and testing are the *qualitative* and *quantitative* approaches. The qualitative approach tends to depend much more on description and the collection of information through direct observation sometimes recorded in field notes. The quantitative approach is empirically based, depending on the collection of some numerical data that are statistically analyzed.

Smith's Six Criteria for Theoretical Legitimacy

VALIDITY
PREDICTABILITY
PRECISION
CONSISTENCY
SCOPE
UTILITY

Qualitative approaches depend more on the data driving the nature of the conclusions and insights made by the researchers. Suppose we want to study romance in the workplace. A qualitative study might proceed through the following steps: The researcher would spend six months or a year in an organization making observations about the interactions, collecting communication artifacts (memos, newsletters), using surveys, and/or conducting interviews with various members of the organization. The researcher then would examine the data for episodes or themes. Finally, the qualitatively based research report would present arguments and evidence in support of the conclusions drawn from the data, often incorporating models or metaphors. Another qualitative approach involves transcribing interactions and doing a content or thematic analysis. In interpersonal communication research this transactional analysis sometimes is applied to naturalistic conversations and includes not only the coding of the content but also the coding of interruptions, pauses, changes in intonation, laughs, and so forth. A recent study by Cissna, Cox, and Bochner (1990) utilized interviews with husbands and wives from nine stepfamilies, each of which had at least two children. Husbands and wives individually responded to questions concerning their relationships to the previous spouses, relationships with the children, and advice on organizing a stepfamily. Conjointly, each couple discussed problems in reorganizing the family, tactics for overcoming the problems, and assessment of their successes. Transcriptions of the interviews were analyzed for common themes. The overriding theme that emerged dealt with the tension between the marital and parental relationship. The authors use examples from the interviews to support several other themes that were discussed, such as efforts to establish marital solidarity as well as stepparent authority.

The qualitative approach provides a great deal of data to be examined, but the manner of examination is not as well defined as in the quantitative approach. The qualitative approach has a narrow scope providing much detail about a specific interaction or situation. The results of a qualitative study are limited in their generalizability (how applicable or true the conclusions would be to different situations or individuals). In the article discussed above, only nine stepfamilies were interviewed. How representative are those nine stepfamilies of stepfamilies in general? The qualitative researcher must convince others that the data were objectively collected and analyzed, that the analysis is an appropriate and accurate one, and that the categories, themes or metaphors used are sufficient and well defined.

The majority of interpersonal communication research is quantitative in nature. The remainder of this chapter is devoted to reviewing approaches generally associated with the quantitative approach. Underlying the quantitative approach is the collection of numerical or empirical assessments of variables and a subsequent statistical analysis. Quantitative studies range from unobtrusive assessments of naturalistic phenomena to controlled laboratory experiments.

A significant challenge raised against quantitative studies concerns the validity with which concepts are assessed or operationalized. For instance, I can define empathy as an emotional response by an individual that is the same as another person's emotional response in a given situation, but how do I measure that? I might operationalize or assess empathy as two individuals having the same changes in the physiological measures of heart rate, respiration, and galvanic skin response. But is that really assessing empathy? Is it a valid measure of that concept? Do we know that emotions necessarily present themselves according to those three physiological indices? Additional problems associated with quantitative studies include controlling extraneous factors that might influence the results and the adequacy and appropriateness of the statistics.

TOWARD RESEARCH

While the ultimate goal of research is to provide explanation and prediction, the first step usually involves description. Describing something is not easy. Try to describe interpersonal communication. What should be included? Do you include only that which is observable? What about that which occurs within the interactants themselves (their thoughts and feelings)? How do you observe or determine those thoughts or feelings? Several definitions/descriptions of interpersonal communication were presented earlier, each based on different arguments forwarded by its advocates. As a reader you judge the merit of the arguments against some criteria, such as those mentioned above, and decide whether a given definition is adequate and acceptable. Descriptions provide the boundaries of a given phenomenon that allow individuals to have a shared understanding of what is being discussed. Descriptions provide us with an understanding of what is included in a given phenomenon and what is not.

Theory building and the development of research begin with defining or describing some phenomenon or occurrence. In interpersonal communication those phenomena can be qualities associated with the interactants, the interactions themselves, or the contexts or cultures in which the interactions occur. *Variables* are phenomena that have different values, properties that are present in varying degrees, or anything with more than one category. Thus such things as sex (male or female), race, height, degree of extroversion, speech fluency, and friendliness are all variables. At the most basic level, research is focused on understanding why things vary; thus there is an attempt to define one or more other variables that affect the first. These cause-and-effect variables are referred to as *independent variables* and *dependent variables*. The independent variable is the one a researcher would manipulate while observing the effect upon the dependent variable. In the statement "Women are more empathic than men," sex is the independent variable and empathy is the dependent variable. Another way of considering the relationship between two variables is to say that by knowing one variable (a person's sex) we can predict another variable (level of empathy). Determining relationships between and among variables leads to fulfilling the goal of research to provide predictability. The in-

dependent variable, the relationship, and the dependent variable make up a *hypothesis* or *research question*.

A hypothesis is a statement of an expected relationship between two or more variables. A research question asks either whether a relationship exists or what the relationship might be between two or more variables. Research reports generally begin with a review of relevant theory and research, building a case for the legitimacy of a particular hypothesis or research question. For the hypothesis there must be sufficient preexisting evidence that a certain relationship should be expected. A research question is posed when there is a lack of clear evidence to indicate the expected nature of the relationship among the variables. In reading research reports you should consider whether a strong enough case (theory) has been established to warrant the proposed hypothesis. Hypotheses are tested to determine the validity of the proposed relationship between the variables. Ideally, the result of investigating a research question would be the development of a testable hypothesis.

Research Validity

The testing of a hypothesis or answering of a research question requires designing a research procedure. Research design involves creating a plan for manipulating the independent variable and assessing the impact on the dependent variable while controlling for the effects of the intervening or extraneous variable. Ultimately the research design needs to provide valid evidence if the hypothesis is to be accepted or the research question answered. Valid means that the researchers really did find what they claim they found. To prove validity a researcher must be able to convince readers that it is highly unlikely any other explanation is probable for the effects on a dependent variable than those created by manipulating the independent variable. There are a number of factors that can undermine the validity of a study (Campbell & Stanley, 1963). To explain these, let us assume we want to prove that taking an introductory interpersonal communication course (independent variable) will improve a student's relational satisfaction (dependent variable measured with some instrument we create). One hundred students enroll in four sections of an interpersonal communication course and are given our relational satisfaction questionnaire. Several weeks after completing the course they complete the questionnaire a second time. Lo and behold, their satisfaction scores are significantly higher after the course. Now, what else might explain the finding besides their having taken the course?

1. The effects of *history* or events occurring during the semester might have affected the scores. For instance, a popular new movie such as *When Harry Met Sally* might have been released during the semester, and the film contained information on establishing relationships that a majority of the class happened to see. Exposure to the film rather than to the course might have heightened the students' sensitivity in relationships and thus created the effect on the dependent variable.

2. *Maturation* is the normal effects that occur within participants with the passage of time—getting hungry, tired, older. In our example, six months might have passed from the first to the second administration of the questionnaire. That's a lot of time during a traditional college student's life, so a certain amount of relational maturity might be

expected to have occurred. If our class sample had many freshmen or sophomores the amount of relational maturation might be even more significant. This produces an effect called *selection-maturation interaction* (Campbell & Stanley, 1963), in which the participants were particularly susceptible to a type of maturation effect.

3. The taking of a test might have an impact on taking the test a second time. Usually students score higher the second time they take certain tests, such as the SAT, ACT, or GRE, not because they have become smarter but because of the effect of *test–retest*. The first test might also increase the respondent's sensitivity to the concepts incorporated in the instrument. Having filled out a questionnaire asking about relational satisfaction, students might become more aware of their relational behaviors in the next six months and therefore their responses in filling out the questionnaire the second time will be biased by this heightened sensitivity.

4. If enrollment in the course was voluntary, then the students taking the course probably have an interest in interpersonal communication. That interest might result in greater self-motivation and improvement than in a more random sample of participants. Resulting increases in scores might not be because of the course, but because of this *selection bias*.

5. During the term students who were not doing very well in the course might have dropped the class. The students who remained and thus completed the follow-up questionnaire might be students who were more motivated to learn and apply the information. This *participant mortality* of the less relationally oriented participants can thus create a biased data set.

The next three variables that can undermine the validity of a research study are caused by variations in research design that are not related to the relational satisfaction example we have been discussing.

6. Sometimes data are generated by using observers or raters to categorize or evaluate some phenomenon. For instance, we might have had observers trained to watch the students in our interpersonal communication course interact and to

---

Sources of Invalidity

1. HISTORY
2. MATURATION
3. TEST–RETEST
4. SELECTION BIAS
5. PARTICIPANT MORTALITY
6. OBSERVER BIAS
7. STATISTICAL REGRESSION
8. ENVIRONMENTAL EFFECTS
9. MULTIPLE TREATMENT INTERACTION

(Adopted from Campbell & Stanley, 1963).

provide an evaluation on some criteria of the students' interpersonal communication effectiveness. *Observer bias* might exist in an observer's categorization of the data. (Have you ever felt an instructor did not give you a fair grade on an essay exam?) The ratings between observers might not be consistent, and changes in observers from one testing period to the second might also create invalid data.

7.   Some studies divide participants into bipolar extremes on the basis of some quality and then compare effects on these two groups. We might take individuals who scored high on relational satisfaction during the beginning of the semester and compare them to students with low scores. There is a statistical effect called *statistical regression* in which the highest scores generally decrease on the second testing and the lowest scores increase as both groups regress to the overall average or mean. This effect would make it look as if those who were not satisfied improved and those who were satisfied got worse.

8.   A major problem in conducting research is creating a naturalistic situation. Any time research participants are placed in a laboratory setting there is a danger that the laboratory setting will cause the participants to act in an artificial manner. Some researchers use microphones and videocameras in a room with the participants and still expect the participants to act normal. Knowing your interaction with another is being recorded probably will affect your behavior. How detrimental are these *environmental effects?* To what degree might these environmental effects account for changes in the dependent variables? As you read the studies included in this text consider the impact the research context might have on the study and see if you can think of alternative ways the data might have been collected.

9.   The final factor that might affect changes in the dependent variables is called the *multiple treatment interaction*. This is an effect caused by the interaction of a prior treatment upon a second or third different type of treatment. This factor is a strong concern in the physical sciences and is why, when new medications are prescribed, your physician or pharmacist needs to know what other

medications you might be taking. The interaction effect of two different medications can be fatal. In communication research this can be a problem when more than one independent variable is being manipulated or examined, though there are statistical means to determine these interaction effects.

Researchers do not actually have to manipulate the independent variable to assess its impact on the dependent variable. Researchers can compare two samples of people in which the independent variable has been present in one and absent in the other or varied to some significant degree. For instance, collecting data from 40-year-old individuals about their educational backgrounds (as the independent variable) and mean incomes (dependent variable) results in the observation that those with more education also have higher incomes. In this example, the researcher does not have to force some people to go to school and prohibit others from attending school in order to manipulate the independent variable.

Research Design

As a general rule, the validity of a claim that a given independent variable is responsible for a change in a dependent variable is undermined whenever there are other variables that potentially could be causing the change. If the same instructor were used in the four sections of the interpersonal communication course, then how much of the impact of the change in students is due to the course content, the instructor, the assignments, or the text? As long as all four of those variables are the same in each class, then it could be argued that any of those variables might be responsible for the observed change. If the desire is to prove that the content of the course produces the change, then sections need to be taught by different instructors covering the same content but with different texts, assignments, and so forth. Any changes in relational satisfaction that occurred consistently across sections could then be attributed to the course content, and the effects of other factors could be examined. To conduct this study successfully probably would require many sections of the course and many instructors; but such variations are not always possible, and researchers therefore must use designs with recognized limitations. Using several instructors is an example of creating a research design that controls some competing variables.

There are a number of possible research designs that can be used. Each design has certain strengths and weaknesses in assuring validity. The choice of research design is often dictated by the nature of the research question and the resources available. One of the strongest designs that allows for determining the effect of many of the above invalidating factors is called the *Solomon Four-Group Design*. In this design participants are randomly assigned to one of four conditions. *Randomness* is a critical factor to most research studies because of both the manner in which it controls other variables and the principles on which many statistics are based. By randomly assigning participants in any study, any nuances associated with any of the participants will be distributed by chance and generally will be fairly equally distributed among the groups. For instance, if in a group of 100 we had 40 seniors, by randomly dividing them into four groups each group should have about the same number (while not assuring exactly the same number in each, any random difference is unlikely to be statistically significant). We could intentionally assign 10 seniors to each group, a step taken when we know a given variable might have an effect. However, rather than try to identify, assess, and divide among a host of confounding variables, we can simply randomly divide the effect of those variables into all the groups.

After dividing the participants into four groups, two groups (A and B) complete a measure of the dependent variable. In our example, groups A and B would fill out our relational satisfaction questionnaire. Two groups (C and D) do not fill out the questionnaire. One of the groups that filled out the questionnaire (A), and one of the groups that did not (C), are manipulated according to the independent variable. We would have students in groups A and C take the course in interpersonal

communication. After the course, groups A and B complete the relational satisfaction questionnaire again, and at this time groups C and D also fill out the questionnaire. If taking the course is responsible for the change, what should we find? The scores for A should increase significantly from the first testing while those for B should not. In addition, group C should have significantly better scores than D. Group A and B both might show increases from their first scores, but if group A increased significantly more than B, then we could still claim a positive effect from taking the course. If all four groups produced about the same scores in the final ratings, then some other factor besides taking the interpersonal course is responsible for the improvement in relational satisfaction. The results of group A compared to C, and B compared to D should not be significantly different unless the first testing biased the second testing.

Some of the same factors controlled for in the Solomon Four-Group Design can be controlled or accounted for by using the simpler *Post-test-only Control Group Design*. In this design only groups C and D from the previous design are used. This eliminates any pretest bias effect and allows for an accounting of other effects between the two groups since both are tested at the end of the research. The control group D provides a baseline for comparison with the treatment group, and the difference between the two is regarded as the amount of change that occurs in a group from before and after the independent variable is manipulated.

Many research questions do not easily lend themselves to an experimental design like the two above. If the researcher is still interested in a statistical proof of a given hypothesis, then some other designs can be utilized. These other designs are not as powerful as the two already presented. Most prevalent among these pre-experimental or quasi-experimental designs are those that involve comparing two or more groups on the basis of their possession of two or more variables. Typically, these are questionnaires or surveys that use either paper and pencil response scales or interviewing to collect data. Generally data are collected on an independent variable and a dependent variable. For our study on the interpersonal course we could survey 500 graduating seniors, dividing them into two groups, those who had taken a course in interpersonal communication and those who had not. We also would have them respond to our relational satisfaction scale. We could then examine the means (averages) of the two groups to see if there is a statistical difference. If we find a difference, we would argue that this supports our claim of the impact of the interpersonal communication course. You should be able to recognize that this method does not control for several of the confounding variables. For one thing, the respondents were not randomly assigned into two groups: those who had taken the course and those who had not. It could be argued that those who had the greatest interest in interpersonal relations (a personality trait) were more likely to take the course, and that it was this interest that led to greater relational satisfaction, not the course.

Among the variations of this questionnaire method is a method that involves assessing a given population on some quality (independent variable), creating two comparison groups by selecting those who scored the highest and lowest, and then comparing their scores on some other dependent variables. We might create two groups of students, those with the strongest relational satisfaction and those with the weakest, and then compare the two groups on a variety of other qualities, such as types of courses they took, major, grade-point average, degree of extroversion, or size of hometown. Remember, any such comparison should be driven by some theoretical expectation of a relationship. Thus, for example, we would have to provide some theoretical explanation or evidence as to why we might expect that the size of an individual's hometown would affect his or her relational satisfaction.

A STATISTICAL PRIMER

This section is meant to provide you with an introduction to some of the most common types of sta-

tistics incorporated in quantitative research. The following discussion is meant only to familiarize you with what the statistics are meant to test since these statistical procedures are mentioned in several of the articles in this text. You should be better equipped after reading this section to understand the research articles.

Statistics Covered in this Section
ANALYSIS OF VARIANCE (ANOVA)
F-TEST
T-TEST
CORRELATION
FACTOR ANALYSIS
REGRESSION ANALYSIS

Comparing and Contrasting Groups

Assume we have administered a questionnaire with the following statement and corresponding choices for responses to 100 students from Alpha University (A), 100 students from Beta University (B), and 100 students from Gamma University (G).

STATEMENT: "I am very satisfied with the quality of my interpersonal relationships."

Respondents indicated how much they agreed or disagreed with the above statement using the following seven possible choices:

	Alpha U.	Beta U.	Gamma U.
1. Strongly disagree	10	0	5
2. Disagree	25	0	10
3. Somewhat disagree	30	10	15
4. Somewhat disagree and somewhat agree	25	25	10
5. Somewhat agree	10	30	5
6. Agree	0	25	20
7. Strongly agree	0	10	35

The number of students from each university responding to the response choices is presented in the columns. We will skip the discussion of the limitations that exist in having a one-item scale and the question of whether this scale validly assesses relational satisfaction (establishing validity of a scale goes beyond the discussion to be presented in this text). In our questionnaire we also collected the following information from the students, with the distribution being the same from all three universities: sex (50 males and 50 females) and year in school (25 freshmen, 25 sophomores, 25 juniors, and 25 seniors).

We now have 300 numbers indicating relational satisfaction. What do the numbers tell us? The numbers in the table need to be simplified or translated into a more digestible and comprehensible form—that is what statistics do. However, every statistical calculation causes us to lose information. For instance, the average or mean for students is 3.0 for Alpha U., 5.0 for Beta U., and 5.0 for Gamma U. We now have translated the 100 responses from each college to a single number. But that tends to be an oversimplification because only 30 of the respondents from A.U. actually indicated a response of 3.0, which means the average is not really the response of 70 students. Therefore we need to look at another significant statistic called *variation*. Variation is essentially how many and how far away the responses are from the mean. A large amount of variation essentially indicates that the mean is not a very reliable indication of the general trend of responses. A small amount of variation indicates that the mean is fairly representative of the scores of the respondents. In our example, 80% of the responses for A.U. and B.U. are within one point, plus or minus, of the mean; however, for G.U., only 35% are within one point. Any assumptions based upon the means from G.U. will be much more suspect—less reliable—than those from A.U. or B.U.

One of the fundamental research questions posed when data are from different samples is whether or not the samples are significantly different. Comparing groups allows for testing of a hypothesized effect of a given variable by exposing one group to the variable while not exposing the other. In this situation a statistical procedure is needed to test for differences between two or more groups. Figure 2.1 is a graphic representation of data from the three universities. From just eyeing the graph would you feel that the students from the three universities are significantly different in their relational satisfaction?

Analysis of variance (Anova) is a statistical method that allows a number of groups to be compared on a given variable. Analysis of variance produces a statistic called an **F-test.** The F value can be examined for the level of significance depending on the number of groups or variables examined. The significance level or confidence level is the likelihood that the statistic generated (F value in this example) would occur purely by chance. A significance level of .05 means that five times out of a hundred the statistic would occur by chance. The smaller the significance number the greater degree of confidence you can have that something has influenced the results other than chance. Thus a level of significance less than .01 means that less than one time out of a hundred would the number occur by accident. In our example of the three universities the F value was 80.00 with a significance level of less than .001; which means that in less than one time in one thousand would you find an F value of 80.00 by chance for the number of variables and groups we had.

So now we know that there is a difference among the three group means, but is there a difference between each pair of universities? A **T-test** is a statistical procedure for determining whether the means of two groups are significantly different. The following are the t values and significance levels associated in the paired comparisons of the three samples:

Alpha-Beta	t = 12.34	significance <.001
Alpha-Gamma	t = 8.64	significance <.001
Beta-Gamma	t = 0.00	significance = 1.00

In our example then, the responses from students at Alpha U. on relational satisfaction were significantly different from students at Beta U. and Gamma U., but the students at Beta U. and Gamma U. were not significantly different. Alpha U. stu-

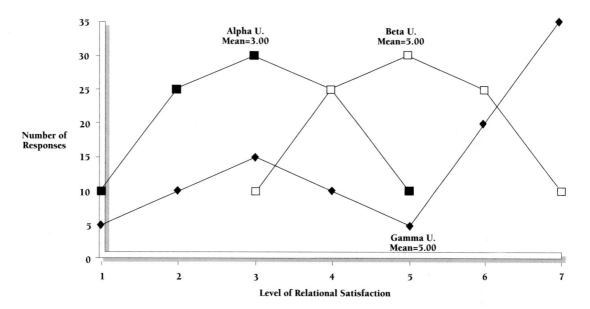

FIGURE 2.1

Distribution of Responses to Level of Relational Satisfaction

Distribution of Resources to
Level of Relational Satisfaction

dents in our sample reported significantly less relational satisfaction than those at the other two universities.

Now comes the tricky part—interpreting the results. If you knew that B.U. and G.U. had a required course in interpersonal communication for all of their students, and A.U. did not, you might be inclined to attribute the difference in responses to that course experience. But such an assumption would need further support because a sample of three universities is not large enough to generalize to other universities. With such a small sample there is a strong possibility that there are other variables affecting the three universities that explain the difference. For instance, maybe A.U. emphasizes engineering and hard sciences and the other two are more liberal arts oriented. Maybe there is a greater ratio of men to women at Alpha compared to the ratios at Beta and Gamma. Claims of differences using the T-test are strongest in those situations where the researcher has manipulated some independent variable applied to two or more groups and then measured the outcome dependent variable.

Research sometimes involves several dependent variables and several independent variables. Having more than one independent variable requires the use of a different type of analysis of variance called **Multiple Analysis of Variance** (Manova). Manova allows for various combinations and interaction effects of the independent variables to be examined for their effect on the dependent variables.

Correlational Analyses

The second major type of statistical analysis involves the degree to which two variables change at the same time, that is, the degree to which they correlate. When one variable changes each time another variable changes and the amount of change in both is proportionally the same, then you have a perfect correlation represented as $r = 1.0$. The correlation coefficient can be positive or negative ranging from 0.00 to 1.00, for example $r = .70$, $r = .50$, $r = .20$, or $r = -.45$. The size of the coefficient might be a bit misleading. One way to appreciate the strength of the correlation is to square the coefficient, giving you the amount of common variance accounted for by the correlation. Thus a correlation of .7 gives us an $r^2 = .49$, meaning that the 49% of the variance in one variable relates to the other variable; subsequently, 51% of the variance is unaccounted for by the other variable. A correlation of .5 gives us $r^2 = .25$ (25% accounted for), and a correlation of .2 produces an $r^2 = .04$ (4% accounted for). The degree of significance is also presented with a correlation, to indicate the degree of confidence that the correlation is not by chance. The degree of significance is not simply based on the size of the correlation coefficient. If the correlations are based on a large number of respondents, then it is possible to have small but significant correlation coefficients. Correlations can be calculated on any two variables, whether independent or dependent, with the correct type of data. One major caution in reading a study that reports correlations is that correlations are not proof of a cause-and-effect relationship. Correlations simply indicate that two variables change at that same time. Both variables could be caused by some other variable that has been overlooked.

An Example In our earlier example on relational satisfaction, we also might have asked respondents to indicate the number of fights or conflicts occurring in a given relationship during a typical week. Suppose we found a strong correlation between relational satisfaction and conflicts, such as $r = -.60$. (This is a negative correlation meaning that when there were more fights there was less likelihood of respondents indicating relational satisfaction.) Does this mean that having fights reduces

relational satisfaction? The answer might be intuitively affirmative, but no answer can be drawn from the correlation. What if we also had measured interpersonal communication competence and found it correlated with relational satisfaction ($r = .80$) and with frequency of conflicts ($r = -.80$). What evolves is the possibility that this third variable, competence, leads to the ability to manage relationships more effectively, thus increasing satisfaction and decreasing conflicts.

The type of analysis represented by correlations is the basis for more complicated statistical procedures, such as partial correlations, multiple correlations, factor analysis, and regression analysis. The last two tend to be the most commonly used of these statistical procedures. A typical *factor analysis* might involve taking a number of items on a given instrument and determining which of those items most closely relate to one another, and then producing a small number of overriding "factors" composed of subsets of those items. For instance, assume we have a 20-item measure of relational satisfaction and we conduct a factor analysis. The factor analysis would create factors composed of those items that are most strongly intercorrelated. We might find that the measure fell into three factors, each with four or five items, with a few of the items not fitting into any factor. We then would look at the content of the items making up each factor and label it accordingly. This analysis might indicate that the concept of relational satisfaction was made up of three elements (the factors), for which we create the labels of dependency needs, emotional satisfaction, and communication.

Regression analysis is a statistical procedure which allows us to predict the value of a variable (Y) when we know the value of another variable (X). The mathematics involved incorporate correlations in developing the best fit of the two variables. (Best fit is the identification of how X needs to be manipulated to produce the most accurate prediction of Y.) The typical regression formula consists of the two variables, a factor by which X is multiplied, plus a constant (K): $Y = a(X) + K$. Let X be a number for the amount of conflicts ranging from 0 to 20 in the relationship and Y be the level of satisfaction with a range from 1 to 10 (10 being high satisfaction). Through regression analysis a formula could be generated that weights the relationships among the variables and might look like this: $Y = -\frac{1}{2}(X) + 10$. Thus someone with a conflict score of 10 (X) would have a predicted relational score of 5 ($Y = -\frac{1}{2}(10) + 10$). Someone with a conflict score of 20 would have a satisfaction score of 0. Regression analysis also provides a correlation coefficient and its square to indicate what portion of variance in Y can be predicted by X as well as a test of significance.

When there are a number of variables for which the scores are known, they can be combined through multiple regression to create a formula for predicting a greater portion of the variance in the dependent variable. We could apply multiple regression analysis in our example to create a formula by which we could predict relational satisfaction on the basis of conflict and communication competence. Regression analysis determines which variables are most important to a predictive equation and weights them accordingly.

CONCLUSION

A variety of other statistical methods exist, each with particular applications, depending upon the nature of the research design and data. The above review should provide you with enough working knowledge of the major statistics employed in the studies you will be reading in this text. As you read the articles you might find it valuable to return to this chapter to review relevant information. Do not become too preoccupied with making sense of the statistics if those statistics exceed your understanding. Instead, focus on the nature of the design. Try putting yourself in the study as a participant and consider the impact of the various measures and conditions as a way of coming to a clearer understanding of the given study. Above all, focus on the concepts and theories represented in the studies, since that is the reason for including the selected articles.

REFERENCES

Campbell, D. T., & Stanley, J. C. (1963). *Experimental and quasi-experimental designs for research.* Chicago: Rand McNally.

Cissna, K. N., Cox, D. E., & Bochner, A. P. (1990). The dialectic of marital and parental relationships within the stepfamily. *Communication Monographs, 57,* (44–61).

Smith, M. J. (1988). *Contemporary communication research methods.* Belmont, CA: Wadsworth.

SUGGESTED FURTHER READING

Anderson, J. A. (1987). *Communication research: Issues and methods.* New York: McGraw-Hill.

Babbie, E. (1986). *The practice of social research* (4th ed.) Belmont, CA: Wadsworth.

Emmert, P., & Barker, L. L. (1989). *Measurement of communication behavior.* White Plains, NY: Longman.

Kerlinger, F. N. (1979). *Behavioral research: A conceptual approach.* New York: Holt, Rinehart and Winston.

Rubin, R. B., Rubin, A. M., & Piele, L. J. (1993). *Communication research: Strategies and sources* (3rd ed.) Belmont, CA: Wadsworth.

Tucker, R. K., Weaver II, R. L., & Berryman-Fink, C. (1981). *Research in speech communication.* Englewood Cliffs, NJ: Prentice-Hall.

Williams, F. (1986). *Reasoning with statistics: How to read quantitative research* (3rd ed.). New York: Holt, Rinehart and Winston.

UNIT II

General Theoretical Approaches
to Interpersonal Communication

The four articles in this section represent a sampling of the theoretical perspectives discussed earlier. The articles incorporate social exchange theory, uncertainty reduction theory, pragmatics, relational development, and constructivism in their discussions of interpersonal communication. You will find a strong interrelatedness among the articles. The authors often use the same blocks to build their theories, but organize those blocks in different ways.

Article 3 by Taylor and Altman applies the notions of social exchange theory to understanding relational development through a process they call "social penetration theory." Taylor and Altman also present a review of research related to their theory. They claim that individuals evaluate relationships on the basis of costs and rewards and will penetrate the relationship further when the rewards or potential rewards are greater than the costs. They include a four-stage model of relational development. Fundamental to this development is the role that self-disclosure plays in moving the relationship to more intimate levels. In their original treatment of social penetration, Altman and Taylor focused on the breadth and depth of self-revelation as it related to relational development. Relationships can be typified by the breadth of knowledge two individuals have of one another as well as the depth of that knowledge. As relationships move toward intimacy the breadth is expanded while moving to deeper levels of disclosure. Such relational development is obviously dependent on interpersonal communication as the means by which information is disclosed.

Like Altman and Taylor, Knapp and Vangelisti are interested in identifying the stages or phases a relationship moves through as it moves toward intimacy. Article 4 is a fairly straightforward presentation of a theory of relational development. The model presented in this article is one of the extended models of relational development, with ten specific stages identified. The model consists of five stages of coming together and five stages of coming apart. Underlying such models of interpersonal development are two basic principles. First, the nature of the interpersonal communication is unique and predictable for each relational stage. Thus, a couple's interpersonal communication reflects the stage of the relationship. Second, interpersonal communication plays a significant role in moving the relationship from one stage to another.

You should be able to identify both similarities and differences between the ten-stage model presented by Knapp and Vangelisti and the four-stage model presented by Taylor and Altman. Like Taylor and Altman, Knapp and Vangelisti incorporate the social exchange approach in their discussion of what motivates movement from one stage to another. Further, they present several principles to explain movement among the various relational stages.

While Taylor and Altman advocate that disclosing information helps advance the intimacy of a relationship, Berger and Bradac in Article 5 focus on the drive by individuals to collect information about others. Gaining information about others is a way of reducing uncertainty and thus increasing an individual's ability to predict and control his or her environment. The more uncertain we are in a given situation the more difficult it is to achieve our goals, especially when we are talking about goals that involve an interpersonal relationship. Berger and Bradac posit that we have a drive to find out information about others so that we can better accomplish goals that are dependent upon others. If you want to form a socially satisfying relationship with others, you need to know how they behave and why they behave the way they do. You want to know what to expect from them in response to your own behavior. Berger and Bradac discuss situations that increase our drive to reduce uncertainty by gaining information and the strategies we employ to gain that information.

Uncertainty can exist both about the other person with whom one is interacting as well as about one's self. Berger and Bradac contend that the desire to reduce uncertainty about ourselves is also a factor in our interactions with others and with our environment. Two specific types of uncertainty identified in interactions are cognitive and behavioral uncertainty. Included in cognitive uncertainty is our knowledge of our own and the other's beliefs, attitudes, and so forth. Behavioral uncertainty concerns the ability or inability to predict our own or another person's behavior in a given situation.

Besides the strategic methods Berger and Bradac present, they also discuss various social cognitive processes, most notably attribution theory. Attribution theory is essentially the explanations we generate to explain another person's behavior. If your teacher in this class walks in and slams her or his books on the desk you probably would make some attribution about why she/he behaved that way. You might infer that the teacher is mad, that the teacher is in a typical bad mood, or that the teacher accidentally put the books down too hard.

The article covers three theories of attribution that have been developed to explain the process by which we make attributions. The authors also discuss the limitations of those theories.

In addition to attribution theory, Berger and Bradac discuss a number of theories related to mindlessness, scripted behavior, self-awareness, self-consciousness, and self-monitoring. All of these theories are examined from the standpoint of their relationship to and impact on uncertainty reduction. These concepts reflect factors that might either diminish or expand the likelihood of seeking to reduce uncertainty.

The final article in this section, Article 6, begins with an overview and critique of Altman and Taylor's social penetration theory as an approach to explaining relational development. In attempting to establish a framework on which to analyze competent relational management, Applegate and Leichty present a constructivist theory of communication. As noted earlier, interpersonal constructs represent cognitive templates that are developed over time through our interactions with others. This article reviews some of the principles underlying constructivism and then applies them to relational development. The constructs are related to the three goals generally attributed to interactions: instrumental (what you are attempting to accomplish), identity (confirmation of who you are), and relational (how you want the relationship to be). It is on this third goal that the authors focus the application of constructivism, as a better theoretical model than social penetration theory, to explain relational development. Little specific research has been done to test the application of constructivism to relational development, but the authors do review some studies that they claim support this approach. Having highly developed construct systems is said to increase an individual's strategic flexibility. Strategic flexibility, then, enhances the ability to meet a variety of interaction goals and to negotiate conflicts in relational expectations.

The four articles in Unit II are only a sampling of some of the theoretical approaches to interpersonal communication. Each has both merits and limitations. The ideal theory is probably one that incorporates qualities from each of these. You should be able to identify the effect of some of the theories reviewed earlier, such as social exchange theory, relational development, symbolic interactionism, and constructivism. As you read the articles, consider how they interrelate, look for similarities and differences, and apply them to explaining your own experiences to see whether the theory rings true.

QUESTIONS TO CONSIDER
FOR EACH ARTICLE:

ARTICLE 3
A. What is the role of interpersonal communication in social penetration theory?

B. What is the relationship among social exchange theory, self-disclosure, and intimacy?

ARTICLE 4
A. How well do your relationships fall within one of the stages identified in the model? What problems are there in identifying the appropriate stage in which to classify your relationship?
B. How mindful do you think people are of the movement among the stages? Why or why not?

ARTICLE 5
A. In what ways do attribution theories relate to strategies for knowledge acquisition?
B. Use your own experiences to identify specific instances that either support or contradict the case for uncertainty reduction theory.

ARTICLE 6
A. How do social penetration theory and constructivism differ in their explanations of relational development?
B. In what ways do constructs relate to an individual's interpersonal communication competence?

3

Communication in Interpersonal Relationships: Social Penetration Processes

DALMAS A. TAYLOR | IRWIN ALTMAN

Communication is critical in developing and maintaining interpersonal relationships. Several studies point to strong association between good communication and the general satisfaction of relationships (Markman, 1981; Murphy & Mendelson, 1973; Navran, 1967). In a longitudinal study of couples prior to and during marriage, Markman (1981) found that couples who had positive communication prior to the marriage were more likely to have happier marriages after five years than couples who had not established positive communication prior to marriage. Good communication or "openness" has also been associated with positive mental health (Jourard, 1964) and liking (Jourard & Landsman, 1960; Jourard & Lasakow, 1958). These studies suggest that making the self accessible to others through self-disclosure is intrinsically gratifying. Gratification, in turn, leads to the development of positive feelings for the other person. Research on married couples by Levinger and Senn (1967) also reveals a positive correlation between marital satisfaction and self-disclosure. In a more recent study of marital satisfaction, McAdams and Vaillant (1982) reanalyzed longitudinal data collected in the 1950s and 1960s on male Harvard graduates. Intimacy motivation (derived from TAT stories) correlated highly with marital happiness. Men high in intimacy motivation in early life were more likely to report happiness and stability in their marriages at midlife than men who were low in intimacy mo-

tivation. Thus communication and disclosure intimacy appear to be the sine qua non of developing satisfying interpersonal relationships. In their theory of social penetration, Altman and Taylor (1973) explicate the role of self-disclosure, intimacy, and communication in the development of interpersonal relationships. Further, their theory describes the role of these variables in the dissolution of relationships—depenetration. In this chapter, we will review the status of social penetration theory using as a backdrop the empirical literature that has emerged since its publication.

More than a decade of research has dealt with issues or topics initially raised in social penetration theory. Many of these studies are somewhat peripheral to the theory, but nonetheless examine concepts that are critical to a further understanding of communication and developing relationships. Some of this literature includes studies testing hypotheses derived from social penetration. The objective of this chapter is to review this research literature as a basis for providing commentary on some of the ideas and concepts that we began to formulate approximately 20 years ago.

The approach employed here is similar to a propositional inventory in that we have organized our discussion around major aspects of the theory, and secondarily around subordinate issues as they relate to the research literature. This approach not only allows us to determine aspects of social

From Roloff, M. E., & Miller, G. R. (Eds.) (1987), *Interpersonal processes: New directions in communication research* (pp. 257–277). Beverly Hills, CA.: Sage.

penetration theory that have been confirmed empirically, but also to ascertain features of the theory that have not been confirmed, as well as those which have been ignored by researchers.

To generate articles for this review, a bibliography consisting of all journal publications that cited "social penetration theory" between the years 1973-1985 was compiled. The *Social Science Citation Index* yielded 193 items. A less useful secondary source was a computer search based on key words from the theory. The chief difficulty with this approach was the inability to key on the term "social penetration." Nonetheless, we generated another 150 articles, many of which had already been identified through the *Social Science Citation Index*. The resulting bibliography contained only studies that reported empirical data—we eliminated theoretical articles and those attempting to develop or validate instruments. Only studies reported in the English language were used, and we omitted books, chapters, technical reports, and dissertation abstracts. Approximately 100, or one-third of the articles identified by this procedure, are included in this review.

The article abstracts included a detailed casting of the hypotheses, both conceptual and operational. A description of the research participant population (sex, age, size, etc.), methods and procedures, and the statistical analyses employed was also included. Finally, results and conclusions were extracted and evaluated. Key words from each article were used to form topical categories reflecting the major variables and categories in social penetration theory. As might be expected, many studies fit into more than one category.

SOCIAL PENETRATION THEORY
Development and Dissolution

Social penetration theory focuses on relationship development. It deals primarily with overt interpersonal behaviors occurring in social interaction and the internal cognitive processes that precede, accompany, and follow relationship formation. The theory is developmental in that it is concerned with the growth (and dissolution) of interpersonal relationships. Social penetration processes proceed in a gradual and orderly fashion from superficial to intimate levels of exchange as a function of both immediate and forecast outcomes. Forecasts involve estimates of potential outcomes in areas of more intimate exchange. This factor causes relationships to move forward in the hope of finding new and potentially more satisfying interactions. For example, people generally move only gradually from discussions of work situations to those concerning their fears, or from comparable superficial issues to details of their sexual problems.

The earliest stage (*orientation*) of interaction is postulated to occur at the periphery of personality in "public" areas. During these initial encounters, individuals make only a small part of themselves accessible to others. At this stage there is very little evaluation; instead, individuals make concerted efforts at conflict avoidance. The overall tone is cautious and tentative, as each party to the relationship scans one another in accordance with socially conventional formulas.

The next stage (*exploratory affective exchange*) represents an expansion of richness of communication in public-outer areas; aspects of personality that were guarded earlier are now revealed in more detail, and less emphasis is placed on caution. Relationships at this stage are generally more friendly and relaxed, and movement toward intermediate areas of intimacy is begun.

Close friendships and romantic relationships characterize the next stage (*affective exchange*) of social interaction. Here, interactive engagements are more freewheeling and casual. Interaction at outer layers of personality is open, and there is heightened activity at intermediate layers of personality. Although some cautions are employed here, generally there is little resistance to open explorations of intimacy. The importance of this stage is that barriers are being broken down and dyad members are learning a great deal about each other. This stage is transitional to the highest level of intimacy exchange possible.

A final stage (*stable exchange*) of development in growing relationships is characterized by continuous openness, as well as richness across all layers of personality. Both public and private communication become efficient—dyad members know one another well and can reliably interpret and predict the feelings and probable behavior of the other. In addition to verbal levels, there is a good deal of nonverbal exchange and environmentally oriented behavior.

The dynamics of the theory include verbal, nonverbal, and environmentally oriented behaviors, each of which has substantive and affective or emotional components. Verbal exchanges include self-disclosure and other communication processes; nonverbal behaviors involve body postures and gestures, smiling, touching, and eye gaze. Environmentally oriented behaviors include use of personal space and physical objects, as well as interpersonal distance, as ways of managing social relationships. The more a relationship approaches friendship and love, the greater the probability that intimate distances will be experienced. Close relationships should permit easier transitions between physical distance, in much the same way that movement to and from intimate and superficial areas on a verbal continuum is easier once barriers have been crossed. Facial expressions and other bodily postures will also have different manifestations in close relationships than in superficial ones. In close relationships, dyad members are more willing to allow each other to use, have access to, or know about very private intimacies and belongings.

Conflict is viewed as an essential part of development. Relationship growth occurs during periods of compatibility, and relationship deterioration occurs in response to crises and other stresses. These conflict processes are hypothesized to operate in accordance with the same factors (reward/cost, personal, and situational) involved in development. However, once set in motion, the exchange processes that occur in the dissolution of an interpersonal relationship are the reverse of those occurring in developmental phases. They are systematic and proceed gradually, this time from inner (intimate) to outer (nonintimate) levels of exchange. In one sense depenetration is a failure of conflict management.

Few studies have directly examined the development process in social penetration. Altman, Vinsel, and Brown (1981) note that the studies done to test the theory "have consistently demonstrated that the growth of relationships follows the hypothesized course of development from peripheral, superficial aspects of personality to more intimate ones. The disclosure of superficial information usually takes place rapidly during the early stages of a relationship whereas exposure of intimate aspects of the self occurs only gradually and at later stages of a relationship" (p. 110).

A good deal of the evidence for this contention is based on inferences from studies that address only the results of relationships, not their development (e.g., Berg, 1983, 1984; Chaiken & Derlega, 1974; McAllister & Bregman, 1983; Morton, 1978; Sabatelli, Buck, & Dreyer, 1982, 1983). For example, two separate studies, one of dating couples (Berg, 1983) and another of college roommates (Berg, 1984), confirmed predictions about the final outcomes of relationships using data that were collected at the initiation of the relationships (early) and again after the passage of several months (later). Using discriminant analysis, Berg found that the late measures were no better predictors of final outcome than were the early measures. He concluded that people make decisions about the nature of their relationships early, and there is insignificant change over time. At both time points persons who were satisfied with their relationships reported a greater number of social exchanges—more communication about the relationship, more problem-solving behaviors, more self-disclosure, and greater satisfaction with the relationship than expected. Aries and Johnson (1983) and Chaiken and Derlega (1974) infer relationship growth or development from distinctions made between casual acquaintances and close (intimate) friends. Similarly, Baxter and Wilmot (1983) extracted information on growth and development from 116 diaries kept by one member of each relationship over a two-week period.

In contrast to the above studies and interpretations, however, there is modest support for a gradual development in relationship building from studies conducted in the context of mate selection (e.g., Kerckhoff & Davis, 1962; Murstein, 1970). This research preceded the publication of social penetration theory, but is quite compatible with its tenets. Potential partners pass through a series of successive stages (called filters) in which initially external characteristics are important, then value consensus, and finally role matching. Although the evidence for this approach has been deemed weak (Rubin & Levinger, 1974), other studies offer stronger support of a gradual development of friendships and romantic relationships (Braiker & Kelley, 1979; Davis, 1976; Hays, 1984, 1985; Levinger & Snoek, 1972).

In a 13-week longitudinal study of college roommates, Taylor (1968) investigated shifts in self-disclosure of intimate and nonintimate behaviors. His findings confirmed several hypotheses derived from social penetration theory: progressive development in exchanges over time, with less rapid development in intimate behaviors than nonintimate ones, and a general slowing down of the process at later time periods. No one has actually studied development directly since Taylor's (1968) study. A laboratory analogue of self-disclosure development (Davis, 1976) and two longitudinal studies on friendship formation by Hays (1984, 1985) constitute partial exceptions to this assertion.

Davis (1976) tested the social penetration hypothesis that there is a monotonic increase over time of the breadth and depth of self-disclosure. However, a more specific interest was to determine whether this monotonic function would apply to the minute-by-minute transaction in a brief encounter. Three general findings confirmed social penetration theory:

1. The intimacy of topics disclosed increased linearly as encounters progressed, without appearing to reach an asymptote. This outcome was interpreted as supporting the temporal features of social penetration theory applicable within a brief encounter just as much as between the encounters of a developing relationship.
2. Partners matched the average intimacy levels of their disclosures and their rates of increase of intimacy, an outcome supportive of the "dyadic effect."
3. The dyadic effect was not due to mutual reciprocity but rather to a role differentiation in which the more disclosing member of the dyad took the lead and the less disclosing one tended to take his or her cue accordingly.

In two separate studies, Hays (1984, 1985) asked new students to select two same-sex others whom they had not known before but with whom they thought they might become good friends during the school year. On three subsequent occasions, at three-week intervals, respondents were asked to report the amount of casual and intimate exchange they had with the target students. The exchanges dealt with communication, companionship, affection, and consideration. Overall behavioral exchange (intimate and nonintimate) increased over time among pairs rated as "close" at the end of the semester but not among those who were rated as "not-close."

For the most part, the studies reviewed above simply address the issue of relationship development by comparing brief samples of people's behavior in long-term versus short-term relationships (e.g., Berg, 1983, 1984), by making inferences based on casual acquaintances compared with intimates (e.g., Chaiken & Derlega, 1974), or by examining verbal and nonverbal communication between short-term and long-term cohabiting couples (Sabatelli et al., 1982). Longitudinal studies of development (e.g., Hays, 1984, 1985), as prescribed by Altman and Taylor (1973), are rare. This has been a neglected approach for the study of relationships by social psychologists and other students of relationships.

The issue of dissolution (depenetration) has received far less attention than has development. Our review uncovered only one study in the literature that attempted to assess the dynamics of relationship dissolution. Tolstedt and Stokes (1984) hypothesized that in depenetration, as intimacy decreased, self-disclosure breadth and depth would decline and the valence of self-disclosure would become more negative, particularly at low levels of intimacy. The correlational results confirmed the reversal hypothesis of social penetration theory for breadth and valence of self-disclosure: As intimacy decreased, so did breadth; similarly, as intimacy decreased, valence became more negative. Contrary to the depenetration hypothesis, however, depth of self-disclosure tended to increase as intimacy decreased for both descriptive and evaluative depth. The latter finding may be due in part to experimental demands and the respondent population.

Tolstedt and Stokes's respondents were facing crisis points in their relationships and were asked to discuss these relationships. In these cases, increased depth was also associated with negative valence. Therefore, the increased depth may be temporary; and as depenetration continues, decreased depth may accompany decreased intimacy. On the other hand, the social penetration prediction for depth may be incorrect. The pain and anger that accompany the loss of an intimate relationship may engender self-disclosures of considerable depth. Such couples, already at such low intimacy levels, could feel that they have less to lose and that communication of negative thoughts and feelings may lead to an improvement in their relationship. Due to the procedural limitations of this study, however, these interpretations must be viewed with some skepticism.

Unfortunately, there are no other studies on depenetration that could provide a basis for evaluating the above conjectures. As noted earlier, a number of studies have confirmed the value of communication in the development and maintenance of interpersonal relationships. More research is needed to inform us of the dynamics of relationship dissolution.

Rewards and Costs

The second broad category of the theory involves a description of the role of rewards and costs in the social penetration process—the dyadic effect. Interpersonal rewards and costs are motivational in that rewards form the basis for maintaining or continuing a relationship to deeper levels of exchange, whereas costs lead to a winding down or dissolution of relationships.

The meaning of rewards and costs in social penetration theory is principally derived from the theories of Thibaut and Kelley (1959) and Homans (1950, 1961). These theories assume that parties in social exchanges seek to maximize gains and to minimize losses. However, since all relationships inevitably involve costs, parties typically evaluate costs relative to the rewards they may obtain. Therefore, the overall outcome of a relationship is a function of both its rewards and its costs:

RELATIONSHIP OUTCOMES = REWARDS − COSTS

Altman and Taylor derived their definition of rewards and costs, in part, from the social psychology of Thibaut and Kelley (1959):

> By rewards, we refer to the pleasures, satisfactions, and gratifications the person enjoys. The provision of a means whereby a drive is reduced or a need fulfilled constitutes a reward. . . . By costs, we refer to any factors that operate to inhibit or deter a performance of a sequence of behavior. . . . Thus cost is high when great physical or mental effort is required, when embarrassment or anxiety accompany the action, or when there are conflicting forces or competing response tendencies of any sort. (pp. 12–13)

Additional inputs to the definition come from a similar approach to rewards and costs. Homans (1950) relies upon economic-based ideas of profit and loss. Rewarding interaction involves a positive exchange of objects, symbolic signs, and attitudes and feelings. Costs come from negative experiences deriving from an aversive stimulus, or from the withdrawal of a pleasant one. Homans's (1961) concept of *distributive justice* deals with interactants' perceptions of equity and fairness in the distribution of rewards and costs:

> A man in an exchange relationship with another will expect that the rewards of each man be proportional to his costs—the greater the rewards, the greater the costs—and that the net rewards, or profits, of each man be

proportional to his investments—the greater the investments, the greater the profits. (p. 32)

For Homans, relationship outcomes are described in terms of profits. The overall evaluation of a relationship is in terms of distributive justice:

$$\text{PROFIT (RELATIONSHIP OUTCOME)} = \text{REWARDS} - \text{COSTS}$$

The combined formulations of rewards and costs by Thibaut and Kelley (1959) and Homans (1950, 1961) have been incorporated into social penetration theory in five propositions:

1) *Reward/cost ratio* refers to the balance of positive and negative experiences in a social relationship (i.e., the relative number of rewards to costs). The greater the number of rewards to costs, the more satisfying the relationship.

2) *Absolute reward and cost properties* involve the absolute magnitude of positive and negative experiences in a relationship. For example, two social relationships might have the same relative reward/cost ratios but differ in absolute amounts of rewards and costs and, consequently, in psychological characteristics.

3) *Immediately obtained rewards and costs* refer to the set of rewards and costs that accrue from a finite, temporally bound, relatively immediate social interaction. The temporal locus is "what just happened."

4) *Forecast rewards and costs* are projections to future rewards and costs. Such forecasts play an important role in propelling relationships foward or in slowing them down and even reversing their growth. The forecasting process is similar to the Thibaut and Kelley (1959) concepts of comparison level (CL) and comparison level for alternatives (CL$_{alt}$) in that one component of forecasting includes a comparison of a present relationship to some standard, or to alternative relationships.

5) *Cumulative rewards and costs* refer to the cumulation of rewards and costs throughout the history of a dyad. Conceptually, they can be represented as a reservoir or pool of positive and negative experiences up to a given point in time and extending back to the point of a relationship's formation.

Thus rewards and costs are consistently associated with mutual satisfaction of social and personal needs. Relationship outcomes are not necessarily the same as satisfaction with a relationship. In order to predict how satisfied persons will be in a relationship, we need to take into account their experiences and expectations. Outcomes received in past experiences are often critical to knowing and understanding the kinds of outcomes expected in the future. Finally, gains and losses from an interpersonal relationship cover a broad spectrum, from anxiety and security to status and power, group identification, and other sociopsychological phenomena.

The greater the ratio of rewards to costs, the more rapid the penetration process. Stated differently, the growth of a relationship will be a direct function of the extent to which good or satisfying aspects of the experience outweigh bad or unfavorable ones. In addition to a proportional analysis of rewards and costs, their absolute magnitude must also be considered. Assuming a similar ratio of favorable to unfavorable experiences, a greater absolute magnitude of rewards should yield a faster-growing, more intimate relationship. In this regard rewards are probably more important than costs in that the driving force that propels relationships forward is most likely the search for and reaction to achieved rewards rather than the avoidance of costs. This assertion does not rule out the importance of cost factors, but only suggests a different subjective emphasis. In maximizing their own reward characteristics, people often make it difficult for others to learn about their negative characteristics. Thus cost assessment is less certain and cost information is in a less accessible form—the positive aspects of each individual are most salient.

The early exchange theorists (i.e., Homans, 1950; Thibaut & Kelley, 1959) were principally concerned with the preconditions of relationship formation, not development. In social penetration theory the concept of reward/cost assessment is viewed as the motivational basis for relationship growth through the various stages of development. Continuous exchanges (communication, self-disclosure, etc.) occur as long as individuals mutually experience a favorable reward/cost balance. Further, as relationships progress, the exchanges become more intimate, a process illustrated in Figure 3.1. If exchange processes are sustained or increased over time, individuals must be "profiting" from the relationship (Taylor, 1968). The process begins with a first encounter in which individuals communicate at fairly superficial levels. These communications are evaluated in terms of rewards and costs, and forecasts are made regarding future exchanges. Two events occur here: (1) a reward/cost assessment, analogous to Thibaut and Kelley's (1959) concept of comparison level (CL); and (2)

an extrapolation that takes into account the projected relationship and alternative relationships—a comparison level for alternatives (CL_{alt}). The process continues throughout the history of the interaction.

Studies uncovered in this review, while ignoring the developmental focus of social penetration, confirm the importance of rewards and costs in social exchanges, similar to early application of these principles. The reinforcement or motivational interpretations of rewards and costs are augmented with cognitive explanations of the assessment of forecasted and retroactive analyses of rewards and costs (see figure below). Rewards are operationalized as positive experiences (e.g., liking, agreement, compatibility) and costs are translated as negative experiences (e.g., dislike, disagreement, tension).

FIGURE 3.1

Interpersonal Reward/Cost Aspects of the Social Penetration Process

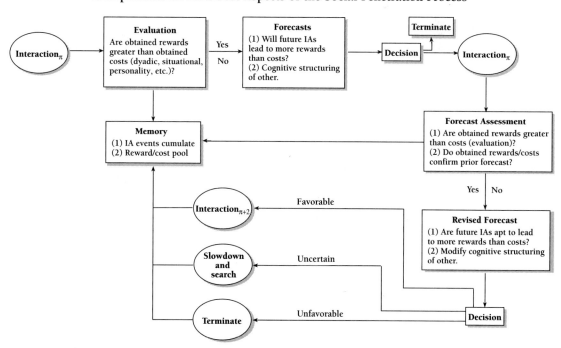

An important application of rewards and costs in an interpersonal context can be found in studies on communication. For example, McLaughlin, Cody, and Rosenstein (1983) describe what they call *account sequences,* a mechanism by which parties to an initial encounter deal with the discovery of dissimilarity and other conversational disagreeables (costs). They conclude that there is a structural preference for agreement in conversations, especially for new acquaintances. Through the use of account strategies parties to a relationship attempt to maintain harmony in conversations. When this is not effective for a particular topic, there is a tendency to drop the subject, or otherwise change the conversation. In more intimate contexts positive correlations have been found between marital satisfaction and verbal, affective, and physical intimacy (Tolstedt & Stokes, 1983); attitude similarity (Hendrick, 1981); quality nonverbal communication (Honeycutt, Wilson, & Parker, 1982; Markman, 1981; Murphy & Mendelson, 1973; Navran, 1967; Sabatelli et al., 1982); and openness as indicated by personal self-disclosure (Levinger & Senn, 1967).

In investigating the matching hypothesis through lonely hearts advertisements, Harrison and Saeed (1977) operationalized attractiveness and financial security as rewards. Rosenfeld (1979) explored cost factors in communication by examining self-disclosure avoidance. Even though self-disclosure has many potential benefits (rewards) and is essential to relationship development, it appears to be a small part of the communication process. Rosenfeld found that males tend to avoid self-disclosure to maintain control over their relationships, whereas females avoid disclosing themselves to prevent personal hurt and other problems. In both instances disclosure appears to be perceived as a cost rather than a reward. This conclusion, however, should be viewed with caution since the finding is not tied to a developmental stage. Taylor and Altman (1966) found that disclosure intimacy is inversely correlated with social desirability and therefore can be potentially rewarding or costly. McAllister (1980), for example, describes

the social reward potential and resulting attraction that could result from sending and receiving communications. Premature and/or inappropriate disclosure intimacy is often costly, whereas disclosure intimacy that is synchronized with target and stage of development can have beneficial effects for a relationship (see Chelune, Sultan, & Williams, 1980). We will return to these considerations later in discussing reciprocity and intimacy.

Taylor, Altman, and Sorrentino (1969) went beyond the demonstration of basic reward/cost effects by exploring expectations (confirmed and disconfirmed) as a function of prior reward/cost experiences; that is, how do individuals react to communications that are consistently favorable (rewarding) and unfavorable (costly) versus those that are initially unfavorable and end up being favorable, and vice versa? Mixed reward/cost experiences seem to produce a contrast effect. Positive messages that immediately follow initially negative ones are enhanced by this context. Evidence for the reverse of this sequence is equivocal. Aronson and Linder (1965) have described this phenomenon as a "gain-or-loss" effect; gains and losses have more impact on attraction than consistent evaluations. McAllister and Bregman (1983) tested an integration theory model against gain-loss theory and found more evidence for integration theory. Integration theory models predict that sequences increasing or decreasing in intimacy should have less impact on attraction than constant intimate or nonintimate disclosures. Although the McAllister and Bregman finding was not interpreted as consistent with social penetration theory, it is consistent with exchange theory. It simply suggests an alternative hypothesis concerning what is more rewarding—constant high intimacy disclosures versus a sequence of increasingly intimate disclosures. More important, these studies show that a reward (or cost) is not an absolute entity but is assessed in relation to its context (Taylor, DeSoto, & Lieb, 1979), potentially or real existing alternatives (Berg, 1984), and sequence (Aronson & Linder, 1965; McAllister & Bregman, 1983; Taylor et al., 1969). Moreover, they provide support for the Thibaut and

Kelley concept of comparison level for alternatives (CL_{alt}).

Reciprocity and Intimacy

A final topic of importance to the social penetration framework concerns the reciprocity of exchange between persons in a relationship. Will one person's disclosure, or behavior, increase the probability that the other person will disclose? According to social penetration theory, one organizing principle for communication in initial encounters is the *norm of reciprocity* (Gouldner, 1960). This norm asserts that we feel obligated or indebted to return disclosures received. A second question for the social penetration process is concerned with whether we like another person because he or she has disclosed to us, or whether we disclose to others because we like them. In social penetration theory, we argued that while a norm of reciprocity seems to exist, it is not the sole determinant of the social penetration process. Further, we speculated that reciprocity derives from the dynamics of the encounter between people, the level of intimacy of topics discussed, the properties of the situation, and the characteristics of the participants. Altman and Taylor (1973) concluded that reciprocity is a set of behavioral events, not necessarily an explanation of those events (p. 56).

Altman (1973) later expanded upon the concept of reciprocity by proposing a model that incorporates the norm of reciprocity and social reward as motivational determinants of mutual disclosure. In this model an obligation to reciprocate disclosure is hypothesized to be more important in early stages of a relationship than in later stages. At early stages, reciprocal disclosure is presumed to occur independent of social consequences. Instead, reciprocal disclosure was postulated as a basis for establishing trust. Once trust has been established, reciprocation is no longer considered important since unilateral disclosures carry little risk of vulnerability. Thus nonintimate disclosure probably operates more in accordance with a norm of social reciprocity than do highly intimate disclosures.

This outcome leads to the prediction of an inverse relationship between stage of relationship and degree of reciprocity. Further, the intimacy of the disclosed topic interacts with the stage of a relationship so that nonintimate reciprocity is at a maximum among strangers and declines as a relationship develops. Conversely, reciprocity of intimate disclosures is predicted to reach a peak in the middle stages of a relationship. At early and late stages reciprocity of intimate disclosures will be minimal or nonexistent. In two separate studies, Won-Doornick (1979, 1985) directly tested and found support for Altman's hypotheses on reciprocity. Evidence from Cohn and Strassberg (1983) corroborates and adds to the generalizability of the disclosure reciprocity effect. In the early stages of relationships reciprocity is thought to be important because it demonstrates and establishes trust (Altman, 1973; Rubin, 1975). This explanation, however, has been challenged by others (Berg & Archer, 1980, 1982; Jones & Archer, 1976; McAllister, 1980).

Jones and Archer (1976) tested modeling versus trust explanations for reciprocity, and added an additional explanation—equitable exchange. Equitable exchange is presumed to operate when a recipient feels obligated to reciprocate personal information to pay for disclosures received. According to these authors a special variant of equitable exchange, personalism, engenders exclusive trust. Personalistic disclosures are held to be more valuable than disclosures shared with others (Taylor et al., 1981). Jones and Archer, therefore, hypothesized that personalistic disclosure leads to liking because the recipient feels that she or he has been singled out as trustworthy and is a candidate for an intimate relationship. Trust was ruled out as a possible mediating variable in disclosure reciprocity. In a series of studies of the special effects of personalism and intimacy, Taylor and his colleagues (Taylor, Gould, & Brounstein, 1981; Taylor & Hinds, 1985) found that highly intimate disclosers were liked most when they attributed their disclosure behavior to characteristics of the disclosers, whereas low-intimacy disclosers who attributed their disclosure to characteristics of the disclosees, were liked least.

Up to now the research studies reviewed give clear evidence that reciprocity in relationship development depends on early reward/cost experiences and intimacy. Participants' perceptions of the impact of their own communication and other exchanges have implications for their understanding of how mutual liking and trust develop, and how these in turn promote increased intimacy (Berg & Archer, 1983; Brewer & Mittelman, 1980; Hill & Stull, 1982; Petty & Mirels, 1981; Shaffer, Smith, & Tomarelli, 1982). Whether the relationship proceeds to an intimate stage depends on the accuracy of perception and the ability of the parties in the relationship to assess and to sustain favorable reward/cost outcomes. There is disagreement, however, among theorists on the application and interpretation of intimacy in interpersonal relationships:

The principles of the interpersonal marketplace are most likely to prevail in encounters between strangers and casual acquaintances, and in early stages of the development of relationships. As an interpersonal bond becomes more firmly established, however, it begins to go beyond exchange. (Rubin, 1973, p. 86)

Others criticize the implications of "emotional bookkeeping" and the crass weighing of rewards and costs in strict conformity with exchange principles (Clark, 1984; Clark & Mills, 1979; Clark, Ouellette, & Milberg, 1984; Mills & Clark, 1982; Murstein, 1971, 1973; Murstein, MacDonald, & Cerreto, 1977; Rubin, 1973). On the other hand, Walster and her colleagues (Walster, Berscheid, & Walster, 1973; Walster, Walster, & Berscheid, 1978) have steadfastly defended exchange interpretations of intimate relationships: "We contend that, even in the most intimate relations, considerations of equity will influence strongly the viability and pleasantness of a relationship" (Walster et al., 1973, p. 170).

Recall that Altman's (1973) hypotheses on reciprocity state that reciprocity will be greater for superficial, nonintimate messages than for intimate ones. Qualifications on equity applications to inti-

mate relationships by Walster et al. (1978) support that distinction. Specifically, intimates are predicted to tolerate more imbalance in exchange than do casual acquaintances. These variable effects in intimacy reciprocity, however, have not been consistently supported in the literature (e.g., Caltabiano & Smithson, 1983; Dalto & Ajzen, 1979; Davis & Perkowitz, 1979). The analysis of intimacy reciprocity by Caltabiano and Smithson (1983) identifies two qualifying variables that may account for the mixture of findings in the research literature: valence and gender. Positive disclosures were seen as more appropriate than negative disclosures, and females were more receptive to disclosure than males.

Patterson (1976) proposed an arousal model of interpersonal intimacy that presumes variations or changes in intimacy produce changes in arousal level. Furthermore, the change in arousal is thought to be a mediating mechanism for adjustments in reciprocated intimacy. If the arousal is labeled negative (e.g., anxiety, discomfort), the resultant behaviors are designed to lessen the negative affective state. If the arousal is perceived as positive (e.g., liking, love, relief), it is predicted that the intimacy will be reciprocated. In two separate studies, Taylor and his colleagues (Moriarty & Taylor, 1986; Taylor & Belgrave, 1986) found that negatively labeled messages diminished the effect of reciprocation. These findings taken together with those of Caltabiano and Smithson (1983) demonstrate that disclosure reciprocity is sensitive not only to the intimacy of received disclosure but also to the valence of that disclosure. Further considerations of reciprocity effects in interpersonal communication should incorporate or examine the impact of valence.

Caltabiano & Smithson's (1983) observation on gender effects and self-disclosure is consistent with a pervasive finding in the literature. Although gender effects were not originally dealt with in social penetration theory, the effect is now one that cannot be ignored. A persistent finding among the studies examining the self-disclosure process in relationship to social penetration theory is that females disclose more, and are more open, than males (Aries & Johnson, 1983; Arlett, Best, & Little, 1976; Chelune, 1976; Cozby, 1973; Little, 1968; McGuire & Padawer-Singer, 1976; Pelligrini, Hicks, Meyers-Winton, & Antal, 1978; Rosenfeld, Civikly, & Herron 1979; Taylor & Hinds, 1985; Thase & Page, 1977; Walker & Wright, 1976). Jourard and his colleagues (Jourard & Lasakow, 1958; Jourard & Richman, 1963) reasoned that females are socialized to be more open, self-disclosing, and empathic than males. The male role, according to Jourard and his associates, requires greater control of emotion and concealment of self-disclosure intimacy, and is therefore a "lethal" role.

Despite the persistence of this finding, it has been challenged and subject to modification by a number of contradictory and/or equivocal findings (Dies & Greenberg, 1976). In a major literature review on sex differences, Maccoby and Jacklin (1974) state that the evidence does not justify concluding that men and women differ in self-disclosure. The differences in self-disclosure between men and women are influenced by the target person's sex (Komarovsky, 1976; Wheeler & Nezlek, 1977), social desirability (Zanna & Pack, 1975), marital status (Booth & Hess, 1974), and topical content (Komarovsky, 1976). Rosenfeld et al. (1979) similarly state, "It becomes clear that the conclusion 'females disclose more than males' is inaccurate" (pp. 108–109). These authors conclude that the consideration of four factors could lead to less equivocal findings regarding male–female disclosure. These factors are anatomical/psychological sex, a clear operational definition of intimacy, control over disclosure topics, and an unambiguous specification of the relationship between subject and target. It may, therefore, be necessary to keep these four considerations in mind as we review sex differences and disclosure in social penetration processes.

Knapp (1978) has extended the social penetration framework to emphasize communication phenomena. Specifically, he proposes going beyond considerations of depth and breadth of exchange to examine synchronized communication and effi-

ciency. Within this context, Baxter and Wilmot (1983) investigated the communication characteristics of relationships of differing growth rates, and looked at how these characteristics vary as a function of the sex of respondent. They found sex differences in several aspects of communication including encounter personalness, topic breadth, encounter importance, and enactment of talk for talk's sake; all were consistent with traditional sex-role socialization described above.

Derlega, Durham, Gockel, and Sholis (1981) conducted a series of experiments on disclosure intimacy and gender that may be responsive to the gender-disclosure issues raised earlier by Rosenfeld et al. (1979). These studies manipulated sex of subject, disclosure topic, intimacy target gender, and degree of friendship. Derlega et al. predicted that males would disclose more than females on traditionally masculine topics; females would disclose more than males on traditionally feminine topics; and males and females would disclose at the same level for "neutral" topics (those considered equally appropriate for either sex). Women did disclose more than men on feminine topics, emphasizing personal concerns and vulnerabilities. However, males did not differ from females on masculine topics or neutral topics. These findings also generalized to strangers as target persons. Therefore, the robustness of the traditional male–female differences was demonstrated in a variety of settings with the kinds of controls advocated by Rosenfeld et al. (1979).

SUMMING UP

We have reviewed literature relevant to social penetration theory and communication and developmental phenomena. The theory is developmental in its concern with the growth and dissolution of interpersonal relationships. Four stages of interpersonal exchange and communication were identified: (1) orientation, (2) exploratory affective exchange, (3) affective exchange, and (4) stable exchange. A second aspect of the theory involves rewards and costs as motivational components of establishing and sustaining stable interpersonal relationships. Finally, the dynamics of reciprocity and intimacy were assessed as to how they influence interpersonal relationships. A large number of studies that referenced social penetration were analyzed as a way of determining the impact of the theory.

The most glaring conclusion to be derived from this review is that many researchers have been influenced by the ideas from social penetration theory, but few have directly tested propositions from the theory. To assess development—the major focus of the theory—researchers need to employ longitudinal research strategies. These approaches are not in vogue in social psychology; moreover, it is difficult to gain access to appropriate populations for research. A direct challenge to the efficacy of the theme of "gradual development in relationship formation" was found in the work of Berg and his colleagues (Berg, 1983, 1984; Berg & Clark, in press). The conclusions from their studies indicate that many aspects of close relationships develop quickly rather than gradually. Berg cites evidence that measures of attraction and social exchange obtained early in a relationship predict the state of the relationship almost as well as the same measures taken later in the relationship. However, Berg also acknowledges the need for further longitudinal research in order to clarify these observations.

Although a number of studies examined development by inference, we were able to find only one study in the literature that attempted to assess the dynamics of relationship dissolution (depenetration). It is quite likely that the same procedural challenges that discourage investigators from making direct tests of developmental hypotheses are at issue here. These omissions point to opportunities in tracking growth and dissolution in interpersonal relationships. The *dyadic effect* has been confirmed by numerous studies, but reciprocity and intimacy analyses have broken new ground with the introduction of Patterson's (1976) intimacy arousal model and studies on personalistic disclosure (e.g., Jones & Archer, 1976; Taylor et al., 1981). It is

hoped that these efforts will not only sharpen and improve our knowledge about reciprocity in interpersonal contexts but will also be used to understand better relationship buildup and breakdown.

REFERENCES

Altman, I. (1973). Reciprocity of interpersonal exchange. *Journal for the Theory of Social Behavior, 3,* 249-261.

Altman, I., & Taylor, D. A. (1973). *Social penetration: The development of interpersonal relationships.* New York: Holt, Rinehart & Winston.

Altman, I., Vinsel, A., & Brown, B. B. (1981). Dialectic conceptions in social psychology: An application to social penetration and privacy regulation. In L. Berkowitz (Ed.), *Advances in experimental social psychology* (Vol. 14, pp. 107–160). New York: Academic Press.

Aries, E., & Johnson, F. (1983). Close friendship in adulthood: Conversational content between same sex friends. *Sex Roles, 9,* 1183-1196.

Arlett, C., Best, J. A., & Little, B. R. (1976). Influence of interviewer self-disclosure and verbal reinforcement on personality tests. *Journal of Clinical Psychology, 32,* 770-775.

Aronson, E., & Linder, D. (1965). Gain and loss of esteem as determinants of interpersonal attractiveness. *Journal of Experimental Social Psychology, 1,* 156-171.

Baxter, L., & Wilmot, W. (1983). Communication characteristics of relationships with differential growth rates. *Communication Monographs, 50,* 264-272.

Berg, J. H. (1983). *Attraction in relationships: As it begins so it goes.* Paper presented at the annual meeting of the American Psychological Association, Anaheim, CA.

Berg, J. H. (1984). Development of friendship between roommates. *Journal of Personality and Social Psychology, 2,* 346-356.

Berg, J. H., & Archer, R. L. (1980). Disclosure or concern: A second look at liking for the norm-breaker. *Journal of Personality, 48,* 245-257.

Berg, J. H., & Archer, R. L. (1982). Responses to self-disclosure and interaction goals. *Journal of Experimental Social Psychology, 18,* 501-512.

Berg, J. H., & Archer, R. L. (1983). The disclosure-liking relationship: Effects of self-perception, order of disclosure and topical similarity. *Human Communication Research, 10,* 269-281.

Berg, J. H., & Clark, M. S. (1986). Differences in social exchange between intimate and other relationships: Gradually evolving or quickly apparent? In V. J. Derlega & B. Winstead (Eds.), *Friendship and social interaction.* New York: Springer-Verlag.

Booth, A., & Hess, E. (1974). Cross-sex friendships. *Journal of Marriage and the Family, 36,* 38-47.

Braiker, H. B., & Kelley, H. H. (1979). Conflict in the development of close relationships. In R. L. Burgess & T. L. Huston (Eds.), *Social exchange in developing relationships* (pp. 135–169). New York: Academic Press.

Brewer, M., & Mittelman, J. (1980). Effects of normative control of self-disclosure on reciprocity. *Journal of Personality, 48,* 89-102.

Caltabiano, M., & Smithson, M. (1983). Variables affecting the perception of self-disclosure appropriateness. *Journal of Social Psychology, 120,* 119-128.

Chaiken, A. L., & Derlega, V. J. (1974). Variables affecting the appropriateness of self-disclosure. *Journal of Consulting and Clinical Psychology, 42,* 588-593.

Chelune, G. J. (1976). A multidimensional look at sex and target differences in disclosure. *Psychological Reports, 39,* 259-263.

Chelune, G. J., Sultan, R. F., & Williams, C. L. (1980). Loneliness, self-disclosure, and interpersonal effectiveness. *Journal of Counseling Psychology, 27,* 462-468.

Clark, M. S. (1984). Record keeping in two types of relationships. *Journal of Personality and Social Psychology, 47,* 549-557.

Clark, M. S., & Mills, J. (1979). Interpersonal attraction in exchange and communal relationships. *Journal of Personality and Social Psychology, 37,* 12-24.

Clark, M. S., Ouellette, R., & Milberg, S. (1984). *Recipient mood, relationship type, and helping.* Paper presented at the Second International Conference on Personal Relationships, Madison, WI.

Cohn, N. B., & Strassberg, D. S. (1983). Self-disclosure reciprocity among preadolescents. *Personality and Social Psychology Bulletin, 9,* 97-102.

Cozby, P. C. (1973). Self-disclosure: A literature review. *Psychological Bulletin, 79,* 73-91.

Dalto, C. A., & Ajzen, I. (1979). Self-disclosure and attraction: Effects of intimacy and desirability on beliefs and attitudes. *Journal of Research in Personality, 13,* 127-138.

Davis, J. D. (1976). Self-disclosure in an acquaintance experience: Responsibility for level of intimacy. *Journal of Personality and Social Psychology, 33,* 787-792.

Davis, D., & Perkowitz, N. T. (1979). Consequences of responsiveness in dyadic interaction: Effects of probability of response and proportion of content-related responses on interpersonal attraction. *Journal of Personality and Social Psychology, 37,* 534-550.

Derlega, V. J., Durham, B., Gockel, B., & Sholis, D. (1981). Sex differences in self-disclosure: Effects of topic content, friendship, and partner's sex. *Sex Roles, 7,* 433-447.

Dies, R., & Greenberg, B. (1976). Effects of physical contact in an encounter group context. *Journal of Consulting and Clinical Psychology, 44,* 400-405.

Gouldner, A. W. (1960). The norm of reciprocity: A preliminary statement. *American Sociological Review, 25,* 161-178.

Harrison, A. A., & Saeed, L. (1977). Let's make a deal: An analysis of revelations and stipulations in lonely heart advertisements. *Journal of Personality and Social Psychology, 35,* 257-264.

Hays, R. B. (1984). The development and maintenance of friendship. *Journal of Social and Personal Relationships, 1,* 75-97.

Hays, R. B. (1985). A longitudinal study of friendship development. *Journal of Personality and Social Psychology, 48,* 909-924.

Hendrick, S. (1981). Self-disclosure and marital satisfaction. *Journal of Personality and Social Psychology, 40,* 1158-1159.

Hill, C. T., & Stull, D. E. (1982). Disclosure reciprocity: Conceptual and measurement issues. *Social Psychology Quarterly, 45,* 238-245.

Homans, G. C. (1950). *The human group.* New York: Harcourt Brace Jovanovich.

Homans, G. C. (1961). *Social behavior: Its elementary forms.* New York: Harcourt Brace Jovanovich.

Honeycutt, J., Wilson, C., & Parker, C. (1982). Effects of sex and degrees of happiness on perceived styles of communicating in and out of the marital relationship. *Journal of Marriage and the Family, 44,* 395-406.

Jones, E. E., & Archer, R. L. (1976). Are there special effects of personalistic self-disclosure? *Journal of Experimental Social Psychology, 12,* 180-193.

Jourard, S. M. (1964). *The transparent self.* New York: Van Nostrand.

Jourard, S. M., & Landsman, M. J. (1960). Cognition, cathexis, and the "dyadic effect" in men's self-disclosing behavior. *Merrill Palmer Quarterly, 9,* 141-148.

Jourard, S. M., & Lasakow, P. (1958). Some factors in self-disclosure. *Journal of Abnormal and Social Psychology, 56,* 91-98.

Jourard, S. M., & Richman, P. (1963). Disclosure output and input in college students. *Merrill Palmer Quarterly, 9,* 141-148.

Kerckhoff, A. C., & Davis, K. E. (1962). Value consensus and need complementarity in mate selection. *American Sociological Review, 27,* 295-303.

Knapp, M. L. (1978). *Nonverbal communication in human interaction* (2nd ed.). New York: Holt, Rinehart & Winston.

Komarovsky, M. (1976). *Dilemmas of masculinity: A study of college youth.* New York: Norton.

Levinger, G., & Senn, D. J. (1967). Disclosure of feelings in marriage. *Merrill Palmer Quarterly, 13,* 237-249.

Levinger, G., & Snoek, J. D. (1972). *Attraction in relationship: A new look at interpersonal attraction.* New York: General Learning Press.

Little, K. B. (1968). Cultural variations in social schemata. *Journal of Personality and Social Psychology, 10,* 1-7.

Maccoby, E. E., & Jacklin, C. N. (1974). *The psychology of sex differences.* Stanford, CA: Stanford University Press.

Markman, H. J. (1981). Prediction of marital distress: A 5-year follow-up. *Journal of Consulting and Clinical Psychology, 49,* 554-567.

McAdams, D., & Vaillant, G. E. (1982). Intimacy motivation and psychosocial adjustment: A longitudinal study. *Journal of Personality Assessment, 46,* 586-593.

McAllister, H. A. (1980). Self-disclosure and liking: Effects for senders and receivers. *Journal of Personality, 48,* 409-418.

McAllister, H. A., & Bregman, N. J. (1983). Self-disclosure and liking: An integration theory approach. *Journal of Personality, 51,* 202-212.

McGuire, W. J., & Padawer-Singer, A. (1976). Trait salience in the spontaneous self-concept. *Journal of Personality and Social Psychology, 33,* 743-754.

McLaughlin, M. L., Cody, M. J., & Rosenstein, N. E. (1983). Account sequences in conversations between strangers. *Communication Monographs, 50,* 102-128.

Mills, J., & Clark, M. S. (1982). Exchange and communal relationships. In L. Wheeler (Ed.), *Review of personality and social psychology* (Vol. 3, pp. 121–144). Newbury Park, CA: Sage.

Morton, T. L. (1978). Intimacy and reciprocity of exchange: A comparison of spouses and strangers. *Journal of Personality and Social Psychology, 36,* 72-81.

Moriarty, B. F., & Taylor, D. A. (1986). *Intimacy and valence effects in self-disclosure reciprocity.* Paper presented at the annual meeting of the Eastern Psychological Association, New York.

Murphy, D. C., & Mendelson, L. A. (1973). Communication and adjustment in marriage: Investigating the relationships. *Family Process, 12,* 317-326.

Murstein, B. I. (1970). Stimulus-value-role: A theory of marital choice. *Journal of Marriage and the Family, 32,* 465-481.

Murstein, B. I. (1971). A theory of marital choice and its applicability to marriage adjustment and friendship. In B. I. Murstein (Ed.), *Theories of attraction and love* (pp. 100–151). New York: Springer.

Murstein, B. I. (1973). A theory of marital choice applied to interracial marriage. In I. R. Stuart & L. E. Abt (Eds.), *Interracial marriage: Expectations and realities* (pp. 19–35). New York: Grossman.

Murstein, B. I., MacDonald, M. G., & Cerreto, M. (1977). A theory of the effect of exchange-orientation on marriage and friendship. *Journal of Marriage and the Family, 39,* 543-548.

Navran, I. (1967). Communication and adjustment in marriage. *Family Process, 6,* 173-184.

Patterson, M. L. (1976). An arousal model of interpersonal intimacy. *Psychological Review, 83,* 235-245.

Pelligrini, R. J., Hicks, R. A., Meyers-Winton, S., & Antal, B. G. (1978). Physical attractiveness and self-disclosure in mixed sex dyads. *Psychological Record, 28,* 509-516.

Petty, R. E., & Mirels, H. L. (1981). Intimacy and scarcity of self-disclosure: Effects on interpersonal attraction for males and females. *Personality and Social Psychology Bulletin, 7,* 493-503.

Rosenfeld, L. B. (1979). Self-disclosure avoidance: Why I am afraid to tell you who I am. *Communication Monographs, 46,* 63-74.

Rosenfeld, L. B., Civikly, J., & Herron, J. (1979). Anatomical and psychological sex differences. In G. J. Chelune & Associates, *Self-disclosure* (pp. 80–109). San Francisco: Jossey-Bass.

Rubin, Z. (1973). *Liking and loving: An invitation to social psychology.* New York: Holt, Rinehart & Winston.

Rubin, Z. (1975). Disclosing oneself to a stranger: Reciprocity and its limits. *Journal of Experimental Social Psychology, 11,* 233-260.

Rubin, Z., & Levinger, G. (1974). Theory and data badly mated: A critique of Murstein's SVR theory and Lewis's PDF model of mate selection. *Journal of Marriage and the Family, 36,* 226-231.

Sabatelli, R. M., Buck, R., & Dreyer, A. (1982). Nonverbal communication accuracy in married couples: Relationships with marital complaints. *Journal of Personality and Social Psychology, 43,* 1088-1097.

Sabatelli, R., Buck, R., & Dreyer, A. (1983). Locus of control, interpersonal trust, and nonverbal communication accuracy. *Journal of Personality and Social Psychology, 44,* 399-409.

Shaffer, D. R., Smith, J. E., & Tomarelli, M. (1982). Self-monitoring as a determinant of self-disclosure reciprocity during the acquaintance process. *Journal of Personality and Social Psychology, 43,* 163-175.

Taylor, D. A. (1968). The development of interpersonal relationships: Social penetration processes. *Journal of Social Psychology, 75,* 79-90.

Taylor, D. A., & Altman, I. (1966). Intimacy-scaled stimuli for use in studies of interpersonal relations. *Psychological Reports, 19,* 729-730.

Taylor, D. A., Altman, I., & Sorrentino, R. (1969). Interpersonal exchange as a function of rewards and costs and situational factors: Expectancy confirmation-disconfirmation. *Journal of Experimental Social Psychology, 5,* 324-339.

Taylor, R. B., DeSoto, C. B., & Lieb, R. (1979). Sharing secrets: Disclosure and discretion in dyads and triads. *Journal of Personality and Social Psychology, 37,* 1196-1203.

Taylor, D. A., Gould, R., & Brounstein, P. (1981). Effects of personalistic self-disclosure. *Personality and Social Psychology Bulletin, 7,* 487-492.

Taylor, D. A., & Hinds, M. (1985). Disclosure reciprocity and liking as a function of gender and personalism. *Sex Roles, 12,* 1137-1153.

Taylor, D. A., & Belgrave, F. Z. (1986). The effects of perceived intimacy and valence on self-disclosure. *Personality and Social Psychology Bulletin, 12,* 247-255.

Thase, M., & Page, R. A. (1977). Modeling of self-disclosure in laboratory and nonlaboratory interview settings. *Journal of Counseling Psychology, 24,* 35-40.

Thibaut, J. W., & Kelley, H. H. (1959). *The social psychology of groups.* New York: John Wiley.

Tolstedt, B. E., & Stokes, J. P. (1983). Relation of verbal, affective, and physical intimacy to marital satisfaction. *Journal of Counseling Psychology, 30,* 573-580.

Tolstedt, B. E., & Stokes, J. P. (1984). Self-disclosure, intimacy, and the depenetration process. *Journal of Personality and Social Psychology, 46,* 84-90.

Walker, L. S., & Wright, P. H. (1976). Self-disclosure in friendship. *Perceptual and Motor Skills, 42,* 735-742.

Walster, E., Berscheid, E., & Walster, G. W. (1973). New directions in equity research. *Journal of Personality and Social Psychology, 25,* 151-176.

Walster, E., Walster, G. W., & Berscheid, E. (1978). *Equity theory and research.* Boston: Allyn & Bacon.

Wheeler, L., & Nezlek, J. (1977). Sex differences in social participation. *Journal of Personality and Social Psychology, 35,* 742-754.

Won-Doornick, M. J. (1979). On getting to know you: The association between the stage of a relationship and reciprocity of self-disclosure. *Journal of Experimental Social Psychology, 15,* 229-241.

Won-Doornick, M. J. (1985). Self-disclosure and reciprocity in conversation: A cross-national study. *Social Psychology Quarterly, 48,* 97-107.

Zanna, M. P., & Pack, S. J. (1975). On the self-fulfilling nature of apparent sex differences in behavior. *Journal of Experimental Social Psychology, 11,* 583-591.

4

Stages of Coming Together and Coming Apart

M. L. KNAPP | A. L. VANGELISTI

We describe our relationships in many ways. Sometimes we rely on conventional intimacy terms like *stranger, acquaintance, buddy, close friend, lover*; sometimes role designations such as *neighbor, boss, hitchhiker, teacher, or pickup* are used; sometimes the nature of the relationship is linked to kinship terms such as *mother, sister, cousin,* or *husband*. Inferences about the nature of the relationship may be made from temporal descriptions—e.g., "known him since high school," "going steady," or "just met her once"; or we may assume a reference to ethnicity or personal characteristics will be a sufficient relationship description—e.g., "brothers" or "we think alike." A reference to joint activities or social organizations may provide the initial relationship description—e.g., "we bowl together," "we're in the same sorority," "I work with him," or "I only see her in class."

TYPES OF RELATIONSHIPS

The preceding relationship descriptions do very little to explain a multitude of personal and societal expectations attendant to these relationships. The type of relationship we develop with another person is heavily influenced by mutual and ongoing expectations for the relationship: What is it? What will it become? What should it be now? What should it become? What behavior is expected? What do most people do? Some expectations for

relationships are held by many people in this culture—e.g., that family members will most likely have close relationships; that male–female friendships are most likely to be romantic in nature; that same-gender relationships will most likely be limited to friendships (rather than romance); that marriage will most likely be the result of highly intimate feelings between the partners; that participants in various role relationships (teacher-student; doctor-patient) will most likely behave according to those roles. The extent to which such expectations are shared and acted upon helps to explain perceived similarities among relationships described as "friend" or "teacher" or "mother."

Sometimes expectations are not shared—with society or with one's relationship partner. Contrary to the expectations and/or wishes of many people, some family members develop distant relationships; some male–female pairs do not pursue romance; some same-gender pairs seek romantic relationships; some people get married who don't feel intense intimacy; and some people don't fulfill the expectations for their role as doctor, teacher, or mother. When we have difficulty establishing a relationship or in changing an established relationship to one of a different type it is often linked to differing expectations for the relationship held by each party.[1]

Sometimes relationship expectations are confusing because more than one relationship is involved.

From Knapp, M. L., & Vangelisti, A. L. (1992). *Interpersonal communication and human relationships* (2nd ed.) (pp. 29-63). Boston: Allyn & Bacon.

You may have several relationships with the same person and it is not always clear which relationship is being performed—e.g., a teacher who is also your teammate in handball. The handball activity may suggest a new set of expectations for the relationship, but if you make a poor shot, you may hear a comment that sounds more like your teacher than your teammate. Families also present a complex set of relationship expectations. An older parent living in his or her adult child's home may occasionally play parent and occasionally play dependent tenant to the adult son or daughter.

Expectations for relationships change with time and circumstances. The expectations for romantic relationships of today seem to include more physical contact and a greater expression of both positive and negative feelings than people expected fifty years ago.[2] As a child reaches adolescence, he or she expects certain relationship changes with his or her parents. We found that people below age 22 expected more personalized and synchronized communication in all types of relationships than did those people over age 41.[3] A man and a woman may be assigned to work on a task in a corporate environment. The expectations for this relationship are formal, task-oriented, and nonintimate. However, when the task relationship occurs for an extended period, when the pair works together several nights a week, and when they discuss various personal aspects of their life during breaks, the relationship expectations may change.[4] Many of our relationship expectations are rooted in the activities we perform together.[5]

We don't always consciously pursue the relationships we have with others. Sometimes we're "thrown together" with people in certain circumstances. Similarly, we may not actively terminate a relationship, but changes in interests, priorities, or geographical location may contribute to a lack of initiative to keep the relationship going. So it fades away due to mindless inattention rather than planned avoidance.

The variety of relationships we have or could have seems quite diverse. There are, however, some basic principles that all types of relationships seem to have in common. These include: (1) Relationship expectations are often altered because of the way people communicate, and the way they communicate often helps to shape the expectations they have for a relationship. This principle establishes the central role of communication behavior in assessing the nature of relationships, but it also recognizes that overt communication behavior may tell only part of the relationship story. (2) Whether our relationships are actively sought or develop out of shared circumstances, each of them reveals fluctuations in closeness or intimacy. Superficial, task-oriented relationships and unfriendly relations can be viewed as less intimate while best friends and lovers are more intimate. With these foundation concepts in mind, we can return to our initial questions: Are there regular and systematic patterns of communication that suggest stages on the road to a more intimate relationship? Are there similar patterns and stages that characterize the deterioration of relationships?

A MODEL OF INTERACTION STAGES IN RELATIONSHIPS

Scientists are forever seeking to bring order to a seemingly chaotic world of overlapping, interdependent, dynamic, and intricate processes. Frequently, the process of systematizing our life and environment is discussed in terms of stages of growth, stages of deterioration, and the forces that shape and act on this movement through stages. For instance, developmental psychologists recount regularized patterns of behavior accompanying stages of infancy, childhood, adolescence, maturity, and old age. Anthropologists and geologists plot the evolutionary stages of human beings and human environments. Biologists note similarities in the life processes of such seemingly diverse organisms as trees and fish. Physical and social scientists talk about affinity and attraction, weak and strong interactions, friction, repulsion, and splitting-up as basic forces acting on matter and people. Rhetorical critics often dissect spoken messages by noting patterns regularly occurring during the introduction, development toward the main points, transitions, and conclusion.

The idea that there are stages in the development of relationships that are characterized by certain patterns of communication is not new.[6] We tried to synthesize as well as expand on this previous work in the development of the model presented in Table 4.1.

Before each stage is described in greater detail, several preliminary remarks about the model are in order. First, we should resist the normal temptation to perceive the stages of coming together as "good" and those of coming apart as "bad." It is not "bad" to terminate relationships nor is it necessarily "good" to become more intimate with someone. The model is descriptive of what seems to happen—not what should happen.

We should also remember that in the interest of clarity the model simplifies a complex process. For instance, the model shows each stage adjacent to the next—as if it was clear when a communicating couple left one stage and entered another. To the contrary. Each stage contains some behavior from other stages. So stage identification becomes a matter of emphasis. Stages are identified by the proportion of one type of communication behavior to another. This proportion may be the frequency with which certain communication acts occur or proportion may be determined by the relative weight given to certain acts by the participants. For example, a couple at the Intensifying Stage may exhibit behaviors that occur at any of the other stages, but their arrival at the Intensifying Stage is because: (1) the most frequent communication exchanges are typical of the Intensifying Stage and/or (2) the exchanges that are crucial in defining the couple's relationship are statements of an intensifying nature. The act of sexual intercourse is commonly associated with male–female romantic couples at the Intensifying or Integrating Stages, but it may occur as an isolated act for couples at the Experimenting Stage. Or it may occur regularly for a couple at the Experimenting Stage, but remain relatively unimportant for the couple in defining the closeness of

their relationship. Thus, interaction stages involve both overt behavior and the perceptions of behavior in the minds of the parties involved. During the formation of a romantic relationship, the couple's overt behavior (to each other and in front of others) may be a good marker of their developmental stage. During periods of attempted rejuvenation of a relationship we may find that the overt behavior is an effective marker of the stage *desired*. However, in stable or long-established relationships, overt behavior may not be a very accurate indicator of closeness. Instead it is the occasional behavior or memories of past behaviors that are perceived by the couple as crucial in defining their relationship. For example, the married couple of fifteen years may spend much of their interaction time engaging in small talk—a behavior typical of an early developmental stage. And even though the small talk does play an important role in maintaining the relationship, it is the less frequent but more heavily weighted behavior that the couple uses to define their relationship, as at the Integrating Stage. Similarly, close friends may not engage in a lot of talk that outside observers would associate with closeness. In some cases, friends are separated for long periods of time and make very little contact with one another. But through specific occasional acts and the memory of past acts, the intimacy of the friendship is maintained.

The dialogue in the model is heavily oriented toward mixed-gender pairs. This does not mean the model is irrelevant for same-gender pairs. Lovers and tennis buddies go down the same road, but lovers go further; business partners and sorority sisters find different topics, but both engage in a lot of small talk. Even at the highest level of commitment, the model may apply to same-gender pairs. The bonding ceremony, for instance, need not be marriage. It could be an act of becoming "blood brothers" by placing open wounds on each other to achieve oneness. Granted, American cultural sanctions against the direct expression of high-level intimacy between same-sexed pairs often serve to inhibit, slow down, or stop the growth of relationships between same-sexed pairs. But when such

TABLE 4.1

A Model of Interaction Stages

PROCESS	STAGE	REPRESENTATIVE DIALOGUE
	Initiating	"Hi, how ya doin'?" "Fine. You?"
	Experimenting	"Oh, so you like to ski . . . so do I." "You do?! Great. Where do you go?"
Coming Together	Intensifying	"I . . . I think I love you." "I love you too."
	Integrating	"I feel so much a part of you." "Yeah, we are like one person. What happens to you happens to me."
	Bonding	"I want to be with you always." "Let's get married."
	Differentiating	"I just don't like big social gatherings." "Sometimes I don't understand you. This is one area where I'm certainly not like you at all."
	Circumscribing	"Did you have a good time on your trip?" "What time will dinner be ready?"
Coming Apart	Stagnating	"What's there to talk about?" "Right. I know what you're going to say and you know what I'm going to say."
	Avoiding	"I'm so busy, I just don't know when I'll be able to see you." "If I'm not around when you try, you'll understand."
	Terminating	"I'm leaving you . . . and don't bother trying to contact me." "Don't worry."

relationships do develop, similar patterns are reported.[7]

The model . . . also focuses primarily on relationships where people voluntarily seek contact with, or disengagement from, one another. But the model is not limited to such relationships. All people drawn into, or pulled out of, relationships by forces seemingly outside their control will like or not like such an event and communicate accordingly. For instance, a child's relationship with his or her parent (involuntary) may, at some point, be very close and loving, at another time be cold and distant, and at another time be similar to relationships with other friends. . . .

INTERACTION STAGES

Initiating

This stage incorporates all those processes enacted when we first come together with other people. It may be at a cocktail party or at the beach; it may be with a stranger or with a friend. As we scan the other person we consider our own stereotypes, any prior knowledge of the other's reputation, previous interactions with this person, expectations for this situation, and so on. We are asking ourselves whether this person is "attractive" or "unattractive" and whether we should initiate communication. Next, we try to determine whether the other person is cleared for an encounter—is he or she busy, in a hurry, surrounded by others? Finally, we search for an appropriate opening line to engage the other's attention.

Typically, communicators at this stage are simply trying to display themselves as a person who is pleasant, likable, understanding, and socially adept. In essence, we are saying: "I see you. I am friendly, and I want to open channels for communication to take place." In addition, we are carefully observing the other to reduce any uncertainty we might have—hoping to gain clarification of mood, interest, orientation toward us, and aspects of the other's public personality. Our conscious awareness of these processes is sometimes very low. "Morning, Bob. How ya doin'?" "Morning, Clayton. Go to hell." "Fine, thanks."

Obviously, specific methods and messages used to initiate communication vary with:

1. The kind of relationship and whether the participants have been through this stage before. *Stranger:* "Hello. Nice to meet you." *Friend:* "Hi dude. What's up?"
2. The time allowed for interaction—passing each other on the street versus a formal appointment.
3. The time since last greeting—re-greeting a person you saw just five minutes before versus greeting a relative at the airport who visits once a year.
4. The situational or normative constraints—meeting in the library versus meeting at a rock concert.
5. The special codes of particular groups—fraternity handshake.

In spite of the possibility for considerable variance of initiating behaviors, people generally exercise a good deal of caution and communicate according to conventional formulas.

Experimenting

Once communication has been initiated, we begin the process of experimenting—trying to discover the unknown. Strangers trying to become acquain-

tances will be primarily interested in name, rank, and serial number—something akin to the sniffing ritual in animals. The exchange of demographic information is frequent and often seems controlled by a norm that says: "If you tell me your hometown, I'll tell you mine." Strangers at this stage are diligently searching for an integrating topic, an area of common interest or experience. Sometimes the strain of this search approaches the absurd: "Oh, you're from Oklahoma. Do you know . . . ?" Obviously, the degree to which a person assists another in finding this integrating topic shows the degree of interest in continuing the interaction and the willingness to pursue a relationship.

Miller and his colleagues have pointed out that we use three bases for predictions in interpersonal encounters.[8] With strangers we may have to rely primarily on *cultural information*. If one's partner is from this culture, they probably share some predictable ways of behaving and thinking. You assume they have knowledge of certain cultural happenings. It is a place to begin, but the potential sources of error are many.

As we gain information about another person, we may begin to use *sociological information* as a basis for conversational strategies and adaptations. This knowledge of a person's reference and membership groups is frequently used in casual social gatherings. When we hear that a person is a feminist, a physician, or a Southern Baptist, we immediately begin scanning associations with these labels that may be useful to us in our conversational pursuits.

The third basis for predictions involves *psychological information*. This information recognizes the individual differences associated with one's conversational partner. It is more likely to occur with conversational partners who are better known to you. These sources of information are important because they will mark differences in the small talk of strangers, people from very different cultures, people who have a close relationship, and people whose relationship is close in name only.

It should be noted that people in established close relationships do spend a lot of time experimenting.

It may be an effort to seek greater breadth, to pass the time, or to avoid some uncomfortable vibrations obtained at a more intense level of dialogue. Both strangers and friends are searching for possible similarities; both are trying to present a desirable "come-on self" ("If you like the label, you might like what's in the container"); both are concerned about setting up the next encounter where consistency of behavior can be examined.

Small talk is the sine qua non of experimenting. It is like Listerine; we may hate it, but we may also take large quantities of it every day. If we hate it, why do we do it? Probably because we are vaguely aware of several important functions served by small talk: (1) It is a useful process for uncovering integrating topics and openings for more penetrating conversation. (2) It can be an audition for a future friendship or a way of increasing the scope of a current relationship. (3) It provides a safe procedure for indicating who we are and how another can come to know us better (reduction of uncertainty). (4) It allows us to maintain a sense of community with our fellow human beings.

Relationships at this stage are generally pleasant, relaxed, overtly uncritical, and casual. Commitments are limited. And, like it or not, most of our relationships probably don't progress very far beyond this stage.

Intensifying

When people achieve a relationship known as "close friends," indicators of the relationships are intensified. Active participation and greater awareness of the process typify this stage when it begins. Initial probes toward intensification of intimacy are often exercised with caution, awaiting confirmation before proceeding. Sitting close, for instance, may precede hugging; holding hands will generally precede holding genitals. Requests for physical or psychological favors are sometimes used to validate the existence of intensity in a relationship. . . .

The amount of personal disclosure increases at this stage and we begin to get a glimpse of some previously withheld secrets—that my father was an alcoholic, that I masturbate, that I pretend I'm a rhino when I'm drunk, and other fears, frustrations, failures, imperfections, and prejudices. Disclosures may be related to any topic area, but those dealing most directly with the development of the relationship are crucial. These disclosures make the speaker vulnerable—almost like an animal baring its neck to an attacker.

Verbally, a lot of things may be happening in the intensifying stage:

1. Forms of address become more informal—first name, nickname, or some term of endearment.
2. Use of the first personal plural becomes more common—"*We* should do this" or "*Let's* do this." One study of married couples found that the use of "we" was more likely to be associated with a relationship orientation while the use of "I" was more likely to be associated with a task orientation or the functional requirements and accomplishments of marriage.[9]
3. Private symbols begin to develop, sometimes in the form of a special slang or jargon, sometimes using conventional language forms that have understood, private meanings. Places they've been together; events and times they've shared; and physical objects they've purchased or exchanged; all become important symbols in defining the nature of developing closeness.[10] Such items or memories may be especially devastating and repulsive reminders if the relationship begins to come apart unless the symbols are reinterpreted ("I like this diamond ring because it is beautiful, not because he gave it to me") or put in a different perspective ("It really was fun when we did _____, but in so many other ways he was a jerk").
4. Verbal shortcuts built on a backlog of accumulated and shared assumptions, expectations, interests, knowledge, interactions, and experiences appear more often; one may request a newspaper be passed by simply saying, "paper."
5. More direct expressions of commitment may appear—"We really have a good thing going" or

"I don't know who I'd talk to if you weren't around." Sometimes such expressions receive an echo—"I really like you a lot." "I really like you, too, Elmer."

6. Increasingly, one's partner will act as a helper in the daily process of understanding what you're all about—"In other words, you mean you're . . ." or "But yesterday, you said you were . . ."

Sophistication in nonverbal message transmission also increases. A long verbalization may be replaced by a single touch; postural congruence may be seen; clothing styles may become more coordinated; possessions and personal space may be more permeable.

As the relationship intensifies, each person is unfolding his or her uniqueness while simultaneously blending his or her personality with the other's.

Integrating

The relationship has now reached a point where the two individual personalities almost seem to fuse or coalesce, certainly more than at any previous stage. Davis discusses this concept, which he calls *coupling:*

> The extent to which each intimate tries to give the other his own self-symbols or to collect the other's self-symbols measure the degree to which he wants to increase their communion.*

The experience of Florida State Senator Bruce Smathers and his fiancée provides one example of movement toward this interpersonal fusion. He switched from Methodist to Presbyterian; she switched from Republican to Democrat. The wire service report indicated this was "a compromise they say will help pave the way for their wedding."

Verbal and nonverbal manifestations of integrating may take many forms: (1) Attitudes, opinions, interests, and tastes that clearly distinguish the pair from others are vigorously cultivated—"We have something special; we are unique." (2) Social circles

merge and others begin to treat the two individuals as a common package—one present, one letter, one invitation. (3) Intimacy "trophies" are exchanged so each can "wear" the other's identity—pictures, pins, rings. (4) Similarities in manner, dress, and verbal behavior may also accentuate the oneness. (5) Actual physical penetration of various body parts contributes to the perceived unification. (6) Sometimes common property is designated—"our song," a joint bank account, or a coauthored book. (7) Empathic processes seem to peak so that explanation and prediction of behavior are much easier. (8) Body rhythms and routines achieve heightened synchrony. (9) Sometimes the love of a third person or object will serve as glue for the relationship—"Love me, love my rhinos."

Obviously, integration does not mean complete togetherness or complete loss of individuality. Maintenance of some separate and distinct selves is critical, and possible, due to the strength of the binding elements. One married woman of ten years told us: "I still hold some of myself back from John because it's the only part of me I don't share, and it's important to have something that is uniquely mine."

Thus, we can see that as we participate in the integration process we are intensifying and minimizing various aspects of our total person. As a result, we may not be fully conscious of the idea but, when we commit ourselves to integrating with another, we also agree to become another individual.

Bonding

Bonding is a public ritual that announces to the world that commitments have been formally contracted. It is the institutionalization of the relationship. There are many kinds of bonding rituals and they characterize several stages of the mixed-sex relationship—going steady, engagement, and ultimately marriage. American society has not sanctioned similar rituals for same-sexed romantic pairs, although some exist in certain sub-cultural groups.

Since bonding is simply the contract for the union of the pair at any given stage of the relationship, one might question why it has been designated as a separate stage. It is because the act of bonding itself may be a powerful force in changing the nature of the relationship "for better or for worse." The institutionalization of the relationship hardens it, makes it more difficult to break out of, and probably changes the rhetoric that takes place without a contract. The contract becomes, either explicitly or implicitly, a frequent topic of conversation. Communication strategies can now be based on interpretation and execution of the commitments contained in the contract. In short, the normal ebb and flow of the informal relationship can be, and often is, viewed differently.

When bonding is an extension of integrating, it is probably seen as a way to help stabilize one's newly formed individuality and integrated selves. It is a commitment to a common future:

One's future in Western society at least, is one's most prized possession (or particularization). To commit it to another is the most important gift one can give.*

Bonding is a way of gaining social or institutional support for the relationship. It enables the couple to rely on law or policy or precedent. Bonding also provides guidance for the relationship through specified rules and regulations.

Differentiating

Literally, to differentiate means to become distinct or different in character. Just as integrating is mainly a process of fusion, differentiating is mainly a process of disengaging or uncoupling. While individual differences are of some concern at any stage in the developing relationship, they are now the major focus and serve as a prelude to increased interpersonal distance. A great deal of time and energy are spent talking and thinking about "how different we really are."

Joint endeavors formerly described by "we" or "our" now assume a more "I" or "my" orientation—a sort of "Please mother, I'd rather do it myself" approach. Previously designated joint possessions often become more individualized—"my friends," "my daughter," or "my bathroom." Communication is generally characterized by what distinguishes the two persons, or how little they have in common. Differences may be related to attitudes, interests, personality, relatives, friends, or to a specific behavior such as sexual needs or picking one's nose. Individuals who persist in interaction at this stage perceive these differences as strongly linked to basic or core values. Hence, we would expect to see less conversation about certain central areas of personality that may reflect these basic values. Persons who move in and out of this stage develop a history of expectations for the manner in which such difficulties will be settled, even if it is simply an agreement to seal off the areas of potential conflict.

When an unusually intense siege of differentiating takes place following bonding, it may be because bonding took place before the relationship achieved sufficient breadth and depth. It may also be due to some unplanned individual or social changes that altered the data upon which the original commitment was made. Advocates of renewable-term marriage argue that couples would be more likely to face, discuss, and work out unexpected changes in their lives if the marriage bond was not a lifelong commitment—if "till death do us part" meant the death of the relationship rather than the death of the participants.

The most visible communication form of differentiating, or affirming individuality, is fighting or conflict, although it is possible to differentiate without conflict. . . . Often conflict is a matter of one person simply testing the toleration of the other for something that threatens the relationship; it ultimately ends up with an explicit or implicit "love me (as I am) or leave me."

* From *Intimate Relations* by Murray S. Davis. Copyright © 1973 by Murray S. Davis. Macmillan Publishing Co., Inc.

Circumscribing

At almost any stage of a relationship we can see some evidence of communication being constricted or circumscribed. In decaying relationships, however, information exchange qualitatively and quantitatively decreases. The main message strategy is to carefully control the areas of discussion, restricting communication to safe areas. Thus, we find less total communication in number of interactions as well as depth of subjects discussed, and communications of shorter duration.

Communication restraint applies to both breadth and depth. As the number of touchy topics increases, almost any topic becomes dangerous because it is not clear whether the new topic may in some way be wired to a previous area of static. When communication does take place, superficiality and public aspects are increasingly the norm. Communications related to one's basic values and hidden secrets may have a history of unpleasantness surrounding them; hence, we see a lot less information exchanged about "who I am and what our relationship is like." A corresponding decrease in expressions of commitment may be seen. When one person ventures such an expression, the echo response may not be so prevalent. "In spite of our differences, I still like you a lot." (Silence)

Familiar phrases typical of this stage include: "Don't ask me about that"; "Let's not talk about that anymore"; "It's none of your business"; "Just stick to the kind of work I'm doing and leave my religion out of it"; "You don't own me and you can't tell me what to think"; or "Can't we just be friends?" The last example is a suggestion that prescribes a whole new set of ground rules for permissible topics in the interaction.

When circumscribing characterizes the relationship, it may also have an impact on public social performances. Sometimes mutual social circles are also circumscribed, sometimes the presence of others is the only time when communication seems to increase—an effort to avoid being seen as not getting along. The following routine is not at all uncommon for some couples: Driving to a party, the two people exhibit mutual silence, empty gazes, and a general feeling of exhaustion. While playing out their party roles we see smiling, witticisms, and an orientation for being the life of the party. The trip home becomes a replay of the pre-party behavior.

Stagnating

To stagnate is to remain motionless or inactive. Rather than orally communicate, participants often find themselves conducting covert dialogues and concluding that since they "know" how the interaction will go, it is not necessary to say anything. At this stage, so many areas are closed off, efforts to communicate effectively are at a standstill. Even superficial areas have become so infected by previous communicative poison that they are generally left untried. In a sense, the participants are just marking time.

Some of the messages that are sent reflect unpleasant feeling states through the medium of non-verbal behavior. Other messages are very carefully chosen and well thought out. Language choices and message strategies seem to come even closer to those used with strangers, and the subject of the relationship is nearly taboo. . . .

Extended stagnating can be seen in many relationships: between parents and children, just prior to divorce, just prior to the termination of a courtship, following unproductive small talk. The main theme characterizing this stage is "There is little sense bringing anything up because I know what will happen, and it won't be particularly pleasant." Experimentation is minimal because the unknown is thought to be known. It is during this time that each partner may engage in "imagined interactions."[11] These imagined dialogues will either take the form of narrative (e.g., "I'll say this and then she'll say this, and then . . .") or actual dialogues (e.g., "I'll do it." "You don't have to." "Ok." "Ok, what?" "Ok, I won't." "Your typical attitude." "And *Your Typical Attitude!*" . . .).

You might legitimately question why people would linger at this stage with so many apparent costs accumulating. Most don't. But when persons continue interacting at this stage they may be getting some rewards outside of the primary relationship, through increased attention to their work or in developing another relationship. They also avoid the pain of terminating the relationship, which they may anticipate will be stronger than the current pain. Others may have hope that they can still revive the relationship. Still others may spend time at this stage because of some perverse pleasures obtained in punishing the other person.

Avoiding

While stagnating, the participants are usually in the same physical environment. Avoiding attempts to eliminate that condition. The rhetoric of avoidance is the antithesis of the rhetoric of initiation. Here, communication is specifically designed to avoid the possibility of face-to-face or voice-to-voice interaction. The overriding message seems to be: "I am not interested in seeing you; I am not interested in building a relationship; and I would like to close the communication channels between us." In this sense, then, avoiding suggests a much more permanent state of separation than that communicated by most people in their everyday leavetaking.

When the need to communicate avoidance results from an intimate relationship gone sour, the particular messages may contain overtones of antagonism or unfriendliness. They are more likely to be direct and to the point. "Please don't call me anymore. I just don't want to see or talk to you." This bluntness may naturally evolve from other conditions as well, such as when one person wants to pursue the relationship and ignores the more subtle avoidance cues. These subtle or indirect cues may take the form of being consistently late for appointments or preceding each encounter with "I can't stay long." Here the avoiding tactics are not motivated so much by dislike of the other as a lack of desire to expend time and energy pursuing a relationship. Sometimes an inordinate number of conflicting engagements can make the point: "I'm so busy I don't know when I'll be able to see you. Friday? I'm going home for the weekend. Monday? I have a sorority meeting. Tuesday? I have to study for a test," etc., etc.

In certain situations physical separation simply cannot be achieved, so a form of avoiding takes place in the presence of the other—it's as if the other person didn't exist. Not surprisingly under such conditions we find the receiver participating less in what interaction is available, not evaluating the other highly, and being less inclined to provide a reward to the other when an opportunity arises. The less obvious result of being ignored is the possibility of a lowered self-concept.[12]

Terminating

Relationships can terminate immediately after a greeting or after twenty years of intimacy. Sometimes they die slowly over a long period of time. The bonds that held the pair together wear thin and finally pull apart. The reasons behind such deterioration may be something obvious like living in parts of the country separated by great distance; or termination may just be the end result of two people growing socially and psychologically at different rates and in different directions. At other times, the threads holding two people together may be abruptly cut. It may be the death of one partner, radically changed circumstances, or an effort by one person to spare both of them the anticipated agony of a prolonged termination period.

Naturally, the nature of the termination dialogue is dependent on many factors: the relative status held or perceived between the two communicators; the kind of relationship already established or desired in the future; the amount of time allowed; whether the dialogue is conducted via the telephone, through a letter, or face to face; and many other individual and environmental factors.

Generally, however, we would predict termination dialogue to be characterized by messages of distance and disassociation. *Distance* refers to an attempt to put psychological and physical barriers between the two communicators. This might take the form of actual physical separation, or it may be imbedded in other nonverbal and verbal messages. *Disassociation* is found in messages that are essentially preparing one or both individuals for their continued life without the other—increasing concern for one's own self-interests, emphasizing differences. Obviously, the amount of distancing and disassociation will vary with the kind of relationship being dissolved, time available, and so on.

We would also predict that the general dimensions of communicative behavior reviewed earlier in this chapter would polarize more than ever around narrow, stylized, difficult, rigid, awkward, public, hesitant, and suspended judgments.

Finally, we would like to take a finding derived from the study of conversations and apply it to relationships. Thus, we would predict that termination dialogue would regularly manifest: (1) a summary statement; (2) behaviors signaling the impending termination or decreased access; and (3) messages that indicate what the future relationship (if any) will be like.[13] A summary statement reviews the relationship's history and provides the rationale for the imminent termination. Decreased-access messages clarify what is happening. Addressing the future avoids awkward interactions after parting. Even when dissolving a long-term relationship, the subject of being future friends or enemies must be addressed. "I'll always respect you, but I don't love you anymore," or "I don't ever want to see you again!" Saying goodbye to a long-term relationship may take longer, especially if one party does not want to end it and seeks to delay the final parting. . . .

MOVEMENT: IN, OUT, AND AROUND STAGES

Let us now return to some of our original questions to explain fully the stages just outlined: What are the forces which help us understand our movement in, out, and around the various stages? What directions for movement are possible at each stage? What is the likely rate of movement through the stages outlined in the model?

The first question focuses on the forces of change. Movement within stages may involve less intense, but possibly more frequent, fluctuations than movement to a new stage—but both involve change. Two theories provide useful perspectives for explaining movement through interaction stages.

Dialectical Theory

From this perspective, change takes place as the result of trying to resolve the inevitable tensions of relationship life. These tensions arise when we are faced with the desire to do two opposite things at the same time. We want to seek togetherness with our partner, but at any given point we may make autonomy and individual needs a priority. The way a couple communicatively manages situations like this provides the measure of how and why their relationship changes. Baxter has identified three dialectical tensions that she believes are central to relationship change.[14]

Autonomy–Connection. Relationships require that each partner remain an individual while at the same time merging that self with his or her partner. Obviously, intimate relationships require more integration than those of casual friends, which, in turn, makes this an especially critical dimension for intimates. When there is too much togetherness or too little of it, this will create the tension, which will initiate change. Questions about autonomy and connection occur at all relationship stages— whether it involves the decision to become a couple, the rules regarding freedom outside the relationship, or pondering whether staying together is worse than separating.

Openness–Closedness. Even though beginning relationships are often characterized as efforts to seek information from another and provide information about yourself to this other, there is also a counterforce that cautions about revealing too much too soon. This kind of reveal–hide tension continues throughout various relationship stages. We know that on the one hand we need openness to achieve intimacy; we also know that we make our self and our relationship more vulnerable with greater openness.

Novelty–Predictability. In order to be comfortable with another person, a certain amount of predictability is necessary. Without predictable patterns there is too much uncertainty and ambivalence for a long-term relationship—that is, having someone you know you can count on in certain predictable ways. But too much predictability (in certain areas or in general) may make the relationship seem stale and prompt a call for something "different."

Each couple may react to the tensions created on these dimensions in different ways, but it can be a complicated process of negotiation. For example, partner A may want a great deal of autonomy and partner B may want only a little less. Partner A thinks that the survival of the relationship will require even more connectedness than partner B wants. But partner B thinks if partner A emphasized togetherness only a little more, they'd have a fine relationship. At this point we are less concerned with how this will be negotiated than we are in pointing out how change or movement in relationships involves: (1) what one person wants for him or herself; (2) what one person wants for the other person; and (3) what both parties want for the relationship. Many times people don't know what they want until they start talking.

Even though autonomy–connectedness, openness-closedness, and novelty–predictability may be at the heart of relationship change, the discussions that affect these dimensions may be on any topic. For example, suppose two intimates disagree about the need to recycle bottles, cans, and newspapers. They discuss it often and each maintains a disagreeable position to the other. Each realizes that the other's position is not likely to change by continued argument that creates unpleasant feelings for both

of them. They develop a tacit agreement not to discuss the issue so often and, when they do, each subscribes to the rule that on this issue they will agree to disagree. The way this couple managed the issue of recycling affected all three central tensions discussed earlier—that is, each can be autonomous on this issue but remain connected; each has agreed to a certain degree of openness when discussing the issue, but each knows it is important to close down the number of times the topic is discussed; and there is a certain predictability to their interaction on this issue, but this could change as each feels the tug of novelty.

Sometimes the responses of a couple to these tensions will produce dialogue that propels them toward greater intimacy, and sometimes toward less intimacy. It is important to remember that these tensions associated with building and maintaining a relationship are natural—part of what relating is all about. It is equally important to understand that one cannot "solve" relationship problems by seeking greater connectedness or openness or predictability, because the very act of moving toward these goals brings into focus the need for the polar opposite. The more you practice closed behavior, for example, the more salient openness becomes.

Social Exchange Theory

Social exchange theory has been used to explain changes in social behavior for many years.[15] Simply put, *social exchange theory* says that social relationships involve the exchange of resources (e.g., love, status, information, money, goods, and services)[16] and that these resources are perceived as positive and/or negative—as a reward and/or cost.

> By rewards, we refer to the pleasures, satisfactions, and gratifications, the person enjoys. The provision of a means whereby a drive is reduced or a need fulfilled constitutes a reward.
>
> By costs, we refer to any factors that operate to inhibit or deter a performance of a sequence of behavior. The greater the deterrents to performing a given act—the greater the inhibition the individual has to overcome—the greater the cost of the act. Thus, cost is high when

great physical or mental effort is required, when embarrassment or anxiety accompany the action, or when there are conflicting forces or competing response tendencies of any sort.[17]

Davis proposes an analogous concept when he discusses giving or not giving favors.[18] Favors may be physical or psychological. Although physical favors may certainly have psychological overtones, they include such behaviors as: giving a monetary loan, satisfying sexual desires, having a person to dinner, protecting against physical harm, providing an extra hand when one person is incapacitated or lazy, or offering some expertise the other person lacks. Examples of psychological favors include feeling an integral part of the other's sorrows and joys, giving support for approved behavior, helping to offset or improve unapproved behavior while still communicating support, and helping the other to justify his or her problems. "You couldn't help it. Everybody goes through the same thing."

When favors are given, it may be because one participant in the relationship: (1) is dependent on the other; (2) is returning a favor received; (3) wants to obligate the other in the future; or (4) is rewarded by seeing the other person enjoy the favor given.

Withholding favors may occur when one person: (1) doesn't think a similar favor will be needed in return; (2) feels the relationship will suffer by granting the favor; (3) doesn't think the favor can be returned; (4) doesn't have the time or resources to give the favor; or (5) doesn't think the other needs or will benefit from the favor.

It would be a mistake to assume that we are constantly evaluating everything that happens to us as a reward or cost. It is more likely that we make such assessments when we feel especially good or bad in an effort to determine how that state came about. We also pay particular attention to the reward/cost ratio when we have strong expectations for favorable or unfavorable outcomes.

When we evaluate and analyze these rewards (or favors) and costs, it may include a combination of the following as they affect the relationship as a whole: (1) the current encounter, (2) past encounters, and (3) future encounters.

Analysis of the Current Encounter. For any given encounter, you might assess the rewards and costs and ask yourself whether the rewards were greater than the cost. Naturally, the greater the ratio of rewards to costs, the more satisfied you are with the relationship. If your own investment is high, you may have to receive a proportionately high return to evaluate the experience favorably.

Sometimes we seek the highest rewards for ourselves with the least cost, a condition which may also increase the costs for the other person. While frequent application of this strategy sometimes works successfully for transient, short-term, or superficial relationships, it does not seem conducive to achieving greater intimacy because one party in the relationship is always "one down." Of course, you can try to keep the other person from knowing about your increased rewards—keeping the other from knowing that he or she is the "loser"—but daily interaction with intimates makes this chore especially difficult.

When a student tells a professor he or she is one of the best teachers in the school and receives a correspondingly high grade (deserved, of course), the situation could be described as rewarding to the student and the professor while incurring minimal costs for both.

Analysis of Past Encounters. In any given situation, we may also ask ourselves how this experience compares with all others we have had with this person. You may have an experience in which the costs are very high, but when compared with the multitude of previous rewarding experiences, it does not seem to be a sufficient cause for slowing down the relationship. Sometimes one person has been almost completely dependent on the other for rewards in certain areas. Then when the other person "doesn't come through" or "takes advantage" it may be quite a shock. Conversely, an extremely rewarding experience may not balance an interpersonal economy that has accumulated many costs. It may, however, be an important first step in causing the relationship to grow again. Close friends, lovers, and spouses are less likely to expect a constant balance of rewards and costs because they antici-pate that the favors given and received will average out during the course of their relationship. But as these relationships experience problems, the de-mand for more immediate rewards may increase—particularly in newer relationships, with insecure partners, etc. Sometimes we perceive something as a cost initially (an intense argument), but the long-term effects are rewarding (important issues for the relationship were openly discussed and mutually agreeable decisions were reached).

This analysis of the cumulative rewards and costs obtained in a relationship also provides val-uable data for comparison with possible alternatives to the current relationship. For example, poor mar-riages often continue because the alternatives—di-vorce proceedings, living alone, division of the children, social criticism—offer potentially greater costs than those currently felt. Thus, not all the re-wards and costs that affect the relationship are de-rived from the partners themselves. Other people in your social network, people you work with, rel-atives—all provide rewards and costs that may im-pact on the two-person relationship.

Analysis of Future Encounters. Finally, we may ask ourselves whether it will be rewarding to inter-act with this person in the future. What will be the relative rewards and costs derived from interacting at our current stage of the relationship? At a less intimate level? At a more intimate level? Such con-siderations have a definite impact on the movement through the various stages of growth and deterio-ration.

One important concept regarding expectations for future encounters concerns the norm of reci-procity.[19] Simply stated, the *norm of reciprocity* sug-gests that there is a strong tendency on the part of human beings to respond in kind to the behavior they receive. Are you willing to give another certain rewards today in the hope that the norm of reci-procity will be activated and you will be "done unto as you did unto them" sometime in the future?

Reciprocity is not likely to be an immediate, un-thinking response, but one that is conscious and

planned. The return volley does not necessarily have to take place immediately following the other's serve—"they had us to dinner last month so we should have them over soon," or "they sent us a Christmas card last year, so maybe we'd better send them one this year." The reciprocated act may not be of exactly equivalent value. A: "You're a great person." B: "I really admire your artistic talent." The exchange may concern two very different objects—trading access to one's genitals for access to the other's money. Or it may involve almost antithetical behavior—for example, dominance provoking sub-missiveness and vice versa.

A closely related phenomenon is known as *imi-tation*. Here, the reciprocated response usually fol-lows soon after the initial response and is generally less conscious. The behavior is similar, but still op-erates within a basic reward-cost framework. Have you ever noticed how jokes seem to lead to more jokes; strokes lead to more strokes? A: "You really did a good job." B: "So did you." Or A: "I love you." B: "I love you, too." Hostility may evoke hostility. I raise my voice and you counter by raising yours. Nonverbal cues like smiling, nodding, silence, and structural dimensions like interruptions or length of utterance are other examples of imitation that have been documented by research. The phenom-enon known as *emotional contagion,* where one per-son's feeling state is assumed and reflected by others present, would also seem to fall within the realm of imitation.

That a norm of reciprocity exists is evident. The exact manner in which it appears, however, is largely dependent on the nature of the relationship. For instance, some feel there is a reciprocity in dis-closing information about oneself. Indeed, during initiation and experimentation stages the obligation for giving tit for tat is high. "I'll tell you my home-town if you'll tell me yours." During intensifying and integrating, the parties to the relationship may feel that they can ask and expect greater reciprocity of intimate information. It's almost like saying: "By revealing part of my inner self to you first, I'm showing my trust. This should give you sufficient reward and increase the possibility that you will trust me with an equivalent secret of yours. And if you do, our relationship will grow." Some, however, would argue that during the integrating process the reciprocity norm becomes muddled because it is hard to analyze an exchange of intimate information between two people who see themselves so often as a single entity. It should be obvious that there are many relationships that do not demand reciprocation for a high degree of disclosure—you don't expect your doctor, psychiatrist, or priest to exchange intimate information with you.

The preceding observations about past, current, and future rewards make it seem like we are always highly conscious of what is a reward and what is a cost. On the contrary, many times we only make such a determination after we have a *feeling* of satisfaction or dissatisfaction. It should also be noted that we don't always react to actual rewards and costs. Instead, we react to the rhetoric of rewards and costs—how people talk about what they do to reward and punish others and how talk itself can be rewarding or costly. We know very little about how partners in a relationship actually talk about rewards and costs.

Rewards and Costs in Enduring Relationships.
Several characteristics of more intimate, long-term relationships affect the way these participants deal with rewards and costs.

First, the value of both rewards and costs tends to increase as the relationship becomes more intimate. "I sure like to spend an evening just talking to you" may be much more powerful from an intimate than an acquaintance; similarly, "You're so rigid in your beliefs" can be a great cost from an intimate and an unimportant opinion from an acquaintance.

Second, intimates exchange a greater variety of resources than casual acquaintances. And seemingly inequitable resources may be equitably exchanged—e.g., a special anniversary dinner is "paid back" by not going to play golf on Sunday. Intimates have had the time to negotiate the relative values of these different resources, but less intimate

pairs have not. As a result, exchanges between acquaintances are often of the same type—e.g., you had us over for dinner so we'll have you over for dinner.

Third, intimates are more likely to tolerate periods where costs exceed rewards than will acquaintances. Since the relationship is expected to continue, the expectation is that losses can be recouped later. In fact, sometimes people will incur considerable costs during the courtship period in order to win the other's approval for marriage. This may create an imbalance that is difficult to restore immediately and gets the marriage off to a rough start.

Fourth, some rewards and costs of intimates may need to be analyzed as a couple rather than two individuals. The wife's career setback or the husband's success in losing weight may more appropriately be considered as costs or rewards for both people rather than the specific individual concerned. If one profits, both are rewarded; if one loses, both are hurt.

Fifth, since intimates in long-term relationships have many events over many years to consider in any assessment of overall rewards and costs, it is likely that intimates may find it more difficult to specifically account for an overall feeling of deficit or surplus in rewards and costs. After how much time does one stop expecting "payment" for something? To what extent can the time we spent together when dating be used to balance the time we are apart now?

Observers of people who have maintained a relationship over a long period of time may tend to believe that it is happiness or intimacy that has sustained the relationship over so many years. Some enduring relationships do manifest a high degree of intimacy over the years, but others are far less intimate. A married couple may stay together because the marriage provides needed security or because separation is perceived as more costly than a marriage with little intimacy. Sometimes the mutual commitment to the institution of marriage—rather than the marital partner—will sustain a marital partnership. In short, the rewards necessary to sustain a relationship over a long period of time may be derived from a variety of sources other than feelings of intimacy for one's partner.

An analysis of the rewards and costs in our everyday interpersonal relations can be very useful for understanding why we choose to pursue some relationships, remain at the same level with others, and terminate still others. Most resources we exchange have both a reward and a cost component to them. And some things are only rewarding because they aren't a cost. Some behaviors considered rewarding at one point in a relationship may be perceived as costs at another point. Just because we are rewarded by another person doesn't mean our relationship will continue to increase in intimacy. You may really like to play tennis with someone, but the rewards derived from this activity alone are not sufficient to bring the partners to a more intimate stage. And even if one partner felt the rewards were sufficient to move toward greater intimacy, the other partner may not.

Any analysis of human relationships in terms of an "economic model" of exchange inevitably causes some to feel that the humanness has been taken out of relationships and that the possibility of behavior that is not self-serving has been eliminated. They point to examples of people running into blazing buildings or freezing rivers to save strangers, donating blood or money without hope of reciprocated gain. Such examples tend to support the contention that altruistic behavior does exist. Altruism, however, is a complex behavior that may have hidden or subtle rewards. Krebs's experiments suggest that some highly empathic people will obtain rewards vicariously by helping others, even if it means jeopardizing their own welfare.[20] Similar good samaritan acts appear to put the helpee in a secondary role while the helper derives satisfaction from the contest between himself or herself and the extant forces of evil.[21] Thus, even though I may be motivated by the accumulation of rewards for myself, this doesn't necessarily mean that I will always act in a selfish manner; maximizing my gains may be achieved by maximizing yours. . . .

Now that we have an idea of two general theories which are useful for understanding why change in

relationships occurs, let's examine our model from another perspective—the directions that are available for movement.

Directions Available for Movement Through Interaction Stages

The following propositions about movement possibilities can be derived from the staircase analogy presented in the Staircase Model:

Movement is generally systematic and sequential.

Movement may be forward.

Movement may be backward.

Movement occurs within stages.

Movement is always to a new place.

Movement Is Generally Systematic and Sequential. Typically, when coming together, people follow a process of moving up the left side of the staircase in Figure 4.1; when coming apart, they commonly move down the right side. This, however, does not suggest that the process is linear or that there is a fixed, unchangeable sequence of movement through stages. We are dealing with a phenomenon that is never at rest, continually moving and in flux. Of course, the participants may perceive the development of a relationship as chaotic or "out of control"—moved by forces "bigger than either one of us." No doubt some relationships develop in a less orderly fashion than others, but many people experience a general sequencing effect because: (1) each stage contains important presuppositions for the following stage; (2) sequencing makes forecasting adjacent stages easier; and (3) skipping steps is a gamble on the uncertainties presented by the lack of information that could have been learned in the skipped step. Some social norms even help to inhibit skipping steps.

Sometimes people skip steps during growth processes. Witness the not unfamiliar pickup routine that moves from "Hi, what's your name?" (Initiat-

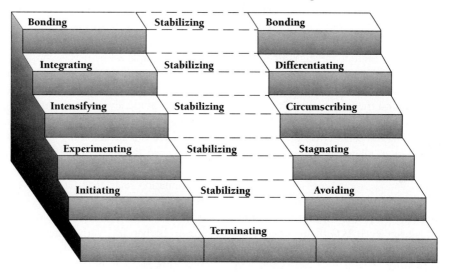

FIGURE 4.1

Staircase Model of Interaction Stages

ing) to "Let's get out of this place and get to know each other better at my apartment" (Intensifying). Another familiar skip is for a couple to reach Intensifying and then move to Bonding—only to find out later that their major problem is the lack of integrating in their relationship. Each person "really loves" the other, but one or both are unwilling to move from a primarily "I" orientation to a "we" orientation—risking the merger of self with another.

The termination of relationships may also violate an orderly sequence, achieving sudden death rather than a slow decay. Sudden death is reflected in the situation where a couple is operating at the integration stage, making plans for marriage, and suddenly one party elopes with another person, never to be heard from again. Returning home to a house empty of furniture and finding divorce papers on the last remaining table is another example. As a general rule, movement is to adjacent stages (vertical or horizontal), but any final-state form can be approached from differing initial conditions and through a variety of paths.

Movement May Be Forward. During phases of coming together, one evaluates the various rewards and costs and may decide to advance the relationship to the next logical step upward. The decision might be one of formalizing one's commitments during integration by moving to the bonding stage. It is, of course, possible to perform bonding rituals at earlier stages, thus having one foot on intensifying and one on bonding. During the phases of coming apart, forward movement means a movement from one of the stairs on the right to one on the left. For instance, a pair may be at the circumscribing stage and, after various efforts at rejuvenation, move back to intensification, and, in time, perhaps move toward integration. Any movement toward greater intimacy is considered *forward*.

Movement May Be Backward. Having once achieved interaction at a level such as intensification, the relationship may not be able to stabilize and slips back to a previous step, in this case, experimenting. The parties may mutually agree that a more superficial relationship is more to their liking. "I like you a lot, Delbert. I still want to go out with you, but I would rather we didn't try to make something out of our relationship which it just isn't right now. Maybe it will develop into something more intimate, but it takes time." Of course, backward movement in the deterioration process is a constant movement down the staircase from differentiation to termination. Backward movement starts laterally, moving from a stair on the left to one on the right. An example is meeting a person at a party and experimenting, inviting the person over several times until stagnation sets in, then avoiding and eventually terminating the relationship.

Movement Occurs Within Stages. The central staircase represents the possibility of stabilizing relationships at a given level. As with any system, we are constantly fighting the law of nature, which says that all things move toward disorganization and death. We constantly try to arrest possible disintegration by achieving some steady state or equilibrium. This might involve brief forays into communication more characteristic of other stages, while generally maintaining the interaction within a given stage. When lovers quarrel, their disagreement can manifest characteristics more central to the deterioration process. Naturally, to maintain the relationship at the stage more appropriate to lovers, certain forces have to be enacted to counter this disruptive force. In some cases, such disruption may not be as harmful as it first appears. Those who study living systems argue that negative feedback is often needed to keep the system functioning. The absence of negative feedback can cause the steady state to vanish and terminate the system. This is probably why intimates are more apt to provide us with evaluative judgments.

There will always be a certain degree of instability associated with any stable relationship. Thus, when patterns fluctuate excessively or when they do not fluctuate at all, a condition of instability exists. To complicate things even more, it is likely that there are progressive steps within the stages—a beginning, middle, and end—for each stage.

Movement Is Always to a New Place. Once something has been worked through, it is different. Once communicators have achieved a certain level of interaction, they can never go back to "the way we were." They may, however, work through the same stages or even more intimate ones. Take, for example, a couple who spends considerable time in the experimenting stage. One person wants to move to the intensifying stage; the other doesn't. As a result, they gradually move toward stagnation and, eventually, to avoiding. Through chance, the couple is later put in adjoining rooms in an experimental coed dorm. Should they choose to renew the relationship and start moving through the experimentation stage again, it will be colored by the previous experiences. It may mean some things can be worked through much more quickly but others have to be handled with patience and sensitivity, perhaps due to the pain incurred in the original decay process. The best predictor of who will be friends after an intimate relationship is whether they were friends prior to the romantic involvement. In addition, the extent to which a partner feels "taken advantage of" or manipulated is also an important factor in determining whether romantic partners can be "just friends" after romance.[22]

Now that we have some idea of the directions followed in developing relationships, a few comments about the rate of growth and deterioration are in order.

Rate of Movement Through Interaction Stages

Movement is usually rapid through stages already achieved or exposed. Intimates or close friends can more easily move through or dispense with small talk (characteristic of experimenting) and move freely into more personal areas.

Movement is usually rapid through areas where positive rewards have been achieved. Those married couples who avoid talking about "why don't you come to church with your family" may be agreeing not to disagree, which may be rewarding in itself. People interested in developing a positive relationship generally avoid conflict (which might elicit high costs or simply provide no reward) until their relationship has a sufficient reward reservoir to manage such conflict.

Movement may be rapid where time is short—for example, summer romances. In a highly mobile and transient society like that in the United States, many efforts are made to short-circuit a lengthy process for getting to know people.

Movement may be facilitated where proximity is high. Seeing someone on a daily basis allows more rapid assimilation of information used in determining whether movement will be forward or backward.

Movement may be facilitated by certain situational features—sensitivity groups, parents-without-partners groups, a newcomer to a block party. In other situations such as attending a church service, movement is inhibited by sanctions regarding what can be talked about.

Movement is generally faster during the early stages. Highly personal information, characteristic of more intimate stages, comes out slowly and acts as a governing agent. In addition, intimates are usually intimates because they have a backlog of rewards. Each reward is tempered by previous rewards, making it harder for dramatic movement to take place as a result of a new reward. "Sure Homer brought me flowers and I appreciate them, but he always does that."

Movement may be slow or rapid depending on individual needs. Two lonely, isolated people with few friends may move quickly; two popular people with a lot of stable friends may move more slowly.

Movement is bound to be slower if only one party to the relationship desires a change, whether it is to advance or retreat.

Movement during deterioration may be rapid if one person violates a particularly sacred part of their covenant. This is particularly true when (1) the offended person has repeatedly taken a strong stand on the issue and has forecast destruction of the relationship, should violation occur; and (2) if the offended person sees no possibility for offsetting the violation.

Movement from courtship to marriage is accelerated by the time spent together in joint activities and the expression of strong feelings for the other. If the couple feels the reasons for their relationship growth are similar to what is generally expected, this also seems to promote faster movement from courtship to marriage.[23]

Sometimes movement is rapid when both parties agree that they have experienced a relationship "turning point." For example, the mutual expression of serious commitment, the energy each puts into making up after a bad fight, or the way each partner handles an external threat to the relationship, can facilitate movement.[24] If one person thinks it is a turning point and the other does not, it is not as likely to stimulate rapid movement.

These are the major forces that determine how fast or how slow we move in and out of interaction stages and relationships in general. There are many other forces as well.

SUMMARY

There are many different types of relationships, but all of them seem to have some characteristics in common. For example, relationship expectations change as a result of communication behavior and communication behavior changes as a result of relationship expectation. In addition, each type of relationship appears to fluctuate along a continuum of intimacy or "closeness." With these features in mind, a model of interaction stages covering the growth and decay of relationships was proposed. The model was based on the idea that certain patterns of communication manifest themselves at different points in the life of a relationship. This evolutionary model of message making from greeting to goodbye included the following stages: initiating, experimenting, intensifying, integrating, bonding, differentiating, circumscribing, stagnating, avoiding, and terminating. An overview of the language, topics, and message strategies relevant to each stage was discussed. The model is closely linked to the eight dimensions of communication. . . . In the last section the concepts of dialectical contradictions and rewards and costs (derived from social exchange theory) were introduced to help explain why, where, and how fast people move through interaction stages. In short, we have taken a quick trip via communication behavior through the birth, adolescence, maturity, sickness, isolation, and death of a relationship.

ENDNOTES

[1] Relationship expectations have been examined from several different perspectives. See R. M. Sabatelli and J. Pearce, "Exploring Marital Expectations," *Journal of Social and Personal Relationships* 3 (1986): 307-321; J. H. Harvey, G. Agostinelli, and A. L. Weber, "Account-making and the Formation of Expectations About Close Relationships." In C. Hendrick, ed., *Close Relationships.* Newbury Park, CA: Sage, 1989, A. L. Vangelisti and J. A. Daly, "Expectations in Close Relationships." Paper presented to the International Communication Association, 1991.

[2] M. Rands and G. Levinger, "Implicit Theories of Relationship: An Intergenerational Study," *Journal of Personality and Social Psychology* 37 (1979): 645-661.

[3] M. L. Knapp, D. G. Ellis, and B. A. Williams, "Perceptions of Communication Behavior Associated with Relationship Terms," *Communication Monographs* 47 (1980): 262-278.

[4] R. E. Quinn, "Coping with Cupid: The Formation, Impact and Management of Romantic Relationships in Organizations," *Administrative Science Quarterly* 22 (1977): 30-45; and J. P. Dillard, "Close Relationships at Work: Perceptions of the Motives and Performance of Relational Participants." *Journal of Social and Personal Relationships* 4 (1987): 179-193.

[5] J. G. Delia, "Some Tentative Thoughts Concerning the Study of Interpersonal Relationships and Their Development," *Western Journal of Speech Communication* 44 (1980): 97-103.

[6] Representative works include: R. Lacoursiere, *The Life Cycle of Groups* (New York: Human Sciences Press, 1980); R. Thornton and P. M. Nardi, "The Dynamics of Role Acquisition," *American Journal of Sociology* 80 (1975): 870-885; I. Altman and D. A. Taylor, *Social Penetration: The Development of Interpersonal Relationships* (New York: Holt, Rinehart & Winston, 1973); B. W. Tuckman, "Developmental Sequence in Small Groups," *Psychological Bulletin* 63 (1965): 384-399; S. W. Duck, *Personal Relationships and Personal Constructs: A Study of Friendship Formation* (New York: John Wiley & Sons, 1973); M. S. Davis, *Intimate Relations* (New York: Free Press, 1973); T. M. Newcomb, *The Acquaintance Process* (New York: Holt, Rinehart & Winston, 1961); C. B. Broderick, "Predicting Friendship Behavior: A Study of the Determinants of Friendship Selection and Maintenance in a College Population" (Doctoral diss. Cornell University, 1956); G. M. Phillips and N. J. Metzger, *Intimate Communication* (Boston: Allyn & Bacon, 1976), pp. 401-403; C. R. Berger and R. J. Calabrese, "Some Explorations in Initial Interaction and Beyond: Toward a Developmental Theory of Interpersonal Communication," *Human Communication Research* 1 (1975): 99-112; C. R. Rogers, "A Process Conception of Psychotherapy," *American Psychologist* 13 (1958): 142-149; G. Simmel, *The Sociology of George Simmel,* trans. K. Wolff (New York: Free Press of Glencoe, 1950); K. Lewin, "Some Social Psychological Differences Between the United States and Germany," *Character and Personality* 4 (1936): 265-293; J. T. Wood, "Communication and Relational Culture: Bases for the Study of Human Relationships," *Communication Quarterly* 30 (1982): 75-83; D. P. McWhirter, and A. M. Mattison, *The Male Couple* (Englewood Cliffs, NJ: Prentice-Hall, 1984); W. J. Dickens and D. Perlman, "Friendship over the Life-Cycle." In S. Duck and R. Gilmour, eds. *Personal Relationships: 2. Developing Personal Relationships.* New York: Academic Press, 1981; C. A. VanLear, Jr. and N. Trujillo, "On Becoming Acquainted: A Longitudinal Study of Social Judgment Processes," *Journal of Social and Personal Relationships* 3 (1986): 375-392; and J. M. Honeycutt, J. G. Cantrill, and R. W. Greene, "Memory Structures for Relational Escalation: A Cognitive Test of the Sequencing of Relational Actions and Stages. *Human Communication Research* 16 (1989): 62-90.

[7] McWhirter and Mattison, *The Male Couple.*

[8] G. R. Miller and M. Steinberg, *Between People: A New Analysis of Interpersonal Communication.* Chicago: Science Research Associates, 1975; G. R. Miller and M. J. Sunnafrank, "All Is for One But One Is Not for All: A Conceptual Perspective of Interpersonal Communication." In F. E. X. Dance, ed., *Human Communication Theory.* New York: Harper & Row, 1982.

[9] H. L. Rausch, K. A. Marshall, and J. M. Featherman., "Relations at Three Early Stages of Marriage as Reflected by the Use of Personal Pronouns." *Family Process* 9 (1970): 69-82.

[10] L. A. Baxter, "Symbols of Relationship Identity in Relationship Cultures." *Journal of Social and Personal Relationships* 4 (1987): 261-280.

[11] Imagined interactions may occur at other points in the relationship as well—and for different purposes. For example, a person may construct an imagined dialogue relative to a forthcoming date or marriage proposal. See J. M. Honeycutt, K. S. Zagacki, and R. Edwards, "Intrapersonal Communication, Social Cognition, and Imagined Interactions." In C. Roberts and K. Watson, eds., *Readings in Intrapersonal Communication.* Birmingham, AL: Gorsuch Scarisbrick, 1989.

[12] D. M. Geller, L. Goodstein, M. Silver, and W. C. Sternberg, "On Being Ignored: The Effects of the Violation of Implicit Rules of Social Interaction." *Sociometry* 37 (1974): 541-556.

[13] M. L. Knapp, R. P. Hart, G. W. Friedrich, and G. M. Shulman, "The Rhetoric of Goodbye: Verbal and Nonverbal Correlates of Human Leave-Taking." *Speech Monographs* 40 (1973): 182-198.

[14] L. A. Baxter, "A Dialectical Perspective on Communication Strategies in Relationship Development." In S. Duck, ed., *Handbook of Personal Relationships.* New York: Wiley, 1988, pp. 257-273; and L. A. Baxter, "Dialectical Contradictions in Relationship Development." *Journal of Social and Personal Relationships* 7 (1990): 69-88.

[15] G. C. Homans, *Social Behavior: Its Elementary Forms* (New York: Harcourt Brace Jovanovich, 1961).

[16] U. G. Foa, "Interpersonal Economic Resources," *Science* 171 (1971): 345-351.

[17] J. W. Thibaut and H. H. Kelley, *The Social Psychology of Groups* (New York: John Wiley & Sons, 1959), pp. 12-13.

[18] Davis, *Intimate Relations,* pp. 131-168.

[19] A. W. Gouldner, "The Norm of Reciprocity: A Preliminary

Statement." *American Sociological Review* 25 (1960): 161-178. T. Leary labeled a similar concept the *interpersonal reflex* in *Interpersonal Diagnosis of Personality* (New York: Ronald Press, 1957). W. J. Lederer and D. D. Jackson provide an interesting treatment of the reciprocity phenomenon in marriage in *Mirages of Marriage* (New York: W. W. Norton, 1968), pp. 177-186.

20 D. L. Krebs, "Empathy and Altruism," *Journal of Personality and Social Psychology* 32 (1975): 1134-1146.

21 T. L. Huston, G. Geis, and R. Wright, "The Angry Samaritans," *Psychology Today* 10 (1976): 61-62, 64, 85.

22 S. Metts, W. R. Cupach, and R. A. Bejlovec, " 'I Love You Too Much to Ever Start Liking You': Redefining Romantic Relationships." *Journal of Social and Personal Relationships* 6 (1989): 259-274.

23 T. L. Huston, C. A. Surra, N. M. Fitzgerald, and R. M. Cate, "From Courtship to Marriage: Mate Selection as an Interpersonal Process." In S. W. Duck and R. Gilmour, eds., *Personal Relationships: 2. Developing Personal Relationships,* 1981, Academic Press: New York. Also see C. A. Surra, "Reasons for Changes in Commitment: Variations by Courtship Type." *Journal of Social and Personal Relationships* 4 (1987): 17-33.

24 L. A. Baxter, and C. Bullis, "Turning Points in Developing Romantic Relationships." *Human Communication Research* 12 (1986): 469-493; and S. A. Lloyd and R. M. Cate, "Attributions Associated with Significant Turning Points in Premarital Relationship Development and Dissolution," *Journal of Social and Personal Relationships* 2 (1985): 419-436.

5

Uncertainty Reduction and the Generation of Social Knowledge

C. R. BERGER | J. J. BRADAC

If we are unable to explain why we and others believe and behave in the ways we do, we become less able to know what to say and how to behave in social situations. Uncertainty lowers our ability to exercise control in the situation and decreases the probabilities that we will obtain our goals in the interaction, whatever these goals may be. [Here, we] will focus upon the strategies and processes we employ to reduce our uncertainties about ourselves and others in social situations. We will begin by describing some specific strategies persons use to gain knowledge about others and strategies that persons might use to remain unknown to others. We will then consider three theories which have been developed by social psychologists to explain how we come to attribute dispositions and causes of actions to ourselves and others. These attribution theories are vitally concerned with the generation of what we have called predictive and explanatory levels of knowledge. Finally, we will consider some potential limitations upon the extent to which persons in social interaction situations can be aware or mindful of the strategies and processes they use to achieve their goals in interaction situations.

KNOWLEDGE ACQUISITION STRATEGIES

In this section we will address two questions. First, under what conditions do persons become espe-cially preoccupied with reducing their uncertainties about others? Obviously, in our everyday lives, there are many persons whom we meet but do not feel the need to get to know well. Thus, we can ask what conditions prompt a heightened concern for uncertainty reduction. Second, given that uncertainty is at a high level and a person wishes to reduce it, what strategies might the person employ to reduce his or her uncertainty?

Conditions Prompting Uncertainty Reduction

Recent studies have suggested that it is only under certain conditions that persons become preoccupied with explaining another's actions. For example, Pyszczynski and Greenberg (1981) found that persons attended to relevant explanatory information about a person only when their expectations of the person's behavior were violated. When their expectations were met, they showed few signs of concern for acquiring relevant information about the person. Their findings suggest the broader proposition that when persons *deviate from norms or expectations,* persons become more concerned with reducing their uncertainties about the person being observed. When persons act 'normally,' observers experience little uncertainty regarding the person observed, and do not concern themselves with knowledge acquisition. Thus, one condition for the creation of uncertainty-reduction concerns

From Berger, C. R., & Bradac, J. J. (1982). *Language and social knowledge: Uncertainty in interpersonal relations* (pp. 14-50). Baltimore: Edward Arnold.

is that of unpredictability or deviation from some kind of standard.

There is evidence, other than the Pyszczynski and Greenberg (1981) study, to suggest that when persons encounter novel or unpredictable behaviors, they behave in ways to reduce uncertainties. For example, Newtson (1973) had subjects look at videotapes of individuals doing mundane tasks by themselves. While they observed the tapes, the individuals were instructed to press a button when they felt that a meaningful action began. The button presses defined what Newtson called 'break points.' Newtson found that when he introduced novel or unpredictable actions into an action sequence, the rate of button pressing increased; that is, observers segmented the ongoing behavior into more perceptual units. When the actor returned to behaving in a 'normal' manner, observers pressed the button fewer times; that is, they segmented the ongoing action into larger units. Newtson (1973, 1976) interpreted these findings as indicating that when persons encountered an unpredictable act in an otherwise normal action sequence, they tried to restore predictability by more closely monitoring the stream of ongoing behavior. Finer unitization of the deviant behavior was an attempt by the observers to gain a better understanding of the behavior. Newtson (1976) also reported that still pictures representing segments where most observers of a group recorded a break point (consensus break points) were more accurately sorted with reference to their actual sequence in a film than were still pictures taken from non-break-point segments of the film. According to Newtson, these findings indicate that break points contain more information than non-break points. It should be pointed out, however, that recently some investigators have questioned what Newtson's break-point measure actually indicates (Ebbesen, 1980). Ebbesen suggests that break points may not be indicative of some kind of basic 'chunking' process involved in the processing of social information.

The above evidence suggests that when persons encounter unexpected events, they tend to engage in actions which are designed to help them reduce their uncertainties. However, when behavioral events occur the way they usually do, persons are not preoccupied with uncertainty-reduction concerns, at least in terms of the person with whom they are interacting or the person whom they are observing.

A second condition which motivates uncertainty reduction is *expectation of future interaction*. When persons expect to interact with each other in the future, they will monitor their present interaction more carefully and try to reduce their uncertainties about each other more. This principle is illustrated by several studies. First, Kiesler, Kiesler, and Pallak (1967) studied the effects of commitment to future interaction on evaluations of persons who conformed to or deviated from social norms. When persons were led to believe that they would be interacting with a norm violator in the future, they rated the norm violator's behavior more negatively than did persons who believed that they would not have to interact with the norm violator in the future. Furthermore, persons who thought that they would be interacting with a person who conformed to norms found that person to be more attractive than did persons who thought that they would not be interacting with the conformer in the future. In short, expectations of future interaction made deviators less attractive and conformers more attractive. Kiesler (1969) has also pointed out that commitment to future behavior can exert considerable influence upon present behavior. Persons who know that they will be interacting in the future are likely to surpress behaviors which might make them less attractive. Persons who know that they will never see each other again may be willing to say and do things which are somewhat less socially desirable.

More directly related to the relationship between anticipation of future interaction and uncertainty reduction is a study by Calabrese (1975). In this study, pairs of strangers were asked to get acquainted with each other. They held a conversation for 13 minutes. Unknown to the conversational participants, their interaction was tape-recorded. Before beginning their conversations, half of the pairs were told that they would be interacting in the future. The remaining pairs were given no such instructions. Calabrese's (1975) analysis of the content of these conversations over the 13-minute period revealed that persons who thought that they would interact in the future exchanged more background information with each other than did persons who believed that they would not converse again. These findings are consistent with the uncertainty model advanced by Berger and Calabrese (1975) which suggests that biographic and demographic information, which dominates initial interactions between strangers, is exchanged in order to reduce uncertainty.

If the notion that anticipated interaction heightens concern for uncertainty reduction is correct, we might expect persons anticipating future interaction with others to be able to remember more about those persons. There are at least two studies which show this to be the case. First, Berscheid, Graziano, Monson, and Dermer (1976) had subjects agree to let the experimenters decide whom they would go out with or date. Some subjects agreed to let the experimenters control their dating choices for a short period of time (1 week), while other subjects agreed to let the experimenters determine their dates for a longer period of time (5 weeks). These investigators then let the subjects view videotaped discussions in which their prospective dates were allegedly participating. After viewing the tapes, persons were asked to recall as many details as possible about the prospective dates. Those persons who expected to date the person for five weeks showed better recall than those persons who expected to date the person for five weeks showed better recall than those persons who expected to date the person for only one week. Harvey, Yarkin, Lightner, and Town (1980) conducted a study in which some persons were led to believe that they would be interacting with one person who was involved in a videotaped discussion which they observed. Other subjects were not led to expect interaction with any person who was part of the discussion. These investigators found that recall for details of the discussion was better for those who anticipated interaction.

Taken together, the results of the above studies suggest that when persons anticipate interaction with others, they act in ways which are likely to reduce their uncertainties about each other. Anticipated interaction increases exchanges of biographic and demographic information during interactions and heightens recall of conversational content as well as details about the persons with whom one is interacting. Also, when persons anticipate interaction, the consequences of norm violations and norm conformity become more pronounced. The available evidence provides strong support for anticipated interaction as a determinant of the magnitude of concern for uncertainty reduction.

A final condition which gives rise to needs for uncertainty reduction is the extent to which the outcomes of an interaction are likely to be rewarding or punishing. There are numerous theories of social interaction which emphasize the rewards and costs exchanged in the relationship as determinants of relationship growth and decline (Adams, 1965; Altman & Taylor, 1973; Blau, 1964; Homans, 1961; Miller & Steinberg, 1975; Thibaut & Kelley, 1959). In brief, these theories assert that persons involved in relationships with others attempt to maintain a balance between ratios of rewards and costs they give and receive in the relationship. When reward/cost ratios for one's self and the other are roughly equal, the relationship remains stable; however, when these ratios are unequal, inequity is felt and steps are taken to correct the inequity. It is important to note that these models do *not* assume that rewards and costs must be equal for equity to be obtained. It is only necessary that the ratios be equal. Also, rewards and costs in relationships go beyond material goods and include emotional satisfactions and dissatisfactions as well as relationships foregone by participation in the present relationship.

Within the context of uncertainty reduction, we postulate that when persons become concerned with the rewards and costs that another person can mediate for them, they will become more concerned about reducing their uncertainties about the other person. By contrast, if the other person does not have the power to reward or punish us in significant ways, then our concerns for reducing our uncertainties about the other person are reduced. In support of this relationship, Berger, Weber, Munley, and Dixon (1977) found that when persons were asked to indicate what factors made specific others attractive to them, they indicated that understanding, rapport, reinforcement, and loyalty were very important. These variables were all associated with a general factor which these authors labeled *supportiveness*. Thus, persons are attracted to those who give them understanding as well as material rewards. While there are no doubt a number of other specific conditions under which persons might become preoccupied with reducing their uncertainties about others, we feel that perceived deviance, anticipated interaction and anticipated rewards and punishments are among the most important general factors which are responsible for heightened uncertainty-reduction concerns.

In addition to the above findings, Giles and Powesland (1975) report that when persons want to exchange rewards with each other or become attractive to each other, they tend to *converge* or become more similar with respect to a number of speech characteristics like accent, dialect, and speech rate. When persons wish to emphasize their differences, they tend to *diverge* along these speech lines. Within the context of uncertainty theory, these findings could be taken as support for the notion that when persons wish to establish a relationship, they reduce their uncertainties about each other by becoming more similar to each other in terms of speech characteristics. However, if persons are not interested in pursuing a relationship, they are likely to maintain or even diverge with respect to speech characteristics in order to discourage the other person from continuing to try to get to know them. This interpretation is further supported by data from a study by Clatterbuck (1979). Clatterbuck (1979) developed a scale called CLUES which is designed to measure persons' subjective feelings of uncertainty about others. Clatterbuck's scale asks the subject to indicate the degree to which he or

she feels able to predict various things concerning a person about whom the subject is thinking. For example, one item asks the subject to indicate how good he or she feels about predicting the way in which the person being thought about would behave in a particular situation. A number of similar items are included in the scale. In a summary of several experiments, Clatterbuck (1979) found that when persons were asked to think of a person whom they liked and to fill out the CLUES scale, they displayed lower levels of uncertainty than when they were asked to fill out the CLUES scale for a person whom they knew well but disliked. When we conclude we dislike a person, we cease trying to get to know them. Thus, there may be a tendency for us to want to reduce our uncertainties about persons who will give us rewards and to not reduce uncertainty about those who might punish us. However, there are circumstances under which it is highly adaptive to 'know your enemy.' So, in all likelihood, uncertainty-reduction concerns are heightened when others can reward or punish us, but perhaps more for those who can reward us.

STRATEGIES FOR KNOWLEDGE ACQUISITION

In the previous section we considered three conditions which give rise to uncertainty-reduction concerns: (1) observation of deviant behavior, (2) anticipated interaction, and (3) high probabilities of receiving rewards and punishments from others. We now assume that one or more of these conditions is present and that we are concerned with reducing our uncertainty about the other. Another way of expressing our desire for uncertainty reduction is to speak of knowledge gaining or knowledge acquisition. The question we will examine in this section concerns the strategies we use to generate knowledge about the other person. In our discussion we will consider three general classes of strategies. *Passive strategies* are those in which we as observers gain knowledge of other persons by observing them without them knowing that we are observing them. These strategies do not involve direct interaction between the observer and the person being observed. *Active strategies* are those ways of gaining information which require the observer to do something to affect the response of the actor but do not involve direct contact between the observer and the actor. Finally *interactive strategies* are those in which the observer gains knowledge about the actor by engaging in face-to-face interaction with the actor. Within each one of these general classes of strategies are specific strategies that can be used to acquire information. We now turn to these strategies.

Passive Strategy I: Reactivity Search

The question being asked as we consider the passive strategies for knowledge acquisition is, what do persons look for in the behavior of others to try to find out things about them? At the most basic level we would contend that observers tend to prefer situations in which the target person being observed is actively engaged in some activity rather than in a passive state. Further, we would argue that observers prefer to watch the target person reacting to other persons rather than to observe the target in solitary situations. This is the case even if the observer is unable to overhear the conversation taking place between the target person and the other person or persons present. We learn more about another person by observing him or her react to others rather than observing the person react to objects or things because the behavior of other persons is considerably more variable than the behavior of most objects. Thus, the variations in the behavior of others is more likely to require similar variations in the behavior of the target person.

There is evidence to support the above reasoning. Berger and Perkins (1978) took color-slide pictures of a target person in a variety of solitary and social situations. In some pictures the target person was reading a book alone or typing alone. Other pictures showed the target person simply in the presence of others or actively talking with

others. Subjects were shown pairs of these slide pictures. In one experiment, one member of the pair of slides was a solitary situation and the other member of the pair was a social situation. Subjects were asked to assume that they wanted to get to know the target person and that they had the opportunity to observe the target person without the target person knowing that he or she was being observed. Subjects were told to assume that they could not talk to the target person. The task for the subjects was to choose the slide which they thought would give them the most information about the target person. The results of this experiment were dramatically clear. For 12 comparisons of social and solitary slides, the minimum percentage of subjects choosing the social slides on any comparison was 70 percent. In general, the percentages of subjects choosing the social slides was considerably higher than 80 percent. Thus, subjects showed an overwhelming preference for social as opposed to solitary situations in terms of their information value.

A second experiment reported by Berger and Perkins (1978) employed only social slides in the judgment task. In this situation, subjects were asked to choose between slides which varied in the extent to which the target person was involved in interactions with others. In some slides the target person was depicted as highly involved in the interaction, in others the target person was shown to be uninvolved in the interaction. In this experiment, subjects overwhelmingly preferred slides in which the target person was actively involved with others for information gaining. However, it was felt that the overwhelming preference for active, social situations might be a product of what Berger and Perkins (1979) called the 'Matthew Effect,' named after the youngest son of the senior author. When the slide pictures were shown to Matthew (when he was 8 years old), he overwhelmingly preferred the active social slides to the inactive social slides or the solitary slides. When asked why he preferred the active slides, he stated that by listening to the persons talk to each other in the interaction slides, he could find out where they live. He could then go to their house, talk to them, and find out more about them.

Berger and Perkins (1979) in another series of experiments attempted to discern whether the overwhelming preferences for active social situations in the previous studies were due to a widespread belief on the part of subjects that they could overhear the target person interacting with the others present in the picture. In one of their experiments, Berger and Perkins (1979) told half of the subjects making judgments that they were to assume they could *not* overhear what the persons in the pictures were saying. The other half of the subjects were not given these instructions. The results of this experiment revealed that regardless of the instructions, the patterns of choices were very similar between the two groups. Both groups preferred slides in which the target person was highly involved with the others present. These findings support the view that persons prefer socially involving situations as sources of information about a target person not because they assume that they can overhear what the target person is saying but because of the kind of reactivity the target person is likely to display while interacting with others.

Passive Strategy II: Disinhibition Search

The research discussed in the previous section consistently showed that persons prefer to gain information about strangers by observing them in social contexts where they are actively involved in conversations. However, there are any number of social contexts within which such conversations might occur. For example, we might have the choice of observing a given target person interacting with a minister after a church service or observing the same person having a conversation with some friends over a few brews at the local pub. One of the more striking differences between these two situations is their formality. We would expect that the conversation with the minister would be more formal in that each person in the interaction would inhibit more behaviors than they would in the pub situation. Certain topics would most likely not be

talked about in the after-church conversation; however, these same topics might be more than acceptable in the pub conversation.

Given the communicative constraints of formal interaction situations, we would argue that observers would find out less about a person as an *individual* by observing him or her within such formal contexts. Obviously, some things can be learned about persons by observing them in formal situations, but the range of things is generally more limited than that provided by informal contexts. Thus, we reasoned that when given the choice, persons would prefer to observe others in informal contexts as opposed to formal contexts for knowledge-gaining purposes. Berger and Douglas (1981) reported a study in which persons again judged the information value of slide pictures of a target person shown in a variety of different situations. In this study, over 200 slide pictures of a target person were taken in different public and private situations. In some of the slides the target person was alone, while in others she was with other persons and interacting with them. In this particular study, persons judged a randomly selected subset of 15 of the slides. Before making their judgments, half of the persons were informed that they would be meeting and talking to the target person shown in the slides after making their judgments. These persons were actually taken to a room where the target person was seated alone reading a book. Persons anticipating interaction with the target were also told that their task would be to try to get the target person to like them as much as possible during their conversation. The other half of the participants were not led to believe that they would interact with the target person.

After reviewing their instructions, all participants made their judgments of the information value of the 15 slide pictures. These judgments were then analyzed using a multidimensional scaling procedure which extracts the perceptual dimensions used by the judges in making their preference judgments for the various slides. The two dimensions found in the multidimensional scaling analyses are shown in Figure 5.1.

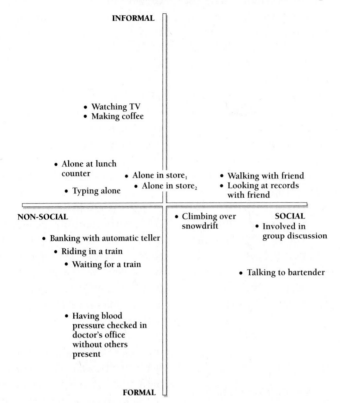

FIGURE 5.1

Locations of 15 Stimulus Pictures in Two-Dimensional Space

As Figure 5.1 indicates, the dimension represented in the horizontal axis is related to the non-social–social dimension discussed in the previous section. The slides on the right side of the axis generally represent situations in which the target person is interacting with others. Those on the left-hand side represent situations in which the target is alone. This dimension underscores the importance of reactivity for knowledge gaining. The vertical axis of Figure 5.1 is related to the issues discussed in this section. The situations in the upper part of the figure are ones in which the target person is depicted in her apartment or in other more informal situations. Those in the lower half of the figure show the target person in public and more formal situations.

The analyses of the judgment data further revealed that persons making the judgments overwhelmingly preferred the slides in which the target person was engaged in social interaction to those in which she was alone. In terms of the formal-informal dimension, there was about an even split between the judges in their preferences. However, there was a significant tendency for those who anticipated interacting with the target person to prefer the informal slides and for those who did not anticipate interacting with the target person to prefer the more formal slides. Furthermore, those who anticipated interacting with the target person rated themselves as more similar to the target than did those who did not anticipate interaction. The similarity rating was completed immediately after the slide judgments were finished. These findings show that when persons anticipate interaction with a stranger and they have the opportunity to observe that stranger in a number of different contexts, they will prefer social to solitary situations and informal situations to formal situations. In addition, it appears that anticipated interaction has the effect of inducing persons to feel more similar to the person with whom they will interact. A study reported by Larsen, Martin, and Giles (1977) also demonstrates the impact that anticipated interaction has on similarity; however, in this case these authors examined perceptions of speech similarity. Their experiment revealed that persons who anticipated interacting with a person whom they heard on a tape judged their speech to be significantly more similar to the person on the tape than did persons who did not anticipate interacting with the person heard on the tape. These effects may be a manifestation of uncertainty reduction about how one will communicate with the target person once the face-to-face meeting occurs.

We should point out that there may be circumstances under which observers might prefer to observe a given individual in a formal as opposed to an informal context. For example, a boss who is interviewing a prospective employee might place the prospective employee in a particular formal situation to see how he or she responds in the situation. Obviously, such a 'test' would tell the employer something about the ability of the prospective employee to cope with the situation, but we believe it would not tell the employer very much about the prospective employee as an *individual*. In some formal contexts, persons may find it necessary to misrepresent themselves or present themselves in ways which are at variance with their actual beliefs and preferences, e.g., misrepresent one's political opinions to agree with the boss so that one will win the favor of the boss. We would argue that formal situations are more likely to encourage such misrepresentations.

The above observational strategies tell us something about the conditions which persons feel will optimize their information gain about a target per-

son. However, the above research does not tell us about *specific* characteristics or attributes about a person which might be important in reducing uncertainty about him or her. For example, the way in which a person is dressed may indicate something about the person's status. Certain facial features may be taken as evidence for a particular kind of personality. Even hair color (redheads have hot tempers) might be used by some to infer something about a target person's temperament. A number of studies have linked such attributes as physical attractiveness (Berscheid & Walster, 1974) to the desirability of persons. Obviously, the way persons dress may be more or less attractive to us; however, the critical question here is what inferences we make about a person given a certain form of dress; that is, what do persons' manners of dress tell us about them? Clearly, the links between various person attributes and the inferences observers make upon observing them is important; for it is on the basis of such inferences that we interact with the person being observed.

Active Strategy I: Asking Others about the Target Person

The passive strategies outlined above do not require the observer to do any more than situate himself or herself in a particular context and observe the target person. By contrast, active strategies demand considerably more activity from the observer. In the present case, the observer tries to find persons who know the target person and to extract information about the target person from them. Notice that as in the case of the passive strategies there is no direct interaction between the observer and the target person; nevertheless, the observer reduces uncertainty about the target by asking others for information about the target.

This information acquisition strategy has not received research attention, but there are some important observations that can be made about it. First, the person who is gaining information by asking others about the target person must be concerned about the possibility that the persons being asked will tell the target person that the observer is asking questions about him or her. If the target person is so informed, considerable embarrassment might be experienced by the question-asking observer. Secondly, if the target person is informed that the observer is asking questions about him or her, the target person might take steps to modify his or her behavior in such a way that he or she is able to effect an unrepresentative self-presentation. Thus, the observer will gain faulty information. Finally, observers must be concerned about the credibility of the information that informants give them about the target person. Such information may be either wittingly or unwittingly distorted, so that the secondhand view of the target person may contain a considerable amount of inaccurate information. An interesting issue here is how and to what extent observers attempt to verify the secondhand reports of informants. How many different informants' reports are sought before the observer is satisfied that he or she has obtained a reasonably accurate assessment of the target person? How does the observer handle conflicting reports from various informants? These issues seem to be worthy of some research attention.

Active Strategy II: Environmental Structuring

In the case of the strategy of environmental structuring, the observer manipulates some aspect of the physical or social environment of the target person, observes the target person react to that physical or social environment, and uses the responses of the target to gain knowledge about the target. One of the best examples of this kind of knowledge gaining strategy is the way in which psychologists and other social scientists study social interaction in laboratory situations. Frequently, naive subjects are placed in particular circumstances and their responses to the circumstances are observed through a one-way mirror. The experimenter is usually interested in comparing the responses of subjects to

different conditions to see if and how various conditions affect the subjects' responses. For example, in a classic study Schachter (1951) examined the effects of deviance from group opinions on communication to the deviant. In some discussion groups a confederate of the experimenter consistently disagreed with various solutions to problems being discussed by the group; while in other groups the experimenter's confederate consistently agreed with the consensus of the group. During the course of these discussions, the amount of communication directed toward the confederate was measured. This study revealed that the deviant received more communication than the conformer up to a point. However, if the deviant continued to disagree, the amount of communication he or she received began to decrease.

From the point of view of knowledge gaining strategies, we can say that in the Schachter experiment some aspect of the social environment was manipulated by introducing either a deviant or conforming confederate. Then, the responses of the naive group members to the confederate were observed and compared. The critical question is whether in our everyday lives we structure environments in ways to gain knowledge about persons whom we do not know. The answer to this question seems to be affirmative. First, in employment interviews, interviewers may arrange the interview situations in such a way that they obtain specific information about the person being interviewed. Staged incidents may be used to see how the person being interviewed reacts to stress. Second, there are occasions in which an observer might strategically arrange seating in order to be able to observe a target person. The target person might be seated next to a person whom the observer knows well so that the observer can ask his or her friend about the target person after the event is over. There are no doubt numerous other situations in which the observer structures either the physical or the social environment in such a way as to gain information about a target. It is important to keep in mind, however, that the notion of environmental structuring does not include direct contact between the observer and the target. The observer structures the environment and then observes the responses of the target person to these stimuli.

Interactive Strategy I: Interrogation

By contrast to the passive and active knowledge gaining strategies, the interactive strategies involve direct contact between the observer and the target. These strategies require that the observer become a participant-observer in the social situation. One great advantage of interactive strategies over passive and active strategies from the observer's point of view is that he or she can do more to probe the target person in order to clarify potential ambiguities that the observer may feel about the target person. However, this benefit comes at some cost. When the observer becomes a participant-observer, he or she must be concerned about his or her self-presentation and give at least some thought to these concerns. Some degree of preoccupation with self-presentation may detract from the amount of attention that the observer can give to the target. Thus, when the observer employs passive or active strategies, he or she may be able to devote almost all of his or her attention to observing the target. In the interactive mode, the observer must divide his or her attention between concerns for self-presentation and concerns for gaining information about the target person.

One of the most obvious ways of gaining information about a stranger is simply to ask the stranger questions about himself or herself. Berger (1973b) and Calabrese (1975) both found that the first few minutes of initial interactions between strangers were dominated by question asking. Most of these questions were concerned with requests for background information, for example, 'Where are you from?' 'What is your main subject?' 'Where do you live?' and so on. After the first two or three minutes, the rate at which questions were asked in these studies showed a marked decline. Part of the reason for this decline is the tendency for persons to spend some time dwelling upon conversation topics on

which they have some degree of shared experience; thus, if two persons find that they are from the same hometown or have both traveled to the same city, they may spend considerable time talking about matters related to these topics. However, initial questions may serve another function. The answers to them may give us hints about other attributes that the person possesses but which we have not yet observed. If we find out that a particular person is a college professor and that another person is a miner, we will most likely make quite different inferences about the preferences and opinions that these two persons have. Such inferences might determine whether or not we will continue to interact with this person.

The importance of information exchanged in the first few minutes of an interaction for the future of the relationship was demonstrated in a study by Berger (1975). In this experiment, students initially filled out an attitude questionnaire which measured their opinions on a variety of issues. In addition, students gave such information as their hometown, major, and number of brothers and sisters in their family. This latter information is the type that is usually exchanged in initial encounters between college students. A few weeks later, students were given a questionnaire on which there was background information about another student. This information had been filled in by the experimenter in such a way that for half of the students the background information was very similar to their own background; for the other half of the students, the background information was very dissimilar. After reading the background information about the other person, the students were asked to guess how the student would fill out the rest of the questionnaire. The remainder of the questionnaire contained a large number of attitude items, some of which the students had filled out several weeks before. The students' own responses to the opinion items were then compared with the opinions they guessed for the other student. This study revealed that the degree of similarity between subjects' own attitudes and the attitudes they guessed for the other students was much higher when they believed that the student was from a similar background. Those students who received the dissimilar background information tended to guess attitudes which were quite discrepant from their own. This study clearly indicates that when we find that our backgrounds differ greatly from those of the persons with whom we are interacting, we are likely to assume, perhaps erroneously, that our opinions are very different from those of the person with whom we are interacting. By contrast, if we find we are from a similar background, we are likely to assume, perhaps erroneously, that our opinions are quite similar to those of the person with whom we are conversing.

While the questions that are asked and answered during an initial interaction between strangers may serve to reduce uncertainty and reveal common ground between interactants, there is most probably a limit to the number of questions which can be asked during such encounters. In formal interview situations, doctor-patient interactions, and other similar communication situations, we expect that one person will do most of the question asking and the other will do most of the answering. However, in an initial encounter between strangers in an informal social context, such asymmetries in question asking would not generally be tolerated. Moreover, it is probable that even if persons asked equal numbers of questions in an informal context, they would not continue to ask questions at a relatively high rate over time. Mutual interrogation is probably just as negatively viewed as unilateral interrogation after a certain point. At this time we cannot say at what point an initial encounter becomes an interrogation because of excess question asking, however, there appears to be such a point. Furthermore, it is evident that the kinds of questions which are asked change as the interaction progresses. Finally, we can ask what happens when one runs out of questions; that is, what other knowledge gaining strategies can be employed when one has asked the 'appropriate' number of questions?

Interactive Strategy II: Self-Disclosure

One possible alternative interactive knowledge gaining strategy to that of interrogation is self-disclosure. Gouldner (1960) and Jourard (1971) both suggest that a norm of reciprocity exists in social interaction situations such that persons of equal status are expected to exchange information about themselves in similar quantities and levels of intimacy. Jourard (1971) labeled this notion the 'dyadic effect' in his self-disclosure research. He found that persons who reported more willingness to disclose personal information about themselves to others also reported that they received more personal disclosures from others. By contrast, persons who were unwilling to disclose personal information about themselves reported that others were unwilling to disclose personal information to them. Other experiments have found evidence for the dyadic effect and the potential negative consequences of non-reciprocated self-disclosure (Worthy, Gary, & Kahn, 1969; Ehrlich & Graeven, 1971; Sermat & Smyth, 1973). Generally these studies indicate that when persons demand disclosures from others and the others comply by giving the information, refusal to reciprocate these disclosures lowers the attractiveness of the nondiscloser. Persons who reciprocate disclosures are generally judged to be more attractive.

The norm of reciprocity and the dyadic effect can be used by the knowledge seeker to glean information from a target. The research cited above implies that when all other things are equal (of course they rarely are), persons will tend to reciprocate information that we are willing to disclose to them about ourselves. Thus, if you wish to find out whether the person with whom you are conversing is afraid of snakes, you might disclose to him or her that you are afraid of snakes and discuss a vivid instance in which you showed such fear. There is the chance that the person will reciprocate at the same level of intimacy but not in the same content category as your disclosure. Thus, the person might respond to your revelation by talking about his or her fear of rabbits or high places. Of course, once the target person begins such a disclosure process, it may be possible for you to interject a question about the specific item of information in which you are interested. For example, after the person describes his or her fear of high places, you might ask something like, 'How do you feel about snakes?'

Detecting Deception

For the most part, our discussion of knowledge gaining strategies has thus far assumed that the target person does not engage in any kind of intentional deception. The possibility of deception is especially problematic when it comes to the interactive strategies. In the case of both interrogation and self-disclosure, the target person may both answer our questions and reciprocate our disclosures; however, it may also be the case that the target person is deliberately giving us false information. The question is how might such deception be detected. First, there is the possibility of changing one's opinion to see if the other person follows suit. For example, assume that you are conversing with a person whom you suspect is agreeing with you in order to ingratiate himself or herself with you. Every time you state a preference or an opinion, the person shows agreement. Once the target person has said that he or she agrees with your opinion on an issue, you might announce a change in your opinion sometime later in the conversation. If the person continues to agree with your 'changed' opinion, you might then assume that the person is simply engaging in indiscriminate agreement with you, probably for some ulterior motive like ingratiation.

There is a large literature on verbal and nonverbal cues that persons emit when they are engaging in deception (Ekman & Friesen, 1969; Knapp, Hart & Dennis, 1974; Bauchner, Kaplan & Miller, 1980). However, while these studies show that when persons engage in deception their verbal and nonverbal behaviors change, these studies do not tell us what *strategies* persons use once they

suspect that deception is taking place. In addition to the strategy of opinion change suggested above, sometimes persons very directly ask whether or not the target person is telling the truth. The success of this deception detection strategy depends upon the ability of the target person to 'lie with a straight face.'

On Remaining Unknown

A final issue to be considered here concerns the kinds of counterstrategies targets might use against observers who wish to gain information about them. There are a number of reasons which might induce a target to try to prevent a person from gaining knowledge about him or her. The target might simply dislike the knowledge seeker for some set of reasons and wish to avoid developing a relationship with the person. Some persons place extremely high values upon personal privacy and do not wish others to invade their personal lives unless those others are invited to do so. Finally, the target might have 'something to hide' in terms of his or her personal life and not wish to risk sharing the 'something' with another person. Obviously, in order for such counterstrategies to be employed, the target must be at least dimly aware that some observer or observers are trying to gain information about him or her. There are a number of possible ways in which persons can avoid being known by others. First, persons can isolate themselves. In a sense, the late American billionaire Howard Hughes employed this strategy for remaining unknown. Popular figures in sports and entertainment sometimes go to great lengths to avoid interaction with others. A second kind of counterstrategy for foiling knowledge gaining attempts is that of non-responsiveness. When persons are approached by others who attempt to engage in conversation, the persons might give minimal responses to questions and generally indicate that they do not wish to interact. A third possibility to avoid being known is to interact within the confines of role-determined action. In work situations, persons can do a very good job of fulfilling the demands of work related roles and essentially remain unknown to their co-workers. These persons limit their communication with co-workers to work related matters and do not discuss their 'personal lives' in the work situation. You may interact with the same person almost every day of your life, e.g., a newspaperman or a store clerk, and not get to know them as individuals because your communication with them is confined to role relationships.

One final possibility for remaining unknown to others is to talk with them but keep the focus of interaction away from one's self. This can be accomplished by chronic joke telling or talking about such topics as the weather or sports. Persons can communicate around such topics for long periods of time and learn little about each other. There may be a considerable volume of talk in such interactions but the type of talk is such that little is learned about the target persons beyond their most superficial preferences. In this regard it is interesting to note that wives are often heard to complain about their husbands' unwillingness to talk about what they consider to be less superficial topics. This complaint may, however, have some basis in fact, since studies show that males are generally lower in self-disclosure than are females (Jourard, 1971).

THREE ATTRIBUTION APPROACHES

Our discussion of knowledge-gaining strategies emphasized specific techniques that persons might employ to find out things about others or to prevent others from gaining knowledge about them. In this section we will try to answer the question how persons process and combine social information once they have obtained it. This question is central to attribution theory. The general aim of the attribution approaches we will consider is to explain how persons arrive at confident estimates of others' dispositions and how persons evaluate the causes of their own and others' actions. By forming our individual accounts of others' dispositions and the causes of their behavior, we make other persons

more predictable and more understandable. This increased understanding enables us to communicate more effectively with others and to achieve our interaction goals—as long as our dispositional and causal attributions are reasonably correct. In everyday life, we generally base our communication behavior on what we *believe* to be the case rather than upon what the case may actually be. The attribution approaches to be discussed now also consider the kinds of conditions which give rise to attributional biases which may in turn interfere with the smooth conduct of social interaction.

Heider's Analysis of Social Action

In his book *The Psychology of Interpersonal Relations,* Heider (1958) considered a number of issues related to how persons perceive and evaluate the actions of others. Heider contended that while most persons may not have the sophisticated knowledge of human behavior that a psychologist might have, in their everyday lives persons do try to make assessments of intentions, motives, and dispositions so that they can predict the behavior of others. Heider also recognized that persons are active perceivers of their environments and not merely passive recipients of experience. Persons actively seek to predict and explain the actions of others; however, Heider noted that it is impossible for persons to perceive social reality accurately. Our perception of social reality may be adversely affected by the presence of *distracting physical stimuli* in the social environment; moreover, our *prior experiences* may also determine how we perceive a person or group of persons. Heider noted that we can usually determine the accuracy with which we perceive physical objects by reference to some kind of physical measurement system; however, it is difficult to provide standards by which to assess the accuracy of our perceptions of others. In the case of social perception, we may rely upon the consensus judgments of a group of persons. The difficulty with this approach is that the group judgment may be totally inaccurate!

Heider pointed out that persons communicate their naive analyses of others' social actions in the form of statements that we hear every day. For example, if a person takes an examination and does well, we might attribute his or her performance to such personal forces as ability or motivation, or some combination of the two. It is also possible, however, that we might attribute the person's outstanding performance in the examination to environmental forces such as task ease or good fortune; that is, the person did well because the examination was easy or the person was lucky, or some of both. Personal or environmental forces could be invoked to explain a poor performance. A low examination score might be attributed to such personal factors as low ability or low motivation, or the same poor performance might be attributed to the inordinate difficulty of the task or to bad luck.

Personal or *internal* forces and environmental or *external* forces as explanations of actions may be viewed in terms of their *stability*. The internal force of ability is a relatively stable attribute of an individual, while the internal force of motivation shows more variation and is therefore less stable. With regard to external causes of action, task difficulty can be viewed as a relatively stable attribute and luck can be viewed as an unstable property of the environment. When we make causal attributions regarding the behavior of others, stable internal attributions might be more difficult to change than unstable internal attributions. The same may hold true for external attributions.

Considerable research has examined how persons attribute causality in response to success and failure. For example, Johnson, Feigenbaum, and Weibey (1964) found that teachers attributed the consistently poor performance of students to the *student's* low levels of motivation and ability. By contrast, when students showed improvement, teachers tended to attribute such improvements to the *teacher's* efforts. Streufert and Streufert (1969) found that persons who were successful at a task tended to attribute their success to internal factors; persons who failed at tasks tended to attribute their failures externally. Feather (1969) found that when persons were initially confident of their ability to do a task, persons attributed success to their ability and failure to bad luck; however, persons who were initially unconfident attributed success to good luck and failure to their lack of ability. In a follow-up study, Feather and Simon (1971) reported that unexpected outcomes were attributed more to unstable environmental factors (luck). Berger (1973a) found that persons were more attracted to those who tended to agree with their attributions of causality for performance. When persons succeeded at a task and others attributed their success to a high level of ability or when persons failed and others attributed their failure to bad luck, the persons receiving the causal assessments from the others indicated that they liked those persons giving the assessment. However, when the others attributed success to good luck or failure to lack of ability, those persons receiving the assessments of the others liked them considerably less.

These studies indicate that when persons evaluate the causes of their own performance, they tend to attribute cause in ways which will enhance their self-esteem. Success is attributed to internal factors (ability/motivation) and failure is attributed to external factors (task difficulty/luck). Thus, there appears to be a kind of attribution bias in assessments of causes for success and failure. Obviously, in any given case of success or failure, one or more of the four possible causal attributions we have discussed might be used to explain performance; however, there is a distinct tendency to weight some factors over others when it comes to explaining our own successes or failures.

Correspondent Inference Theory

Jones and Davis (1965) extended Heider's (1958) initial thinking on attribution to the area of dispositional attributions. These investigators were interested in answering the question of what factors are responsible for our willingness to take persons' actions as reliable indicators of their underlying dispositions. For example, if a person behaves in a friendly way toward us, we might ask whether the person's behavior is an indicator of a friendly disposition or whether the friendly behavior might simply be a temporary state and not really indicative of the person's true disposition. What we as observers can see regarding other persons are their actions and the effects of their actions. By observing their actions and the effects of their actions we make inferences about their dispositions. When we take actions to be reliable indicators of dispositions, we have, according to Jones and Davis, made a *correspondent inference*. When we have low levels of confidence that persons' actions are true indicators of their dispositions, it is not possible to make correspondent inferences.

Before we can draw correspondent inferences from observing actions, we must first determine whether the person intended to produce a particular effect by his or her actions. For example, if you observe a person strike another person, you would need to know whether or not the person intended to strike the other before you would be willing to impute a hostile disposition to the person doing the striking. It could be that the person hit the other person by accident, and if you believed this to be the case, you would most probably not attribute the disposition of hostility to the person doing the striking. Even if you did believe that the striking behavior was intended, you still might not be willing to attribute a disposition of hostility to the striker. Let us say that you found out that just before the striking incident occurred, the person who was struck had insulted the striker in some significant way. Given this piece of information, you might attribute the aggressive actions of the striker to external factors, rather than to some disposition of the striker. However, if you found out that the striker hit the other person without provocation, you would then be more likely to attribute a hostile disposition to the striker.

Once we have solved the intent problem, according to Jones and Davis (1965) there are four factors which determine whether or not we will draw correspondent inferences from observing actions and their effects. First, we can observe the *choices* that the person makes and the effects of these choices. For example, let us assume that a person is in the process of choosing between two jobs. Let us further assume that a number of effects of the person's choice would be similar for both of the two jobs. Perhaps both jobs are with large corporations which are located in warm climates. Additionally, the jobs might involve approximately equal levels of responsibility and authority. However, the one effect they do *not* hold in common might be that one job is located in a city where the job applicant's intimate friend is also located while the other job is in a city far away from the location of the intimate friend. In the terms of Jones and Davis (1965) the effect of being close to or far away from an intimate friend is a *non-common* effect of the choice. No matter which job the person chooses, we as observers of the choice and its effects will generally base our attributions concerning the disposition of the person making the choice upon the non-common effects of the choice. In our example, the non-common effect of relative proximity to the intimate friend gives us considerable information about the choice-maker's disposition. Jones and Davis (1965) argue that choices which have *few* non-common effects give rise to correspondent inferences, while choices which have a large number of non-common effects do not give rise to correspondent inferences. Thus, if the two jobs were dissimilar with respect to size of company, climate of the job location, levels of responsibility and authority as well as proximity to the intimate friend, it would be much more difficult for us as observers of the choice and its effects to confidently explain the job seeker's choice. There are too many plausible alternative explanations; however, when just one effect is 'non-common,' we are more likely to assert confidently that the location of the intimate friend played the critical role in the person's choice.

A second factor which influences the confidence with which we will make dispositional attributions from observations of actions is that of *assumed desirability* of the actions and their effects. If a person behaves in a very friendly way toward us, if a political candidate advocates a position which is popular with the audience, or if a person compliments us on some achievement, there are a number of potential attributions which we can generate for those behaviors. In all of the above cases, the persons might be saying what they are saying or behaving the way they are in order to ingratiate themselves with us for some reason, e.g., getting our vote. However, it is also possible that the positive or agreeing actions might be sincere expressions of feelings and beliefs. By contrast, *socially undesirable* actions like criticizing, snubbing, and taking an unpopular stand on an issue tend to have *fewer* plausible alternative explanations. When someone snubs us or criticizes us, we can eliminate ingratiation as a possibility and assume that these negative expressions are true indicators of the person's dispositions, that is, the person is a 'critical' person or a 'snob.' Furthermore, if a political candidate advocates a position which is unpopular with his audience, we are more likely to take his arguments as true expressions of his beliefs.

A study done by Schulman (1976) demonstrates this relationship quite nicely. Schulman (1976) constructed three bogus transcripts of an alleged conversation between a male and a female who had just met at a party for the first time. The conversations were identical except that one version contained no compliments, a second version contained two compliments, and a third version contained eight compliments. Persons read one of the three versions of the conversation and then rated the participants in the conversation on a number of scales. These ratings revealed that the compliment giver was judged to be most attractive when he gave two compliments and least attractive when he gave eight compliments. The attractiveness of the person in the no-compliment conversation was greater than the attractiveness of the person who gave eight compliments but less than the attractiveness of the person who gave just two compliments. Paralleling these results were uncertainty ratings. Persons who read the two-compliment transcript felt the least uncertain about the person who gave the two compliments. Those who read the other transcripts expressed the most uncertainty. These results suggest that very positive behavior may make a person less attractive because the socially desirable behavior makes observers of that behavior less certain concerning the motives for the behavior. Remember, uncertainty increases as the number of alternatives in the situation increase. Socially desirable behavior may lead to more plausible alternative attributions than socially undesirable behavior because of the possibility of ulterior motives like ingratiation.

A third factor which influences the extent to which we will judge a person's actions to be reliable indicators of their underlying dispositions is the *hedonic relevance* of the person's actions to us as observers. If we perceive that a person's actions have a direct bearing on whether we will or will not receive rewards or punishments in a given situation, the person's actions become hedonically relevant to us. According to Jones and Davis, as the hedonic relevance of the actor's behavior increases, our tendency to attribute the actor's behavior to his or her underlying dispositions also increases. Thus, for example, in an employment situation we would expect employees to make a large number of correspondent inferences about their bosses, since the bosses have the power to reward or punish the employees. By contrast, bosses would be less likely to make correspondent inferences on the basis of observing employees' actions, since the employees do not have much power to mediate rewards and punishments for their bosses.

A final factor which influences the making of correspondent inferences is that of *personalism*. Personalism refers to the belief on the part of the observer that the actor is adjusting his or her actions for the sake of the observer; that is, the actor is 'personalizing' his or her behavior for the observer. When the observer is in the actor's presence, the actor behaves in one way; however, when the observer is not present, the actor behaves in another way. It is assumed that as personalism increases, the tendency to make correspondent inferences also increases. So, if you believe that a close friend of yours treats you in a 'special' way, you are more likely to take the person's actions as true indicators of his or her underlying dispositions.

Kelley's Attribution Approach

The final attribution approach we will consider here is that of Kelley (1967, 1971, 1972). In one sense, Kelley's attribution concerns are somewhat broader than those of correspondent inference theory. While correspondent inference theory seeks to explain the confidence with which persons will infer personality dispositions from observations of actions, Kelley's model is concerned with the broader issue of causal attribution in general. This causal attribution problem is best illustrated by a simple example. Let us say that you observe John watching a television variety show. A comedian appears on the screen and tells several jokes. By the end of the comedian's act, John is on the floor laughing. Now, as a naive scientist you are interested in answering the question, 'Why did John laugh so much?' According to Kelley's analysis, there are three possible explanations for John's behavior. First, John may have laughed so much because of the comedian (a stimulus attribution). Second, John may have laughed so much because John has a sense of humor (a person attribution). Third, John's laughter may be explained by something about the circumstance in which John viewed the comedian (a circumstance attribution). Of course, there is the possibility that some combination of these factors may have produced John's laughter.

Kelley (1972) has advanced three basic principles of causal attribution which are relevant to the problem of establishing the basis of causality in our example. The first of these principles is that of *covariation*. The covariation principle simply states that effects are attributed to causes with which they covary over time. So, if John is a very serious person unless he is watching a comedian, as observers we are likely to attribute John's laughter to the presence of the comedian, since when the comedian is absent, John tends to be very serious. A second principle relevant to causal attribution is that of *discounting*. If we as observers perceive a *number* of causes for John's laughter rather than just one, we are less likely to see any one cause as having a great influence in producing John's laughter. The more

potential causes we perceive for a given effect, the less we weigh the influence of each cause. Finally, the *augmentation* principle asserts that if a given cause must overcome countervailing influences in order to produce an effect, we are likely to see the cause as more influential. Thus, if John is watching television in a public place where loud laughter is perceived to be inappropriate but John laughs very loudly in spite of the normative proscription against loud laughter, we are more likely to judge the cause of John's laughter to be extremely powerful. By contrast, if we observed John watching television in the privacy of his own home where such social prohibitions against loud laughter would be fewer, and John laughed loudly, we would not judge the cause of his laughter to be as powerful, since the cause did not have to overcome countervailing influences of various kinds.

Although the covariation, discounting, and augmentation principles tell us how causes are associated with effects and how causes, once established, are differentially weighted, the three principles do not directly address the issue of what factors are responsible for attributions to stimuli (the comedian), persons (John), or circumstances (watching television). Kelley (1967) has provided an analysis which details what *patterns* of data will give rise to these three *loci* of attribution or combinations of them. It is to this analysis that we now turn.

According to Kelley (1967) there are three types of information which help us to determine whether to attribute a given effect to the stimulus, person, circumstance, or a combination of the three. These three types of information are distinctiveness, consensus, and consistency. *Distinctiveness* information refers to uniqueness of the response to the particular stimulus. In our example of John's response to the comedian, distinctiveness information would indicate to us how John responded to a number of other comedians. Does John generally laugh at all comedians, or does John only laugh at the comedian he is currently watching and no other? When John's responses are similar across a large number of comedians, his pattern of behavior is displaying low distinctiveness. When John laughs at only one of many comedians, his behavior is highly distinctive.

Consensus information refers to the way in which other persons respond to the stimulus. Again in our example, if most persons found the comedian very funny, there would be high consensus among observers. However, if most observers found the comedian to be relatively unfunny, there would be low consensus. *Consistency* information takes into account the interaction of the person with the stimulus over time and situations. If John laughs a great deal when he sees this particular comedian on different occasions and in different situations, for example on television and in person, John is exhibiting considerable consistency in his response to the comedian. By contrast, if John's response to the comedian varies over time and situations such that sometimes he finds the comedian funny and sometimes not, then John's responses to the comedian exhibit considerable inconsistency.

According to Kelley's analysis, it is combinations of distinctiveness, consensus, and consistency information which determine whether attributions will be made to the stimulus, person or circumstance. Table 5.1 summarizes the various combinations of the three information factors and the attribution outcomes that they produce.

As the table shows, when all three of the information factors are high, the observer is likely to attribute the person's response to the stimulus. Thus, when you as the observer find out that John laughs only at the comedian he is watching and at no other comedians (high distinctiveness), and that most persons who see this comedian laugh at him or her (high consensus) and that every time John encounters this comedian he has the same response (high consistency), you are likely to conclude that it is the comedian (stimulus) which is causing John's laughter.

The table also indicates, however, that when you as the observer of John's laughter learn that John laughs at all comedians (low distinctiveness), that almost no one laughs at this particular comedian that John is watching (low consensus), and that John consistently laughs at this comedian (high consistency), then you are more likely to attribute John's laughter to something about John himself rather than to something about the comedian. Finally, if you find out that John laughs at only this comedian and no other (high distinctiveness), that most other persons do not laugh at this comedian (low consensus), and that sometimes John laughs at this particular comedian but at other times he does not (low consistency), you are likely to attribute John's behavior to something about the situation.

The three information patterns shown in Table 5.1 can be thought of as basic schemata or mental templates that persons use to arrive at causal explanations for behavior. It is also important to notice that each of the three patterns has *one* unique informational element. Looking down the columns of Table 5.1, notice that *low distinctiveness* is unique to the person attribution. *High consensus* is unique to a stimulus attribution, and *low consistency* is unique to a circumstance attribution. This property

TABLE 5.1

Information Patterns and the Attributions They Produce

	TYPE OF INFORMATION		
	Distinctiveness	Consensus	Consistency
Stimulus Attribution	High	High	High
Person Attribution	Low	Low	High
Circumstance Attribution	High	Low	Low

of these three causal schemata suggests that they can each be used when we have less than complete information on each of the three information dimensions. For example, if we find out that John laughs at all comedians in addition to the one he is watching (low distinctiveness), we are likely to conclude that John's response to the particular comedian we are observing him watching is the product of something about John, for example, his sense of humor. By contrast, if we only learn that almost all persons who view this particular comedian find him funny (high consensus), we are likely to attribute John's response to the 'funniness' of the comedian. Finally, on the basis of low consistency information alone (John sometimes finds this comedian funny), we are likely to conclude that John's reaction to the comedian is being produced by something about the situation. Thus, in order to make one of the three attributions it is not necessary to have complete information on the distinctiveness, consensus, and consistency dimensions.

In an important test of Kelley's attribution model, Leslie McArthur (1972) constructed a number of situations similar to our John example, varied the three information dimensions, and asked persons to indicate whether the person's behavior was caused by the stimulus, person, circumstance, person and stimulus together, or some other combination. For example, McArthur created situations such as, 'George translates the sentence incorrectly' or 'Professor Jones compliments student Smith.' Following each of these statements she gave the three types of information in differing patterns. After the sentence 'George translates the sentence incorrectly' persons might be told 'George always translates sentences like this incorrectly' (low distinctiveness), 'Most persons translate the sentence correctly' (low consensus) and 'George has not been able to translate this sentence correctly in the past' (high consistency). After reading the situation and the three pieces of information, McArthur's subjects were asked to indicate whether George's response (incorrectly translating the sentence) was due to the sentence, George, the situation, the sentence and George together, or some other combination. In

this particular situation we would expect persons to attribute George's inability to translate the sentence to George rather than to something about the sentence or something about the circumstance.

By varying the information patterns and situations, McArthur found support for Kelley's model; the predictions shown in Table 5.1 were generally confirmed. Two additional findings from the McArthur study are of importance. First, McArthur's results showed that subjects most frequently made *person* attributions, that is, they more frequently judged the person's behavior to be a product of factors residing in the person than factors outside of the person (the stimulus or the circumstance). Second, she reported that of the three types of information, consensus had the least impact upon attributions. Distinctiveness and consistency information showed more influence in the making of the causal attributions.

Later studies have essentially confirmed McArthur's findings. Orvis, Cunningham, and Kelley (1975) used situations similar to those employed by McArthur (1972) to determine whether the same effects that McArthur observed could be produced with more limited information. For example, in the situation in which George fails to translate the sentence, what kind of attribution would be made regarding George's performance if we learned only that George was never able to translate any sentence (low distinctiveness)? Given this one piece of distinctiveness information, we would most likely attribute George's failure to George himself; that is, he lacks ability, motivation, or both. If we were only told, however, that along with George, most persons failed to translate the sentence (high consensus), we would be more likely to attribute George's failure to something about the sentence rather than to George himself. Orvis et al. (1975) generally found that just one critical piece of information would lead persons to the same attribution as would a complete set of information on all three dimensions. This finding led them to conclude that the three information patterns shown in Table 5.1 are fundamental and that persons first look for the critical information on each information dimension in order to make an attribution. So, if you encounter low distinctiveness information when you are trying to make a causal attribution, you are likely to make a person attribution as long as information on the other two dimensions does not contradict the information pattern for the person attribution. If, however, you first receive low distinctiveness information and then receive high consensus and low consistency information, a pattern which does not fit with a person attribution pattern, then you will make some kind of combination attribution; that is, the person's behavior was caused by the person, the stimulus, and the circumstance. Of course, it takes much less cognitive work to make the attribution based upon the low distinctiveness information itself.

Attribution Biases

The three attribution approaches we have discussed appear to make persons quite rational decision-makers when they are interested in explaining others' actions and linking actions to dispositions. We did note, however, in our discussion of Heider's (1958) work, that several studies have revealed the tendency for persons to attribute their successes to internal sources like ability and motivation and to attribute failures outward to such factors as bad luck or inordinate task difficulty. This tendency can be thought of as a kind of ego-defensive attributional bias; that is, persons make these biased attributions in order to preserve a positive image of themselves.

In addition to the ego-defensive or self-serving attributional bias, other work has demonstrated additional biases which may interfere with the generation of accurate causal or dispositional attributions. Jones and Nisbett (1971) have noted that actors and observers tend to make differing attributions because of their different perspectives in interaction situations. They suggest that actors tend to see external factors as causes of their actions while observers of actors tend to perceive the actors' actions as internally caused. This bias arises because

the perceptual fields of observers are flooded or engulfed by actors' actions. Actors are oriented outward toward the environment rather than to themselves. Thus, they tend to explain their own behavior in terms of conditions they perceive in the environment. Storms (1973) has shown how videotape replays of interactions can be used to modify these actor-observer differences. By watching one's self on videotape, thus becoming an observer, environmental attributions for behavior can be changed to internal or dispositional attributions for behavior.

Given the predisposition of observers to attribute the actions of others to their internal dispositions, it should come as no surprise that a number of studies have shown that when persons engage in interpersonal conflict or experience the dissolution of their relationships, they frequently attribute their relational difficulties to some internal disposition of their relational partner rather than to themselves or to some aspect of the environment (Harvey, Wells, & Alverez, 1978; Kelley, 1979; Orvis, Kelley, & Butler, 1976; Sillars, 1980a). Kelley, (1979) has noted that relational partners have great difficulty specifying relational problems in terms of specific behavior, for example, 'I don't like him because he fails to greet me sometimes.' Rather, persons are more prone to couch complaints in terms of undesirable personal dispositions of the other, for example, 'I don't like her because she is just plain unfriendly.' Because of the tendency to see relational problems as a product of the other person's negative personality dispositions, it becomes difficult to modify specific behaviors in such relationships. Sillars (1980a) found that when persons attribute the causes of conflict to the undesirable personality characteristics of their partners, they are less likely to try to negotiate a solution to their problems. Instead, they are more likely to avoid their partners. This avoidance strategy makes some sense since if one assumes that it is a personality trait of the other that is causing the conflict, it might be difficult or impossible to change such a trait. Thus, the most efficient way to deal with the conflict is to avoid the person. Of course, the problem with this reasoning is that it is based upon the questionable assumption that the conflict is solely caused by some undesirable personality trait the other person possesses. It is probably the case that in most conflicts *both parties* share some responsibility for the difficulties experienced.

A final kind of bias we will consider here is one which has been labeled the *negativity effect* (Kanouse, 1971; Kanouse & Hanson, 1971). These researchers present evidence which suggests that when persons are presented with both positive and negative information about a person, the negative information assumes an inordinate weight in the formation of an overall impression of the person. Thus, one negative attribute in a sea of positive attributes will lower an overall impression to a greater extent than one positive attribute in a sea of negative attributes will improve on overall impression. Another way of looking at this effect is to say that equal amounts of positive and negative information about a person are likely to produce a somewhat negative overall impression of the person. Wegner and Vallacher (1977) have suggested two explanations for this effect. One of these states that since persons expect positive things to occur in their everyday lives, negative instances tend to stand out more. A second explanation asserts that persons are sensitive to potential threats in their environments for purposes of survival.

Regardless of the explanation for the negativity effect, it is important to note that it can exert considerable impact upon relationship development and change. When persons first meet, there may be conscious attempts to suppress negative behaviors in order to project a positive social self to the other person. When persons date they tend 'to put their best foot forward.' However, after relationships develop and persons become closer, some negative aspects of behavior may no longer be masked. The unmasking of negative behaviors may have a very negative impact upon the relationship. These instances of unmasking lead persons to say such things as 'I never knew that he could be so nasty' or 'I can't believe how sloppy she is' and so on. The potential problems created by this attributional bias

suggest that persons could try to counterbalance it by consciously thinking about positive attributes of their relational partners.

Other information-processing biases have been discussed with reference to social judgment and decision making. Several of these shortcomings have been noted by Nisbett and Ross (1980). These authors suggest that frequently persons are willing to make inferences on the basis of incomplete information or biased samples of information. Furthermore, they note that persons may be unaware of factors which may have been responsible for their reaching a particular decision. Thus, even though we may strive to gain an understanding of another person, various biases and limitations in information-processing capacity may interfere with our ability to gain an accurate explanation for his or her actions.

Limitations of Attribution Theories

Several recent studies have suggested some limits upon the generality of attribution principles. These studies do not totally refute correspondent inference theory or the Kelley model, but they do suggest that the theories may be somewhat more limited than first supposed. Enzle, Harvey, and Wright (1980) tested what they argued is a contradiction between correspondent inference theory and the Kelley model. Specifically, as we saw earlier, Jones and Davis (1965) assert that the more an observer believes that an actor is varying his or her behavior for the benefit of the observer (high personalism), the more likely the observer is to take the actor's actions as representative of the actor's underlying dispositions. High personalism leads to a person or dispositional attribution. By contrast, Kelley's model predicts that such variations in behavior (high distinctiveness) do not lead to person attributions. It is when the response is similar across stimuli and distinctiveness is low that we tend to attribute the response to the person. These investigators confronted these conflicting predictions in a study which involved an interviewing situation.

After an interview, the interviewee was given high or low distinctiveness information about the interviewer's past interviewing behavior. Unknown to the interviewee, observers watched the interview and were given the same set of distinctiveness information that the interviewee received after participating in the interview. The findings of this study showed support for Kelley's prediction that low distinctiveness leads to person attributions and little support for Jones and Davis's personalism prediction. However, it is crucial to note that these findings held only for those persons who *observed* the interview. The interviewees themselves were not influenced one way or the other by the distinctiveness information about the interviewer. Persons who were *actively involved* in the communication situation did not behave in line with either of the theories. These findings suggest that not only is the personalism prediction of correspondent inference theory in need of revision, but more importantly that both of the attribution models may only hold for observers of social interaction rather than for participant-observers. This latter finding may not be as surprising as it might first appear, since the theories which were tested were developed by persons whose business it is to be keen *observers* of social interaction! It may be considerably more difficult for social scientists to develop theories of human action from the point of view of the *participant-observer*.

A second limitation of these attribution approaches is suggested by another study (Major, 1980). In her experiments, Major allowed subjects to seek distinctiveness, consensus, and consistency information rather than giving this information to subjects as had been done in the McArthur and Orvis et al. studies. Major (1980) found that when given the choice, persons acquired more consistency information than distinctiveness or consensus information in order to establish a causal attribution; however, persons utilized relatively little of the total information available to them to make their attributions. Persons were willing to make attributions on the basis of relatively limited samples of available information. These findings suggest that

persons may not do as thorough a job of acquiring critical information as would scientists.

A third limitation of attribution models stems from the work of Pyszczynski and Greenberg (1981). These investigators led subjects to expect that another person would either give help or refuse to give help when asked to do a favor. For some subjects their expectations were confirmed; that is, the person did what they expected the person to do. Other subjects observed the person engage in behavior which disconfirmed their expectations. Subjects were then given the opportunity to acquire additional information, some of which was relevant to their expectations and some of which was irrelevant to their expectations. Results showed that persons whose expectations were disconfirmed chose more information relevant to their expectations than did persons whose expectations were confirmed. These findings indicate that persons will become active information processors, seeking the causes of behavior, when unexpected or unpredictable events occur. When the expected happens, persons may not process information the way attribution theories suggest.

A final limitation to the generalizations of attribution theory has been suggested by Hewstone and Jaspars (in press). These authors point out that attribution models have a distinct 'individualistic' bias in that they focus upon the information-processing strategies of isolated individuals. They assert that persons respond very differently when they perceive themselves to be connected with social groups than when they perceive themselves as individuals. One difference the individual versus group emphasis might make in terms of attribution is in the extent to which consensus information influences attributions of causality. In two studies, McArthur (1972, 1976) found that when compared with distinctiveness and consistency information, persons generally under-utilized consensus information. In these studies, however, persons responded to the various situations as individuals, that is, their memberships in social groups were not made salient to them. One implication of the Hewstone and Jaspars (in press) critique of attribution models is that if group memberships were made salient to individuals, consensus information might assume a much greater role in determining their attributions; in this case it would be the consensus of the group which would strongly influence the individual's attribution.

As we noted at the beginning of this discussion, the limitations to attribution models outlined above do not totally invalidate them; however, they do suggest that there are potentially significant limits to the conditions under which attribution theories are likely to work in terms of prediction and explanation. At present, we will have to wait and see whether attribution theories can be modified successfully to take into account these limitations or whether other theories will take their places. In the section which follows, we will examine some other approaches to the processing of social information which might at least partially supplant or significantly augment the attribution models we have considered.

THOUGHT AND TALK:
HOW AWARE ARE WE?

Our examination of the various attribution approaches and knowledge-gaining strategies carries with it the implication that persons are highly conscious and thoughtful when they prepare for and engage in social interactions with others. We did note in our discussion of attribution that recent research has shown that persons engage in attribution making only under a limited number of conditions. Also, it was suggested that persons become concerned with knowledge-gaining strategies when they observe deviant actions, anticipate future interactions, and believe that others can reward or punish them. The question we will address in this section concerns the extent to which persons are aware of their communicative actions during social interactions. There are a number of research areas which suggest that for a variety of reasons, persons may be more or less conscious of what they are doing within the context of a particular social situation. We will

examine four of these areas: (1) Scripts and mindlessness, (2) Objective self-awareness, (3) Self-consciousness, and (4) Self-monitoring.

Scripts and Mindlessness

For most of us, our lives consist of a number of routine activities which vary little from day to day. Consider the sequence of actions involved in your getting up and preparing yourself to face yet another day at the academy; or consider the sequence of actions in which you must engage in order to purchase an article at a clothing store. While there may be minor variations from day to day in your 'getting up' sequence and some differences in the routine involved in buying clothing, these kinds of action sequences are generally routine. Not only do we participate in these kinds of routine sequences of actions, but we also observe others participating in them. Much of the entertainment fare on American television is written according to various 'formulas' or standard story lines. The same situation holds for movie plots. For example, there is the standard story consisting of male meets female; male and female are attracted to each other; adverse circumstances intervene in their relationship; the problems are solved; and male and female live happily ever after. Even conflict situations can become routine. Husband complains that wife doesn't keep house clean; wife complains that husband does not make enough money to support family; husband begins to drink heavily; wife accuses husband of ignoring her for the sake of drink; husband physically attacks. And so it goes.

The above examples are but a small sample of the kinds of routine action sequences which persons either actively participate in or observe in their everyday lives. There are two questions which we can ask about how persons deal with such routine sequences. First, how do persons *know* when they are involved in a particular kind of sequence? Second, once a person can identify the kind of situation that they are in, how do they know what to *do* or how to *act?* These two questions are answered, in part, by the notion of *scripts*. Abelson (1976) defines a cognitive script as 'a coherent sequence of events expected by the individual, involving him either as a participant or as an observer' (p. 33). According to Abelson (1976), scripts are cognitive structures which enable us to gain an understanding of the situation in which we find ourselves. Scripts also serve as guides to the actions that we should display in the situation. A cognitive script enables us to predict what will happen in a given situation. In this sense we can say that *scripts enable us to reduce uncertainty about the situation in which we find ourselves*—as long as we have an appropriate script for understanding and acting in the situation.

Abelson (1976) and Schank and Abelson (1977) point out that scripts are learned by direct participation in event sequences of various kinds or they may be acquired by observing others participate in various event sequences. For example, when we go to a restaurant, we may be seated by a host or a hostess, approached by a waiter or a waitress, given a menu, asked to order, be given our food, eat our food, leave a gratuity and pay the bill. This rather typical sequence may be learned by going to a number of restaurants for meals or by observing others go to restaurants, perhaps in plays or in television productions. In either case, repeated exposure to the sequence produces a cognitive structure or script which allows us to understand what to expect in future restaurant trips and allows us to know what to do when we are in a restaurant. Obviously, while there are similarities among restaurants, the routines which we go through from restaurant to restaurant may vary. For example, in some restaurants there may be no host or hostess to seat us. If we are in a so-called 'fast food' establishment, we will not be served at all and we will not leave a tip. These variations in routines are accounted for by the idea that any given script like a restaurant script may contain several tracks to account for these variations.

According to Abelson (1976) and Schank and Abelson (1977), by adulthood we have acquired thousands of scripts for the understanding of various routine action sequences: Once this large file

of scripts is developed, the problem for the human understander facing a particular situation is: (1) to determine whether he or she has a script to fit the particular situation being faced, and (2) if there is a script, what role he or she will play in it. Once these issues are resolved in an affirmative way, the person can enact the sequence of behavior involved in the routine without paying much attention to what he or she is doing. Thus, once a well-formulated script is learned, the necessity for thinking about the details involved in the sequence decreases.

There is considerable research which demonstrates the role that scripts play in our abilities to recall action sequences. For example, Chiesi, Spilich, and Voss (1979) found that persons who had high levels of knowledge about the principles and strategies of baseball were better than their low-knowledge counterparts at: (1) recognizing information changes in verbal descriptions of action sequences of baseball games and (2) recalling event sequences which followed a normal order. In a related study, Spilich, Vesonder, Chiesi, and Voss (1979) found that when high and low baseball-knowledge persons were presented with a one-half-inning narrative of a baseball game, high knowledge-level persons were better able to: (1) recall information that was related to the goals of the game (scoring, runs, etc.), (2) integrate sequences of goal-related actions, and (3) recall more information in the appropriate order. Finally, Bower, Black, and Turner (1979) conducted a series of experiments in which persons were asked to respond in a variety of ways to a number of different scripted sequences of actions. Their research revealed that when persons were asked to recall scripted sequences after reading them, they tended to fill in details which were *not* given to them in the original script. Thus, scripts can cause persons to 'recall' events of an action sequence they have observed when the events actually did not take place but are part of the cognitive script they use to process the action sequence. The Bower, Black, and Turner (1979) study also demonstrated that persons were better at recalling actions which deviated from scripted expectations than they were at recalling actions that were consistent with the script. We are more likely to recall the waiter who spills his tray of food all over us than we are to remember the waiter whose actions are like those of all other waiters. A study by Graesser, Gordon, and Sawyer (1979) also showed that script-deviant actions are better recalled than are script-congruent actions.

While the above research shows how scripts influence the recall of routine action sequences of various kinds, there is another important consequence of scripted activities. Langer (1978) has argued that when persons develop scripts for routine action sequences, they enact these sequences with little attention to the details of how they actually carry out the sequence. For example, when persons learn to brush their teeth, they pay little attention to the various angles and strokes they use to accomplish toothbrushing. When persons drive their cars over the same routes many times, they may end up at their destinations and not be aware of exactly how they arrived there. When action sequences become overlearned or scripted, persons tend to become *mindless* with respect to those activities according to Langer (1978). In this context, mindlessness can mean at least two things. First, mindlessness can refer to a situation in which a person is doing one thing but thinking about another, for example, thinking about a date while washing dishes. With respect to the actions involved in dish washing, one is mindless. In the second sense of mindlessness, the person is engaging in some kind of action but not thinking about anything. Watching television might be an example. According to Langer (1978) most of our daily social interactions are so routinized that we are generally mindless with respect to them, even though we may give the appearance of being actively involved in them. Persons may look like they are engaged in thoughtful conduct, but may in fact be mindless.

Langer, Blank, and Chanowitz (1978) reported a series of experiments which demonstrate the operation of mindlessness. In one of them, individuals about to make copies on a xerox machine were approached by a confederate of the experimenter. The confederate asked the persons about to use the machine if they would allow him or her to make copies first. The confederate told half of the persons waiting that he or she had to make five copies (small favor), while the other half of those waiting were told that the confederate needed to make 20 copies (large favor). In addition, the request was followed by three kinds of justifications. Some of the waiting persons were given no justification for the request. A second group was told that the person needed to make copies because he or she was in a hurry (real justification). A final group was told that the person needed to use the xerox machine in order to make some copies (placebic justification). Obviously, the placebic justification is no justification at all. Langer et al. (1978) reasoned that the request for the small favor would induce little mindfulness in the receiver so that a placebic justification would be as effective as a real justification. However, in the large-favor situation, the person receiving the request would become more mindful and recognize the absurd nature of the placebic justification, thus reducing the effectiveness of the placebic justification. This study revealed that within the small-favor group, 93 percent of those given the placebic justification allowed the confederate to make his or her copies first and 94 percent of those given the real justification complied. Of those given no justification, 60 percent granted the favor. Of those persons who were asked for a large favor, 42 percent of those given the real justification complied with the request, while only 24 percent of those given the placebic justification complied. For those given no justification for the request, 24 percent complied.

The findings of the above study provide support for the operation of mindlessness. When a small favor was requested, an absurd justification was just as effective in gaining compliance as was a reasonable justification; however, when a large favor was involved, the placebic justification was no more effective in gaining compliance than was no justification. In the second experiment of their study, Langer et al. (1978) surveyed secretaries' wastepaper baskets to determine the general form of memos sent to the secretaries. Their survey revealed that the structure of these memos was generally an unsigned request as opposed to a signed demand. Armed with this knowledge of the structure of the typical memo, Langer et al. (1978) devised a memo which requested that the receiver of the memo return the memo to a non-existent room in the office building. The message was obviously silly; why would a person send a memo to someone and ask that they return the piece of paper to a particular room? Langer et al. devised four forms of the memo. In some cases the memo was written in a request form while in others it was written in a demand form. Some of the memos were signed by the sender and others were not signed. The researchers reasoned that memos of the typical form (unsigned request) would be processed in a mindless manner, and more of these memos would be returned; however, memos which were unusual in form, for example signed demands, would induce more mindfulness and the reader would become aware of the absurdity of the content of the memo, thus lowering compliance in the group. The results of this study supported these predictions. Of those secretaries who received the memos of the typical form (unsigned requests) 90 percent returned them to the non-existent room. By contrast, only 60 percent of those secretaries who received the most structurally deviant memos (signed demands) returned them.

It is interesting to speculate why the 60 percent who received the memos of the most structurally deviant form still complied with the absurd request. Presumably, the form of the memos they received would make them more mindful, thus making them aware of the ridiculous nature of the content of the message. However, it is also possible that since the memo was both in the form of a demand and signed, some secretaries might have over estimated its importance and paid little attention to the content of the message. This latter possibility would suggest that some secretaries in the signed-demand group might have also been mindless with reference to the content of the message because their attention was drawn *away* from it by the message's structural characteristics.

Many of our everyday interactions with family, friends, and co-workers are routine in nature. The findings of the above studies indicate that while scripts may aid us in getting through these conversations in a relatively smooth manner, Langer's research indicates that this increased efficiency may come at a price. Certainly there are situations in which misunderstandings develop between friends and family members because of mindlessness. On the basis of minimal cues, persons *assume* that the person providing the cues is beginning a particular kind of script (e.g., a conflict script). On the basis of this assumption, the person receiving the cues becomes angry or overreacts in some way and begins to 'run through' the script. The other person who innocently provided the 'wrong cues' is now offended and also 'gets into' the conflict script and a ritualized fight then ensues which neither party can stop until the script plays itself out. This approach explains why in some close relationships persons may wish to avoid conflicts but cannot.

Lest the preceding discussion lead the reader to believe that we are always mindless during social interactions, Langer (1978) has cited a number of conditions which are likely to make us more mindful of our actions in social situations. Increased mindfulness occurs when:

1. We encounter a novel situation for which we have no script.
2. The enactment of scripted behavior becomes effortful for some reason.
3. The enactment of scripted behavior is interrupted by external factors which prevent its completion.
4. We experience consequences which are discrepant with the consequences of prior enactments of the same script.
5. The situation does not permit sufficient involvement.

Any one or a combination of these factors will increase mindfulness in a given situation.

Scripts are functional in that they allow us to perform various action sequences without having to attend closely to what we are doing. This condition frees our mind to think about things that are more important than what we are doing. However, scripts can introduce distortion into recall such that we assume that events took place which actually did not. Moreover, scripts can cause us to become inattentive to nuances and details in interactions which may provide important cues to the understanding of the other person's feelings and emotions. In short, scripts are useful for dealing with mundane situations with 'prototypic' others. However, when we wish to deal with persons as *individuals,* scripts may become dysfunctional and counterproductive to achieving satisfaction with the relationship.

Objective Self-Awareness

Our discussions of knowledge acquisition strategies and attribution models painted a picture of persons as relatively self-conscious, rational information processors. The research on scripts and mindlessness indicated that the degree to which persons attend to what they are doing in social interaction situations varies as a function of the extent to which scripts are relied upon to process information. Another area of theory and research directly addresses the issue of self-awareness. Duval and Wicklund's (1972) theory of objective self-awareness states that persons experience two states of consciousness: objective self-awareness and subjective self-awareness. When in the objective state, the person's consciousness is dominated by his self or her self; that is, attention is focused inward on the self as an object of experience. In the subjective state, attention is focused outward, away from the self as an object. The self blends in with the surrounding environment. Duval and Wicklund (1972) argue that when persons are objectively self-aware, they experience discomfort and attempt to become subjectively self-aware. The discomfort produced by objective self-awareness is due to the fact that when attention is focused upon the self, persons become aware of the discrepancies between what they would ideally like to be (ideal self) and the way they actually are (real self). Awareness of these discrepancies produces discomfort and the desire to focus attention away from the self toward the environment. Duval and Wicklund (1972) also contend that the two states of consciousness are binary in nature: a person is either objectively or subjectively self-aware. Movement between these two states can be rapid, but at any point in time a person is either objectively or subjectively self-aware.

Objective self-awareness is induced by self-reflecting stimuli in the person's environment. Mirrors, tape recordings of one's own voice, watching videotapes of one's self and anticipating delivering a speech to an audience are some ways in which objective self-awareness can be created. It has also been suggested that when a person holds an opinion which is discrepant with those of other group members, the discrepant member is likely to feel objective self-awareness. Ickes and Wicklund (1971) found that persons who completed questionnaires designed to measure their self-esteem made more negative ratings of themselves when they listened to a tape recording of their own voice than did persons who completed the self-ratings when they heard the voice of another person. The difference between the two groups in their self-esteem ratings disappeared over time, most probably because persons who listened to their own voice devised ways in which to divert their attention away from themselves and become subjectively self-aware.

Another study which demonstrates the aversive nature of objective self-awareness was done by Duval, Wicklund, and Fine (1971). These researchers informed some persons that they had performed poorly on a test relative to other students. Other research participants were told that they had done very well on the test compared with other students. All research participants were then asked to wait for another study to begin, but were told that after waiting for about five minutes, they should seek out the experimenter if he did not appear. Some subjects waited at a table facing a mirror, while other subjects waited at the same table with the mirror covered. When the lengths of time that subjects in the various groups were willing to wait were compared, it was found that subjects who had been informed that they had done poorly relative to others who were also seated in front of the mirror waited significantly less time than did those persons who did poorly but who did not see themselves in the mirror. For those subjects who had done well, there were no differences in waiting times between those persons who were exposed to the mirror and those who were not. These findings indicate that the mirror created more aversion for those who did poorly, presumably because of increased objective self-awareness. In a later discussion of objective self-awareness theory and research, Wicklund (1975) has asserted that objective self-awareness might not always produce aversive reactions. While it is probable that if we think about ourselves for a long enough period of time, we will become aware of various shortcomings, it is also true that sometimes we do better than we expected in various activities. Becoming aware of positive discrepancies should not be at all aversive.

Other research in this area has shown that when persons are made objectively self-aware they tend to react more extremely to stimuli which produce positive or negative emotional reactions (Scheier & Carver, 1977). Persons who filled out questionnaires about themselves while objectively self-aware were more likely to behave in ways which were consistent with their questionnaire responses than were persons who completed the questionnaires while subjectively self-aware (Pryor, Gibbons, Wicklund, Fazio, & Hood, 1977). Finally Duval and Wicklund (1972) suggest that when persons receive information which they know they will have to pass on to others at some later time, they will do a better job of integrating that information than when they believe that they will not have to transmit the information to others. Thus, when persons are preparing to give a speech to an audience, they are likely to become more objectively self-aware; however, once involved in the process of actually giving the speech, the focus of attention will shift to the audience and subjective self-awareness will become more prevalent.

In general, objective self-awareness theory and research indicates that our attention to ourselves as objects in the environment can be influenced by a number of self-reflecting stimuli. When we become objectively self-aware we are likely to experience some discomfort. This discomfort can be reduced by turning our attention outward to the environment. When we prepare to communicate with others, we are likely to experience objective self-awareness; moreover, when we are in a communication situation, certain stimuli may induce objective self-awareness. Not only might the presence of mirrors make us objectively self-aware but remarks made about us in our presence might induce objective self-awareness. The frequently observed awkwardness that many persons display when they receive compliments from others may be the product of objective self-awareness induced by the compliments. In special communication situations, for example, psychotherapy, attentional focus upon one's self may be both easy and desirable; however, outside of such special situations, we can say that objective self-awareness may interfere with the smooth conduct of social interaction.

Self-Consciousness

Objective self-awareness can be created by a variety of environmental stimuli; it is a more or less transient state. By contrast, self-consciousness is conceived as a relatively enduring personality characteristic which is relatively slow to change (Fenigstein, Scheier, & Buss, 1975). According to Fenigstein et al. (1975), self-consciousness has at least two different components. First, *private* self-consciousness occurs when the self is focused upon as an object, much like objective self-awareness. Second *public* self-consciousness is created when we become aware that other persons are focusing their attention upon us. This type of self-consciousness might be experienced during some kind of public performance before an audience. A dimension related to these two self-consciousness factors is social anxiety. There have been a number of studies which have examined the impacts of these three dimensions upon various aspects of behavior.

Scheier and Carver (1977) found that persons scoring high in private self-consciousness reacted more extremely to emotionally arousing stimuli than did persons who scored low in private self-consciousness. In this respect, the highly private self-conscious individuals reacted much like persons who were made objectively self-aware. Also similar to the objective self-awareness findings was the finding that persons high in private self-consciousness gave more accurate self-reports about their future behavior than did persons low in private self-consciousness (Turner, 1978). Fenigstein (1979) observed that females with high levels of public self-consciousness were more likely to react negatively to rejection by a group. These persons were also more likely to quit the group.

These research findings suggest that persons with high levels of private self-consciousness behave as if they were in a state of objective self-awareness with all of the attendant difficulties of being in that state. We can only speculate that persons who have high levels of private self-consciousness may feel less affiliative toward others than their low private self-consciousness counterparts. Unfortunately, we have no research which links private self-consciousness to communication behavior. It does appear, however, that persons with high public self-consciousness are sensitive to the reactions of other persons to them. Persons with high levels of self-consciousness in the public sense might find face-to-face interactions difficult and communication with large audiences even more unnerving. Again, because of the relative youth of the self-consciousness research, it is difficult to talk about these links to communicative conduct with any degree of certainty. However, this area of theory and research suggests that persons may be chronically more or less aware of themselves and their conduct in social interaction situations, depending upon their levels of self-consciousness.

Self-Monitoring

Like public and private self-consciousness, self-monitoring is conceived of as a relatively enduring personality disposition of an individual (Snyder, 1974). According to Snyder (1974, 1979), high self-monitors are persons who are generally concerned with making favorable impressions on others. Because of this concern, they possess two general characteristics. First, they are sensitive to the behavior of others for cues which will enable them to gain an understanding of the person with whom they are interacting. High self-monitors are more socially perceptive. Secondly, high self-monitors have better developed acting skills. They can affect a particular 'personality' when they wish to do so. This means that high self-monitors might not express their inner feelings or beliefs in order to avoid offending the person with whom they are interacting. By contrast, low self-monitors are persons who 'tell it the way they feel it.' They are less concerned with the impressions they make on others and because of this lowered concern for impression management, low self-monitors are not as sensitive to cues which others provide which might be used to guide their conduct.

Since Snyder (1974) created the self-monitoring construct, there have been numerous studies which have contrasted the behavior of high and low self-monitors. Snyder (1974) developed a 25-item scale to measure self-monitoring and found that actors scored higher on self-monitoring than did college students, and college students scored higher than did mental patients. Snyder (1974) also found that high self-monitors were better able to enact different emotional states when requested to do so. When they thought that they would be interacting with a stranger, high self-monitors spent more time studying information about the stranger than did low self-monitors who also thought they would meet the stranger.

Subsequent research has generally supported the differences between high and low self-monitors. In the study described earlier, Bersheid, Graziano,

Monson, and Dermer (1976) asked students to agree to let the experimenter determine their dating choices for varying periods of time. The students were then given the opportunity to watch a videotaped discussion in which their prospective date was a participant. After watching the videotape, the students were asked to make various ratings of the persons in the tape. This study revealed that students who were high self-monitors: (1) recalled more details about their prospective dates, (2) made more confident trait ratings about their prospective dates, and (3) liked their prospective dates more than did students with low levels of self-monitoring. Elliott (1979) found that persons with high self-monitoring levels were willing to spend more money than lows to purchase information about a person to whom they were asked to misrepresent their opinions on an issue. Geizer, Rarick, and Soldow (1977) reported that high self-monitors were better than lows at being able to pick out persons who misrepresented themselves within the context of a television game show. All of these studies provide support for the notion that high self-monitors are both more sensitive to the actions of others and are more concerned with uncertainty reduction when they know they will be interacting with a stranger who may determine whether or not they will reach their interaction goals—whatever these goals may be.

Other research supports the idea that high self-monitors are better able to change their behavior in response to changes in situational demands. Snyder and Monson (1975) found that high self-monitors changed their levels of conformity in response to changes in situations to a greater extent than did low self-monitors. Lippa (1976) had high and low self-monitors enact the roles of introverted and extroverted teachers. This study revealed that the behavior of the high self-monitors changed more when they shifted from one role to the other than did the behavior of low self-monitors. In addition, persons who observed the role playing were better able to identify the intended personality style when it was played by high self-monitors. Thus, high self-

monitors were not *only more flexible across roles*, but they did a more 'convincing' job of enacting the assigned role. In all likelihood, these differences stem from the kinds of social knowledge bases that high and low self-monitors use to guide their self-presentations. Research reported by Snyder and Cantor (1980) suggests that high self-monitors use prototypic conceptions of *others* as guides to their self-presentations in social interaction situations. Low self-monitors use their *self-images* as guides for their self-presentations. Since we generally see more variations in the behavior of others and tend to see ourselves as less 'variable,' it is not surprising that the range of potential self-presentations that the low self-monitor can display is more limited than the range that the high self-monitor can generate.

SUMMARY

At the beginning of this reading we raised the questions of how persons go about gaining information from others and how persons process that information in order to develop predictive and explanatory knowledge for the purpose of reducing their uncertainties about themselves and others. We also indicated that uncertainty reduction is a critical prerequisite for the exercise of control in social interactions. Finally we recognized that our discussion of knowledge acquisition strategies and attribution models was biased in the direction of assuming that persons engage in considerable thought and planning when they interact with others. We considered a number of different research areas which suggest that when persons enact routine sequences of action, they may be relatively inattentive to the details of their performances.

Our discussion of knowledge acquisition strategies revealed that persons may gather information about others by: (1) observing them unobtrusively, (2) studying their reactions to a set of conditions set up by the observer, or (3) engaging in interaction with them. Within each one of these general classes of strategies, we considered a number of more specific strategies which might be employed to gain knowledge. We considered the problem of assessing the veracity of information gleaned by these methods and counterstrategies that might be employed to foil knowledge gaining attempts.

We then turned to a discussion of various models of attribution. These models attempt to explain how persons arrive at characterizations of others' dispositions and how persons arrive at causal explanations for others' actions. These models are concerned with uncertainty reduction at the predictive and explanatory levels. We saw how a number of factors influence the extent to which we are willing to take a person's actions as representative of his or her dispositions (correspondent inference theory) and we indicated how different kinds of information influence the ways we attribute causality (Kelley's approach). We suggested several limitations of these attribution models. We then considered some other approaches to social knowledge. Our discussion of scripts indicated that when persons engage in the same or similar patterns of interaction over time, they are likely to become less mindful of the details of their performances. We also found that stimuli in the immediate environment of the individual can make him or her more or less self-aware. Finally, we considered approaches to self-awareness and self-monitoring which conceive of these attributes as enduring traits which persons possess. We saw how various facets of social interaction and social judgment are influenced by these attributes.

Communication is not only something which we receive from others, it is a tool we use to gain knowledge. . . . Moreover, employing language to exert control in relationships may also be a way of reducing our uncertainties both about the other person in the relationship and ourselves.

6

Managing Interpersonal Relationships: Social Cognitive and Strategic Determinants of Competence

JAMES L. APPLEGATE | GREGORY B. LEICHTY

Perhaps no aspect of human existence is as perplexing as our social relationships. These relationships can be sources of security or anxiety, material success or failure, happiness or sorrow. Given their importance it is not surprising that considerable popular writing and scientific research has been devoted to studying how social relationships are developed, maintained, and dissolved. In this chapter we describe and critique a large body of relationship research tied to Altman and Taylor's (1973) social penetration model of relationship development. Following this we briefly describe a "constructivist" theory of communication and argue for its utility as an approach to relational studies in overcoming many of the limitations of traditional relationship research. We believe the later perspective provides a more comprehensive theoretical base from which to study the general social cognitive and communicative processes that undergird the competent negotiation of social relationships.

We should note that our review of traditional relationship research focuses on studies of relationship development. Growing numbers of researchers are turning their attention to the processes of relationship dissolution or disengagement (e.g., see Duck, 1982a; Knapp, 1978). We feel our criticisms research on development are applicable to dissolution research adopting a model of dissolution that is basically social penetration in reverse (see Duck,

1982b, for a critique of these positions). Some recent work has pointed to the need to ground dissolution research in more basic understandings of the communication processes which characterize it (Duck, 1983; Duck et al., forthcoming; McCall, 1982). Such research is consistent with our general argument that relationship development, maintenance, disengagement, and dissolution are best seen as implicit accomplishments within multifunctional communicative interactions. Competent relationship management is dependent upon individuals' ability to effectively integrate relationship goals within everyday communications designed as well to inform, persuade, comfort, and/or manage impressions of relational partners.

THE SOCIAL PENETRATION MODEL OF RELATIONAL DEVELOPMENT

While a number of approaches are available for the study of acquaintance and relational development, the social penetration theory of Altman and Taylor (1973) has received more theoretical elaboration than its competitors. The framework of this theory is also broad enough to encompass a number of smaller theories that are confined to particular stages of acquaintance, or focus on specific behavioral developments such as self-disclosure or reciprocity of

From Bostrom, R. N. (Ed.) (1984). *Competence in communication* (pp. 33-55). Beverly Hills, CA: Sage.

exchange. This discussion incorporates attribution perspectives and filter theories of information processing under the umbrella of the social penetration paradigm. Even though these smaller theories are usually considered separately, they are compatible with and subject to the weaknesses of social penetration theory.

Altman and Taylor (1973) characterize initial exchange between strangers as narrow and superficial. Strangers initially talk on a rather narrow set of topics and are careful only to disclose the outer nonintimate layers of their personalities. As a relationship between two persons develops, however, the exchange characteristically broadens and includes the disclosure of increasingly intimate or core aspects of one's personality. The quantitative and qualitative transformations of this exchange facilitate the mutual penetration of personalities as a relationship progresses. Relational partners are presumed to acquire increasing amounts of intimate and nonintimate information about each other as the relationship proceeds through the developmental cycle. The process of information exchange is thought to proceed more quickly in the early stages of relational development. Exchange of intimate information tends to involve greater risks and is done with greater discretion (Altman & Taylor, 1973).

According to social penetration theory, persons anticipate rewards from mutual association that they are unable to attain individually and are thus motivated to form social relationships. From this perspective a relationship represents "mutual agreement, implicit or explicitly, between people to interact in order to maximize rewards" (Roloff, 1976, p. 182). While the types of rewards sought in relationships are quite varied, the theory assumes that a relationship will be maintained only for as long as each relational partner anticipates that his or her desired rewards will be available at reasonable costs in the future. Concurrently, the impetus to form relationships or to escalate existing ones, can fluctuate as a function of several factors. The potential rewards of relational escalation may become more salient to an individual following changes in loca-

tion, personal crises, or changes in one's self-concept (Miller & Steinberg, 1975).

From this perspective the formation, maintenance, and dissolution of relationships depends on how the relational partners calculate the reward/cost ratios of existing and anticipated interaction. Persons presumably make relational decisions on the basis of whether or not these ratios are favorable. In theory, a person evaluates the rewards and costs of the present interaction with the intent of determining whether the rewards are greater than the costs. In addition, the person forecasts or assesses the probable reward/cost ratios of future interaction with the same person at the next more intimate relational stage. If both the evaluation of present interaction and the forecasts of future interaction with a person are favorable, the individual should decide to proceed to the next level of intimacy. Of course, actual relational escalation is always contingent on the other person's acceptance of the move.

Social penetration theory assumes that the calculation of profit/cost ratios continues for the duration of a social relationship, and that these calculations are the basis for each movement toward or away from a given level of intimacy. If either of the ratios becomes unfavorable at some point, the individual has a number of options depending on the stage of the relationship. If this occurs early in interaction, the other person can easily be filtered out of a field of potential partners. A relationship can also be frozen at the existing stage of development or it can be de-escalated. According to social penetration theory, the individual progressively chooses a few intimates from a large field of potential intimates via these processes of evaluation and forecasting the costs and rewards of interaction.

Given the importance of these calculation processes, a considerable amount of attention has been given to *how* persons calculate reward/cost ratios and decide whether they are favorable or unfavorable. This has included research into how decision making may be qualitatively different depending on the stage of a relationship. A second line of research has examined how persons go about changing a relational trajectory once they have made a decision to do so.

Under the first line of research, Thibaut and Kelley (1959) developed a conceptual framework to describe how a person evaluates reward/cost ratios and forecasts. According to Thibaut and Kelley, this is done by comparing ratios and forecasts to two standards, a comparison level (CL), and a comparison level of alternatives (CLalt). An individual's comparison level represents what a person feels she or he should receive in a relationship based on her or his past experience. A person's comparison level of alternatives represents the lowest profit ratio a person is willing to accept on the basis of his or her estimate of rewards available in other relationships. Using these variables we can predict the stability of a relationship and the satisfaction that each partner derives from the relationship. This is done by comparing each person's present and anticipated outcomes with each individual's CL and CLalt (Miller & Parks, 1982; Roloff, 1981).

Considerable attention has also been directed to how persons process information while they construct profit ratios and forecast the relative rewardingness of future interaction. Person perception research has shown that forecasts frequently appear to be made on the basis of very limited amounts of stimulus information about the other person (see the review of research in Schneider et al., 1979). Such information often consists of a mere scanning of the other person's appearance, a brief observation of the person's behavior in one or two social contexts, or utilization of information that has been received about the person from third parties. Person-perception researchers have been particularly interested in how persons use such limited information sets to create an overall impression of the other person and make additional inferences about the target person's response characteristics.

Impression formation research suggests the construction of profit forecasts are made possible by the use of implicit theories of personality (Bruner & Tagiuri, 1954). These implicit theories are beliefs about sets of perceived relationships between behaviors and underlying invariances in persons' personalities. Persons are thought to use these theories to infer personality traits from observed appearances and behaviors. Future behaviors of the target person are then forecast from these personality traits. The implicit personality theories help the perceiver infer additional information about the other person, as well as to organize the accumulated beliefs into an overall impression that can be evaluated.

Most relational development research assumes that assessment of the specific response propensities of the other person are heavily influenced by initial evaluations of the other person (i.e., interpersonal attitudes). The perceiver's global affective evaluation of the stimulus person is thought to serve as the primary determinant of whether a person decides to pursue, escalate, freeze, or retreat from a given relationship. Attitude research posits that persons will make positive forecasts of future interaction for persons they like and negative forecasts of future interaction with people they dislike (see O'Keefe, 1980, for an analysis of this research).

Given the theoretical importance of interpersonal attitudes, an extensive body of research has sought to determine what sorts of attributes lead to an overall positive evaluation of a person. A number of studies indicate that we tend to be attracted to persons whom we believe possess attitudes, interests, beliefs, and values similar to our own (Morton & Douglas, 1981). However, several competing theories exist to explain *why* similarity is attractive.

Reinforcement theory suggests that cognitive similarity is attractive because it provides an individual with social validation of his or her beliefs and opinions about social reality (Duck, 1976). Alternatively, balance theory suggests that similarity is attractive because it keeps persons' interpersonal cognitions comfortably balanced (Heider, 1958). Others suggest that similarity is attractive because it makes for easier communication and synchronization of interaction, or that similarity makes understanding and prediction of the other person easier (Schneider et al., 1979).

These conclusions about the attractiveness of similarity, however, are tempered with the recognition that interpersonal attraction is not a unitary phenomena. The attractiveness of an attribute also depends on the developmental stage of a relationship. Levinger and Snoek (1972) point out that criteria for liking based on a first impression are qualitatively different from liking assessments based upon rewarding interactions with a person over an extended period of time. It also is apparent that acquaintance can be treated as a process with qualitatively different stages. These stages are characterized by the kinds of information that persons in a relationship attend to and give off (Duck, 1973, 1976).

The developmental view of relational information processing suggests that the perceiver uses the level of information that fits with his or her purposes at the given stage of interaction. Early in interaction, decisions are made on the basis of physical appearance and status cues that are readily available. In the latter stages of acquaintance, information about the other person's underlying personality is increasingly sought and inferred. This developmental view of information processing recognizes that interpersonal attraction is not a simple function of any kind of information. The informativeness of a given type of information at a particular stage of acquaintance must also be taken into account.

The developmental view of acquaintance also highlights the necessity of treating acquaintance as a skilled performance. Mutual attraction alone does not guarantee that relational escalation will occur. Each person must skillfully encode and decode information in a way that is appropriate to the given stage of a relationship. Researchers generally have abandoned the relatively simple assumption that individuals form relationships by matching up with persons on factors that are antecedent to the acquaintance process itself. Accordingly, increasing attention has been given to how individuals strategically control the rate of relational escalation.

Self-disclosure has received enormous attention as one of the primary mechanisms that individuals use to manage self-presentation and control the trajectory of a relationship (Deregla & Grzelak, 1979). A person wanting to escalate a relationship must simultaneously convey a positive image of self and still convey his or her intentions of being trusting and trustworthy. Early conceptions that free self-disclosure would automatically escalate a relationship were abandoned as it became apparent that indiscriminate disclosure often does more harm than good. In any case of disclosure of potentially negative information, there is a trade-off between the benefits one gains by disclosing and conveying that one is honest and trusting and the potential negative impact of the information disclosed (Ajzen, 1977).

It has also become clear that self-disclosure is not a discrete variable. The context of self-disclosure changes and the goals of disclosure can be pursued with a large number of strategies (Roloff, 1976). These discoveries pointed to the importance of considering communication strategies within the context of situated interaction. The person wanting to disclose information needs to be able to do so in ways that are consistent with the norms that apply to a given context. The discloser must also be able to forecast whether positive or negative attributions will result from the disclosed information.

A CRITIQUE OF THE TRADITIONAL MODEL

The social penetration account of relational development has become increasingly sophisticated as developmental processes of relationships have been considered. A reasonable amount of empirical data supporting the theory has also accumulated. Recently, however, a number of the assumptions of the model have been seriously challenged (Applegate, 1983; Berger & Roloff, 1982; Burke & Springer, 1981; Crockett & Friedman, 1980; Delia, 1980; Duck et al., forthcoming). We offer a selective review of these criticisms and offer an alternative view of relationship development suggested by them.

Relationship Development
Is an Implicit Process

The most prevalent criticism of mainstream relationship research is that it paints an overly conscious and rationalistic picture of relational negotiation. The heavy use of laboratory investigations and experimental methods that force individuals to explicitly consider relational variables has helped to foster such a view. They also have deprived the area of rich descriptive data depicting historical, cultural, and individual variations in the ways various types of relationships (especially nonintimate ones) emerge as an implicit feature of daily activities (Berger & Roloff, 1982; Delia, 1980; Deaux, 1978; Duck, 1980; Hinde, 1979; Kimmel, 1979).

An inordinate amount of research has been devoted to studying attraction issues based on initial impressions in first encounters. The "longitudinal" research that does exist has originated for the most part in retrospective accounts of the development of commitment in heterosexual relationships. Moreover, little attention has been given to the frequency with which the phenomena typically studied in controlled settings actually occur in everyday life. Without such frequency data we have little indication of whether a particular phenomena has much relevance to an explanation of recurring behaviors in relationships.

We believe that longitudinal analyses of relationships in everyday life will, and common sense does, suggest that the vast majority of our relationships are developed and maintained as implicit features of daily activities. Some theorists have offered perspectives addressing relationship development in such a way (see Berger & Roloff, 1982; Delia, 1980; McCall, 1970). However, the bulk of relationship research has ignored the fact that the majority of relationships we establish (e.g., plumbers and homeowners, doctors and patients, students and teachers, supervisors and subordinates) are not dependent for their existence on traditional relational variables like self-disclosure, increasing intimacy, or even positive affect. Rather, competent management of such relationships requires the ability to implicitly negotiate a variety of types of relationships in the course of communicating about healing, teaching, repairing pipes, and turning a profit. To analyze many everyday relationships with these traditional variables is to impose dimensions on interactants' communication that are at best tangential to the actual organization of their interactions.

Moreover, even in relationships where intimacy, positive global affect, relational control, and so on might have expected relevance (e.g., with close friends, spouses, dating couples) these qualities of relationships typically are implicitly accomplished and maintained as we communicate in the course of deciding what restaurants to frequent, cleaning house, and/or dressing the children for school. Individuals' ability to integrate relational goals for intimacy, supportiveness, and love within strategic performance that comfort, inform, instruct, persuade, and manage impressions is, in our view, central to relationship development and the maintenance of mutuality in relationship definitions. We know little about what enables people to construct such integrated strategic efforts or how they are constructed largely because of the tendency in traditional research to extract relationships from the social contexts in which they exist and make them explicit foci for subjects.

Relationships Follow Multiple Trajectories

Traditional relationship research, tied to the notion of social penetration, has fostered a narrow conception of the differing forms relationship development may take. A survey of the bulk of relationship research would suggest that all relationships follow the same trajectory. Like astronauts strapped into a fully automated rocket, relational partners are seen as locked into a trajectory carrying them from impersonal to personal levels: from acquaintance to intimacy. Progress is fueled by increasing self-disclosure and positive affect. Partners' only choices are to provide the appropriate mix of self-disclosure and affect for different stages of the flight or bail out. Implicit in this idea of relationship development is the notion that relationships are driven by a strain toward total integration of partners' selves. The function of relationships is to convince persons of the genuineness, dependability, and reality of other persons. Persons are led inevitably to integrate greater portions of their selves into the foci of the relationship making the relationship less vulnerable to unmasking. In addition, this strain toward totality and intimacy is motivated by a need to conserve cognitive energy. It is argued a few intimate relationships provide a more efficient method of gaining dependable support for our various role-identities. Hence, it is easier to satisfy our identity-support and relational needs in a few relationships than in a large number of them.

While there is no doubt that some relationships reflect a path of development similar to that outlined in traditional theory, we find the model deficient in at least two respects. First, the model encourages researchers to treat communication as epiphenomenal to the process of relational development. That is, communication behaviors are studied as realizations of a particular relational trajectory rather than as the medium through which relational goals and paths to those goals are negotiated and pursued. We argue (and this argument is developed in detail in the latter half of this article) that adequate explanation of the process of relationship negotiation should begin with analyses of the communicative goals of interactions. The multifunctional nature of communication is a well-documented truism. Clark and Delia (1979) suggest that every interaction is organized around at least three types of goals: instrumental (e.g., persuasive, informational, instructional), identity/impression management, and relational. Research in social cognition and communication suggests the specific nature of the goals embodied in our definitions of social situations directly influence the organization of strategic behavior (Cohen, 1981; Higgins et al., 1981; McCann & Higgins, forthcoming; O'Keefe & Delia, 1982). Moreover, there

is evidence of group and individual differences in the importance assigned to different types of goals (e.g., instrumental vs. relational) as well as to types of instrumental, identity, and relational goals typically informing interaction (McCann & Higgins, forthcoming).

Such research suggests that studies of the relational function of communication begin with assessments of the *variety* of relational goals informing communication as well as their explicitness and salience in relation to other types of communicative goals—this, rather than assuming the goal of social penetration as a salient feature of most (if not all) communication in relationships. Some theorists have offered perspectives which explicitly address relational goals and definitions as negotiated products of multifunctional communications rather than treating communications as the product of a particular relational trajectory (e.g., McCall, 1970). Such an orientation allows study of relationships in which goals of intimacy and intimacy and penetration are explicit but casts such relationships within a broader framework, treating relational trajectories themselves as variables for study.

Our second objection to the narrow conception of relational trajectories encouraged by traditional research is that it encourages a much too orderly conception of development even for those relationships in which intimacy and social penetration are the general goals (e.g., dating couples thinking about marriage). Huston, Surra, Fitzgerald, and Cate (1981) have found a variety of developmental patterns for courtship relationships and in the way self-disclosure, perceived similarities, conflict, and mutual participation in different types of activities affect the pattern of development. Moreover, Duck, Miell, and Miell (forthcoming) argue that individual differences in social cognitive and communicative ability affect the way in which intimacy is achieved or whether or not it is achieved at all. Again, the argument here is that even relationships generally oriented to social penetration evidence various paths of development is partly due to the differences in communicative ability of interactants.

Relational Development Is an Accommodative Process

O'Keefe and Delia (1982) argue that most impression formation research reflects an assimilative bias emphasizing the role of the perceiver's cognitive system in reconstructing, inferring, and organizing information about others. Such a bias has led researchers to neglect the role of situations and the behavior of others in determining what dimensions of judgment perceivers deem salient for a situation and in effecting change in the nature and organization of perceivers' cognitive organization that facilitate accommodation to new information across time. A similar criticism can be leveled at traditional approaches to relationship development.

Traditional relationship research has focused on how perceivers' reconstruct information about others and attempted to identify the criteria applied to make relationship decisions (e.g., similarity, reward/cost potential). Typically such approaches have implied a static conception of perceivers' self-concepts and goals. The result is conceptions of relationship development closely tied to matching and filtering hypotheses.

This orientation has led researchers to neglect the central role of communication in negotiating identities and relationships. We know little about how particular situational constraints, instrumental goals, and types of behavior by partners affect the elicitation and modification of perceivers' relational goals or their decisions about which aspects of self to disclose in a given context, or relationship. We have little to say about how and why relational partners alter their self-concepts or their beliefs and strategic responses to one another in accommodating to new information provided in communication. Finally, and perhaps most disturbing, we have little knowledge about what contributes to differences in individuals' strategic flexibility in meeting the changing demands of an ongoing relationship. Any adequate approach to relationship development must offer a way of explaining accommodation and change as well as differences in individuals' ability to strategically make such accommodations.

A related criticism of traditional models of relationship development is their tendency to disregard social-structural constraints to which individuals must accommodate. Much writing on interpersonal attraction assumes that persons have a great deal of choice about whom to interact with. While this assumption may be fairly accurate in a high school, it does not apply to many contexts. We frequently find it necessary to establish friendly relations with persons we don't particularly like (Kurth, 1970). Kin relationships also involve very little choice but are still very important relationships for most people. Friendship patterns are affected as well as the number of social roles one acquires. Marriage and parenthood both appear to significantly alter a person's friendship network (Dickens & Perlman, 1981). A more realistic model of relational development would presumably devote at least some attention to how persons accommodate to these social-structural constraints.

AN ALTERNATIVE FRAMEWORK FOR RELATIONSHIP STUDIES

We now briefly overview a "constructivist" theory of communication and argue for its utility in studying relationship development in a way that overcomes many of the limitations of traditional relationship research outlined earlier. Over the last 15 years, constructivist theory has spawned an important research tradition in the field of speech communication (for a comprehensive overview see Delia et al., 1982). The thrust of this work has been the integration of research on interpersonal construct system development within the general study of social cognition and communication behavior. Communication, by this account, is not epiphenomenal to construal processes but rather an independent phenomena influenced by and influencing application and development of personal constructs, social scripts, perspective-taking processes, and the like (for recent work offering similar interactive accounts of the relationship between social cognition and communication, see Athay &

Darely, 1981; Duck et al., forthcoming; McCann & Higgins, forthcoming.)

The logic of the constructivist epistemology is hierarchic and developmental in nature embracing the comparative conception of development forwarded by Werner (1957; also see Werner & Kaplan, 1963), which is captured succinctly in his orthogenetic principle: "Whenever development occurs, it proceeds from a state of relative globality and lack of differentiation to a state of increasing differentiation, articulation, and hierarchic integration" (1957, p. 126). Specific assessments of relationships between and individual differences in the quality of communication behavior and social cognition are approached through comparative analysis within a series of parallel developmental axes derived from this principle. The analysis of social cognition is grounded in an integration of Kelly's (1955) theory of interpersonal constructs with Werner's developmental approach. An elaboration of this conception of communication and its relationship to interpersonal constructs follows.

Communication as Functional Behavior

At the heart of the constructivist conception of communication is the contention that messages *do* things. People typically do not communicate to be listener-adaptive, evidence the behavioral correlates of labile cognitive structure, and so on. Rather, talk is directly tied to interaction goals such as comforting, persuading, or negotiating relationships (O'Keefe & Delia, 1982). The functions communication messages serve may be explicit (closely tied to the intentions of the interactants) or implicit (embedded in tacit situational knowledge).

Constructivist theory has integrated aspects of symbolic interactionist theory in sociology, including W.I. Thomas's conception of the "definition of the situation" (see Ball, 1972; Blumer, 1969) and a variety of sociolinguistic analyses (e.g., Bernstein, 1974; Halliday, 1973; Hymes, 1974) to construct a beginning taxonomy of communicative functions. Clark and Delia (1979) argue that every commu-

nicative transaction involves the overt and/or tacit negotiation of identities and relationship definitions between interactants. Moreover, the transaction may (and typically does) involve pursuit of instrumental goals (e.g., persuading, comforting, transmitting information).

Utilizing a variety of data gathering techniques including naturalistic observation, structured interactive communication tasks, and open-ended responses to hypothetical situations, researchers have generated a corpus of strategies employed by children, adolescents, and adults to accomplish interaction goals. Hierarchic coding systems have been derived from analysis of these strategies reflecting axes of development consistent with Wernerian developmental theory. This work has provided a picture of developmental and individual differences in (1) the listener-adaptiveness of persuasive strategies (e.g., Applegate, 1982a; Clark & Delia, 1977; Delia & Clark, 1977; Delia et al., 1979; B. O'Keefe & Delia, 1979); (2) the referential adequacy of information giving strategies (e.g., Hale, 1980, 1982); (3) the person-centeredness of regulative and interpersonal comforting strategies (e.g., Applegate, 1980a, 1980b; Applegate et al., forthcoming; Applegate & Delia, 1980; Burleson, 1982); and (4) the relative sophistication of impression management strategies in meeting cultural guidelines for politeness and "face" needs (for a general analysis of such strategic demands see Brown & Levinson, 1978; for constructivist applications see Kline, 1981; Kline & Ceropski, forthcoming; also see Applegate, 1982a, 1982b). Such developmental differences have been found across a variety of social contexts for all ages (e.g., the family, school, peer groups, work settings).

Interpersonal Constructs and Communication

Constructivist theory suggests that differences in the quality of strategic behavior are strongly influenced by the quality of communicators' understanding of people. That "person knowledge" is in turn largely achieved through application of constructs. The bulk of research (including that referenced above) has attempted to establish relationships between interpersonal construct system development along particular axes (e.g., globality-differentiation, concreteness-abstractness, diffuseness-integration) and strategic behavior.

In contrast to the limited success of research attempting to relate communication behavior to global measures of empathy, perspective-taking, and/or role-taking (see the general review of Shantz, 1981), constructivist research efforts have evidenced consistent success in relating developmental differences in the quality of child and adult communication strategies to specific developments in the differentiation, abstractness, integration, and comprehensiveness, and so on, of the interpersonal construct system. For example, in the research referenced previously, individuals with more differentiated, abstract (dispositionally oriented) and comprehensive constructs have been shown to use a greater number of alternative strategies that are more listener-adaptive in pursuing persuasive goals. Parents with more advanced systems employ more person-centered strategies in regulating children's behavior and helping them deal with interpersonal problems—strategies that better recognize and elaborate individual feelings, beliefs, and the like as salient features of social contexts and encourage the child to engage in autonomous reflection. Increased differentiation and abstractness of constructs also has been tied to greater awareness of and strategic sophistication in impression management.

Researchers recently have acknowledged the influence of various types of social cognitive schemes, scripts, and the like on communication (e.g., O'Keefe & Delia, 1982; O'Keefe et al., 1980). However, personal constructs still are viewed as central structures underlying social perception processes (e.g., social inference and evaluation, perspective-taking, impression organization) and thus a central foundation for the foundation of communication strategies.

Interaction Goals and the "Definition of the Situation"

While previous research has consistently found direct relationships between interpersonal construct system development and communication behavior, it has led also to a theoretical explanation for that relationship that is somewhat more complex. It is an extremely suggestive explanation for investigation of ties between personal constructs, communication, and the development of interpersonal relationships—one that enlarges the scope of the theory and enables it to address many of the limitations of current approaches to relationship development.[1]

In this view, communication behavior is most directly influenced by situated communication-relevant beliefs organized within the interactant's "definition of the situation." One usually has some expected definition as one enters the situation that is modified as one accommodates to the behavior of others. Included in this changing definition are impressions of self and other, a definition of the relationship that exists with the other, and beliefs about type of context, expectations for behavior in that context, and the like. Also included either as explicit intentions or tacitly embedded in beliefs about self, other, and/or the situation, are identity, relational, and instrumental interaction goals (Clark & Delia, 1979). Moreover, the interactant typically has some beliefs about his or her partner's definition of the situation (e.g., the other's impression of him or her, self-concept, goals).[2]

Not all beliefs embodied in situational definitions are communication-relevant. Only those that suggest interaction goals means of achieving and/or obstacles to those goals and hence have implications for strategic behavior are relevant. That Joe's socks do not match and that I believe him to be sloppy may not be relevant for strategic behavior designed to persuade him to loan his Mercedes. On the other hand much of the person knowledge acquired through application of personal constructs is communication-relevant. Moreover, differences in the quality of person knowledge produced by application of a more differentiated, integrated construct system should enable the individual to recognize more of what could or should be influencing his or her goals and strategic behavior. A more advanced perceiver might understand that Joe's socks are part of a general behavior pattern that reflects not only sloppiness but also a desire to be seen as nonmaterialistic. That information, unavailable to a less integrative perceiver, could be relevant to the persuasive effort. More advanced person knowledge can affect not only how interaction goals are pursued but what goals are perceived. If the persuader understands that Joe feels his friends are more attracted to his possessions than to him, the persuader would understand that in addition to trying to persuade Joe it would be good to reassure Joe that their friendship is not materially based. Such understandings lay the foundation for a more complex, integrated, multifunctional strategic effort. It is in this somewhat indirect way—through its potential influence on the number and quality of communication-relevant beliefs—that construct development is thought to influence strategic behavior.

To date there has been little effort to relate personal construct development to the quality of situated communication-relevant beliefs (cf. O'Keefe et al., 1983). Some previous research has indirectly addressed the issue by asking subjects to provide rationales for the strategies they employ (e.g., Applegate, 1980a, 1980b, 1982b). Such rationales display the goals that inform behavior and beliefs about self, others, situation and the like, which are perceived as useful or obstructive to goal attainment. These studies show that individuals with more advanced interpersonal construct systems more consistently tend to (1) point to beliefs about the subjective perspectives of others (e.g., their self-image, perception of the subject, feelings) as influential in strategic organization; and (2) recognize multiple goals in the situation (e.g., spontaneously indicate that identity and relationship goals were also influential in the formulation of persuasive strategies).

Future research that (1) directly examines the impact of differences in the quality of person knowledge produced by construct system development on communication-relevant beliefs (of which interaction goals are themselves a subset) and (2) casts analysis of strategic behavior in terms of the multiple implicit and explicit functions it fulfills can enlarge the scope of our analysis of communication in at least two ways. First, we take seriously the multifunctional nature of communication and orient toward strategic *complexity* and *integration* as important variables for research. Here the concern is not the degree of listener-adaptation or self-disclosure evidenced in the form of a particular strategy but rather the extent to which that strategy and others employed in the situation reflect an integrated effort to meet the multiple implicit and explicit identity, relational, and instrumental goals presented by/perceived in the situation (e.g., relative sophistication in organizing a strategic effort so as to persuade a peer to reform his drinking behavior while maintaining the existing supportive, equalitarian relationship, and without spoiling his self-image as a good parent).

Obviously situations vary in the types and number of goals and obstacles they present. Similarly, individuals will vary in the typical types and number of goals and obstacles they typically perceive as present and in their ability to construct integrated strategic responses to what they perceive. It is just those individual differences that we now study in their own right as they are influenced by construct system development.

Second, this framework points to strategic *flexibility* as a central feature of communication ability. Obviously, when we consider the variety of goals interactants have and the variation in situational constraints they confront we recognize that no one form of strategy is consistently functional. At times tying persuasive requests to the individual needs of the persuadee (i.e., being highly listener-adaptive) may be less sensible than simply issuing a command. Similarly, having the strategic skills necessary to self-disclose appropriately does not preclude recognizing the need to "stonewall" information skillfully at times.

Individual differences in strategic flexibility

should be expected not only in behavior across contexts but also within contexts as interactants are confronted with new information requiring strategic accommodation. Such variations in behavior within and across situations are common and reflect ability to range across the possible levels/types of persuasive, identity management, and relational strategies to accomplish situated goals. Such flexibility as a product of development is suggested in Werner's principle of "developmental stratification" (the ability to operate at different levels depending on situational demands). It argues for accepting Tschudi and Rommetiveit's (1982) suggestion that Kelly's sociality corollary might (and we would argue should) be interpreted as meaning, "To the extent that one person construes the construction process of another, he may, *if he so chooses,* play a role in a social process involving the other" (p. 257). That choice, implemented in strategic behavior, will be a product of goals and other communication-relevant beliefs embodied in the individual's definition of the situation.

We have suggested that application of this conception of personal constructs, interaction goals, and strategic organization would be useful for researchers interested in an analysis of relationship development. We now attempt to make good that claim.

AN APPLICATION TO RELATIONSHIP RESEARCH

Longitudinal studies of different types of relationships examining the effect of interpersonal construct system development on communication-relevant beliefs/goals and strategic behavior can address systematically the implicit, multipathed, accommodative features of relationship development outlined here. Direct examination of relationship-relevant goals and beliefs can define the multiple trajectories of relationships. Leichty's (1983) comparison of attributions to friendship and supervisor-subordinate relationships suggests, for example, that in work relationships (unlike friend-

ships) subordinates incorporate almost no "person-centered" qualities (e.g., mutual emotional support, self-concept validation, partners' personal qualities) in their descriptions of the focus of the relationship regardless of the length of association with the supervisor. Yet comparison across the two types of relationships reflects similar levels of relational satisfaction. The results suggest different paths as well as different determinants of development. Such differences can only be captured through direct examination of relationship-relevant goals and beliefs embodied in situational definitions.

Study of group and individual differences in the paths and determinants of particular types of relationship development related to social cognitive and communicative skill in producing more functionally complex, integrated, and flexible strategic behavior is another important area of research. The development of many types of relationships (those heavily scripted by straightforward, simple cultural and institutional norms) may be unaffected by differences in development. However, in less scripted relationships the quality of personal constructs and person knowledge may affect the nature of development. Leichty (1983) found that while offering activity-centered and instrumental goals for friendships, more advanced perceivers tended over time to incorporate person-centered (see above) goals as well. The latter goals were seldom included in the relational attributions of their less advanced peers. In Burke and Springer's (1981) study construct differentiation related significantly to the variability of behavioral intentions toward friends and roommates. More generally, advanced perceivers evidence greater explicit concern for relationship maintenance/development in their definitions of communicate situations (Applegate, 1980b, 1982a). Research in this area is limited and very exploratory, but encourages further investigation of relationship between personal construct development and the types of goals and information that individuals define as relevant to relationship development.

In addition, some past research defining the role of personal construct quality in social perception processes suggests possible individual differences in determinants of relationship development. For example, differentiated perceivers are less reliant on global evaluations in the organization of their beliefs about others (O'Keefe & Delia, 1981; O'Keefe, 1980). This may explain in part Burke and Springer's (1981) finding that increasingly global evaluations of relational partners (liking) is a less salient determinant of relationship development for differentiated perceivers.

Other impression-formation research has related construct development and ability to integrate inconsistent information to accommodate to basic differences in values and background between self and others, and to less use of simplifying social schemes in understanding patterns of interpersonal relationships (see Delia et al., 1982). These findings alone suggest at least two important questions for research on relational development. Do these abilities to accommodate to inconsistencies and dissimilarities in others reduce the salience of "similarity" as a determinant of development, or at the least orient more advanced perceivers to different types of similarity? Second, does construct development produce relational definitions and goals (especially in institutional settings) that are more frequently at variance with cultural/institutional norms (i.e., are less scripted)?

Such research questions, examining the effects of personal constructs on the nature of communication-relevant (and more specifically relationship relevant) beliefs are one important part of a constructivist agenda for research on relationship development. A second, equally important item is analysis of communication behavior itself.

The same methods of strategy elicitation and analysis used successfully to identify the quality of persuasive, comforting, and referential efforts individually can be used to assess differences in the degree to which and the ways in which relational goals are addressed in strategic messages. Typically such goals will be implicit features of multifunctional messages. The findings of Applegate (1980b, 1982a) and Kline (1981) suggest systematic relationships between construct development, interac-

tion goals, and the formulation of more complex strategic efforts that incorporate relationship and identity goals as implicit features of persuasive messages. Continued examination of relationship development in the context of multifunctional messages will allow researchers to capture its implicit accomplishment in everyday talk and assess the impact of individual differences in ability to construct complex and integrated messages on that process. Moreover, differences in the degree to which individuals and social groups explicitly address relational concerns becomes, in itself, an interesting relational variable (see Komarovsky, 1962; Philipsen, 1975).

Multifunctional analyses also allow researchers to assess the impact of differences in strategic skill in pursuing other communicative goals on relational development. Clark (1979) has shown how relational concerns affect the form of persuasive strategies. Conversely, differences in the way impressions are managed, comfort is offered, persuasive goals are pursued, and/or information is transmitted should be expected to dramatically affect relationships between individuals—often in ways at odds with their particular relational goals. Differences in strategic ability in these areas has been related to construct development. However, their implications for relationship development have not been addressed.

Let us conclude with one final advantage of this particular constructivist conception of relationships. It focuses attention on individual differences in strategic flexibility in (1) accommodating to the variety of goals that emerge across and within relationships and (2) negotiating conflicts between the relational expectations of self, others, and those embedded in cultural and institutional contexts. There is no more important variable for research examining relationship development.

Explorations of the contribution of interpersonal construct system development on this accommodative skill are called for. Given the demonstrated relation of construct quality to perspective-taking, ability to integrate diverse and inconsistent information about people, listener-adaptive communication skills, and awareness of communication-relevant cultural rules outlined previously, relationships between strategic flexibility and construct differentiation, abstractness, integration, permeability, and comprehensiveness should be expected.

However, research on flexibility and accommodation must not neglect the ways in which exposure to varieties of relationships, immersion in relational conflicts, and confrontation with particular behavior patterns serve to alter relational goals and definitions, the application of constructs, and ultimately the content and structure of the construct system itself. The effect of contexts and communication on individuals' self-concepts, constructs for perceiving others, and their relational definitions and goals has been neglected in research on relationship development. A focus on the causes and effects of strategic flexibility and accommodation will at least allow researchers to address the issue.

This application of constructivist theory to the study of relationship development is admittedly brief and speculative. Nevertheless, the general success of the theory . . . and the conceptual tools it offers for tackling the limitations of traditional research on relationships argue for its viability as an alternate framework within which to cast future research. It ties competent relationship management to the development of (1) social cognitive skills producing situational definitions with a more complex and integrated understanding of communication-relevant factors and (2) the ability to construct more integrated and flexible strategic responses to others in the negotiation of the implicit and explicit instrumental, identity, *and* relational goals of situated actors.

ENDNOTES

[1] In analysis of this issue and its implications for relationship research we are indebted to B. O'Keefe and Delia (1982) for the insights provided by their general exploration of relationships between social cognition and message production.

[2] Several researchers (e.g., Laing et al., 1966) have shown metacognition to operate at even more abstract levels involving assessments of "what I think you think *I* think," "what I think you think I think you think," and the like.

REFERENCES

Ajzen, I. (1977). Information processing approaches to interpersonal attraction. In S. W. Duck (Ed.), *Theory and practice in interpersonal attraction.* New York: Academic Press.

Altman, I., & Taylor, D. (1973). *Social penetration: The development of interpersonal relationships.* Chicago: Holt, Rinehart & Winston.

Applegate, J. L. (1980a). Person and position-centered teacher communication in a day-care center: A case study triangulating interview and naturalistic methods. In N. K. Denzin (Ed.), *Studies in symbolic interaction* (vol. 3). Greenwich, CT: JAI Press.

Applegate, J. L. (1980b). Adaptive communication in educational contexts: A study of teachers' communicative strategies. *Communication Education, 29,* 158-170.

Applegate, J. L. (1982a). The impact of construct system development on communication and impression formation in persuasive contexts. *Communication Monographs, 49,* 277-289.

Applegate, J. L. (1982b). *Construct system development and identity-management skills in persuasive contexts.* Paper presented at the meeting of the Western Speech Communication Association, Denver.

Applegate, J. L. (1983). *Constructs, interaction goals, and communication in relationship development.* Paper presented to the Fourth International Congress on Personal Construct Psychology, Boston.

Applegate, J. L., Burke, J. A., Burleson, B. R., Delia, J. G., & Kline, S. L. (Forthcoming). Reflection-enhancing parental communication. In I. E. Sigel (Ed.), *Parental belief systems: The psychological consequences for children.* Hillsdale, NJ: Erlbaum.

Applegate, J. L. & Delia, J. G. (1980). Person-centered speech, psychological development, and the contexts of language usage. In R. St. Clair & H. Giles (Eds.), *The social and psychological contexts of language.* Hillsdale, NJ: Erlbaum.

Athay, M., & Darley, J. M. (1981). Toward an interaction-centered theory of personality. In N. Cantor & J. F. Kihlstrom (Eds.), *Personality, cognition, and social interaction.* Hillsdale, NJ: Erlbaum.

Ball, D. W. (1972). The definition of the situation: Some theoretical and methodological consequences of taking W. I. Thomas seriously. *Journal for the Theory of Social Behavior, 2,* 61-82.

Berger, C. R., & Roloff, M. E. (1982). Thinking about friends and lovers: Social cognition and relational trajectories. In M. E. Roloff & C. R. Berger (Eds.), *Social cognition and communication.* Beverly Hills: Sage.

Bernstein, B. (1974). *Class, codes, and control: Theoretical studies towards sociology of language* (Rev. ed.). New York: Schocken Books.

Blumer, H. (1969). *Symbolic interactionism: Perspective and method.* Englewood Cliffs, NJ: Prentice-Hall.

Brown, P., & Levinson, S. (1978). Universals in language usage: Politeness phenomena. In E. N. Goody (Ed.), *Questions and politeness: Strategies in social interaction.* Cambridge: Cambridge University Press.

Bruner, J. S., & Tagiuri, R. (1954). Person perception. In G. Lindsay (Ed.), *Handbook of social psychology* (vol. 2). Reading, MA: Addison-Wesley.

Burke, J. A., & Springer, E. V. (1981). *Roommate relations: On the variability of behavioral intentions.* Paper presented at the meeting of International Communication Association, Minneapolis.

Burleson, B. R. (1982). The development of comforting skills in childhood and adolescence. *Child Development, 53,* 1578-1588.

Clark, R. A. (1979). The impact on selection of persuasive strategies of self-interest and desire for liking. *Communication Monographs, 46,* 257-273.

Clark, R. A. & Delia, J. G. (1977). Cognitive complexity, social perspective-taking and functional persuasive skills in second to ninth-grade children. *Human Communication Research, 3,* 128-134.

Clark, R. A., & Delia, J. G. (1979). Topoi and rhetorical competence. *Quarterly Journal of Speech, 65,* 187-206.

Cohen, C. E. (1981). Goals and schemata in person perception: Making sense from the behavior stream. In N. Cantor & J. F. Kihlstrom (Eds.), *Personality cognition and social interaction.* Hillsdale, NJ: Erlbaum.

Crockett, W. H., & Friedman, P. (1980). Theoretical explorations of the processes of initial interactions. *Western Journal of Speech Communication, 44,* 86-92.

Deaux, K. (1978). Looking at behavior. *Personality and Social Psychology Bulletin, 4,* 207-211.

Delia, J. G. (1980). Some tentative thoughts concerning the study of interpersonal relationships and their development. *Western Journal of Speech Communication, 44,* 97-103.

Delia, J. G., & Clark, R. A. (1977). Cognitive complexity, social perception, and the development of listener-adaptive communication in six-, eight-, ten-, and twelve-year-old boys. *Communication Monographs, 44,* 326-345.

Delia, J. G., Kline, S. L., & Burleson, B. R. (1979). The development of persuasive communication strategies in kindergarteners through twelfth-graders. *Communication Monographs, 46,* 241-256.

Delia, J. G., O'Keefe, B. J., & O'Keefe, D. J. (1982). The constructivist approach to communication. In Frank E. X. Dance (Ed.), *Human communication theory.* New York: Harper & Row.

Derlega, V. J., & Grzelak, J. (1979). Appropriateness of self-disclosure. In Gordon Chelune (Ed.), *Self-disclosure.* San Francisco: Jossey-Bass.

Dickens, W. J., & Perlman, D. (1981). Friendship over the life-cycle. In S. Duck & R. Gilmour (Eds.), *Personal relationships 2: Developing personal relationships.* New York: Academic Press.

Duck, S. (1973). *Personal relationships and personal constructs: A study of friendship formation.* New York: John Wiley.

Duck, S. (1976). Interpersonal communication in developing acquaintance. In G. R. Miller (Ed.), *Explorations in interpersonal communication.* Beverly Hills, CA: Sage.

Duck, S. W. (1980). Personal relationships research in the 1980's: Towards an understanding of complex human sociality. *Western Journal of Speech Communication, 44,* 114-119.

Duck, S. W. (Ed.). (1982a). *Personal relationship 4: Dissolving personal relationships.* New York: Academic Press.

Duck, S. W. (1982b). A topography of relationship disengagement and dissolution. In S. W. Duck (Ed.), *Personal relationships 4: Dissolving personal relationships.* New York: Academic Press.

Duck, S. W. (1983). *Attraction, acquaintance, filtering and communication . . . but not necessarily in that order.* Paper presented

to the Fourth International Congress on Personal Construct Psychology, Boston.

Duck, S. W., Miell, D. E., & Miell, D. K. (Forthcoming). Social cognitive and communicative aspects of relationship growth and decline. In H. E. Sypher & J. L. Applegate (Eds.), *Interpersonal communication in children and adults.* Beverly Hills, CA: Sage.

Hale, C. L. (1980). Cognitive complexity-simplicity as a determinant of communication effectiveness. *Communication Monographs, 47,* 304-311.

Hale, C. L. (1982). An investigation of the relationship between cognitive complexity and listener-adapted communication. *Central States Speech Journal, 33,* 339-344.

Halliday, M. A. K. (1973). *Explorations in the functions of language.* London: Edward Arnold.

Heider, F. (1958). *The psychology of interpersonal relations.* New York: John Wiley.

Higgins, E. T., Fondcaro, R., & McCann, C. D. (1981). Rules and roles: The "communication game" and speaker-listener processes. In W. P. Dickson (Ed.), *Children's oral communication skills.* New York: Academic Press.

Hinde, R. (1979). *Towards understanding relationships.* New York: Academic Press.

Huston, T. L., Surra, C. A., Fitzgerald, N. M., & Cate, R. M. (1981). From courtship to marriage: Mate selection as an interpersonal process. In S. Duck & R. Gilmour (Eds.), *Personal relationships 2: Developing personal relationships.* New York: Academic Press.

Hymes, D. (1974). *Foundations of sociolinguistics: An ethnographic approach.* Philadelphia: University of Pennsylvania Press.

Kelly, G. A. (1955). *The psychology of personal constructs* (2 vols.). New York: Norton.

Kimmel, D. (1979). Relationship initiation and development: A life-span developmental approach. In R. Huston & R. Burgess (Eds.), *Social exchange and developing relationships.* New York: Academic Press.

Kline, S. L. (1981). *Individual differences in the accomplishment of face-support in persuasive communication.* Unpublished doctoral dissertation, University of Illinois at Urbana-Champaign.

Kline, S. L., & Ceropski, J. M. (Forthcoming). Person-centered communication in medical practice. In J. T. Wood & G. M. Phillips (Eds.) *Human decision-making.* Carbondale: Southern Illinois University Press.

Knapp, M. L. (1978). *Social intercourse.* Boston: Allyn & Bacon.

Komarovsky, M. (1962). *Blue-collar marriage.* New York: Vintage.

Kurth, S. B. (1970). Friendship and friendly relations. In G. J. McCall, M. M. McCall, N. K. Denzin, G. D. Suttles, & S. B. Kurth (Eds.), *Social relationships.* Chicago: Aldine.

Laing, R. D., Phillipson, H., & Lee, H. R. (1966). *Interpersonal perception.* New York: Springer.

Leichty, G. (1983). *The effects of interpersonal construct system development on attributions to two types of interpersonal relationships.* Unpublished M. A. thesis, University of Kentucky.

Levinger, G., & Snoek, D. (1972). *Attraction in relationships: A new look at interpersonal attraction.* Morristown, NY: General Learning Press.

McCall, G. (1982). Becoming unrelated: The management of bond dissolution. In S. W. Duck (Ed.), *Personal relationships 4: Dissolving personal relationships.* New York: Academic Press.

McCall, M. (1970). Boundary rules in relationships and encounters. In G. McCall (Ed.), *Social relationships.* Chicago: Aldine.

McCann, C. D., & Higgins, E. T. (Forthcoming). Individual differences in communication: Social cognitive determinants and consequences. In H. E. Sypher & J. L. Applegate (Eds.), *Interpersonal communication in children and adults.* Beverly Hills, CA: Sage.

Miller, G., & Parks, M. (1982). Communication in dissolving relationships. In S. Duck (Ed.), *Personal relationships 4: Dissolving personal relationships.* New York: Academic Press.

Miller, G., & Steinberg, M. (1975). *Between people: A new analysis of interpersonal communication.* Palo Alto, CA: Science Research Associates.

Morton, T., & Douglas, M. (1981). Growth of relationships. In S. Duck & R. Gilmour (Eds.), *Personal relationships 2: Developing personal relationships.* New York: Academic Press.

O'Keefe, B. J., & Delia, J. G. (1979). Construct comprehensiveness and cognitive complexity as predictors of the number and strategic adaptation of arguments and appeals in a persuasive message. *Communication Monographs, 46,* 231-240.

O'Keefe, B. J., & Delia, J. G. (1982). Impression formation processes and message production. In M. E. Roloff & C. R. Berger (Eds.), *Social cognition and communication.* Beverly Hills, CA: Sage.

O'Keefe, B. J., Delia, J. G., & O'Keefe, D. J. (1980). Interaction analysis and the analysis of interactional organization. In N. K. Denzin (Ed.), *Studies in symbolic interaction* (vol. 3), Greenwich, CT: JAI Press.

O'Keefe, B. J., Murphy, M., Meyers, R., & Babrow, A. (1983). *The development of persuasive communication skills: The influence of developments in interpersonal constructs on the ability to generate communication-relevant beliefs and on level of persuasive strategy.* Paper presented at the meeting of the International Communication Association, Dallas.

O'Keefe, D. J. (1980). The relationship of attitudes and behavior: A constructivist analysis. In D. P. Cushman & R. McPhee (Eds.), *Message-attitude-behavior relationship.* New York: Academic Press.

O'Keefe, D. J., & Delia, J. G. (1981). Cognitive complexity and the relationship of attitudes and behavioral intentions. *Communication Monographs, 48,* 146-157.

Philipsen, G. (1975). Speaking like a man in teamsterville: Cultural patterns of role enactment in an urban neighborhood. *Quarterly Journal of Speech, 61,* 13-22.

Roloff, M. (1976). Communication strategies, relationships, and relational change. In G. Miller (Ed.), *Explorations in interpersonal communication.* Beverly Hills, CA: Sage.

Roloff, M. (1981). *Interpersonal communication: The social exchange approach.* Beverly Hills, CA: Sage.

Schneider, D., Hastorf, A., & Ellsworth, P. (1979). *Person perception* (2nd ed.). Reading, MA: Addison-Wesley.

Shantz, C. U. (1981). The role of role-taking in children's referential communication. In W. P. Dickson (Ed.), *Children's oral communication skills.* New York: Academic Press.

Thibaut, J., & Kelley, H. (1959). *The social psychology of groups.* New York: John Wiley.

Tschudi, F., & Rommetveit, R. (1982). Sociality, intersubjectivity, and social processes: The sociality corollary. In J. C. Mancuso & J. R. Adams-Wevver (Eds.), *The construing person.* New York: Praeger.

Werner, H. (1957). The concept of development from a comparative and organismic point of view. In D. B. Harris (Ed.), *The concept of development.* Minneapolis: University of Minnesota Press.

Werner, H., & Kaplan, B. (1963). *Symbol formation.* New York: John Wiley.

Unit III

Relationship Preliminaries: Attraction, Initiation, Affinity Seeking, Cognition, and Nonverbal Immediacy

In this unit the readings take a more relational perspective. The five articles deal with factors significant to the beginnings of relationships. A large body of literature has been developed that examines the initiation of relationships. Most of these studies attempt to explain why we are attracted to certain individuals as well as the process by which we begin moving toward friendship and intimacy. In general, the studies have dealt with what generates attraction for another and then the manner in which we exhibit that attraction for another. The first two articles represent an attempt to explain attraction and the initial development of relationships. One impetus for these attempts is the limitation in the methodology employed in the past to test attraction theories. Many of the earlier studies on attraction utilized fairly static testing procedures where participants were given written descriptions of other people and asked how attractive they found the others. Researchers have varied such qualities as attitudes in the descriptions of the target person to be similar to or different from the respondents. This method has generated such theories of attraction as similarity, matching, and complementarity of needs. In article 7 Sunnafrank points out that such methods ignore the effect of actually communicating with another. Some studies that have included interaction appear to be artificial and contrived. In these studies, participants filled out questionnaires about their attitudes and then were matched with a stranger whose attitude was similar or contrasting.

The two participants were then told to discuss only that issue of controversy. Such a manipulation does not seem to be very reflective of the natural course of how we become acquainted. How many of us begin our interaction with a stranger by talking about capital punishment, abortion, or some other controversial issue?

A second major limitation to prior research and theory on attraction and relational development has been the failure to recognize that what might have led you to be initially attracted to another person is not necessarily the same factor that causes you to move to and remain in an intimate relationship with that person. Consider your best friend: 1) What initially caused the two of you to interact? and 2) Why is she or he now your best friend? Your answers probably will be something like: (1) She lived in the apartment next door and we kept running into each other in the hallway, and (2) Because she accepts me for who I am.

In article 7, Sunnafrank combines the importance of communication in the initiation of relationships with goal attainment. One goal we have in our initial interactions with others is to maintain control and predictability of our environment. Disagreement with another undermines such goal attainment and therefore, Sunnafrank argues, we are unlikely to pursue disagreements with strangers. Sunnafrank created four interaction conditions (conversational sequence) and two conditions of similar or dissimilar attitudes. In reading the results of his study, pay particular attention to the means for the amount of attraction in each of the eight cells. The higher the mean the greater the attraction, with means reported ranging from a high of 11.76 to a low of 8.35. He uses the F-test and t-test to compare both among and between the groups. By examining the means you can compare the relative attraction of the eight conditions.

Article 8 represents a proposed modification of uncertainty reduction theory in light of the research on initial interactions. Sunnafrank argues that the predicted-outcome-value of an interaction mediates the effect of uncertainty reduction. Sunnafrank argues that it is the prediction of the outcome value associated with a relationship that affects an individual's continuation of the relationship. The problem with uncertainty reduction is that gaining more information about another is supposed to increase predictability and attraction. But if that information leads to the prediction of a negative outcome in the relationship, an individual is more likely to restrict or terminate the relationship.

As you read Sunnafrank's predictive outcome value article remember that the axioms he discusses are the original statements concerning uncertainty reduction generated by Berger and Calabrese, and that the propositions are Sunnafrank's proposed modifications of those axioms. In addition, Sunnafrank presents 15 hypotheses concerning Predicted Outcome Value Theory. The first nine of these hypotheses are presented with a corresponding uncertainty reduction theorem with which it conflicts. The last six of these hypotheses are in agreement with an uncertainty reduction theory counterpart.

Articles 7 and 8 deal with some of the factors that affect our attraction toward others. The next step, once attraction occurs, might be to get the other to reciprocate and be attracted to you. How you get someone to like you or have "affinity" toward you is the subject of article 9 by Bell and Daly. Affinity seeking is defined as "the active social-communicative process by which individuals attempt to get others to like and to feel positive toward them." You will find a list of 25 affinity-seeking strategies that were derived from the input of several brainstorming groups. A number of research methods and statistics are reported in this article. Correlations are used to see how much the responses to self-report instruments related to one another. Specifically, the authors correlated the number of affinity strategies respondents felt were used by a specific other person with how much the respondents liked the other person, and with how satisfied the respondents thought the other person was with his or her life. Correlations also were used in analyzing the relationship between various personality measures and affinity seeking. Finally, the authors used a method called cluster analysis, which essentially determines which strategies were most closely related to one another. Cluster analysis provides a graphic picture for how similar or dissimilar the strategies are. Each cluster is then labeled according to some quality the authors feel is commonly shared by the strategies comprising the element.

In article 10 Baxter proposes that we have relational expectancies that affect the way we interpret and behave in relationships. Baxter talks about relational expectancy violations as an indirect way of communicating a change in the relationship. Baxter claims individuals have relationship process cognitions about the manner in which a relationship should progress (relationship trajectories) and preexisting strategies for how we might accomplish various relational goals, such as moving toward intimacy or dissolving a relationship.

One way to approach this article is to attempt to see whether the descriptions of the various cognitions fit your own life experiences. For instance, do you have an expectation about what behavior is appropriate or inappropriate on a first date? If the person you have been dating stops calling you as frequently as she or he had been, what does this usually mean to you? What expectations (cognitions) do you have for how much time you spend with your best friend in a given week?

Several notions are presented by Baxter that might be good to preview. The phrases "relational schema" and "trajectory schema" are used to reflect some preexisting collection of thoughts about relationships. The trajectory schema represent principles we process and apply to our interpretation of relational activity. Trajectories are essentially our conceptualization of the growth and dissolution of interpersonal relationships. Two trajectory schema are identified by Baxter: Friendship First and Whirlwind. Friendship First trajectory is a schema for those situations in which intimate romantic relationships start out as friendships and escalate over time. The Whirlwind trajectory is a schema for explaining love at first sight.

Baxter discusses an interesting aspect of how we communicate to others changes in the relationship that are dependent upon the application of another's relational cognitions or schemata to behavior. We are often reluctant to communicate directly our intentions about the relationship. One classic faux pas is, after meeting someone for the first time, to tell the person you think you could have a meaningful relationship with her or him. The reason this is problematic is because, for most of us, it violates our cognition about first-meeting behavior. Instead of directly communicating that message we usually use indirect strategies. These indirect strategies allow us and the other to save "face." Face is a term used to describe the self-image we wish to have accepted and confirmed by others. If I indicate I want a meaningful relationship on a first date, and the other says she never wants to see me again, I lose face (my feelings are hurt, I'm embarrassed). On the other hand, if I use some indirect method—holding hands and putting my arm around my date—I might be indirectly communicating the desire for escalating the relationship. However, if my date picks up on these cues and directly asks me if I'm looking for a more meaningful relationship, I can deny such an intention and save face. My date's interpretation of my behavior is based on her cognitions about what those behaviors might mean at that point in a relationship.

The last article in this section, by Burgoon and Hale, applies some of the same notions discussed about uncertainty reduction and relational expectations in articles 8 and 10 to nonverbal communication. One of the principles presented in article

8 by Sunnafrank on Predictive Outcome Value dealt with the relationship between nonverbal affiliative cues, such as nods and gestures, with both uncertainty reduction and predictive outcome values in initial interactions. Burgoon and Hale in article 11 also look at attraction and "immediacy" in interactions with friends and strangers as related to nonverbal behaviors. Specifically they present a model of "nonverbal expectancy violation," which is based on our having expectations about what are appropriate or inappropriate nonverbal behaviors in a given relationship.

Similarly to Baxter's relational expectations in article 10, Burgoon and Hale claim that we expect certain nonverbal behaviors in our interactions with others. When these expectations are violated (someone unexpectedly hugs you), it arouses our awareness of the other and the interaction. Violations do not necessarily mean that we have a negative reaction. For instance, we might want the other person to hug us, but just not expect it. When he or she gives us a hug, it might be an important positive signal, as when a child receives an unexpected hug from a parent. The positive or negative impact of such a violation is referred to in this article as "valence."

Burgoon and Hale specifically focus on the nonverbal behaviors associated with immediacy. The notion of "immediacy" was used by Wiener and Mehrabian (1968) to reflect a variable in language in which a person communicates some sense of distance or inclusion about an object (often another person). For instance, using "we" instead of "you and me" would be more immediate; or "Someone should clean this up" is less immediate than "You should clean this up." Mehrabian (1971) reasoned that if we are drawn toward people and things we like or prefer we will exhibit nonverbal behaviors associated with immediacy. Thus we spend more time with the people we like and less time with people we do not like. We lean toward a person who is saying something of interest to us, and lean back when the subject is boring.

Burgoon and Hale specifically examined the violation of expectation of nonverbal immediacy behaviors between friends and strangers. In their study, individuals interacted with a friend and with a stranger. One member of the pair was a confederate of the researchers and was instructed to engage in one of three sets of behaviors: (1) normal immediacy (expected), (2) nonimmediacy (increase distance, etc.) (expectancy violation), and (3) high immediacy (increase closeness, etc.) (expectancy violation). The results of several measures were used to test variations among these three conditions to determine the effect of violating immediacy expectancies.

QUESTIONS TO CONSIDER
WHILE READING

ARTICLE 7
A. How does a goal-oriented approach to attraction differ from other attraction theories?
B. In what ways does communication affect attraction?

ARTICLE 8
A. What is the "Predicted-Outcome-Value" perspective?
B. How does predicted-outcome-value relate to uncertainty reduction theory?

ARTICLE 9
A. How valid do you think the affinity-seeking construct is? How accurate and complete do you think the list of affinity-seeking strategies is?

B. What might the role of affinity seeking be in attraction, relational development, relational maintenance, and relational disengagement?

ARTICLE 10
A. Drawing on the article, generate a list of cognitions or schemata we have about relationship formation, maintenance, and dissolution. Which of these match or do not match your own experiences?
B. Under what conditions are we most likely to use direct strategies and indirect strategies in relationship talk?

ARTICLE 11
A. As you read through the discussion of the nonverbal expectancy violations model, try to think of examples from your own experience that either confirm or contradict the authors' claims. For example, a lengthy stare at someone is okay if it is done by a high-reward communicator. This would mean that having your boss or an attractive stranger stare at you would be okay. Is that true?
B. Try the methodology of the study on your own. Try to violate the nonverbal expectancies in your interactions with two of your friends. For one situation use high immediacy, for the other nonimmediacy. After ten minutes ask your friends how they felt about your interaction up to that point. How do the two compare? How did you feel in the two situations?

REFERENCES
Mehrabian, A. (1971). *Silent messages.* Belmont, CA: Wadsworth.
Wiener, M., & Mehrabian, A. (1968). *Language within language: Immediacy, a channel in verbal communication.* New York: Appleton-Century-Crofts.

7

A Communication-Based Perspective on Attitude Similarity and Interpersonal Attraction in Early Acquaintance

MICHAEL SUNNAFRANK

This study examines past conflicting evidence on the relationship of attitude similarity and interpersonal attraction in early acquaintance. The results suggest that the conflict in the findings is due to differences in the communicative environments used in research. In the present study, attitude similarity and interpersonal attraction were positively related only in highly atypical communicative relationships. These results are interpreted as generally supporting a goal-oriented perspective on the similarity-attraction association over traditional social validation and balance perspectives.

Discovering consistent patterns of interpersonal attraction has proven difficult for researchers. New or retreaded variables appear promising for a time but upon closer examination their promise is seldom fulfilled. One of the few associates of attraction which has survived considerable scrutiny is attitude similarity. Attitude similarity has been shown to be positively related to attraction in hundreds of studies encompassing several types of relationships and research situations.

The predominant focus of attitude similarity research over the past few decades has been on attraction between unacquainted individuals (Byrne, 1961, 1971; Byrne, London, & Griffitt, 1968; Clore & Baldridge, 1968; Griffitt, 1969; Seta, Martin, & Capehart, 1979). These efforts consistently employ the bogus-stranger technique popularized by Byrne (1971). This method produces results indicating that when individuals are made aware a stranger is attitudinally similar to them, they are more predisposed to be attracted to that stranger than when the stranger is attitudinally dissimilar.

This research has been conducted primarily as a means of testing various theories of social perception. In the process, these studies appear to have isolated, in attitude similarity, a strong potential influence on preacquaintance attraction in normally occurring relationships. This research typically provides participants with fairly precise information on a number of attitudinal topics, a situation not usually encountered during preacquaintance. In normal situations, individuals often possess only vague information about another's attitudes on a few topics.

Recent research focusing on interpersonal goals in early acquaintanceship indicates that this sort of imprecise attitudinal information on a few relevant topics is sufficient to produce the usual positive similarity-attraction association during the preacquaintance period (Sunnafrank, 1983; Sunnafrank & Miller, 1981). However, this research also indicates that the association is ephemeral; once communicative contact is established in the form of typical get-acquainted conversations, the usual

From Sunnafrank, M. (1984). *Communication Monographs, 51,* 372–380.

influence of attitude similarity on attraction is largely eliminated. Further evidence from these studies shows that even when the relevant attitudinal topics are discussed after get-acquainted conversations, no influence attributable to attitude similarity is observed.

These findings conflict with past research pursued from traditional social reinforcement and balance perspectives that indicates that relative strangers are more attracted to attitudinally similar than dissimilar others after initial communicative encounters as well as during preacquaintance (Brewer & Brewer, 1968; Byrne, Ervin, & Lamberth, 1970; Byrne & Griffitt, 1966). These apparently contradictory findings may be due to a crucial conceptual and methodological divergence between the two sets of studies.

The research by Sunnafrank adopts a goal-oriented, communication-based perspective on attraction. It examines the influence of normal communication and likely attitude information available during early acquaintance. In contrast, the research generated by the social validation and balance perspectives focuses on the influence of attitude similarity on attraction without considering communication. Since communication is not the focus of this research, communication during acquaintance is not realistically portrayed. Rather than allowing the participants to engage in a normal get-acquainted conversation, they are involved in a discussion of controversial attitude topics from the beginning of their communicative relationship.

The research reported here addresses the conceptual and methodological differences in the two sets of studies. It confirms that the positive relationship between attitude similarity and attraction, reported in many past studies, occurs only when normal acquaintance conversations are not allowed to take place.

Several reinforcement explanations of the positive attitude similarity-attraction relationship have been proposed. Byrne's research generally follows Festinger (1954) in proposing that a major source of reinforcements stems from the social testing of objectively unverifiable attitudes: Attitudinal agreement from another provides positively reinforcing social validation for one's attitudinal positions leading to greater attraction to the other as the source of this reinforcement, while attitudinal disagreement provides invalidation, negative reinforcement, and subsequent lower attraction. Brewer and Brewer (1968) propose a balance explanation (Heider, 1958) of this relationship, which indicates that in an attempt to achieve cognitive consistency individuals may become more attracted to attitudinally similar than dissimilar others.

In evaluating a stranger one will never meet, as in bogus-stranger research, social validation and balance pressures emanating from perceived similarity or dissimilarity on several variables, including attitudinal positions, may be the major attraction influences. No conceptual conflict between these perspectives and the goal-oriented perspective exists at this level since the scope of the goals perspective does not include situations in which individuals are aware communicative contact will not occur. Once the likelihood or actual occurrence of communicative contact is introduced, conflict over theoretical explanations of, and in many cases, predictions regarding attraction is raised.

Social validation and balance perspectives differ on their explanation of the attraction process but make essentially the same predictions regarding attraction in the situations pertaining to the current research. During preacquaintance, partners aware of the state of their attitude similarity should be more attracted when similar than dissimilar. This attraction influence should continue after initial communicative encounters between partners. When this initial communicative contact proceeds to discussions of the attitudinal topics composing the partner's similarity state, the positive similarity-attraction association will again be manifested. No predictions regarding differences between attraction in these various early acquaintance situations are made. The research of Brewer and Brewer (1968) and Byrne, Ervin, and Lamberth (1970) appears to support these predictions.

The present goal-oriented perspective, discussed in greater detail in Sunnafrank (1983) and Sunnafrank and Miller (1981), raises serious doubts about the accuracy of these theoretical orientations and the generalizability of the research generated by them when applied to communicative relationships. Briefly, it is proposed that individuals strive to achieve a stable, predictable, and controllable environment and it is the satisfaction of these goals which assumes preeminence in determining attraction in potential or actual communicative environments. During preacquaintance, individuals aware of their similarity state should be more attracted to similar than dissimilar partners because similarity produces goal satisfaction and dissimilarity is goal-threatening. These attraction differences should be overcome when partners take the opportunity to engage in normal conversational processes. Participating in normal, nonthreatening, get-acquainted conversations provides the individuals with a mutually experienced stable, predictable, and controllable environment. This experience should lead individuals to perceive that future contact is likely to proceed in a manner that will satisfy these goals. This goal satisfaction, both as experienced in the communicative past and perceived in the future, should lead to high levels of attraction, regardless of the similarity state. If partners begin to communicate on attitude topics after achieving goal satisfaction, they should proceed in a manner calculated to maintain stability, predictability, and control leading to high and equal levels of attraction for similar and dissimilar partners. This goal-oriented explanation of the attraction process makes the same predictions as social validation and balance perspectives for preacquaintance attraction. The predictions regarding attraction after normal communicative contact differ drastically. In addition, the goals perspective offers an explanation and predictions regarding attraction differences between preacquaintance and later communicative stages. The research of Sunnafrank (1983) and Sunnafrank and Miller (1981) appears to support this interpretation.

The current research attempts to resolve the conflict produced by the contradictory findings of the research supporting the goal-oriented perspective and the social validation and balance perspectives as well as to clarify the relative strength of support for these orientations. Although the research of Brewer and Brewer (1968) and Byrne, Ervin, and Lamberth (1970) can be taken as support for the balance and social validation perspectives on attraction in early acquaintance, the fact that these studies appear to circumvent normal communication processes by explicitly or implicitly producing initial conversations on controversial attitudinal topics renders this support questionable.

In atypical initial conversations concerning attitudinal topics, the similarity of the participants' attitudes on the topics would be likely to influence goal satisfaction and subsequent attraction. Participating in an initial conversation about attitude topics is a situation rarely encountered by individuals. Such encounters themselves should be enough to heighten threats to stability, predictability, and control goals for the individuals involved. Information indicating the participants in this seldom-occurring transaction are attitudinally similar with respect to the topics involved should produce goal satisfaction, provided the conversations continue to generally reinforce this perception.

Conversely, information indicating the participants are dissimilar with respect to the topics involved in the conversation should continue to produce a goal-threatening state. These individuals find themselves participating in a potentially unstable, unpredictable, and uncontrollable conversation with a disagreeing stranger at the very beginning of their communicative relationship. Achieving a stable, predictable, and controllable environment should remain a central focus of the attitudinally dissimilar individuals involved in this atypical communicative situation. The threat to these goals will likely lead individuals to employ communicative strategies designed to produce greater likelihood of goal satisfaction. Such strategies could involve sending messages indicating that the participants are willing to agree to disagree and to respect one another's opinion rights. If these strategies are at least partially successful in alleviating the threat, then attraction should increase in proportion to the amount of success achieved.

Even so, this unprecedented situation should make it difficult for the individuals involved to fully satisfy their goals during the course of the conversation. Continued threat to the goals of dissimilar partners should produce lower attraction between them than between their attitudinally similar counterparts. Thus, the goal-oriented perspective agrees with the social validation and balance perspectives regarding attraction predictions during initial communicative contact, but only when this contact originates with and continues to focus on a discussion of attitudinal topics.

If this prediction is accurate, it could possibly resolve the conflicting findings produced by the research on these traditional perspectives and the goal-oriented perspective. Such conflicting findings may be due to differences in the degree to which the studies employed normal communication processes, with those studies employing more typical processes supporting the goal-oriented perspective over social validation and consistency perspectives. Moreover, even the social validation and consistency supporting findings of Brewer and Brewer (1968) and Byrne, Ervin, and Lamberth (1970), which appear to have been generated in this atypical situation, can be viewed as generally supporting the goal-oriented perspective in light of the above explanation.

The goal-oriented prediction regarding attraction differences between attitudinally similar and dissimilar partners who have engaged in an initial conversation regarding their relevant attitudes, and the prediction regarding differences in attraction between this conversational situation and the more normal early acquaintance situations, is tested through the following hypothesis:

Among individuals who are aware of the state of their similarity on relevant attitude topics, attitudinally similar individuals will be more attracted to one another than attitudinally dissimilar individuals prior to conversing and after an initial conversation concerning these topics, but not after an initial get-acquainted conversation or such a conversation followed by a discussion of the relevant attitude topics. Moreover, attitudinally dissimilar individuals will be least attracted to one another prior to conversing, more attracted after an initial conversation concerning the relevant topics, and most attracted after an initial get-acquainted conversation or such a conversation followed by an attitudinal discussion.

This hypothesis has been partially tested in Sunnafrank (1983) and the results of that test have been discussed above. Added here is the prediction regarding attraction differences between similar and dissimilar partners engaged in initial conversations on relevant attitude topics which tests the explanation offered for the conflict in past research. Sunnafrank's previously reported findings for pre-acquaintance, get-acquainted conversations, and get-acquainted conversations followed by attitudinal discussions are again reported here to provide a test of the goal-oriented perspective's predictions regarding differences in attraction between these conditions and the conditions involving initial attitudinal discussions. The following section concentrates on describing the method used to collect data for the initial conversations on attitudinal topics, which, except for the experimental manipulation of conversational stage, are identical to those reported in Sunnafrank (1983). Some additional participants were included in the attitudinally dissimilar pre-conversation situation during this new collection and the results obtained are reported here along with those previously reported.

METHOD

SELECTION OF PARTICIPANTS AND ATTITUDE TOPICS

The topics of the construction of nuclear power plants and capital punishment were chosen for the attitude similarity manipulation, in order to make the topics consistent with those employed in Sunnafrank (1983) and to render the results comparable. Two hundred and forty-five students at a Western university participated in the total study. Dyads were formed of previously unacquainted individuals of the same sex during each of several experimental sessions.

PROCEDURES

Upon arrival each participant was placed in a separate room to prevent interaction among participants. All participants were told they would be engaging in a project with another student involving their ability to make accurate predictions about others based on limited information. They were told that to accomplish the task they would be asked to exchange their general opinions on a few topics with their partners prior to meeting him or her. In addition, they were informed they would have the opportunity to get acquainted with their partner and to discuss the exchanged opinion topics during the course of the study. Finally, they were informed that at some point during the project they would be asked to make predictions about their partner based on the information they had acquired up to that point.

After reading the instructions, participants responded to a dichotomous measure of their attitudes toward the two selected topics. These responses were then examined by the researcher to determine the distribution of responses across participants during that session. Whenever possible, individuals who had similar responses to both topics were selected as partners for the attitudinally similar conditions and individuals who had dissimilar responses to both topics were selected as partners for the attitudinally dissimilar conditions. In some instances partners might agree on one topic and disagree on the other. When this occurred, the researcher would assign the partners to either an attitudinally similar or dissimilar condition. The researcher then manufactured responses, which either agreed completely with each participant's responses or disagreed completely. These manufactured responses were then exchanged by the researcher.

After receiving their partners' responses, participants were left alone for five minutes to study the responses. Participants were then escorted to a conference room with their partners.

Participants were then informed they would be spending the next five minutes in a conversation with one another on one of the exchanged opinion topics. The researcher reminded them that the purpose was to determine if this sort of discussion would influence predictive accuracy. Dyads who were in agreement or disagreement on both topics were asked to discuss one of the two topics chosen randomly by the experimenter. Dyads who were unknowingly in agreement on one topic and in disagreement on the other were asked to discuss whichever topic they were actually in agreement or disagreement on respectively. In all cases the dyads were instructed to discuss only the assigned topic and not the other opinion topic or any other topic.

After receiving their initial conversation instructions, all participants were asked if they would mind having their conversations taped to allow a more accurate assessment of how the type of information exchanged during their conversations might influence predictive accuracy. All participants agreed to be taped and the researcher placed an audiotape machine on the conference table before them. Each dyad was reminded to discuss only the assigned topic as the researcher turned on the machine and left the room.

After completing their conversational assignments, all participants were returned to their rooms and given a questionnaire to fill out. Participants were reminded they would later have the opportunity to discuss the remaining opinion topic with their partners.

The conversational conditions reported in Sunnafrank (1983), which are reported again here to make the comparisons called for, were collected using methods identical to these except for the following introductions of the conversational conditions to participants. In the get-acquainted conversation conditions, participants were asked to discuss what they would normally discuss when first meeting another.

In the get-acquainted conversations followed by attitudinal discussions participants were given these same instructions to engage in initial get-acquainted conversations. After completing this conversation they were given additional instructions to discuss a chosen attitude topic. In the pre-conversation conditions participants filled out the questionnaire after studying their partners' responses for five minutes. As in the current conditions, all participants were led to expect future communicative contact(s) with their partners during the course of the experiment.

The questionnaire all participants responded to contained several items, including the measure of interpersonal attraction. This measure consisted of two items measured by seven-point scales adopted from Byrne's Interpersonal Judgment Scale. Responses to these two items were summed to produce the attraction measure. An alpha coefficient (Cronbach, 1951) of .70 was obtained for this measure, indicating an acceptable degree of internal consistency among items.

After completing the questionnaire, all participants were informed of the purpose of the study and it was determined that none of the participants had fathomed its actual purpose. All participants in the attitudinally similar conditions believed their partners to be completely similar on the two topics while those in the attitudinally dissimilar conditions believed their partners to be completely dissimilar.

With the addition of the conversational conditions from Sunnafrank (1983), a 4-by-2 independent groups design with four levels of conversational sequence (pre-conversation, attitudinal discussion only, get-acquainted conversation only, and get-acquainted plus attitudinal conversation) and two levels of attitude similarity (complete similarity and dissimilarity) was employed. The number of participants in each condition ranged from 24 to 54.

RESULTS

For all statistical tests the .05 significance level was employed.

As a preliminary step, a two-way analysis of variance employing unweighted means was conducted. A significant interaction effect was observed

for the conversational sequence and attitude similarity variables ($F = 12.74$, $df = 3/237$). Significant main effects were observed for conversational sequence ($F = 5.95$, $df = 3/237$) and attitude similarity ($F = 21.50$, $df = 1/237$). An estimate of the amount of variance ($Omega^2$) explained by each of these effects indicated that the sequence by similarity interaction accounted for 10% of the variance; the main effect of conversational sequence for 4%, and attitude similarity for 6%.

An inspection of the attraction means for conversational sequence by attitude similarity (Table 7.1) reveals a pattern that generally conforms to the hypothesized interaction effect: Attitudinally similar partners appeared to be more attracted to one another both prior to conversing and after an initial attitudinal discussion but not after an initial get-acquainted conversation nor after such a conversation followed by an attitudinal discussion. Among attitudinally dissimilar partners, the lowest attraction level was observed for the pre-conversation condition followed by the initial attitudinal discus-

---

TABLE 7.1

Means and Standard Deviations for Attraction Toward Similar and Dissimilar Participants by Conversational Sequence

CONVERSATIONAL SEQUENCE	SIMILARITY CONDITION	
	Similar	Dissimilar
Pre-Conversation	M = 11.76	M = 8.55
	s = 1.13	s = 2.21
	n = 25	n = 42
Attitudinal Discussion	M = 11.65	M = 10.78
	s = 1.57	s = 1.87
	n = 26	n = 54
Get-Acquainted Conversation	M = 11.23	M = 11.16
	s = 1.28	s = 1.27
	n = 26	n = 24
Get-Acquainted and Attitudinal Conversations	M = 11.13	M = 11.25
	s = 1.04	s = 1.51
	n = 24	n = 24

sion condition, with both the get-acquainted conversation only and the get-acquainted plus attitudinal conversation producing the highest attraction levels. An additional unhypothesized difference may involve attraction among similar partners. Attraction levels for similars in the pre-conversation and initial attitudinal discussion conditions were higher than for the get-acquainted only and get-acquainted plus attitudinal conversation conditions.

The hypothesized differences were directly tested by subjecting the cells involved in the prediction to further analysis. This analysis revealed that attitudinally similar partners were more attracted to one another than attitudinally dissimilar partners in the pre-conversation ($t = 6.68$, df $= 237$) and attitudinal discussion only ($t = 2.06$, df $= 237$) conditions, but not in the conditions involving get-acquainted conversations only ($t < 1$, df $= 237$) or get-acquainted plus attitudinal conversations ($t < 1$, df $= 237$). The major new test here involves the attraction differences between attitudinally similar and dissimilar partners who engaged in attitudinal discussion only. The findings for this condition relative to the other conversational sequence conditions support this study's hypothesis. As predicted, initial attitudinal discussions, as well as pre-conversational situations, result in an attitude similarity-attraction influence not present in normal conversational sequences.

The prediction involving attraction between attitudinally dissimilar partners was only partially supported. Dissimilar partners in the pre-conversation condition were, as predicted, less attracted to one another than dissimilars in the remaining conversational sequences. Participants in the attitudinal discussion only condition, who had the next lowest mean attraction level, were still more attracted to their dissimilar partners than individuals in pre-conversation ($t = 5.35$, df $= 237$). Contrary to the prediction, no differences in attraction were observed between dissimilar partners involved in initial attitudinal discussions only and the two conditions involved in get-acquainted conversations ($F < 1$, df $= 2237$). While each of these

three conversational sequences produced increased attraction among dissimilars over pre-conversation, the continued attraction difference between similar and dissimilar partners in the attitudinal discussion only condition cannot be attributed to lower levels of attraction to dissimilars alone. The conjoint attraction influences of conversational sequence and attitude similarity cannot be explained without including the elevated attraction levels for attitudinally similar partners in the pre-conversation and attitudinal discussion only conditions relative to the conditions involving get-acquainted conversations.

DISCUSSION

The current findings provide partial support for the hypothesis advanced. As predicted, attitude similarity was positively related to attraction during the preconversation period and in atypical initial attitudinal discussions but not after either more typical communicative sequence. The finding that attraction to dissimilars increases from pre-conversation levels after initial attitudinal discussions provides further support for the hypothesized relationships. However, no support was observed for the final prediction concerning greater attraction among dissimilars in normal get-acquainted sequences than in atypical initial attitudinal discussions.

The finding that the atypical conversational sequence of initiating communicative relationships with attitudinal discussions results in a positive similarity-attraction association not present in normal conversational sequences supports the explanation concerning the conflicting research results of the goal-oriented perspective (Sunnafrank, 1983; Sunnafrank & Miller, 1981) and social validation and balance perspectives (Brewer & Brewer, 1968; Byrne, Ervin, & Lamberth, 1970). Apparently, the conflict between these studies is largely due to the presence or absence of get-acquainted conversations in the communication environments employed.

The finding that attraction among dissimilars is greater after initial attitudinal discussions than during pre-conversation again supports a goal-oriented perspective. Apparently, the preeminence individuals place on satisfying stability, predictability, and control leads them to communicate in ways which reduce preconversation threats to these goals in initial attitudinal discussions. Contrary to expectations, the increase in attraction among dissimilars engaged in initial attitudinal discussions was equal to that of dissimilars who engaged in get-acquainted sequences. This finding suggests that initial communicative contact, even on topics involving attitudinal dissimilarities, reduces the negative pre-conversation influence of disagreement.

The findings cannot be explained as a function of conversational sequence or attitude dissimilarity alone. Get-acquainted sequences produce both large increases in attraction to dissimilars and slight decreases in attraction to similars in comparison to the pre-conversation stage, while initial attitudinal discussions produce large increases in attraction to dissimilars but no change in attraction to similars in relation to pre-conversation. This results in slightly lower attraction to dissimilars and slightly higher attraction to similars for initial attitudinal discussions relative to get-acquainted sequences.

Despite the lack of support for one hypothesized outcome, the overall pattern of findings supports the major contention of this paper. The results supported goal-oriented predictions in all four conversational sequences, but social validation and balance perspectives were supported only for pre-conversation and initial attitudinal discussions. Thus, the goal-oriented perspective appears to pre-dict the influence of attitude similarity in a broader and more realistic range of early communicative relationships.

REFERENCES

Brewer, R. E., & Brewer, M. B. (1968). Attraction and accuracy of perception in dyads. *Journal of Personality and Social Psychology, 8,* 188-193.

Byrne, D. (1961). Interpersonal attraction and attitude similarity. *Journal of Abnormal and Social Psychology, 62,* 713-715.

Byrne, D. (1971). *The attraction paradigm.* New York: Academic Press.

Byrne, D., Ervin, C. R., & Lamberth, J. (1970). Continuity between the experimental study of attraction and "real life" computer dating. *Journal of Personality and Social Psychology, 16,* 157-165.

Byrne, D., & Griffitt, W. (1966). Similarity versus liking: A clarification. *Pychonomic Science, 6,* 295-296.

Byrne, D., London, O., & Griffitt, W. (1968). The effect of topic importance and attitude similarity-dissimilarity on attraction in an intra-stranger design. *Psychonomic Science, 11,* 303-304.

Clore, G. L., & Baldridge, B. (1968). Interpersonal attraction: The role of agreement and topic interest. *Journal of Personality and Social Psychology, 9,* 340-346.

Cronbach, I. J. (1951). Coefficient alpha and the internal structure of tests. *Psychometrika, 16,* 167-188.

Festinger, L. (1954). A theory of social comparison processes. *Human Relations, 7,* 117-140.

Griffitt, W. (1969). Attitude-evoked anticipatory responses and attraction. *Psychonomic Science, 14,* 153-155.

Heider, F. (1958). *The psychology of interpersonal relations.* New York: John Wiley.

Seta, J. J., Martin, L., & Capehart, G. (1979). Effects of contrast and generalization on the attitude similarity-attraction relationship. *Journal of Personality and Social Psychology, 37,* 462-467.

Sunnafrank, M. (1983). Attitude similarity and interpersonal attraction in communication processes: In pursuit of an ephemeral influence. *Communication Monographs, 50,* 273-284.

Sunnafrank, M., & Miller, G. R. (1981). The role of initial conversations in determining attraction to similar and dissimilar strangers. *Human Communication Research, 8,* 16-25.

8

Predicted Outcome Value During Initial Interactions: A Reformulation of Uncertainty Reduction Theory

MICHAEL SUNNAFRANK

This article presents an expansion and reformulation of uncertainty reduction theory. Past research indicates that support for the basic axioms of the uncertainty perspective is weak, especially with regard to initial interaction processes. It is suggested that uncertainty reduction is not the primary concern of individuals during this entry phase, as previously posited. Rather, uncertainty reduction is cast as subordinate to the more central concern of increasing positive relational outcomes. During initial interactions, uncertainty reduction is expected to enhance individuals' perceived ability to forecast future relational outcomes. Important initial interaction behaviors and decisions are presumed to follow from the values these forecasted outcomes take. Several major revisions of uncertainty axioms and theorems are generated.

Several theoretical perspectives on human behavior in general and communicative behavior in particular assume that individuals attempt to increase predictability or reduce uncertainty about their relationships with others (Heider, 1958; Kelley, 1973; Miller & Steinberg, 1975). Uncertainty reduction theory (Berger, 1979; Berger & Bradac, 1982; Berger & Calabrese, 1975), the most formally articulated theoretical treatment of this position in communication, proposes that a key element in relational development is individuals' uncertainty level concerning knowledge and understanding of selves and others. The original uncertainty perspective (Berger & Calabrese, 1975) focused exclusively on potential influences of uncertainty and uncertainty reduction during beginning acquaintance. More recent revisions attempt to extend the theory to include later relational stages, as well as adding new variables and propositions (Berger, 1979; Berger & Bradac, 1982; Gudykunst, Yang, & Nishida, 1985; Parks & Adelman, 1983).

This perspective generates a unifying explanation for previously diverse research findings. Although this ability to explain past results is a desirable characteristic, the crucial test of uncertainty reduction theory is the predictive accuracy of its unique proposals. Novel propositions and implications from this perspective have generated a substantial amount of research on the antecedents and consequents of uncertainty. However, research results have provided only mixed support for the theory. Some of this research examines aspects of uncertainty reduction theory in a manner that does not entail direct tests of its basic axioms and theorems and, therefore, produces only implicit support for these propositions (Berger & Douglas, 1981; Berger & Perkins, 1978; Sherblom & Van Rheenan, 1984). Works that do involve relatively direct tests of theoretic relationships normally provide only partial and weak support (Clatterbuck, 1979; Gudykunst & Nishida, 1984; Gudykunst, Yang, & Nishida, 1985).

Mixed support justifies neither a complete acceptance nor rejection of uncertainty reduction

From Sunnafrank, M. (1986). *Human Communication Research, 13,*(1), 3-33. © 1986 International Communication Association.

theory. Rather, findings indicate that both more critical tests and theoretical modifications may be in order. This article proposes one such modification in an effort to increase the uncertainty perspective's explanatory and predictive utility. This change involves altering the theory to reflect a potentially important relationship between uncertainty about another and individuals' perceptions of future relational rewards and costs to be obtained with the other. Recent revisions of Berger and Calabrese's (1975) perspective acknowledge that a relationship between uncertainty and the perceived outcome value of relations with others may exist, but give it only a minor role in the theory. Both Berger (1979) and Berger and Bradac (1982) propose that incentives provided by rewards and costs controlled by another may trigger or increase individuals' attempts to reduce uncertainty, while leaving the original theoretical propositions intact.

The present proposal accords individuals' perceptions of future relational reward and cost outcomes a more encompassing role. Several perspectives assume that individuals make predictions to increase the potential for achieving positive relational outcomes (Altman, 1974; Lott & Lott, 1974; Miller & Steinberg, 1975). Within these perspectives uncertainty reduction would not be the primary concern of individuals, but only a means to achieving the more central goal of maximizing outcomes. The major focus of this article involves incorporating individuals' perceptions of these relational outcomes into the uncertainty framework. Prior to examining this position, it is necessary to review previous uncertainty formulations and research results.

UNCERTAINTY REDUCTION THEORY

Berger and Calabrese (1975) propose seven axioms detailing the relationship of uncertainty level to amount of verbal communication, nonverbal affiliative expressiveness, information seeking, intimacy level of communicative content, reciprocity rate, similarity, and liking. Also specified are 21 theo-

rems concerning the interrelation of these variables through uncertainty. Consistent with various attribution perspectives (Heider, 1958; Jones & Davis, 1965; Kelley, 1973), Berger and Calabrese propose that uncertainty regards both prediction of future behaviors and explanation of present and past behaviors. Prediction involves a proactive process of determining the most likely future relational behavior of partners, and selecting appropriate self-behavior given this prediction. Explanation involves a retroactive process of determining the perceived causes of the observed behaviors of self and others.

Berger (1979) and Berger and Bradac (1982) propose a further distinction between two types of uncertainty: cognitive and behavioral. Cognitive uncertainty encompasses uncertainty that individuals have about their own and relational others' beliefs and attitudes. Behavioral uncertainty refers to predictability of behavior in particular circumstances. These two types of uncertainty may often be highly related, especially when behavioral predictions are rooted in perceived knowledge of the relating individuals' cognitions. However, in some circumstances behavioral uncertainty may be strongly influenced by knowledge of situational constraints on behavior that have little relation to cognitive uncertainty. In ritualized communicative encounters, such as those occurring in the beginning of initial interactions or in formal role relationships, behavior may be highly predictable due to situation-relevant norms and rules. Knowledge of these behavioral constraints would likely reduce behavioral uncertainty in the immediate situation, but should be little related to cognitive uncertainty about the beliefs and attitudes of the interaction partners, although information exchanged during the encounter may influence these cognitive uncertainty levels. Uncertainty reduction theory is primarily concerned with how we come to know others as individuals; as such, uncertainty formulations focus on the cognitive element of uncertainty.

Berger and Calabrese (1975) originally proposed that uncertainty-reduction processes apply to all initial interaction situations. Later formulations add three conditions, any of which should increase the likelihood of activating the reduction of uncertainty (Berger, 1979; Berger & Bradac, 1982). First, individuals are more likely to engage in uncertainty reduction when others have high incentive value; that is, if others are perceived as likely to provide rewards or costs to them. Second, if the behavior of others deviates from what is normally expected, increased uncertainty-reduction efforts are expected. Third, uncertainty-reduction efforts should become more pronounced as the perceived probability of future interaction increases.

These elaborations of uncertainty reduction theory also propose three general categories of information-seeking strategies individuals employ to reduce uncertainty: passive, active, and interactive. Passive strategies involve unobtrusive observation of target individuals to obtain information about them. Active strategies necessitate intervention in the form of seeking information from third parties or through manipulation of the target person's environment. Interactive strategies involve obtaining information directly from the target person through such communicative methods as interrogation and self-disclosure.

Research on uncertainty reduction has advanced along three main related lines within this general conceptual framework. One line of research examines the use of information-seeking strategies, but generally does not directly test basic uncertainty axioms and theorems. Other research focuses on extending and modifying Berger and Calabrese's (1975) original theory to include relational stages beyond early acquaintance. Finally, some research directly tests Berger and Calabrese's propositions in beginning relationships.

Research on information-seeking strategies generally supports uncertainty expectations. Research on the use of passive strategies provides support for the expectation that individuals prefer to observe strangers in those situations that provide greater potential for gathering uncertainty-reducing information (Berger & Douglas, 1981; Berger & Perkins, 1978). However, these investigations do not directly examine the relation of passive-strategy use

to uncertainty level, nor do they test uncertainty-reduction axioms and theorems.

Gudykunst et al. (1985) report research including more direct evidence on theoretic propositions regarding information seeking, as well as other variables related to uncertainty reduction. These researchers applied an uncertainty model to acquaintance, friend, and dating relationships in three cultures, and found that the overall model provided an acceptable description of the data. However, tests of several hypotheses resulted in mixed support for specific uncertainty-reduction predictions. Only one of seven hypotheses regarding information-seeking strategies received consistent support. Little support was provided for Berger and Bradac's (1982) proposals regarding the influence of self-monitoring and self-consciousness on information seeking. Tests of four axioms and four theorems, beyond those employed to derive hypotheses concerning interactive strategy use, resulted in consistent support for one axiom, no support for one theorem, and various degrees of partial support in the remaining cases.

Further investigations of uncertainty propositions in established relationships have resulted in inconsistent support. Parks and Adelman (1983) tested an expansion of uncertainty reduction theory with premarital partners and found support for several predictions regarding communication networks that were unique to their expansion. However, only partial support was provided for the uncertainty axioms tested in this research. Prisbell and Anderson's (1980) examination of uncertainty in established relationships produced partial support for one uncertainty-reduction axiom and equivocal support for one axiom and one theorem. Overall, research examining uncertainty reduction theory within established relationships provides mixed support for uncertainty-reduction propositions, with partial and weak support being the typical finding.

A few studies have examined uncertainty propositions in the entry-level relationships addressed by the original theory. Gudykunst and Nishida (1984) asked participants from Japan and the

United States how they would behave in an imagined meeting with a stranger. Results provided consistent support for only one axiom out of the four axioms and six theorems tested. Clatterbuck (1979) reports a reanalysis of seventeen studies employing attributional confidence measures of uncertainty level, including several that appear to involve beginning relationships. The results of this reanalysis produced partial support for three uncertainty axioms. In short, research on the entry phase has provided only limited support for uncertainty reduction theory.

Two general conclusions can be drawn from a review of uncertainty-reduction research. First, uncertainty axioms and theorems have yet to be tested under optimal conditions specified by the theory. Studies clearly meeting the incentive condition, deviance condition, or probability of future interaction condition proposed by Berger (1979) and Berger and Bradac (1982) all appear to involve relationships beyond the early acquaintance stage that is the theory's initial scope. Conversely, studies focusing on beginning relationships do not explicitly address the incentive, deviance, and future interaction probability conditions. It seems reasonable that the initial encounters employed in most of these studies should produce uncertainty concerns even in the absence of these conditions, though these concerns might be minimized. Still, these antecedents should be included in future tests to provide maximum likelihood of detecting uncertainty-related processes, if present.

Second, the low level of support for uncertainty propositions, even under these less than optimal conditions, requires further explanation. Tests of 16 of the 28 axioms and theorems proposed by Berger and Calabrese (1975) have been conducted in the research reviewed above. Well over 100 individual tests have been performed in this research, with only approximately half resulting in theoretical support. With few exceptions, this support has been in the form of weak associations between the variables examined. Though future research employing more optimal conditions may produce greater consistency and strength of support, the current pattern of results suggests that theoretic modifications may also be required.

The remainder of this article attempts to supply such modifications. The focus is limited to the initial interactions addressed by the original theory, though some implications for later relational stages are discussed. Given the weak support thus far obtained for uncertainty reduction theory in early-acquaintance research, this limitation appears to be justified. Moreover, the present formulation is restricted to initial interaction situations involving individuals who will or can, with minimal effort, be in physically proximate settings in the future. Most established relationships begin in such initial contact situations. It is also apparent that these proximate situations produce a broad range of communicative relationships, from relations involving no further or very restricted contact through highly developed social relationships. Given the focus of this inquiry on beginning relational development, the present formulation examines the possible role of initial interactions in producing this relational variation.

PREDICTED OUTCOME VALUE

Berger and Calabrese (1975) propose that the central concern of strangers upon meeting is the reduction of uncertainty about the self and other in the relationship. The predicted-outcome-value perspective posits that a more primary goal is the maximization of relational outcomes. These two goals may be complementary: The reduction of uncertainty may aid individuals to achieve more positive experiences in the relationship. Prior to exploring this possible connection and the resultant modifications of uncertainty reduction theory, it is necessary to outline the predicted-outcome-value position.

Various theoretical perspectives and related research programs support the view that individuals seek to increase the positiveness of their outcomes in relationships with others. Several communication perspectives posit that an individual's experience with outcome values during interactions is a primary factor in relational development processes (Miller & Steinberg, 1975; Roloff, 1981; Sunnafrank & Miller, 1981). Related social psychological orientations on social exchange (Homans, 1961, 1974; Kelley & Thibaut, 1978; Thibaut & Kelley, 1959), social penetration (Altman & Taylor, 1973), social reinforcement (Byrne, 1961, 1971; Byrne & Nelson, 1965), and equity (Adams, 1963; Walster, Berscheid, & Walster, 1973, 1976; Walster, Walster, & Berscheid, 1978) take similar positions on the centrality of outcome values in social relationships. These perspectives share the assumptions that individuals desire to maximize their outcomes and are more likely to form relationships with available others who enable them to do so.

The typical outcome-value explanation of relational development concentrates on individuals' past and present relational experiences. However, some perspectives discuss the potential influence of the value of forecasted outcomes on this process, especially during the beginning stages of relationships. Altman and Taylor (1973) posit that relationships develop because partners expect that the rewards of this development will outweigh the costs. Although the social exchange perspective is largely based on experienced outcome values, Thibaut and Kelley (1959) do propose that individuals employ experienced outcomes to predict future outcome potential for relationships. Sunnafrank and Miller (1981) propose that a major determinant of attraction between relative strangers is the perception of how future interactions will proceed.

The importance of predicted outcome value in beginning relationships is due to the limited outcome experiences typically available during initial interactions, and the tendency for these experiences to be markedly similar across relationships. Berger and Bradac (1982) note that communication during this stage is highly structured and routinized: Individuals normally exchange limited demographic information, followed by conversations on topics with little likelihood of producing obvious relational or personal consequences. As Altman and Taylor (1973) note, rewards and costs obtained at this beginning level are relatively low in magnitude. Moreover, the routinized nature of initial interactions would appear to produce somewhat similar outcome-value experiences in most relationships.

Although relatively little variance in outcome-value experiences should be evident in beginning relationships, differences in the demographic and low-consequence information provided through this conversational routine would distinguish between the interaction partners' individuals meet. Berger's (1975) research demonstrates that this information strongly influences individuals' perceptions of the cognitive disposition of others, suggesting that impressions of partners will vary greatly as a result of information available during initial interactions. This view is consistent with uncertainty positions (Berger, 1979; Berger & Bradac, 1982; Berger & Calabrese, 1975), as well as with the attribution formulations from which they are derived (Heider, 1958; Jones & Davis, 1965; Kelley, 1973).

The current perspective assumes that these impressions are employed to forecast outcomes likely to be obtained in the future, an assumption shared with other perspectives on relational development (Altman & Taylor, 1973; Miller & Steinberg, 1975). Obviously, these varying impressions would produce different estimates of future outcome values. Given the relatively minor outcome differences from initial interaction experiences, these forecasted values should be of critical importance to relational-development decisions. Individuals should employ these predictions in making decisions about whether to avoid, restrict, or seek further relational contact, as well as how to proceed with the interaction given these predictions. The primary consideration in such decisions should be the individual's desire to maximize future outcomes.

Given this framework, several propositions regarding beginning relationships are possible. Those introduced here have relatively direct implications for uncertainty reduction theory, as is detailed in the following section. First, individuals should be more attracted to partners and relationships when greater predicted outcome values are expected in the relational future. Second, increasingly positive predicted outcomes will produce more communicative attempts to extend initial interactions and establish future contact. Conversely, increasingly negative predicted outcomes will result in communicative attempts to terminate or curtail the conversation and future contact. Finally, individuals will attempt to guide conversations toward topics expected to result in the most positive predicted outcomes.

PREDICTED OUTCOME VALUE AND UNCERTAINTY

Both uncertainty-reduction and predicted-outcome-value processes may have important, related roles in beginning communicative relationships. Exploring the affinity between these perspectives should produce a broader understanding of relational development. This connection rests on the assumption that uncertainty reduction increases individuals' perceived outcome-maximization potential, an assumption that leads to several alterations in basic uncertainty-reduction axioms (Berger & Calabrese, 1975).

Berger (1979) and Berger and Bradac (1982) acknowledge a possible uncertainty-outcome value association in proposing that another person's incentive value influences uncertainty-reduction efforts. Additionally, increased deviance and probability of future interaction, proposed by these authors as also increasing uncertainty, should be related to outcome-value concerns: Deviant behavior by others indicates that future outcomes will be difficult to determine, whereas increased probability of future interaction increases the relevance of future outcomes. Increased uncertainty concerns under these conditions may reflect perceptions that reduced uncertainty is required to determine future outcome values.

Further support for this association may be derived from the posited relationship between cognitive and behavioral uncertainty. Though uncertainty reduction theory explicitly focuses on cognitive uncertainty, key connections to the behavioral component are provided by most formulations. Berger (1975) and Berger and Bradac (1982) propose that reduced uncertainty about the cognitive dispositions of others should reduce behavioral uncertainty in nonroutine situations. The behavioral predictions arrived at in this process may be used to estimate the value of outcomes to be received in the relational future.

Given the highly routinized structure of initial interaction, it might appear that the relation between cognitive and behavioral uncertainty would not apply to this relational stage. Although the structure and general behaviors of partners during beginning communicative contact are largely governed by external guidelines, conversational behavior and topics beyond the first, brief, demographic exchanges are increasingly determined by partners' cognitive dispositions. This suggests that even during initial interactions, cognitive uncertainty levels are related to uncertainty about the behavioral reactions of others to the introduction of conversational topics. Cognitive uncertainty reduction should also provide a basis for predicting future behaviors of others in even less routine encounters beyond this beginning phase. Both of these possibilities support the view that an important function of cognitive uncertainty reduction during initial interactions is the reduction of future behavioral uncertainty.

From the predicted-outcome-value perspective, these uncertainty-reduction efforts would result from individuals' desires to maximize relational outcomes. Reducing uncertainty concerning future behaviors allows individuals to determine likely outcome-value alternatives for the relationship. These behavioral predictions and associated outcome values provide a means of determining how to proceed with the interaction and relationship to realize the most positive outcomes.

At a general level, these projections should allow individuals to determine if the most positive course of action would be to continue the interaction and relationship at the entry level, attempt to terminate or restrict the interaction and relationship, or seek to escalate the interaction and relationship. At a more specific level, predictions regarding likely future behavioral alternatives and associated outcome values should allow individuals to determine how to communicate in attempting to realize the most positive results. Given this goal, individuals presumably would introduce conversational behaviors and topics expected to produce these positive outcomes. Several such communicative strategies are addressed under individual axioms.

This proposed outcome-value function of reducing cognitive and future behavioral uncertainty provides the foundation for modifying uncertainty-reduction axioms. The relationships formulated in the original axioms generally postulate a linear association between uncertainty and specified variables (Berger & Calabrese, 1975). Although there may be a linear component to these relationships, the predicted-outcome-value perspective suggests greater complexity. If individuals are motivated to reduce uncertainty in order to increase the value of their outcomes, reduced uncertainty with regard to either negative or positive outcomes should be useful to those individuals, though these outcome differences would result in substantially different relational consequences. For example, decreased uncertainty that future behavior will result in generally negative outcomes should produce attempts to terminate or restrict the relationship. Conversely, more attempts to continue or increase contact with the relational partner should be produced by decreased uncertainty that future behavior will result in generally positive outcomes. This indicates that the linear relationships specified by uncertainty axioms require modification based on predicted-outcome-value levels: Decreased uncertainty may produce one set of results when predicted outcome values are positive, and an opposite set when these values are negative. The specific modifications regarding each of the axioms follow.

MODIFICATION OF AXIOMS

Amount of Verbal Communication

Axiom 1 of uncertainty reduction theory posits a reciprocal causal relationship between amount of verbal communication and uncertainty:

> *Axiom 1:* Given the high levels of uncertainty present at the outset of the entry phase, as amount of verbal communication increases, the level of uncertainty for each interactant in the relationship will decrease. As uncertainty is further reduced, the amount of verbal communication will increase. (Berger & Calabrese, 1975)

Berger and Calabrese (1975) draw empirical support for this relationship from Lalljee and Cook (1973) and Berger and Larimer (1974). Lalljee and Cook found that as initial interactions proceed, the number of words uttered per minute increases. This research also demonstrated that uncertainty, as indicated by filled pause and speech rates, decreases during these interactions. No direct evidence of a positive association between uncertainty reduction and amount of verbal communication is provided by these findings, as the measure of uncertainty employed verbal indicators that were also used to assess amount of verbal communication. However, these results are consistent with Axiom 1. Berger and Larimer found that amount of verbal communication decreases when feedback between partners is not allowed. Berger and Calabrese suggest this lack of feedback maintains high uncertainty levels producing decreases in amount of verbal communication. Although no measure of uncertainty was provided, these results appear consistent with Axiom 1.

Subsequent tests provide mixed support for the posited relationship between uncertainty and amount of verbal communication. Only four of eleven tests involving relationships beyond the entry stage are consistent with Axiom 1 (Gudykunst et al., 1985; Parks & Adelman, 1983). Initial interaction tests are limited to Clatterbuck's (1979) reanalysis, which provides consistent support for a weak, positive association between amount of time spent together and uncertainty reduction. Overall, empirical evidence provides only indirect support for Axiom 1 during initial interactions, and more direct, but weak and inconsistent, support beyond this relational state. No evidence concerning the reciprocal causal nature of this relationship has been provided.

The predicted-outcome-value perspective leads to a modified verbal communication-uncertainty relationship. This perspective is in general agreement with Berger and Calabrese's (1975) expectation that uncertainty reduction and amount of verbal communication are positively related in the beginning phase of initial interactions, though these perspectives differ substantially on the relation of uncertainty and verbal communication subsequent to this period. The current perspective assumes that during initial interactions individuals attempt to acquire information about partners to enable them to predict future outcome values. Information-seeking strategies likely to be employed in these situations, such as interrogation and self-disclosure, involve verbal communication. Information-seeking and intimacy processes (to be discussed later) indicate that these strategies produce increasingly lengthy speaking turns with fewer speaker and topic switches as initial interactions proceed. This would result in a more constant flow of verbal communication during the course of the conversation, and reduced uncertainty as more information is made known.

Uncertainty reduction allows individuals to form tentative judgments of the outcomes to be obtained from partners' likely future behaviors. When associated predicted outcome values are positive, individuals should seek continued interaction to realize these outcomes. The more positive the predicted outcome values, the greater the likelihood of attempted continuation. When successful, these attempts should lead to further increases in the rate of verbal communication and in uncertainty reduction through the above processes. In addition, the lengthened interaction period would produce an increase in the total amount of verbal communication during the conversation.

When behavioral uncertainty reduction produces tentative judgments that future outcomes will be negative, individuals should attempt to terminate or restrict the interaction. The more negative predicted outcome values, the more likely these attempts. One method of attempting termination or restriction would be to reduce the amount of verbal communication. Individuals should produce briefer comments and ask fewer questions requiring briefer answers as they seek to curtail the conversation. Unless partners respond by engaging in substantially longer speaking turns, this would result in reduced amounts of verbal communication. In addition, when attempts to end the conversation are successful, the overall amount of verbal communication during the conversation will be lower as a result of early termination.

The expected relationship between amount of verbal communication (both rate and total quantity), uncertainty reduction, and predicted outcome value is summarized in the following proposition:

Proposition 1: During the beginning stage of initial interactions, both the amount of verbal communication and uncertainty reduction increase. Further increases in amount of verbal communication occur when uncertainty reduction results in positive predicted outcome values, whereas decreases in amount of verbal communication follow from negative predicted outcome values.

The apparent contradiction between this proposition and the results reported by Lalljee and Cook (1973) and Clatterbuck (1979) can perhaps be explained: Both of these studies indicate that amount of verbal communication may increase as initial interactions proceed. It may be that initial interactions more typically produce positive than negative predicted outcomes. This would produce an overall pattern of increasing verbalization when predicted outcome value is not considered. Because neither of these studies provides a measure of predicted outcome value, the present explanation remains speculative.

The methods employed in these studies may also explain the apparent inconsistency. As Clatterbuck (1979) indicates, the validity of his use of time in a relationship as a measure of amount of verbal communication is problematic. Rates of verbal communication could vary widely in conversations, but length of relational time would not necessarily measure such variation. Additionally, many of the initial interaction studies analyzed by Clatterbuck (1979), as well as Lalljee and Cook's (1973) research, employ conversational time periods set by the experimenters, which effectively eliminates participants' opportunities to terminate the interaction. It also seems likely that participants' abilities to curtail the conversation may be restricted in such experimentally produced situations. Participants generally find themselves in dyadic situations with little to do but converse with their assigned partner. Conversation is experimentally induced, no alternative conversational partners are available, and participants are generally unable to engage in other activities. Typical initial interaction situations enable individuals to make choices in these areas, providing acceptable options for curtailing the conversation. All of the above procedures indicate that the results of these studies cannot be applied to the current proposition, which assumes normal termination and curtailment possibilities. Clearly, future research employing adequate measures and procedures is needed to test Proposition 1.

Nonverbal Affiliative Expressiveness

Axiom 2 of uncertainty reduction theory posits a reciprocal causal relationship between nonverbal affiliative expressiveness and uncertainty levels:

Axiom 2: As nonverbal affiliative expressiveness increases, uncertainty levels will decrease in an initial interaction situation. In addition, decreases in uncertainty level will cause increases in nonverbal affiliative expressiveness. (Berger & Calabrese, 1975)

The empirical base Berger and Calabrese (1975) provide for this axiom rests on the work of Mehrabian (1971) and Mehrabian and Ksionzky (1971). These studies indicate that a number of nonverbal affiliative behaviors are related to amount of verbal communication. These findings coupled with Axiom 1 suggest an association between nonverbal affiliative expressiveness and uncertainty. Gudykunst

and Nishida's (1984) research tested this association directly, with results providing no support in one test and support for a weak association in another. No tests of the reciprocal causal nature of this relationship have been reported.

If nonverbal affiliative expressiveness and amount of verbal communication are positively related, the earlier proposed alteration of the verbal communication-uncertainty relationship suggests changes in Axiom 2. Aside from Mehrabian's (1971) and Mehrabian and Ksionzky's (1971) findings, there are grounds for expecting a positive association between nonverbal affiliative expressiveness and amount of verbal communication. Speakers regularly employ nonverbal affiliative cues, such as head nods and arm gestures, to complement and emphasize verbal messages. Listeners generally provide nonverbal feedback or backchanneling (Duncan, 1975), including head nods and smiling, during partners' speaking turns. This backchanneling may provide reinforcement to the speaker that induces longer speaking turns and greater self-disclosure (Burgoon & Saine, 1978). These tendencies to provide nonverbal affiliative cues during verbal exchanges support the view that amounts of these variables should be positively related. This association alone should provide sufficient reason to expect an uncertainty-nonverbal affiliation relationship similar to the posited relationship regarding amount of verbal communication.

A more direct relation between uncertainty and nonverbal affiliative expressiveness is suggested by the predicted-outcome-value perspective. During initial interactions, uncertainty reduction may be related to the reinforcement properties of nonverbal expressions of affiliation from listeners. Increasingly lengthy speaker turns and self-disclosures in response to this nonverbal reinforcement would provide interactants with substantially more information about one another, with associated reduction in uncertainty levels. Individuals may employ such cues in an attempt to acquire information, though this reinforcement may often just represent an attempt to appear agreeable. As McLaughlin,

Cody, and Rosenstein (1983) note, partners prefer to convey such agreement during initial interactions. In either case, the result would be increased information acquisition and reduced uncertainty.

When predictions of positive outcomes are arrived at through this process, further increases in nonverbal affiliative expressions are likely. This increase would be partially due to the increases in amount of verbal communication expected in these positive situations. Moreover, partners should employ these expressions of affiliation to attempt to continue the interaction and potential relationship. The more positive predicted outcome values, the greater the increase of nonverbal affiliative expressiveness should be.

Conversely, when negative predicted outcomes result from cognitive and behavioral uncertainty reduction, decreases in nonverbal affiliative expressiveness should occur. The expected decrease in amount of verbal communication in negative situations would suggest this. Additionally, decreased affiliative cues are likely when individuals attempt to terminate or curtail interactions with negative predicted outcome values. The more negative these values, the more pronounced this reduction should be.

The proposed relationship between nonverbal affiliative expressiveness, uncertainty reduction, and predicted outcome value leads to the following proposition:

Proposition 2: During the beginning stages of initial interactions, increases in listeners' nonverbal affiliative expressiveness produce reduction in their uncertainty levels. When this uncertainty results in positive predicted outcome values, further increases in nonverbal affiliative expressiveness occur. Uncertainty reduction associated with negative predicted outcome values produces decreases in nonverbal affiliative expressiveness.

Information Seeking

Uncertainty reduction theory proposes a reciprocal causal relationship between information seeking and uncertainty, partially reflected in the following axiom:

Axiom 3: High levels of uncertainty cause increases in information seeking behavior. As uncertainty levels decline, information-seeking behavior decreases. (Berger & Calabrese, 1975)

Berger and Calabrese (1975) derive empirical support for this formulation from Frankfurt's (1965) finding that the number of questions asked during simulated conversations declined over time. Berger and Calabrese also suggest that several demographic questions, likely to produce brief responses, occur in the beginning of initial interactions. The resulting rapid exchange of speaking roles should produce a high number of questions relative to later stages of initial interaction involving more prolonged responses. Although this axiom is based primarily on the use of interrogation as an information-seeking technique, Berger's (1979) introduction of self-disclosure as a strategy to obtain information about partners appears compatible with Axiom 3.

Direct tests of this relationship are limited to the two performed in Gudykunst and Nishida's (1984) study of hypothetical conversations: one test resulted in support for a weak association and the other produced no support. Gudykunst, Yang, and Nishida's (1985) work with developed relationships provided mixed support for a derivative of this axiom. No tests of the reciprocal causal nature of this relationship have been reported.

Prior to examining the predicted-outcome-value perspective on information seeking, a few relevant points concerning this variable need to be addressed. First, it should be clear that individuals may both seek information without receiving it and obtain information that is not sought. It seems reasonable to expect that individuals will provide more unsolicited information as positive interactions proceed, reducing the need for the use of interrogation and self-disclosure as information-seeking methods. Second, information-seeking attempts may be directed at soliciting differing amounts of information. A request for demographic information may be expected to produce rather limited information, but subsequent questions may require more extensive information from partners. Just considering the number of questions asked ignores the amount of information requested. It may well be that as initial interactions proceed, explicit information-seeking requests may decrease in number but increase in the amount of information that is sought. Finally, the earlier discussion of nonverbal affiliative expressiveness suggests that these cues may be used as an additional information-seeking strategy. The use of this strategy should increase as positive initial interactions progress toward longer speaking turns, perhaps replacing interrogation and self-disclosure strategies to a degree. The inclusion of this potential strategy indicates that the type of information-seeking behavior may change in the course of initial interactions.

Within this broadened conceptual framework, information-seeking behavior is viewed as occupying a central position in outcome-maximization processes. Given the highly limited information possessed about others at the outset of initial interactions, explicit information-seeking behavior should begin almost immediately. The rapid exchange of speaker and listener roles at this stage may reflect a high rate of demographically directed information-seeking attempts. This information should reduce uncertainty to a degree, but only lead to tentative impressions of future outcome values. In order to increase the perceived accuracy and validity of these impressions, individuals should begin to seek more detailed information about the cognitive dispositions of partners. Demographic information obtained earlier may suggest topics likely to produce such information. This more detailed information should result in further uncertainty reduction and more stable predictions of future outcome values.

When this uncertainty reduction is associated with positive predicted outcomes, continued information-seeking attempts to further test these predictions and possibly achieve the positive outcomes seem likely: The more positive predicted outcome values, the more likely such attempts. Conversely, uncertainty reduction associated with negative predicted outcomes should result in decreased information-seeking behavior. Because individuals are

expected to terminate or curtail these interactions, further information seeking that would produce prolonged conversation should be avoided. The more negative the predicted outcome values, the more pronounced the reduction in information-seeking behavior.

The predicted-outcome-value perspective thus leads to the following proposition regarding the relation of uncertainty to information-seeking behavior:

Proposition 3: High levels of uncertainty produce increased information-seeking behavior in beginning initial interactions. Decreased uncertainty, when associated with positive outcome values, produces increased information-seeking behavior. When associated with negative predicted outcome values, reduced uncertainty produces decreased information-seeking behavior.

Intimacy Level of Communication Content

Uncertainty reduction theory predicts that uncertainty level has a negative influence on intimacy level of communication content.

Axiom 4: High levels of uncertainty in a relationship cause decreases in intimacy level of communication content. Low levels of uncertainty produce high levels of intimacy. (Berger & Calabrese, 1975)

Berger and Calabrese (1975) review several studies supporting the position that as initial interactions and relationships proceed, intimacy level of communication content increases (Berger, 1973; Cozby, 1972; Ehrlich & Graeven, 1971; Sermat & Smyth, 1973; Taylor, Altman, & Sorrentino, 1969; Taylor, Altman, & Wheeler, 1973). Subsequent research by Berger, Gardner, Clatterbuck, and Shulman (1976) provides further support for increased topic intimacy as initial interactions proceed. Together, these studies indicate that initial interactions begin with conversations focused on demographic topics that are followed by discussions of more intimate but peripheral "attitudinal" information. Further relational development is associated with generally increasing levels of content intimacy. If uncertainty level generally decreases while intimacy level increases over time in a relationship, a negative association between these variables should be observed.

Gudykunst et al.'s (1985) study of established relationships provides evidence for this negative association. This study indicates that higher levels of uncertainty are associated with either lower levels of own self-disclosures or partners' self-disclosures. Berger, Gardner, Parks, Schulman, and Miller (1976) report results indicating that level of content intimacy in initial interactions has no influence on uncertainty. However, no direct evidence regarding Axiom 4 is provided by this research because the posited influence of uncertainty level on content intimacy was unexamined.

Berger and Calabrese (1975) note that the results of past intimacy studies are generally interpreted as supporting Altman and Taylor's (1973) position that as relationships become more rewarding, increasingly intimate discussions occur. Altman and Taylor stipulate that these more intimate discussions will focus on topics projected to produce further rewards. Berger and Calabrese propose a different explanation of this phenomena, reflected in Axiom 4. The predicted-outcome-value perspective suggests that a composite of these positions may produce the most useful view of changes in intimacy level during initial interactions.

The current explanation of the movement of the content of initial interaction from general demographic information to more detailed information about individual partners is addressed in the previous section. This movement can be conceptualized as proceeding along an intimacy continuum: Demographic exchanges provide highly superficial information about group membership, whereas subsequent exchanges produce more intimate information about partners' cognitive dispositions. This change is expected to increase individuals' perceived ability to accurately predict outcome-value alternatives through cognitive and behavioral uncertainty reduction.

Increasing content intimacy should involve topics related to demographic information acquired in the beginning interaction phase. Cognitive and future behavioral uncertainty regarding these topics should be high. However, uncertainty regarding topics unrelated to known demographic categories should be higher still. Given this, individuals should perceive greater accuracy in predicting outcomes for demographically suggested topic areas. When the discussion of some such topics is expected to result in positive outcomes, more intimate conversations on these topics should occur. This discussion would further reduce uncertainty and increase the perceived accuracy of predicting future outcomes. If continued predictions of positive outcomes result, increasingly intimate content should be exchanged. The more positive the predicted outcome values, the more likely the attempts at increasing intimacy level.

Conversely, it is possible that none of the topics suggested by early demographic exchanges leads to acceptable outcome values. This should result in either continued demographic and superficial exchanges or attempts to terminate the conversation. A similar process should occur when more intimate conversations result in negative predicted outcomes. Individuals should attempt to terminate these interactions, move the content of discussion back to less intimate levels, or attempt to discuss other topics suggested by known demographic categories. In any case, increasing content intimacy would not result from negative outcome-value predictions. The more negative these values, the more likely attempts at conversational termination or restriction to low intimacy levels.

The expected relationship between content intimacy, predicted outcome value, and uncertainty is summarized in the following proposition:

Proposition 4: Given high uncertainty levels at the onset of initial interactions, communication content is low in intimacy. When subsequent uncertainty reduction is associated with positive predicted outcome values, intimacy level of communicative content increases. When uncertainty reduction is associated with negative predicted outcome values, intimacy level is maintained at or decreases to low levels.

Reciprocity Rate

Uncertainty reduction theory posits a positive causal relationship between uncertainty levels and reciprocity rates:

Axiom 5: High levels of uncertainty produce high rates of reciprocity. Low levels of uncertainty produce low reciprocity rates. (Berger & Calabrese, 1975)

Several studies demonstrate that conversational exchanges between equal status partners are reciprocal in nature. Partners generally match speech rates (Matarazzo, Wiens, & Saslow, 1965), amount of information disclosed (Worthy, Gary, & Kahn, 1969), and intimacy level of communicative content (Jourard, 1960). Violating this norm of reciprocity tends to reduce attraction to violators during initial contact situations (Sermat & Smyth, 1973). In subsequent research, Berger, Gardner, Parks, Shulman, and Miller (1976) report that reciprocity of content intimacy in initial interactions leads to lower uncertainty levels than nonreciprocity. However, research has yet to test the relationship between uncertainty level and reciprocity rates.

Berger and Calabrese (1975) propose that reciprocal behavior is due to concerns about the distribution of informational power in relationships: Reciprocal exchanges help assure that neither interaction partner will obtain an informational advantage over the other. Given the relative lack of partner information available during beginning initial interactions, even moderate differences in amount or intimacy of information could lead to large power imbalances. Only small amounts of information should be provided in beginning speaking turns to avoid such imbalances. The result of this should be the brief comments and rapid exchanges of speaking roles which characterize this stage. As the information base about partners increases, relative balance could be maintained with greater amounts of information provided during individual speaking turns.

Alternatively, the predicted-outcome-value perspective explains reciprocal information exchange during initial interactions as due to partners' mutual attempts to maximize their outcomes. The central role of possessing information about partners in producing outcome maximization has been discussed extensively. Partner cooperation in providing the needed information is clearly required in these beginning interactions. In order to solicit such behavior from partners, individuals should demonstrate their own willingness to cooperate. When mutual decisions to cooperate are coupled with the information-seeking and intimacy-level processes discussed earlier, a general matching on amount and intimacy of information would be expected.

This reciprocal *behavior* should continue as long as partners choose to cooperate. Continued cooperation would result from uncertainty reduction associated with positive predicted outcome values, though reciprocity *rates* should decline as a result of increasing length of speaking turns. Such continued cooperation should convey the individual's desire to maintain the interaction and relationship. When negative predicted outcome values are associated with reduced uncertainty, attempts to reciprocate should be discontinued or severely curtailed as a method of terminating or restricting the conversation and relationship.

The following proposition reflects this predicted-outcome-value view of the uncertainty-reciprocity rate relationship.

Proposition 5: During the beginning stage of initial interactions, high uncertainty levels are associated with high rates of reciprocity. When uncertainty reduction is associated with positive predicted outcome values, reciprocity rate declines. When uncertainty reduction is associated with negative predicted outcome values, greater decreases in reciprocity rate occur.

Similarity

Uncertainty reduction theory posits a positive causal relationship between similarity and uncertainty reduction:

Axiom 6: Similarities between persons reduce uncertainty, whereas dissimilarities produce increases in uncertainty. (Berger & Calabrese, 1975)

Berger and Calabrese (1975) propose that uncertainty level mediates between similarity and liking. Much of their empirical evidence for Axiom 6 is drawn from studies demonstrating a positive attitude-similarity/attraction association (Berscheid & Walster, 1969; Byrne, 1971). In addition, Berger and Calabrese cite evidence demonstrating that individuals provide more explanations for not liking others than for liking them (Koenig, 1971), and more explanations for dissimilarities between people than for similarities (Berger, 1975). These differences in number of explanations are taken as an indication that uncertainty levels are higher under conditions of dissimilarity or disliking than of similarity or liking.

Subsequent tests of the uncertainty-similarity relationship have yielded mixed support for Axiom 6. In studies of established relationships, Parks and Adelman (1983) report weak support for the uncertainty-similarity association, Prisbell and Anderson (1980) report support with some forms of similarity but not with others, and Gudykunst et al.'s (1985) research indicates support in only four of nine tests. Studies of initial interactions find equally ambiguous support. Clatterbuck's (1979) reanalysis of several studies consistently supports a weak perceived similarity-uncertainty relationship though providing no support for actual similarity. Gudykunst and Nishida (1984) report no relationship between the uncertainty and similarity variables.

Contrary to the uncertainty reduction position, initial interaction information indicating either similarity or dissimilarity should generally reduce cognitive and future behavioral uncertainty, as long as individuals have previous knowledge of others who display these same similarities or dissimilarities. When individuals have formed impressions of others from certain demographic groups or who hold particular low-risk cognitive dispositions, information indicating their partner is aligned with that group or disposition would reduce uncertainty. As Miller and Steinberg (1975) indicate, individuals are likely to apply these impressions to early-acquaintance partners through a process of stimulus generalization. This stimulus generalization should reduce uncertainty levels, regardless of whether the information employed indicates similarity or dissimilarity. In some cases, individuals may have greater familiarity with and, therefore, more well-formed impressions of others from similar demographic groups than from dissimilar ones. Information indicating similarity should result in greater uncertainty reduction in such situations, though dissimilar information would still reduce uncertainty.

This perspective on the similarity-uncertainty association is summarized in the following proposition:

Proposition 6: Both similarities and dissimilarities between persons reduce uncertainty. Greater uncertainty reduction will result from similarities when dissimilarities reflect groupings that are not highly familiar to individuals.

Liking

Uncertainty reduction theory proposes a negative causal relationship between uncertainty level and liking:

Axiom 7: Increases in uncertainty level produce decreases in liking; decreases in uncertainty level produce increases in liking. (Berger & Calabrese, 1975)

Berger and Calabrese (1975) base this axiom primarily on the assumption that uncertainty mediates between similarity and liking. Gudykunst et al. (1985) report consistent support for the uncertainty-attraction relationship from nine tests on developed relationships. However, research on the initial interaction stage provides inconsistent support. Clatterbuck (1979) reports support for an uncertainty-attraction relationship in some studies but not in others. Gudykunst and Nishida's (1984) research provides no support for this relationship. In addition, recent work indicates that the previously accepted positive attitude similarity-attraction relationship does not apply to normal initial interactions (Sunnafrank, 1983, 1984, 1985; Sunnafrank & Miller, 1981), suggesting that the basis of Axiom 7 may be in error.

The predicted-outcome-value perspective expects that higher forecasted outcome values will produce higher levels of attraction. The current application of this perspective to uncertainty-related variables makes it clear that uncertainty reduction could be associated with either negative or positive predicted outcome values. When cognitive and future behavioral uncertainty reduction leads to positive predicted outcome values, increased liking should result. However, uncertainty reduction associated with negative predicted outcome values should produce opposite attraction influences. The relationship between uncertainty, liking, and predicted outcome value is formally stated in the following proposition:

Proposition 7: When decreased uncertainty is associated with positive predicted outcome values, liking increases. When associated with negative predicted outcome values, liking decreases.

HYPOTHESES

Berger and Calabrese (1975) deduce 21 theorems from their original seven axioms. To further clarify differences between uncertainty reduction and predicted-outcome-value theories, corresponding hypotheses are derived from the current propositions. Fifteen such hypotheses are presented. The derivation of these hypotheses is based on the assumption that predicted outcome value is influencing the consequent variables, as previously indicated in six of the propositions. (Because Proposition 6 does not specify a relationship involving predicted outcome value, it was not employed in this process.) Nine of these hypotheses predict different associations from those expected by uncertainty-reduction theorems. These hypotheses are presented first, along with the corresponding theorems. Critical comparisons of the two theories will require investigation of these conflicting predictions, as well as those present in the seven pairs of axioms and propositions. Given this, a brief discussion of empirical evidence relevant to these hypotheses is provided. Finally, the six hypotheses that are in agreement with uncertainty-reduction theorems are presented.

Conflicting Predictions

Hypothesis 1 (POV): Amount of verbal communication and information-seeking behavior are positively related.

Theorem 3 (URT): Amount of communication and information-seeking behavior are inversely related. (Berger & Calabrese, 1975)

Hypothesis 2 (POV): Nonverbal affiliative expressiveness and information-seeking behavior are positively related.

Theorem 8 (URT): Nonverbal affiliative expressiveness and information seeking are inversely related. (Berger & Calabrese, 1975)

Hypothesis 3 (POV): Intimacy level of communication content and information-seeking behavior are positively related.

Theorem 12 (URT): Intimacy level of communication content and information seeking are inversely related. (Berger & Calabrese, 1975)

Hypothesis 4 (POV): Information-seeking behavior and reciprocity rate are inversely related when predicted outcome values are positive, and positively related when predicted outcome values are negative.

Theorem 16 (URT): Information seeking and reciprocity rate are positively related. (Berger & Calabrese, 1975)

Hypothesis 5 (POV): Information-seeking behavior and liking are positively related.

Theorem 17 (URT): Information seeking and liking are negatively related. (Berger & Calabrese, 1975)

Hypothesis 6 (POV): Amount of verbal communication and reciprocity rate are inversely related when predicted outcome values are positive, and positively related when predicted outcome values are negative.

Theorem 4 (URT): Amount of communication and reciprocity rate are inversely related. (Berger & Calabrese, 1975)

Hypothesis 7 (POV): Nonverbal affiliative expressiveness and reciprocity rate are inversely related when predicted outcome values are positive, and positively related when predicted outcome values are negative.

Theorem 9 (URT): Nonverbal affiliative expressiveness and reciprocity rate are inversely related. (Berger & Calabrese, 1975)

Hypothesis 8 (POV): Intimacy level of communication content and reciprocity rate are inversely related when predicted outcome values are positive, and positively related when predicted outcome values are negative.

Theorem 13 (URT): Intimacy level of communication content and reciprocity rate are inversely related. (Berger & Calabrese, 1975)

Hypothesis 9 (POV): Reciprocity rate and liking are inversely related when predicted outcome values are positive, and positively related when predicted outcome values are negative.

Theorem 19 (URT): Reciprocity rate and liking are negatively related. (Berger & Calabrese, 1975)

All of these conflicting hypothesis/theorem pairs involve reciprocity rate, information-seeking behavior, or both. Currently, there is no empirical basis for assessing the relative accuracy of reciprocity-rate hypotheses and theorems. Direct comparisons will require inclusion of the predicted-outcome variable in future research. Lack of research on reciprocity-rate theorems renders even an indirect evaluation of the contrasting prediction impossible. Though some uncertainty-reduction research examines various aspects of reciprocity (for example, see Berger, Gardner, Parks, Schulman, & Miller, 1976), none directly tests these theorems.

However, research evidence does allow a direct comparison of two information-seeking hypothesis/theorem pairs. Gudykunst and Nishida's (1984) research on the initial interaction situations addressed by both theories provides support for predicted-outcome-value predictions. Their results demonstrate a positive association between information

seeking and nonverbal affiliative expressiveness, as well as between information seeking and liking. These findings are consistent with Hypotheses 2 and 5 respectively, and in opposition to Theorems 8 and 17. This limited evidence suggests that future research on conflicting uncertainty-reduction and predicted-outcome-value predictions will prove useful.

Concordant Predictions

- *Hypothesis 10* (POV): Amount of verbal communication and nonverbal affiliative expressiveness are positively related (URT Theorem 1).
- *Hypothesis 11* (POV): Amount of verbal communication and intimacy level of communication content are positively related (URT Theorem 2).
- *Hypothesis 12* (POV): Amount of verbal communication and liking are positively related (URT Theorem 5).
- *Hypothesis 13* (POV): Nonverbal affiliative expressiveness and intimacy level of communication content are positively related (URT Theorem 7).
- *Hypothesis 14* (POV): Nonverbal affiliative expressiveness and liking are positively related (URT Theorem 10).
- *Hypothesis 15* (POV): Intimacy level of communication content and liking are positively related (URT Theorem 14).

CONCLUSION

Prior to the development of uncertainty reduction theory, the primary frameworks for studying interpersonal communication were generally provided by various social psychological theories of interpersonal relations. Berger and Calabrese (1975) note that although such frameworks are relevant to interpersonal communication, they rarely focus directly on important communication concerns. Uncertainty reduction theory responded to this shortcoming by making communication processes and constructs its central focus. Their formulation rejected the dominant rewards-costs analysis of interpersonal relations, and proposed uncertainty reduction as the major explanatory factor in interpersonal communication processes. The focus of uncertainty reduction theory on communication clearly represented a major theoretical advance. However, empirical evidence provides inconsistent and generally weak support for the posited role of uncertainty reduction, suggesting that major theoretical modifications are needed.

Predicted-outcome-value theory attempts to provide these modifications, though maintaining Berger and Calabrese's (1975) focus on communication processes. This perspective acknowledges the potential complementary nature of uncertainty-reduction and rewards-costs orientations. The resulting theoretical integration assumes that uncertainty is not the central goal of individuals in beginning relationships, but only an important vehicle for the primary goal of achieving positive relational outcomes.

Predicted-outcome-value theory proposes 22 propositions and hypotheses; the preponderance conflict with corresponding uncertainty-reduction predictions. These propositions and hypotheses have the potential to resolve many inconsistent uncertainty-reduction findings. In the few cases in which direct empirical evidence exists, findings support predicted-outcome-value expectations over those of uncertainty-reduction theory. Given this, research designed to test these contrary predictions seems warranted. This testing process will obviously require research methods that adequately reflect the current perspective. Developing valid measures and manipulations of predicted outcome value will be particularly crucial. Such attempts might initially concentrate on individuals' global perceptions of predicted-outcome-value levels, an approach that would be sufficient to test the formal relationships posited here.

In addition to research on the formal predicted-outcome-value propositions and hypotheses, several other potentially fruitful research possibilities are suggested by the current perspective. Research questions concerning the use of nonverbal affilia-tive expressiveness as an information-seeking strategy, and the relationship of predicted outcome value to reciprocal communication behavior (other than reciprocity rate), among other questions, are clearly raised by predicted-outcome-value theory. This formulation may also have the potential to help explain theoretically inconsistent results from uncertainty-reduction research on communication-network variables (Parks & Adelman, 1983), cultural context (Gudykunst & Nishida, 1984), as well as self-consciousness and self-monitoring (Gudykunst et al., 1985). Finally, potential connections between predicted-outcome-value theory and several seemingly compatible perspectives should be explored. For example, work on account sequences in initial interactions (McLaughlin, Cody, & Rosenstein, 1983), affinity-seeking strategies (Bell & Daly, 1984), and interpersonal goals (Sunnafrank & Miller, 1981) all address communication variables and processes that appear to be particularly relevant to the predicted-outcome-value perspective. Research that explicitly examines these potential connections may prove highly useful.

In closing, it should be noted that if tests of predicted-outcome-value theory are sufficiently supportive, attempts to expand the theory to include relational stages beyond initial interactions would be reasonable. Such attempts must confront several issues raised by critiques of relational development perspectives (for example, see Bochner, 1978). Although it is not within the scope of the present article to address all of these concerns, the issue of specifying causal mechanisms of relational change is particularly relevant, given the current formulation. Predicted-outcome-value theory proposes that predicted-outcome-value levels are the primary determinant of change in initial interactions. However, when relational contact continues beyond beginning interactions, further change may be more influenced by how these levels compare to those projected for alternative relationships, when such alternatives are readily available. For example, highly positive predicted outcome values should not result in further relational escalation when more positive alternative relationships exist. (For a more complete development of the idea of comparing outcomes for alternative relationships see Thibaut and Kelley, 1959, Chapter 6.) Future expansions of predicted-outcome-value theory should give serious consideration to this comparison process as a component of relational change in continuing relationships.

Further speculation on possible expansions of predicted-outcome-value theory would be premature at this point. The immediate task is to begin empirical examination of the current perspective. At a minimum, these tests will lead to theoretical modifications. It is hoped that the present formulation provides both an adequate conceptual grounding and sufficient justification for beginning this testing process.

REFERENCES

Adams, J. S. (1963). Toward an understanding of inequity. *Journal of Abnormal and Social Psychology, 67,* 422-436.

Altman, I. (1974). The communication of interpersonal attitudes. In T. E. Huston (Ed.), *Foundations of interpersonal attraction* (pp. 121-142). New York: Academic Press.

Altman, I., & Taylor, D. A. (1973). *Social penetration: The development of interpersonal relationships.* New York: Holt, Rinehart & Winston.

Bell, R. A., & Daly, J. A. (1984). The affinity-seeking function of communication. *Communication Monographs, 51,* 91-115.

Berger, C. R. (1973, November). *The acquaintance process revisited: Explorations in initial interaction.* Paper presented at the annual convention of the Speech Communication Association, New York.

Berger, C. R. (1975). Proactive and retroactive attribution processes. *Human Communication Research, 2,* 33-50.

Berger, C. R. (1979). Beyond initial interaction: Uncertainty, understanding, and the development of interpersonal relationships. In H. Giles & R. N. St. Clair (Eds.), *Language and social psychology* (pp. 122-144). Oxford: Basil Blackwell.

Berger, C. R., & Bradac, J. J. (1982). *Language and social knowledge: Uncertainty in interpersonal relations.* London: Edward Arnold.

Berger, C. R., & Calabrese, R. J. (1975). Some explorations in initial interaction and beyond: Toward a developmental theory of interpersonal communication. *Human Communication Research, 1,* 99-112.

Berger, C. R., & Douglas, W. (1981). Studies in interpersonal epistemology III: Anticipated interaction, self-monitoring, and observational context selection. *Communication Monographs, 48,* 183-196.

Berger, C. R., Gardner, R. R., Clatterbuck, G. W., & Schulman, L. S. (1976). Perceptions of information sequencing in relationship development. *Human Communication Research, 3,* 29-46.

Berger, C. R., Gardner, R. R., Parks, M. P., Schulman, L., & Miller, G. R. (1976). Interpersonal epistemology and interpersonal communication. In G. R. Miller (Ed.), *Explorations in interpersonal communication* (pp. 149-172). Beverly Hills, CA: Sage.

Berger, C. R., & Larimer, M. W. (1974, April). *When beauty is only skin deep: The effects of physical attractiveness, sex and time on initial interaction.* Paper presented at the annual convention of the International Communication Association, New Orleans.

Berger, C. R., & Perkins, J. W. (1978). Studies in interpersonal epistemology I: Situational attributes in observational context selection. In B. D. Rubin (Ed.), *Communication yearbook 2* (pp. 171-184). New Brunswick, NJ: Transaction.

Berscheid, E., & Walster, E. H. (1969). *Interpersonal attraction.* Reading, MA: Addison-Wesley.

Bochner, A. (1978). On taking ourselves seriously: An analysis of some persistent problems and promising directions in interpersonal research. *Human Communication Research, 4,* 179-191.

Burgoon, J. K., & Saine, T. (1978). *The unspoken dialogue: An introduction to nonverbal communication.* Boston: Houghton Mifflin.

Byrne, D. (1961). Interpersonal attraction and attitude similarity. *Journal of Abnormal and Social Psychology, 62,* 713-715.

Byrne, D. (1971). *The attraction paradigm.* New York: Academic Press.

Byrne, D., & Nelson, D. (1965). Attraction as a linear function of proportion of positive reinforcements. *Journal of Personality and Social Psychology, 1,* 659-663.

Clatterbuck, G. W. (1979). Attributional confidence and uncertainty in initial interaction. *Human Communication Research, 5,* 147-157.

Cozby, P. C. (1972). Self-disclosure, reciprocity and liking. *Sociometry, 35,* 151-160.

Duncan, S. (1975). Interaction units during speaking turns in dyadic, face-to-face conversations. In A. Kendon, R. Harris, & M. Key (Eds.), *Organization of behavior in face-to-face interaction* (pp. 199-213). The Hague: Mouton.

Ehrlich, H. J., & Graeven, D. B. (1971). Reciprocal self-disclosure in a dyad. *Journal of Experimental Social Psychology, 7,* 389-400.

Frankfurt, L. P. (1965). *The role of some individual and interpersonal factors on the acquaintance process.* Unpublished doctoral dissertation, American University.

Gudykunst, W. B., & Nishida, T. (1984). Individual and cultural influences on uncertainty reduction. *Communication Monographs, 51,* 23-36.

Gudykunst, W. B., Yang, S. M., & Nishida, T. (1985). A cross-cultural test of uncertainty reduction theory: Comparisons of acquaintance, friends, and dating relationships in Japan, Korea, and the United States. *Human Communication Research, 11,* 407-455.

Heider, F. (1958). *The psychology of interpersonal relations.* New York: John Wiley.

Homans, G. C. (1974). *Social behavior: Its elementary forms* (2nd ed.). New York: Harcourt Brace Jovanovich.

Jones, E. E., & Davis, K. E. (1965). From acts to dispositions. In L. Berkowitz (Ed.), *Advances in experimental social psychology* (Vol. 2, pp. 219-266). New York: Academic Press.

Jourard, S. (1960). Knowing, liking, and the "dyadic effect" in men's self-disclosure. *Merrill Palmer Quarterly of Behavior and Development, 6,* 178-186.

Kelley, H. H. (1973). The process of causal attribution. *American Psychologist, 28,* 107-128.

Kelley, H. H., & Thibaut, J. W. (1978). *Interpersonal relations: A theory of interdependence.* New York: John Wiley.

Koenig, F. (1971). Positive affective stimulus value and accuracy of role perception. *British Journal of Social and Clinical Psychology, 10,* 385-386.

Lalljee, M., & Cook, M. (1973). Uncertainty in first encounters. *Journal of Personality and Social Psychology, 26,* 137-141.

Lott, A. J., & Lott, B. E. (1974). The role of reward in the formation of positive interpersonal attitudes. In T. E. Huston (Ed.), *Foundations of interpersonal attraction* (pp. 171-192). New York: Academic Press.

Matarazzo, J. D., Wiens, A. N., & Saslow, G. (1965). Studies of interview speech behavior. In L. Krasner & L. P. Ullman (Eds.), *Research in behavior modification: New developments and implications* (pp. 179-210). New York: Holt, Rinehart & Winston.

McLaughlin, M. L., Cody, M. J., & Rosenstein, N. E. (1983). Account sequences in conversations between strangers. *Communication Monographs, 50,* 102-125.

Mehrabian, A. (1971). Verbal and nonverbal interaction of strangers in a waiting situation. *Journal of Experimental Research in Personality, 5,* 127-138.

Mehrabian, A., & Ksionzky, S. (1971). Factors of interpersonal behavior and judgment in social groups. *Psychological Reports, 28,* 483-492.

Miller, G. R., & Steinberg, M. (1975). *Between people.* Chicago: Science Research Associates.

Parks, M. R., & Adelman, M. B. (1983). Communication networks and the development of romantic relationships: An expansion of uncertainty reduction theory. *Human Communication Research, 10,* 55-79.

Prisbell, M., & Anderson, J. F. (1980). The importance of perceived homophily, level of uncertainty, feeling good, safety, and self-disclosure in interpersonal relationships. *Communication Quarterly, 28,* 22-33.

Roloff, M. E. (1981). *Interpersonal communication: The social exchange approach.* Beverly Hills, CA: Sage.

Sermat, V., & Smyth, M. (1973). Content analysis of verbal communication in the development of a relationship: Conditions influencing self-disclosure. *Journal of Personality and Social Psychology, 26,* 332-346.

Sherblom, J., & Van Rheenen, D. D. (1984). Spoken language indices of uncertainty. *Human Communication Research, 11,* 221-230.

Sunnafrank, M. (1983). Attitude similarity and interpersonal attraction in communication processes: In pursuit of an ephemeral influence. *Communication Monographs, 50,* 273-284.

Sunnafrank, M. (1984). A communication-based perspective on attitude similarity and interpersonal attraction in early acquaintance. *Communication Monographs, 51,* 372-380.

Sunnafrank, M. (1985). Attitude similarity and interpersonal attraction during early communicative relationships: A research note on the generalizability of findings to opposite-sex relationships. *Western Journal of Speech Communication, 49,* 73-80.

Sunnafrank, M., & Miller, G. R. (1981). The role of initial conversations in determining attraction to similar and dissimilar strangers. *Human Communication Research, 8,* 16-25.

Taylor, D. A., Altman, I., & Sorrentino, R. (1969). Interpersonal exchange as a function of rewards and costs and situational factors: Expectancy confirmation-disconfirmation. *Journal of Experimental Social Psychology, 5,* 324-339.

Taylor, D. A., Altman, I., & Wheeler, L. (1973). Self-disclosure in isolated groups. *Journal of Personality and Social Psychology, 26,* 39-47.

Thibaut, J. W., & Kelley, H. H. (1959). *The social psychology of groups.* New York: John Wiley.

Walster, E., Berscheid, E., & Walster, G. W. (1973). New directions in equity research. *Journal of Personality and Social Psychology, 25,* 151-176.

Walster, E., Walster, G. W., & Berscheid, E. (1978). *Equity: Theory and research.* Boston: Allyn & Bacon.

Worthy, M., Gary, A. L., & Kahn, G. M. (1969). Self-disclosure as an exchange process. *Journal of Personality and Social Psychology, 13,* 59-64.

9

The Affinity-Seeking
Function of Communication

ROBERT A. BELL | JOHN A. DALY

A model of the affinity-seeking function of communication is introduced and explicated. The affinity-seeking construct describes ways people get others to like and feel positive about them. The research is grounded in the presumption that people attempt to generate liking by using various communication strategies. Four questions were addressed in six studies: (1) How do people attempt to generate liking? (2) What is the relationship of affinity-seeking to interpersonal attraction? (3) How do individual differences and situational contingencies constrain affinity-seeking? and (4) What is the multivariate structure of affinity-seeking? An inductively-devised typology of affinity-seeking strategies provided a reliable operationalization of the construct. Affinity-seeking was strongly and positively related to interpersonal attraction, life satisfaction, and social effectiveness. In addition, strategy knowledge and strategy preferences were related to various personality variables and situational contingencies. The final investigation reported in this article identified three dimensions underlying the typology and seven general clusters of strategies.

People expend considerable social energy attempting to get others to like and to appreciate them. Whether their aim is developing friendships, forging romantic attachments, achieving positive evaluations from superiors, or broadly seeking the approval of others, generating affinity is an ubiquitous social process. The ability to evoke positive feelings is a favorably regarded and often envied skill. Furthermore, developing and maintaining affinity is an important function of communication. When other people indicate by their words and actions that they like a person, that individual's sense of personal worth is substantially enhanced. Inability to generate positive feelings is, on the other hand, a severe social concern. A person who is unable to gain affection, support, attention, and other social reinforcements is likely to suffer from a variety of social and personal turmoils. People know this; one of the most widely translated and circulated books in publishing history focuses on how people can "win" friends (Carnegie, 1937). Nor does Carnegie stand alone: Bookstore counters are dotted with literature offering advice on seeking affinity which ranges from what to say after you say, "Hello," to how to communicate effectively in boardroom and bedroom.

The process of generating affinity, while ever present and central to social exchanges, has not been systematically examined. How do people get others to like them? What strategies do people use? What techniques are successful? These are questions largely lacking reliable answers. This article introduces the concept *affinity-seeking*, systematically identifies the major strategies available to individuals, and reports several investigations of the construct and typology. Affinity-seeking is defined as the active social-communicative process by which individuals attempt to get others to like and to feel positive toward them.

A recent trend in communication research has been the identification and investigation of the functions communication serves in meeting basic human needs. Attention has focused on such functions as compliance-gaining, relational disengage-

From Bell, R. A., & Daly, J. A. (1984). The affinity-seeking function of communication. *Communication Monographs, 51,* 91-115.

ment, deception, and information-seeking and -giving. Affinity-seeking, like compliance-gaining, information-giving, and other communicative functions, plays an important role in social interaction. Unlike these functions, affinity-seeking has received little systematic exploration. This is surprising, for there are few social needs that are more critical to life satisfaction and success than feeling liked by others. Affinity-seeking is inherently a communicative function. It is impossible to imagine an attempt to generate liking that does not require verbal or nonverbal messages. It is primarily through talk and carefully controlled actions that people influence the level of attraction others feel toward them.

Previous research relating to affinity-seeking takes two major forms. The first emphasizes the *static characteristics* affecting people's likability. In this approach, characteristics of people are identified or manipulated and others' reactions to them are assessed. Particularly noteworthy are studies of attitude similarity and physical appearance. A large literature suggests that attitudinal similarity increases the probability that individuals will like each other (Byrne, 1971). Likewise, physically attractive individuals are better liked than physically unattractive ones (Berscheid & Walster, 1974). Research has also examined the role of proximity, background similarity, and a variety of person perceptions (e.g., credibility) in shaping interpersonal attraction and liking (Berscheid & Walster, 1978). These studies take a passive approach to how people generate liking: An individual is or is not similar, is or is not physically attractive, etc. Although this paradigm has been valuable in guiding research into attraction processes, it misses an important consideration. Individuals often go beyond static characteristics when generating affinity; they strategize and labor to get others to like them. They may highlight their similarity, credibility, or physical attractiveness, but they surely do more. Indeed, even when their static characteristics do not foreshadow liking (for example, when they are physically unattractive), people persevere in their attempts to generate affinity.

Not all research has been so static. A second perspective emphasizes the *social requirements and skills* associated with generating affinity. This approach specifies what an individual must know and do to be likable (e.g., Argyle, 1972). It also recognizes that people vary considerably in their ability to be attracting. An example of this kind of research comes from Davis (1973) who, in his analysis of the typical pickup routine, identifies six tasks that must be executed skillfully if a person wishes to induce another individual to enter into an intimate relationship. Reflecting the active nature of this perspective is an enormous self-help industry which provides a wealth of instruction about ways people can curry affection and liking. Though the social requirements and skills literature describes a number of potentially effective behaviors, it unfortunately fails to provide a systematic account of the various options people have available when they want others to feel affinity for them.

MODELING AFFINITY-SEEKING

Our research approaches the generation of affinity differently than previous investigations. We systematically explicate various behavioral options available to individuals who want to get others to like them. Aside from the broad proposition that affinity-seeking is an important communication skill, two basic assumptions guided this research. First, affinity-seeking is a strategic activity; individuals can and do elicit liking from others through the manipulation of certain social behaviors. This view contrasts with passive, static approaches to interpersonal attraction. Our focus is consistent with a growing concern by communication researchers for the strategies social actors employ to meet personal objectives (e.g., Clark & Delia, 1979; Roloff, 1976). The term *strategy* describes an abstract category of largely symbolic behaviors that, when enacted, are expected to lead to greater affinity. Nested within a strategy are *tactics,* those specific behaviors that *operationalize* a strategy. For example, the junior executive who believes she can win the admiration of her superior by being perceived as dynamic might act physically animated and talk in an enthusiastic manner. The animation and enthusiasm *tactics* implement a *strategy* of dynamism.

Our second assumption is that various affinity-seeking strategies are available to individuals at any point in time. Thus, the processes underlying strategy choices ultimately are quite important. A tentative model of affinity-seeking is presented in Figure 9.1. The model facilitates the understanding of the choice-making process that people engage in when seeking affinity. The model posits four issues that should be considered when investigating affinity-seeking: *antecedent factors, constraints, strategic activities,* and *target responses.*

Antecedent Factors

The phrase "antecedent factors" is used to refer to the myriad considerations that characterize the interaction within which affinity is sought. A partial listing of antecedent factors includes the goals of the interactants, the motives of the affinity-seekers and the level of consciousness with which affinity is sought. People usually interact with goals in mind. One might, for instance, initiate an encounter to generate liking, acquire information, express oneself, or gain compliance. Presumably, these interaction goals influence the nature of affinity-seeking in yet-to-be-determined ways. While affinity-seeking can be the sole goal of an interaction, it can also be the means to other goals. Information-gathering, for example, might better be accomplished if the potential informant feels affinity toward the questioner.

A second antecedent factor is the motives underlying an individual's desire to generate affinity. One may seek affinity for many reasons. The junior executive mentioned earlier might wish to be liked for professional gain, relational development, politeness, or some combination of these motives. Other motives for affinity-seeking no doubt exist.

A third antecedent factor involves the level of consciousness with which affinity-seeking takes place. In many situations, affinity-seeking is conscious, deliberate, and intentional. For example, one or both parties on a first date may carefully plan their actions and comments well in advance so as to make a good impression. In other contexts, however, affinity-seeking strategies may be enacted with little or no conscious thought. Through years of social experience, people develop behavioral repertoires that can be executed with little deliberation. Just as we can walk, eat, and drive a car without contemplating every action, so we can use affinity-seeking strategies without considering their minute components.

Constraints

A second feature of the model is the "constraints" individuals operate under when seeking affinity. In any situation, people's affinity-seeking options are constrained by both personal and contextual characteristics. Examples of individual factors that constrain affinity-seeking include people's dispositions, social skills, and past experiences. For instance, communicatively apprehensive people may attempt to generate liking in ways that differ from nonapprehensive people. Individuals with poor social skills or deficient social experiences probably seek affinity in less effective ways than socially skilled and experienced individuals. Contextual constraints include, but are certainly not limited to, the purposes of the encounter (compare affinity-seeking at a party with affinity-seeking at a business meeting), the characteristics of the target person, the amount of prior familiarity with the target person, the role relations between the person seeking affinity and the target person, and the setting where affinity-seeking takes place. Obviously, individual and contextual constraints can interact in numerous ways.

Strategic Activity

The outcomes of these antecedent factors and constraints are strategic activities designed to generate

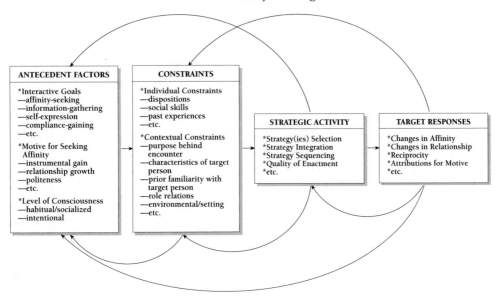

FIGURE 9.1

A Model of the Affinity-Seeking Process

affinity. The model addresses four issues pertinent to these activities. First, individuals seeking affinity must decide on an optimal strategy or strategies in a given situation. Thus, an important concern is how people choose one strategy or combination of strategies over others. Second, multiple overlapping strategies varying in their length of enactment probably are often combined by communicators to form an integrated approach. Certain strategies may be quite continuous and prolonged, while others are discrete and immediate. Contrast certain nonverbal immediacy cues that may be performed without interruption for several minutes with such short-lived actions as complimenting and laughing.

Affinity-seeking strategies not only need to be integrated, they must also be sequenced. A reasonable premise is that people generate affinity by using a number of temporally ordered strategies. Indeed, the sequencing of strategies may be just as critical as the selection of strategies. One ordering of strategies may produce liking while another or-

dering of the same strategies may lead to failure. For example, individuals who disclose personal information about themselves when seeking affinity would probably be well-advised to use less intimate strategies initially—at least if they are interacting within the context of a noninterpersonal relationship.

A final issue relevant to strategic activity in affinity-seeking is the quality with which affinity-seeking strategies are enacted. In some situations, the mere activity of affinity-seeking may result in liking regardless of the quality of the efforts. In other situations, the quality of strategy enactment may take precedence over the frequency with which affinity-seeking behaviors are initiated.

Target Responses

Investigations of affinity-seeking must also take into account the effects of people's strategic activities.

The affective, behavioral, and cognitive responses of the target person must be assessed. Affective responses include changes in the affinity that the target person feels toward the individual attempting to generate liking and the emotional tone of the relationship. Behavioral responses include the physical and verbal actions elicited by the affinity-seeking activities. For example, a target person may respond reciprocally to a particular affinity-seeking enactment. Affinity-seeking is also likely to trigger cognitive responses. The target person might, for instance, make attributions about the motive of the affinity-seeker's behaviors. Individuals on the receiving end of affinity-seeking may also change their evaluations of the affinity-seeker; evaluations of self may also change.

The model is recursive insofar as people's affinity-seeking behavior influences their future affinity-seeking attempts. The results of a given attempt shape future antecedent conditions and constraints. For instance, the responses elicited by particular strategies affect future strategy-selection decisions. If, for example, the target person responds negatively to a particular strategy, the affinity-seeker may try another approach or give up altogether. The constraints and antecedent factors under which individuals seek affinity are, in part, a function of their earlier strategic activities and the responses these strategies elicited. Individuals may improve their skills at affinity-seeking as they acquire social experiences. They may also become more familiar with the target person's dispositions, permitting more accurate behavioral predictions. Moreover, the constraints imposed on affinity-seeking may change the antecedent factors when affinity is sought in future situations. A person might, for example, enter an encounter with the goal of generating affinity, but conclude that the setting does not allow realization of this goal. Finally, the target person's responses to the strategies employed can change the antecedent factors under which affinity is sought in future interactions. If, for example, people continually accuse someone of having ulterior motives, he or she may become less likely to seek affinity for manipulative reasons.

The centrality of affinity-seeking to social interaction and human relationships gives rise to a number of basic issues. For instance, how do people attempt to generate liking? If affinity-seeking is conceptualized as a strategic communicative activity, the strategies defining this activity must be identified. Second, what is the relationship of affinity-seeking to interpersonal attraction? Presumably, individuals who can enact the various strategies skillfully should be better liked than people who cannot. Third, what factors influence the ways people seek affinity? Probably people's personalities exert a major impact on the strategies they select when seeking affinity. Likewise, the situations in which people find themselves probably influence the effectiveness and appropriateness of the various strategic options. Finally, what is the multivariate structure of affinity-seeking? Can general categories of strategic behaviors be identified? What dimensions differentiate the strategies available to people? This article summarizes six studies that addressed these four issues. Space limitations preclude a highly detailed description of the results of each investigation, but a full account of the studies can be found in Bell and Daly (1984).[1]

QUESTION 1: HOW DO PEOPLE SEEK AFFINITY?

To address the question of how people seek affinity, we developed a typology of affinity-seeking strategies based on the responses of 22 small brainstorming groups to one of two tasks. Ten of these groups were composed of adults enrolled in a summer workshop in instructional communication. The remaining 12 groups were made up of undergraduates. The adult participants were told to "produce a list of things people can say or do to get others to like them." Six of the groups of undergraduates were given the same task. The remaining six groups were asked to "produce a list of things people can say or do to get others to *dislike* them." It was felt that if some of the groups focused on the generation of *negative feelings,* unique insights about affinity-seeking strategies might be discovered.

The responses from these groups were content analyzed. Categories of affinity-seeking behaviors were developed based on two criteria. First, we required that the behaviors encompassed by a category be communicative. By "communicative" we meant that a category had to refer to messages and/or alterations of a person's self-presentation for the purpose of achieving the liking of another. Second, the specific tactics that composed each category had to occur consistently across the groups to justify its importance. Based on the lists produced by these groups, a typology of 25 strategies was developed (see Table 9.1). Rather than describing each, the strategies will be discussed as they become relevant to later parts of this article.

QUESTION 2: WHAT IS THE RELATIONSHIP OF AFFINITY-SEEKING TO INTERPERSONAL ATTRACTION?

The most basic question one can ask about the typology is: Do the strategies actually generate affinity? Presumably, individuals who use the strategies skillfully will be more positively evaluated than individuals who enact them ineffectively. Indeed, the construct assumes a positive relationship between affinity-seeking and interpersonal attraction.

The relationship of affinity-seeking to interpersonal attraction was assessed in a study involving 150 undergraduates enrolled in basic communication classes. The participants were asked to think of an individual they knew within a specified relationship and to complete questionnaires asking for

---

TABLE 9.1

A Typology of Affinity-Seeking Strategies

1. *Altruism.* The affinity-seeker strives to be of assistance to the target in whatever she or he is currently doing.
   Example: The affinity-seeker is generally available to run errands for the target.
2. *Assume Control.* The affinity-seeker presents himself or herself as a person who has control over whatever is going on.
   Example: The affinity-seeker takes charge of the activities engaged in by the target and herself or himself.
3. *Assume Equality.* The affinity-seeker strikes a posture of social equality with the target.
   Example: The affinity-seeker avoids one-up games and behaving snobbishly.
4. *Comfortable Self.* The affinity-seeker acts comfortable and relaxed in settings shared with the target.
   Example: The affinity-seeker ignores annoying environmental distractions, seeking to convey a "nothing bothers me" impression.
5. *Concede Control.* The affinity-seeker allows the target to assume control over relational activities.
   Example: The affinity-seeker permits the target to plan a weekend that the two will share.
6. *Conversational Rule-Keeping.* The affinity-seeker adheres closely to cultural rules for polite, cooperative interaction with the target.
   Example: The affinity-seeker acts interested and involved in conversations with the target.
7. *Dynamism.* The affinity-seeker presents herself or himself as an active, enthusiastic person.
   Example: The affinity-seeker is lively and animated in the presence of the target.
8. *Elicit Other's Disclosures.* The affinity-seeker encourages the target to talk by reinforcing the target's conversational contributions.
   Example: The affinity-seeker queries the target about the target's opinions regarding a significant personal issue.
9. *Facilitate Enjoyment.* The affinity-seeker tries to maximize the positiveness of relational encounters with the target.
   Example: The affinity-seeker enthusiastically participates in an activity the target is known to enjoy.
10. *Inclusion of Other.* The affinity-seeker includes the target in the affinity-seeker's social groups.
    Example: The affinity-seeker plans a party for the target which numbers friends of the affinity-seeker as guests.
11. *Influence Perceptions of Closeness.* The affinity-seeker engages in behaviors that cause the target to perceive the relationship as closer than it has actually been.
    Example: The affinity-seeker uses nicknames and talks about "we," rather than "you and I," when discussing their relationship with the target.

TABLE 9.1

Continued

12. *Listening.* The affinity-seeker listens actively and attentively to the target.
Example: The affinity-seeker asks the target for frequent clarification and elaboration, and verbally recalls things the target has said.

13. *Nonverbal Immediacy.* The affinity-seeker signals interest in the target through various nonverbal cues.
Example: The affinity-seeker smiles frequently at the target.

14. *Openness.* The affinity-seeker discloses personal information to the target.
Example: The affinity-seeker reveals some social insecurity or fear to the target.

15. *Optimism.* The affinity-seeker presents himself or herself to the target as a positive person.
Example: The affinity-seeker focuses on positive comments and favorable evaluations when discussing mutual acquaintances with the target.

16. *Personal Autonomy.* The affinity-seeker presents herself or himself to the target as an independent, free-thinking person.
Example: The affinity-seeker demonstrates a willingness to express disagreement with the target about personal and social attitudes.

17. *Physical Attractiveness.* The affinity-seeker tries to look and dress as attractively as possible in the presence of the target.
Example: The affinity-seeker always engages in careful grooming before interacting with the target.

18. *Present Interesting Self.* The affinity-seeker presents herself or himself to the target as someone who would be interesting to know.
Example: The affinity-seeker discreetly drops the names of impressive or interesting acquaintances in the presence of the target.

19. *Reward Association.* The affinity-seeker presents himself or herself in such a way that the target perceives the affinity-seeker can reward the target for associating with him or her.
Example: The affinity-seeker showers the target with gifts.

20. *Self-Concept Confirmation.* The affinity-seeker demonstrates respect for the target and helps the target to "feel good" about herself or himself.
Example: The affinity-seeker compliments the target frequently.

21. *Self-Inclusion.* The affinity-seeker arranges the environment so as to come into frequent contact with the target.
Example: The affinity-seeker plans to have afternoon cocktails at the same time and place as the target.

22. *Sensitivity.* The affinity-seeker acts in a warm, emphatic manner toward the target.
Example: The affinity-seeker sympathizes with the target regarding a personal problem the target is experiencing.

23. *Similarity.* The affinity-seeker seeks to convince the target that the two of them share many similar tastes and attitudes.
Example: The affinity-seeker often points out things to the target that the two of them have in common.

24. *Supportiveness.* The affinity-seeker supports the target in the latter's social encounters.
Example: The affinity-seeker sides with the target in a disagreement the target is having with a third party.

25. *Trustworthiness.* The affinity-seeker presents herself or himself to the target as an honest, reliable person.
Example: The affinity-seeker consistently fulfills commitments made to the target.

their perceptions of, and feelings toward, this person. Six kinds of relationships were included in the investigation: work supervisor, romantic partner, close friend, acquaintance, roommate, and neighbor. Twenty-five participants responded to each kind of relationship. In one questionnaire, participants were asked to rate how characteristic it was for their selected person to use each of the strategies in his or her interactions with other people. These judgments were made on seven-point scales ranging from "extremely uncharacteristic" to "extremely characteristic." The other questionnaire included Rubin's (1970) liking and loving scales, which provided indications of how much participants liked and loved the individuals they selected. In addition, two three-item scales assessed perceptions of how satisfied their selected person was with his or her life and how effective he or she was at developing relationships.[2]

Participants' reports of how much they like and love the individuals they selected and their judgments of these individuals' *life satisfaction* and *social effectiveness* were correlated with the ratings for the 25 strategies in four separate multiple correlation analyses. The resulting correlations were large and significant: liking ($R = .74, p < .001$), loving ($R = .63, p < .001$), life satisfaction ($R = .56, p < .001$), and social effectiveness ($R = .58, p < .001$). These correlations clearly suggest that the more likely people are to use affinity-seeking strategies, the more positively they are viewed by those who know them. The results support our entering assumptions of the importance of affinity-seeking behaviors for social integration.

It is important to note that the very large multiple correlations obtained between each of the four dependent measures and the strategies were based on participants' judgments of how characteristically their selected person used the strategies *in general*. These correlations might be higher were participants to report the extent to which their selected person used each strategy when personally interacting with *them*. We suspected that when the level of behavior judgment is matched with the level of affective judgment, the relationships may be stronger than when the two are incongruent. A follow-up investigation involving a different group of 150 students was undertaken to test this possibility. The procedures for this investigation were identical to those used in the preceding study, with one exception: We asked participants to indicate whether or not ("Yes" or "No" response) their selected person used each of the strategies with *them personally*. Participants also completed the questionnaire consisting of Rubin's (1970) liking and loving scales and the measures of life satisfaction and social effectiveness.

Participants' scores on the four measures were correlated with the ratings for the 25 strategies in four separate multiple correlation analyses. The multiple correlations were once again very large and statistically significant: liking ($R = .80, p < .001$), loving ($R = .78, p < .001$), life satisfaction ($R = .73, p < .001$), and social effectiveness ($R = .67, p < .001$). As expected, these correlations were substantially larger than those obtained in the preceding investigation. The reason for this increase seems obvious: Affinity-seeking has its largest impact on the target individual. Taken together, these two studies provide strong support for a link between affinity-seeking and interpersonal attraction, life satisfaction, and social success.

QUESTION 3: HOW DO INDIVIDUAL DIFFERENCES AND SITUATIONAL CONTINGENCIES SHAPE AFFINITY-SEEKING?

In line with the model in Figure 9.1, we must account for factors that shape people's affinity-seeking behaviors. Earlier, we suggested that two especially important categories of constraints are individual differences and situational features. This section summarizes two studies that examined the relationship of affinity-seeking to several communication-related predispositions and to two situational parameters. The first study pertained to affinity-seeking *competence*—to what people *know* about affinity-seeking. The second study addressed the constraining influence of situations and personality on people's strategy *preferences*.

Strategy Competence (Knowledge)

A fundamental aspect of affinity-seeking concerns people's knowledge of the strategies: How do different people think they could generate affinity in various settings? It is unlikely that knowledge about affinity-seeking is invariant across situations or people; rather, both situational differences and personality variables probably affect the affinity-seeking strategies people generate. To probe this issue, we identified 10 individual differences that seemed especially relevant to the generation of affinity: communication apprehension (McCroskey, 1977); social anxiety, public and private self-consciousness (Fenigstein, Scheier, & Buss, 1975); Machiavellianism (Christie & Geis, 1970); interaction involvement (Cegala, 1980); self-monitoring (Snyder, 1974, 1979); assertiveness (Lorr & More, 1980); communicator style (Norton, 1978), and biological sex. Each characteristic has been related in numerous studies to important social and communication behaviors.

A comprehensive understanding of affinity-seeking must also address the role of situational characteristics in the selection of strategies. The appropriateness, effectiveness, and even the meaning of messages and actions are contingent upon the situations in which they occur (e.g., Forgas, 1979). We identified two situational dimensions suspected to affect the means by which people seek affinity: the social- or task-oriented context of the situation and the relative status of the individuals involved in the interaction. These dimensions are two of the four dimensions of situations identified by Wish, Deutsch, and Kaplan (1976).

One hundred and twenty undergraduates enrolled in basic communication courses participated in this study. Initially, the students were given one of four hypothetical situations varying on context (social versus task) and status dimensions (same-status other versus higher-status other). Status was manipulated by telling participants to assume they were interacting in a hypothetical situation with either a fellow student (same-status other condition) or one of their professors (higher-status other condition). The context dimension was operationalized by locating participants' hypothetical interactions at either a party (social context) or at a meeting (task context). After the situation was described, each student was told to:

come up with every technique possible that you think would generate liking in this setting. Don't pick out only the best ones or the ones that you always do—rather, list every technique you can think of.

After writing down the ways they could generate affinity in the particular situation, the students completed measures of the nine personality constructs discussed above and indicated their sex. Communication apprehension was measured with McCroskey's (1978) PRCA (*alpha* = .93). Social anxiety, public self-consciousness, and private self-consciousness were measured with Fenigstein, Scheier, and Buss's (1975) scales (*alphas*: .75, .89, .82, respectively). Machiavellianism was measured with the Mach-IV scale developed by Christie and Geis (1970) (*alpha* = .81). Interaction involvement was measured with Cegala's (1980) Interaction Involvement Scale (IIS), which taps three dimensions of interaction involvement: responsiveness (*alpha* = .88), attentiveness (*alpha* = .87), and perceptiveness (*alpha* = .84). Self-monitoring was measured with Snyder's (1974) self-monitoring scale (*alpha* = .84). Assertiveness was measured using Lorr and More's (1980) scale, which includes subscales for directiveness (*alpha* = .93), social assertiveness (*alpha* = .93), defense of rights and interests (*alpha* = .89), and independence (*alpha* = .88). Finally, communicator style was measured with Norton's (1978) ten-dimensional communicator style measure (average *alpha* = .79).

Participants generated 1,020 descriptions of affinity-seeking. Two coders independently coded 250 responses from 40 of the participants to assess the completeness and reliability of the typology. One coder classified the remaining responses. The coders classified each response as a particular strategy. Only 4.4 percent of the responses were unclassifiable, suggesting that the typology reflects the vast majority of affinity-seeking behaviors generated by the students. The coders agreed in 89 percent of the cases, indicating that the typology can be reliably employed.

Table 9.2 reports the cell and marginal frequencies, as well as the multiplier effects, for the coded responses in the form of a 25 × 2 × 2 (strategy × context × status) contingency table.[3] There were substantial differences in the frequencies with which the strategies were generated. Tests of significance based on z-scores ($p < .05$) indicated that

TABLE 9.2

Frequencies of Occurrence of Strategies[1]

| STRATEGIES | CONDITION (N = 120) | | | | SUBTOTALS | | | | TOTALS | |
| | Social (n = 60) | | Task (n = 60) | | Context | | Status | | | |
	Same (n = 30)	Higher (n = 30)	Same (n = 30)	Higher (n = 30)	Social	Task	Same	Higher	ʃ	Multiplier
Altruism	20	14	7	0	34	7	27	14	41	1.76
Assume Control	0	1	2	0	1	2	2	1	3	.13
Assume Equality	2	4	2	5	6	7	4	9	13	.56
Comfortable Self	7	9	7	7	16	14	14	16	30	1.29
Concede Control	1	0	0	0	1	0	1	0	1	.04
Conversational Rule-Keeping	74	46	70	55	120	125	144	101	245	10.52
Dynamism	5	1	3	5	6	8	8	6	14	.60
Elicit Other's Disclosures	22	20	16	31	42	47	38	51	89	3.82
Facilitate Enjoyment	17	11	15	4	28	19	32	15	47	2.02
Inclusion of Other	7	6	1	1	13	2	8	7	15	.64
Influence Perceptions of Closeness	0	1	1	0	1	1	1	1	2	.09
Listening	7	8	20	13	15	33	27	21	48	2.06
Nonverbal Immediacy	19	10	20	14	29	34	39	24	63	2.70
Openness	7	9	14	12	16	26	21	21	42	1.80
Optimism	5	3	11	8	8	19	16	11	27	1.16
Personal Autonomy	2	10	5	8	12	13	7	18	25	1.07
Physical Attractiveness	5	1	7	17	6	24	12	18	30	1.28
Present Interesting Self	12	11	5	7	23	12	17	18	35	1.50
Reward Association	2	4	5	1	6	6	7	5	12	.52
Self-Concept Confirmation	19	37	28	16	56	44	47	53	100	4.29
Self-Inclusion	28	15	8	5	43	13	36	20	56	2.40
Sensitivity	6	1	5	1	7	6	11	2	13	.56
Similarity	6	3	2	2	9	4	8	5	13	.56
Supportiveness	4	1	9	6	5	15	13	7	20	.86
Trustworthiness	3	14	8	11	17	19	11	25	36	1.55
TOTALS ʃ	280	240	271	229	520	500	551	469	1020	
Multiplier					1.02	.98	1.08	.92		.92

[1] The values under Condition are cell frequencies. The values under Subtotals are sums associated with each other. The marginal values are overall totals.

nine strategies were generated significantly more frequently than would be expected by chance. These strategies were, beginning with the most frequent strategy: *conversational rule-keeping, self-concept confirmation, elicit other's disclosures, nonverbal immediacy, self-inclusion, listening, facilitate enjoyment, openness,* and *altruism.* Three strategies were reported less frequently than would be expected by chance: *concede control, influence perceptions of closeness,* and *assume control.* There were no significant differences between the two levels of the context dimension or the two levels of the status dimension in the number of strategies generated.

The contingency table was subjected to a log-linear analysis (Bishop, Fienberg, & Holland, 1975) to assess the effects of the context and status manipulations on the production of strategies. In addition, the analysis assessed the association between the context and status dimensions, collapsing across the 25 strategies. A test of the independence model revealed a substantial amount of association in the table ($G^2 = 184.31$, df = 73, $p < .001$; G^2, the likelihood ratio statistic, tests the statistical significance of the association among dimensions in a contingency table). The interaction between the strategy and context dimensions accounted for over 47% of the association in the table ($p < .01$). This means that the frequency with which specific strategies were reflected in the participants' responses was dependent upon the context (social versus task). The strategy by status interaction accounted for an additional 26.8% of the association in the table ($p < .01$), indicating that the status of the target person affected the affinity-seeking strategies generated by the students. Together, the strategy by context and strategy by status interactions accounted for over 73% of the total association in the table. The context by status interaction accounted for less than 1% of the association in the table. The remaining association was accounted for by the saturated model, which includes all parameters. Thus, it appears that the differing frequencies are primarily a function of the strategy by context and strategy by status interactions.

To assess more precisely the nature of the two major interactions, chi-square tests of significance were computed for each strategy comparing: (1) the frequency of responses generated in the social setting to the frequency of responses generated in the task setting and (2) the frequency of responses generated in the same-status other condition to the frequency of responses generated in the higher-status other condition. For the strategy by context association, the participants in the social setting condition generated significantly ($p < .05$) more examples of *altruism, inclusion of other,* and *self-inclusion* than did participants in the task condition, but significantly fewer examples of *listening, physical attractiveness,* and *supportiveness.* For the strategy by status association, participants in the same-status other condition generated significantly more examples of *conversational rule-keeping, facilitate enjoyment, self-inclusion,* and *sensitivity* than did participants in the higher-status other condition, but significantly fewer responses representing the strategies *personal autonomy* and *trustworthiness.* The pattern of results strongly indicates that people's notions of appropriate affinity-seeking strategies are affected by situational characteristics.

The relationship of individual differences to affinity-seeking knowledge was examined by correlating the participants' scores on the personality measures with both the absolute number of classifiable responses generated (range: 1 to 28) and the number of strategies reflected in these responses (range: 1 to 14). The first measure is a productivity index assessing the number of behaviors respondents can come up with to generate liking. The second variable taps the breadth of respondents' knowledge—the number of affinity-seeking constructs (strategies) they describe. Several of the personality indices correlated significantly ($p < .05$) with the productivity and breadth measures. Self-monitoring was positively related to both productivity ($r = .22$) and breadth ($r = .20$) of affinity-seeking behavior, implying that socially sensitive people have a broad repertoire of strategies. Conversely, communication apprehension was negatively related to both productivity ($r = -.28$) and breadth ($r = -.24$), indicating that communication apprehension may be marked by a limited repertoire of affinity-seeking strategies. There was also an inverse relationship between social anxiety and the productivity index ($r = -.18$). Thus, one correlate of a limited construct system for generating affinity-seeking strategies may be generalized anxiety toward social situations, rather than simply toward communicating. The responsiveness subscale of the communicator style measure correlated positively with the productivity ($r = .17$) and breadth ($r = .16$) measures. Likewise, the directiveness subscale of the assertiveness measure correlated positively with productivity and breadth ($r = .16$ for both). The group means for males and females did not differ significantly on either the productivity or breadth variables.

Strategy Preferences

Two additional issues were investigated in a second study of factors affecting affinity-seeking decisions. First, we examined how the 10 personality constructs described above related to people's reports of how likely they are to use specific strategies. Note that this is a very different issue than the one raised in the preceding study where personality was related to people's knowledge of the strategies. Second, we continued to assess the shaping effects of situational characteristics on affinity-seeking, but this time we emphasized the self-reported likelihood of strategy use.

One hundred and sixty undergraduates enrolled in basic communication courses participated in the study. The students received a description of one of the four hypothetical situations used in the preceding investigation. After reading it, participants read randomly ordered descriptions of the 25 strategies and rated their likelihood of using each strategy on 7-point Likert scales with response options ranging from "very unlikely" to "very likely." Note how this study differs from the previous one. In the earlier study, participants generated lists of affinity-seeking behaviors, which were then coded into the typology. In this study, participants were given descriptions of the strategies, which were then eval-

uated for their likelihood of use in the assigned situation. After the students completed the likelihood ratings, they were given a booklet consisting of the personality measures used in the preceding investigation.

Numerous statistically significant relationships were found between the individual differences measures and strategy preferences. We will report only a few to illustrate the point that personality influences affinity-seeking behavior (see Bell & Daly, 1984, for the complete results). Communication apprehension was positively correlated with the strategy *concede control* ($r = .39$), and negatively correlated with the strategies *assume control* ($r = -.25$) and *dynamism* ($r = -.30$). Social anxiety was also negatively correlated with *dynamism* ($r = -.25$). As communication apprehension and social anxiety increase, there is also an increasing tendency to rely on strategies that place the other individual in charge of the interaction. Public self-consciousness was positively correlated with nine strategies, most notably *conversational rule-keeping* ($r = .28$) and *supportiveness* ($r = .32$), suggesting that as one's consciousness about self as a public object increases, so does the tendency to be positive toward other interactants. Private self-consciousness correlated significantly with *trustworthiness* ($r = .22$), indicating that introspecting individuals may highlight their dependability and reliability when attempting to generate affinity.

Machiavellianism related positively to respondents' likelihood ratings for *reward association* ($r = .28$), which is in line with the manipulative style of interaction defining the Machiavellianism construct. All three subscales of the interaction involvement construct were significantly correlated with some of the strategies. Responsiveness, for example, was negatively related to the likelihood ratings for *concede control* ($r = -.32$) and *supportiveness* ($r = -.24$), while perceptiveness and attentiveness were positively correlated with *listening* ($r = .21$ and .20, respectively). There were significant correlations between the likelihood ratings for nine strategies and self-monitoring, including *dynamism* ($r = .22$)

and *facilitate enjoyment* ($r = .32$). Thus, high self-monitors not only have more strategic constructs than their low-self-monitoring counterparts, as was found in the preceding study, they also report a greater likelihood of using many of these strategies.

All four subscales of Lorr and More's (1980) assertiveness measure had significant and readily interpretable relationships with the likelihood ratings. Directiveness, for instance, was positively correlated with *assume control* ($r = .24$) and *dynamism* ($r = .32$), and negatively correlated with *concede control* ($r = -.25$). Among other strategies, social assertiveness correlated positively with *dynamism* ($r = .30$). Defense of rights and interests was positively correlated with *assume control* ($r = .22$) and *personal autonomy* ($r = .29$), but was negatively correlated with *concede control* ($r = -.24$). Independence correlated negatively with *concede control* ($r = -.32$) and *supportiveness* ($r = -.32$). In short, all four dimensions of assertiveness correlated positively with active strategies and negatively with passive strategies.

All subscales of Norton's (1978) communicator style measure correlated significantly with the likelihood ratings of some strategies. Openness was positively correlated with *dynamism* ($r = .28$) and *openness* ($r = .43$). Friendliness was positively related to *conversational rule-keeping* ($r = .38$), *optimism* ($r = .36$), and *supportiveness* ($r = .32$). Animated was positively associated with *nonverbal immediacy* ($r = .28$) and *dynamism* ($r = .22$). Communicator image was also positively correlated with *dynamism* ($r = .31$), and impression leaving correlated positively with *dynamism* ($r = .29$). Attentive was positively related to *listening* ($r = .32$), *nonverbal immediacy* ($r = .29$), and *optimism* ($r = .27$). Dominant correlated positively with *assume control* ($r = .25$), *dynamism* ($r = .34$), and *openness* ($r = .26$). Dramatic was positively associated with *dynamism* ($r = .26$), *facilitate enjoyment* ($r = .30$), and *present interesting self* ($r = .29$). Finally, contentious related positively to *openness* ($r = .41$) and *personal autonomy* ($r = .28$). Together, these results suggest that people's preferences for strategies are strongly influenced by their general style of communicating.

Sex differences in the students' ratings of how likely they would be to use each of the 25 strategies were examined using *t*-tests ($p < .05$). Females reported being significantly more likely to use the strategies *conversational rule-keeping, elicit other's disclosures, listening, sensitivity,* and *similarity*. These strategies are characterized by their strong orientation toward the other person, conforming with commonly held sex role stereotypes.

The question of the extent to which likelihood ratings for the various strategies are dependent upon situational characteristics was probed through a 2 × 2 × 25 (context × status × strategies) repeated factor analysis of variance. The analysis of variance yielded four significant effects: a main effect for status (F, 1/156 df $= 32.28, p < .00001$), a main effect for strategy (F, 24/3744 df $= 61.35, p < .00001$), an interaction between strategy and context (F, 24/3744 df $= 3.19, p < .00001$), and an interaction between strategy and status (F, 24/3744 df $= 14.43, p < .00001$). None of the other effects was statistically significant. Examination of the means associated with the main effect for status suggested that when students supposed they were interacting with an individual of equal status they were more likely to use affinity-seeking strategies than when they were conversing with someone of higher status. The main effect for the repeated strategies factor indicates that there were large differences in likelihood of use ratings among the 25 strategies.

The significant interaction between strategy and context was probed in several ways. Rather than reporting all observed characteristics, a few will be highlighted (see Table 9.3 for all mean values). Participants reported greater likelihood of use of *openness* and *dynamism* in the task context than in the social setting. Alternatively, they were more likely to use *inclusion of other, assume equality,* and *concede control* in the social than in the task setting. The likelihood ratings for the remaining strategies were unaffected by context.

TABLE 9.3

Means and Standard Deviations (in parentheses) for the Likelihood Ratings[1]

| | CONDITION (N = 160) | | | | SUBTOTALS | | | | |
| | Social (n = 80) | | Task (n = 80) | | Context | | Status | | |
STRATEGIES	Same (n = 40)	Higher (n = 40)	Same (n = 40)	Higher (n = 40)	Social	Task	Same	Higher	MARGINALS
Altruism	4.00 (2.18)	4.80 (1.74)	4.25 (1.86)	5.08 (1.69)	4.40 (2.00)	4.66 (1.81)	4.13 (2.02)	4.94 (1.71)	4.53 (1.91)
Assume Control	3.68 (1.64)	4.38 (1.72)	3.13 (1.68)	4.05 (1.71)	4.03 (1.71)	3.59 (1.75)	3.40 (1.67)	4.21 (1.71)	3.81 (1.74)
Assume Equality	2.65 (1.58)	4.98 (2.01)	3.43 (2.01)	5.70 (1.70)	3.81 (2.14)	4.56 (2.17)	3.04 (1.84)	5.34 (1.88)	4.19 (2.18)
Comfortable Self	5.13 (1.53)	5.10 (1.39)	5.10 (1.46)	5.20 (1.70)	5.11 (1.46)	5.15 (1.56)	5.11 (1.49)	5.15 (1.54)	5.13 (1.51)
Concede Control	4.28 (1.78)	2.90 (1.86)	4.63 (1.53)	3.70 (1.87)	3.59 (1.94)	4.16 (1.76)	4.45 (1.66)	3.30 (1.90)	3.88 (1.87)
Conversational Rule-Keeping	6.08 (1.38)	5.35 (1.46)	5.70 (1.81)	5.23 (1.81)	5.71 (1.55)	5.46 (1.80)	5.89 (1.75)	5.29 (1.66)	5.59 (1.70)
Dynamism	4.98 (1.66)	5.08 (1.46)	4.43 (1.81)	4.53 (1.81)	5.03 (1.55)	4.48 (1.80)	4.70 (1.75)	4.80 (1.66)	4.75 (1.70)
Elicit Other's Disclosures	4.18 (1.91)	5.95 (1.30)	4.88 (1.77)	5.95 (1.17)	5.06 (1.85)	5.41 (1.59)	4.53 (1.86)	5.95 (1.23)	5.24 (1.73)
Facilitate Enjoyment	3.73 (1.89)	5.33 (1.51)	4.50 (1.55)	5.20 (1.70)	4.53 (1.88)	4.85 (1.65)	4.11 (1.76)	5.26 (1.60)	4.69 (1.77)
Inclusion of Other	2.30 (1.56)	5.48 (1.61)	3.75 (1.64)	6.18 (1.01)	3.89 (2.24)	4.96 (1.82)	3.03 (1.75)	5.83 (1.39)	4.43 (2.11)
Influence Perceptions of Closeness	2.40 (1.41)	3.78 (1.87)	2.05 (1.50)	3.98 (1.79)	3.09 (1.78)	3.01 (1.91)	2.23 (1.46)	3.38 (1.82)	3.05 (1.84)
Listening	5.95	5.68	5.73	5.40	5.81	5.56	5.84	5.54	5.69

TABLE 9.3
(Continued)

| STRATEGIES | CONDITION (N = 160) | | | | SUBTOTALS | | | | MARGINALS |
| | Social (n = 80) | | Task (n = 80) | | Context | | Status | | |
	Same (n = 40)	Higher (n = 40)	Same (n = 40)	Higher (n = 40)	Social	Task	Same	Higher	
Nonverbal Immediacy	5.35 (1.41)	5.43 (1.23)	4.75 (1.22)	5.60 (1.45)	5.39 (1.32)	5.18 (1.33)	5.05 (1.32)	5.51 (1.34)	5.28 (1.33)
Openness	3.20 (1.67)	4.13 (1.80)	2.62 (1.81)	3.20 (1.45)	3.66 (1.72)	2.91 (1.68)	2.91 (1.76)	3.66 (1.62)	3.29 (1.70)
Optimism	5.75 (2.05)	6.08 (1.87)	5.93 (1.66)	6.35 (1.90)	5.91 (2.01)	6.14 (1.79)	5.84 (1.88)	6.21 (1.06)	6.03 (1.93)
Personal Autonomy	3.48 (1.39)	4.20 (1.01)	3.63 (1.28)	4.08 (1.10)	3.84 (1.22)	3.85 (1.21)	3.55 (1.34)	4.14 (1.74)	3.84 (1.22)
Physical Attractiveness	5.58 (1.85)	5.78 (1.71)	5.50 (1.48)	6.18 (1.79)	5.68 (1.81)	5.84 (1.81)	5.54 (1.83)	5.97 (1.38)	5.76 (1.80)
Present Interesting Self	4.18 (1.71)	3.90 (1.48)	3.65 (1.26)	4.70 (1.26)	4.04 (1.59)	4.18 (1.41)	3.91 (1.59)	4.30 (1.72)	4.11 (1.50)
Reward Association	2.13 (1.81)	2.93 (1.61)	2.33 (1.77)	2.85 (1.76)	2.53 (1.71)	2.59 (1.83)	2.23 (1.80)	2.89 (1.61)	2.56 (1.77)
Self-Concept Confirmation	4.68 (1.62)	4.97 (1.53)	4.70 (1.51)	4.85 (1.70)	4.83 (1.61)	4.78 (1.62)	4.69 (1.56)	4.91 (1.70)	4.80 (1.61)
Self-Inclusion	2.58 (1.75)	4.50 (1.61)	3.18 (1.40)	5.18 (1.80)	3.54 (1.67)	4.18 (1.61)	2.88 (1.57)	4.84 (1.75)	3.86 (1.63)
Sensitivity	4.83 (1.48)	5.78 (2.01)	4.95 (1.86)	6.00 (1.39)	5.30 (2.01)	5.48 (1.92)	4.89 (1.70)	5.89 (1.17)	5.39 (1.99)
Similarity	4.13 (1.72)	4.00 (1.33)	4.10 (1.57)	4.40 (.99)	4.06 (1.60)	4.25 (1.41)	4.11 (1.64)	4.20 (1.92)	4.16 (1.50)
Supportiveness	4.68 (1.83)	4.30 (1.96)	4.90 (1.63)	5.13 (1.89)	4.49 (1.88)	5.01 (1.76)	4.79 (1.72)	4.71 (1.72)	4.75 (1.82)
Trustworthiness	6.35 (1.67)	5.90 (1.70)	5.70 (1.30)	5.88 (1.65)	6.13 (1.68)	5.79 (1.48)	6.03 (1.49)	5.89 (1.72)	5.95 (1.60)
MARGINALS (across strategies) means	4.25 (.77)	4.83 (1.46)	4.30 (1.22)	4.98 (1.24)	4.54 (1.19)	4.64 (1.23)	4.27 (1.07)	4.90 (1.35)	4.59 (1.21)
standard deviations	(1.74)	(1.64)	(1.54)	(1.60)	(1.70)	(1.68)	(1.69)	(1.63)	(1.88)

¹ The values under Condition are individual cell means and standard deviations. The values under Subtotals are main effects and standard deviations while the Marginal values are overall means and standard deviations.

The significant interaction between strategy and status was also probed. Participants indicated they were significantly more likely ($p < .05$) to use the following strategies when interacting with the same-status individual than with the higher-status person: *altruism, assume control, assume equality, elicit other's disclosures, facilitate enjoyment, influence perceptions of closeness, inclusion of other, openness, optimism, personal autonomy, reward association, self-inclusion,* and *sensitivity.* On the other hand, they were significantly more likely to use *conversational rule-keeping* and *concede control* when interacting with a higher-status individual. Use of other strategies did not vary due to level of status. The two significant interactions suggest that people are sensitive to situational differences in their estimates of how likely they would be to use different strategies. Moreover, they reliably differentiate among strategies given varying situational characteristics.

This second investigation of situational and personality influences on affinity-seeking yielded additional information about the nature of the process. First, there are broad and meaningful relationships between communication-oriented individual differences and self-reported estimates of the likelihood of using various strategies. Second, individuals adjust their likelihood of using the strategies to meet differing situational demands.

QUESTION 4: WHAT IS THE MULTIVARIATE STRUCTURE OF AFFINITY-SEEKING?

The final question addressed in this article concerns the structure of the affinity-seeking typology. An understanding of the structure of the typology is important for two reasons. First, it is a step in reducing the size of the typology so as to explain more parsimoniously affinity-seeking processes. Obviously, it would be useful to develop eventually a typology of more general, overarching strategies. Second, it is important to identify basic dimensions that undergird the 25 strategies, for discovery of

these dimensions offers substantial explanatory power. Participants in this final investigation were 327 undergraduates enrolled in basic communication courses. Two hundred and sixty-eight of the students participated in Phase I, while the remaining 59 participated in Phase II.

Phase I: Assessment of Strategy Similarity

To obtain measures of the perceived similarities among the strategies, each participant received an envelope containing 25 randomly ordered cards, each describing a different strategy. Participants sorted the cards into piles of similar strategies, using whatever unstated criteria for assessing similarity they felt were appropriate. No limit was placed on the number of piles that could be formed. The resulting co-occurrence data were converted into a 25×25 matrix of dissimilarity judgments with cell entries representing the proportion of times every pair of strategies was placed into separate piles. The matrix was subjected to nonmetric multidimensional scaling (MDS) using the Statistical Analysis System (SAS, Reinhardt, 1980) version of the ALSCAL procedure (Takane, Young, & De Leeuw, 1976). Solutions for one to six dimensions were derived, based on a Euclidean model. The optimal configuration was determined by comparing the stress values and interpretability of the six solutions. Stress is an index of the "badness-of-fit" between the MDS model and the original data. Although stress was small enough to justify selection of the two-dimensional solution (stress $= .17$), the three-dimensional solution had a somewhat better fit (stress $= .12$). The four-, five-, and six-dimensional solutions were not substantially better fits than the three-dimensional solution. Because the three-dimensional solution appeared to offer no advantages in interpretation over the more parsimonious two-dimensional configuration, the two-dimensional representation was chosen as the optimal solution. This solution, reported in Figure 9.2, accounted for 87% of the variance of the disparities, suggesting a good fit.

FIGURE 9.2

Two-Dimensional Configuration Obtained by the ALSCAL Program for Perceived Similarity Among 25 Affinity-Seeking Strategies. Vectors for the Rating Scales Defining the Dimensions Were Determined by Linear Regression Analyses.

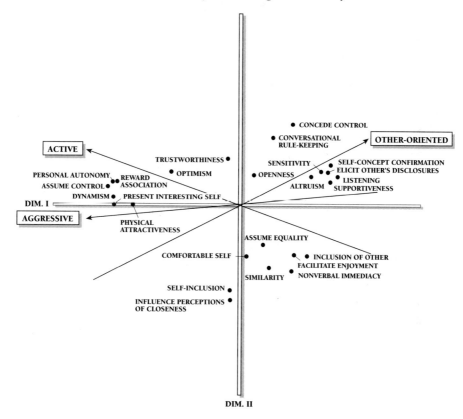

Phase II: Interpretation

Directions in the space. The two-dimensional solution was interpreted using two complementary procedures. The first was a linear regression procedure outlined by Kruskal and Wish (1978), which identified directions in the configuration. A direction represents an underlying dimension of meaning that accounts for the positioning of points in the MDS configuration. Identifying directions in the multidimensional space provides insight into the underlying characteristics of the strategies the re-

spondents found salient when assessing strategy similarity. Furthermore, it helps explain the location of each strategy in the configuration, relative to other strategies.

Fifty-nine students rated each strategy on 14 seven-point semantic differential scales which were considered potentially relevant to affinity-seeking—e.g., passive-active, manipulative-not manipulative, and ineffective-effective. For each of the 14 scales, ratings on every strategy were averaged across the 59 raters to obtain a measure of the strategy's perceived passivity, manipulation, etc. The coordinate axes were then used as independent variables to predict the means of the strategies on each of the 14 ratings in 14 separate analyses. A semantic differential scale is generally considered to provide a good interpretation of the stimulus space of an MDS solution if the multiple correlation (R) resulting from the regression of the rating on the coordinates is statistically significant at $p < .01$ and exceeds .80. If a given rating has a sufficiently high multiple correlation with the coordinates of the MDS solution, the standardized regression weights for the dimensions are converted to direction cosines. The inverse cosines of these values are then determined to plot a vector through the configuration that represents the direction of the semantic differential scale.

The three external criteria with sufficiently high multiple correlations with the coordinates were active-passive ($R = .83$), aggressive-unaggressive ($R = .94$), and self-oriented–other-oriented ($R = .79$). Their projection onto the space is represented in Figure 9.2. An ordering of the strategies along the active-passive vector can be found by visually projecting a perpendicular line from the points representing each strategy to the vector. When this is done, the strategies *assume control, personal autonomy, reward association, dynamism, present interesting self,* and *physical attractiveness* emerge as very active strategies. These strategies are generally characterized by taking control of an interaction and by physical activity. On the other end of the continuum are such passive strategies as *listening, inclusion of other, supportiveness, elicit other's disclosures,* and *facilitate enjoyment.*

The location of the aggressive-unaggressive vector indicates that the strategies *assume control, dynamism, personal autonomy, present interesting self, reward association,* and *physical attractiveness* were perceived to be very aggressive; the strategies *listening, supportiveness, elicit other's disclosures,* and *self-concept confirmation* fell on the unaggressive end of the line. The aggressiveness vector better differentiates the strategies in the upper right-hand corner of the configuration from the strategies in the lower right-hand corner than does the activity vector.

Though the strategies *listening, supportiveness, elicit other's disclosures,* and *self-concept confirmation* were perceived to be about as active as the strategies *inclusion of other, nonverbal immediacy,* and *facilitate enjoyment,* the latter strategies are perceived as being more aggressive, a finding that jibes intuitively.

The final significant rating occurred for orientation. The strategies judged to be active and aggressive focused, by and large, on the person attempting to generate liking. Conversely, behaviors such as *elicit other's disclosures, listening,* and *supportiveness* were perceived as being other-oriented. The strategies that are perpendicular to the middle region of this vector include *assume equality, inclusion of other, trustworthiness, facilitate enjoyment, nonverbal immediacy,* and *similarity.* These strategies appear to be both self- and other-oriented. For example, the person who uses *trustworthiness* is essentially saying, "You can trust me"; *similarity* communicates, "I am like you"; and *assume equality* says, "You and I are of equal status and worth."

Overall, the regression analyses suggest that respondents attended to the activity level of the strategies, the aggressiveness of the strategies, and the individual upon whom the strategies were focused when making similarity assessments. Possibly the underlying structure of the typology includes other unidentified directions.

Cluster Analysis. The second procedure used was a hierarchical clustering of the coordinates of each strategy on the two dimensions of the final MDS solution. This approach is helpful in understanding the meaning of regions in the space. Such regions, sometimes referred to as "neighborhoods," are particularly useful in identifying characteristics shared by sets of stimuli included in a study.

The results of the hierarchical cluster analysis of the coordinates for the two-dimensional solution are reported in Figure 9.3. From the standpoint of interpretability, the optimal clustering solution yielded seven clusters, with only the *optimism* strategy failing to cluster. Beginning at the left region of the space, there is a clustering of the following strat-

FIGURE 9.3

Results of a Hierarchical Clustering Analysis of the Coordinates for the Two-Dimensional Representation of 25 Affinity-Seeking Strategies. The Figure Represents Clustering Through Step 17.

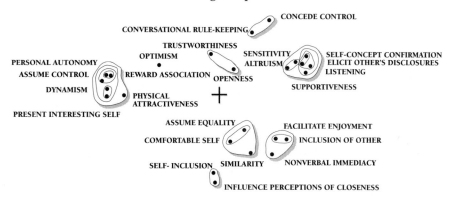

egies: *personal autonomy, reward association, assume control, dynamism, present interesting self,* and *physical attractiveness.* These six strategies involve aggressive action to either obtain control over another person, the function of the first three strategies, or to become highly visible, a primary function of the latter three. This cluster was labeled CONTROL AND VISIBILITY.

Moving clockwise, the strategies *trustworthiness* and *openness* join together to form a single cluster. The development of trust is apparently the shared characteristics of these two strategies. *Trustworthiness* involves an attempt to present oneself as "trustable," while *openness* functions to suggest that one is "trusting" enough to disclose to the other. This cluster was labeled MUTUAL TRUST.

A third cluster includes the strategies *conversational rule-keeping* and *concede control.* Because both are characterized by a high degree of adaptability to another individual, this cluster was labeled POLITENESS.

A second cluster of other-oriented strategies can be found nearby. This fourth cluster includes strategies that communicate CONCERN AND CARING

to another individual: *self-concept confirmation, elicit other's disclosures, listening, supportiveness, sensitivity,* and *altruism.*

Moving to the lower right-hand corner of the space, two clusters pertain to sociability. The first cluster was labeled OTHER INVOLVEMENT because it includes strategies that seek to draw another person into one's social activities and to signal interest. The strategies in this cluster are: *facilitate enjoyment, inclusion of other,* and *nonverbal immediacy.* Nearby, there is a grouping of the strategies *self-inclusion* and *influence perceptions of closeness.* These two strategies function to integrate oneself into the activities of another person and to signal a desire for a relationship. This cluster was referred to as SELF-INVOLVEMENT.

The strategies in the last cluster focus on the COMMONALITIES between the individual attempting to generate liking and the target person. This is accomplished by pointing to *similarities* between oneself and the other, by *assuming equality* between oneself and another, and by acting very casual and at ease with the other party (*comfortable self*).

What is the multivariate structure of the typology? At one level, the study identifies three dimensions (directions) underlying the typology. At another level, it suggests the existence of meaningful clusters of affinity-seeking behavior of a higher generality than are found in the present typology. These clusters may eventually serve as the basis for a reduced typology, one that identifies a smaller set of more general, but conceptually distinct strategies.

GENERAL DISCUSSION

Affinity-seeking is the process by which individuals attempt to get other people to like and to feel positive toward them. This article introduced the affinity-seeking concept, proposed a model of the process, argued for its importance as a critical communication concern, and explored some of its important features. Our studies can be summarized as follows: First, the 25-strategy typology developed to address the preliminary question operationalized the affinity-seeking construct thoroughly and reliably. Second, people who were thought to use many affinity-seeking strategies were judged likable, socially successful, and satisfied with their lives. Third, personality and situational features influence both the number of strategies a person produces and the self-reported likelihood of using each strategy. Fourth, at least three dimensions underlie the affinity-seeking construct: the *activity level* of the strategies, the *aggressiveness* of the strategies, and the *focus* of the strategies. Moreover, the strategies cluster into seven more general groupings that eventually may serve as a basis for a refined typology.

How does the affinity-seeking construct fit within the overall scheme of communication inquiry? Affinity-seeking offers an integrative concept highlighting a function shared by many communication behaviors. Moreover, affinity-seeking relates to numerous other communication variables. The strategies reflect behaviors of long-standing interest to communication researchers. In addition, communicator characteristics such as communication apprehension, assertiveness, and communicator style influence both the choice and effectiveness of affinity-seeking messages. Perhaps most important, the affinity-seeking construct provides a dynamic, communication-based approach to a topic that has long been of central concern to social scientists—interpersonal attraction. Unlike much of the earlier theory and research in this area, the affinity-seeking construct recognizes that *how* people feel toward us is, in part, a function of our own communication behaviors—behaviors that we can, and often do manipulate to facilitate liking.

The implications of individual studies were highlighted in earlier sections. Rather than repeat these comments, we now raise some general issues about the affinity-seeking construct and sketch a preliminary plan for future work. For the sake of clarity, our discussion of these issues is organized around the four components of the affinity-seeking model.

The first set of questions raised by the model pertains to the antecedent factors which foreshadow affinity-seeking. Investigations of these factors should prove quite fruitful. A number of issues come to mind; most obvious, the reasons people seek affinity should be explored. When and why do people attempt to generate liking? What are the characteristics of situations that motivate affinity-seeking? In focusing on these questions, the influence of culture merits consideration. Culture doubtless exerts a major influence on people's values about affinity-seeking: when it is right, appropriate, important, etc.

The motivation for seeking affinity within established relationships also should be explored. The present research assumed that affinity-seeking is a major interactional goal in the initiation of interpersonal relationships. Although this assumption is sound, it should be beneficial to broaden the focus of affinity-seeking to examine its importance in more intimate relationships. How does the decision to seek affinity change as relationships move from acquaintanceship to intimacy? Probably people shift their goals away from affinity-*seeking* to affinity-*maintaining*. Are the behaviors that sustain good feelings markedly different from those that foster amity? These questions are the focus of in-progress studies of affinity-seeking in marriage and in the classroom.

A related question concerns the role of affinity-seeking in relational disengagement. We suspect that relationships which are coming apart may be characterized not so much by negative exchanges as by neutral behavior; in other words, people may signal a desire for relationship termination by suspending affinity-seeking behaviors. If this suspicion is accurate, the relevance of affinity-seeking to interactional goals ranging from relational initiation to cessation needs to be examined. Some preliminary data also suggest that the kinds of strategic enactments change. As a relationship begins to falter, certain strategies disappear from the exchange and others appear. Some simple, almost etiquette-perfect strategies become paramount as people, failing in intimacy, move to a more polite, less personal level.

The relationship of affinity-seeking to other social objectives also merits attention. Liking can be both an end in itself and a means to other communicative goals. One obvious illustration is compliance-gaining (Marwell & Schmitt, 1967); though the pursuit of compliance is clearly distinct from the pursuit of liking, there are interesting overlaps between the two. People often attempt to generate liking when seeking compliance. Likewise, compliance-gaining attempts sometimes generate liking. Compliance-gaining attempts may, thus, function as affinity-seeking strategies. Other examples readily come to mind. Affinity-seeking strategies can be used to conceal deception, and deception can be used to generate affinity. Affinity-seeking can help communicators obtain information, and information can be elicited to generate affinity. Affinity-seeking no doubt interrelates with numerous communicative functions and goals.

The constraints placed on affinity-seeking also warrant investigation. Our studies demonstrate the influence of personality, status, and context on affinity-seeking behavior; however, other constraints should also be addressed. Most notably, the nature

of affinity-seeking competence needs examination. People doubtless vary in their ability to generate liking. Concern for affinity-seeking competence underlines the importance of developing instruments for assessing ability in this critical realm of social interaction. The free generation technique we have used to measure knowledge of affinity-seeking shows promise as an assessment tool, but more research is required to assess its reliability and validity. It may also prove beneficial to develop a self-report measure of people's general skills at affinity-seeking. Such work is in progress.

If deficiencies in affinity-seeking are associated with negative personal and social outcomes, the teachability of these skills becomes important. Can people be taught to generate affinity more effectively? Social skills training programs probably can be developed to help individuals master some of the affinity-seeking strategies. Implicit in this concern for people's affinity-seeking abilities is the question of how individuals learn to generate liking in the first place. Some strategies represent little more than socialized etiquette, but others are very different. Their etiology poses an interesting question.

The third issue suggested by the affinity-seeking model concerns the nature of the strategic activities enacted during attempts to generate liking. Most pressing is the need for studies dealing with the behavioral manifestations of affinity-seeking within ongoing interactions. It is important to devise coding schemes of affinity-seeking behaviors for use in future research. Development of a behavioral scheme within the framework of the present typology, while possible, raises thorny problems. Communication acts are often multifunctional, and the behaviors that generate affinity are no different. Moreover, individual behaviors may be less important than *patterns* of action representing a particular strategy. Some strategies also involve discrete acts while others are characterized by continuous displays of behaviors. Nonetheless, identifying behavioral indicators is a crucial next step.

Studies of the sequential and longitudinal aspects of affinity-seeking should also prove insightful.

Affinity-seeking can be conceptualized as a multiple-act phenomenon which typically occurs over time (see Jaccard & Daly, 1980). While recognizing that affinity-seeking often involves multiple acts, it was necessary to first explore characteristics of the specific strategies before moving to examine the ways they are integrated and sequenced. Studies of the sequencing and integration of strategies within an encounter, as well as the use of strategies across encounters, are in order. Are there, for example, "introductory strategies" and "strategies of last resort"? Is there a grammar of affinity-seeking? How does strategy use change over time as individuals build a relationship? Does affinity-seeking proceed in a stage-like manner?

The last issue raised by the model concerns the consequences, or target responses, of affinity-seeking. Studies will, we believe, demonstrate convincingly that effective affinity-seekers have more personal relationships characterized by stronger ties. Of particular importance are studies of the evaluative consequences of affinity-seeking. What are the consequences of affinity-seeking behavior in situations such as a job interview or an initial social encounter? How do people react to enactments of the different strategies? Are some strategies more positively regarded than others? In general, people should react more positively to persons who enact affinity-seeking displays readily. There may, however, be important and interesting exceptions. For instance, when an individual's affinity-seeking behavior is attributed to an ulterior motive, these actions may be labeled as "ingratiation" and become ineffective, if not counterproductive. Finally, the dyadic nature of affinity-seeking should be considered in future work, since any sophisticated account of the process must recognize that an individual's affinity-seeking behaviors both influence and are influenced by the party from whom liking is desired.

Most researchers recognize the value of a functional approach to the study of human communication. In this article we have explored the nature and some of the correlates of another function of communication—one that is extremely important in everyday life. An account of affinity-seeking processes is important both in its own right and because such an account can shed light on other aspects of communication.

ENDNOTES

[1] Copies of this paper are available from the authors whose address is: Department of Speech Communication, University of Texas, Austin, TX 78712.

[2] Items composing the life satisfaction scale were: "This person seems to have a very happy and satisfying life," "This person is a very lonely individual," and "This person is usually very happy." Items composing the social effectiveness scale were: "This person has difficulty making friends," "This person could have almost anyone for a friend that s/he so desired," and "This person is not very popular." Participants indicated their level of agreement with each of the six items on seven-point Likert scales. The alpha reliabilities of both these scales were .77.

[3] A multiplier effect represents the standardized value of a row, column, or subtable effect against the general level of the table. A multiplier effect of 1.0 indicates the effect is no larger or smaller than expected, given the general level of the table. A multiplier of, say, .50 indicates the effect is only half the expected size given the general level of the table. Similarly, a multiplier effect of 1.5 indicates the effect is 50% larger than expected given the general level of the table.

REFERENCES

Argyle, M. (1972). *The psychology of interpersonal behavior* (2nd ed.). Harmondsworth: Penguin.

Bell, R. A., & Daly, J. A. (1984) Affinity-seeking: Its nature and correlates. Paper presented at the annual convention of the International Communication Association, San Francisco.

Berscheid, E., & Walster, E. (1978). *Interpersonal attraction.* Reading, MA: Addison-Wesley.

Berscheid, E., & Walster, E. (1974). Physical attractiveness. In L. Berkowitz (Ed.), *Advances in experimental social psychology.* (Vol. 7, pp. 158-216). New York: Academic Press.

Bishop, Y. M. M., Fienberg, S. E., & Holland, P. W. (1975). *Discrete multivariate analysis.* Cambridge, MA: MIT Press.

Byrne, D. (1971). *The attraction paradigm.* New York: Academic Press.

Carnegie, D. (1937). *How to win friends and influence people.* New York: Simon & Schuster.

Cegala, D. J. (1980). Interaction involvement: A cognitive dimension of communicative competence. *Communication Education, 30,* 109-121.

Christie, R., & Geis, F. L. (1970). *Studies in Machiavellianism.* New York: Academic Press.

Clark, R. A., & Delia, J. (1979). Topoi and rhetorical competence. *Quarterly Journal of Speech, 65,* 187-206.

Crowne, D. P., & Marlowe, D. (1964). *The approval motive: Studies in evaluative dependency.* New York: Wiley.

Daly, J. A., & Stafford, L. (1984). Correlates and consequences of social-communicative anxiety. In J. A. Daly & J. C. McCroskey (Eds.), *Avoiding communication: Communication apprehension, reticence, and shyness* (pp. 125-144). Beverly Hills, CA: Sage.

Davis, M. S. (1973). *Intimate relations.* New York: Free Press.

Fenigstein, A., Scheier, M. F., & Buss, A. H. (1975). Public and private self-consciousness: Assessment and theory. *Journal of Consulting and Clinical Psychology, 43,* 522-527.

Forgas, J. P. (1979). *Social episodes: The study of interaction routines.* London: Academic Press.

Jaccard, J., & Daly, J. (1980). Personality traits and multiple-act criteria. *Human Communication Research, 6,* 367-377.

Kruskal, J. B., & Wish, M. (1978). *Multidimensional scaling.* Sage University Paper series on Quantitative Applications in the Social Sciences, Series No. 07-011. Beverly Hills, CA: Sage.

Lorr, M., & More, W. W. (1980). Four dimensions of assertiveness. *Multivariate Behavioral Research, 15,* 127-138.

McCroskey, J. C. (1977). Oral communication apprehension: A summary of recent theory and research. *Human Communication Research, 4,* 78-96.

McCroskey, J. C. (1978). Validity of the PRCA as an index of oral communication apprehension. *Communication Monographs, 25,* 192-203.

Marwell, G., & Schmitt, D. R. (1967). Dimensions of compliance-gaining behavior: An empirical analysis. *Sociometry, 30,* 350-364.

Norton, R. (1978). Foundations of a communicator style construct. *Human Communication Research, 4,* 99-112.

Reinhardt, P. S. (1980). *SAS supplemental library user's guide.* Raleigh, NC: SAS Institute.

Roloff, M. E. (1976). Communication strategies, relationships, and relational change. In G. R. Miller (Ed.), *Explorations in interpersonal communication* (pp. 173-195). Beverly Hills, CA: Sage.

Rubin, Z. (1970). Measurement of romantic love. *Journal of Personality and Social Psychology, 16,* 265-273.

Snyder, M. (1974). The self-monitoring of expressive behavior. *Journal of Personality and Social Psychology, 30,* 526-537.

Snyder, M. (1979). Self-monitoring processes. In L. Berkowitz (Ed.), *Advances in experimental social psychology* (Vol. 12, pp. 85-128). New York: Academic Press.

Takane, Y., Young, F., & De Leeuw, J. (1976). Nonmetric individual differences multidimensional scaling: An alternating least squares method with optimal scaling features. *Psychometrika, 42,* 7-67.

Wish, M., Deutsch, M., & Kaplan, S. (1976). Perceived dimensions of interpersonal relations. *Journal of Personality and Social Psychology, 33,* 409-440.

10

Cognition and Communication in the Relationship Process

LESLIE A. BAXTER

For the past six years, I have been researching how people communicatively accomplish romantic relationship development, maintenance and repair, and disengagement (Baxter, 1979, 1982, 1983, 1984, 1985, in press; Baxter & Bullis, in press; Baxter & Philpott, 1980, 1982; Baxter & Wilmot, 1983, 1984, 1985; Bullis & Baxter, 1986; Dindia & Baxter, 1986; Wilmot & Baxter, 1983, 1984; Wilmot, Carbaugh, & Baxter, 1985). To a large extent, personal relationships research has mirrored other social scientific work in viewing communication as a mere conduit of more causally forceful psychological and sociological factors (Pearce & Cronen, 1980). By contrast, a view of relationships as communicative accomplishments presumes that communication is a central force in its own right. The significant role accorded communication in creating the social order can be traced to the later Wittgenstein's (1953) focus on language-in-use. However, a view of relationships as communicative accomplishments should not be taken as a deterministic stance toward the power of communication. Rather, communication and the social order relate dialectically with communication constructing people's conceptions of the social order just as the constructed social order frames our understanding of communication. The dialectic or reflexive relationship between communication and the social order also has its roots in the later Wittgenstein's (1953) work, in particular his metaphor

of "language games." Language-in-use (i.e., communication) gains its meaning because of the context in which it is framed, and simultaneously such language use enacts the contextual frame. For example, the choice of a given chess move is made in the context of knowing the rules of the game of chess and the move gains its meaning only through that contextual frame; simultaneously, the particular chess move accomplishes and makes real a game of chess. The Wittgensteinian assumptions that frame my research program are evident in several contemporary social theories, including the Coordinated Management of Meaning (Pearce & Cronen, 1980), symbolic interaction (Blumer, 1969; Mead, 1934), language action (Frentz & Farrell, 1976), ethogeny (Harré, 1980), and structuration (Giddens, 1979).

Collectively, my program of research affords insights into two aspects of relationship cognitions or knowledge. First, this research suggests that relationship parties have a cognitive repository of relationship process knowledge in addition to their conceptions of various static relationship types. Such process cognitions or schemata serve to frame any given communicative action, thereby assisting actors in their communicative choice-making and in making sense of such communicative actions. Second, this research program gives insights into the functions and uses of relationship cognitions in the communicative interaction between relation-

From Baxter, L. A. (1987). Cognition and communication in the relationship process. In R. Burnett, P. McGhee, & D. Clarke (Eds.), *Accounting for relationships: Explanations, representation, and knowledge* (pp. 192–212). New York: Methuen & Co.

ship parties. Specifically, the argument will be advanced that relationship process knowledge allows relationship parties to use ambiguous communicative actions to their advantage in creating certain relational outcomes.

Extant work in social cognition and relationships focuses largely on one type of relationship knowledge: cognitive conceptions of various relationship types (Argyle & Henderson, 1984, 1985; Davis & Todd, 1982, 1985; La Gaipa, 1979; Rands & Levinger, 1979; Wish & Kaplan, 1977; Wright, 1985). Although researchers in this domain may differ on the form such relationship knowledge takes, i.e., whether it is in the form of prototypes, systems of behavioral rules, or underlying dimensions (cf. Planalp, 1985), they collectively give us insight into people's conceptions of such relationship types as acquaintanceship, platonic friendship, and the romantic relationship. Insightful as this body of work is, however, it generally affords us a static state view of relationships, in contrast to a dynamic view of processes of relationship emergence and change. Relationship types do not materialize instantaneously but rather are constructed over time through the interactions of the relationship parties. Further, once a given relationship type has formed, it is not static but typically is ever changing and fluid. In short, extant work in social cognitions of relationships has deemphasized relationship processes in favor of relationship products. It is a primary thesis of this article that interactants are guided by relationship process cognitions in addition to their conceptions of various static relationship types. Relationship process cognitions appear to be organized into two orders of specificity: (1) cognitions relevant to various relationship trajectories, i.e., conceptions of how relationships typically develop and dissolve; and (2) cognitions relevant to relationship-ing, i.e., conceptions of strategic actions by which to accomplish various relational outcomes.

In addition, existing work in social cognitions of relationships deals largely with the psychological functions of such cognitions for the individual, rather than the social and communicative functions

(Clark & Delia, 1979). Although we know that relationship cognitions affect the person's information acquisition and retrieval functioning (Planalp, 1985; Roloff & Berger, 1982), relatively less attention has been given to how this relationship knowledge is communicatively used in interaction between relationship parties (the substantial research program by Berger and his colleagues is a notable exception). It is a second thesis that relationship cognitions allow relationship parties to rely heavily on indirect cueing to accomplish much of their relationship interaction, rather than using direct communication about their relationship. Contrary to the popular stereotype encapsulated in the expression "What we need is communication" (Katriel & Philipsen, 1981), the typical relationship process is not dominated by open, direct relationship communication, but rather involves the construction of a web of ambiguity by which parties signal their relationship indirectly.

With this overview in mind, the chapter first turns to a discussion of the two types of relationship process knowledge that have surfaced in the research program. Process trajectory knowledge provides a general framework of what growth and dissolution processes are like; it provides a cognitive backdrop for the more particularized knowledge relationship parties have of strategic actions that can be performed during these processes. Reciprocally, however, such strategic actions are the "stuff" of which relationship trajectories are constituted. Thus, cognitive knowledge of process trajectories and strategic actions mutually inform one another and jointly reveal what people think of relationship *processes*.

RELATIONSHIP PROCESS KNOWLEDGE: TRAJECTORIES AND STRATEGIC ACTIONS

Process Trajectory Cognitions

Several of the studies in this research program suggest that people have cognitive schemata, i.e., coherent conceptual frameworks (Craik, 1979), for the ways relationships grow and disengage. Built on the basis of observation and experience, these relationship trajectory schemata allow the relationship parties to make sense of the sequence of episodes that occur when relationships are forming and breaking up. In the formative state of romantic relationship growth, for instance, the parties' growth trajectory schemata allow them to gauge whether the relationship's progress is "on course," to predict which sorts of events should occur next in the trajectory sequence, and to make retrospective sense of episodes that have occurred already in the relationship's interaction history. Such trajectory schemata are distinct from the parties' relationship type schemata; whereas the former address the issue of how romantic relationships form (or decline), the latter address the issue of what constitutes the romantic relationship type.

Process trajectory schemata have been derived from two types of data across several studies in the research program: respondent reactions to hypothetical relationship situations, and respondent verbal accounts of their own relationship experiences. In response to hypothetical scenarios, the assumption is that respondents "call up" their schemata of the ways in which such situations play themselves out in real life (Harré & Secord, 1973). In providing accounts of their own relationship experiences, the assumption is that respondents use their schemata as a guide to sense-making, focusing on features of their experience that are salient in their own schemata. Both types of data affirm the author's belief in the subjectively constructed nature of social life. Thus, no claims are made about objectifiable behaviors enacted by relationship parties in actual relationship encounters. Based on the assumption that reality is subjectively constructed, actors' perceptions and schemata are valid sources of data about relational life. Obviously, however, a useful complement to the research in this program would be observation of relationship interaction in order to determine how relationship knowledge plays itself out in actual communicative action.

In an attempt to determine whether people have growth trajectory and disengagement trajectory schemata, Wilmot and Baxter (1983) presented 263 subjects with hypothetical conversations that were attributed to one of two relationship types (cross-sex friends or cross-sex romantic partners) and to one of two relationship trajectories (growing closer or growing apart). Although the conversational stimuli were identical for all subjects and afforded substantial specificity of information, subjects interpreted the relational meaning of the conversations quite differently depending on the process trajectory in which the conversations were framed. The growth trajectory frame produced perceptions of the conversations as more disclosive, honest, and direct than the conversations framed in the dissolution trajectory. The relationship type did not affect perceptions of the conversations, suggesting that process trajectories do not differ for these two relationship types. The results of this study support the claim that people do indeed have process trajectory schemata, which they use to interpret relationship interactions. Further, these schemata point to disclosive and direct communication as an important feature that differentiates growth and dissolution trajectories.

Additional work in the research program has elaborated on both the growth trajectory and dissolution trajectory schemata. In an attempt to move beyond hypothetical relationships and to expand our understanding of the growth trajectory schema, the relationship partners from forty cross-sex romantic couples were interviewed independently for all of the significant turning-points that occurred in the development of their relationships (Baxter & Bullis, in press; Bullis & Baxter, 1986). Because the extant analyses of these turning-point interviews have focused on facets of the relationship other than the growth trajectory schema, I will use this occasion to delve into this account data in some detail.

It is apparent that two mutually exclusive pattern variations exist in people's growth trajectory schema: the proverbial love-at-first-sight, which we labeled the Whirlwind trajectory, and the gradual Friendship First trajectory. Both of these thematic variations featured reported increases in disclosure and directness over time, but both were heavily punctuated by instances of indirectness and incomplete disclosures as well.

Only a minority of the respondents actually reported experiencing the Whirlwind trajectory, yet several verbal accounts made reference to this type of commonly known growth trajectory. One female respondent indicated surprise in experiencing a Whirlwind trajectory because she didn't think "it" happened that way: "We got together at a party, no big deal, and then he kissed me goodnight. And then the next day I saw him and it just happened. Those kinds of things usually never happen. I mean, if something happens at a party it's usually disastrous. It usually never works out." By contrast, a male respondent expressed pleasant surprise that his romantic relationship did not experience a Whirlwind trajectory but instead typified the second type of growth trajectory people made reference to, the Friendship First trajectory:

[The relationship] was totally different. . . . It just doesn't seem like what you're supposed to do. You're supposed to catch her first glance and fall in love, but this was more like the 6000th glance. . . . I think it's real important to a relationship to grow the way we did, a gradual year of becoming real good friends and then deciding that there might be something more that you want to experience.

The most frequently reported growth trajectory was the gradual progression from friendship to romantic involvement. For some respondents, this Friendship First trajectory reflected the opinion expressed above by the male respondent that friendship was a desirable antecedent foundation for a romantic relationship. For other respondents, the Friendship First trajectory occurred out of necessity, as when the other party was hesitant to commit to a romantic relationship due to a third party rival or general caution against involvement. For yet other respondents, the Friendship First trajectory was a safe and secure way to continue enjoying one another's company without worrying about loss of autonomy in becoming a couple.

In addition to the basic conceptual distinction between Whirlwind and Friendship First trajectories, three secondary themes emerged in respondent accounts: perceived symmetry of involvement, perceived effortfulness, and perceived degree of autonomy separate from the couple relationship. These secondary themes were evident in the accounts of both Whirlwind and Friendship First trajectories. The theme of symmetry of involvement captures whether both relationship parties were in agreement on the progress of their relationship (the symmetrical condition), in contrast to the asymmetrical state in which one party wanted a romantic relationship more than the other party. The asymmetrical state was described by respondents in terms of distinct pursuer-pursued roles, as this verbal account excerpt from a male indicates: "I was kind of surprised to find us caught up in the whole pursuit thing. I was the definite pursuer and she was the pursuee. I thought I was in a commanding portion of the market. Then I was invaded by a competitor [a rival] and needed to reanalyze my strategies."

Although unequal involvement creates an effortful situation for the more involved party, the effortful–effortless theme surfaced in other respondent accounts, as well. In general, this dimension captures whether or not the growth trajectory is conceived of as an inherently problematic phenomenon that necessitates interactional work to overcome difficulties. One female indicated the presence of the effortfulness feature in her growth schema by expressing surprise that her relationship's history had been so problem-free:

We got to know each other *really* quickly. And spent a lot of time together. . . . It seems like things are too perfect sometimes and they shouldn't be like that. It [the relationship] just keeps elevating itself and I don't know if there are any specific times . . . we haven't had any times when things have declined.

A male respondent repeated the effortfulness theme in his declaration that "All relationships have their ups and downs." Yet another female respondent supported the same theme in her statement that

"All relationships are kind of crazy at first; everything's so idealized. Then reality catches up." In contrast, several respondents revealed that the presence of effort and interactional work signaled that the relationship "just wasn't meant to be" or that it "wasn't natural." As one male expressed the effortless theme: "In my view of relationships, you can't push and you can't hold back. You just 'be.' Some people are lucky and they have similar backgrounds and environments—they just fit real well together. For others, it just won't work out."

The third theme captures the degree of individual autonomy the relationship parties maintained during their relationship's growth. Some couples' growth trajectories were characterized by limited autonomy, or what one female respondent aptly referred to as the "glue couple syndrome." Other relationship histories were characterized by greater independence by the relationship parties, either throughout the entire relationship's history or after experiencing an intensive "glue syndrome" stage. One female respondent referred to this more independent trajectory as "knowing that you're always two separate individuals apart from the relationship that's forming."

Given that the majority of relationships described in the turning-point interviews illustrated the Friendship First trajectory, it is useful to inquire whether respondents have clear conceptions of how the transformation from friendship to romantic partners occurs. The transformation issue is an important one, given that there are fuzzy boundaries between the cross-sex friendship and cross-sex romantic relationship types with many attributes in common (Davis & Todd, 1982; Wilmot & Baxter, 1984). Relationship parties do have clear conceptions of what events transform the relationship to one of romantic involvement. The first display of physical affection (Wilmot & Baxter, 1984) and the first "date," as opposed to simply "spending time together" (Bullis & Baxter, 1986), are the salient schema features that transform a relationship from platonic friendship to romantic involvement.

In sum, two basic growth trajectory schemata are suggested: the Whirlwind trajectory and the Friendship First trajectory. These two basic patterns capture how quickly the relationship parties become romantically involved. In addition, three secondary schema themes surfaced in people's talk about relationship growth: symmetry of involvement, degree of effort, and degree of autonomy the parties maintain outside the relationship. These three secondary themes emerged with both of the two basic trajectory types.

Two studies in the research program have further explored the dissolution trajectory schema. Baxter and Philpott (1980) presented respondents with a story completion task whose story start involved a couple desiring unilateral or bilateral disengagement. In completing the story the way they thought it would really happen, two break-up patterns were evident. One trajectory was characterized by themes of procrastination, equivocation, and indirect hinting by the breaker-upper, leading to several escalatory exchanges between the parties of increasing frustration, hurt, and anger to both parties. Labeled the Protracted Indirectness trajectory, this pattern matches quite closely the schema of reduced disclosure and directness found in the Wilmot and Baxter (1983) study reported above. The second trajectory, labeled the Swift Directness trajectory, featured a less protracted exchange between the parties with direct expression of wants and desires. Although negative emotional reactions were present in this trajectory as well, they were generally envisioned as less intense than in the Protracted Indirectness trajectory.

Although these two dissolution trajectories were created in response to hypothetical relationship situations, they match quite closely the accounts respondents have provided in making sense of their own relationship break-ups (Baxter, 1984). In analyzing the accounts of ninety-seven romantic relationship break-ups, Baxter (1984) noted the salience of four schema themes: (1) whether the break-up was unilaterally or bilaterally desired; (2) whether the dissolution was negotiated directly or indirectly; (3) whether the dissolution was relatively swift as opposed to protracted with several cycles or rounds of negotiation; and (4) whether the parties experienced ambivalence and sought repair actions at some point. The most common pattern was a unilateral, protracted, and indirect trajectory, a finding that bears close resemblance to the Protracted Indirectness trajectory noted above. That is, the typical disengagement was reported as one-sided in which the breaker-upper sought to signal his/her desire to end the relationship through indirect cues such as hinting; such hinting usually failed, which led to additional "rounds" of signaling from the breaker-upper to the broken-up-with. Much less common was a pattern of swift and direct dissolution.

On the whole, many of the themes evident in the dissolution trajectory schema appear similar to those for the growth trajectory schema. The protracted–swift rate of dissolution accomplishment appears to parallel the gradual–immediate distinction noted in the growth trajectories for onset of romantic involvement. The symmetry of involvement theme noted for the growth trajectory schema bears close resemblance to the unilateral–bilateral desire to seek dissolution. Effortfulness appears to be pervasive in all variations of the break-up trajectory schema, perhaps with the single exception of the bilateral, direct, and swift scenario (Baxter, 1984), whereas growth trajectories allowed both effortful and effortless variations. Last, the ambivalence experienced during dissolution bears on the issue of autonomy versus interdependence that was noted for the growth trajectory schema. In short, people appear to make sense of relationship beginnings and endings by using the same basic set of relational themes.

The growth trajectory and dissolution trajectory schemata that have emerged in this research program are quite general in nature. They do not entail a detailed sequence of events but rather capture the overall themes of the two processes. Subsequent work is needed to determine whether people have detailed event-by-event sequential conceptions of these processes. Work is needed, as well, on people's conceptions of the "middle process" between the end-points of growth and dissolution. Do people have schemata of the process dynamics once

relationship parties have established a mutually acceptable relationship state? The next section discusses an initial piece of research related to this stage of relational life, but much more work is needed. Research also needs to address people's schemata for relationships "at risk." What conceptions do people have of what a troubled relationship looks like? Obviously, this middle process between formation and dissolution holds enormous importance for how the parties choose to function in established relationships.

This section has addressed people's general trajectory schemata of what relationship growth and dissolution processes are like. It has painted a broad portrait of how people regard these processes. The next section attempts to fill in some of the details of this broad portrait in discussing people's conceptions of strategic actions during the processes of relationship growth, maintenance and repair, and dissolution. Although cognitions of strategic actions are at a different level of specificity than the trajectory schemata just discussed, they obviously hold relevance to people's process knowledge of relationships.

Strategic Action Cognitions

Many of the studies in this research program have probed people's conceptions of the strategic actions that collectively comprise the relationship processes of developing, maintaining and repairing, and dissolving romantic relationships. "Strategic action" refers to the rational means–ends nature of communicative activity regardless of whether the parties are consciously aware of their strategic choice-making at the time of its enactment. Indeed, as Duck (1985) suggests, relationship parties probably do not invest much conscious cognitive effort in their day-to-day relationship encounters. Baxter and Philpott (1985) have found that conscious strategic choice-making occurs only in circumstances of high importance, difficulty, or unpredictability. Conceptualization based on rational means–ends rather than cognitive effort locates strategic action as a social as opposed to psychological phenomenon. That is, from a Wittgensteinian view, communicative action takes on the meaning of "strategic" based on properties of the social context in which it is embedded. Cognitive structures about strategic action have been variously referenced in the literature, e.g., scripts (Abelson, 1981), memory organization packets (Schank, 1980), and procedural records (Greene, 1984). Greene's (1984) action assembly theory posits a hierarchical order of specificity to such cognitive structures, with four basic levels of abstraction:

1. The interactional representation, i.e., a general conception of how current interaction goals are to be achieved.
2. The ideational representation, i.e., the level at which the specific content of discourse is conceived.
3. The utterance representation, where syntactic, lexical, and phonological features are conceived.
4. The sensorimotor representation, the most specific of the levels, in which the action is actually produced.

The strategic action work discussed in this section can best be captured at the interactional representation level.

Individuals usually have multiple goals in any given encounter. What are the types of goals most salient in relationship dynamics? Consistent with Berger's uncertainty reduction theory (Berger & Bradac, 1982; Berger & Calabrese, 1975), relationship parties seek to acquire information relevant to the current situation before them in order to reduce uncertainty. Second, as articulated in the politeness theory of Brown and Levinson (1978), relationship parties seek to maintain the face of self and the other. A useful distinction has been drawn between two types of face: (1) positive face, i.e., one's desire to be liked, respected, and valued; and (2) negative face, i.e., one's desire to maintain a sense of control or freedom from constraint (Brown & Levinson, 1978). Third, the relationship parties seek to estab-

lish their desired relational outcomes, whether formation of a mutually acceptable romantic relationship, maintenance and repair of same, or dissolution of the relationship.

In order to expedite the discussion of strategic action interactional representations, research will be organized around the three process stages of relationship formation, maintenance and repair, and dissolution.

Relationship Formation

The person seeking to form a specific relationship with another faces several informational burdens. As articulated elsewhere (Baxter & Philpott, 1982), this person must establish two critical attributional perceptions in the other party: (1) that one is interested in having the relationship with the other party; and (2) that one is worthy of the other party's investment in such a relationship. Clearly, these two perceptions are not entirely independent of one another, as one's interest in the relationship can constitute evidence of one's worth. The critical feature about these attributions is their conjunctive nature, i.e., both are necessary. How the person strategically establishes these two perceptions in the other party is dependent on what information has been obtained about the other party relative to: (1) his or her realization that one is interested; and (2) his or her realization that one is worthy and that the relationship is desirable.

Direct relationship communication affords the most efficient strategic action for both acquiring information on the other party's current perceptions and for altering those perceptions. Direct talk maximizes clarity, thereby reducing the likelihood of misunderstandings. However, strategic action during the growth trajectory is not typified by direct relationship communication, but rather features highly selective instances of directness embedded in a dominant pattern of indirectness. Such indirectness, if appropriately enacted, allows the relationship parties to acquire and present information "off the record," thereby reducing risk to positive and negative face (Brown & Levinson, 1978). If a person indirectly indicates his or her desire for romantic involvement with the other party and is rebuffed, the person's face nonetheless can be maintained. An indirect "bid" for involvement entails sufficient "slippage" to allow the person to deny the attributed meaning. Indirect as opposed to direct self-presentation of oneself as a worthy relationship partner also maintains the person's face; excessive directness runs the risk of being disliked because of too little modesty. In addition, a rebuff from the other party would probably occur indirectly as well, further contributing to the person's face-saving. Further, indirect strategic action maintains the other party's face as well. A "bald on record" declaration of one's desire for romantic involvement or a direct inquiry about feelings puts the other party "on the spot" by demanding an answer, potentially threatening his or her negative face.

Several studies in the research program document the salience of indirect strategic action over direct relationship communication during the relationship development period. In a study of "taboo" topics in opposite-sex relationships, Baxter and Wilmot (1985) found that the status of the relationship was a pervasive topic partners avoided, especially if the relationship was in a transition between platonic friendship and a romantic relationship. The reasons given by respondents for avoiding direct relationship talk shed insight into their conceptions of the relationship growth process. The most frequent reason expressed by respondents for a taboo against relationship talk was the threat such directness would pose for the relationship. Many respondents perceived that commitment levels were not yet equal; explicit talk about the relationship would force recognition of this discrepancy, thereby jeopardizing the relationship's future. Interestingly, the concern over a discrepancy in commitment levels was equally present for both the more committed and the less committed parties; the more committed did not want the less com-

mitted to feel pressured by the discrepancy in feelings, and the less committed did not want the more committed to become angry by the imbalance. Clearly, these respondents perceived themselves embedded in the asymmetrical involvement trajectory presented above. The second most frequent reason for the relationship talk taboo was vulnerability to the individual's face posed by the possibility of something the other party would say. The third reason expressed against direct relationship talk was the perceived effectiveness of tacit strategic action. Fourth, some respondents expressed a taboo against relationship talk because it constituted interactional work in what was ideally conceived as an effortless process, reflecting the effortful–effortless theme discussed above. Last, respondents avoided direct relationship talk because it was premature, appropriate only in already close relationships. The last reason is quite consistent with the turning-point data discussed above, in which respondents reported avoiding relationship talk about significant turning-points in the early stages of development (Baxter & Bullis, in press).

The perception that increased disclosure and directness characterize the relationship growth process, as reported above, appears to be contradicted by the avoidance of direct talk about the state of the relationship. The contradiction may be more apparent than real. Direct relationship talk may be used for symbolic purposes to confirm and validate relationship closeness once the parties have assured that closeness through tacit and indirect strategic actions, in contrast to use of direct relationship talk as a strategy of negotiating greater closeness. This analysis is consistent with the final reason expressed above for avoidance of direct relationship talk. This almost ritualistic use of relationship talk has also been noted by others (Katriel & Philipsen, 1981).

In addition to the avoidance of direct talk about the state of the relationship, the taboo topics study (Baxter & Wilmot, 1985) revealed other subject areas that are strategically avoided in developing relationships. Activities outside the relationship, prior romantic relationships, relationship norms (especially sexual norms), and known issues of disagreement were also taboo because of their perceived threat to the relationship's growth potential. Collectively, people's taboo topics strongly suggest a conception of relationship growth as a fragile endeavor best handled through the perceived safety afforded by indirect strategic actions.

But what indirect actions are likely to be employed? Baxter and Wilmot (1984) found a rich repertoire of strategic actions that relationship parties reported employing to discern the other party's perceptions. Labeled "secret tests," these strategies are unknown to the partner and test his or her relational feelings concerning the worth of the relationship investment. Most commonly reported were endurance tests that reduce the other's rewards in order to determine his or her depth of commitment. For instance, the person might create a situation in which the partner must choose between the relationship and something else that is desired. Second most frequently mentioned were triangle tests, in which the person creates a situation with a real or hypothetical third party where the other party can be checked for fidelity or jealousy. For example, one might create a fictitious rival in order to see whether or not the partner displays jealousy. To test fidelity one might strategically monitor how the partner behaves with an attractive member of the opposite sex in a party situation. Respondents also reported use of separation tests in which contact with the other party is broken in order to monitor whether and when the other initiates reuniting. Other indirect secret tests mentioned less frequently than the strategic actions just mentioned include: (1) inquiry with third parties who might have information about the partner's feelings; (2) public presentation as "a couple" in order to check the partner's reaction to the presentation; and (3) a variety of "testing the water" tests through hints, jokes, etc. Taken as a whole, these secret test strategies suggest that evidence of commitment is exceedingly important to the growth trajectory. In fact, many of the significant turning points people identified in the growth of their relationships revolved around this salient feature (Bullis & Baxter, 1986).

People also have a repertoire of indirect strategies for conveying their interest in the other party and in convincing the other party to become involved in a relationship. Baxter and Philpott (1982) found that strategies for relationship initiation can be reduced to five basic types:

1. *Other Enhancement:* the giving of compliments or other signals that demonstrate that one thinks highly of the other.
2. *Similarity Display:* the demonstration of commonality with the other.
3. *Self-Presentation:* the presentation of a unique and favorable image of oneself to the other.
4. *Favor Rendering:* the doing of favors or giving of rewards.
5. *Inclusion:* activity that brings the other person into one's interaction proximity.

The strategies of Other Enhancement and Inclusion appear most directly related to the perceptual attribution that one is interested in and likes the other. Similarity Display and Self-Presentation permit one to display attributes by which to prove one's worthiness to the other party. Favor Rendering would seem to contribute simultaneously to both key attributions—that one is interested and that one is appealing. Because a display that one likes the other is nothing more than positive face work, the detailed set of positive politeness tactics presented by Brown and Levinson (1978) has direct relevance to the relationship initiation process. Recent work in affinity-seeking (Bell & Daly, 1984) also holds relevance.

Although the various elaborations of strategic action repertoires that have emerged in the research differ in detail and labels, they collectively affirm that relationship parties seek to establish the two critical attributes of liking the other and being likable. Further, these various strategy repertoires support the strong role that indirect cueing plays during the growth trajectory process.

Relationship Maintenance and Repair

As noted above, this research program has not yet examined people's maintenance and repair trajectory schemata. However, some initial work has recently been completed on people's strategic actions for maintenance and repair, and the findings of this research shed some beginning insight on the conceptions people hold of this middle process between relationship formation and dissolution. An initial study with both partners from forty-five marriages followed by a replication with fifty marital couples (Dindia & Baxter, 1986) revealed a rich repertoire of over fifty strategies by which parties attempt to maintain and repair the marital relationship, which conceptually reduce to a much smaller set of basic strategy types. The respondents in this study, married an average of fourteen years, were asked to list all the things they did when attempting to accomplish preventive maintenance, i.e., to keep their relationship healthy, and to accomplish restorative repair, i.e., to restore their relationship's health in the presence of problems. Space limitations preclude an exhaustive review of all of the study's findings, but the most frequently listed strategy types merit discussion for what they reveal about people's conceptions of maintenance and repair processes. Overall, the most frequently reported strategies were increased time spent together and increased general interaction (e.g., talk about the day). The conception of relational difficulty implicit in these two strategies appears to be a drifting apart of the relationship partners. In other words, these strategies suggest relational drift as a central theme in people's cognitive schemata of the middle period of relational life.

Spending more time together and general interaction perhaps offset such relational drift. However, if the sorts of difficulties experienced by marital partners are more complex than relational drift, as the literature on marital complaints would suggest (Harvey, Wells, & Alvarez, 1978; Kelley, 1979; Kitson & Sussman, 1982), general talk and increased contact might be quite ineffective if not counterproductive. Research is needed on the actual efficacy of strategic repertoires used by relationship parties in maintaining and repairing their own relationship.

Although maintenance and repair goals shared several strategies in common, including the two mentioned above, specialized strategies emerged for each type of goal. Specifically, direct relationship talk was likely to be used for repair purposes and strategically avoided for relationship maintenance. By contrast, relationship maintenance was significantly more likely than repair to involve the strategies of introducing novelty to offset routine and more responsible execution of one's marital role obligations (e.g., lawn work, house cleaning, etc.). This partial specialization of strategies suggests that preventive maintenance and restorative repair are related but different processes as conceived by these respondents. Additional work is needed to tease out the similarities and differences in these processes. As Duck (1984) has recently argued, coping with relational difficulty is not a monolithic phenomenon but rather a complex set of processes that vary in important ways. The findings of this study support Duck's analysis.

At a minimum, the ability of these marital partners to generate strategies of maintenance and repair is suggestive of their conception of the middle period of relationships as inherently effortful with ongoing interactional work. More particularly, the strategies suggest a perceived need to counter the problem of relational drift. Finally, the strategies suggest that preventive and restorative interactional work are perceived as partially similar but also distinct processes.

Relationship Dissolution

Many studies in this research program have been devoted to strategic actions by which parties dissolve their relationships (Baxter, 1979, 1982, 1983, 1984, 1985, in press; Baxter & Philpott, 1982; Baxter & Bullis, in press; Wilmot, Carbaugh, & Baxter, 1985). Following Duck's (1982) stage model of dissolution, Baxter (in press) suggests that strategic actions vary depending on where the parties are in the dissolution phase.

The initial stage of dissolution, the so-called private decision-making stage, involves a private assessment of the other party and of the relationship as sources of satisfaction and dissatisfaction. The party's primary goal is to decide whether or not to dissolve the relationship. This period is high in uncertainty (Duck, 1982), motivating the person to strategically acquire information about the other party's likelihood of resisting a dissolution "bid," the other's motivation to make changes necessary to make the relationship more satisfying, and the possible reactions of social network members to a dissolution of the relationship. Direct relationship talk potentially affords the greatest efficiency of action, just as it does during the growth trajectory. However, relationship parties who are contemplating dissolution opt instead for indirectness, largely because its threat to face is less than the threat posed by bald-on-record directness (for a detailed discussion of this point, see Baxter [in press]). Thus, this preliminary phase of dissolution is conducive to indirect secret test strategies, as noted above for the growth trajectory. However, the purpose of such tests is obviously different than during the relationship development stage.

Assuming that a person concludes the private decision-making stage with a decision to dissolve the relationship, the information burden shifts to that of informing the other party of one's desire and persuading him or her to accept it. Baxter and Philpott (1982) argue that dissolution at this stage involves the mirror opposites of the conjunctive attributions discussed above for relationship initiation. That is, the two critical attributions to create for the other party are: (1) that one no longer is interested in the relationship; and (2) that one no longer is worthy of the other's continued investment in the relationship. However, unlike relationship initiation in which the counterparts of these attributions function conjunctively, Baxter and Philpott (1982) suggest that one of these attributions may suffice to accomplish dissolution. That is, one could employ strategic actions that signal

one no longer is interested in the relationship *or* one could employ strategies so costly to the other party that he or she initiates dissolution action. In practice, these two attributions often overlap at the level of strategic action. The mere realization that one's partner doesn't wish to continue creates relational spoilage that is often sufficient evidence that the relationship is no longer worthy of continued investment (McCall, 1982). Further, as discussed above under the dissolution trajectory schema, how one signals the first attribution often convinces the other party of one's lack of worth.

Although many levels of specificity could be discussed in terms of reported strategic dissolution actions (see in particular Baxter [1982, 1984, 1985]), the functional thrust of these strategic actions is their relevance to these two critical attributions. Because it is generally less stressful psychologically to view oneself as the breaker-upper rather than the broken-up-with (Hill, Rubin, & Peplau, 1976), most of the strategic actions concentrate on the first attribution, i.e., conveying that one no longer is interested in a relationship with the other.

Basically two clusters of strategic action have emerged concerning this first attributional task (Baxter, in press). The first, labeled Distance Cueing, involves a variety of indirect signals to the other party that convey loss of interest, e.g., reduced breadth, depth, and valence of self-disclosure. The second cluster involves direct relationship talk with the other about one's feelings. These two clusters of strategies hold implications for both parties' face. Because of the likelihood that directness will be met with anger and hostility from the other party, the disengager's positive face is better served by the indirectness of Distance Cueing. Relationship talk is perceived as more effortful than Distance Cueing, thus evoking greater threat to the disengager's negative face in his or her desire for freedom from constraints. Unfortunately, face-saving on behalf of the disengager is often at odds with the other party's face. The other's positive face is threatened under any circumstance, but the threat is probably greatest with Distance Cueing for it doesn't even show the basic courtesy of a face-to-face accounting (Wilmot, Carbaugh, & Baxter, 1985). Similarly, the other party's negative face is likely to be more threatened with Distance Cueing; at least a direct talk allows the other party some sense of control in the situation.

As noted above, indirectness is a frequent strategic choice by the disengager, who clearly opts for his or her own face instead of face-saving on the other's behalf. However, directness does become more likely under some circumstances: when the other is not culpable in the relationship's demise (Baxter, 1982), when future contact with the other party is anticipated (Baxter, 1982), and, most importantly, when the prior relationship was very close (Baxter, in press). The greater likelihood of directness in very close relationships may imply that parties' close relationship schemata obligate face work on the other's behalf as just compensation for the former good times once experienced in the relationship. Alternatively, directness may be employed in close relationships simply because the web of interdependence is so complex that indirectness is inadequate to the dissolution task (e.g., determining who gets which household goods).

The second attribution, which involves giving the other party sufficient cause to seek dissolution himself or herself, is accomplished by a myriad of tactics, which collectively are labeled Cost Escalation (Baxter, 1985). Such actions as becoming hypercritical toward the other may drive the other party to the conclusion that the relationship is no longer worth the investment. However, Cost Escalation is probably a strategy of last resort for two reasons. First, as noted above, it is more desirable to be perceived as the breaker-upper than as the broken-up-with. Second, in light of the costly face implications for the other party that accompany the Distance Cueing strategies, these frequently employed strategies targeted at the first critical attribution simultaneously accomplish the second critical attributional task as well.

Taken collectively, the dissolution strategies research supports the dissolution trajectory schema presented above in featuring reduced disclosure and reduced directness. Although directness is ev-

ident in some selected circumstances, indirectness is a prevalent strategic action. Both Distance Cueing and Cost Escalation fall short of directly confronting the other party with one's dissolution desire.

Although direct relationship talk may afford the greatest efficiency in accomplishing one's relationship goals due to its clarity, the strategic action research consistently suggests that relationship parties opt instead for a variety of indirect actions. Such indirectness serves the face work needs of the user. The final section addresses the functional value of relationship process cognitions in allowing such heavy reliance on indirect cueing actions.

THE FUNCTIONS OF
SOCIAL COGNITIONS IN
RELATIONSHIP INTERACTION

The central argument of this section is that it is people's well-developed relationship process cognitions that allow indirectness to be employed quite efficiently in relationship interaction. In turn, such indirectness reduces the face threat otherwise present in direct communication; because indirect meanings are not formally codified, the user has some "slippage" through which to deny attributed intentions if they prove damaging or ineffectual. Certainly, indirectness lacks the explicit clarity of bald-on-record direct talk and thus is not as efficient as directness; indirectness does increase the likelihood of misunderstandings because it is more ambiguous by definition. But relationship parties, heavily reliant on indirectness, *do* manage to accomplish relationship-ing. If misunderstandings were omnipresent, indirectness would be totally inefficient and relationship parties would be incapable of conducting their relational lives. Obviously something intervenes to prevent ubiquitous misunderstanding of indirect signals. That "something" is commonly understood relationship process knowledge.

As King and Sereno (1984) argue, the relational meaning derived from any action is based on Grice's (1975, 1978) principle of implicature. In

Grice's view, implicated meaning is triggered when a communicative act violates what is expected for the situation at hand. Thus "the date" evokes the implicated meaning that the relationship is being transformed from platonic to romantic; the event violates the norm of platonic relationships and makes relational sense only at the implicated level. Similarly, a Distance Cueing tactic such as reduced self-disclosure violates an expectation that romantic partners disclose openly to one another; this violation triggers the implicated meaning that the relationship is being transformed to one of reduced closeness. Our ordinary language use is characterized by many instances of strategic implicature that have become conventionalized through frequent and recurring use. Similarly, many of the indirect signals used in relationship-ing can be regarded as conventionalized. They are commonly used and commonly understood, composing the substance of our process cognitions about how relationship processes work. However, because such implicated relational meanings are not formally codified by the culture, the user has the "slippage insurance," which assures him or her reduced threat to face. It is difficult to deny meaning that is directly coded; implicatures, by contrast, can be denied if this is useful. In short, then, our relationship process cognitions consist of many conventionalized implicatures about relational meaning. Conventionalization produces the efficiency of indirect cueing. Thus, indirectness is interaction work designed to "have one's cake and eat it, too": sufficient efficiency with minimized threat to face.

However, it is important to challenge the assumption that all misunderstandings constitute inefficiency. As Sillars and Scott (1983) observe in their review of the perceptual agreement research in close relationships, not all perceptual disagreements harm the relationship. Baxter and Bullis (in press), for example, noted the absence of a significant correlation between current satisfaction with the relationship and whether or not the two partners agreed in the perceptions of important turning-points in their relational history. The crucial issue is whether the discrepant cognitions are compatible with one another or whether they block one another's constructions of social reality (Sillars & Scott, 1983).

Indirect cueing, which involves compatible but different process schemata between the two relationship parties, may be quite functional to the relationship, especially early in the developmental process. Early on, the two parties lack a stockpile of relational investments and rewards necessary to cope effectively with difference and conflict (Altman & Taylor, 1973). Direct relationship talk at that point would force premature realization of cognitive differences, whereas indirect cueing allows the parties to maintain the illusion of agreement so long as the parties' schemata do not block one another. Thus, indirect cueing may "buy time" for the relationship parties, allowing them to construct a relational foundation sufficient to cope at a later point in time with differences and conflicts surrounding how relationships can and should function.

REFERENCES

Abelson, R. P. (1981). Psychological status of the script concept. *American Psychologist, 36,* 715-729.

Altman, I., & Taylor, D. (1973). *Social penetration: The development of interpersonal relationships.* New York: Holt, Rinehart & Winston.

Argyle, M., & Henderson, M. (1984). The rules of friendships. *Journal of Social and Personal Relationships, 1,* 209-235.

Argyle, M., & Henderson, M. (1985). The rules of friendships. In S. Duck & D. Perlman (Eds.), *Understanding personal relationships* (pp. 63-84). London: Sage.

Baxter, L. (1979). Self-disclosure as a relationship disengagement strategy: An exploratory investigation. *Human Communication Research, 5,* 215-222.

Baxter, L. (1982). Strategies for ending relationships: Two studies. *Western Journal of Speech Communication, 46,* 223-241.

Baxter, L. (1983). Relationship disengagement: An examination of the reversal hypothesis. *Western Journal of Speech Communication, 47,* 85-98.

Baxter, L. (1984). Trajectories of relationship disengagement. *Journal of Social and Personal Relationships, 1,* 29-48.

Baxter, L. (1985). Accomplishing relationship disengagement. In S. Duck & D. Perlman (Eds.), *Understanding personal relationships* (pp. 243-265). London: Sage.

Baxter, L. (in press). Self-disclosure and relationship disengagement. In V. J. Derlega & J. Berg (Eds.), *Self-disclosure: Theory, research and therapy.* New York: Plenum.

Baxter, L., & Bullis, C. (in press). Turning points in the development of romantic relationships. *Human Communication Research.*

Baxter, L., & Philpott, J. (1980, November). Relationship disengagement: A process view. Paper presented at the Speech Communication Association.

Baxter, L., & Philpott, J. (1982). Attribution-based strategies for initiating and terminating friendships. *Communication Quarterly, 30,* 217-224.

Baxter, L., & Philpott, J. (1985, February). Conditions conducive to awareness of communication activity. Paper presented at the Western Speech Communication Association Convention.

Baxter, L., & Wilmot, W. (1983). Communication characteristics of relationships with differential growth rates. *Communication Monographs, 50,* 264-272.

Baxter, L., & Wilmot, W. (1984). Secret tests: Social strategies for acquiring information about the state of the relationship. *Human Communication Research, 11,* 171-201.

Baxter, L., & Wilmot, W. (1985). Taboo topics in close relationships. *Journal of Social and Personal Relationships, 2,* 253-269.

Bell, R. A., & Daly, J. A. (1984). The affinity-seeking function of communication. *Communication Monographs, 51,* 91-115.

Berger, C. R., & Bradac, J. (1982). *Language and social knowledge: Uncertainty in interpersonal relations.* London: Edward Arnold.

Berger, C. R., & Calabrese, R. (1975). Some explorations in initial interaction and beyond: Toward a developmental theory of interpersonal communication. *Human Communication Research, 1,* 99-112.

Blumer, H. (1969). *Symbolic interactionism: perspective and method.* Englewood Cliffs, NJ: Prentice-Hall.

Brown, P., & Levinson, S. (1978). Universals in language usage: Politeness phenomena. In E. Goody (Ed.), *Questions and politeness: Strategies in social interaction* (pp. 56-289). New York: Cambridge University Press.

Bullis, C., & Baxter, L. (1986, February). A functional typology of turning point events in the development of romantic relationships. Paper presented at the Western Speech Communication Association Convention.

Clark, R. A., & Delia, J. G. (1979). Topoi and rhetorical competence. *Quarterly Journal of Speech, 65,* 187-206.

Craik, F. I. M. (1979). Human memory. *Annual Review of Psychology, 30,* 63-102.

Davis, K., & Todd, M. (1982). Friendships and love relationships. In K. E. Davis & T. O. Mitchell (Eds.), *Advances in Descriptive Psychology,* vol. 2 (pp. 79-122). Greenwich, CT: JAI Press.

Davis, K., & Todd, M. (1985). Assessing friendship: Prototypes, paradigm cases and relationship description. In S. Duck & D. Perlman (Eds.), *Understanding personal relationships* (pp. 17-38). London: Sage.

Dindia, K., & Baxter, L. (1986, May). Strategies used by marital partners to maintain and to repair their relationship. Paper presented at the International Communication Association Convention.

Duck, S. (1982). A topography of relationship disengagement and dissolution. In S. Duck (Ed.), *Personal relationships 4: Dissolving personal relationships* (pp. 1-30). New York: Academic Press.

Duck, S. (1984). A perspective on the repair of personal relationships. In S. Duck (Ed.), *Personal relationships 5: Repairing personal relationships* (pp. 163-184). New York: Academic Press.

Duck, S. (1985). Social and personal relationships. In G. Miller & M. Knapp (Eds.), *Handbook of interpersonal communication* (pp. 655-686). Beverly Hills: Sage.

Frentz, T., & Farrell, T. (1976). Language-action: A paradigm for communication. *Quarterly Journal of Speech, 62,* 333-349.

Giddens, A. (1979). *Central problems in social theory.* Berkeley, CA: University of California Press.

Greene, J. O. (1984). A cognitive approach to human communication: An action assembly theory. *Communication Monographs, 51,* 289-306.

Grice, H. P. (1975). Logic and conversation. In P. Cole & J. L. Morgan (Eds.), *Syntax and semantics: Speech acts,* vol. 3 (pp. 41-58). New York: Academic Press.

Grice, H. P. (1978). Further notes on logic and conversation. In P. Cole (Ed.), *Syntax and pragmatics: Pragmatics,* vol. 9 (pp. 113-128). New York: Academic Press.

Harré, R. (1980). *Social being.* Totowa, NJ: Littlefield, Adams.

Harré, R., & Secord, P. (1973). *The explanation of social behavior.* Totowa, NJ: Littlefield, Adams.

Harvey, J., Wells, G., & Alvarez, M. (1978). Attributions in the context of conflict and separation in close relationships. In J. Harvey, W. Ickes, & R. Kidd (Eds.), *New directions in attribution theory,* vol. 2 (pp. 235-260). Hillsdale, NJ: Lawrence Erlbaum.

Hill, C. T., Rubin, Z., & Peplau, L. A. (1976). Breakups before marriage: The end of 103 affairs. *Journal of Social Issues, 32,* 147-168.

Katriel, T., & Philipsen, G. (1981). "What we need is communication": "Communication" as a cultural category in some American speech. *Communication Monographs, 48,* 301-317.

Kelley, H. H. (1979). *Personal relationships: Their structures and processes.* Hillsdale, NJ: Lawrence Erlbaum.

King, S. W., & Sereno, K. K. (1984). Conversational appropriateness as a conversational imperative. *Quarterly Journal of Speech, 70,* 264-273.

Kitson, G., & Sussman, M. (1982). Marital complaints, demographic characteristics, and symptoms of mental distress in divorce. *Journal of Marriage and the Family, 44,* 87-101.

La Gaipa, J. (1979). A developmental study of the meaning of friendship in adolescence. *Journal of Adolescence, 2,* 201-213.

McCall, G. J. (1982). Becoming unrelated: The management of bond dissolution. In S. Duck (Ed.), *Personal relationships 4: Dissolving personal relationships* (pp. 211-231). New York: Academic Press.

Mead, G. H. (1934). *Mind, self, and society.* Chicago: University of Chicago Press.

Pearce, W. B., & Cronen, V. E. (1980). *Communication, action, and meaning: The creation of social realities.* New York: Praeger.

Planalp, S. (1985). Relational schemata. *Human Communication Research, 12,* 3-29.

Rands, M., & Levinger, G. (1979). Implicit theories of relationship: An intergenerational study. *Journal of Personality and Social Psychology, 37,* 645-661.

Roloff, M. E., & Berger, C. R. (1982). *Social cognition and communication.* Beverly Hills, CA: Sage.

Schank, R. C. (1980). Language and memory. *Cognitive Science, 4,* 243-284.

Sillars, A., & Scott, M. (1983). Interpersonal perception between intimates: An integrative review. *Human Communication Research, 10,* 153-176.

Wilmot, W., & Baxter, L. (1983). Reciprocal framing of relationship definitions and episodic interaction. *Western Journal of Speech Communication, 47,* 205-217.

Wilmot, W., & Baxter, L. (1984, February). Defining relationships: The interplay of cognitive schemata and communication. Paper presented at the Western Speech Communication Association Convention.

Wilmot, W., Carbaugh, D., & Baxter, L. (1985). Communicative strategies used to terminate romantic relationships. *Western Journal of Speech Communication, 49,* 204-216.

Wish, M., & Kaplan, S. J. (1977). Toward an implicit theory of interpersonal communication. *Sociometry, 40,* 234-246.

Wittgenstein, L. (1953). *Philosophical investigations.* New York: Macmillan.

Wright, P. H. (1985). The acquaintance description form. In S. Duck & D. Perlman (Eds.), *Understanding personal relationships* (pp. 39-62). London: Sage.

11

Nonverbal Expectancy Violations: Model Elaboration and Application to Immediacy Behaviors

JUDEE K. BURGOON | JEROLD L. HALE

Nonverbal expectancy violations theory holds that positive violations produce more favorable communication outcomes than conformity to expectations, while negative violations produce less favorable ones, and that reward characteristics of the communicator mediate the interpretation and evaluation of violations. The factors affecting expectancies and the consequences of violating them are reviewed and compared to other models (discrepancy-arousal, arousal-labeling, arousal-valence, sequential functional) employing similar assumptions and mediating variables. An experiment extending the model domain to immediacy violations and to interactions with familiar as well as unfamiliar others had friend and stranger dyads (N = 82) engage in discussions during which one member of each pair significantly increased immediacy, significantly reduced it, or conformed to normal levels. Nonimmediacy violations produced lower credibility ratings than high immediacy or conformity to expectations for both friends and strangers. Nonimmediacy was interpreted as communicating detachment, nonintimacy, dissimilarity and more dominance than normal immediacy, while high immediacy expressed the most intimacy, similarity, involvement, and dominance. Implications for the role of ambiguity in violations are discussed.

Communication literature is rife with the assumption, and often the explicit dictum, that the road to success lies in conformity to social norms. One perspective that challenges that notion is nonverbal expectancy violations theory (Burgoon, 1978, 1983, 1985; Burgoon, Coker, & Coker, 1986; Burgoon & Jones, 1976; Burgoon, Stacks, & Woodall, 1979). The basic thesis of the model is that there are circumstances under which violations of social norms and expectations may be a superior strategy to conformity. Given the frequency with which we encounter others who deviate from expected behaviors in their daily transactions, it becomes an important communication issue to determine if and when such violations have favorable as opposed to detrimental consequences. The rise in interest in strategic communication behavior and communication competence also endorses the value of examining how violations may be used as strategic, goal-attaining acts.

Originally designed to explain terminal consequences of conversational distance changes during interpersonal interactions, the expectancy violations model has been revised and extended to apply to a greater range of nonverbal behaviors and communication outcomes (see Buller & Burgoon, 1986; Burgoon & Aho, 1982; Burgoon, Coker, & Coker, 1986; Burgoon, Manusov, Mineo, & Hale, 1985; Burgoon, Stacks, & Burch, 1982). Numerous tests of the model, along with empirical results from other research that can be reinterpreted within the expectancy framework, have yielded support for many of the model's propositions (cf. Burgoon, 1983; Hale & Burgoon, 1984). At the same time, inconsistent findings across studies suggest a need for further elaboration and/or revision of the theory. Especially important is to distinguish how this model differs from others designed to predict the communication consequences of changes in nonverbal behavior. The scope of the model also

From Burgoon, J. K., & Hale, J. L. (1988). Nonverbal expectancy violations: Model elaboration and application to immediacy behaviors. *Communication Monographs, 55*, 55-79.

remains indeterminate, having been applied primarily to manipulations of single nonverbal cues in interactions with strangers, but theoretically having the potential to apply to a wide range of cues and cue patterns and to interactions with familiar others as well as strangers.

The purposes of the current monograph are therefore threefold: (1) to offer a more complete and modified explication of the model that resolves some previous uncertainties, (2) to clarify how the expectancy violations model compares with other similar theoretical models, and (3) to present results of an experiment that broadens the model's domain and advances its explanatory underpinnings.

THE NONVERBAL EXPECTANCY VIOLATIONS MODEL

In overview, the model posits that people hold expectations about the nonverbal behaviors of others. Violations of these expectations are posited to trigger a change in arousal, which heightens the salience of cognitions about the communicator and behavior. The valenced evaluation of the communicator, implicit messages associated with the violation behavior(s), and evaluations of the act combine to determine whether a violation is positive or negative, which in turn influences communication outcomes. The key elements in the process, then, are *expectancy violations, arousal, communicator reward valence, behavior interpretation and evaluation,* and *violation valence.*

At many junctures, the expectancy violations model shares assumptions with such other arousal and cognitive labeling approaches to nonverbal behavior as Andersen's (1985) arousal-valence model, Cappella and Greene's (1982) discrepancy-arousal model, Patterson's earlier (1976) arousal-labeling model, and his more recent (1982, 1983) sequential functional model. The model differs from these, however, in the underlying explanatory system that is advanced, in the directionality of its predictions, in the broader domain of nonverbal behaviors to

which it is potentially applicable, and in its broader scope of applying to both the interaction exchange process and outcomes. A primary focus of the other models is predicting immediate, micro-level compensatory or reciprocal responses to changes in a partner's level of intimacy or involvement, with reciprocity predicted under nonaversive circumstances and compensation predicted under aversive ones. Not only does the expectancy violations model produce conflicting predictions and explanations for compensation and reciprocity exchange processes (see Hale & Burgoon, 1984), it attempts to predict and explain terminal communication consequences, such as attraction and persuasion, as well as more macro-level exchange patterns. It also has the potential to account for the effects of other nonverbal phenomena beyond intimacy and involvement signals.

Elements of the Model

Expectancies. The theoretical framework begins with the assumption that in interpersonal encounters, interactants develop expectancies and preferences about the nonverbal behaviors of others, an assumption that is also relatively central in the discrepancy-arousal, arousal-valence, and sequential functional models. The models differ in the extent to which they explain the origins of those expectancies and treat them as cognitive, affective, and/or behavioral.

According to the expectancy violations model, expectancies may include cognitive, affective, and conative components and are primarily a function of (1) social norms and (2) known idiosyncracies of the other. With unknown others, the expectations are identical to the societal norms and standards for the particular type of communicator, relationship, and situation. That is, they include judgments of what behaviors are possible, feasible, appropriate, and typical for a particular setting, purpose, and set of participants (cf. Kreckel, 1981, for more detailed analysis of situational features that may impinge on expectations).

As illustration, conversational distance norms are based on a combination of communicator characteristics (e.g., gender, age, personality, style), relational characteristics (e.g., degree of acquaintance, status inequality, liking, relational history), and contextual factors (e.g., environmental constraints, definition of the situation or task, communication functions being accomplished). Thus, female friends in a social situation expect to interact at a closer distance than two males of different status and age in a work environment. All else being equal, interacting at moderately close range is also preferable to interacting at a greater distance because it heightens sensory involvement and carries such culturally approved meanings as equality and affiliation.

Although the pre-interactional and interactional factors dictating norms and preferences are complex in themselves, individuals appear to have little difficulty arriving at a net expectancy of how others should behave and recognizing deviations from that pattern. Research shows, for example, that people experience discomfort, compensate for, and rate as inappropriate and unexpected nonverbal interaction patterns that deviate from intermediate levels of distance, gaze, and sensory involvement (Argyle & Cook, 1976; Burgoon, 1978; Burgoon & Coker, in press; Burgoon & Jones, 1976; Rosenfeld, Breck, Smith, & Kehoe, 1984; Smith & Knowles, 1979; Sundstrom & Altman, 1976; Thompson, Aiello, & Epstein, 1979). This ability to recognize violations of expected behaviors and sequences is evident even in infants (Gibson, Owsley, & Johnston, 1978; Haith, Kiesen, & Collins, 1969) and by adulthood becomes formalized into entire patterns of expected action—what some have labeled interaction scripts or behavioral programs (Abelson, 1981; Schank & Abelson, 1977; Scheflen, 1974; Street & Cappella, 1985)—that serve as standards against which to compare a given interaction.

Expectancies are not exclusively norm-based. Known idiosyncratic differences based on prior knowledge of the other, relational history, or observation may be factored in to yield person-specific expectations. For example, one may expect more vocal animation from a highly gregarious friend or closer conversational distance from someone who has impaired hearing. Idiosyncratic expectancies, then, reflect the extent to which the expectancies for a particular communicator deviate from the socially normative ones.

Expectancies also operate within a range, rather than representing some specific behavior. The expected distance for a personal conversation, for example, may range from two to four feet. This concept of range acknowledges that norms are not precise themselves but rather have some degree of variability associated with them. According to the original conceptualization of the expectancy violations model, there is a threshold or limen of recognition that must be passed before a deviation from the norm becomes a violation (Burgoon & Jones, 1976). Any discrepancies within the socially tolerated range of variability will be perceptually assimilated as part of the expected behavior pattern.

Based on one's own habitual behavior and that of others within a society, one comes not only to anticipate that others will behave in a particular fashion but also to assign evaluations, or *valences,* to these actions:

> People who interact develop expectations about each other's behavior, not only in the sense that they are able to predict the regularities, but also in the sense that they develop preferences about how others *should* behave under certain circumstances. (Jackson, 1964, p. 255)

This is the affective component of expectations. Jackson (1964, 1966) has shown that norms and role expectations can be scaled along two continua: a behavioral dimension (the frequency with which associated role behaviors might occur) and an approval dimension (subjective ratings of approval-disapproval, which Jackson equates with expectations). The same principle applies to communicative expectations. Although individual preferences color affective reactions to behaviors, valences are undoubtedly most strongly influenced by the society's standards or ideals for competent communication performance. Thus, one expects normal speakers to be reasonably fluent and coherent in their discourse, to refrain from erratic movements or emotional outbursts, and to adhere to politeness norms. Generally, normative behaviors are positively valued. If one keeps a polite distance and shows an appropriate level of interest in one's conversational partner, for instance, such behavior should be favorably received. In Jackson's (1966) terminology, the expected behaviors tend to be those that fall within the range of tolerable behavior (i.e., above the indifference threshold) and which become "crystallized" into consensually recognized norms.

The difficult question to answer is how deviations from expectations are evaluated. Most sociological writings on norms, rules, and roles implicitly assume that any form of violation is negative. While the nonverbal interaction models allow for the possibility of moderate deviations producing positive reactions, they also assume that extreme violations or extremely arousing events, which may be the result of violations, are negatively valenced. For example, the discrepancy-arousal model holds that large discrepancies produce large changes in arousal which in turn produce negative affect. As intuitively appealing as this position is, it may be incorrect. It is possible to imagine violations that are positively valenced, as in the case of a highly fluent, witty speaker or an intimate overture from the object of one's romantic fantasies. One form of positive violation is implicit in Aronson and Linder's (1965) gain-loss theory: Initially cold behavior from a communicator (which presumably sets the expectations), followed by warm behavior (a positive violation), is hypothesized to produce more favorable consequences than a warm-warm sequence (which entails no violation). Given the possibility that positive as well as negative violations may occur, what is needed is clarification of what qualifies as a positive versus a negative violation and how such violations compare to expectancy conformity in affecting communication processes and consequences.

According to the expectancy violations model, if one's interaction partner conforms to expectancies, the expectancies themselves and the nonverbal behaviors they govern should operate largely out of awareness, and communication outcomes should depend on such pre-interactional and interactional factors as communicator and relational characteristics, the definition of the situation, and the intrinsic meaning of the verbal and nonverbal behaviors being exchanged. This assumption parallels Patterson's (1983) argument in his functional model that behavior matching expectations serves to maintain stable exchanges. (The arousal-valence and discrepancy-arousal models make similar arguments.)

Violations and Arousal. If, however, the communicator violates expectancies to a sufficient degree for the deviation to be recognized (i.e., exceeds a limen of socially tolerated variability or receiver sensitivity), the violation is posited to heighten the violatee's arousal. All the models subscribe to the principle that noticeably deviant or discrepant behavior by a communicator produces a change in a partner's arousal level. All are also primarily focused on predicting and explaining how such deviations or instability-producing changes affect communication behaviors and evaluations. The expectancy violations, arousal-labeling, arousal-valence, and functional models contend that heightened arousal results in some cognitive-affective assessment of the situation and/or behavior. (The discrepancy-arousal theory moves cognitive processes to the role of antecedents to arousal change, but also treats affective changes as a consequent of arousal change.)

In the case of the violations model, the arousal change is posited to cause an alertness or orienting response that diverts attention away from the ostensive purpose of the interaction and focuses it toward the source of the arousal—the initiator of the violation. This position is consistent with Newtson's (1973) observation that introduction of an unexpected activity in the midst of a prolonged behavior episode results in finer-grained observations of behavior, that is, subsequent behavior is decomposed into smaller meaningful units. It is also consistent with the notion that deviant characteristics or behavior make people more mindful of specific details about the deviant (Langer, 1978; Langer & Imber, 1980). King and Sereno (1984) propose that unexpected language use shifts attention from the content level of an interaction to the relational implicature. The expectancy violations model makes essentially the same argument. It proposes that the attentional shift to the relational level makes communicator and message/behavior characteristics more salient, causing the violatee to engage in a two-stage interpretation and evaluation process that results in the violation act being defined as either a positive or negative violation of expectations. The explanation which follows separates expectancy violations from the other cognitive models, which fail to articulate precisely how the cognitive labeling process operates to yield a positive or negative valence.

Communicator Reward Valence. The first factor to influence the valencing of a violation as positive or negative is the reward value of the violator. Reward is a function of all those static and initial, or preinteractional, communicator and relationship characteristics (such as gender, personality, physical attractiveness, reputation, status, and anticipated future interaction) and all those derived, interactional behaviors (such as possessing tangible rewards, having an amusing communication style, or giving positive feedback) that cause the communicator to be perceived, on balance, as someone with whom it is desirable to interact.[1] It is the net valence of all the relevant communicator and relationship characteristics that can be judged on an evaluative continuum. Put in exchange theory terms, it means the benefits of interacting with the communicator outweigh the costs.

Behavior Interpretation and Evaluation. Communicator reward value influences the valencing of a violation in two ways. First, it may affect *interpretation* of the violation. Many nonverbal behaviors carry implicit relational messages and other social meanings (Burgoon, Buller, Hale, & de Turck, 1984; Burgoon et al., 1986; Burgoon et al., 1985; Burgoon & Saine, 1978). Often a given act carries multiple interpretations among which several alter-

natives are plausible. Here is where regard for the communicator may influence selection of meaning. For example, increased proximity during conversation may be taken as a sign of affiliation if committed by a high reward person but as a sign of aggressiveness if committed by a low reward person. To the extent that multiple interpretations are possible, expectancy violations theory holds that more favorable ones will be given to the act when it is committed by a high reward than a low reward violator.

Where the meaning of the behavior is unequivocal, reward may mediate the *evaluation* of the violation. Although there are some nonverbal behaviors that may produce uniformly negative or positive evaluations regardless of who commits them (e.g., displaying an insulting gesture), the affective reaction to many behaviors depends on their source. For example, even if a behavior such as continuous gaze carries the same interpretation (e.g., high involvement) for both high and low reward violators, that level of gaze may be welcome from a high reward communicator and unwelcome from a low reward one. Thus, deviant gaze is favorably evaluated in the case of a high reward communicator and unfavorably evaluated in the case of a low reward one.

One other possibility is that the behavior is disregarded, either because it is seen as externally caused or because it has no discernible meaning. In both instances, the behavior is noncommunicative and is discounted.

Violation Valence. Positively evaluated behaviors, either because they originate from a positively valued communicator, are assigned positive interpretations, or have consensually assigned positive value within a speech community, should qualify as positive violations and produce favorable communication patterns and consequences. Negatively interpreted and evaluated deviations should qualify as negative violations and generate unfavorable interaction patterns and consequences. However, in contrast to the other nonverbal interaction models, the expectancy violations model predicts that an extreme violation, if committed by a high reward communicator, can be positively valenced, producing reciprocal communication patterns and positive outcomes such as higher credibility and attraction. The other models predict that an extreme violation produces compensatory interaction patterns. They do not address terminal communication outcomes (i.e., those resulting from an entire episode).

This interpretation and evaluation process as filtered through communicator reward is depicted in Figure 11.1. For simplicity, reward, expectancies, and violation valences have been dichotomized as positive or negative, although they should be understood as continua. In the case of a violation, the arousal change triggers the interpretive process. If the meaning of the behavior(s) is initially ambiguous, one must first decide if a positive or negative interpretation is to be selected. Once this decision is made, the interpreted message is evaluated—simply put, does the recipient like or dislike receiving it? The assignment of a behavior as a negative (or positive) violation can occur at either the interpretive or evaluative stage: at the interpretative stage, if the interpreted message is considered inappropriate or negatively valued *by society,* which results in an automatic unfavorable evaluation; at the evaluative stage, if the message is negatively valued *by the recipient* for this particular occasion or communicator. This valencing process need not entail cumbersome or lengthy cognitive effort. Indeed, to the extent that evaluations have been conditioned to the behaviors and interpretation is a habitual, overlearned activity, the valencing process may occur almost automatically.

Noteworthy is that a high reward communicator may commit a negative violation, either by engaging in an act which has an unambiguous negative interpretation (e.g., displaying complete disinterest in what one's partner has to say), or engaging in a positively interpreted act that the partner nevertheless finds unpleasant or undesirable (e.g., using too much affiliative touch). A low reward communicator may also engage in a positive violation, although the opportunities for such are more limited. A positive violation will be attributed to a poorly

regarded communicator only when the violation carries an unambiguously positive interpretation *and* a socially positive evaluation.

The double pluses and minuses designate that violations produce more pronounced effects than conformity to expectations. A positive violation produces more favorable consequences, and a negative violation, more unfavorable ones, than adhering to the expected behavior pattern. This proposed intensification of response is bolstered by Langer and Imber's (1980) finding that characteristics of deviants were perceived as more extreme and evaluated more extremely than those of "normal" individuals.

The foregoing discussion is not meant to imply that interpretations and evaluations are made in an absolute fashion. Rather, it is more likely that they are judged relative to the expectancy and can be placed with it along an evaluative continuum. Thus, ultimately the *direction* and *magnitude* of a violation dictate its type and consequences. If the actual (violation) behavior is more positively valenced than the expected behavior(s), a *positive violation* occurs and should produce more favorable communication outcomes than conforming to the expected (normative) pattern.[2] Conversely, if the actual behavior is more negatively valenced than the expected behavior, a *negative violation* is said to occur and should yield more negative consequences than conforming to expectations. The magnitude of discrepancy dictates whether a violation is actually perceived and how significant it is. The greater the magnitude of deviation from expectancy, the greater the impact on communication outcomes.

Because people may hold higher standards or more stringent expectations for a high reward person than for a low reward one, it is possible for a high reward person to commit a more grievous violation. For example, gaze aversion tends to carry uniformly negative interpretations and evaluations. If a well-liked person avoids gaze, this may be a more serious negative violation than if a disliked person does it, because one expects the well-liked person to reciprocate affiliative behavior but may hold no such expectations for the low reward com-

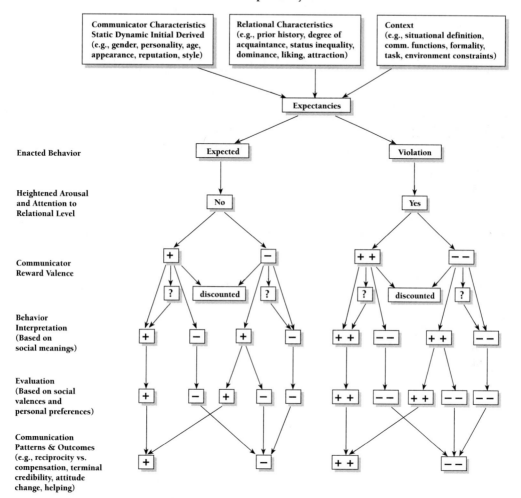

FIGURE 11.1

Nonverbal Expectancy Violations Model

Note: For simplicity, communicator reward valence, behavior interpretation, and behavior evaluation valence have been dichotomized into positive and negative but should be understood to represent continua. Double pluses and minuses denote greater magnitude of effect.

municator. Therefore, the gap between the actual and expected behavior could be much greater for the high than the low reward person.

Figure 11.2 illustrates several examples of small and large positive and negative violations. It should be noted that for strangers, the expected behavior is the same as the socially normative behavior. Otherwise, the relevant expectancy is the one held for

the specific individual. The significance of the societal expectation is that it provides a basis for judging how large a violation is. For example, a low reward person, reputed to be a terrible speaker, who exhibits far greater fluency than is common, may be committing a large positive violation by not only exceeding the individual expectation but also the social norm (Case 2). Or a high reward person

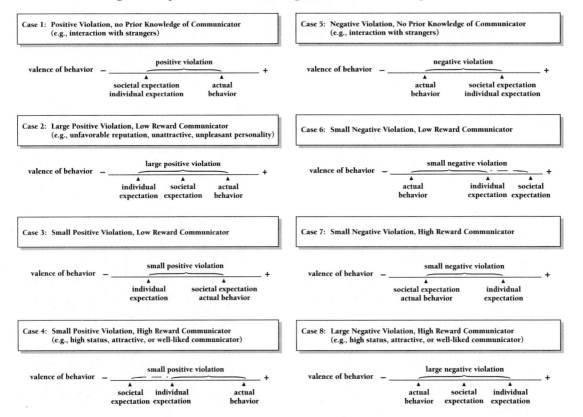

FIGURE 11.2

Eight Examples of Positive and Negative Violations of Expectations

for whom one has high expectations may commit a small negative violation merely by conforming to the societal norm (Case 7).

Empirical Support for the Model

The accumulated research evidence relevant to the nonverbal expectancy model has produced support for the following conclusions:

1. *Interactants develop expectations about the distancing and immediacy behavior of others.* As noted earlier, people are most comfortable with, and re-

gard as most appropriate and expected, intermediate levels of conversational distance, gaze, and sensory involvement.

2. *Communicator behaviors and characteristics that contribute to interpersonal rewards mediate communication outcomes.* All of the following have been defined as bases for reward and shown to influence outcomes: positive and negative feedback, physical attractiveness, smiling, head nods, task competence, socioeconomic status, purchasing power, and attitudinal similarity (Burgoon, 1978; Burgoon & Aho, 1982; Burgoon et al., 1982; Burgoon et al., 1979; Schiffenbauer & Schiavo, 1976; Smith &

Knowles, 1979; Stacks & Burgoon, 1981; Storms & Thomas, 1977).

3. *For conversational distance, rewarding communicators frequently accrue the most favorable communication outcomes by violating rather than conforming to expectancies.* The beneficial consequences result from both close and far violations and not only benefit the violator in an absolute sense but also relative to another, nondeviating interactant (Baron, 1978; Burgoon, 1978; Burgoon & Aho, 1982; Burgoon et al., 1982; Burgoon et al., 1979; Donohue, Diez, Stahle, & Burgoon, 1983; Ickes, Patterson, Rajecki, & Tanford, 1982; Imada & Hakel, 1977; Schiffenbauer & Schiavo, 1976; Smith & Knowles, 1979; Stacks & Burgoon, 1981; Storms & Thomas, 1977).

4. *For conversational distance, nonrewarding communicators frequently accrue their optimal communication outcomes by conforming to distance expectancies rather than violating them.* Violations by poorly regarded others tend to produce more negative consequences for the violator and have the effect of conferring greater credibility, attraction, and perceived influence on other, nonviolating interactants (Baron, 1978; Burgoon, 1978; Burgoon & Aho, 1982; Burgoon et al., 1982; Burgoon et al., 1979; Ickes et al., 1982; Konecni, Libuser, Morton, & Ebbeson, 1973; Schiffenbauer & Schiavo, 1976; Smith & Knowles, 1979; Stacks & Burgoon, 1981; Storms & Thomas, 1977).

5. *For eye gaze, rewarding communicators achieve greatest attraction, credibility, and endorsement for hiring by engaging in nearly continuous gaze or normal gaze; gaze aversion produces negative consequences.* A high degree of gaze is interpreted as expressing intimacy, affiliation, trust, interest, involvement, relaxation, composure, and possibly depth and similarity. These favorable interpretations may qualify it as a positive violation when committed by a high reward person. Gaze aversion, by contrast, is interpreted as detached, cold, nonintimate, tense, untrustworthy, dissimilar and superficial, causing it to serve as a negative violation (Burgoon et al., 1986; Burgoon et al., 1985; Manusov, 1984).

6. *Violations are arousing and distracting.* Distance violations and changes in nonverbal intimacy often produce physical manifestations of activation and discomfort and have been shown to shift attention away from the task or topic of discussion (Burgoon & Aho, 1982; Galle, Spratt, Chapman, & Smallbone, 1975; Konecni et al., 1973; Smith & Knowles, 1979; Stacks & Burgoon, 1981).

EXTENSION TO IMMEDIACY BEHAVIORS

The empirical evidence so far lends some credence to the model. However, until recently, the nonverbal and relational domains of the theory have been rather narrow, confined to single nonverbal behaviors (conversational distance and gaze), manipulated in carefully controlled ways, during encounters among strangers. Although single-cue tests with strangers have been necessary in the early stages of model-testing to insure adequate experimental control and to eliminate extraneous sources of variance such as relational history, the result has been to limit the generalizability and ecological validity of the model. To extend it more broadly to the types of interactions that typify daily communication transactions requires examining complexes of simultaneous nonverbal cues in interactions among acquainted as well as unacquainted individuals.

The need to examine multiple simultaneous nonverbal behaviors rests in the abundant evidence that distance and gaze are but two of several immediacy behaviors that work in concert with one another (e.g., Andersen, Andersen, & Jenson, 1979; Argyle & Cook, 1976; Burgoon et al., 1984; Coutts & Ledden, 1977; Mehrabian, 1971) and should therefore be studied as a set. It is bolstered further by the observation in previous tests of the expectancy model that confederates had difficulty manipulating just one cue and often found themselves resisting the urge to manipulate several at once. In fact, confederates may have inadvertently compensated for their own violations by altering other immediacy cues, thereby weakening the experimental manipulation. Use of a set of interrelated cues has the added advantage of producing a more powerful manipulation capable of yielding more detectable changes in communication outcomes.

A further rationale for using multiple nonverbal cues is to test the explanation that ambiguous nonverbal cues produce different patterns of results than nonambiguous ones. With conversational distance, a tentative explanation offered for the positive consequences of a far violation by a high reward person is that adjustments in conversational distance are ambiguous, permitting the receiver to select a favorable interpretation of the act, and hence, to respond positively to it. With gaze, the explanation offered for the negative consequences of gaze aversion is that, unlike far distance, gaze avoidance carries rather unambiguous negative interpretations and hence yields negative consequences. Simultaneous manipulation of a set of congruent immediacy behaviors should be even less ambiguous than gaze adjustments. Results under low immediacy should therefore parallel the pattern for gaze violations rather than distance violations, if the ambiguity interpretation is correct.

However, rather than leave the interpretive process as a hypothetical construct, this investigation sought empirical evidence of this intervening process. Because violation acts are posited to carry social meaning, the relational message interpretations assigned to them are one appropriate index of whether such acts carry favorable or unfavorable interpretations and, hence, should qualify as positive or negative violations. A major objective of this investigation was to determine if violations do in fact carry the meanings that have been attributed to them in past explanations of the model and whether they also carry surplus meanings that may affect the ultimate valencing of violations.

These concerns and objectives led to the design of an experiment in which communicators violated or conformed to their own pre-established level of nonverbal immediacy in interactions with friends and strangers. The inclusion of friendship interac-

tions permitted examination of whether the same interpretive-evaluative processes would operate in established relationships as in unfamiliar ones, or whether friends would find ways to discount and excuse the violation behaviors of their partners. To increase ecological validity, violations were committed by untrained participants rather than trained confederates to see if the model's predictions would hold in spite of individual differences in execution of the manipulations. To explore the ambiguity issue, relational meanings associated with immediacy behaviors were assessed. Finally, the impact of violations on both immediate nonverbal responses and terminal communication consequences were assessed. The results pertaining to compensation and reciprocity of nonverbal immediacy adjustments are reported in Hale and Burgoon (1984); the effects on terminal evaluations of the violator and on relational message interpretations are reported here.

HYPOTHESES

The potential for reward to mediate interpretations and evaluations hinges on differential reward being present between communicators. Because the present experiment was designed to extend the expectancy model to friends, the question arises as to whether interacting with friends is itself more rewarding than interacting with strangers. Research indicating that friends use more intimate, inclusive, reciprocal, and constructive verbal and nonverbal communication styles with one another than do strangers (e.g., Cupach, 1980; Little, 1965; Rosenfeld et al., 1984; Traynowicz, 1982; Willis, 1966) supports the common belief that interactions with friends are more rewarding occasions than interactions with strangers and should result in more favorable perceptions of one's friend than of a stranger. This expectation formed the basis for the first hypothesis:

H1: Friends are perceived as (a) more attractive, (b) more credible, and (c) expressing more intimate/similar, nonaroused/composed, nondominant, and immediate relational communication than strangers.

Research on the interpretations that are associated with immediacy suggests that immediacy communicates greater involvement, interest, affiliation, trust, and caring and sometimes composure, relaxation, and dominance while nonimmediacy communicates the opposite (Burgoon et al., 1984). While this might lead to the prediction that non-immediacy is negative valenced and immediacy is positively valenced, regardless of communicator reward, the expectancy violations model requires taking evaluations into account. Such evaluations may be mediated by reward. A significant increase in level of involvement should be regarded as desirable when committed by a friend but possibly excessive and discomfiting when presented by a stranger. Thus, such a deviation from a normal immediacy level should constitute a positive violation when committed by a friend and a negative violation when committed by a stranger. Conversely, a significant decrease in involvement by a friend should be disconcerting and unpleasant, carrying as it does messages of rejection and disinterest. Such a violation should qualify as a negative violation. Such behavior by a stranger should likewise carry negative relational meanings and should engender unfavorable evaluations and consequences, although the effect might be less severe than when committed by a friend because the person has less invested in the relationship:

H2: In interactions with friends, a substantial increase in immediacy yields (a) more attraction and (b) more credibility than does conformity to normative levels of immediacy.

H3: In interactions with strangers, a substantial increase in immediacy yields (a) less attraction and (b) less credibility than does conformity to normative levels of immediacy.

H4: In interactions with friends or strangers, a substantial decrease in immediacy yields (a) less attraction and (b) less credibility than does conformity to normative levels of immediacy.

Finally, because past research on the meanings associated with immediacy was conducted in an observer rather than a participant paradigm, a research question was posed regarding interpretations:

R1: What relational messages are attributed to changes in nonverbal immediacy?

METHOD

Participants

Participants were pairs of undergraduate students, one of whom was enrolled in a communication course at a large midwestern university; the other was a friend of his or her choice (excluding spouses and relatives). Each person engaged in two interactions, one with the friend and one with a stranger, for a total of 82 dyads (33 male-male pairs, 15 female-female pairs, 17 male confederate–female subject pairs, and 17 female confederate–male subject pairs).[3] Participation was voluntary and earned course credit.

Procedures

Participants, who reported to the experiment in pairs, were immediately separated to complete a communication reticence scale used for another study and to receive instructions. They were then informed that the current study was designed to examine naturalistic, face-to-face interactions between friends and strangers. They were to engage in two ten-minute discussions, one with the friend and one with a stranger, on two (out of four possible) social-moral problems, and to agree upon one of the alternative solutions for each. The four topics (the pregnancy of one's unmarried, Catholic sister; theft of a friend's possession by a sibling; the infidelity of a close friend's fiance; and an impending visit by the unsuspecting parents of a cohabiting couple) were randomly assigned, with order counterbalanced across conditions. Participants were told the interactions would be videotaped and followed by completion of questionnaires.

In each dyad, the communication student was enlisted as a confederate for the manipulation of immediacy. In the *normal immediacy* (expected) conditions, confederates were merely told to initiate the discussion and to maintain as normal an interaction pattern as possible. They were then ushered into the discussion room in advance of the naive participant. In the *nonimmediacy* condition, confederates were instructed "to violate the normal behavior patterns by increasing the distance between you and the other person as much as possible without making it obvious that you are trying to violate them. Once you are in the interviewing room, your attitude is one of remoteness. You are distant, uninvolved, and unreceptive. That is not to say that you are in high disagreement with the person's views but that you are not very open to his/her position." Confederates were further told to initiate the conversation and to begin the violation after about one minute of discussion. To assist them in accomplishing the violation, they were encouraged to (1) gradually double the distance between themselves and the other, (2) adopt an indirect body orientation, (3) lean backward, (4) cross their arms, and (5) decrease eye contact compared to the first minute. They were urged to maintain these body movements throughout the entire conversation. In the *high immediacy* condition, confederates were also instructed to violate after one minute of normal interaction but to increase closeness and a sense of interest and involvement. Specifically, they were told to (1) halve the distance between themselves and their partner, (2) maintain a direct body orientation, (3) lean forward, (4) assume an open posture, and (5) increase eye contact compared to the first minute. Confederates practiced the manipulations before the naive participant entered the discussion room and conducted the same violation with a stranger and with a friend. The order of interactions was counterbalanced.

Naive participants were always ushered to the same corner chair, which had restricted backward mobility. This insured that the subject could not "escape" the violation and that it would be sustained throughout the interaction. Following the discussion, participants were separated to complete dependent measures on credibility, attraction, and relational messages. Confederates also rated their success in conducting the manipulation. All participants were debriefed after the second discussion.

Dependent Measures

Violator credibility was measured by the naive participant's ratings of the violator on five subscales comprised of three seven-interval semantic differential scales developed by McCroskey, Jensen, and Valencia (1973) to measure the *competence, character, sociability, composure,* and *dynamism* dimensions of peer credibility. Coefficient alpha reliabilities for the five subscales were .83, .78, .84, .83, and .79, respectively.

Violator attraction was measured by naive participants' ratings on three subscales, each comprised of four Likert-type items, developed by McCroskey and McCain (1974) to measure *social, physical,* and *task attraction.* Alpha reliabilities were .68, .73, and .75, respectively.

Relational message themes were measured on a 32-item, Likert-type scale developed by Burgoon and Hale (1987) to reflect as many as twelve topoi of relational communication. The four orthogonal clusters used in this investigation were *intimacy/similarity, detachment, emotional arousal/receptivity,* and *dominance.*[4] Reliabilities were .81, .56, .70, and .72.

Manipulation Checks

All confederates rated themselves as successful at manipulating distance, eye contact, posture, leg and arm positions, and overall violation. An assistant who observed all interactions in progress through a one-way mirror also confirmed that the assigned conditions were carried out. Subsequently, a panel of observers who were blind to the conditions reviewed all the videotapes and recorded whether the confederate appeared to engage in high, normal, or low immediacy. They showed 99% agreement with the assigned condition. Finally, participants rated confederates as significantly more detached in the nonimmediacy than in the normal and high immediacy conditions, $F(2,38) = 4.38, p < .05$ (respective means = 3.68, 2.81, 2.85), and as increasingly intimate across the three conditions, $F(2,38)$ = 3.50, $p < .05$ (means = 4.27, 4.72, 4.92).

RESULTS

All hypotheses were tested by 3 × 2 (high/normal/low immediacy by friend/stranger reward level) repeated measures multivariate analyses of variance with subjects nested within immediacy condition. Groups of related variables (the five credibility dimensions, three attraction dimensions and four relational message dimensions) were analyzed separately. Univariate analyses of variance were then probed. Fisher's modified Least Significant Differences test was used for planned comparisons.

Hypothesis 1

All three parts of the hypothesis received support. Significant multivariate effects obtained for reward on ratings of the confederate's attraction, A = .68 approx. $F(3,36)$ = 5.58, $p < .01$, R^2 = .32, and relational communication, A = .50, approx. $F(4,35)$ = 12.03, $p < .01$, R^2 = .50. Significant univariate effects appeared on social attraction, $F(1,38)$ = 13.30, $p < .01$, physical attraction, $F(1,38)$ = 7.49, $p < .05$, intimacy/similarity, $F(1,38) = 32.71, p < .01$, and detachment, $F(1,38)$ = $p < .05$, and a near significant effect obtained on task attraction, $F(1,38)$ = 3.90, $p < .06$. A trend toward a significant multivariate effect also obtained on credibility, A = .77, approx. $F(5,34)$ = 2.05, $p < .10$, R^2 = .23, with a significant univariate effect on competence, $F(1,38)$ = 10.69, $p < .05$, and a trend toward significance on dynamism, $F(1,38)$ = 3.22, $p < .10$. Consistent with Hypothesis 1, friends were seen as more socially, physically, and task attractive, as more credible in terms of competence (and possibly dynamism), and as expressing more relational intimacy/similarity and less detachment. (See Table 11.1 for means.) However, despite friends' receiving more positive evaluations than strangers did, the means revealed that the ratings given to strangers were also above the

midpoints of the attraction, credibility, and relational messages scales. These terminal ratings suggest that strangers may have qualified as nonrewarding in a relative sense but not an absolute sense. Because initial ratings were not obtained, this speculation is untestable.

Hypotheses 2, 3, and 4

The combined hypotheses proposed that for friend interactions, as immediacy increases, so does attraction and credibility (i.e., a positive linear relationship), while for stranger interactions, deviations toward either increased or decreased immediacy reduce credibility and attraction (i.e., a nonlinear, inverted U pattern). If high immediacy produces differential effects for friends versus strangers, it should be confirmed through a reward by immediacy interaction. Exclusively main effect findings may support the negative consequences of a nonimmediacy violation but imply that reward does not mediate the effects of a high immediacy violation.

The MANOVA for attraction (Hypotheses 2a, 3a, 4a) produced a trend toward a significant interaction, A = .74, approx. $F(6,70)$ = 1.93, $p < .10$, R^2 = .26, and no significant main effect for immediacy, but there were no significant univariate interaction effects. Low power due to sample size probably accounted for this failure: Power was approximately .58. In the absence of significant univariate interaction effects, it is probably unwise to speculate about the meaning of the multivariate interaction; however, it is worth noting that the means showed nonimmediacy consistently to produce more negative attraction ratings for both high and low reward communicators than normal or high immediacy. The high variance accounted for indicates that with a slightly larger sample size, this effect would become significant.

The MANOVA on credibility yielded a significant main effect for immediacy, A = .59, approx. $F(10,66)$ = 2.04, $p < .05$, R^2 = .41, with significant univariate effects on character, $F(2,38)$ = 6.49, $p < .01$, sociability, $F(2,38)$ = 5.65, $p < .01$,

TABLE 11.1

Main Effect and Interaction Means for Credibility, Attraction, and Relational Communication Dependent Measures

	IMMEDIACY CONDITION			REWARD CONDITION		IMMEDIACY × REWARD					
	High	Normal	Low	Friend	Stranger	FH	FN	FL	SH	SN	SL
	(n = 26)	(n = 28)	(n = 28)	(n = 41)	(n = 41)	(n = 13)	(n = 14)	(n = 14)	(n = 13)	(n = 14)	(n = 14)
Credibility Dimensions											
Competence	5.74	6.21	5.54*	6.05	5.61*	6.00	6.49	5.74	5.49	5.94	5.36
Character	5.80	6.48	5.59*	6.00	5.92	5.90	6.56	5.52	5.71	6.34	5.64
Composure	5.54	5.23	5.05	5.27	5.21	5.55	5.39	4.92	5.52	5.06	5.17
Sociability	6.13	6.48	5.58*	6.18	5.90	6.29	6.78	5.57	5.88	6.18	5.60
Dynamism	5.41	5.26	4.95	5.29	5.11**	5.55	5.61	5.02	5.26	4.94	4.83
Attraction Dimensions											
Physical	5.64	5.77	5.35	5.88	5.29*	5.97	6.31	5.36	5.31	5.24	5.33
Social	5.76	6.24	5.88	6.36	5.57*	5.92	6.79	6.33	5.59	5.69	5.43
Task	5.65	5.73	5.31	5.76	5.36**	6.03	5.81	5.48	5.28	5.64	5.14
Relational Communication Dimensions											
Intimacy/Similarity	4.92	4.72	4.27*	5.19	4.07*	5.58	5.44	4.58	4.26	4.01	3.95
Detachment	2.85	2.81	3.68*	2.78	3.46*	2.36	2.38	3.57	3.33	3.24	3.79
Arousal/Receptivity	5.77	6.11	5.67	5.88	5.82	5.83	6.10	5.70	5.71	6.11	5.64
Dominance	4.02	3.11	3.52*	3.69	3.38	3.91	3.37	3.81	4.12	2.84	3.23

* Groups differed significantly from one another ($p < .05$).
** Near-significant differences obtained ($.05 < p < .10$).

and competence, $F(2,38) = 3.90, p < .05$. The main effect means (Table 11.1) indicate that both friends and strangers were seen as most credible in the normal and high immediacy conditions and least so in the nonimmediacy condition. High immediacy did not differ significantly from normal immediacy except on character, $t = 2.61, p < .05$; high immediacy yielded lower scores.

The presence of only main effects and no interactions on credibility mitigated against supporting differential patterns for friends and strangers (Hypotheses 2b and 3b) in the high immediacy condition. However, the cell means revealed a pattern consistent with predictions in the friend conditions for the dependent measures of composure and dynamism, and for the stranger conditions for competence, character, and sociability.

Finally, the data strongly supported Hypothesis 4b. Nonverbally nonimmediate confederates were seen as significantly less competent, $t = -2.23, p < .05$, less trustworthy, $t = -3.42, p < .01$, and less sociable, $t = -3.03, p < .05$, than those who maintained normal levels of immediacy. The means for composure and dynamism were also in line with predictions.

Research Question

A multivariate effect for immediacy obtained on relational communication, $A = .68$, approx. $F(6,70) = 2.55, p < .05, R^2 = .32$. Significant univariate main effects appeared on three dimensions: intimacy/similarity, $F(2,38) = 3.16, p = .05$; detachment, $F(2,38) = 3.85, p < .05$; and dominance, $F(2,38) = 3.68, p < .05$. As expected, nonimmediate nonverbal behavior communicated far more detachment than high immediacy, $t = 2.76, p < .05$. High immediacy also communicated more intimacy and similarity than nonimmediacy, $t = 2.50, p < .05$. Finally, both types of violations—increases and decreases in immediacy—communicated greater dominance than conformity to the normative level of immediacy, with high immediacy being significantly more dominant, $t = 2.84, p < .05$ (see Table 11.1).

DISCUSSION

The present experiment sought to extend the domain of nonverbal expectancy violations theory to multiple nonverbal behaviors and to familiar as well as unfamiliar relationships. The results suggest that the extension is appropriate and offer partial support for some of its predictions and explanatory framework. Hypothesis 1 was supported, demonstrating that reward includes familiarity with a partner. Friends were rated as more attractive and credible and as expressing more favorable relational messages than strangers (based on the multivariate analyses). In particular, friends were seen as more physically and socially attractive, as more competent, and as communicating more intimacy, similarity, and involvement. Moreover, friends were sensitive to communicative violations, in some cases more so than strangers, and derogated their violating friend for such infractions. This justifies concluding that the nonverbal expectancy violations model generalizes beyond relationships among strangers.

As for the hypothesized arousal and valencing process, ratings by trained coders (reported previously in Hale & Burgoon, 1984) confirmed that violatees exhibited greater arousal than nonviolatees and that those in the nonimmediacy condition were the least composed, providing evidence that violations did produce activation. Another experiment conducted subsequent to this one that also manipulated multiple nonverbal cues in the form of conversational involvement (Burgoon & Coker, in press) likewise found that the introduction of a violation increased apparent arousal and distraction, as judged by raters. Based on these external manifestations, it can be inferred that violations heightened arousal.

The current results also demonstrate that the two types of violations were interpreted differently. Decreases in nonverbal immediacy (via conversational distance, gaze, body orientation, lean, and postural openness) communicated detachment, nonintimacy, dissimilarity, and dominance, while increases in immediacy communicated more involvement, intimacy, and similarity and moderate dominance. (The nonviolation condition was seen as the least dominant.)[5] The combination of relational meanings associated with nonimmediacy should have been especially undesirable, making nonimmediacy a potent negative violation.

This was the case. Consistent with Hypothesis 4, nonimmediacy violations produced more negative communication consequences than a nonviolation. Reducing immediacy produced lower ratings on competence, character, and sociability for both friends and strangers and violations accounted for a substantial 41% of the variance in credibility ratings. Although attraction failed to achieve a significant effect, Burgoon and Coker (in press) did find that decreased involvement also undermined attractiveness ratings, and the means from the current study are all in line with predictions. Thus, the nonsignificant effect in the current study may be attributable to low statistical power.

The consistent negative effects of a nonimmediacy violation, contrasting as they do with the previous finding for distance violations among highly rewarding persons, argue persuasively that a multiplicity of cues carrying the same, redundant message will not be assigned a positive interpretation, even when committed by a highly regarded other (such as a friend). It appears that the reward value of the communicator can only affect the labeling process when the cue in question is ambiguous and subject to a range of interpretations. The present findings, then, add explanation to the previous counterintuitive findings that far violations often produce more favorable communication outcomes than conforming to the norm. They strongly imply that such violations must have been sufficiently ambiguous to allow assigning positive meanings to the violations (such as greater status or composure) when they were committed by a high reward communicator.

Moreover, these findings confirm that even high reward communicators may engage in a negative violation of expectations. This finding refutes the argument that violation valence is simply a function of reward value and that the reward-violation va-

lence link produces a tautology. Reward valence alone does not dictate whether a violation is a positive or negative one. The social meaning of the violation behavior must also be taken into account. Both factors together influence the consequences of violations.

The only failure of the current experiment is the lack of support for differential effects of a high immediacy violation. The absence of significant interactions meant that friends and strangers did not show materially different patterns of response. Main effect means showed slight but nonsignificant decrements in the high immediacy condition compared to the normal condition. These findings run contrary to previous results showing that increases in single immediacy cues such as distance and gaze are positive violations by high reward communicators and produce more positive consequences than conforming to expectations. They are also slightly at odds with Burgoon and Coker (in press), who found that increased involvement was a positive violation for both high and low reward communicators. It was argued in the current experiment that friends would find an increase in immediacy a positive communicative pattern, while strangers would find such intensity of involvement and affiliativeness unwelcome. Although the relational message interpretations confirm that increases in immediacy communicated greater intimacy and involvement, friends and strangers both tended to respond to such increases in the same way. One explanation resides in the friends data. Among friends, some increment in intimacy is desirable, but too much at once may overwhelm the recipient, produce discomfort and suspicion, and lead to some reduction in positive evaluations of the violating friend. This would suggest that large increases along a single behavioral dimension such as proximity or gaze serve as positive violations, as do moderate increases in a set of behaviors, but large, simultaneous increases along several dimensions begin to turn the communication into a negative violation. Certainly, equilibrium theory (Argyle & Cook, 1976; Argyle & Dean, 1965) would argue this is the case. Research by Scherwitz and

Helmreich (1973) also supports this interpretation. They found that female dyads, who usually desire more affiliative types of interactions than males, experienced discomfort when high topic intimacy was coupled with high degrees of eye contact, compared to high eye contact and an impersonal topic. Scherwitz and Helmreich interpreted the high immediacy condition as constituting a violation of expectations. Hence, excessive immediacy along several kinesic and proxemic behaviors may be a risky communication strategy even among high reward communicators, despite some research arguing to the contrary (e.g., Imada & Hakel, 1976). Although it did not result in significant declines in attraction and credibility, the consistent pattern among means reveals that some decrements were occurring. It is possible that a more prolonged interaction would have produced more pronounced decreases.

As for the effects among nonreward communicators, if high immediacy began to show detrimental effects among friends, it should have shown more serious consequences among strangers. Yet it did not. A possible explanation for this anomaly is that, while strangers in general were less favorably evaluated than friends, their absolute credibility and attraction ratings were still relatively favorable. A plausible interpretation is that participants did not find interaction with a stranger truly nonrewarding. The pattern of communication consequences for them could therefore be expected to more closely approximate those among friends. It did.

One possible criticism that could be lodged against the current experiment and the model in general is that it might only be applicable to extreme types of violations. This criticism can be answered on both methodological and theoretical grounds. Methodologically, the types of violations employed here and in previous tests have been designed to be large enough to exceed a limen of recognition and to arouse the recipient but to be nonblatant. In this case, confederates were told to make their adjustments gradually so that they would not be obvious to the recipient. The fact that confederates were untrained and unrehearsed meant that they did not engage in the kinds of ex-

cessive violations that more experienced, motivated confederates might employ. Other experiments have similarly attempted to create violations that approximate the kinds of behaviors people might exhibit during routine encounters. More important, however, the theory itself applies to the full range of violations, from those that are barely deviant to those that are extreme, and predicts that the magnitude of the consequences will be a function of the magnitude of the violation. Experimental tests must necessarily operate within the range of moderate to large violations if statistically significant results are to be obtained; to attempt to detect small effect sizes would necessitate much larger samples and extremely labor-intensive research efforts. Equally important, it is with the larger types of violations that the differences between the violations model and other arousal-based interaction models become apparent. All the other models implicitly or explicitly claim that large violations produce compensatory responses and negative consequences. Only the nonverbal expectancy violations model proposes that certain kinds of large violations may produce reciprocal responses and favorable consequences. This experiment substantiates this claim.

While the present results add to the base of support for the nonverbal expectancy violations model, a question that remains unanswered and merely assumed at this stage is what kinds of relational messages are preferred from what kinds of sources. For example, do people positively or negatively value an affiliative overture from a stranger? And to what extent are dominance displays liked or disliked when exhibited by friends or strangers? These preferences and evaluations would provide the necessary valences to predict which types of violations should be positive ones and which negative ones. Future research along these lines should significantly advance understanding of the effects of nonverbal expectancy violations.

ENDNOTES
[1] There are actually three types of reward that can be distinguished. *Initial reward* is the communicator's net valence at the outset of an interaction; *derived reward* is that which develops during the course of an interaction; *terminal reward* is that

which exists at the conclusion of an interaction. (These distinctions follow those made for source credibility.) The operationalizations of reward are all forms of initial or derived reward.

[2] This can occur when the most favorably evaluated behavior, what Jackson (1964, 1966) calls the *point of maximum return,* is not the same as the norm or expectation. This position is the ideal and defines the extreme big end of the evaluative continuum. Monotonic increases in behavior need not correspond to monotonic increases in positive valence. Thus, it is possible to have "too much of a good thing." An extreme degree of some behavior—say, paying compliments—may be less positively valenced than a moderate degree. The important thing to recognize is that degrees of a given behavior or behavioral set can be scaled along an evaluative continuum.

[3] Apart from space considerations, the imbalance between males and females and among the four gender combinations, especially across the three experimental conditions, argued against including gender as a variable in this study. Gender effects can be relevant, however, and are analyzed in more detail in Burgoon and Aho (1982), Burgoon et al. (1984), and Burgoon et al. (1986), in which confederate gender was equally balanced. In Burgoon et al. (1984), males were judged as more dominant and detached than females. In Burgoon et al. (1986), male confederates were consistently rated more favorably than female confederates on credibility and attraction. On relational interpretations, receptivity effects were more pronounced for female confederates, who were seen as especially receptive using high gaze and least receptive using gaze aversion. Finally, dominance interpretation differed by gender in the high reward condition such that high or normal gaze was seen as dominant when exhibited by males but as submissive when exhibited by females. These interpretation differences did not alter the main effects of gaze on attraction and credibility.

[4] Elsewhere, the detachment dimension is labeled as an immediacy dimension, but to avoid confusion with the independent variable, we have preserved the detachment label here.

[5] Burgoon and Coker (in press) found similar interpretations were assigned to increased and decreased involvement. Greatly increased involvement communicated being very immediate, receptive, and equal; somewhat composed/relaxed; and neither similar nor dissimilar. If the communicator was highly rewarding, increased involvement also was perceived as somewhat dominant, but if the communicator had lower reward value, it was perceived as somewhat submissive. Decreased involvement expressed nonimmediacy, dissimilarity, neutral receptivity, moderate equality, and moderate submissiveness if the communicator had high reward value, and considerable submissiveness if the communicator had low reward value.

REFERENCES

Abelson, R. P. (1981). Psychological status of the script concept. *American Psychologist, 36,* 715-729.

Andersen, J. A., Andersen, P. A., & Jensen, A. D. (1979). The measurement of immediacy. *Journal of Applied Communication Research, 7,* 153-180.

Andersen, P. A. (1985). Nonverbal immediacy in interpersonal communication. In A. W. Siegman & S. Feldstein (Eds.), *Multichannel integrations of nonverbal behavior* (pp. 1-36). Hillsdale, N J: Lawrence Erlbaum.

Argyle, M., & Cook, M. (1976). *Gaze and mutual gaze.* Cambridge: Cambridge University Press.

Argyle, M., & Dean, J. (1965). Eye contact, distance, and affiliation. *Sociometry, 28,* 289-304.

Aronson, E., & Linder, D. (1965). Gain and loss of esteem as determinants of interpersonal attractiveness. *Journal of Experimental Social Psychology, 1,* 156-171.

Baron, R. A. (1978). Invasions of personal space and helping: Mediating effects of invader's apparent need. *Journal of Experimental Social Psychology, 14,* 304-312.

Buller, D. B., & Burgoon, J. K. (1986). The effects of vocalics and nonverbal sensitivity on compliance: A replication and extension. *Human Communication Research, 13,* 126-144.

Burgoon, J. K. (1978). A communication model of personal space violations: Explication and an initial test. *Human Communication Research, 4,* 129-142.

Burgoon, J. K. (1983). Nonverbal violations of expectations. In J. M. Wiemann & R. P. Harrison (Eds.), *Nonverbal interaction* (pp. 77-111). Beverly Hills, CA: Sage.

Burgoon, J. K. (1985, May). *Expectancies, rewards, violations and outcomes: Applications to the instructional environment.* Paper presented at the annual meeting of the International Communication Association, Honolulu.

Burgoon, J. K. & Aho, L. (1982). Three field experiments on the effects of conversational distance. *Communication Monographs, 49,* 71-88.

Burgoon, J. K., Buller, D. B., Hale, J. L., & de Turck, M. A. (1984). Relational messages associated with nonverbal behaviors. *Human Communication Research, 10,* 351-378.

Burgoon, J. K., & Coker, D. A. (in press). Nonverbal expectancy violations and conversational involvement. *Journal of Nonverbal Behavior.*

Burgoon, J. K., Coker, D. A., & Coker, R. A. (1986). Communicative effects of gaze behavior: A test of two contrasting explanations. *Human Communication Research, 12,* 495-524.

Burgoon, J. K. & Hale, J. L. (1987). Validation and measurement of the fundamental themes of relational communication. *Communication Monographs, 54,* 19-41.

Burgoon, J. K., & Jones, S. B. (1976). Toward a theory of personal space expectations and their violations. *Human Communication Research, 2,* 131-146.

Burgoon, J. K., Manusov, V., Mineo, P., & Hale, J. L. (1985). Effects of gaze on hiring, credibility, attraction and relational message interpretation. *Journal of Nonverbal Behavior, 9,* 133-146.

Burgoon, J. K., & Saine, T. (1978). *The unspoken dialogue: An introduction to nonverbal communication.* Boston: Houghton-Mifflin.

Burgoon, J. K., Stacks, D. W., & Burch, S. A. (1982). The role of interpersonal rewards and violations of distancing expectations in achieving influence in small groups. *Communication, 11,* 114-128.

Burgoon, J. K., Stacks, D. W., & Woodall, G. W. (1979). A communicative model of violations of distancing expectations. *Western Journal of Speech Communication, 43,* 156-167.

Cappella, J. N., & Greene, J. O. (1982). A discrepancy-arousal explanation of mutual influence in expressive behavior for adult-adult and infant-adult interaction. *Communication Monographs, 49,* 89-114.

Coutts, L. M., & Ledden, M. (1977). Nonverbal compensatory reactions to changes in interpersonal proximity. *Journal of Social Psychology, 102-103,* 283-290.

Cupach, W. R. (1980, November). *Interpersonal conflict: Relational strategies and intimacy.* Paper presented at the annual meeting of the Speech Communication Association, New York.

Donohue, W. A., Diez, M. E., Stahle, R., & Burgoon, J. K. (1983, May). *The effects of distance violations on verbal immediacy: An exploration.* Paper presented at the annual meeting of the International Communication Association, Dallas.

Galle, A., Spratt, G., Chapman, A. J., & Smallbone, A. (1977). EEG correlates of eye contact and interpersonal distance. *Biological Psychology, 3,* 237-245.

Gibson, E. J., Owsley, C. J., & Johnston, J. (1978). Perception of invariants by five-month-old infants: Differentiation of two types of motion. *Developmental Psychology, 14,* 407-415.

Haith, M. M., Kiesen, W., & Collins, D. (1969). Response of the human infant to level of complexity of intermittent visual movement. *Journal of Experimental Child Psychology, 7,* 52-69.

Hale, J. L., & Burgoon, J. K. (1984). Models of reactions to changes in nonverbal immediacy *Journal of Nonverbal Behavior, 8,* 287-314.

Ickes, W., Patterson, M. L., Rajecki, D. W., & Tanford, S. (1982). Behavioral and cognitive consequences of reciprocal versus compensatory responses to pre-interaction expectancies. *Social Cognition, 1,* 160-190.

Imada, A. S., & Hakel, M. D. (1977). Influence of nonverbal communication and rater proximity on impressions and decisions in simulated employment interviews. *Journal of Applied Psychology, 62,* 285-300.

Jackson, J. (1964). The normative regulation of authoritative behavior. In W. J. Gove & J. W. Dyson (Eds.), *The making of decisions: A reader in administrative behavior* (pp. 213-241). New York: Free Press.

Jackson, J. (1966). A conceptual and measurement model for norms and roles. *Pacific Sociological Review, 9,* 35-47.

King, S. W., & Sereno, K. K. (1984). Conversational appropriateness as a conversational imperative. *Quarterly Journal of Speech, 70,* 264-273.

Konecni, V. J., Libuser, L., Morton, H., & Ebbesen, E. B. (1973). Effects of a violation of personal space on escape and helping responses. *Journal of Experimental Social Psychology, 11,* 288-299.

Kreckel, M. (1981). *Communicative acts and shared knowledge as natural discourse.* New York: Academic Press.

Langer, E. (1978). Rethinking the role of thought in social interaction. In J. H. Harvey, W. J. Ickes, & R. F. Kidd (Eds.), *New directions in attribution research* (Vol. 2, pp. 35-58). Hillsdale, NJ: Lawrence Erlbaum.

Langer, E. J., & Ember, L. (1980). Role of mindlessness in the perception of deviance. *Journal of Personality and Social Psychology, 39,* 360-367.

Little, K. B. (1965). Personal space. *Journal of Experimental Social Psychology, 1,* 237-247.

Manusov, V. L. (1984). *Nonverbal violations of expectations theory: A test of gaze behavior.* Unpublished master's thesis, Michigan State University.

McCroskey, J. C., Jensen, T., & Valencia, C. (1973). *Measurement of the credibility of peers and spouses.* Paper presented at the annual meeting of the International Communication Association, Montreal.

McCroskey, J. C., & McCain, T. A. (1974). The measurement of interpersonal attraction. *Speech Monographs, 41,* 261-266.

Mehrabian, A. (1971). *Silent messages.* Belmont, CA: Wadsworth.

Newtson, D. (1973). Attribution and the unit of perception of ongoing behavior. *Journal of Personality and Social Psychology, 28,* 28-38.

Patterson, M. L. (1976). An arousal model of interpersonal intimacy. *Psychological Review, 83,* 235-245.

Patterson, M. L. (1982). A sequential functional model of nonverbal exchange. *Psychological Review, 89,* 231-249.

Patterson, M. L. (1983). *Nonverbal behavior: A functional perspective.* New York: Springer-Verlag.

Rosenfeld, H. M., Breck, B. E., Smith, S. H., & Kehoe, S. (1984). Intimacy-mediators of the proximity-gaze compensation effect: Movement, conversational role, acquaintance, and gender. *Journal of Nonverbal Behavior, 8,* 235-249.

Schank, R. C., & Abelson, R. P. (1977). *Scripts, plans, goals and understanding.* Hillsdale, NJ: Lawrence Erlbaum.

Scheflen, A. E. (1984). *How behavior means.* Garden City, NY: Anchor Books.

Scherwitz, L., & Helmreich, R. (1973). Interactive effects of eye contact and verbal content on interpersonal attraction in dyads. *Journal of Personality and Social Psychology, 25,* 6-14.

Schiffenbauer, A., & Schiavo, R. S. (1976). Physical distance and attention: An intensification effect. *Journal of Experimental Social Psychology, 26,* 332-346.

Smith, R. J., & Knowles, E. S. (1979). Affective and cognitive mediators of reactions to spatial invasions. *Journal of Experimental Social Psychology, 15,* 537-552.

Stacks, D. W., & Burgoon, J. K. (1981). The role of nonverbal behaviors as distractors in resistance to persuasion in interpersonal contexts. *Central States Speech Journal, 32,* 61-73.

Storms, M. D., & Thomas, G. C. (1977). Reactions to physical closeness. *Journal of Personality and Social Psychology, 35,* 412-418.

Street, R. L., Jr., & Cappella, J. N. (1985). Sequence and pattern in communicative behaviour: A model and commentary. In R. L. Street & J. N. Cappella (Eds.), *Sequence and pattern in communicative behaviour* (pp. 243-276). London: Edward Arnold.

Sundstrom, E., & Altman, I. (1976). Interpersonal relationships and personal space: Research review and theoretical model. *Human Ecology, 4,* 47-67.

Thompson, D. E., Aiello, J. R., & Epstein, Y. M. (1979). Interpersonal distance preferences. *Journal of Nonverbal Behavior, 4,* 113-118.

Traynowicz, L. L. (1982, May). *Communication and relationship: The small talk of intimates and strangers.* Paper presented at the annual meeting of the International Communication Association, Boston.

Willis, F. N., Jr. (1966). Initial speaking distance as a function of the speakers' relationship. *Psychonomic Science, 5,* 221-222.

UNIT IV

Relationship Talk: Conversations, Turning Points, and Self-Disclosure

In the previous unit you read articles dealing with attraction and the initiation of relationships. This unit examines the processes associated with the continued development of relationships. Specifically, the three articles in this unit deal with the manner in which we carry on talk in relationships. The unit includes studies of how daily conversations vary, how we communicate changes in the relationship, and a summary of some of the research about how we disclose information about ourselves to others. As you read the articles, think about what each has to offer toward better understanding the nature of the way we talk with one another. Realize that these three articles are three small but significant pieces in a large puzzle. You might think about what other pieces are needed to complete the picture of relational talk.

Duck, Rutt, Hurst, and Strejc in article 12 apply a diary methodology to the collection of data on everyday conversations. Little research has been done on variations in the way we communicate in our everyday interactions. The study reported in article 12 focuses on three areas—sex differences, relational differences, and temporal differences (variations according to the day of the week)—in everyday conversations. The authors describe the development of an instrument created to assess various aspects of everyday communication. The results from three specific studies are presented in the article. Each study uses a different set of respondents and is designed to test a different research question. The first study provided the initial data pool needed to establish the factors that compose the instrument. The authors used factor analysis to tease out the underlying components of everyday talk. They found that the items composing their scale fell predominantly into four factors, which they labeled: **communication quality, value** of the interaction, **degree** of change caused by the interaction, and **control** of the interaction. The researchers report a statistic called Cronback's alpha, which tells how well the items making up each of the measures interrelate to one another. The closer the numbers are to 1.0, the stronger the relationship among the items; alphas ranging from .70 to .90 are generally considered good.

The data from the initial set of self-reports were also used to examine variations in these four factors and the three areas mentioned earlier. The authors report the results of MANOVA (multiple analysis of variance) and univariate analysis (ANOVA). In MANOVA the variation in one independent variable is compared to the variations in a number of dependent variables. For instance, in article 12 the effect of the sex of the respondents was examined on the four communication factors and the effect (called the main effect) was found to be significant. What this means is that there were differences in communication factors based on whether the respondent was male or female. Univariate analysis is used after MANOVA to examine the impact of the dependent variable on each independent variable, one at a time. In this study, the sex of the respondent affected two of the four factors, quality and change.

The article includes two additional studies, with smaller samples than the first study, that were designed to test specifically the nature of everyday conversations by relationship and by day of the week.

Baxter and Bullis's article on turning points (article 13) represents a good test of relational development stage theory. Forty couples completed an instrument in which they graphed changes in the level of commitment over the duration of the relationship. Each individual was then interviewed and asked questions about significant events associated with those commitment changes. The participants also provided information about relational satisfaction. The interview responses were coded by the researchers according to a categorization of 26 turning points. The researchers collapsed these 26 categories into 14 groups, which they called "supratypes."

There were five research questions addressed in the article. The statistics in this article are generally similar to those in some of the previous articles, including ANOVA and *t*-tests. For a number of variables the authors use percentages to indicate frequency of occurrence. The authors utilize a statistical procedure, chi-square, to determine whether the percentage distribution is by chance. According to chance, the percentages should be equally distributed. Chi-square determines whether the obtained data are significantly different from chance distribution.

The final article in this section, article 14 by Bochner, examines the early history of self-disclosure research and theory, and ultimately questions the wisdom of openly sharing information about ourselves. This article was written in 1982, after a decade in which total openness and self-disclosure were advocated. In this article, Bochner challenges the value and effectiveness of being totally open about ourselves when interacting with others. In his review of the research he provides evidence indicating that cultural norms make it generally detrimental to a developing relationship to disclose either too much information or negative information about one's self. This article includes a discussion of some of the methodological problems associated with the research on self-disclosure that make it difficult to form general conclusions about self-disclosure. These problems include the tendency of individuals to self-report higher levels of disclosure than they actually disclose, and the inadvisability of generalizing on the basis of experimental manipulation of information.

You should notice strong connections between this article and the articles on uncertainty reduction, social exchange theory, predicted outcome value, and the initiation of relationships. Self-disclosure is one type of information we can make available in our interactions. Providing self-disclosure would seem to help another reduce uncertainty, and thus be beneficial to relational development. However, Bochner points out that if we are attracted to someone during the initiation of the relationship, we are likely to be very guarded about disclosing information that might alienate the other. There appear to be two contrary forces at work during initial interactions: the desire to reduce uncertainty about another, which is countered by a reluctance to share information about one's self. Think about whether such tension exists in your own experiences.

QUESTIONS TO CONSIDER WHEN READING

ARTICLE 12
A. What findings reported in the studies confirm your own experiences in everyday conversations? What findings contradict your experiences?
B. The findings in this study are based almost entirely on the responses of single college students. How do you think the findings might differ if the respondents had been older and/or married?

ARTICLE 13
A. How do the results of this study fit into a model of relational development like that in the Knapp and Vangelisti article?
B. Try to apply the procedures described in the article to

one of your own intimate relationships. Draw a graph showing the pattern of changes in the level of commitment and try to identify the events associated with each level.

ARTICLE 14

A. Decide whether you agree or disagree with Bochner's contention that openness is overrated. What are your reasons for agreeing or disagreeing?

B. Develop a set of rules for self-disclosure, based on the research reported in the article, that you would share with someone from another culture who is unfamiliar with our disclosure norms.

12

Some Evident Truths About Conversations in Everyday Relationships: All Communications Are Not Created Equal

STEVE DUCK | MARGARET HOY HURST
DEBORAH J. RUTT | HEATHER STREJC

This article presents a program of studies that map out daily conversations and so establish a geography of everyday communication. A new method (the Iowa Communication Record) is offered to extend research using diary methods and focus the researcher on communication in daily life. Three studies collectively show (a) consistent sex differences in the quality and nature of conversations across different types of relationships, (b) a consistent rank ordering of relationship types that differs from that intuitively included in previous models of relationship formation, and (c) a consistent difference between conversations held on different days of the week, with Wednesdays associated with greater degrees of conflictive communication. Self-disclosure is much less frequent in everyday life than assumed on the basis of laboratory work, and the predominant form of communication in intimate relationships is not only nonintimate but not simply distinguishable from communication in other relationship types. Communication quality distinguishes female from male partners, suggesting that previous findings on preference for female partners are truly founded in communication variables, which have previously been underrated. The article shows that closer attention must in future be paid to communicative variations created by daily events and circumstances, and the role of routine communication in daily life must be explored in future studies of social participation.

Recently, it has become apparent that routine, mundane, everyday life behaviors influence a range of psychological and communicative dimensions of interpersonal interaction, such as maintenance of relationships (Baxter & Dindia, 1990), coping with stressors (Bolger, DeLongis, Kessler, & Schilling, 1989), and many aspects of social participation (Reis, Wheeler, Nezlek, Kernis, & Spiegel, 1985; Wheeler & Nezlek, 1977). Accordingly, theorists have called for greater attention to everyday life behaviors, particularly as these affect feelings about one's partner, conduct of emotional life, and exercise of power and control (Baxter, 1987; Duck, 1986, 1988; Hays, 1989; Wiemann & Busch, 1990).

Despite this growing interest, work to date has not focused with any directness on *communication* in everyday life. To the extent that communication is even mentioned in most psychological studies, it is treated only as an idle medium through which cognition is expressed or "delivered." By contrast, when communication is studied directly, it is rarely studied as an everyday life phenomenon, and the true significance of minor environmental circumstances on common routines has not been empirically assessed. Instead, laboratory studies implicitly treat all everyday life communications as essentially equivalent and have paid little attention to day-to-day variation within or between given types of relationship or as a function of daily events.

From Duck, S., Rutt, D. J., Hurst, M. H., & Strejc, H. (1991). Some evident truths about conversations in everyday relationships: All communications are not equal. *Human Communication Research, 18*(2) 228–267. © International Communication Association.

Furthermore, although researchers have drawn important distinctions and similarities between processes in developing relationships, on one hand, and deteriorating relationships, on the other (Montgomery, 1988), or between different types of a given class of relationship (e.g., Fitzpatrick, 1988), we have paid scant attention to the underlying dynamics of stability or change in communication in different types of relationships as moderated by daily experience.

This picture is further complicated by three common research practices: first, aggregating different communication occurrences from different varieties of relationships into summary measures for analytic purposes; second, treating any instance of communication in a given relationship type as an indicator of the distribution of communication activity in the relationship as a whole; and third, treating data gathered on any day or in any life circumstances as equivalent to data gathered on any other day or in other circumstances. Thus respondents who meet a criterion of "close relationship" by reporting involvement in relationships that may range in length from as little as 2 weeks to several years are nevertheless typically regarded as equivalent (see Clark & Reis, 1988; Duck & Montgomery, 1991); or in a search to characterize the communicative features of a given class of relationship, specifically focused single studies of communication in dating (e.g., Tolhuizen, 1989), friendship (e.g., Hays, 1989), or marriage (e.g., Fitzpatrick, 1988) are often taken by other scholars to be studies of the general nature of communication and used as the basis for broad summary claims about both relationships and communication (Argyle & Henderson, 1985); or researchers have treated communication as essentially cognitively driven and have assumed as constant those surrounding circumstances of everyday life that might actually moderate a person's communication on a particular occasion as, for example, a function of mood (Barbee, 1990) or daily events (Bolger et al., 1989).

In sum, researchers have thus far been less successful at careful study of the routine variance that occurs in communication within a type of relationship under different circumstances or across time

in the real world than they have at depicting, as it were, the mean of those relationships. Thus while we have learned a certain amount about all of these things indirectly, there is still much to be learned about the ways in which relational contexts modify communication and about the dynamics of those contexts in real life.

Placed alongside this research is nevertheless a body of studies showing that on structural and psychological dimensions, different sorts of relationships have different features when broad aggregational data sets are compared. Thus Davis and Todd (1982) distinguished friendship from romantic relationships by using a paradigm case formulation procedure and found that romantic relationships involve more exclusiveness and fascination, with a greater criterial demand for loyalty and willingness to help, than do friendships. Also, Berger, Weber, Munley, and Dixon (1977) showed that close friends feel more fully understood by one another than do pairs of lovers. This clearly suggests differences in both the style and content of communication between pairs of individuals in these two classes of relationships taken as a whole. Using a role-playing technique, Knapp, Ellis, and Williams (1980) had respondents imagine what communication would be like in different hypothetical relationships and showed that persons could efficiently differentiate relationship types, given these instructions. There are thus grounds for believing that there are psychological differences in the character of relationships and that these differences are mirrored in communication.

A stronger theoretical argument for exploring such hypothesized differences was offered by Duck and Pond (1989), who saw conversation as a way for persons to present inner symbolic life in relationships. Some have argued that relationships are created and developed by strategic means (Baxter & Wilmot, 1984; Berger, 1988)—indeed, this approach seems to be the dominant one in present research on relational communication (Montgomery, 1988). Such a view lends itself to interpretation within a communicative framework that relies on Aristotelian agentic models of compliance gaining, where one person actively seeks to lure, beguile, or persuade a partner into a deeper level of relationship. Contrasted with this view is the claim that everyday talk embodies relationships through Burkean rhetorical means. In this argument, conversations in everyday life have symbolic force for creating, sustaining, and manifesting relationships over and above any direct but incidental effects that they may have on the stylistic "shape" or character of the relationship. Duck and Pond (1989) argued that in their everyday talk, individuals are essentially dealing with their relationship in symbolic ways that serve to enhance identification and consubstantiality. Talk functions to assure the continuation of the relationship into the future by projecting a rhetorically forceful image of continuance not only through its language but through its very occurrence. In such a model, relationships are essentially unfinished business that needs to be perpetuated through regular mundane relational communication (Duck, 1990).

By tapping the ways in which persons actually conduct their conversation in a daily-life context, researchers could explore not only the ways in which representation of relational reality assists in the construction and differentiation of relationships but a variety of other issues in interpersonal interaction or routine social support (Leatham & Duck, 1990). In other words, discovery of the geography of communication will help us to determine the role of conversation in creating relational stabilities while also aiding us in answering important questions about the role of discourse in relationships (Duck & Pond, 1989). What remains is the need to test this possibility through the raw data of real-life interaction, where everyday communication is the direct topic of assessment.

If relationships are founded in everyday life communication (Duck & Pond, 1989), then, taken with the forgoing argument, previous findings from laboratory or hypothetical contexts suggest that there will be important differences in the daily communication within different sorts of relationships and that there will be communicative as well as psychological features on which such relationships can be differentiated. One obvious suggestion would be that the more intimate the relationship,

the more intimate will be the conversations that take place in the relationship; indeed, such a suggestion is often felt to be so obvious that it is taken for granted without being tested (for a discussion of this, see Helgeson, Shaver, & Dyer, 1987). Another presumption would be that self-disclosure, well-studied in laboratory settings and found to be important in relationships development (e.g., Derlega & Winstead, 1986), should occur more often in intimate relationships than in less intimate ones. Again, such a presumption is sometimes seen as so obvious that it is taken for granted (cf. Helgeson et al., 1987).

Although these are reasonable predictions to make on the basis of laboratory work, there are some pieces of data that conflict with this pattern. Dindia, Fitzpatrick, and Kenny (1989) found that in naturally occurring conversations, self-disclosure does not appear with anything like the frequency that is indicated in the laboratory research, and Duck and Miell (1986) suggested that most conversations between friends are mundane and nonintimate. One research question then concerns the extent to which data from everyday conversations reflect both the intimacy and the self-disclosure levels that might be expected on the basis of laboratory-based research programs:

> RQ1: Do everyday conversations show the graduations of intimacy and self-disclosure, as between one relationship type and another, that some previous research on relational communication would lead one to expect?

This question has important ramifications if these variables are not as significant in real-life relationships as they have been assumed to be in theory (and in textbooks!). Finally, if established relationships differ, in relative terms, from others that are still in flux, development, or process, then there should be greater variability in the latter sorts of conversations than in the former. In other words, a stability should be found in *conversational* measures in well-established relationships (over and above the usual *emotional* stability), and this will not be apparent in relationships of lesser equilibrium.

A second set of research questions focuses on issues raised in previous work by psychologists on "social participation," which has shown interesting patterns of difference between the sexes. For instance, Wheeler and Nezlek (1977) found that females engage in talk for talk's sake more than males do. Such differences have been consistently found by other workers also (e.g., Baxter & Wilmot, 1986). Hays (1989) reported that both sexes claimed to receive comparable amounts of benefits in their interactions but that females reported offering friends more emotional and informational support. Further, Wheeler, Reis, and Nezlek (1983) and Hays (1989) found that females reported more satisfaction with their same-sex friendships than did males, while males reported more costs in their interactions than did females. If we add communication to such analysis, then we should not only readily replicate such findings but extend them to the conversational dynamics and patterns in which the two genders participate. For example, the *communications* of females, rather than the mere presence of females as companions, should be preferred. Support for such a proposal came from Baxter and Wilmot (1986), who found such differences, but in their study, respondents were constrained to compare one same-sex and one cross-sex relationship rather than mapping their general conversation patterns both within and outside such targeted relationships. The larger question thus still remains unanswered:

RQ2: Do communications in everyday life show the same sorts of sex differences as those demonstrated by researchers focusing on other features of social participation? In particular, are females different from males in the functions to which they put everyday conversation?

Although almost no laboratory work on psychological or communicative processes in relationships takes specific account of such factors as the effects of day of the week on responses that are assessed, some theorists, such as McCall (1988), have argued specifically that "literature [should] turn scholarly attention from a dyad's [or individual's] 'internal locus of control' to a greater recognition of vital environmental influences" (p. 484). While some have shown (e.g., Barbee, 1990) that both respon-

dents' and their partners' moods are a significant influence on socially supportive transactions, for instance, others have claimed that day of the week is an influence on mood to the extent that weekends are more positive and less negative than any other day of the week (Stone, Hedges, Neale, & Satin, 1985). We are aware of no studies that have explored the communicative geography of different days of the week. Communication theory usually relies on the evidently untested assumption that any day (including weekends) is the same as any other day as far as communicative processes are concerned. The studies that follow made it possible for us to assess the validity of this untested assumption:

RQ3: Are everyday communications all the same, or are persons systematically influenced by exterior events, such as the "Blue Monday effect" or the alleged relaxing effects of weekends?

In sum, then, our research questions focus on relationship type, sex difference, and day of the week, our main purpose being to draw a geography of everyday communication and to test whether communication phenomena such as intimate talk and self-disclosure occur in everyday life as often as supposed in theory based on laboratory work. We sought to achieve these specific goals by assessing everyday communication, but we wished to focus on the subjective aspects of everyday conversation for theoretical reasons.

Given our practical concern and our research questions, a method based on observation would seem to be satisfactory in principle, even if nightmarish in practice (Sillars, 1991). However, we were particularly interested, for theoretical reasons spelled out earlier and elsewhere (Duck, 1990, 1991; Duck & Pond, 1989), in the role of subjective experience of conversation in the creation and maintenance of relationships. From this standpoint, closely based on rhetorical approaches, everyday talk was construed as a representation of persons' realities and the intermingling of such realities (a concept similar to Stephen's, 1984, term "symbolic interdependence") as fundamental to the existence of relationships. Thus we saw a person's representation of talk as being fundamental to relationships processes (Duck, 1990), and our methodology needed to reflect the assumption that there are important elements to relational communication that are necessarily subjective.

TOWARD A NEW TECHNIQUE FOR THE STUDY OF EVERYDAY COMMUNICATION

A recent significant advance in the study of everyday social participation in general has been the use of "diary" report forms introduced by Wheeler and Nezlek (1977) and now generally known as the Rochester Interaction Record (RIR). These are subjective self-reports of interaction completed soon after the actual encounter itself, and they have been used by many different investigators in a variety of forms and circumstances (Baxter & Wilmot, 1986; Bolger et al., 1989; Duck & Miell, 1986; Hays, 1989; Reis, Nezlek, & Wheeler, 1980). Such accounts avoid the problem of retrospective recall by being completed near the time of the recorded events and are minimally intrusive measures of social participation. Since it was introduced, the RIR has been used to understand underlying aspects of social participation. For example, Reis et al. (1980) depicted the empirical relationship between physical attractiveness and social participation rates and showed not only quantitative differences in the social participation of the physically attractive and the less attractive but related qualitative differences. Using the same technique, Reis et al. (1985) were able to depict the aspects of social interaction that have a specific impact on health and showed that interactants who meet more females tend to report a higher health status.

Because they can be used over extended periods of time with the same individuals, diaries can also be used to gather raw data about the dynamics of roles and relationships that in other work can seem static (e.g., Duck & Miell, 1982, 1986). By repeatedly tapping the interactions of the same person or of a person with the same others over time, diaries give researchers the chance to study change and variation (e.g., Hays, 1989) so that they can rule out stable personality or environmental factors as hidden third variables in the causal patterns identified (Duck, 1991).

The RIR has been employed by communication researchers and used to good effect to test out theories of the development of relationships (Baxter & Wilmot, 1986; Duck & Miell, 1986). Nonetheless, it is striking that apart from asking whether self-disclosure occurred, the RIR includes not a single question assessing communication in any form whatsoever. Its specific interest is to delineate the rates of participation in social interaction rather than to explore the interior dynamics or communicative content of those interactions. In the service of this goal, the RIR implicitly treats conversation as a mere conduit for cognition and neither explores nor credits the complex dynamics of talk in real-life discourse.

What is clearly needed is a diary method that focuses directly and explicitly on communication (Baxter & Wilmot, 1986). Such a diary format would not merely be different from the RIR on a point of methodological nicety but would correct the emphasis in the RIR that treats communication implicitly as unimportant in social interaction and as a simple medium for "more important" processes. Not only would an extended method allow communication researchers to add to the store of knowledge about social participation by adducing raw data on communication, but it would also permit psychologists to account for some of their findings through the medium of communication. For example, if, as indicated earlier, social interactions with females are associated with improved health status, then communication research could perhaps isolate the specific features of females' conversations that contribute to such effects.

Given the undoubted fact that in the social sciences, students are often the basis for theoretical claims extended to a wider humanity, it is useful to begin by building up a geography of student conversations with different sorts of people—if only as one first step toward extending such description to a larger population. At the very least this will begin to provide a geography of the real lives of our standard subjects that could serve as a useful reference point for future laboratory-based work using such individuals. As a first step, we should also find considerable similarity between the RIR results and those based on a communication diary record (since part of our purpose is conceptual replication).

Against this background, the present article reports on part of a program of studies. The basic measurement technique is the same in all studies, in that respondents filled out diary report forms for the specified interactions. What differs between successive studies is the precise schedule that subjects were given for completing their reports, whether unconstrained, daily, or focused on different relationship types.

METHOD

The Iowa Communication Record

The Iowa Communication Record (ICR) is a structured self-report form on which respondents record their recollection of conversations. Its primary purpose is to provide a means of replicating and extending work with previous diary records so as to include communication variables as an explicit focus of measurement (Duck, 1991). For this reason, several of the scales are adapted directly from the RIR and assess basic interaction raw data, such as age and sex of individuals and partner, and time, place, and duration of the interaction. A number of other factual items were also chosen for inclusion on the basis of previous work on typologies of relationships (e.g., Davis & Todd, 1985) that have shown the importance of differentiating such matters as length of time the respondent has known the partner and the nature of the relationship between them (stranger, acquaintance, friend, best friend, lover, or relative [including spouse]).

The remaining scales measure features of the talk and its context along with subjective assessments

of its quality, impact, value, and potential for changing the relationship. Past research (e.g., Baxter & Wilmot, 1986; Knapp et al., 1980; McLaughlin, 1983; Norton, 1983; Rogers & Farace, 1975) has identified a number of features of talk that are of consistent interest to communication theorists, such as judgment/evaluation dimensions, dominance and control/power issues, efficiency, synchrony, and style. We also included nine scales that Baxter and Wilmot (1986) developed to assess relational communication dimensions of Personalness, Smoothness, and Efficiency, important to Knapp et al.'s (1980) model of relational change. On the basis of such work and a series of pretests with earlier forms of the ICR, we devised scales that were intended to assess these features. (In the appropriate section of this article, we report that factor analysis of the results of Study 1 yielded a structure consistent with the belief that we measured at least the judgment/evaluation, style/quality, and dominance/power/control elements of conversation. Given the self-report nature of the ICR, efficiency and synchrony cannot be assessed in studies with the general survey design used here, but there is no reason why the ICR could not be used in conjunction with other techniques to assess self-reports of such elements in relation to other raw data on these issues.)

Because the ICR was designed to be a general instrument whose use and value in communication and psychological research need not be restricted to the sorts of questions tested here, a number of other items were also included on the form. These assessed conversational context, that is to say, questions concerning the partners' activities immediately preceding conversation, during conversation, and after conversation. As can be seen in the appendix, these activities included such items as watching TV, studying, and eating a meal.

The ICR thus combines some of the measures of quantitative aspects of interaction (also assessed by the RIR) with some direct measures of communicational elements of the interaction (cf. Baxter & Wilmot, 1986) and measures of qualitative aspects of the interaction. A full copy of the ICR is shown in the appendix. The ICR consists of 33 questions or rating scales and generally takes about 20 minutes to complete on the first occasion but is completed much more rapidly on subsequent occasions. Individuals completing the ICR, as do subjects completing the RIR, report that it is a meaningful and involving task that they take seriously, a report borne out by checks on the reliability of some of the responses on "factual" matters, such as the number of persons spoken with during a week where alpha coefficients are typically in the .80s and .90s (see the Analyses and Results section for each study).

Our long-term goal is to apply the method in various different settings using as wide a sample of respondents as possible, but for reasons outlined in the introduction, we chose to begin by providing a data base for students that would provide useful comparison data for laboratory-based studies of similar populations. Also, given our long-term goals, we should really conduct immense studies of every facet of communicative life! However, even the longest journey begins with a single step, and the series of studies here each takes a different sampling solution to help create the beginnings of a picture of the phenomena that we seek to understand.

STUDY 1

Respondents

In Study 1, 1,585 students from a large midwestern university were recruited as respondents as part of class exercises and, in their own time out of class, completed an ICR report of a social interaction. They were told that they should do this as soon as possible after the interaction. Part of our intention was extension and conceptual replication of the work of Wheeler and Nezlek (1977). Following their lead, on which this work is based, an interaction was defined as an encounter (of any length) with another person in which the participants attended to one another, conversed (whether face-to-face or by telephone), and adjusted their behavior in response to one another. Using Wheeler and

Nezlek's examples, it was indicated that sitting next to someone on the bus or in class did not count nor did mere exchange of greetings unless conversation occurred and the person felt that the encounter was notable. In Study 1, respondents were unconstrained as to length of interaction selected, the day of the week which they selected, or the time of that day when they chose to report the interaction, although later studies reported here varied these instructions according to design.

Of the 1,585 respondents, 828 were female and 757 male, 12 were married, and the mean age was 21 years, 1 month.

Analyses and Results

As the first of the program of studies, Study 1 bears much of the weight of the arguments advanced earlier for descriptive work. Before reporting the full analytic procedures, then, a brief description of the findings is in order. We found that (a) 52% of reported interactions were with a female partner, (b) the average length of acquaintance with the conversational partner was 16 months, and (c) the modal interaction was with a friend and lasted for 30 minutes. Most interactions took place with a person to whom the respondent spoke for about 19% of all interactions in the week and resulted in a satisfaction level of 2.98 on a 9-point scale (1 = *high*, 9 = *low*), a perceived value of 4.4 (same anchors), and a value for the future of the relationship of 5.27. On average, then, the reported conversations were essentially routine, reasonably satisfying interactions that had little impact on the relationship. It is worth noting even at this early stage that this description notably contradicts the characterization of social interaction implicit in much existing research literature, especially as regards those studies that suggest most interactions have a direct impact on relationship outcomes—as indeed they may when studied in the laboratory or made the focus of a specific battery of research questions.

The items on the ICR were subjected to a principal components factor analysis with Varimax rotation. This produced a clean factor structure with nine factors having eigenvalues of greater than 1 and accounting together for 62.7% of the variance. Some have argued (McCroskey & Young, 1979) that this criterion, of itself, is not adequate for theoretical work and have urged researchers to attend to other criteria, such as (a) at least two items should load above .50 on a factor, (b) the factor should be interpretable and theoretically meaningful, and (c) the factor should pass Cattell's (1966) scree test. This latter test indicates a break in eigenvalues after the sixth factor, the six together accounting for 53% of the variance. Application of the other criteria makes it clear that all but two are factors of major interest that are readily interpretable conceptually and consistent with previous work. The two factors that were dropped each contained only one item that loaded above .50. The first retained factor contains almost all of the items that assess Communication Quality and can safely be given that label. The second factor comprises two scales assessing the Value of the interaction, one assessing the talk-task nature of the interaction and the other qualitatively assessing depth. Task-related, deep conversations were associated with higher value for present and future, while the degree to which the interaction was just "for talk's sake" loaded highly negatively on that factor. The third factor contains most of the scales assessing the degree of Change brought about by the interaction. The fourth factor contains three items dealing with Control of the interaction. These four factors accounted for 46% of the variance and were the subject of the remaining analyses in all three studies.

Cronbach's alpha for the nine contributing measures of Quality was .88. The measures of amount of Change that respondents felt had been brought about by the interaction showed a Cronbach's alpha of .81. The Value scale rendered an alpha of .77, while the items measuring Control yielded a Kendall's $W = .102, p < .001$. These four factors are thus acceptably reliable and are used as basic analytic elements henceforward.

The factor structure was also derived for the two sexes separately and indicated close parallelism. In both sexes, the same initial nine factors were obtained, and the same four major factors were derived by the same criteria, using Quartimax rotation (see Table 12.1). Cronbach's alphas for the four factors for the sexes separately showed Quality: .84 (males) and .90 (females); Change: .78 (males) and .81 (females); and Value: .75 (males) and .78 (females); with Kendall's W for Control $= .07$ (males) and .118 (females), both $ps < .001$.

Sex Differences

To assess effects of Sex of Respondent and Sex of (conversational) Partner, the factor items were submitted to two MANOVAs. In the case of Sex of Respondent, a significant main effect was found ($F = 5.88$; $df = 2, 1585$; $p < .01$; Pillai's trace $= .22$). Further univariate analyses revealed that Sex of Respondent significantly affected both ratings of communication Value ($F = 7.22$; $df = 1, 1583$; $p < .01$; eta$^2 = .05$), with males ($M = 5.24$) rating value lower than females ($M = 5.06$—higher scores indicate lower value) and Change ($F = 32.05$, $df = 1, 1583$, $p < .001$, eta$^2 = .19$), with females ($M = 9.53$) reporting significantly more change after an interaction than did males ($M = 7.13$). Because Value essentially assesses the value of the interaction for the future of the relationship, these results suggest that males are more likely to see relational stability implicit in a given conversation, whereas females are more likely to see conversations as changing their opinion of the person and hence destabilizing the likely future of the relationship.

In the analysis of effects of Sex of Partner, the MANOVA revealed a significant main effect ($F = 3.57, df = 2, 1582, p < .002$, Pillai's trace $= .013$), and subsequent univariate analyses showed that Communication Quality accounted for the effect ($F = 9.57, df = 1, 1583, p < .01$, eta$^2 = .06$), with a female partner being rated significantly higher than a male by both sexes. This finding is consistent with but extends the work of Reis (1986) and Wheeler et al. (1983), who showed that females

TABLE 12.1

Factor Structure and Details for Study 1

ITEM[a]	LOADINGS FOR STUDY 1 (WHOLE SAMPLE)				LOADINGS FOR STUDY 1 (MALES ONLY)				LOADINGS FOR STUDY 1 (FEMALES ONLY)			
	F1	F2	F3	F4	F1	F2	F3	F4	F1	F2	F3	F4
QRELAX 21a	.805				.755				.832			
QPERSNL 21b		.516										
QATTENT 21c	.510					.513			.612			
QFORMAL 21d	.400				.512							
QDEPTH 21e		.796				.643				.726		
QDIFF 212f	.851				.849				.862			
QOPEN 21g	.788				.827				.795			
QUNDER 21H	.853				.844				.863			
QBKDWN 21i	.853				.819				.867			
QCONFLT 21j	.822				.714				.850			
QINTRST 22	.553				.523				.608			
OSATISF 23	.813				.765				.842			
OVALUP 24		.798				.808				.819		
OVALUF 25		.725				.721				.752		
PURTALK 10a		−.617				−.662				−.665		
PURTASK 10b		.536				.707				.532		
RELCHG 30			.770				.805				.776	
ATTCHG 26			.739				.528				.746	
EMOCHG 29			.738				.679				.757	
ATTRACT 31			.772				.798				.721	
COGCHG 28			.647								.710	
BEHCHG 27			.534				.508				.499	
START 18				.716				.681				.711
CONTRL 19				.707				.655				.751
STOP 20				.593				.678				.538
Variance accounted for (in percentage):												
Original nine factors		62.7				65.3				65.0		
Factors passing scree test		53.0				54.3				54.7		
Remaining four factors		46.0				45.1				47.0		

[a] The number after an item refers to the number of the question on the ICR (see appendix).

yield more positive ratings as partners in social interaction. The contribution of the present finding is to raise the possibility that the nature of the communication is the variable that makes the difference in these general ratings of social participation and thus to contradict an alternative explanation in terms of a "mere presence" effect. In particular, as Table 12.2 shows, it seems that male partners were seen as more likely to engage in conflictive communication and also in more variable communication. Further detailed and specific attention to these sex differences in conversational geography could be used to confirm whether the previously observed effects in social participation (such as those demonstrated by Reis, 1986, on lonely persons) are similarly based in the geography of everyday communication in ways previously missed by the earlier methodology.

Relationship Type

A similar MANOVA with Relationship Type as a factor indicated a significant main effect for Relationship Type ($F = 18.38, df = 6, 1578, p < .001$, Pillai's trace $= .07$), and subsequent univariate analyses showed significant effects on all the dependent variables in the analysis (Value: $F = 22.07, df = 6, 1579, p < .001$, eta^2 $= .065$; Control: $F = 5.96, df = 6, 1579, p < .001$, eta^2 $= .02$; Change: $F = 18.93, df = 6, 1579, p < .001$, eta^2 $= .06$; and Communication Quality: $F = 39.06, df = 6, 1579, p < .001$, eta^2 $= .11$). These findings showed that interactions with acquaintances were seen as the least valued (relatives, highest), and communication quality was rated highest in interactions with best friends and lowest with strangers. Interactions with lovers created greatest change and those with relatives the lowest. These results are summarized in the Table 12.2. Curiously, conversations with lovers were rated as of lesser quality than were those with relatives, best friends, and friends, despite the claim that lovers were met most often for relational purposes. One possibility here is that lovers got together to talk about relational problems. We were able to check this possibility more directly by examining the scores on conflict. Conversations with lovers scored higher on conflict than conversations with friends and best friends, but lower than conversations with acquaintances (Table 12.2). This argues against the idea that there is a unique tendency for lovers to talk about relationship problems.

Another possibility to account for these unexpected and intriguing findings is that in a student population, the relationships classified by respondents as "lovers" were not all that long-lasting and so we may have been tapping a population whose "love relations" were still developing. When this was checked, however, it was found that the mean length for the lover relationships was 39.07 months, which tends to refute the possibility.

These findings were corroborated by analysis of the variability of ratings that was attributed to each type of relationship. ANOVA analysis of Variability × Relationship Type showed a highly significant effect ($F = 38.81, df = 6, 1759, p < .001$, eta^2 $= .33$), and Duncan's Multiple Range Test ($p = .05$) indicated that variability of ratings was greatest with strangers and least with best friends (Table 12.2). This suggests that variability of experience of conversations is a reflection of the nature of the relationship between the two persons, as predicted, but it is especially interesting that best friend and relative are the two relationship types with the least variable communication patterns, with lovers being significantly more variable than either of these other two. Since researchers often regard lovers operationally as the most intimate relationship (e.g., Kelley, 1983), one might have expected greater consistency in the experiences of conversations with lovers as partners.

Day of the Week

MANOVA analysis of the effects of Day of Week indicated a significant effect ($F = 3.69, df = 7, 1577, p < .001$, Pillai's trace $= .14$), which further analysis showed to be attributable to univariate effects on Value ($F = 7.05, df = 6, 1578, p < .01$, eta^2 $= .26$), Change ($F = 4.13, df = 6, 1578, p < .01$, eta^2 $= .015$), and Communication Quality ($F = 2.708, df = 6, 1578, p < .01$, eta^2 $= .01$). Further inspection of this result (Duncan's MRT, $p = .05$) showed that communication quality was rated best on the weekends, which confirms commonly held views, and lowest on Tuesdays and Fridays, which does not (Table 12.2). An analysis of the subscales of Communication Quality, however, showed a significant tendency for there to be higher degrees of *conflict* in conversations conducted on a Wednesday ($F = 2.82, df = 6, 1578, p < .01$, eta^2 $= .09$; see Table 12.2). The value of interactions was judged lowest on Mondays, an oblique confirmation of the "Blue Monday" stereotype (but cf. Stone et al., 1985). These results indicate that different elements of communication contribute to the different experience of relationships on days of the week.

TABLE 12.2

Mean Scores and Univariate Fs for Main Effects of Study 1

	CHANGE	VALUE†	QUALITY†	CONTROL‡	CONFLICT	VARIABILITY
Sex of Respondent						
Males	4.97 (4.50)	5.25 (1.33)	2.93 (0.93)	2.39 (0.83)	2.81 (1.87)	21.01 (9.52)
Females	6.58 (5.83)	5.07 (5.83)	2.87 (1.01)	2.46 (0.78)	2.82 (2.13)	20.39 (10.43)
Univariate F	32.05***	7.22**	n.s.	n.s.	n.s.	n.s.
Sex of Partner						
Male	6.12 (5.75)	5.18 (1.35)	1.97 (0.96)	2.44 (0.80)	2.93 (2.02)	21.42 (9.92)
Female	5.92 (5.18)	5.08 (1.28)	1.82 (0.99)	2.43 (0.79)	2.71 (2.05)	19.87 (10.25)
Univariate F	n.s.	n.s.	9.58**	n.s	4.49*	9.25**
Relationship Type						
Stranger	6.89 (4.63)	5.42$_b$ (1.44)	3.08$_b$ (1.11)	2.44 (1.65)	2.86 (2.21)	32.89$_b$ (11.66)
Acquaintance	7.22$_c$ (6.25)	5.66$_b$ (1.28)	2.45$_b$ (1.20)	2.18$_{bc}$ (1.93)	3.42$_{bc}$ (2.25)	26.53$_b$ (12.46)
Friend	5.45$_{bd}$ (5.05)	5.30$_b$ (1.29)	1.81$_b$ (0.84)	2.44$_{bd}$ (0.88)	2.55$_{bd}$ (1.78)	19.91$_b$ (8.69)
Best friend	4.79$_{bd}$ (4.62)	5.23$_b$ (1.14)	1.47$_a$ (0.83)	2.62$_{ad}$ (1.44)	2.16$_{ad}$ (1.64)	16.48$_a$ (8.45)
Lover	8.13$_a$ (6.14)	4.71$_a$ (1.33)	2.02$_b$ (1.06)	2.48$_d$ (1.65)	3.29$_b$ (2.32)	21.78$_b$ (10.78)
Relative	4.52$_{bd}$ (4.46)	4.65$_a$ (1.21)	1.59$_a$ (0.76)	2.42$_{bd}$ (0.81)	2.94$_{bd}$ (2.17)	17.49$_a$ (7.73)
Univariate F	18.93***	22.073***	39.06***	5.96**	13.14***	38.81***
Day of the Week						
Monday	5.44$_a$ (5.12)	5.48$_a$ (1.33)	1.90 (0.96)	2.81 (1.65)	2.73$_b$ (1.98)	20.99 (9.88)
Tuesday	6.39 (5.61)	5.26$_c$ (1.31)	2.03$_a$ (1.07)	2.85 (1.68)	2.81 (2.04)	22.05$_a$ (10.98)
Wednesday	7.01$_b$ (5.45)	5.04$_{bc}$ (1.29)	1.91 (0.91)	2.52 (1.89)	3.13$_a$ (1.95)	20.77 (9.40)
Thursday	5.26$_a$ (5.18)	4.76$_{bd}$ (1.42)	1.82$_b$ (0.95)	2.72 (1.59)	2.42$_{bd}$ (2.06)	19.82$_b$ (9.74)
Friday	6.48 (6.19)	5.20$_{bc}$ (1.27)	1.96$_d$ (1.04)	2.74 (1.91)	2.90$_c$ (2.01)	21.37$_c$ (10.68)
Saturday	5.25$_a$ (4.67)	5.08$_{bc}$ (1.28)	1.75$_{bc}$ (0.95)	2.96 (1.82)	2.80 (2.07)	19.16$_{bd}$ (9.73)
Sunday	5.47$_a$ (4.96)	5.01$_b$ (1.11)	1.69$_{bc}$ (0.98)	2.65 (2.03)	2.76 (2.25)	18.70$_{bd}$ (9.97)
Univariate F	4.126**	7.045**	2.708**	n.s.	2.82**	2.71**

NOTE: In any given block of the table, those means sharing a common subscript within a column are not significantly different from each other. Standard deviations are shown in parentheses.

† Lower scores on these scales represent ratings of *higher quality* or value.

‡ Higher scores on this scale represent greater mutual or shared control.

*$p < .05$; **$p < .01$; ***$p < .001$.

These findings are interpretable, we believe, yet we also recognize that the design of the present study is not ideal because subjects were not constrained to report data from particular days equally. The effects are, however, particularly intriguing and do raise the possibility that the nature of communication in everyday life is not constant nor independent of subjects' general experience of their mundane daily life.

DISCUSSION

The findings on sex differences are interesting confirmation and extension of previous work. The findings essentially suggest that males are unaffected by details that could actually create change in the relationship—or to put it another way, that even at the level of individual conversations, women monitor their relationships more seriously than do men. This presents a communicative extension of a finding widely accepted in the literature that has looked at the broad psychological characteristics of the two sexes in relating (e.g., Helgeson et al., 1987).

The findings on Relationship Type are also interesting in that they show clear and strong differences in the conversations of groups that are conceptually as close as friends and best friends, let alone lovers—groups that have often been treated as operationally equivalent in studies of intimacy. The relative qualities of these groups further suggest an intriguing rank-order for Communication Quality in different relationships that is not strictly correspondent with intuitive intimacy levels (as the sequence stranger-acquaintance-friend-best friend-lover-family might be). Rather, the sequence of quality judgments demonstrated in this study (from lowest to highest) was stranger-acquaintance-lover-friend-relative-best friend, whereas the sequence for value was acquaintance-stranger-friend-best friend-lover-relative. If such findings were to be shown robust, then theories of intimacy would need to take direct account of the role of conversation in operationalizing intimacy. It appears that behavioral, communicative, or conversational realities of intimacy do not clearly accord with the graduated ways in which intimacy might be represented through intuitively ordered relationship labels based on emotion or commitment alone.

The findings on Day of the Week are puzzling from the point of view of dominant cognitively based theories that do not assume an impact of daily hassles and other life circumstances on cognitive processing as McCall (1988) urged that we should. Work on daily hassles (Bolger et al., 1989) has not examined day of the week as a specific factor but has looked, for instance, at "number of days past a given hassle" as an influence on its effect on mood. Common wisdom nevertheless suggests that many people find Mondays and the midweek to be more stressful than other days (Stone et al., 1985), and indeed we show that conversations on Mondays are seen as relatively worthless compared to other days, while communicative conflict is greater on Wednesday. These results are theoretically puzzling but suggest the need to temper purely cognitive theories of communication with attention to factors of cyclicity and daily humdrum were such results to turn out to be robust.

Results from Study 1 are thus suggestive of a number of intriguing further questions and both confirm and extend previous research. In particular, they are supportive of previous work by social psychologists, but they open up the possibility of explaining some of these previously reported findings by reference to communication variables.

Of course, we acknowledge that the design of this study was not perfect for addressing all such questions in depth. Thus although the suggestions are intriguing, these results are only suggestive and point clearly to at least two follow-up studies that would deal directly with particular aspects of conversations. In Study 2, therefore, respondents reported on six different relationship types in order to verify and clarify the differences suggested in this first study, and in Study 3, they reported on every day of the week in order to verify and clarify the suggestions of difference in conversations on different days of the week.

STUDY 2

In Study 2, 97 undergraduates were initially recruited and as part of a class exercise during the week were instructed to complete for any one day six ICR forms covering interactions with one each of a stranger, an acquaintance, a friend, a best friend, a lover (boyfriend/girlfriend), and a family member. The original pool contained 51 males and 46 females, but in the event, only the data of the 85 respondents who returned complete forms were analyzed. This group comprised 44 males and 41 females, all unmarried, whose average age was 21 years, 4 months.

Analyses and Results

Because of the size of the sample, factor analysis was inappropriate in this study. For purposes of comparison with the factor analytic results of Study 1, alpha reliabilities were examined for the various indices developed in Study 1, both overall and within groups (males vs. females, and relationship types) to see whether reliabilities were comparable both within groups and also as compared to Study 1. Cronbach's alphas for Quality (.89), Change (.81), and Value (.80) were acceptable in the sample as a whole, and Kendall's W for Control was .12, p < .001. Analysis of the alphas assessed by Sex revealed no notable deviations from this pattern (males: Quality, .88; Value, .79; Change, .79; and Control: W = .11, p < .001; females: Quality, .90; Value, .80; Change, .82; and Control, W = .14, p < .001). Equally, alphas computed for Relationship type were similar (Quality: stranger, .83; acquaintance, .91; friend, .86; best friend, .88; lover, .88; and relative, .86; Value: stranger, .75; acquaintance, .80; friend, .79; best friend, .60; lover, .83; and relative, .91; Change: stranger, .69; acquaintance, .84; friend, .79; best friend, .90; lover, .77; and relative, .78; Control W: stranger, .18; acquaintance, .12; friend, .08; best friend, .05; lover, .22; and relative, .14, all ps < .05). Taken as a whole, this pattern is encouragingly consistent.

Sex Differences

As in Study 1, effects of Sex of Respondent and Sex of Partner were assessed by separate MANOVAs. In the case of Sex of Respondent, a significant main effect of sex was found (F = 2.48, df = 2, 507, p < .02, Pillai's trace = .029), which subsequent univariate analyses indicated to be attributable to an effect on Change (F = 8.22, df = 1, 508, p < .01, eta^2 = .02), with females again reporting more change than males (M = 6.69 and M = 5.32, respectively).

These results (Table 12.3) are quite similar to those reported in Study 1 in two respects. First, they again indicate systematic sex differences in perception of everyday communication, and second, these are in the direction of females seeing daily conversations as having more potential for changing their behavior in, or beliefs about, relationships than do males. This study, however, where Relationship Type was constrained, showed that females also have a general tendency to report higher quality in conversation. In the previous study, where Relationship Type was not constrained, this difference was not evident, suggesting that when given a free choice, subjects of the two sexes in that study chose to report, in general, on a conversation of equal quality. It is true that the present finding is more directly consistent, however, with previous studies in psychology, suggesting that females generally experience interaction as of higher quality than do males (e.g., Reis et al., 1985). The present study, however, again indicates the likelihood of communication variables being at the hidden root of such findings.

In the analysis of the effects of Sex of Partner, a main effect was again found (F = 3.72, df = 2, 507, p < .001, Pillai's trace = .05). Further univariate analyses showed a significant difference in perception of the single scale assessing concurrent locus of control of the conversation (as distinct from the factor for Control as a whole), with the males seeing it as more under their own control and females seeing it as more likely to be mutually

TABLE 12.3

Mean Scores and Univariate Fs for Main Effects of Study 2

	CHANGE	VALUE†	QUALITY†	CONTROL‡	CONFLICT	VARIABILITY
Sex of Respondent						
Males	5.33 (5.08)	5.18 (1.45)	2.00 (0.99)	2.53 (0.76)	2.93 (1.83)	21.84 (10.27)
Females	6.69 (5.67)	5.10 (1.47)	1.94 (1.08)	2.49 (0.76)	2.63 (1.90)	21.17 (11.18)
Univariate F	8.22*	n.s.	n.s.	n.s.	n.s.	n.s.
Sex of Partner						
Male	5.99 (5.54)	5.19 (1.55)	2.04 (1.11)	2.52 (0.75)	2.85 (2.00)	22.31 (11.52)
Female	5.98 (5.29)	5.09 (1.36)	2.90 (0.95)	2.82 (0.76)	2.72 (1.72)	20.72 (9.79)
Univariate F	n.s.	n.s.	2.39, p = .11	n.s.	n.s.	n.s.
Relationship Type						
Stranger	6.87$_b$ (5.11)	5.59$_a$ (1.24)	3.05$_{ad}$ (1.18)	2.47$_b$ (0.79)	3.54$_a$ (2.37)	32.66$_{ad}$ (12.40)
Acquaintance	7.15$_b$ (6.17)	5.13$_b$ (1.60)	1.95$_{bd}$ (0.99)	2.37$_b$ (0.84)	2.46$_b$ (1.62)	21.25$_{bd}$ (10.39)
Friend	5.01$_{ad}$ (4.97)	5.42$_c$ (1.39)	1.93$_{bd}$ (0.87)	2.48$_b$ (0.83)	2.64$_b$ (1.66)	21.21$_{bd}$ (8.97)
Best friend	4.95$_{ad}$ (5.13)	5.09$_b$ (1.03)	1.41$_{bc}$ (0.76)	2.53$_b$ (0.77)	2.28$_{bd}$ (1.33)	15.84$_{bc}$ (7.76)
Lover	8.26$_{bc}$ (5.84)	4.78$_{bd}$ (1.50)	1.84$_{bd}$ (0.86)	2.77$_a$ (0.55)	2.98$_{bc}$ (2.06)	19.91$_{bd}$ (8.54)
Relative	3.66$_{ad}$ (3.67)	4.85$_{bd}$ (1.76)	1.66$_b$ (0.67)	2.48$_b$ (0.68)	2.82$_b$ (1.77)	18.27$_b$ (6.97)
Univariate F	9.25**	4.115*	32.988**	6.12*	5.00*	33.03**

NOTE: In any given block of the table, those means sharing a common subscript within a column are not significantly different from each other. Standard deviations are shown in parentheses.

† Lower scores on these scales represent ratings of *higher* quality or value.

‡ Higher scores on this scale represent greater mutual or shared control.

*p < .01; **p < .001.

controlled ($F = 4.99$, $df = 1, 508$, $p < .05$, eta^2 = .09). Duck, Cortez, and Strejc (1988) reported that first dates where persons saw control as exerted by either party more than the other were also rated as of much lower overall quality, and this result and the foregoing result, taken together, are consistent with that. However, it is interesting that in this present study, there was no overall tendency for female partners to be rated as higher-quality communication partners than males, as there was in Study 1, although the results did tend in that direction ($F = 2.39$, df = 1, 508, p = .11, n.s.).

Relationship Type

The main interest in this study derives from the differences in communication in different types of relationships, and these comparisons were made by MANOVA, with subsequent univariate analyses. There was a significant main effect of Relationship Type ($F = 8.42$, $df = 6, 503$, $p < .001$, Pillai's trace = .093), and this was again shown by univariate analyses in respect of all four items (Value: $F = 4.12$, $df = 4, 505$, $p < .01$, eta^2 = .039; Control: $F = 6.124$, $df = 4, 505$, $p < .01$, eta^2 = 0.57; Change: $F = 9.26$, $df = 4, 505$, $p < .001$, eta^2 = .084; and Quality: $F = 32.99$, $df = 4, 505$, $p < .001$, eta^2 = .246). Post hoc comparisons using Duncan's MRT ($p = .05$) revealed interesting differences between relationship types (see Table 12.3). When individuals reported on all relationship types, conversation with lovers was rated most valuable and with strangers the least valuable. Surprisingly, conversations with friends are also rated rather low (Table 12.3). Control was seen as most mutually balanced with lovers and most unbalanced with strangers and acquaintances. Conversations with lovers effected the greatest degree of Change and those with relatives the least. Quality of communication, as in Study 1, was best with best friends and least with strangers, with whom (presumably for reasons of reduced familiarity) greater amounts of conflictive difference were observed. Once again, quality of communication with lovers

was *less* than with relatives and best friends. Also, as in Study 1, further analyses revealed no tendency for lovers to score higher on Conflict than other relationship types, except for best friend (Table 12.3), and no tendency for lover relationships to be of a short duration that would suggest continued development ($M = 19.21$ months).

There was again a significant difference in variability ($F = 33.03$, $df = 5, 504$, $p < .001$, eta^2 = .50), and Duncan's MRT ($p = .05$) showed that the order was, from lowest to highest, best friend ($M = 15.84$), relative ($M = 18.27$), lover ($M = 19.91$), friend ($M = 21.21$), acquaintance ($M = 21.25$), and stranger ($M = 32.66$). Once again, with the exception of scores for lovers, the endpoints were more or less what would be expected, with least consistency in conversations with strangers and most with best friends, but the relative positioning of the center of the sequence was not necessarily one that would be predicted either from work typologizing relationships in terms of psychological variables alone (e.g., Davis & Todd, 1985) or from the operational definition of intimacy presently current in the psychological literature (see Acitelli & Duck, 1987; Reis & Shaver, 1988). In particular, and in confirmation of Study 1, lovers occupied a somewhat anomalous position in the sequence and thus raise problems for the assumption of a linear intimacy gradient from stranger to lover.

DISCUSSION

The results from this study confirm and extend, in most respects, the main thrust of those in Study 1. Once again, it is clear that there are systematic sex differences in daily communication and that relationship types differ from one another in respect both of their internal conversational dynamics and the ways in which these are interpreted. Males rated communication quality lower overall than did females, and once again, females were shown to attend to potential for change and to review conversations more with a view to relational future than did males. In Study 1, females were rated as higher-quality partners than were males, but in the present study, this result merely approached significance. We believe that this points to a possible methodological and theoretical issue. Where subjects are unconstrained as to the choice of relationship type, they seem to choose to describe interaction and conversation with a female, whereas when they are constrained to describe different types of relationship equally, the strength of their preference for a female partner is evidently reduced. This suggests that people generally prefer females but not necessarily in all sorts of relationships.

Perhaps researchers also need to query the usual operational assumption of an intuitively derived ordering of relationship intimacy in two respects. First, these results show that acquaintances emerge as "less than" strangers in important ways, while lovers also appear to be "less than" best friends. One possibility for further study would be that acquaintances, being known but to some extent already "disregarded" as "mere acquaintance" (Rodin, 1982), are less involving than are those partners to whom one is already committed (such as friends, lovers, and relatives) and also than those who are to some extent mysterious and of uncertain potential for relationships (i.e., strangers). A second emerging feature is that there are certain important ways in which conversations with lovers are rated lower than one would expect intuitively, especially relative to those involving best friends. This finding is confirmed in separate types of analysis and indicates, at the very least, the theoretical potential of future study of the daily conversational dynamics of lovers' relationships specifically.

Also of particular interest was the relative independence of measures of change, value, and quality of communication across the different types of relationships, suggesting that there is no simple communicative engine for the growth and development of relationships but, instead, a complex of interacting and independent parts that, presumably, must all be managed individually and collectively as relationships grow. Such a possibility offers some support for Miell's (1987) finding that different dimensions of growth in relationships develop at independent rates, a finding also reported recently by Huston (1990). Researchers have often treated commitment and intimacy as not only equivalent and operationally interchangeable measures of relationships' growth but as entities that grow in step. We begin to suspect that this assumption may be unwarranted.

STUDY 3

Respondents and Procedures

In Study 3, 79 persons (35 males and 44 females) were asked to report on one interaction for each day of a specified 14-day period, without constraints on the type of relationship reported on. Of the 79, 66 (28 males and 38 females) returned complete and correctly filled out data and are the respondents used in the analysis, providing the 924 records that are reported here. All were unmarried undergraduates, and their mean age was 20 years, 2 months.

Analyses and Results

Once again, factor analysis was inappropriate in this study, and thus for comparison with Studies 1 and 2, we inspected the alpha reliabilities for the indices previously developed, both for the whole sample and also in subgroups (males vs. females, days of the week). These alpha coefficients were once more satisfactory for all scales and comparable to those of Study 2 in all respects (Quality, .86; Change, .71; Value, .73; and Control, $W = .06$, $p < .001$), and once again, the subsets of the data revealed no important deviations from this pattern. Alphas for the subsets of male and female respondents were as follows: Quality: males, .87, females, .85; Change: males, .72, females, .70; Value: males, .76, females, .72; and Control: males, $W = .04$, females, .08, both $p < .001$. Day of the Week alphas were as follows: Quality: Monday, .86, Tuesday, .87, Wednesday, .80, Thursday, .85, Friday, .87, Saturday, .86, and Sunday, .89; Change: Monday, .62, Tuesday, .79, Wednesday, .75, Thursday, .64, Friday, .74, Saturday, .72, and Sunday, .76; Value: Monday, .70, Tuesday, .77, Wednesday, .73, Thursday, .70, Friday, .77, Saturday, .68, and Sunday, .73; and Control: Monday, $W = 0.15$, Tuesday, .11, Wednesday, .02, Thursday, .03, Friday, .05, Saturday, .04, and Sunday, .03, all $p < .05$.

Sex Differences

Sex of Respondent and Sex of Partner were submitted to separate MANOVA analyses and yielded respective main effects of $F = 4.74$, $df = 2, 921$, $p < .001$, Pillai's trace $= .03$ and $F = 3.34$, $df = 2, 921$, $p < .003$, Pillai's trace $= .021$. Univariate analyses of the Sex of Respondent data showed a significant effect of Change ($F = 12.4$, $df = 1, 922$, $p < .001$, eta$^2 = .13$) in the same direction as in the previous two studies: Once again, females ($M = 6.533$) saw significantly more potential change for the relationship resulting from a given conversation than did males ($M = 5.38$). This reconfirms the notion that females review the impact of individual conversations on a whole relationship more than males do and should alert us to the need to pay closer attention to females' reviewing of individual conversations as an influence on relationship dynamics.

As to Sex of Partner, univariate tests indicated a significant effect of Change ($F = 9.93$, $df = 1, 921$, $p < .01$, eta$^2 = .01$) and a near significant effect of Communication Quality ($F = 3.325$, $df = 1, 921$, $p < .07$). Female partners were rated as inducing more change than were males ($M = 6.61$ and $M = 5.58$, respectively), and quality was rated nonsignificantly higher in interactions with females than with males. These results are in the direction consistent with the previous two studies and with suggestions of previous psychological studies that did not assess communication characteristics of social participation.

Day of the Week

The main purpose of the present study was to test Day of the Week effects suggested in Study 1. MANOVA analysis on the four factors produced a significant main effect of Day of the Week ($F = 1.7$, $df = 7, 916$, $p < .006$, Pillai's trace $= .01$), but subsequent univariate analyses on the four factors produced no significant effects. However, when the scale measuring Conflict was separately analyzed, as in Study 1, a main effect of Day of the Week was again observed ($F = 2.22$, $df = 6, 917$, $p < .03$, eta$^2 = .03$), and as in Study 1, Wednesday was the day producing the highest mean score (3.15; population mean, 2.76), Duncan's MRT ($p = .05$) showing it to be rated significantly differently from other weekdays, Monday ($M = 2.62$), Tuesday ($M = 2.6$), and Thursday ($M = 2.45$). This result closely resembles that found in Study 1 (see Table 12.2) and again indicates that at least as far as communication variables are concerned, all weekdays are not equivalent.

DISCUSSION

This study confirmed the previous patterns in three important respects. First, it showed consistent sex differences in conversation and in the communications of the two sexes in their daily conversations. Second, it showed that the sex of the conversational partner leads to consistent differences of ratings of communications and daily conversations. Third, it showed that there is something about a typical Wednesday that leads to higher conflict in the communications in which persons are involved. The patterns of results in this study are largely confirmatory of those in the previous two studies.

GENERAL DISCUSSION

The results of these three studies have the general effect of showing (a) robust and interpretable sex differences in everyday conversation; (b) robust and interpretable differences in the types of everyday communication that occur in different types of relationships, some of them directly predictable but so far untested in the context of existing theory and some of them not (in particular, the results are consistently different from the widely used intuitive ordering of intimacy gradients given to different sorts of relationships in operational definitions of intimacy); and (c) robust findings that the communications that occur on different days of the week are *not* simply equivalent, with a marked, consistent and significant tendency for there to be greater amounts of conflict within personal relationships on Wednesdays.

This program of studies has demonstrated the value of extending research on everyday behaviors to include communication behavior and not only has shown some unusual effects of everyday activity on communication but suggests a role of communication variables in the explanation of some of the findings on social participation previously reported by social psychologists and explained without reference to such variables. Study 1 showed that routine communication is largely uninfluential in relationships even when it is rated as important for the relationship, and the remaining two studies confirmed the observation in Study 1 that females are more likely than are males to rate specific conversations as likely to create change in or impact on the relationship. Other sex differences were found to confirm and extend previous work indicating qualitative differences in men's and women's relationships. The studies together extend these findings to communication variables that may serve a likely mediating function in explaining why females are preferred to males as communication partners, irrespective of the type of relationship that is involved or the sex of the person doing the rating.

Relationship types were found to be different from one another in terms of communication characteristics but also, rather intriguingly, to be rated in orders different from those typically adopted by researchers on intimacy. One important contribution of the present studies was assessing the ways in which the several relationship types are experienced day by day. It is clear that the relationship types are subjectively different from one another, in that persons conduct them differently and view them as of different weight and significance, but also that these differences are not necessarily identical to those that are supposed intuitively by researchers.

The present program of work certainly indicates that the differences in "conversational geography" between different types of relationships are in urgent need of further exploration. The work further suggests that once the interior dynamics of daily conversations that typify different relationships are fully understood, we shall see that various elements previously collated in linear models of intimacy growth are actually distinct for all practical purposes as persons carry out their daily lives. Coupled with existing evidence (Duck & Miell, 1986) that such elements as intimacy, similarity, and liking often develop independently of overall relationship growth patterns, such findings send a loud warning bell to researchers who presently view intimacy, commitment, and communicative development as not only all linear but as all developing interdependently. There is clearly considerable room for clarification of the exact processes of relationship development in daily lives outside the laboratory.

Day of the Week proved to be an influence on conversations in ways not predicted by existing cognitively driven theories of communication. The results clearly indicate the value of accounting for communication not merely as decontextualized message but as a wider activity in persons' lives that is influenced by what else is going on in those lives. For communication researchers to be sure that general statements about communication really do apply across all life contexts, there is a need for thorough exploration of the nature of, and reasons for, daily variation in communication, particularly as they influence relationship experiences and dynamics. We urge future researchers to attend to the fact that data gathered on different days may be influenced by some underlying patterning influences not yet fully comprehended.

A final lesson to be drawn from this program of research is that communication workers would be well advised to replicate and extend existing work using diary techniques, as this has previously been typically carried out by social psychologists who have not included communication variables on the diary reports that they normally use. Not only is it undesirable to have the complex operations of communication represented as if it were merely an inert medium for externalizing cognitive processes but the communication variables identified in the present program of work have the potential to explain some of the previously discovered "psychological" effects, such as the relative differences of social participation in men and women or lonely and non-lonely persons.

Like longitudinal studies, descriptive work is often called for but less often done and is frequently seen narrowly as atheoretical. A measure such as the ICR which is clearly focused on communication factors in daily life not only offers a handy way of replicating and extending previous descriptive work but its use can be grounded theoretically.

First, it is widely recognized that communication theorists seek to explain the commonplace as well as the unusual and dramatic, but perhaps atypical, aspects of human communication (Berger & Chaffee, 1987), and some, such as Cappella (1988), have argued strongly for attention to interaction patterns and dynamics. Further, Hinde (1981, 1989) argued that description of the patterns of interaction in relationships is a key way to ensure that researchers do not focus on matters that are merely peaks of experience in a continuous graph of other experiences that are less dramatic. The risk is that by focusing on the unusual, we gain only a skewed comprehension of the commonplace. Hinde emphasized that in order, for example, to show personality, cognitive structural, or strategic effects on relationships, it is necessary to explore the characteristic patterns of interaction that an individual reports and to assess the nature of that individual's experiences across a variety of situations.

There is a second theoretical reason for comprehending daily communication in terms that apply specifically to relationships. If relationships are embodied in the talk of the participants, then this notion can partially explain the differences between the interactions that occur in different relationship types and in different daily contexts, such as those found here. Such thinking is especially important to develop in the theoretical explanation of the role of communication in social support, based as it is in everyday life in ways too widely overlooked to date (Leatham & Duck, 1990). A comprehensive theoretical understanding of such activity requires a fuller picture of the geography of everyday conversation, and this series of studies points the way to several important challenges in the future, both for descriptive work and for theory.

There is clearly much to be learned about relationship development, relationship maintenance, and even relationship decline by using such a tool. Nonetheless, its primary benefits will undoubtedly be found in its ready attention to those communicative behaviors and conversational geographies that will help us to map out more clearly the ways in which conversation and communication in everyday life should be theoretically understood. At any rate, the present series of studies shows that communication researchers should not assume that all communications are equally important, either practically in persons' daily lives or theoretically in our understanding of those lives.

APPENDIX

Iowa Communication Record

Your I.D.: _____

Age: _____

Sex: M or F (circle one)

1. Date of Interaction: _____   _____
                                   mo.   day

2. Time of Interaction: _____   AM or PM
                                 hour   (circle one)

3. Length of Interaction: _____   _____
                                    hour   min

4. Description of Interactional Partner:

   _____   _____   M or F (circle one)
      Initials   Age

5. Length of time you have known partner in years and months:

   _____   _____
      year   month

6. How would you describe the nature of your relationship? (circle one)

1	2	3
Stranger	Acquaintance	Friend

4	5	6	
Best Friend	Lover	Relative	Other _____

7. What type of communication? (circle one)

1	2	3
Face-to-Face	Long-Distance Telephone	Local Telephone

8. Would you consider the interaction public or private?
   (circle one and state place)

1	2	_____
Public	Private	Where

9. Were others present?   Yes or No

10. What was the role of talk? Indicate the extent to which you agree with the following:

This was just talk for talk's sake.

1	2	3	4	5	6	7	8	9

Strong   Strong
Agreement   Disagreement

Main purpose of talk was to accomplish some task. (Such as gaining information to complete a project, or solve a problem.)

1	2	3	4	5	6	7	8	9

Strong   Strong
Agreement   Disagreement

Main purpose of talk was to facilitate some social objective. (Such as talk surrounding sports activity or party.)

1	2	3	4	5	6	7	8	9

Strong   Strong
Agreement   Disagreement

Main purpose of talk was to facilitate the relationship. (Such as talk to become better acquainted or resolve differences.)

1	2	3	4	5	6	7	8	9

Strong   Strong
Agreement   Disagreement

11. Describe the main topic of talk:

_____

12. Were there other topics: Yes or No

    If yes, indicate the number of topics you think were addressed in the talk:

_____

13. What were you doing *right before* the conversation occurred? (circle one or more)

        working   eating   driving   study

    childcare   housework   watching TV   reading

        listening   talking to   _____
        to music   someone else   other

14. Were you involved in any activities *during* the conversation?   Yes or No

    If yes, please indicate which of the above:

_____

15. What did you do *after* the conversation (as above)?

_____

16. Was the interaction *planned* or *unplanned?* (circle one)

17. If planned, indicate the extent to which you were looking forward to the meeting:

1	2	3	4	5	6	7	8	9

Looking Forward to Meeting   Dreading Meeting

18. Who initiated the talk? (circle one)

    You   Partner   Seemed Mutual   Accidental   Not Clear

19. Who seemed to control the conversation; for example, who decided topics of talk?

    You   Partner   Seemed Mutual   Accidental   Not Clear

20. Who made moves to end the conversation?

    You   Partner   Seemed Mutual   Accidental   Not Clear

21. Describe the quality of communication:

1	2	3	4	5	6	7	8	9

Relaxed   Strained

1	2	3	4	5	6	7	8	9

Impersonal   Personal

1	2	3	4	5	6	7	8	9

Attentive   Poor Listening

1	2	3	4	5	6	7	8	9

Formal   Informal

1	2	3	4	5	6	7	8	9

In-depth   Superficial

1	2	3	4	5	6	7	8	9

Smooth   Difficult

1	2	3	4	5	6	7	8	9

Guarded   Open

1	2	3	4	5	6	7	8	9

Great Deal of
Understanding

Great Deal of
Misunderstanding

1	2	3	4	5	6	7	8	9

Free of Communication
Breakdowns

Laden with Communication
Breakdowns

1	2	3	4	5	6	7	8	9

Free of Conflict

Laden with Conflict

22. Indicate the extent to which you think the talk was interesting:

1	2	3	4	5	6	7	8	9

Interesting

Boring

23. Indicate the extent to which you came away satisfied with the interaction:

1	2	3	4	5	6	7	8	9

Satisfied

Not Satisfied

24. How valuable was this conversation to you for your life right now?

1	2	3	4	5	6	7	8	9

Extremely Important

Not Important at All

25. How valuable was this conversation to your future?

1	2	3	4	5	6	7	8	9

Extremely Important

Not Important at All

26. Indicate the extent to which this talk resulted in a change of your attitude:

-3	-2	-1	0	$+1$	$+2$	$+3$

Negative Change

No Change

Positive Change

27. Indicate the extent to which this talk resulted in a change of your behavior:

-3	-2	-1	0	$+1$	$+2$	$+3$

Stopped Behavior

No Change

Increased Behavior

Describe behavior change: _____

28. Indicate the extent to which this talk changed your *thinking* or *ideas:*

1	2	3	4	5	6	7	8	9

No Change   Great Change

Describe change in thinking/ideas: _____

_____

29. Indicate the extent to which this talk resulted in a change of your feelings:

-3	-2	-1	0	$+1$	$+2$	$+3$

Negative Change   No Change   Positive Change

Describe change in feelings: _____

_____

30. Indicate the extent to which this talk resulted in a change in your relationship:

-3	-2	-1	0	$+1$	$+2$	$+3$

Much More Distant   No Change   Much More Close

31. Indicate the extent to which this talk changed your attraction toward partner:

-3	-2	-1	0	$+1$	$+2$	$+3$

Greatly Decreased   No Change   Greatly Increased
Attraction   Attraction

32. On an average day how may people do you talk to? _____

33. Out of the total amount of time you spend conversing per week, what percentage of that time do you think is spent talking with this person?

_____ %

The ICR (Iowa Communication Record; copyright G. Leatham and S. W. Duck) is from *Personal Relationships and Social Support* (pp. 23-27), edited by S. W. Duck, 1990. London: Sage. Copyright 1990 Sage Publications Ltd. Adapted by permission.

REFERENCES

Acitelli, L. K., & Duck, S. W. (1987). Intimacy as the proverbial elephant. In D. Perlman & S. W. Duck (Eds.), *Intimate relationships* (pp. 297-308). Newbury Park, CA: Sage.

Argyle, M., & Henderson, M. (1985). *The anatomy of relationships*. London: Heinneman.

Barbee, A. (1990). Interactive coping: The cheering up process in close relationships. In S.W. (Ed., with R. C. Silver), *Personal relationships and social support* (pp. 46-65). London: Sage.

Baxter, L. A. (1987). Symbols of relationship identity in relationship cultures. *Journal of Social and Personal Relationships, 4,* 261-279.

Baxter, L. A., & Dindia, K. (1990). Marital partners' perceptions of marital maintenance strategies. *Journal of Social and Personal Relationships, 7,* 187-208.

Baxter, L. A., & Wilmot, W. (1984). Secret tests: Social strategies for acquiring information about the state of the relationship. *Human Communication Research, 11,* 171-201.

Baxter, L. A., & Wilmot, W. (1986). Interaction characteristics of disengaging, stable and growing relationships. In R. Gilmour & S. W. Duck (Eds.), *Emerging field of personal relationships* (pp. 145-159). Hillsdale, NJ: Lawrence Erlbaum.

Berger, C. R. (1988). Uncertainty and information exchange in developing relationships. In S. W. Duck, D. F. Hay, S. E. Hobfoll, W. Ickes, & B. Montgomery (Eds.), *Handbook of personal relationships* (pp. 239-256). Chichester: Wiley.

Berger, C. R., & Chaffee, S. H. (1987). The study of communication as a science. In C. R. Berger & S. H. Chaffee (Eds.), *Handbook of communication science* (pp. 15-19). Newbury Park, CA: Sage.

Berger, C. R., Weber, M. D., Munley, M. E., & Dixon, J. T. (1977). Interpersonal relationship levels and interpersonal attraction. In B. D. Rubin (Ed.), *Communication yearbook 1* (pp. 245-261). New Brunswick, NJ: Transaction Books.

Bolger, N., DeLongis, A., Kessler, R. C., & Schilling, E. A. (1989). Effects of daily stress on negative mood. *Journal of Personality and Social Psychology, 58,* 808-818.

Cappella, J. N. (1988). Personal relationships, social relationships and patterns of interaction. In S. W. Duck, D. F. Hay, S. E. Hobfoll, W. J. Ickes, & B. M. Montgomery (Eds.), *Handbook of personal relationships* (pp. 325-342). Chichester: Wiley.

Cattell, R. B. (1966). The meaning and strategic use of factor analysis. In R. B. Cattell (Ed.), *Handbook of multivariate experimental psychology* (pp. 174-243). Chicago: Rand McNally.

Clark, M. S., & Reis, H. T. (1988). Interpersonal processes in close relationships. *Annual Review of Psychology, 39,* 609-672.

Davis, K. E., & Todd, M. (1982). Friendship and love relationships. In K. E. Davis & T. O. Mitchell (Eds.), *Advances in descriptive psychology* (Vol. 2, pp. 79-122). Greenwich, CT: JAI.

Davis, K. E., & Todd, M. (1985). Assessing friendship: Prototypes, paradigm cases and relationship description. In S. W. Duck & D. Perlman (Eds.), *Understanding personal relationships* (pp. 17-38). London: Sage.

Derlega, V. J., & Winstead, B. A. (1986). *Friendship and social interaction.* New York: Springer-Verlag.

Dindia, K., Fitzpatrick, M. A., & Kenny, D. A. (1989, May). *Self disclosure in spouse and stranger interaction: A social relations analysis.* Paper presented at the annual meeting of the International Communication Association, New Orleans.

Duck, S. W. (1986). *Human relationships.* London: Sage.

Duck, S. W. (1988). *Relating to others.* Monterey, CA: Dorsey/Brooks/Cole.

Duck, S. W. (1990). Relationships as unfinished business: Out of the frying pan and into the 1990s. *Journal of Social and Personal Relationships, 7,* 5-28.

Duck, S. W. (1991). Diaries and logs. In B. M. Montgomery & S. W. Duck (Eds.), *Studying interpersonal interaction* (pp. 141-161). New York: Guilford.

Duck, S. W., Cortez, C. A., & Strejc, H. J. (1988, May). *Successful and unsuccessful dates as a function of loneliness.* Paper presented at the annual meeting of the International Communication Association, New Orleans.

Duck, S. W., & Miell, D. E. (1982). *Charting the development of personal relationships.* Paper presented at the Second International Conference on Personal Relationships, Madison, WI.

Duck, S. W., & Miell, D. E. (1986). Charting the development of personal relationships. In R. Gilmour & S. W. Duck (Eds.), *Emerging field of personal relationships* (pp. 133-144). Hillsdale, NJ: Lawrence Erlbaum.

Duck, S. W., & Montgomery, B. M. (1991). The interdependence among interaction substance, theory, and methods. In B. M. Montgomery & S. W. Duck (Eds.), *Studying interpersonal interaction* (pp. 3-15). New York: Guilford.

Duck, S. W., & Pond, K. (1989). Friends, Romans, countrymen, lend me your retrospective data: Rhetoric and reality in personal relationships. In C. Hendrick (Ed.), *Review of social psychology and personality, Vol. 10: Close relationships* (pp. 3-27). Newbury Park, CA: Sage.

Fitzpatrick, M. A. (1988). *Between husbands and wives: Communication in marriage.* Newbury Park, CA: Sage.

Hays, R. B. (1989). The day-today functioning of close versus casual friendship. *Journal of Social and Personal Relationships, 7,* 21-37.

Helgeson, V. S., Shaver, P. R., & Dyer, M. (1987). Prototypes of intimacy and distance in same-sex and opposite-sex relationships. *Journal of Social and Personal Relationships, 4,* 195-233.

Hinde, R. A. (1981). The bases of a science of relationships. In S. W. Duck & R. Gilmour (Eds.), *Personal relationships 1: Studying personal relationships* (pp. 1-22). London: Academic Press.

Hinde, R. A. (1989, May). *Individual characteristics and relationships.* Paper presented at the Second International Network Conference on Personal Relationships, Iowa City.

Huston, T. L. (1990, May). *The PAIRS Project data: A progress report.* Paper presented at the Third International Network Conference on Personal Relationships Graduate Workshop, Iowa City.

Kelley, H. H. (1983). Love and commitment. In H. H. Kelley, E. Berscheid, A. Christensen, J. Harvey, T. L. Huston, G. Levinger, D. McClintock, L. A. Peplau, & D. Peterson, (Eds.) *Close relationships* (pp. 265-314). San Francisco: Freeman.

Knapp, M. L., Ellis, D., & Williams, B. (1980). Perceptions of communication behavior associated with relationship terms. *Communication Monographs, 47,* 262-278.

Leatham, G., & Duck, S. W. (1990). Conversations with friends and the dynamics of social support. In S. W. Duck (Ed.), *Personal relationships and social support* (pp. 1-29). London: Sage.

McCall, G. J. (1988). The organizational life cycle of relationships. In S. W. Duck, D. F. Hay, S. E. Hobfoll, W. J. Ickes, & B. M. Montgomery (Eds.), *Handbook of personal relationships* (pp. 467-486). Chichester: Wiley.

McCroskey, J. C., & Young, T. J. (1979). The use and abuse of factor analysis in communication research. *Human Communication Research, 5,* 373-382.

McLaughlin, M. (1983). *How talk is organized.* Beverly Hills, CA: Sage.

Miell, D. E. (1987). Remembering relationship development: Creating a context for interaction. In R. Burnett, P. McGhee, & D. Clarke (Eds.), *Accounting for relationships* (pp. 60-73). London: Methuen.

Montgomery, B. (1988). Quality communication in personal relationships. In S. W. Duck, D. F. Hay, S. E. Hobfoll, W. Ickes, & B. Montgomery (Eds.), *Handbook of personal relationships* (pp. 343-362). Chichester: Wiley.

Norton, R. W. (1983). *Communicator style.* Beverly Hills, CA: Sage.

Reis, H. T. (1986). Gender effects in social participation: Intimacy, loneliness and the conduct of social interaction. In R. Gilmour & S. W. Duck (Eds.), *The emerging field of personal relationships* (pp. 91-105). Hillsdale, NJ: Lawrence Erlbaum.

Reis, H. T., Nezlek, J., & Wheeler, L. (1980). Physical attractiveness and social interaction. *Journal of Personality and Social Psychology, 38,* 604-617.

Reis, H. T., & Shaver, P. (1988). Intimacy as an interpersonal process. In S. W. Duck, D. F. Hay, S. E. Hobfoll, W. J. Ickes, & B. M. Montgomery (Eds.), *Handbook of personal relationships* (pp. 367-390). Chichester: Wiley.

Reis, H. T., Wheeler, L., Nezlek, J., Kernis, M. H., & Spiegel, N. (1985). On specificity in the impact of social participation on physical and psychological health. *Journal of Personality and Social Psychology, 48,* 456-471.

Rodin, M. (1982). Non-engagement, failure to engage and disengagement. In S. W. Duck (Ed.), *Personal relationships 4: Dissolving personal relationships* (pp. 31-50). London: Academic Press.

Rogers, L. E., & Farace, W. V. (1975). Analysis of relational communication in dyads: New measurement procedures. *Human Communication Research, 1,* 222-239.

Sillars, A. L. (1991). Behavioral observation. In B. M. Montgomery & S. W. Duck (Eds.), *Studying interpersonal interaction* (pp. 197-218). New York: Guilford.

Stephen, T. D. (1984). Symbolic interdependence and post break-up distress: A reformulation of the attachment construct. *Journal of Divorce, 8,* 1-16.

Stone, A. A., Hedges, S. M., Neale, J. M., & Satin, M. S. (1985). Prospective and cross-sectional mood reports offer no evidence of a "Blue Monday" phenomenon. *Journal of Personality and Social Psychology, 49,* 129-134.

Tolhuizen, J. H. (1989). Communication strategies for intensifying dating relationships: Identification, use and structure. *Journal of Social and Personal Relationships, 6,* 413-434.

Wheeler, L., & Nezlek, J. (1977). Sex differences in social participation. *Journal of Personality and Social Psychology, 35,* 742-754.

Wheeler, L., Reis, H. T., & Nezlek, J. (1983). Loneliness, social interaction, and sex roles. *Journal of Personality and Social Psychology, 45,* 943-953.

Wiemann, J. M., & Busch, J. D. (1990, June). *Communication and equality in relationships.* Paper presented to the annual meeting of the International Communication Association, Dublin, Ireland.

13

Turning Points in Developing Romantic Relationships

LESLIE A. BAXTER | CONNIE BULLIS

The 80 partners from 40 romantic relationships were independently interviewed using the RIT procedure with regard to the turning points of their respective relationships; 26 types of turning points were found, which reduced to 14 supra-types. These supra-types differed in their association with relational commitment, with some events strongly positive, some strongly negative, and others relatively modest in reported change in commitment. About half of the turning points involved explicit metacommunication between the relationship parties, but the likelihood of relationship talk varied by turning point type. About half of the 759 identified turning points were agreed upon by relationship partners, but agreement differed depending on turning point type. Neither partner agreement nor the presence of explicit metacommunication was related to the respondent's current satisfaction with the relationship. However, the proportion of total turning points that were negative correlated negatively with current satisfaction. Two turning point events, Exclusivity and Disengagement, individually differentiated more from less satisfied relationship parties.

Almost 25 years ago, Bolton (1961) argued the centrality of the "turning point" as a unit of analysis in understanding developmental processes in romantic relationships. However, to date only a handful of studies have examined relational turning points, and a basic descriptive profile is still lacking of what events are associated with relational change. As Hinde (1981) has observed, a descriptive base is crucially important if the study of relationships is to advance. The purpose of this study is to provide such a descriptive base for relational turning points.

The turning point is a unit of analysis that potentially affords a rich understanding of relationship processes. Conceptualized as any event or occurrence that is associated with change in a relationship, the turning point is central to a process view of relationships. Turning points are the substance of change. Yet despite an increased focus by relationship researchers on process issues of growth and decay (see Duck & Perlman, 1985), the

field cannot yet answer such fundamental questions as "What events are related to positive or negative change in relationships?"

Other features of turning points also hold heuristic value. Do relationships progress in a series of small, incremental, and positive shifts in commitment, as the positively sloped line envisioned by Altman and Taylor (1973) would suggest? In contrast, perhaps relationships progress through a series of discrete events each of which results in a major escalation in commitment, as the staircase metaphor advanced by Knapp (1984) would suggest. As yet a third alternative conception of relationship progress, relationships may develop dialectically with both positive and negative changes occurring as the parties construct their joint history (Altman, Vinsel, & Brown, 1981). Examination of the intensity, valence, and sequencing of turning points offers the promise of insight into the basic nature of relationship dynamics.

From Baxter, L. A., & Bullis, C. (1986). Turning points in developing romantic relationships. *Human Communication Research, 12,* 469-493.

Last, studying relationship dynamics through the turning point unit of analysis affords communications researchers a useful lens by which to examine communication and meaning in relationship development. Turning points, by definition, afford insight into events and actions that are steeped in metacommunicative or relational meaning. A description of what phenomena comprise turning points may shed important insight into people's implicit theories of relationships (Davis & Todd, 1982; Rands & Levinger, 1979; Wilmot & Baxter, 1984). In addition to insights about implicit metacommunication, turning point analysis allows opportunity to examine instances when explicit metacommunication, or direct relationship talk, is enacted. In contrast to the common folk myth, which regards relationship talk as both pervasive and significant (Katriel & Philipsen, 1981), work in explicit metacommunication suggests that relationship talk is both infrequent (Wilmot, 1980) and unrelated to couple adjustment (Gottman, Markman, & Notarious, 1977). This apparent inconsistency between folk myth and research findings may be the result of a highly selective role performed by relationship talk. Relationship talk may be central to some turning points and not others. The turning point unit of analysis potentially allows researchers to sort out occasions in which relationship talk is a salient feature of relationship development.

In short, the turning point is a conceptually rich tool by which to understand relationship processes, a tool that has been underutilized to date by researchers. This study seeks to extend our understanding of relationship development through the examination of five research questions, detailed below.

Although the turning point has not been frequently studied, a handful of investigations have been undertaken. However, these studies are collectively limited in several ways. Several studies have employed the turning point unit of analysis, but typically the use was directed toward acquisition of information other than the content of turning points per se. The studies summarized by Huston, Surra, Fitzgerald, and Cate (1981), for ex-

ample, have focused exclusively on the rates of change in relationship progress, typically producing multiple trajectories to reflect rapid versus slow progress. Although these studies make an important contribution in demonstrating the range in rates of progress, they fail to examine the specific phenomena themselves that are related to these changes.

Several studies have considered turning point phenomena but are overly reductionistic in their analyses. Two studies (Lloyd & Cate, 1984; Surra, 1984) categorized respondent reasons for turning points into four basic categories: (1) dyadic, that is, reasons rooted in the interaction between the parties; (2) individual, that is, reasons rooted in the parties' personal belief systems; (3) network that is, reasons attributed to interactions with third parties; and (4) circumstantial, that is, reasons that suggest that the parties had no control over the event. Reasons for turning points may not be equivalent to the turning point events themselves, but apart from this conceptual issue, the four-category coding scheme lacks sufficient richness. The "dyadic" category, for example, subsumes everything from "having a fight," to "having sex," to "getting engaged." A finer-grained analysis seems warranted.

Some research has been overly reductionistic by concentrating on units of analysis larger than the turning point. Braiker and Kelley (1979), for example, focused on the relationship stage or period, identifying the themes of love, conflict, maintenance (i.e., openness), and ambivalence. However, relationship stages or periods may consist of multiple turning point events that merit a finer-grained analysis. The theme of love, for example, may involve the turning point events of "first kiss," "first sex," and "expression of 'I love you'" all embedded in the Serious Dating stage.

If some studies have erred on the side of insufficient detail, others have erred on the side on noncomprehensiveness. Several studies have examined isolated types of events without embedding these types into a holistic view of turning points characteristic of romantic relationship histories. Planalp and Honeycutt (1985), for instance, have investigated the subset of events that increase uncertainty in relationships. To the extent that uncertainty is negatively regarded (Berger & Calabrese, 1975), these events are likely candidates to emerge as negative turning points in relationships. Similarly, the work in expressed reasons for relationship disengagement (Baxter, in press; Cody, 1982) poses likely candidates to emerge as negative turning points. Work on the single events of "expressing 'I love you' " (Nydick & Cornelius, 1984) and "first physical affection" (Wilmot & Baxter, 1984) suggest these two events as likely candidates to emerge as positive turning points in relationship histories. All of these studies provide detailed looks at isolated event types, but none is comprehensive in determining how these events fit in the broader portrait of turning points in relationship progress.

In sum, extant work is either too reductionist or lacking in comprehensiveness, resulting in the absence of a complete profile of the phenomena that comprise relationship turning points. Thus, our first research question:

RQ1: What phenomena comprise relationship turning points in the perceptions of romantic relationship partners?

The second research question examines the role that metacommunication or relationship talk plays in a relationship's turning points. The question has inherent appeal from a communications perspective, yet it has been investigated in only one of the studies that have dealt with turning points. Braiker and Kelley (1979) observed the theme of maintenance in their respondent accounts of courtship stages. Unfortunately, the operationalization of maintenance employed in the researchers' work was muddied; items referenced self-disclosure, relationship talk, and proactive behavior to make the relationship work, all of which may be conceptually distinct from one another. Thus, it is difficult to know how to interpret the Braiker and Kelley (1979) finding that maintenance activity increases over the courtship stage. This finding may be the result of increased personal self-disclosure alone, increased relationship talk alone, increased proac-

tive work and effort alone, or any combination of the above. Extant work in relationship talk suggests that relationship parties are cautious in its use. Although Baxter and Wilmot (1984) found direct talk about the relationship in people's repertoire of strategies by which to discern the state of the relationship, the strategy was far outweighed by many more indirect "secret tests." The prevalence of indirectness may be accounted for by people's beliefs about the consequences of direct relationship talk. Baxter and Wilmot (1985) found that direct talk about the state of the relationship was the most frequently reported "taboo topic" among developing romantic couples, which the partners attributed to the fragility of developing relationships and the resultant risk entailed in going "on record" with relationship talk. Given its apparent risk, relationship talk may be used quite selectively in relationship development, occurring only for certain types of turning points. The role of direct relationship talk in developing relationships is examined in the study's second research question:

RQ2: Do turning point types differ in their likelihood of involving relationship talk between the partners?

Although a relationship is a jointly realized social entity, each relationship party holds his or her own perceptions of that construction process. Indeed, a substantial research history supports the claim that the two parties to a relationship occupy separate phenomenological worlds (see Sillars & Scott, 1983). Although substantial research has examined the issue of perceptual congruence between relationship partners in a variety of attitude domains (see Sillars & Scott, 1983), additional work is needed on the basic building block of a relationship, that is, the turning point. On the one hand, one might argue that turning points constitute the relationship's history, thereby suggesting a high correlation in partner perceptions. Extant work on turning points has found a remarkably high correlation (.80) between partners' month-by-month relationship commitment levels (Huston et al., 1981). However, partners could agree about their basic levels of affective involvement and still disagree about the events associated with those changes. The research on spouse monitoring of day-to-day events in their marriage suggests substantial discrepancy in the perceptions of the marital partners (Christensen & Nies, 1980; Jacobson & Moore, 1981). The third research question examines partner agreement about turning points:

RQ3: To what extent do relationship partners agree in their identification of turning point types?

Despite Bolton's (1961) suggestion that turning points may range from trivial to dramatic in their effects on relationships, extant work has not examined the issue of differential turning point intensities. The studies summarized by Huston et al. (1981) have come closest to this question by examining differential *rates of change* in the likelihood of marriage. However, rate of change as a measure confounds the intensity of change in relationship commitment with change in time. Further, as mentioned above, turning point types were not systematically analyzed in the Huston et al. (1981) research. The issue of intensity is important, for it will shed insight into whether relationship dynamics proceed by modest increments or larger bursts. Thus, the fourth question under investigation in this study is:

RQ4: Do turning point types vary in their perceived intensity?

In addition to the consideration of perceived intensity of turning points, it seems useful to consider the possibility of delayed, cumulative, or long-term effects of turning points through assessment of the current relationship status. Relationship satisfaction, and its companions of dyadic relationship quality, adjustment, and success, are without doubt the single most frequently studied aspect of close relationships (Lewis & Spanier, 1979). Despite the plethora of variables that researchers have correlated with relationship satisfaction (see Spanier & Lewis, 1980), no comprehensive study exists that considers the association of current satisfaction with a relationship's turning point history. The effects of isolated events (e.g., the birth of a first child) have been considered, but it is useful to embed the effects of isolated turning point phenomena within the larger framework of the relationship's total history of change. Given the centrality of the turning point as a unit of change in relationships, it seems only reasonable to expect that some association might be present with current relationship satisfaction.

Several features about a relationship's turning point history merit particular attention with regard to current relationship satisfaction. First, it seems useful to investigate the overall relationship between satisfaction and the proportion of negative turning points. Despite the common folk myth that crisis brings a couple closer, it seems reasonable to expect satisfaction to correlate negatively with the proportion of a relationship's turning points that are negative.

The degree to which the partners agree on their relationship's turning points also merits examination with regard to satisfaction. Sillars and Scott (1983) have advanced the guarded conclusion that some association between perceptual congruence and adjustment (satisfaction) appears evident in the research literature but that there are many exceptions, particularly when perceptual congruence is unnecessary for compatible interaction between the partners. Sillars and Scott (1983) urge researchers to begin sorting out the instances when congruence is and is not likely to correlate with adjustment. This study examines the association between current relationship satisfaction and the proportion of a partner's identified turning points that were present in the other's account.

As mentioned above, openness in communication is often viewed as the *sine qua non* of relationship quality or satisfaction. However, recent thinking has challenged this commonly held belief (Bochner, 1982; Parks, 1982). Similar to the mixed findings on perceptual congruence and satisfaction, it strikes us as important to sort out what kinds of communication are and are not related to satisfaction. This study examines the possible relationship between satisfaction and the proportion of turning points that involve relationship talk.

The final facet of a relationship's turning point history relevant to satisfaction is whether the presence or absence of a given turning point type is related to current satisfaction. There may be certain events from which parties find it difficult to recover. For example, events such as physical separation that are often devastating to relationships (Wilmot, Carbaugh, & Baxter, 1985) may negatively correlate with current relational satisfaction. Similarly, there may be turning points whose function is so important to the bonding of the couple that their absence per se is linked with reduced satisfaction.

The discussion in terms of current relationship satisfaction can be summarized in this final research question:

RQ5: To what extent does turning point type, partner agreement on the identification of turning points, relationship talk surrounding turning points, and the proportion of negative turning points correlate with current relationship satisfaction?

METHODS

Sample of Respondents

The sample was composed of the romantic partners from 40 romantic relationships, producing a final N of 80 respondents. The researchers employed several methods in acquiring the sample of couples. First, a story about the research project was placed in the weekly college newspaper. Second, volunteers were solicited from the lower-division classes of the researchers. Third, the majority of the sample came from using "network sampling" (Granovetter, 1976) with the student interviewing team that collected the data for the study. Team members were asked to generate the names of all the romantic pairs in their social network, and interviewers were then randomly assigned in pairs to romantic couples unknown to them personally. Upon completion of their interviews, these romantic couples were asked to identify other couples in their respective social networks who might be interested in participating. No couple was included in the sample unless its history as a romantic relationship

exceeded an arbitrary length of 6 months. The average duration of relationships included in the study was 22.1 months. All respondents were taken from the student population of a private college, the vast majority of whom were 18-22 years of age.

Measures

Turning point data were acquired using the Retrospective Interview Technique (RIT), a frequently employed methodology in the study of turning points (Huston et al., 1981). The RIT asks each individual respondent to identify all of the turning points in his or her relationship since time of first meeting, plotting these points on a graph whose abscissa axis represents monthly intervals from time of first meeting until the time of the interview and whose ordinate axis reflects some index of relationship commitment, most commonly the estimated likelihood of marriage from 0% to 100% (Huston et al., 1981). At each identified turning point, the interviewer probes for additional information about that particular point. In asking subjects to keep weekly graphs as well as retrospective graphs, Miell (1984) found that people were remarkably accurate in their recall of turning point phenomena, thus lending some validity to the technique.

The interview schedule that accompanied the graphing procedure was adapted from Lloyd (1983). After an introduction that explained the study's purpose and assured confidentiality, respondents were initially asked to construct the graph's abscissa and ordinate axes. First, the respondent was asked to recall the first time that the two partners met; these data were placed on the abscissa of the graph and monthly intervals were marked from that point until the time of the interview. Second, respondents were asked to construct the ordinate axis of the graph by indicating what "100% commitment," "50% commitment," and "0% commitment" meant for a relationship. The ordinate axis was marked off in intervals of 10% and keywords generated by the respondent were written beside the 0%, 50%, and 100% markers to serve as reminders. Although Lloyd (1983) used the "likelihood of marriage" from 0-100%, we opted instead for the more general term "100% commitment" based on our feeling that marriage may not be fully meaningful to our sample of college romances. In fact, we found that our respondents overwhelmingly defined "100% commitment" as a serious and exclusive relationship that was projected to continue into the forseeable future but need not end in marriage.

Next, respondents proceeded to fill in the graph's turning points. Respondents were first asked to plot the relationship's commitment level at the point of first meeting and to plot the current level of relationship commitment to provide markers by which to calibrate the plotting of turning points in between these two endpoints. Respondents were then asked to go back to the first time the relationship partners met and to "plot in all of the times when there were changes in the joint commitment level that you can recall." After each point had been plotted, interviewers probed with questions designed to solicit information on the following: the event associated with the commitment change; whether the event was anticipated in advance of its occurrence; whether the event was intentionally created by one or both of the parties and, if so, to whom the event initiation was attributed and why; whether the turning point involved relationship talk; and last, anything else surrounding the turning point that the respondent felt important to mention in helping the interviewer understand what was going on at this turning point. After completing these probes, the interviewer asked the respondent to connect the prior point with the most recently plotted point and to explain the nature of the connecting line. The point connection information was used to check the incrementalism of commitment change. This cycle was repeated as the interviewer and the respondent worked their way chronologically along the graph's abscissa axis. After all turning points were identified, the interviewer asked the respondent to take "a minute or two to look over the graph and think about [the] discussion of the relationship." Respon-

dents were allowed to make any alterations they thought appropriate at this time.

Current relationship satisfaction was assessed using Norton's (1983) six-item quality index. Although described as a measure to assess marital satisfaction, it draws heavily from the Dyadic Adjustment Scale (Spanier, 1976) designed for any close romantic relationship.

Procedures

Interviewers were trained in the RIT procedure for three 2-hour sessions. They were then assigned to work in pairs, each interview pair responsible for interviewing a specified number of couples from among those they were randomly assigned after controlling for interviewer familiarity with potential couple participants. Interviewers contacted couple partners to determine if they would be interested in participating in the study. In order to prevent the couple partners from contaminating one another's data, the two partners were interviewed at the same time but in separate locations by the two interviewers. Interviews took approximately 1½–2 hours each. Following the completion of a given couple's interviews, interviewers turned in to the researchers the RIT graphs, respondents' satisfaction measures, and written versions of the taped interviews.

Data Analysis

The researchers inductively derived a set of 26 turning point types from the interview data (see Results section) and independently coded a 20% sample of interviews, reaching an absolute agreement of .79 on the identification of turning point types (Cohen's, 1960, kappa = .78, p < .000). Deeming this an adequate level of reliability, each researcher coded turning point types for half of the remaining interviews.

The researchers developed a three-category coding of partner agreement in the identification of turning points: (1) agree; (2) disagree; (3) agree on point identification but disagree on the point's valence. An independent coding of a 20% sample of interviews produced an absolute agreement of .83 in coding partner agreement (kappa = .66, p < .000), and the researchers equally divided the coding of the remaining interviews. A three-category code was derived for the role of communication in the turning points: (1) not mentioned at all; (2) mention of content-level communication only; and (3) mention of relationship talk. The absolute agreement between the researchers across a 20% sample of interviews was .79 (kappa = .61, p < .000), allowing each researcher to code independently half of the remaining interviews.

The internal reliability of the current satisfaction scale using Cronbach's alpha was .88. A respondent's satisfaction score was the sum across all six of the satisfaction items. Satisfaction correlated r = .80 (p < .000) with current relationship commitment, lending credence to the measure's validity for nonmarital romantic relationships.

Change in commitment level was derived directly from respondent graphs: commitment at current turning point minus commitment at immediately prior turning point. Positive turning points were those with a commitment difference score greater than zero; negative turning points were those with difference scores less than zero.

RESULTS

Research Question #1 inquired about the phenomena that comprise turning points in romantic relationships. The interview data revealed a rich array of events that were associated with change in relationship commitment. A total of 759 turning points were identified, with a mean of 9.5 events per respondent account and a range of 3–20 events. The researchers inductively derived 26 different types of events whose frequency distribution is reported in Table 13.1. Because 26 categories were too cumbersome for data analysis purposes, the texts of respondent interviews were examined in order to derive groupings of turning point types that were

TABLE 13.1		
Distribution of Turning Point Types		
SUPRA-TYPES AND SUBTYPES	FREQUENCY N = 759)	%
I. Get-to-Know Time	144	19.0
A. First Meeting	80	10.5
B. Activity Time	46	6.1
C. First Date	18	2.4
II. Quality Time	117	15.4
A. Quality Time	85	11.2
B. Meet the Family	17	2.2
C. Getting Away Time	15	2.0
III. Physical Separation	76	10.0
IV. External Competition	70	9.2
A. New Rival	39	5.1
B. Competing Demands	16	2.1
C. Old Rival	15	2.0
V. Reunion	57	7.5
VI. Passion	48	6.3
A. First Sex	23	3.0
B. First Kiss	10	1.3
C. "I love you"	9	1.2
D. Whirlwind Phenomenon	6	.8
VII. Disengagement	46	6.1
VIII. Positive Psychic Change	42	5.5
IX. Exclusivity	34	4.5
A. Joint Exclusivity Decision	23	3.0
B. Dropping All Rivals	11	1.4
X. Negative Psychic Change	29	3.8
XI. Making Up	25	3.3
XII. Serious Commitment	24	3.2
A. Living Together	13	1.7
B. Marital Plans	11	1.4
XIII. Sacrifice	23	3.0
A. Crisis Help	14	1.8
B. Favors or Gifts	9	3.2
XIV. Other	24	3.2

talked about in similar ways. The resulting 14 supra-types are summarized in Table 13.1.

The supra-type of "Get-to-Know Time" was the most frequently mentioned by respondents, consisting of three turning point events that facilitate the parties getting to know one another. "First Meeting" refers to the first time the two relationship parties ever met. "Activity Time" captures the time early in the relationship when the parties spent time together enacting various activities, such as studying together. Based on respondent accounts, it was apparent that this time was valued for its quantity, not necessarily the quality of the activity. "First Date" refers to the first time the respondent regarded the two of them going on a boy-girl date.

The supra-type of "Quality Time" also consists of three turning point types, all of which are special occasions for the pair to appreciate one another and their relationship for its own sake. "Quality Time" captures the time the relationship parties spent together as a couple just enjoying each other's presence and their relationship without the necessary presence of some activity to be enacted and not necessarily for a large quantity of time. The event of "Meeting the Family" afforded the relationship parties an opportunity to focus on their coupleness in the presence of family members. "Getting Away Time" refers to occasions when the parties broke the routine of school and work and went away to be together.

"Physical Separation" is the only turning point event in the supra-type of the same label. This event refers to separation generated by vacations, school breaks, and overseas trips rather than separations that result from a disengagement or break-up of the relationship. The fact that the sample was drawn from a college population contributes to the relatively high quantity of physical separations experienced by the romantic couples.

The supra-type of "External Competition" consists of three turning event types. "New Rival" refers to the appearance of a third-party rival for the affection of one of the parties. In contrast, "Old Rival" refers to the reemergence of an old boyfriend or girlfriend. "Competing Demands" captures nonromantic competition for the parties' time and attention, typically school, work, or sports. Because respondents often suspected the presence of a romantic rival in such circumstances, however, this event type is logically grouped with the two romantically based competing demands.

"Reunion" is a single-event supra-type that refers to reunion after Physical Separation. The disparity in the frequency of this event and the frequency of the Physical Separation event underscores the fact that not all reunions constituted turning points. Further, some physical separations did not affect

commitment but the reunion event did have an impact on the parties' commitment. Thus, there is no necessary one-to-one correspondence between Physical Separation and Reunion events in these data.

The supra-type of "Passion" refers to four events that involve physical/emotional affection between the parties. "First Kiss" and "First Sex" were important marker events for these respondents in affecting or signaling relationship commitment. Similarly, the expression of "I love you" constituted an important turning point. The "Whirlwind Phenomenon" refers to the proverbial love-at-first-sight experience.

"Disengagement" is a single-event supra-type that refers to any deescalation in the relationship, including total break-up or dissolution. "Making Up" refers to events in which the parties repaired their relationship after its disengagement or break-up. As was the case with the events of Physical Separation and Reunion, the "Disengagement" and "Making Up" events bear no necessary one-to-one correspondence in the data. For some respondents, the disengagement was eventful but the make-up was not; for others, the disengagement was relatively uneventful but the making up was significant.

The single-event supra-types of "Positive Psychic Change" and "Negative Psychic Change" refer to intrapsychic changes of attitude for the respondent. Unlike other turning points, these two lack perceived external events as catalysts to change that respondents could recall.

"Exclusivity" is a supra-type that consists of two turning point events. The "Joint Exclusivity Decision" refers to a joint decision by the relationship parties to be romantically involved with only each other. "Dropping All Rivals" refers to default exclusivity by breaking romantic involvement with all others except the partner.

The supra-type of "Serious Commitment" involves two turning point events. "Living Together" refers to the parties' decision to move in together as a couple. "Marital Plans" refers to the joint decision to marry, typically the event of getting engaged.

"Sacrifice" is a supra-type that consists of two turning point events. "Crisis Help" refers to assistance provided by the other party when the respondent was experiencing some personal problem. "Favors or Gifts" refers to a sacrifice made by the other party or by the respondent in the form of gifts or favors.

Overall, 3.2% of the turning point events could not be classified into 1 of the above 25 types or 13 supra-types. These "Other" events captured a miscellany of experiences, none of which occurred with sufficient frequency to warrant the addition of another turning point type category.

The second research question probed the role of explicit metacommunication in turning point events. The three-category coding scheme described above was dichotomized by collapsing the first two categories into a single category of "No Relationship Talk." Overall, 55.1% of the turning point events involved relationship talk. However, relationship talk was not equally likely for all types of turning point events. Table 13.2 presents the proportions of each type of turning point that entailed relationship talk. A chi-square test indicated that differences were significant beyond the p = .0000 level (χ^2 = 117.07, df = 12; C^2 = .17). Get-to-Know Time, Physical Separation, and Sacrifice were least likely to involve relationship talk. In contrast, the turning point types of Exclusivity, Making Up, Disengagement, Serious Commitment, and Passion were most likely to involve talk about the relationship.

The third research question inquired about partner agreement in the identification of turning point events. For purposes of analysis, the three-category coding scheme described above was reduced to two categories by collapsing the general disagreement category with the valence disagreement category. Overall, 54.5% of all turning points were agreed upon by relationship partners. Table 13.3 summarizes the proportions of each turning point supra-type about which relationship partners agreed. A chi-square test indicated a significant departure from chance at beyond the p = .0001 level (χ^2 = 39.16, df = 12; C^2 = .05). Partner agreement in

TABLE 13.2

Turning Point Types That Involved Relationship Talk

TURNING POINT TYPE	%
Get-to-Know time	19.8
Quality Time	59.4
Physical Separation	37.3
External Competition	59.0
Reunion	50.0
Passion	76.7
Disengagement	79.1
Positive Psychic Change	65.2
Exclusivity	90.9
Negative Psychic Change	61.9
Making Up	86.4
Serious Commitment	77.3
Sacrifice	20.0
Overall	55.1

TABLE 13.3

Turning Point Types About Which Partners Agreed

TURNING POINT TYPE	%
Get-to-Know Time	68.8
Quality Time	45.3
Physical Separation	53.9
External Competition	42.0
Reunion	63.2
Passion	50.0
Disengagement	56.5
Positive Psychic Change	38.1
Exclusivity	67.6
Negative Psychic Change	48.3
Making Up	56.0
Serious Commitment	75.0
Sacrifice	30.4
Overall	54.5

identifying turning points was notably low with External Competition, Positive Psychic Change, Sacrifice, and Quality Time. Partner agreement was especially evident for Reunion, Exclusivity, Serious Commitment, and Get-to-Know Time. In order to determine whether systematic gender differences were at play in the 45% discrepant cases, a chi-square test was performed on the frequency of supra-types reported by males and females. No systematic gender difference was found (χ^2 = 9.86, 12 df, p = .63; power estimated at beyond .99 for a medium effect size at alpha = .05; Cohen, 1969).

The fourth research question asked if turning point types varied in their intensity. A one-way ANOVA was conducted on the 13 supra-types (excluding "Other") with reported change in commitment level serving as the dependent variable. The means and standard deviations are reported in Table 13.4. The main effect on turning point type was significant at beyond the .001 level (F = 27.45, df = 12, 650; eta^2 = .34).[1] The turning point types are composed of three major negative change events—Disengagement, External Competition, and Negative Psychic Change—none of which differs from the other two but all of which differ from the positive change events based on subsequent Scheffé tests. The most positive events are Serious Commitment, Making Up, Get-to-Know Time,

TABLE 13.4

Means and Standard Deviations for Change in Relationship Commitment Level by Turning Point Types

TURNING POINT TYPE	MEAN CHANGE COMMIT- MENT	STANDARD DEVIATION
Get-to-Know Time	+21.13	17.50
Quality Time	+15.18	13.07
Physical Separation	−0.30	22.69
External Competition	−13.44	23.83
Reunion	+10.72	21.28
Passion	+20.35	17.56
Disengagement	−23.28	26.74
Positive Psychic Change	+18.98	20.00
Exclusivity	+19.21	21.91
Negative Psychic Change	−9.00	13.96
Making Up	+21.60	+28.85
Serious Commitment	+23.26	24.78
Sacrifice	+17.61	14.70
Other	−1.04	22.36

Passion, Exclusivity, and Positive Psychic Change, none of which differs from the other five events based on subsequent Scheffe tests.

The fifth research question explored a variety of possible associations between turning points and current relationship satisfaction; with N = 80 and a two-tailed alpha of .05, the correlation statistic employed in these analyses had an estimated power of .78 for a medium effect size (Cohen, 1969). An insignificant correlation was found between a respondent's current satisfaction with the relationship and the proportion or his or her identified turning points with which the partner agreed (r = .08; p = .25). The pattern of association of satisfaction with partner agreement in the identification of turning points remained insignificant when positive turning points were examined separately from negative turning points (r values of .06 and .19, respectively). Current relationship satisfaction was not significantly correlated with the proportion of turning point events that involved relationship talk (r = .09, p = .22). The absence of a relationship between explicit metacommunication and satisfaction held when negative turning points and positive turning points were analyzed separately (r values of .10 and .04, respectively). Current satisfaction with the relationship correlated significantly with the proportion of a respondent's identified turning points that were negative (r = −.39, p < .000).

In order to discern which turning point events were associated with current satisfaction level, a series of t-tests was performed that compared satisfaction level between respondent accounts in which a given turning point type was present versus absent. Significant differences emerged for the Exclusivity turning point event (t = 2.39, df = 78, p = .019; r^2_{pb} = .07) with satisfaction greater for those respondents who identified this turning point in their relationship. The presence of the Disengagement event produced less satisfaction for respondents than was the case for respondents whose relationships lacked a Disengagement event (t = 2.57, df = 78, p = .012; r^2_{pb} = .08). The presence or absence of the remainder of the turning point types was not significantly related to satisfaction (power of the t-test estimated at .60 for two-tailed alpha = .05 and medium effect size; Cohen, 1969).

DISCUSSION

This research has explored Bolton's (1961) turning point as a lens through which to examine relationship change. Researchers should profit from the discoveries that the set of turning points is finite yet diverse enough to capture richly relational change and that participants are able to identify those turning points that they consider meaningful in their relational histories. In contrast to the image of relationship development as a process of creeping incrementalism with indistinguishable points of change, these findings provide tentative support for a view of relationship growth as a series of discrete events that are accompanied by positive or negative explosions of relational commitment. However, respondents provided their relational histories retrospectively, and the possibility exists that creeping incrementalism may nonetheless capture relationship change as it is experienced at the time; cognitive reframing into discrete events may simply be a memory artifact. Such events are self-contained "packages" of salient and concrete actions, perhaps easier to recall than nondistinct incremental changes. The possibility exists also that the RIT procedure biased the data in favor of discrete turning point events. However, the interviewers observed informally that their respondents had little difficulty in recalling turning point events. Such events may be salient to relationship parties because they provide useful "story lines" about which the parties can reminisce or present their relationship to others. Future work needs to monitor relationship development longitudinally to address the issue of how change actually is experienced at the time in relationships as opposed to how such change is recalled after the fact.

Because this study dealt with perceived changes in commitment associated with turning point phenomena, it is impossible to determine causality. Conceptually, however, it would appear useful to distinguish capstone or marker turning points from causal events. In some instances, an internalized change in commitment may produce a turning point. Such a turning point serves to formalize or mark the felt change in commitment, constituting a capstone event. The declaration of exclusive commitment, for example, is likely to serve as such a capstone event in going "on record" about the parties' already changed feelings about one another. Other turning point events may serve a more direct causal function, producing change in felt commitment. Sacrifice events, for example, were always reported as turning points that produced a change in commitment. The display of sacrifice by the other party on one's behalf resulted in increased commitment toward the other. The distinction between capstone and causal turning points is somewhat artificial, however, for reciprocal causality between event and commitment is likely for both types of turning point events. Capstone events may formalize an internalized affective change in commitment, but once such events have occurred, they likely serve as causal forces in propelling further commitment. Similarly, some causal turning points probably involve a prior internalized affect change in one of the parties. Sacrifice, for instance, probably involves some prior affective change in the other to motivate the sacrificial act.

The turning point framework was helpful in probing instances of direct relationship talk. Overall, 55% of the turning points involved relationship talk, a figure that may seem high given that extant work reports the infrequency of explicit metacommunication. This discrepancy is tempered by the realization that turning points themselves occur relatively infrequently; the typical relationship party reported about one turning point every two months or so.

The fact that relationship talk was not equally distributed across turning point types supports the selective use of explicit relationship talk in romantic couples. Some of the events associated with direct metacommunication, especially Exclusivity, Making Up, and Serious Commitment, appear to be events that, by definition, would be difficult to accomplish in the absence of relationship talk. Our Passion category may tap a set of events that is critical to defining the relationship, is accomplished mutually, and provides meaningful events ripe for explicit relationship talk. The fact that Disengagement was strongly associated with relational talk fails to support prior work in relationship break-up that has found indirectness a pervasive strategy (see Baxter, 1985). However, these relationships were still intact, in contrast to the dissolved relationships that have been studied in extant disengagement work. Perhaps relationship talk prevents disengagement events from turning into complete dissolutions.

Other turning point events are noteworthy because of the absence of relationship talk. Get-to-Know Time may tap an initial stage when the relationship is particularly vulnerable and thus direct relationship talk is avoided for fear of destroying the relationship (Baxter & Wilmot, 1985). Similarly, Physical Separation is associated with relational vulnerability and may also be avoided in direct metacommunication. In short, the presence or absence of relationship talk may depend on the specific type of turning point event.

An association between explicit metacommunication and overall relational satisfaction was not evident in this study, consistent with the conclusion drawn by critics of the talk-as-elixir folk myth. It may be that relationship talk is related to satisfaction but in a complex way not tapped in the relatively crude presence-absence distinction employed in this study. Explicit metacommunication might differ in quantity, content, context, strategies, and outcomes depending on the specific turning point. The relationship between metacommunication and overall satisfaction may be mediated by these intervening contingencies.

Partner agreement in reported turning points was about 55%. This figure is comparable to that noted by other researchers in assessing partner agreement in monitoring day-to-day behavior (Christensen & Nies, 1980; Jacobson & Moore, 1981). Further, this behavioral monitoring research has reported the greatest partner agreement with objective behaviors as opposed to behaviors which involve subjectivity by the observer (Christensen & Nies, 1980; Jacobson & Moore, 1981). A comparable pattern was found in this study for partner agreement in reported turning points; agreement was higher for events that appear to be most objectively verifiable and lower for subjectively experienced events. The types of turning points most characterized by low partner agreement appear to be highly individualized as experienced and interpreted by relational partners. For example, the experience of Positive Psychic Change is by definition an internal psychological phenomenon. Quality Time and Sacrifice may also occur predominantly in one individual's interpretation. When one partner experiences External Competition, she or he may withhold the experience from the other (Baxter & Wilmot, 1985), thereby creating a unilateral and subjectively realized turning point. In contrast, those events most characterized by partner agreement (Reunion, Exclusivity, Serious Commitment, and Get-to-Know Time) are events that are more easily externally verifiable.

If accounts of turning points are regarded as objective records of relational histories, the relatively low partner agreement found in this study fails to meet minimum standards of measurement reliability between partner observers. However, if partner reports of the events in their relationship are regarded as important in their own right, rather than as reliable observations about objective events, it becomes moot to cast partner agreement in terms of measurement reliability. Instead, a focus on the phenomenology of relationship partners makes differences in partner reports a theoretically interesting issue. The relatively low agreement between partners suggests that relationship parties indeed coexist in separate phenomenological relationship worlds. However, these differences do not neatly fit into "his" and "her" social realities, for no systematic gender differences were observed for the types of reported turning points.

Partners who experienced more agreement were not found to be more satisfied with their relationships. This suggests that perceptual consensus may not be necessary for overall relationship success, a conclusion consistent with the argument by Sillars and Scott (1983) discussed above. As those researchers noted, the compatibility of the partners' disparate perceptions may be a more predictive indicator of relationship success. That is, partners may successfully function in their relationship despite different cognitive constructions of their history so long as those constructions do not obstruct one another.

Further explorations of agreement need to use diverse measurement methods. For example, in this study, agreement occurred only when both partners' independent accounts of their relationship included the same event. Different measurement methods such as joint interviews or having partners verify one another's accounts should be employed as well.

Turning points were shown to differ in their associated levels of commitment change. Although some turning point events were clearly very positive or very negative in impact, other events, such as Physical Separation, were relatively unclear in their impact. It is likely that events such as Physical Separation are either positive or negative, depending on how the parties manage the event (Wilmot et al., 1985). In general, the turning points highest in reported commitment change (in either a positive or negative direction) were also those turning points likely to be highest in partner agreement and likely to involve relationship talk. This finding suggests that partners share a partially common phenomenological reality, perhaps enhanced through relationship talk, on those turning point events regarded as most significant to the relationship. Alternatively, events that are discussed and agreed upon may simply be accorded more importance retrospectively.

Given that the proportion of events that were negative correlated inversely with overall relational satisfaction, turning points may function in a cumulative manner to affect current relational satisfaction. Alternatively, more satisfied relationship parties may simply fail to recall many negative events for their relationship. Only 2 of the 13 supra-

types were individually related to current satisfaction with the relationship: Disengagement and Exclusivity. This finding suggests that there may be some specific events whose presence or absence during relationship development may differentiate between more and less satisfied partners, regardless of the total proportion of negative (and positive) events in a relational history.

The specific turning point types that emerged in this study provide some confirmatory insights into people's implicit relationship theories. The early event type of Get-to-Know Time contrasted with the later event of Quality Time suggests that quantity may be an important indicator of an early romance whereas the quality criterion becomes more important to a closer romantic relationship. Hays (1984) has observed a similar transformation from quantity to quality criteria in the development of same-sex friendships. The Sacrifice event suggests the salience of demonstrable caring on the other's behalf as an important indicator of romantic involvement. Displays of physical affection (the Passion event) appear important in transforming a platonic opposite-sex relationship into a full-blown romantic relationship type, a finding consistent with prior work (Wilmot & Baxter, 1984). The turning point events of External Competition and Exclusivity point to the salience of loyalty and fidelity to people's implicit theories of romantic relationships, qualities that have emerged in extant work as well (Baxter, in press; Davis & Todd, 1982; Wilmot & Baxter, 1984).

In summary, the turning point should provide a fruitful construct for relationship research. Participants retrospectively cast their relationship development as a series of positive and negative turning points. Turning point analysis is valuable as an approach to explicit metacommunication, partner congruence of perspectives, overall satisfaction, and relational commitment levels. Future research should examine possible differences in turning point accounts for relationships that experience different trajectories of growth (Huston et al., 1981). Work in relationship cultures should consider the role that turning points play in maintaining the relationship through consideration of reminiscing interaction. Because turning points constitute useful story lines, with self-contained "chunks" of a relationship's history, their role in the public presentation of the relationship by its parties should be considered as well.

ENDNOTE

[1] Bartlett's test of homogeneity of variance was $F = 6.01$, $p < .001$, indicating that the various turning point supra-types had different variances. However, Keppel (1973) observes that analysis of variance is sufficiently robust to perform with variances even more divergent than those found here. Nonetheless, the nonparametric Kruskal-Wallis one-way analysis of variance test was performed on supra-type differences in change in commitment, with $H = 261.45$, $p < .000$. The pattern of mean ranks replicated the pattern found with the ANOVA findings. That is, Disengagement, External Competition, and Negative Psychic Change composed the least positive events, and the six most positive events were as reported in the text of the article.

REFERENCES

Altman, I., & Taylor, D. (1973). *Social penetration: The development of interpersonal relationships.* New York: Holt, Rinehart & Winston.

Altman, I., Vinsel, A., & Brown, B. (1981). Dialectic conceptions in social psychology: An application to social penetration and privacy regulation. In L. Berkowitz (Ed.), *Advances in experimental social psychology* (Vol. 14). New York: Academic Press.

Baxter, L. (1985). Accomplishing relationship disengagement. In S. Duck & D. Perlman (Eds.), *Understanding personal relationships: An interdisciplinary approach.* London: Sage.

Baxter, L. (in press). Gender differences in the heterosexual relationship rules embedded in break-up accounts. *Journal of Social and Personal Relationships.*

Baxter, L., & Wilmot, W. (1984). "Secret tests": Social strategies for acquiring information about the state of the relationship. *Human Communication Research, 11,* 171-201.

Baxter, L., & Wilmot, W. (1985). Taboo topics in close relationships. *Journal of Social and Personal Relationships, 2,* 253-269.

Berger, C. R., & Calabrese, R. (1975). Some explorations in initial interaction and beyond: Toward a developmental theory of interpersonal communication. *Human Communication Research, 1,* 99-112.

Bochner, A. P. (1982). On the efficacy of openness in close relationships. In M. Burgoon (Ed.), *Communication yearbook 6.* New Brunswick, NJ: Transaction Books.

Bolton, C. D. (1961). Mate selection as the development of a relationship. *Marriage and Family Living, 23,* 234-240.

Braiker, H. B., & Kelley, H. H. (1979). Conflict in the development of close relationships. In R. L. Burgess & T. L. Huston (Eds.), *Social exchange in developing relationships.* New York: Academic Press.

Christensen, A., & Nies, D. C. (1980). The spouse observation checklist: Empirical analysis and critique. *American Journal of Family Therapy, 8,* 69-79.

Cody, M. (1982). A typology of disengagement strategies and an examination of the role intimacy, reactions to inequity and relational problems play in strategy selection. *Communication Monographs, 49,* 148-170.

Cohen, J. (1960). A coefficient of agreement for nominal scales. *Educational and Psychological Measurement, 20,* 37-48.

Cohen, J. (1969). *Statistical power analysis for the behavioral sciences.* New York: Academic Press.

Davis, K. E., & Todd, M. J. (1982). Friendship and love relationships. In K. E. Davis & T. Mitchell (Eds.), *Advances in descriptive psychology* (Vol. 2). Greenwich, CT: JAI Press.

Duck, S., & Perlman, D. (1985). *Understanding personal relationships: An interdisciplinary approach.* London: Sage.

Gottman, J., Markman, H., & Notarious, C. (1977). The topography of marital conflict. *Journal of Marriage and the Family, 39,* 461-478.

Granovetter, M. S. (1976). Network sampling: Some first steps. *American Journal of Sociology, 81,* 1287-1303.

Hays, R. (1984). The development and maintenance of friendship. *Journal of Social and Personal Relationships, 1,* 75-98.

Hinde, R. A. (1981). The bases of a science of interpersonal relationships. In S. Duck & R. Gilmour (Eds.), *Personal relationships 1: Studying personal relationships.* New York: Academic Press.

Huston, T. L., Surra, C., Fitzgerald, N. M., & Cate, R. (1981). From courtship to marriage: Mate selection as an interpersonal process. In S. Duck & R. Gilmour (Eds.), *Personal relationships 2: Developing personal relationships.* New York: Academic Press.

Jacobson, N. S., & Moore, D. (1981). Spouses as observers of the events in their relationship. *Journal of Consulting and Clinical Psychology, 49,* 269-277.

Katriel, T., & Philipsen, G. (1981). "What we need is communication": "Communication" as a cultural category in some American speech. *Communication Monographs, 48,* 301-317.

Keppel, G. (1973). *Design and analysis.* Englewood Cliffs, NJ: Prentice-Hall.

Knapp, M. (1984). *Interpersonal communication and human relationships.* Boston: Allyn and Bacon.

Lewis, R. A., & Spanier, G. B. (1979). Theorizing about the quality and stability of marriage. In W. Burr et al. (Eds.), *Contemporary theories about the family* (Vol. 1). New York: Macmillan.

Lloyd, S. (1983). *A typological description of premarital relationship dissolution.* Unpublished doctoral thesis, Oregon State University.

Lloyd, S., & Cate, R. (1984). *Attributions associated with significant turning points in premarital relationship development and dissolution.* Paper presented at the Second International Conference on Personal Relationships, Madison, WI.

Miell, D. (1984). *Strategies in information exchange in developing relationships: Evidence for a unique relational context.* Paper presented at the Second International Conference on Personal Relationships, Madison, WI.

Norton, R. (1983). Measuring marital quality: A critical look at the dependent variable. *Journal of Marriage and the Family, 45,* 141-151.

Nydick, A., & Cornelius, R. (1984). *What we talk about when we talk about love.* Paper presented at the Second International Conference on Personal Relationships, Madison, WI.

Parks, M. R. (1982). Ideology in interpersonal communication: Off the couch and into the world. In M. Burgoon (Ed.), *Communication yearbook 6.* New Brunswick, NJ: Transaction Books.

Planalp, S., & Honeycutt, J. (1985). Events that increase uncertainty in personal relationships. *Human Communication Research, 11,* 593-604.

Rands, M., & Levinger, G. (1979). Implicit theories of relationships: An intergenerational study. *Journal of Personality & Social Psychology, 37,* 645-661.

Sillars, A., & Scott, M. (1983). Interpersonal perception between intimates: An integrative review. *Human Communication Research, 10,* 153-176.

Spanier, G. B. (1976). Measuring dyadic adjustment: New scales for assessing the quality of marriage and similar dyads. *Journal of Marriage and the Family, 38,* 15-28.

Spanier, G. B., & Lewis, R. A. (1980). Marital quality: A review of research in the seventies. *Journal of Marriage and the Family, 42,* 825-839.

Surra, C. (1984). *Attributions about changes in commitment: Variations by courtship style.* Paper presented at the Second International Conference on Personal Relationships, Madison, WI.

Wilmot, W. (1980). Metacommunication: A re-examination and extension. In D. Nimmo (Ed.), *Communication yearbook 4.* New Brunswick, NJ: Transaction Books.

Wilmot, W., & Baxter, L. (1984). *Defining relationships: The interplay of cognitive schemata and communication.* Paper presented at the Western Speech Communication Association Annual Convention, Seattle, WA.

Wilmot, W., Carbaugh, D., & Baxter, L. (1985). Communication strategies used to terminate romantic relationships *Western Journal of Speech Communication, 49,* 204-216.

14

On the Efficacy of Openness
in Close Relationships

ARTHUR P. BOCHNER

The term "expressive communication" refers to messages that signify emotive and subjective experiences such as feelings, private sentiments, and personal qualities. Since the 1960s expressive communication has been extensively discussed and vigorously researched. Indeed expressive communication has been conceptualized not only as a function of interpersonal communication but also as a relational ideology (O'Neill & O'Neill, 1972), a rhetorical vision (Kidd, 1975), a philosophical doctrine (Buber, 1958; Johannesen, 1971), and a school of thought (Hart & Burks, 1972).

At issue here is how to play the games of life. How far can one extend the informal logic of public conduct into the realm of private relationships? The literature germane to these questions draws a sharp contrast between two ends of the continuum of social interaction: openness vs. closedness, frankness vs. restraint, dialogue vs. monologue, and so on. While the origins of this rigid dichotomizing are varied and complex, the countercultural movement of the late 1960s must be given considerable credit for polarizing social conduct into the two camps. The popular sociocultural critiques of that period— Roszak's *The Making of a Counterculture* (1969), Reich's *The Greening of America* (1970), Slater's *The Pursuit of Loneliness* (1970)—shared the sentiment that traditional American ideals inhibited emotional gratification by promoting inflexible role definitions, encouraging egocentric drives, discour-

aging expression of feelings, subverting spontaneity, and failing to prepare people for change. Concurrently, the third revolution in psychology (Matson, 1964) offered the counterculture a "humanizing" alternative to the social conventions they deplored. Maslow's *Toward a Psychology of Being* (1962), Jourard's *The Transparent Self* (1964), Bugental's *The Search for Authenticity* (1965), Buber's *I And Thou* (1958), and Schutz's *Joy* (1967) were among the many books that endorsed the fine-sounding principles of "openness," "self-disclosure," and "dialogue" and embraced the exhilarating ideals of "oceanic joy," "peak experience," and "being-cognition." In tandem with injunctions to "tell it like it is," "let it all hang out," and "do your own thing," these buzz-words and catchy phrases became symbolic of the utopian ideals of the counter-culture so vividly captured by Jameson (1976: 122):

> [T]he Sixties . . . held out the ultimate Utopian vision of a life space in which people could meet face to face in some absolute and unmediated sense, beyond all status or conventions, without recourse to preliminary identifications and independent of all the traditional formulas of conversational ritual, in short, utterly divested of all those abundant cues with which the older social groupings hedged and defused the anxieties implicit in the encounter with the Other.

Broadly disseminated by the media to all sectors of American society, the Utopian vision of life es-

From Bochner, A. P. (1982). On the efficacy of openness in close relationships. In M. Burgoon (Ed.), *Communication Yearbook 5* (pp. 109-124). New Brunswick, NJ: Transaction Books.

poused by the counterculture got distilled into a vision of interpersonal relationships that the masses could accept. Virginia Kidd's study of the popular magazines of the period shows the extent to which relational norms were altered by transforms of the Utopian vision. In sources ranging from *Cosmopolitan* to *Reader's Digest* and from *Ebony* to *New York Times Magazine*, periodicals that reach over 1,000,000 people, Kidd (1975: 32) found abundant evidence of a striking shift in perspectives "appearing sporadically in the early Sixties, gaining impetus in the late Sixties and assuming a major position in the last few years."

Kidd calls the period falling between the early 1950s and the mid-1960s "Vision I." The Vision I relationship typically assumed an unchanging world, certainty, predictability, and a single standard for sex-role behavior. It emphasized the virtue of compliments, the value of courtesy, and the necessity of togetherness. Partners were advised to act strategically, even to use duplicity, in order to make the other person happy; the other came first even if it meant putting one's own feelings aside.

The conversion from Vision I to Vision II coincided with the emergence of the counterculture. Bearing the stamp of Utopian ideals, Vision II partners valued honest talk, freedom of expression and absence of convention. Vision II assumed that "life was everchanging and so were relationships . . . so was meaning" (Kidd, 1975: 35). In contrast to Vision I's concern for restraint, strategic communication, and the primacy of the other, Vision II sanctified talking about problems, openly revealing feelings, and magnifying self-importance. The priority it placed on the communication process, says Kidd, was both its great strength and its glaring weakness.

The prescription for interpersonal relations dispensed to readers of popular magazines documents the shift from an instrumental to an expressive orientation to communication that took hold in the early 1970s. That this transfiguration occurred has never been disputed; that it was obviously a change for the best, however, is quite another matter, one that has been the subject of spirited debate.

In 1972 Hart and Burks waged a forceful attack on the school of expressivism. Sensing that the die had been cast in favor of the unpremediated style of the expressivist, Hart and Burks defended the instrumentalist's "rhetorical approach" to social life. Capitalizing on the excesses of an approach they admitted was "complex and disparate . . . and incompletely articulated" (1972: 75), Hart and Burks implied that the expressivist was unwilling to undergo the strain of adaptation, unconstrained by the presence of the other, unable to understand that an idea can be expressed in multiple ways, disinclined to accept role-taking as part of the human condition, and indisposed to calculate responses prior to communicating them.

If these charges are valid, and if the instrumentalist is indeed more sensitive to the taboos and customs that prevent interaction from being short-circuited, then the rhetorical approach undoubtedly "is more universally appropriate to our everyday interactions than are the dictates of expressive utterance" (Hart & Burks, 1972: 91). Yet even if we accept Hart and Burk's baffling extrapolation of the premises of "expressionism," we must keep in mind that, as Clifford Geertz (1980: 4) says, "there is still a difference between testing a hypothesis and embroidering it." Hart and Burks rely only on stalking arguments, not acid tests. Thus nagging questions remain about the force of expressive communication on social relations. Insufficient as they may prove to be, empirical studies of self-disclosure and other aspects of expressive communication may offer the firmest basis for addressing these questions.

SELF-DISCLOSURE

The expression of private feelings, thoughts, and characteristics commonly is termed *self-disclosure*. Interest in the empirical study of self-disclosure was inspired by a series of books published by Sidney Jourard in the 1960s (1964, 1967, 1968) and by Jourard's own attempt to construct a valid instrument for measuring self-disclosure as an enduring personality trait (Jourard, 1971). The first decade of research on self-disclosure was confined mainly to correlational studies in which subjects' scores on Jourard's Self-Disclosure Questionnaire (JSDQ) were correlated with their scores on demographic variables, measures of liking for target persons, physical contact, and psychological well-being. In the second decade the focus of research shifted to the study of self-disclosure as an interactional exchange process and the locus of research moved to the experimental laboratory. Altman and Taylor's (1973) theory of social penetration raised interesting questions about the function of self-disclosure over the course of an interpersonal bond, and their methodological innovations (Taylor & Altman, 1966) made it possible for researchers to study how self-disclosure affected the initiation and maintenance of a bond and/or how other variables impinged upon subjects' self-disclosures.

Jourard introduced the term "self disclosure" in *The Transparent Self* (1964) without defining it rigorously. Self-disclosure, he said, was "the act of making yourself manifest, showing yourself so others can perceive you" (1964: 19). A few years later he recalled choosing the term "self-disclosure" over "real-self communication" because it was "a more neutral descriptive term . . . to describe the act of revealing personal information to others" (Jourard, 1971: 2). Cozby (1973) classified Jourard's application of the term as equivalent in meaning to "verbal accessibility" (Polansky, 1965) and "social accessibility" (Rickers-Ovsiankina, 1956).

After two decades of scholarship on self-disclosure, uses of the concept are still vague and/or inoperable. One recent reviewer, Chelune (1979: 3), found "serious inconsistencies in the conceptual definitions used in self-disclosure research," and another, Archer (1979: 57), referred to "the concept of disclosure itself" as "the weakest point in the basic super-structure of self-disclosure research." Investigators have not achieved consensus on the empirical referents of self-disclosure. While most agree that a message qualifies as self-disclosure if it is verbal, pertains to the self, and passes from a source to a target, they disagree about whether *any* verbal message concerning the self should count.

Some insist that the message must be communicated *intentionally* and reveal something *inaccessible* by other means. This is the basis for Miller and Steinberg's (1975) distinction between *apparent* and *genuine* disclosure. All self-disclosures are apparent, but only some are genuine.

Of course it is one thing to say that "any information about himself which person A communicates verbally to person B" (Cozby, 1973: 73) is self-disclosure, and quite another to limit it to what "one person tells another person . . . about himself which the other person is unlikely to know or to discover from other sources" (Pearce & Sharp, 1973: 414). Where Cozby's definition provides only a general standard for measuring disclosure and does not discriminate among such vastly different forms of self-reference as slips of the tongue, confessions, and impression management strategies, Pearce and Sharp's imposes rigorous operational requirements that are nearly impossible to carry out validly in the absence of an objective basis for determining intentionality and/or accessibility. Neither is satisfactory. Perhaps that is why self-disclosure has become a term more closely tied to the vernacular than to a specific set of empirical operations. There is little consensus about how to define it conceptually and even less about how to investigate it empirically. Yet self-disclosure remains one of the most appealing and widely researched subjects in the study of interpersonal bonding.

Dimensions of Self-Disclosure

Jourard's original attempts to measure self-disclosure were largely unsuccessful. Treating self-disclosure as a personality variable, he constructed measurement scales that required subjects to report how often, to whom, and about what topics they disclosed. Although Jourard and his followers conducted more than 100 studies with various forms of the JSDQ scales, validity was never firmly established. In fact Cozby's review (1973: 73) of this research concluded that "the JSDQ does not accurately predict self-disclosure" and "situational variables may outweigh individual differences in disposition to disclose."

As it became obvious that self-disclosure was significantly affected by the situations in which subjects were placed, researchers turned their attention to the task of describing the dimensions of self-disclosing messages and the factors that affect or are affected by them. Four dimensions have been identified: (1) *breadth,* the number of topics a person discloses (Altman & Taylor, 1973); (2) *depth* or *personalness,* the extent to which disclosure is intimate (Taylor & Altman, 1966); (3) *duration,* the length of disclosure (Cozby, 1973); and (4) *valence,* whether disclosure is positive or negative (Gilbert, 1976). Wheeless and Grotz's (1976) factor analysis of self-disclosure scales produced three additional "dimensions" which they labeled honesty, intent, and relevance, and Chelune (1975) included affective manner of presentation and flexibility of disclosure pattern. These are not dimensions of messages, however, since they cannot be measured reliably without taking into account much more than the messages themselves.

Self-Disclosure over the Course of a Relationship

Though the literature on self-disclosure is enormous (see Rosenfeld, 1979), only a few studies have collected and examined the kind of cross-sectional or longitudinal evidence germane to the scope of this chapter. We must rely, therefore, on studies that are not ideally suited to the goal of drawing conclusions about how interpersonal bonds are affected by self-disclosure. These studies are extremely difficult to comprehend and synthesize for several reasons: (1) *Studies that assess patterns of self-disclosure from subjects' self-reports are not directly comparable to studies in which self-disclosure is manipulated experimentally or measured as a message variable.* In the self-report studies, researchers have asked subjects to think about several of their actual relationships differing in longevity, knowledge of

the other and liking for the other, and to report how frequently and about what topics they disclose to these target persons. In the controlled studies, researchers have manipulated and/or controlled levels and degrees of self-disclosure by training confederates to choose particular topics, reveal preselected information at preselected points in a conversation with unacquainted subjects, and then measured the extent to which subjects reciprocate in kind and/or become attracted to the confederate. (2) *Self-report measures of self-disclosure are poor indicants of actual self-disclosing behavior.* The validity of self-disclosure questionnaires has never been conclusively established. It is likely that such instruments are excessively affected by the social-desirability biases and demand characteristics built into questionnaires, but these invalidating factors rarely have been examined systematically. Since there is substantial doubt about whether these measures are capable of predicting self-disclosing behavior adequately and since many contraindicating factors affect subjects' responses, we must urge a healthy skepticism about what, if anything, these instruments can tell us about self-disclosing behavior. (3) *Experimental studies of self-disclosure generally are not comparable to each other.* Some experiments have had subjects respond to tape-recorded messages, others to written messages; some to content-free disclosures, others to content-restricted disclosures; some to confederates they could hear but not see, others to confederates whom they met face-to-face, others to bogus strangers they were asked to imagine; some in which subjects conversed freely with confederates, others in which they had to speak in prolonged intervals without interruption; some in which the topic counted as the measure of disclosure, others in which the statements about the topic counted as the measure of disclosure. The variability in experimental procedures would not pose such a barrier to the task of comparing studies if there were some data about what differences these differences make. There are none. No studies have been conducted in which several of these conditions were varied systematically to determine how inferences about the effects of self-disclosure are affected by experimental procedures and operational definitions; and little, if any, effort has been made by some investigators to replicate the procedures and findings of others. Moreover researchers often have drawn conclusions about the effects of self-disclosure *as if* variability in procedures made no difference at all, though Morton (1978), as one example, has shown that subjects can trivialize intimate topics and personalize mundane issues. If many studies had reached the same conclusions about the effects of self-disclosure over the course of a relationship, the problem we are pointing to would be minor. Unfortunately, they have not and it is not.

Any attempt to extrapolate generalizations about interpersonal bonding from research on self-disclosure must proceed with extreme caution. The most rigorous studies have taken place in interactional settings with the least generalizability. The studies most pertinent to long-term bonds, on the other hand, have relied on loosely conceived and highly questionable measures of self-disclosure, poor sampling techniques, and inadequate research designs (Chelune, 1979). Nevertheless the review which follows seeks to draw some reasonable conclusions from both sets of studies about how self-disclosure functions over the course of a relationship. In the interests of conserving space, the review is restricted to three classes of studies: (1) landmark studies, (2) studies that treat self-disclosure as a message variable, and (3) studies carried out in the context of long-term relationships. More exhaustive analyses of this literature are available in the reviews of Cozby (1973), Altman (1973), Gilber (1976), Pearce and Sharp (1973), Goodstein and Reinecker (1974), Chelune (1979), Kelinke (1979), Derlega and Grzelak (1979), and Taylor (1979).

Empirical studies of self-disclosure have focused primarily on two questions: (1) Under what conditions do people respond *positively* to others who make disclosures to them? (2) Under what conditions do people reveal themselves to others? The first question is an extension of Jourard's (1959) hypothesis that disclosure leads to liking, attraction, and positive character attributions. The second questions concerns "the dyadic effect," the hypothesis that disclosures tend to be reciprocated.

Disclosure and Positive Reactions

There are three variants of the hypothesis that disclosure is connected causally to liking: (1) self-disclosure leads to liking (positive reactions); (2) liking leads to self-disclosure; (3) self-disclosure and liking form a positive feedback loop in which liking begets self-disclosure which begets greater liking and so on.

The early studies of self-disclosure were bivariate investigations in which measures of liking for a target person were correlated with measures of self-disclosure patterns. Jourard's studies produced evidence of an association between liking and self-disclosure for women but not for men. Jourard and Lasakow (1958) reported a significant positive correlation between liking for parents and self-disclosure to them for a sample of 31 nursing students. This finding was replicated by Jourard (1959) with an older sample of women faculty and their dean at a nursing college and by Fitzgerald (1963) with female college students.

In one of the first studies using male subjects and taking into account a possible mediating variable, Jourard and Landsman (1960) found that the relationship between liking and self-disclosure was attenuated by knowing. Patterns of disclosure for these men were more significantly affected by knowing than by liking. In fact, when subjects' responses were statistically controlled for knowing, the connection between liking and self-disclosure became relatively insignificant.

The studies conducted by Jourard and his associates relied on reports about past disclosures among previously acquainted subjects. These procedures were modified in a study conducted under controlled conditions by Worthy, Gary, and Kahn (1969). Female undergraduates were divided into groups of four and given ten minutes to get acquainted before completing confidential ratings of their liking for other members of the group. Then, on each of ten trials, subjects exchanged responses to questions from lists that had been previously scaled for intimacy. At the conclusion of the experiment subjects again reported their liking for their co-workers. The results showed that these women initially sent responses to the most intimate questions to persons whom they liked most. Subsequently, they showed the most liking for women from whom they received responses to the most intimate questions. Liking led to disclosure and, subsequently, disclosure led to liking.

After Taylor and Altman (1966) made a corpus of intimacy-scaled stimuli available for research on self-disclosure, researchers began to employ confederates trained to manipulate levels of disclosure systematically. Ehrlich and Graeven (1971) found that the level of intimacy of a male confederate's disclosure had *no measurable effect* on subject's rating of attraction to the confederate. Their results must be interpreted cautiously, however, since subjects were forced to speak in two-minute intervals and a host of confounding variables—nonverbal behaviors, physical attractiveness, fatigue of the confederate—were left uncontrolled. Derlega, Walmer, and Furman (1973) adopted similar procedures, matching a female confederate with female subjects. They also found no connection between confederate's level of disclosure and the subjects' ratings of liking.

Critelli, Rappaport, and Golding (1976) analyzed the verbal behavior of male subjects who role-played conversations with four male persons from their own life. The persons were chosen by the subjects on the basis of different categories of knowing and liking imposed by the researchers. Coding each message either as personal or impersonal, the researchers found that "liking is a more crucial determinant of personal disclosure than knowing, while they do not differ in relative control over impersonal disclosure" (Critelli, Rappaport, & Golding, 1976: 89). However, subjects generally self-reported that knowing was more important in determining the persons to whom they would disclose personally.

Cozby (1972) found strong support for a curvilinear relationship between intimacy of disclosure and liking. Female subjects were given information about the topics of self-disclosure chosen by one of a pair of female subjects in a previous experiment and then asked to play the role of the other person by choosing items to reveal. This process was repeated for a low, medium, and high self-disclosing other. Subjects reported the most liking for others who wanted to converse about topics of high intimacy.

The curvilinear relationship between liking and self-disclosure reported by Cozby (1972) led other researchers to contemplate that the link between the two may be mediated by the timing of a disclosure. Wortman, Adesman, Herman, and Greenberg (1976) reasoned that a self-disclosure occurring early in a conversation would be judged as less attractive than one presented later in the conversation because the receiver would be less likely to attribute the disclosure to the source's positive sentiments toward the receiver. A disclosure is perceived most positively, they suggested, when it is *personalized.* The test of this hypothesis involved a confederate revealing that his girl friend was pregnant either very early or near the end of a conversation with a male subject. Subjects indicated significantly more interest in getting to know the late discloser than the early one and significantly greater liking for him as well. "All in all," say the researchers, "the results imply that if one is tempted to reveal something quite personal to a new acquaintance, one should try to restrain himself for a least 8 or 10 minutes" (Wortman, Adesman, Herman, & Greenberg, 1976: 189). Gilbert's (1976) research showed that high self-disclosure by a female confederate in an initial interaction was significantly less attractive than low self-disclosure thus adding further support for the mediating role of timing and the personalism explanation.

Jones and Archer (1976) expressed doubt about whether such results mean that receivers are more attracted to targets when they believe they are being singled out as trustworthy persons. Although a disclosure presented early in a conversation with a stranger may be perceived as unattractive because it embarrasses the receiver, "the embarrassment may indeed by increased by . . . evidence that the recipient is being exclusively given some intimate knowledge" (Jones & Archer 1976: 181). According to Jones and Archer, the personalism/trust hypothesis—disclosure leads to positive attributions when the receiver perceives that he or she has been singled out for disclosure—had not been adequately tested in previous studies because "the typical disclosure experiment provides no information concerning the personalism of disclosures. Subjects are left to infer whether subjects disclosing to them would also disclose to others" (Jones & Archer 1976: 191). To ensure a more definitive test of the personalism hypothesis, Jones and Archer told subjects about a confederate's personal and family problems and then exposed them to audio- and videotapes in which the confederate either did or did not mention his depression and his father's alcoholism. In a subsequent interaction between the confederate and a subject, the same information either was disclosed or withheld. The results showed that "there is nothing unique about subjects' affective responses to the partner who discloses only to them. . . . [T]he distinctive condition is that in which the partner discloses neither to others nor to the subject; here he is relatively disliked and perceived to be threatening and untrustworthy. . . . [T]he consistent discloser is seen as highly trustworthy but he is not particularly liked" (Jones & Archer, 1976: 191). Trust did not mediate the link between disclosure and liking; the personalistic discloser was not perceived as more trustworthy than the nonpersonalistic discloser. Given the negative reactions to the consistently undisclosing confederate, Jones and Archer concluded, contrary to Wortman et al. (1976), that "the best ingratiation strategy for disclosing negative self-information . . . is to disclose the information as soon as possible—at least if it is going to be disclosed at all" (1976: 192).

Taylor (1976) described an unpublished study conducted by Gould, Brounstein, and Taylor (1978) that strongly supported the personalism hypothesis. A female target disclosed either at a high

or low level of intimacy. Female subjects were subsequently informed that the target attributed her disclosure to dispositional characteristics, traits of the subject, or the situation. Attraction was highest in the condition in which high intimacy disclosures were attributed to characteristics of the subject and lowest when low intimacy disclosures were attributed to traits of the subject.

The methodological differences among studies pertinent to the personalism hypothesis make it difficult to explain the contradictory finding. Jones and Archer (1976) provided subjects with background information one rarely possesses in an initial interaction. While these procedures resulted in a rigorous test of the personalism hypothesis, they also created an interpersonal situation that was qualitatively distinct from other experimental settings in which personalism has been tested. Other tests of personalism have been restricted to settings in which subjects lack prospective knowledge about the confederate's personal problems, a situation more typical of initial interactions. Moreover, the disclosures revealed by Jones and Archer's male confederates were highly discrediting, whereas Gould, Brounstein, and Taylor's (1978) female target disclosed information that, though intimate, was considerably less threatening.

Perhaps the valence of a disclosure is a telling factor. Few studies have bothered to manipulate the valence dimension systematically. Most investigations have introduced one standardized disclosure or varied the level of intimacy of a disclosure without altering its valence. There is some doubt in our minds, therefore, about how far the results of these studies can be extended to interpersonal contexts in which a broader range of disclosures are exchanged. Consider for example the evidence that valence of a disclosure makes a substantial difference in subjects' attributions toward the discloser. Nelson-Jones and Strong (1976) found that attraction was strengthened by negative disclosures when they took place in the first episode of interaction between British males and a confederate. Negative disclosures occurring in the second round, however, were viewed less favorably than positive ones, and shifts from positive to negative or negative to positive patterns of disclosure were rated less approvingly than a consistent pattern whether positive or negative. Gilbert and Horenstein (1975) reported that valence was a more powerful determinant of attraction than was level of intimacy of the disclosure. Subjects expressed greater attraction toward a male confederate when the valence of his disclosures was positive than when they were negative regardless of the level of intimacy of the disclosures.

Several studies of marital communication have tested the hypothesis that self-disclosure is positively correlated with marital satisfaction. Levinger (1965) unexpectedly found that more satisfied spouses reported less disclosure of negative feelings toward their mates than did less satisfied couples. The same pattern of responses emerged in a follow-up study. Marital satisfaction was more strongly related to the proportion of pleasant than to that of unpleasant disclosure (Levinger & Senn, 1967). Consequently Levinger and Senn (1967) suggested that "perhaps 'talking about one's feelings' does not necessarily refer to spilling out everything. For the average couple, *selective disclosure* of feelings seems more beneficial to marital harmony than indiscriminate catharsis" (p. 246).

Cutler and Dyer's (1965) study of the adjustment problems reported by young married couples lends further support to the selective disclosure thesis. About half of the nonadjustive responses described by these couples resulted from expressions of negative reactions to the partner. Accordingly Cutler and Dyer concluded that "contrary to what may be expected an open talking about the violation of expectations does not always lead to adjustment" (1965, p. 201). More recently, Burke, Weir, and Harrison (1976) found that for dual career couples disclosure decreases over time; the longer the marriage, the less the disclosure. Collectively, these studies strongly suggest that over time couples must become discriminate disclosers. Uncensored self-disclosure can pose a serious threat to the viability of a long-term bond. This is true not only of marriage but of friendship as well. For instance, Taylor (1968) reported that over the course of a semester roommates who increased the most in disclosure decreased the most in liking. Apparently the risk that familiarity will breed contempt increases as two persons get to know each other better.

What can be concluded from these studies about when, how, and with what results people self-disclose? Keeping in mind the inconsistent use of the term self-disclosure, the absence of a precise empirical referent for the concept, and the numerous idiosyncrasies in experimental manipulations across studies, I offer the following speculative conclusions.

1. People believe it is appropriate to engage in high amounts of self-disclosure with others whom they like. When people are asked to report how much they disclose to some targets as compared to others they will express higher rates of disclosure toward the better liked others. It is commonly assumed that one *should* not withhold private thoughts and feelings from others one likes. This premise does not establish that people actually *do* disclose more frequently to others whom they like. Nor does it show that liking causes higher rates of disclosure. In fact the evidence we have examined suggests that liking imposes constraints on disclosure, a point to be discussed extensively below.

2. *People overestimate the extent to which they self-disclose to others whom they like.* Few studies have addressed this issue directly, though interpretations of reported self-disclosure typically assume that subjects' reports are accurate. Shapiro and Swenson (1969) found, however, that husbands and wives overestimated how much they disclosed to each other. Not only does it seem unlikely that past self-disclosure can predict future self-disclosure accurately (Chelune, 1979; Cozby, 1973), but it appears equally unlikely that subjects' present reports about past disclosures will be accurate.

3. *Self-disclosure does not cause liking.* When impressions already are positive, self-disclosure

may reinforce or enhance liking. On the other hand, self-disclosure produces mistrust, dislike, and other negative impressions if it violates rules of proper conduct. The research on self-disclosure during initial interactions makes me doubt that it is ever wise to disclose to a stranger one expects or hopes to see again. This research is highly supportive of Goffman's (1959: 9) conception of initial interactions as ceremonial rituals in which "each participant is expected to suppress his immediate heartfelt feelings, conveying a view of the situation which he feels the others will be able to find at least temporarily acceptable." Any substantial deviation from a highly ritualized pattern will produce negative attributions. Unless one person has gained access to discrediting information about the other beforehand, as in the Jones and Archer (1976) experiment, verbal disclosure of discrediting information is unlikely to be perceived favorably regardless of when it is introduced. Unfortunately, the studies of initial interaction that we have examined have little relevance to the question of how disclosure functions in forming or maintaining bonds because such studies create a context that is highly atypical even of initial interactions. If two unacquainted people interact under conditions in which they expect or intend to see each other again, it is unlikely that they will take the risk of disclosing highly intimate or discrediting information unless, perhaps, they share a strong physical attraction to each other. In situations where people have an opportunity to form a long-term relationship, the implicit goal of an initial interaction will be to establish a positive context for learning about each other. It is unlikely that people can establish long-term relationships without sharing a fairly wide range of information about themselves, some of it positive and some of it negative. Once a positive context is set for integrating and interpreting disclosures, the risk that a discrediting disclosure will harm the relationship is substantially reduced (though it is never entirely eliminated). Although none of the research

on self-disclosure has attempted to establish a baseline for describing how much or what type of disclosure typically occurs during an initial interaction, the common assumption that self-disclosure is an indicant of closeness leads to the expectation that casual or highly ritualized encounters of this sort will not be characterized by frequent and intimate self-disclosure. The research conducted in the past has resulted in the obvious conclusion that the more appropriate and well-timed the disclosure the more likely it will produce positive attributions about the source. But the important question—what makes a disclosure appropriate and well-timed—has not been addressed systematically. I contend that "genuine" self-disclosure is inappropriate during initial interaction and, though some will be perceived more negatively than others, all such disclosures will lead to negative attributions *unless* some initial attraction—physical, attitudinal, etc.—already exists.

4. *Liking inhibits self-disclosure.* Jourard (1964) contended that "the optimum in a marriage relationship, as in any relationship between persons, is a relationship between I and Thou, where each person discloses himself without reserve" (p. 46). Empirical studies of self-disclosure, on the other hand, suggest that uncensored candor is an insidious idea. In some circles the premise that lovers should tell each other everything they feel, think and do is an immutable idea. As social scientists, however, we cannot allow pedestrian wisdom to cloud our evaluation of the evidence. The research we have reviewed indicates that discriminating disclosers are more satisfied and more likely to remain attractive to their partners than are indiscriminating disclosers. Unless there exists a larger gap between reality and report than is commonly assumed, we are forced to conclude that a rhetorical approach to self-disclosure is usually the best approach for expanding or maintaining liking.

By endorsing assertiveness, embracing spontaneity, emancipating expressiveness, and enlarging the meaning of cohabitation, the counterculture's spiritual and intellectual leaders may have unintentionally placed a veil over our understanding of the function of expressiveness in enduring relationships. But the stark reality of relational life forces us to press the examination further. It is my opinion that people in long-term relationships cannot afford to throw caution to the winds with respect to self-disclosure because they have too much to lose. People will not go out on a limb if they think the branch may break. This was demonstrated in a study conducted by Barrell and Jourard (1976). When asked to describe the conditions under which they were reluctant to self-disclose to others whom they like, subjects reported that it was the fear of damaging the relationship that prevented them from disclosing. Subjects also reported that they refrained from disclosing to disliked persons when they believed the other(s) could threaten their future. Assuming that they wish to maintain their relationship, we would not expect husbands and wives to disclose freely if they think the disclosure will threaten the viability of the bond: nor would we expect subordinates in formal organizations to make discrediting disclosures to their superiors.

When would we expect people to tell the truth? Jules Henry (1971) proposed two conditions under which truth emerges, assuming "that we know the truth and can reveal or withhold it by an act of will" (p. 107). The first is when there is nothing to be afraid of; the second, when one person wants to hurt another. From these Henry (1965: 108) deduced three kinds of ethical truth relevant to human relationships:

The first is routine truth, the innocuous truth whose telling could not possibly hurt or offend anyone. This may be a purely hypothetical class of truth, with no adherents at all; at one time or another we are probably all put out by even the most obvious ethical truth. The second is the truth of courage, and the third is the truth of rage and hate. It is clear . . . that they make very different contributions to happiness.

Truth of courage and truth of rage are rare in satisfying relationships because honesty is not an unqualified virtue. In fact there is abundant evidence that long-term relationships are maintained by illusions of truth, exaggerations of goodness (Bochner & Krueger, 1979), and less than full communication. Recently writers have stressed the potentially positive benefits of conflict (Altman & Taylor, 1973; Simons, 1972). Braiker and Kelly (1979, p. 166), however, were "not able to find any systematic evidence relating to the positive role of conflict." Reported conflict has frequently been associated with relational unhappiness (Bircher, Weiss, & Vincent, 1975; Gurin, Veroff, & Feld, 1960; Orden & Bradburn, 1968; Ort, 1950). When conflict occurs, it is not uncommon for nondistressed couples to lie, withhold from, and otherwise deceive each other. Ryder and Goodrich (1966) found that newlyweds lied to each other to avoid conflicts or reinterpreted their earlier statements so as to deny that any disagreement existed.

Raush, Barry Hertel, and Swain (1976) expressed surprise at the many instances of what they considered communication pathology—disqualifying the other's or one's own statements, double-binding, mystifying—among presumably normal couples participating in their study of quasi-naturalistic conflict. Contrary to their expectations, the researchers became convinced by their data that "optimal communication, in the psychologist's sense, is not essential to what is perceived as a good relationship for all couples. To place a demand for a particular style of communication on all couples is an imposition of values" (p. 211).

Other writers also have found reason to question the validity of popular assumptions about "good" communication in marriage. Following a series of studies designed to describe the interactional variables discriminating distressed from non-distressed couples, Gottman (1979) concluded that the importance of self-disclosure and the direct examination of feelings so highly valued in the clinical literature was not borne out by the data: "Couples in nondistressed marriages are indirect; they mindread rather than directly asked about feelings" (p. 123).

Thus self-disclosure appears to be a highly overrated activity. Perhaps the time has come to lift the fog of ideology surrounding the concept. The fact that there has been only mild (Gilbert, 1976), if any, opposition to the thesis that "openness leads to better and more satisfying relationships" suggests to us that some investigators have been lulled into an uncritical acceptance of an untenable proposition. Clearly there is no firm empirical basis for endorsing unconditional openness. A critical evaluation of the evidence suggests, at most, a restrained attitude toward the efficacy of self-disclosure.

Knowledge about the other is undoubtedly necessary for the development of an interpersonal bond. But the knowledge one accumulates about the other is based more on the other's behavior than on self-disclosure (Shapiro & Swensen, 1969). Actions still speak louder and more forcefully than words. Even if we wanted to we could not completely, spontaneously, and faithfully disclose our inner reality to others. Even if we tried to do so, others would always know something more about us than what we disclose to them. As Simmel (1950: 323) eloquently wrote:

[I]n fragmentary beginnings and unexpressed notions, all of human intercourse rests on the fact that everybody knows something more about the other than the other voluntarily reveals to him; and those things he knows are frequently matters whose knowledge the other person (were he aware of it) would find undesirable.

I do not doubt that faith in the other's honesty ordinarily promotes satisfying relationships, particularly intimate ones. That self-disclosure necessarily produces such an outcome has never been demonstrated. Also, it probably is true that one must show respect for the other, and here self-disclosure becomes problematic. How can one show ample respect for the other without a certain measure of restraint? On the other hand how can one maintain faith and confidence in the other without a measure of openness? Where to draw the line cannot be determined for all cases. What does seem to be suggested by research is that the greater risk lies on the side of frequent self-disclosure of negative feelings and characteristics. Pineo (1961, 1969) has argued

that marriage is characterized by a natural process of deterioration. Over time partners discover that they weren't as similar as they initially assumed—idealizations are subjected to the acid test of experience. This natural deterioration may make it increasingly difficult for partners to perceive each other's self-disclosures positively. While it may seem an overly pessimistic view, the association between low self-disclosure and attraction/satisfaction strongly suggests that even in close relationships being opaque is more effective than being transparent. Taking all the mystery out of a relationship is a risky business. I cannot find any empirical evidence to contest Simmel's incisive commentary on this issue:

Portions even of the persons closest to us must be offered us in the form of indistinctness and unclarity, in order for their attractiveness to keep on the same high levels. . . . The fertile depth of relations . . . is only the reward for that tenderness and self-discipline which . . . allows the right to be questioned to be limited by the right to secrecy.

REFERENCES

Altman, I. Reciprocity of interpersonal exchange. *Journal for the Theory of Social Behavior*, 1973, *3*, 249-261.

Altman, I. and D. A. Taylor. *Social penetration: The development of interpersonal relationships.* New York: Holt, Rinehart & Winston, 1973.

Archer, R. L. Role of personality and the social situation. In G. J. Chelune (ed.) *Self-disclosure,* San Francisco: Jossey-Bass Publishers, 1979.

Barrell, J. and S. Jourard. Being honest with persons we like. *Journal of Individual Psychology,* 1976, *32,* 185-193.

Birchler, G. R., Weiss, R. L., and Vincent, J. P. Multimethod analysis of social reinforcement exchange between maritally distressed and nondistressed spouse and stranger dyads. *Journal of Personality and Social Psychology,* 1975, *31,* 349-360.

Bochner, A. & D. I. Krueger. Interpersonal communication theory and research: An overview of inscrutable epistemologies and muddled concepts. In D. Nimmo (ed.), *Communication Yearbook 3.* New Brunswick, NJ: Transaction Books-ICA, 1979.

Buber, M. *I and thou.* New York: Scribner's, 1958.

Bugental, J. F. *The search for authenticity: An existential-analytic approach to psychotherapy.* New York: Holt, Rinehart & Winston, 1965.

Burke, R., T. Weir, and D. Harrison. Disclosure problems and tensions experienced by marital partners. *Psychological Reports,* 1976, *38,* 531-542.

Chelune, G. J. Self-disclosure: An elaboration of its basic dimensions. *Psychological Reports,* 1975, *36,* 79-85.

Chelune, G. J. Measuring openness in interpersonal communication. In G. J. Chelune (ed.) *Self-disclosure,* San Francisco: Jossey-Bass Publishers, 1979.

Cozby, P. C. Self-disclosure, reciprocity and liking. *Sociometry,* 1972, *35,* 151-160.

Cozby, P. C. Self-disclosure: A literature review. *Psychological Bulletin,* 1979, *79,* 73-91.

Critelli, J. W., J. Rappaport, and S. L. Golding. Role played self-disclosure as a function of liking and knowing. *Journal of Research in Personality,* 1976, *10,* 89-97.

Cutler, B. R. and W. G. Dyer. Initial adjustment processes in young married couples. *Social Forces,* 1965, *44,* 195-201.

Derlega, V. J., and J. Grzelak. Appropriateness of self-disclosure. In G. J. Chelune (ed.), *Self-disclosure,* San Francisco: Jossey-Bass Publishers, 1979.

Derlega, V. J., J. Walmer, and G. Furman. Mutual disclosure in social interactions. *Journal of Social Psychology,* 1973, *90,* 159-160.

Ehrlich, H. J., and D. B. Graeven. Reciprocal self-disclosure in a dyad. *Journal of Experimental Social Psychology,* 1971, *7,* 389-400.

Fitzgerald, M. P. Self-disclosure and expressed self-esteem, social distance and areas of self revealed. *Journal of Psychology,* 1963, *56,* 405-412.

Geertz, C. Sociosexology. *The New York Review of Books,* 1980, *21,* 3-4.

Gilbert, S. J. Empirical and theoretical extensions of self-disclosure. In G. R. Miller (ed.), *Explorations in interpersonal communication,* Beverly Hills: Sage, 1976.

Gilbert, S. J., and Horenstein, D. The communication of self-disclosure: Level versus valence. *Human Communication Research,* 1975, *1,* 316-322.

Goffman, E. *The presentation of self in everyday life.* New York: Doubleday, 1959.

Goodstein, L. D., and V. M. Reinecker. Factors affecting self-disclosure: A review of the literature. In B. A. Maher (ed.), *Progress in experimental personality research,* New York: Academic Press, 1974.

Gould, R., P. Bounstein, and D. A. Taylor. A reexamination of personalistic disclosure. Paper presented at 86th annual meeting of American Psychological Association, Toronto, August 1978.

Gurin, G., Veroff, J., and Feld, S. *Americans view their mental health.* New York: Basic Books, 1960.

Gottman, J. *Marital interaction: Experimental investigations.* New York: Academic Press, 1979.

Hart, R. P. and D. M. Burks. Rhetorical sensitivity and social interaction. *Speech Monographs,* 1972, *39,* 75-91.

Henry, J. *Pathways to madness.* New York: Vintage Books, 1971.

Jameson, F. "On Goffman's frame analysis." *Theory and Society,* 1976, *3,* 119-133.

Johannesen, R. L. The emerging concept of communication as dialogue. *The Quarterly Journal of Speech,* 1971, *57,* 373-382.

Jones, E. E., and R. L. Archer. Are there special effects of personalistic self-disclosure? *Journal of Experimental Social Psychology,* 1976, *12* (2), 180-193.

Jourard, S. M. Healthy personality and self-disclosure. *Mental Hygiene,* 1959, *43,* 499-507.

Jourard, S. M. *The transparent self.* New York: D. Van Nostrand, 1964.

Jourard, S. M. *To be or not to be: Existential-psychological perspectives on the self.* Gainesville: University of Florida Press, 1967.

Jourard, S. M. *Disclosing man to himself.* New York: D. Van Nostrand, 1968.

Jourard, S. M. *Self-disclosure: An experimental analysis of the transparent self.* New York: Wiley, 1971.

Jourard, S. M., and R. Friedman. Experimenter-subject "distance" and self-disclosure. *Journal of Personality and Social Psychology,* 1970, *15,* 278-282.

Jourard, S. M., and M. J. Landsman. Cognition, cathexis, and the "dyadic effect" in men's self-disclosing behavior. *Merrill Palmer Quarterly,* 1960, *6,* 178-186.

Jourard, S. M., and P. Lasakow. Some factors in self-disclosure. *Journal of Abnormal and Social Psychology,* 1958, *56,* 91-98.

Kidd, V. Happily ever after and other relationship styles: Advice on interpersonal relations in popular magazines, 1951-1973. *Quarterly Journal of Speech,* 1975, *61,* 31-39.

Levinger, G. "A comparative study of marital communication." Unpublished paper, 1965.

Levinger, G., and D. J. Senn. Disclosure of feelings in marriage. *Merrill Palmer Quarterly,* 1967, *13,* 237-249.

Maslow, A. H. *Toward a psychology of being.* Princeton, NJ: Van Nostrand, 1962.

Matson, F. *The broken image: Man, science and society.* New York: G. Braziller, 1964.

Miller, G. R., and M. Steinberg. *Between people: A new analysis of interpersonal communication.* Palo Alto, CA: Science Research Associates, 1975.

Morton, T. L. Intimacy and reciprocity of exchange: A comparison of spouses and strangers. *Journal of Personality and Social Psychology,* 1978, *36,* 72-81.

Nelson-Jones, R., and S. R. Strong. "Positive and negative self-disclosure, timing, and personal attraction." *British Journal of Social and Clinical Psychology,* 1976, *15,* 323-325.

O'Neill, N., and G. O'Neill. *Open marriage.* New York: Evans, 1972.

Orden, S. R., and N. A. Bradburn. Dimensions of marriage happiness. *American Journal of Sociology,* 1968, *73,* 715-731.

Ort, R. S. A study of role-conflicts as related to happiness in marriage. *Journal of Abnormal and Social Psychology,* 1950, *45,* 691-699.

Pearce, W. B., and S. M. Sharp. Self-disclosing communication. *Journal of Communication,* 1973, *23* (4), 409-425.

Pineo, P. C. Disenchantment in the later years of marriage. *Journal of Marriage and Family Living,* 1961, *23,* 3-11.

Pineo, P. C. Developmental patterns in marriage. *The Family Coordinator,* 1969, *18,* 135-140.

Raush, H. L., W. A. Barry, R. K. Hertel, and M. A. Swain. *Communication, conflict, and marriage.* San Francisco: Jossey-Bass, 1974.

Reich, C. *The greening of America.* New York: Random House, 1970.

Rickers-Ovsiankina, M. A. Social accessibility in three age groups. *Psychological Reports,* 1956, *2,* 283-294.

Rosenfeld, L. B. Research bibliography. In G. J. Chelune (ed.), *Self-disclosure,* San Francisco: Jossey-Bass Publishers, 1979.

Roszak, T. *The making of a counterculture,* Garden City, NY: Doubleday, 1969.

Ryder, R. G., and D. W. Goodrich. Married couples responses to disagreement. *Family Process*, 1966, *5*, 30-42.

Schutz, W. *Joy*. New York: Grove Press, 1967.

Shapiro, A., and C. H. Swensen. Patterns of self-disclosure among married couples. *Journal of Counseling Psychology*, 1969, *16*, 179-180.

Simmel, Georg. *Soziologie* (4th ed.) (edited & translated by K. H. Wolff). Glencoe, IL: Free Press, 1950 [1908].

Simons, H. "Persuasion in social conflicts: A critique of prevailing conceptions and a framework for future research." *Speech Monographs*, 1972, *29*, 227-247.

Slater, P. *The pursuit of loneliness*. Boston: Beacon Press, 1970.

Taylor, D. A. The development of interpersonal relationships: Social penetration process. *Journal of Social Psychology*, 1968, *75*, 79-90.

Taylor, D. A. Motivational bases. In G. J. Chelune (ed.), *Self-disclosure*, San Francisco: Jossey-Bass Publishers, 1979.

Taylor, D. A., and I. Altman. Intimacy-scaled stimuli for use in studies of interpersonal relations. *Psychological Reports*, 1966, *19*, 729-730.

Wortman, C. B., P. Adesman, E. Herman, and R. Greenberg. Self-disclosure: An attributional perspective. *Journal of Personality and Social Psychology*, 1976, *33*, 184-191.

Wheeless, L. R., and J. Grotz. Conceptualization and measurement of self-disclosure. *Human Communication Research*, 2, 1976, 338-346.

Worthy, M., A. L. Gary, and G. M. Kahn. Self-disclosure as an exchange process. *Journal of Personality and Social Psychology*, 1969, *13*, 59-63.

UNIT V

Relating and Responding to the Other: Conversational Sensitivity, Empathy, and Confirmation/Disconfirmation

In the relational perspective the previous two units presented, you read articles on the initiation of relationships and the nature of the talk in those relationships. This unit examines specific skills or behaviors that are associated with successful relational management: conversational sensitivity, empathy, and confirmation. Article 15 presents the development and testing of a measure of conversational sensitivity. The other two articles, 16 and 17, tend to be reviews of other theory and research in support of a particular theme or perspective. The three articles in this section can be placed into a model of communication skills that progresses from input (conversational sensitivity) to process (empathy) to output (confirming responses).

As an input skill, conversational sensitivity represents an individual's sensitivity to what is occurring in a social interaction. High conversationally sensitive people are described as being attentive, interested in the conversation, nonverbally sensitive, active listeners, and empathic. In essence, these qualities have to do with our perceptiveness of conversational information. The article on conversational sensitivity represents the development of a theory concerning a communication skill and an instrument to assess that skill. The development of the instrument follows a methodology that involves developing the set of response items and then validating the instrument. One way validation is accomplished is by comparing the responses on the new instrument with other measures of related

constructs (**convergent validity**) and unrelated or negatively related constructs (**discriminant validity**). Another way validation is achieved is by the use of the instrument to predict an anticipated outcome. The conversational sensitivity study compares certain behavioral outcomes with the scores on the new instrument to establish **predictive validity.**

The conversational sensitivity items were generated by having students generate items after hearing a description of the concept. The original pool of items was refined, tested and factor analyzed (tested for item interrelatedness). The items fell into seven factors, and an eighth factor was created by writing additional items.

The validation of the conversational sensitivity instrument incorporates correlations with other instruments for which an expected correlation might be found. T-tests and analysis of variance are used to compare the responses of the highest scores with the lowest scores on various qualities and behaviors.

The development of a measure must follow a fairly standard and rigorous testing of validity if it is to be accepted and applied by others. However, the purpose for including article 15 is to introduce the concept of conversational sensitivity. As you read the description of the concept and the related behaviors, see if that concept matches your own personal insights into the process of interpersonal communication. Are some people more aware and cognizant than others of what goes on in interpersonal conversations? Does that awareness increase interpersonal communication effectiveness? Answering these questions is the fundamental reason for including this article.

After the input gained from conversational sensitivity, we then can move on to ways in which that input can be processed. The article on empathy discusses a number of ways to take the information we have perceived about others and use that information in an empathic way. As a result of empathizing with others we can increase the likelihood of accomplishing our communication goals. The article examines the functions empathy plays in our social interactions. A variety of functions that have strong implications for our interpersonal communication effectiveness are identified. This wide variety of functions is probably one of the reasons empathy is often identified as critical to communication competence and effectiveness. In addition to presenting these functions, an argument is presented for a broader conceptualization of empathy called *decentering*. The article includes a discussion of the problems and inconsistencies found in the empathy research. The overriding problem is the use of the same term *empathy* for phenomena that are inherently different. What those phenomena do have in common is argued to be more accurately reflected in the broader concept of decentering.

Among the reactions or outputs of empathy are confirming responses. The final article in this unit specifically discusses responses to others, which have the impact of either confirming or disconfirming another person's sense of self-worth. Article 17 by Cissna and Sieburg presents an extensive list of those behavioral indicators of confirmation and disconfirmation. The underlying principle of confirmation and disconfirmation is that every response

we have toward others can either enhance their self-worth, detract from their self-worth, or be neutral. Imagine a child who grows up in a household where every time she tried to speak to her parents she was ignored or told they did not have time to talk with her. Her sense of importance and self-worth undoubtedly would be seriously harmed.

The article presents a variety of subcategories of confirming and disconfirming responses by which behaviors can be classified. However, the research into confirmation and disconfirmation has been hampered by the lack of an effective methodology. A number of these research problems are discussed in the article.

QUESTIONS TO CONSIDER WHILE READING

ARTICLE 15
A. Would you expect anyone who is high in conversational sensitivity to be more interpersonally effective and satisfied in his or her relationships? Why or why not?
B. Mentally step back from the article after finishing it and address this question: Are you convinced by the evidence presented by the authors that conversational sensitivity really exists and that their instrument effectively measures it?

ARTICLE 16
A. What functions are you most adept at in utilizing empathy? Which are you least adept at? Why?
B. How often do people really empathize with others? Under what conditions do you suppose you are most likely to try to empathize with others?

ARTICLE 17
A. Think about your own exposure to disconfirming and confirming responses. How much of an impact have they really had on you?
B. If most communication is confirming, and there is a serious question about the true negative impact of disconfirming responses, then why is understanding and studying confirmation important?

15

The Nature and Correlates of Conversational Sensitivity

JOHN A. DALY
ANITA L. VANGELISTI
SUZANNE M. DAUGHTON

People differ in their sensitivity to what happens during conversations: Some individuals enjoy listening to social exchanges, pick up hidden meanings in conversations, can generate optimal ways of saying things in interactions, and are generally "savvy" about the different sorts of power and affinity relationships exhibited in conversations. In this article we explore the nature and correlates of conversational sensitivity. People high in sensitivity make more high-level inferences when listening to social exchanges, unitize conversation in smaller chunks, emphasize conversation characteristics in their memories of interactions, and make more self-referents about conversations than less sensitive individuals. In addition, conversational sensitivity is positively related to self-monitoring, private self-consciousness, perceptiveness, self-esteem, assertiveness, empathy, and social skills. It is inversely related to communication apprehension, receiver apprehension, and social anxiety. In a final study, conversational sensitivity is construed not as an individual difference but as situational response: In some settings under some conditions, people become more sensitive to what happens in conversation.

Go into any meeting, observe any conversation, discuss previous conversations with others, and you will probably find that people seem to differ in their sensitivity to what occurs in interactions. Some people seem very "savvy" about social interaction: they sense what is "really" being said in conversations, who is truly in charge, who likes whom, and so on. They find conversations both stimulating and memorable. Given the centrality of social interaction to them, they are often quite sophisticated about what happens in social exchanges. At the other extreme are people far less sensitive about phenomena involved in conversations. They take conversations at face value, seldom wondering about the underlying assumptions, relationships, and meaning implicit in every social exchange. Our goal in the research described in this article is to describe empirically the nature and correlates of this construct, which we choose to label "conversational sensitivity."

Conceptually, the idea of conversational sensitivity can be couched within J. J. Gibson's (1966, 1979) broader theoretic framework of social affordances. Gibson argues that the perceptual systems of different species have evolved so that information of particular relevance to survival is "picked up" from the environment. Affordances involve conjunctions between the properties of the organism and the environment within which that organism resides. Thus, for the dolphin, the ability to detect high-frequency sonic sounds is an essential property given its environment. For humans, who reside in a conversation-centered world, spontaneous communication is a major social affordance (Buck, 1984), involving the production as well as the reception and interpretation of such messages.

People differ in the degree to which they have optimized their utilization of various affordances. For instance, in the case of social perceptions, the difference between a skilled and a naive perceiver

From Daly, J. A., Vangelisti, A. L., & Daughton, S. M. (1987). The nature and correlates of conversational sensitivity. *Human Communication Research, 14*(2), 167-202.

lies in the fact that the former can extract more information from stimuli, detecting features and higher-order structures to which the naive perceiver is not sensitive (Gibson, 1969). Similarly, the degree to which people have developed a sensitivity to social interaction varies. The conversational sensitivity construct attempts to tap these differences. In broad terms, conversational sensitivity is the propensity of people to attend to and interpret what occurs during conversations. Greater sensitivity, in other words, represents more optimal use of an important aspect of the social affordance of communication.

While numerous strands of communication scholarship center on the production of conversations, including many that emphasize differences among people in producing social discourse (e.g., communication competence, communication apprehension), far fewer investigations examine differences in the ways people attend to social interaction. The research that is available, however, clearly indicates that people differ in their attainment of various forms of such sensitivity. Most of this work falls into two clusters: (1) the recognition and interpretation of both nonverbal and verbal messages and (2) personality traits that include an aspect of sensitivity in their formulation.

Research on nonverbal decoding abilities focuses on personality correlates of nonverbal sensitivity (e.g., Hall, 1978; Isenhart, 1980), the direct assessment of such sensitivity (Buck, 1976, 1983; Rosenthal, Hall, DiMatteo, Rogers, & Archer, 1979), and people's accuracy in decoding different aspects of a person's behaviors (e.g., Archer & Akert, 1977; Sabatelli, Buck, & Dreyer, 1982). Similarly, work on listening skills (e.g., Petrie & Carrel, 1976), as well as on personality correlates that affect listening comprehension (e.g., Beatty & Payne, 1984), indicate that people vary in both their willingness and ability to listen effectively in social interaction. While research on nonverbal decoding skills and listening in actual social conversation is limited, the literatures clearly suggest that people reliably differ in their sensitivity to social interaction.

Allusions to conversational sensitivity are implicit in a number of socially centered personality constructs, notably self-monitoring, empathy, and rhetorical sensitivity. Falling under the rubric of social intelligence (Walker & Foley, 1973) or social acuity (Funder & Harris, 1986), these personality characteristics have sensitivity to conversational behavior as implicit themes. When contrasted with low *self-monitors,* high self-monitors are well attuned to their social environment. They have better developed cognitive schemes for others (Snyder & Cantor, 1980) as well as for what occurs in conversations (Douglas, 1984). This enhanced sensitivity results in a greater adaptability by high self-monitors both to other interactants and to the social demands of the situation. *Empathic skills* demand, as a precursor, something akin to conversational sensitivity. Taking the role of another requires attention to what is said and what is meant in an interaction as well as an understanding of the potentially different interpretations people have of any social act (Davis, 1983; Johnson, Cheek, & Smither, 1983). One major characteristic of *rhetorical sensitivity* (Hart & Burks, 1972; Hart, Carlson, & Eadie, 1980) is interaction consciousness (Goffman, 1967) or the tendency of speakers to adapt to the situation and other people. To do so effectively demands something akin to conversational sensitivity since judgments about what is socially appropriate require sensitivity to what has gone on in the conversation.

Most directly relevant to the sensitivity construct is *interaction involvement* (Cegala, 1981, 1984; Cegala, Savage, Brunner, & Conrad, 1982). Composed of three dimensions (perceptiveness, attentiveness, and responsiveness), the research comparing high and low involved individuals has found that highly involved people remember more from conversations, have more positive feelings about social interactions, are more effective at managing conversations, and make fewer body-focused gestures than less involved people. Conceptually, conversational sensitivity and interaction involvement, especially the perceptiveness dimension of interaction involvement, should be related. However, interaction involvement is so broadly construed that the specific components that make people differentially perceptive in conversations are not clearly delineated.

Two general conclusions can be drawn from the related literatures. First, people differ in how sensitive they are to what goes on in social interactions; some people are more nonverbally sensitive, more active in their listening, and more predisposed to focus on conversations than others (e.g., those high in self-monitoring, empathy, rhetorical sensitivity, and interaction-involvement). Second, while extant literature clearly hints at the nature of conversational sensitivity, there is no clear, empirically grounded definition of the construct. It may include a tendency to enjoy listening to social interaction; it may be a knack for picking up hidden meanings in what people say; it may be a proclivity for remembering what is uttered in conversations. While all of these are obvious candidates for inclusion in a definition of conversational sensitivity, are there other components? Answering this question was one focus of the studies that follow. We sought to enumerate empirically the major elements of conversational sensitivity. After describing these elements, we sought to tie sensitivity to memory for social interaction, the ways people organize their impressions of conversations, and a number of other variables that play significant roles in social interaction. Finally, we propose that conversational sensitivity can also be conceived of as a reaction or response to a variety of contextual characteristics.

STUDY I

For the first study, a group of graduate students in communication (n = 21) were given a general description of conversational sensitivity and asked to generate items to include in a measure of the characteristic. The group generated more than 150 items that, when pruned for redundancies and obviously inappropriate items, left 73 items. In total, 149 undergraduate students then responded on five-step scales (bounded by strongly agree and strongly disagree) to the 73 items. Their responses

were factor analyzed. Given the preliminary nature of the items and the small sample size, results of this factor analysis were used to refine the item pool. These results led to the deletion of some items, construction of additional items potentially tapping dimensions hinted at by the factor analysis, and development of other items representing dimensions that seemed appropriate to the construct but were not tapped by the original item pool. A total of 443 undergraduate students then completed the revised, 58-item questionnaire and their responses were factor analyzed (principal components with an orthogonal rotation). The optimal solution appeared to be a seven factor one. The seven factors included: (1) Detecting Meanings, (2) Conversational Memory, (3) Conversational Alternatives, (4) Conversational Imagination, (5) Conversation Enjoyment, (6) Interpretation, and (7) Perceiving Affinity. After settling on the dimensional structure, some additional items were written for factors that had very few items and an eighth dimension was created to tap subjects' sensitivity about power relationships in social interactions. The specific items tapping each of the eight factors are presented in the accompanying Table 15.1. The factor loadings from the main factor analyses are also presented in the table.

A major purpose of this project was to delineate the structure of conversational sensitivity. The first investigation, based on responses to a wide variety of items tapping potential dimensions of sensitivity, reveals that the major components of sensitivity include: (1) perceptiveness in finding deeper and often multiple meanings in what others say; (2) a capacity to remember, better than most, what is uttered; (3) a sense of conversational tact—being able to come up with alternatives in conversations that are particularly well suited to a given situation; (4) a proclivity to imagine conversations; (5) a strong liking for listening to conversations, even when not participating; (6) an ease in conversational word play (e.g., punning, paraphrasing); (7) a sense of who likes whom in conversational settings; and (8) a skill in determining power or control relationships in conversations. While there may

TABLE 15.1

Items in Final Sensitivity Measure

1. (10) I often find myself detecting the purposes or goals of what people are saying in conversations. (1; .49; .42)
2. (12) Many times, I pick up from conversations little bits of information that people don't mean to disclose. (1; .48; .18; .54; .44)
3. (25) I can often understand why someone said something even though others don't see that intent. (1; .60; .19; .45; .38)
4. (35) In conversations I seem to be able to often predict what another person is going to say even before he or she says it. (1; .60; .20; .48; .42)
5. (40) I often hear things in what people are saying that others don't seem to even notice. (1; .61; .22; .60; .57)
6. (43) I often find hidden meanings in what people are saying in conversations. (1; .65; .23; .79; .53)
7. (52) I often notice double meanings in conversations. (1; .59; .29; .56; .50)
8. (33) I often have a sense that I can forecast where people are going in conversations. (1; .53; .27)
9. (18) I think I remember conversations I participate in more than the average person. (2; .63; .28; .68; .45)
10. (21) I'm terrible at recalling conversations I have had in the past. (2; .75; .26; .70; .46)
11. (38) If you gave me a few moments I could probably easily recall a conversation I had a few days ago. (2; .76; .16; .71; .55)
12. (41) I have a good memory for conversations. (2; .89; .14; .98; .50)
13. (44) I can often remember specific words or phrases that were said in past conversations. (2; .55; .25; .55; .52)
14. (2) I have the ability to say the right thing at the right time. (3; .55; .21; .58; .44)
15. (23) If people ask me how to say something I can come up with a number of different ways of saying it. (3; .46; .24; .68; .40)
16. (34) I am very good at coming up with neat ways of saying things in conversations. (3; .76; .16; .69; .41)
17. (46) I am good at wording the same thought in different ways. (3; .89; .14; .77; .43)
18. (56) In virtually any situation I can think of tactful ways to say something. (3; .60; .17; .62; .40)
19. (19) I like to think up imaginary conversations in my head. (4; .75; .13; .82; .38)
20. (51) I often make up conversations in my mind. (4; .74; .24; .94; .43)
21. Compared to most people, I don't spend much time inventing "make-believe" conversations. (.59; .39)
22. (13) I would enjoy being a fly on the wall listening in on other people's conversations. (5; .52; .19; .72; .18)
23. (28) Conversations are fascinating to listen to. (5; .68; .28; .63; .23)
24. (36) I really enjoy overhearing conversations. (5; .54; .19; .86; .27)
25. I'm less interested in listening to others' conversations than most people. (.58; .29)
26. (17) I'm usually the last person in a conversation to catch hidden meanings in puns and riddles. (6; .53; .15; .55; .32)
27. (49) I often have difficulty paraphrasing what another person said in a conversation. (6; .44; .29; .72; .30)
28. (57) I'm not very good at detecting irony or sarcasm in conversations. (6; .61; .20; .63; .28)
29. (16) Often, in conversations, I can tell whether the people involved in the conversation like or dislike one another. (7; .53; .25; .74; .37)
30. (45) I can tell in conversations whether people are on good terms with one another. (7; .34; .32; .90; .35)
31. (48) I can often tell how long people have known each other just by listening to their conversation. (7; .39; .20)
32. I'm not very good at figuring out who likes whom in social conversations. (.43; .25)
33. I can often tell when someone is trying to get the upper hand in a conversation. (.69; .29)
34. I'm often able to figure out who's in charge in conversations. (.84; .37)
35. Most of the time, I'm able to identify the dominant person in a conversation. (.78; .35)
36. In group interactions, I'm not good at determining who the leader is in the conversation.

NOTE: The number in parentheses at the beginning of each item is the number of the item as it appeared in the original factor analysis. The first three numbers at the end of the item represent the factor the item is associated with, the loading of the item on that factor, and the highest secondary loading the item has, respectively. The fourth value is the primary loading of the item in a factor analysis of the measure in Study II. The final value is the item-total correlation using the sample in Study II. Items 21, 25, 32, 33, 34, and 35 were created after the first major factor analysis. The two values following each of these items are the primary loadings from Study II and the item-total correlation from Study II. Item 36 was not used in either investigation.

be additional components imaginable, the eight identified here very likely represent much of what is central to conversational sensitivity.

In the studies described in this article, sensitivity was treated as a unidimensional construct although there appeared to be underlying factors. This was done for a number of reasons: First, the question raised about conversational sensitivity focused on the general construct rather than its more specific components. In the studies that follow, we wanted to link sensitivity, in its broadest sense, to a number of communication-related behaviors and personal characteristics. Second, it can be argued that a composite index is appropriately used when the relationship of that measure to the dependent variable(s) under examination is typically stronger than the relationships of the underlying factors to the same variable(s) (Snyder & Gangestad, 1986). The results of the studies reported here indicated that this was the predominant pattern. Moreover, in most cases, the patterns of correlation using the different subscales were such that their direction seldom varied from the direction of the composite measure. Third, provided that the composite index is sufficiently reliable, collapsing across dimensions is a commonly used procedure in personality research both in communication (e.g., Cegala, 1984; McCroskey, 1984) and psychology (e.g., Fletcher, Danilovics, Fernandez, Peterson, & Reeder, 1986). When all the items composing the sensitivity measure are taken together as a single composite, the internal consistency estimates (*alpha*) are always above .80. That magnitude of reliability is reasonable for the investigations reported in this article.

It is important to note that our primary aim was not to develop a highly reliable, multifactor instrument tapping the sensitivity construct. Instead, we sought to explicate empirically the general construct. We do not argue that the operationalization of sensitivity used in the studies reported here is the optimal assessment for tapping the construct. Rather, the measure is a first attempt—one that can serve as a sufficiently reliable indicator of the construct to demonstrate its existence and importance. Future scholarship on the topic may broaden and refine the construct by devising highly reliable measures of the different factors and by exploring their individual correlates. With these caveats in mind, we do, where appropriate, summarize the relationships of the various dimensions to the different variables examined. These relationships hint at possible additional questions.

The studies that follow focus on three major concerns: personality correlates of conversational sensitivity (Study II and Study III), behavioral indicators of the construct (Studies IV and V), and the nature of sensitivity as a response to various contextual characteristics (Study VI). Taken together, the investigations clarify the nature of the construct, as well as its role in some important communication processes.

STUDY II

This study examines a number of personality correlates of conversational sensitivity. The rationale for conducting the study is twofold. First, we wanted to examine the relationship between sensitivity and a variety of personality variables that have, in the past, been related to important communication outcomes. By examining these correlations, we gain a sense of how sensitivity relates to other important communication variables. For instance, a good deal of scholarly work in communication has explored the correlates of communication apprehension (e.g., Daly & McCroskey, 1984). Are apprehensive individuals more sensitive to what happens in conversations? Competing hypotheses seem plausible. One might argue that apprehensive individuals are more sensitive to what happens in social exchanges because they participate less in the ongoing talk—they are, instead, quiet observers. On the other hand, one could suggest that apprehensive individuals, given their tendency to avoid participating in conversations, would, if from nothing more than a lack of familiarity, be less sensitive to what happens during interaction. Second, it is important to determine if the sensitivity construct is redundant with previously established personality dimensions relevant to communication. If correlations among sensitivity and other variables are high, then we are not introducing a distinct construct but are instead simply rediscovering, under a different label, an already established construct. Duplicative constructs are not particularly useful and before any further work was completed it seemed important to ensure the relative independence of sensitivity from other constructs. If we discover that sensitivity is relatively independent, then the patterns of association will provide preliminary evidence of the construct's convergent and discriminant validity. There are, in other words, some variables sensitivity ought to correlate with and others it should not.

We entered the investigation with some expectations, the most general of which was that sensitivity ought to correlate positively with various personality traits associated with greater, and more positive, experiences in communication as well as with measures tapping social acuity, "the ability and inclination to perceive the psychological state of others" (Funder & Harris, 1986, p. 530). For instance, conversational sensitivity should correlate positively with *self-monitoring*. The self-monitoring construct implicitly contains aspects of conversational sensitivity and taps a person's social acuity. Individuals who are highly sensitive to conversations ought to be more adept at determining when and how they should behave in social situations. Similarly, *communication apprehension* (McCroskey & Beatty, 1986) and *social anxiety* (Fenigstein, Scheier, & Buss, 1975) should be inversely related to sensitivity. To the extent that highly apprehensive people avoid social interactions, their experiences in social exchanges should be relatively few, and this decreased experiential base should result in lower sensitivity to conversations. In addition, people who are less sensitive to social exchanges are also less likely to receive the various rewards that can accompany social interaction. The lack of such rewards certainly should not reduce anxiety, and may even increase it. Conversationally sensitive individuals, who have a strong tendency to enjoy listening to conversations, should not score high on a measure of *receiver apprehension*, which taps people's tendencies to dislike and avoid receiving messages (Wheeless, 1975). Instead, there should be an inverse relationship. Finally, *empathy*, or the ability to see another's point of view, is inherently a social exercise as well as a mark of social acuity. As such, there should be a positive relationship between empathy and conversational sensitivity.

In addition to assessing the relationship among conversational sensitivity and a variety of communication-related traits, we wanted to ensure that responses to the sensitivity instrument were not systematically biased by a tendency to respond in a socially desirable way. To test this subjects completed a measure of social desirability.

Methods

In total, 230 undergraduate students enrolled in introductory communication courses participated in this project. Each received a packet containing a variety of personality measures. The order of the measures was random. Measures included the sensitivity scale (see Table 15.1); McCroskey's (McCroskey & Beatty, 1986) Personal Report of Communication Apprehension (which has subcomponents assessing communication apprehension in the public speaking, meeting, small group, and conversation settings); Davis's (1983) four-factor empathy scale that includes measures of perspective-taking, empathy, fantasy, and distress; the revised UCLA Loneliness scale (Russell, Peplau, & Cutrona, 1980); Snyder's self-monitoring measure (Snyder, 1974, 1979), which was also considered, in this study, as a three-factor measure tapping dimensions of acting, extroversion, and other-directedness (Briggs, Cheek, & Buss, 1980); Lorr and More's (1980) four-factor measure of assertiveness, which includes dimensions of defense of rights, directiveness, independence, and social assertiveness; Rosenberg's (1965) measure of self-esteem; Wheeless's (1975) receiver apprehension measure; Hart et al.'s (1980) measure of rhetorical sensitivity composed of three subscales measuring what they labeled noble selves, rhetorical reflectors, and rhetorical sensitives; Fenigstein et al.'s (1975) measures of public and private self-consciousness as well as their instrument assessing social anxiety; and Crowne and Marlowe's (1964) measure of social approval seeking.

Results

Reliabilities. Table 15.3 summarizes the *alpha* reliabilities associated with the measures. Reliabilities ranged from a high of .93 for the communication apprehension measure to a low of .53 for the rhetorical reflector dimension of the rhetorical sensitivity scale.

The sensitivity measure was factor analyzed and an eight dimension, orthogonal solution was chosen as optimal. The primary loadings from the analysis are shown in Table 15.1. By and large, the loadings were as expected. In every case, the strongest loading for an item fell on the expected factor. In addition, item-total correlations of each item with the total measure were calculated. They are also reported in Table 15.2.

Correlational Analysis. For reasons of both space and interest, only the correlations with the total sensitivity measure are presented in Table 15.3[1]. By and large, the magnitudes and directions of the correlations were as anticipated. First, none of the personality measures had sizable (in terms of magnitude) associations with the sensitivity construct. This is important since some of the measures, notably the receiver apprehension instrument and the various empathy measures, might, at first glance, be expected to tap the sensitivity construct. Second, the statistically significant correlations were, in most cases, quite interpretable. People with greater sensitivity ought to be more experienced with conversation. To the degree that social anxiety, receiver apprehension, and communication apprehension tap experience, inverse correlations between these personality dimensions and sensitivity would be anticipated. That was found. An interesting pattern emerged in the correlations among sensitivity and the different aspects of communication apprehension. Since sensitivity is conversation focused, no meaningful relationship with public speaking anxiety should be expected. But the other three dimensions (meeting, group, and conversation) should correlate significantly with sensitivity. That was what was found. Definitionally, sensitivity and empathy ought to be related, and they were: The correlations were both positive and significant. In addition, greater sensitivity was associated with more private self-consciousness, greater self-esteem, and more assertiveness. The self-esteem re-

TABLE 15.2

Factor Analysis and Item-Total Correlations of Sensitivity Measure in Personality Correlates Study

ITEM	r WITH TOTAL	I	II	III	IV	V	VI	VII	VIII
2	.44		.54						
3	.38		.45						
4	.42		.48						
5	.57		.60						
6	.53		.79						
7	.50		.56						
9	.45	.68							
10	.46	.70							
11	.55	.71							
12	.50	.98							
13	.52	.55							
14	.44			.58					
15	.40			.68					
16	.41			.69					
17	.43			.77					
18	.40			.62					
19	.38					.82			
20	.43					.94			
21	.39					.59			
22	.18				.72				
23	.23				.63				
24	.27				.86				
25	.29				.58				
26	.32								.55
27	.30								.72
28	.28								.63
29	.37							.74	
30	.35							.90	
32	.25							.43	
33	.29						.69		
34	.37						.84		
35	.35						.78		

NOTE: In this investigation, items 1, 8, 31, and 36 (see the preceding table) were not used. They did not load well on their expected dimensions.

lationship is particularly interesting. The sensitivity construct could be seen as tapping something akin to conversation-focused self-esteem. Individuals who respond positively to the sensitivity measure may be reflecting a general positive self-regard for their conversational skills.

Conversational sensitivity was unrelated to public self-consciousness, other-directedness (as

TABLE 15.3

Summary of Correlational Analyses

MEASURE	*alpha* RELIABILITY	r WITH SENSITIVITY
Sensitivity	.82	
PRCA	.93	− .35[c]
Conversation	.85	− .28[c]
Group	.87	− .42[c]
Meeting	.90	− .34[c]
Speaking	.81	− .05
Self-Monitoring	.64	.19[b]
Extroversion	.65	.27[b]
Acting	.58	.33[b]
Other-Directed	.63	− .01
Rhetorical Sensitivity		
Noble Self	.82	.28[c]
Rhetorical Reflector	.53	− .04
Rhetorical Sensitivity	.84	− .24[c]
Receiver Apprehension	.83	− .22[c]
Social Approval Seeking	.82	.01
Self-Consciousness		
Social Anxiety	.69	− .21[c]
Private Self-Consciousness	.80	.24[c]
Public Self-Consciousness	.83	.07
Loneliness	.89	− .07
Self-Esteem	.83	.20[b]
Assertiveness	.87	
Defense of Rights	.76	.27[c]
Directiveness	.85	.39[c]
Social Assertiveness	.86	.22[c]
Independence	.68	.29[c]
Empathy		
Empathy	.75	.18[b]
Fantasy	.77	.21[c]
Perspective-Taking	.71	.12[a]
Distress	.81	.22[c]

[a] $p < .05$
[b] $p < .01$
[c] $p < .001$

measured in the self-monitoring measure), loneliness, and social approval-seeking. This last correlation, between approval-seeking and sensitivity, is especially important. The measure tapping approval-seeking is often used to assess the social desirability of a self-report instrument. Finding no correlation suggests that, at least in terms of personality dispositions, the sensitivity measure is not confounded by respondents' generalized tendencies to seek social approval. The correlations with the rhetorical sensitivity measure raise some questions.[2] There was a positive relationship between sensitivity and the "noble self" dimension and an inverse relationship between sensitivity and the dimension called "rhetorical sensitivity." An examination of the scoring routine used for the measure presents a possible explanation. Scoring high on the rhetorical sensitivity dimension means that one answers items on the questionnaire with midrange responses (e.g., frequently true, sometimes true, infrequently true) and avoids extreme responses (e.g., almost always true, almost never true). Underlying this scoring scheme is the assumption that individuals who are very sure of their feelings about communication are not "rhetorically sensitive." It might be argued that people who have the savvy and concern for conversation that is represented by high scores on the sensitivity measure might respond with extremes to many of the rhetorical sensitivity items. People less sure about their feelings about social interaction (i.e., high "rhetorical sensitives") may be less conversationally centered and thus would score lower on the sensitivity measure. In addition, the rhetorical sensitivity measure is focused primarily on the construction of messages. Conversational sensitivity, on the other hand, has as its primary focus the reception of messages. It is quite possible for people to be highly sensitive to conversations yet be less than entirely articulate in producing their own messages.

STUDY III

In the preceding study, good convergent and discriminant validities in terms of communication-related personality variables were found. Sensitivity had low correlations with other personality indices and, in general, had statistically meaningful associations with only those variables one would expect it to. A hypothesis arose at this point about the relationship between conversational sensitivity and general social skills: The greater one's conversational sensitivity, the better one's social skills ought to be. The development of sensitivity should, in all likelihood, co-occur with the development of social skills as much of social skill acquisition is probably tied to involvement in, and sensitivity to, what happens in conversations—the most social of activities. In this study we sought to examine, in a preliminary way, the relationship between conversational sensitivity and social skills.

Methods

A total of 73 undergraduate students enrolled in basic communication courses completed the 36-item conversational sensitivity measure and a recently reported measure of social skills (Riggio, 1986). Riggio's social skills inventory taps seven dimensions of basic social skills: emotional expressivity, emotional sensitivity, emotional control, social expressivity, social sensitivity, social control, and social manipulation. Taken as a composite, the scale purportedly measures an individual's basic level of social skills.

Results

Reliabilities. The seven dimensions of the social skills index were all sufficiently reliable for further analysis (emotional expressivity: .67; emotional sensitivity: .79; emotional control: .77; social expressivity: .87; social sensitivity: .84; social control: .89; social manipulation: .71; total score: .85). The reliability of the sensitivity measure was .87.

Correlations. Conversational sensitivity was positively and significantly related to emotional expressivity ($r = .25$, $p < .02$), emotional sensitivity ($r = .47$, $p < .001$), and social control ($r = .21$, $p < .04$). Overall, the total score for social skills was positively and significantly associated with conversational sensitivity ($r = .39$, $p < .001$).

These results suggest a positive relationship among conversational sensitivity and a variety of social skills. The strongest correlation was between conversational sensitivity and what Riggio (1986)

labels emotional sensitivity. A close reading of the description of emotional sensitivity suggests that of all the social skills dimensions, this is the one most related to the reception of social stimuli. Many of the other dimensions emphasize the opposite issue—production of socially skillful messages and behaviors. These, if they correlate at all with conversational sensitivity, have much smaller associations.[3]

STUDY IV

The previous two studies demonstrated that conversational sensitivity has some convergent validity—it correlates with other related personality variables in the manner expected. What remains is to demonstrate the construct's predictive validity: Is it associated with actual behavioral differences important in social interaction?

One of the most likely behavioral correlates of conversational sensitivity is the remembrances people take away from interactions. Since sensitivity emphasizes people's receptivity to conversation, memory measures represent a likely behavioral indicator of the construct. In other words, we would anticipate that high and low sensitive individuals would differ in the ways they remember conversations. Given their stronger focus on conversation and their reported tendency to find multiple meanings in most utterances, highly sensitive people should draw more inferences from interactions than their counterparts, low in sensitivity. Less sensitive individuals, if asked about what occurred in a conversation, ought to emphasize more surface features of the text since they report not making as many inferences about what goes on in conversations, whether it has to do with meanings, relationships, or words. In addition, high sensitive people should be more accurate in what they remember about conversations than low sensitive individuals. Given the greater centrality of social interaction to highly sensitive individuals, they should also find stronger personal relevance in conversations than those low in sensitivity. In essence, the cognitive scheme of high sensitive individuals for conversations should be deeper and more personal. This should be reflected in the ways they remember social interaction.

Methods

Subjects. Undergraduate students enrolled in a large introductory communication course completed the sensitivity measure at the start of the semester. From the group, 19 individuals who scored one standard deviation above the mean and 17 who scored one standard deviation below the mean were asked to participate in an extra-credit project on communication five to six weeks after completing the instrument.

Procedures. Subjects participated in the project in small groups composed of both high and low sensitive individuals. Each group viewed short portions of two movies first released more than fifteen years ago. Two movies were used to avoid confounding due to such things as familiarity or involvement. For instance, had only one movie been used, results would be limited to that movie. With two, assuming that there are little or no differences in results between the two movies, conclusions can be more general. The two movies, *In the Heat of the Night* and *Who's Afraid of Virginia Woolf?*, were selected for three reasons. First, both were primarily "conversational movies": physical action was minimal. Second, each contained sequences where conversation moved quickly from, in the case of *In the Heat of the Night*, openness and self-disclosure to acrimony and, in *Who's Afraid of Virginia Woolf?*, pleasantness to anger. Third, neither movie was familiar to undergraduates (only four subjects said they had seen either movie). After watching each excerpt, subjects summarized what they had seen. The specific instructions were as follows:

Now that you've seen the short excerpt we would like you to write down all your impressions, memories, and thoughts about the excerpt and especially about the conversations you saw in the excerpt. You might write down things like what was said, why it was said, how it was said, what the people really meant by what they said, and so on. Be analytic, if you want, but understand that there are no right or wrong answers.

The order in which subjects saw the two movie excerpts was random. After completing the memory task for the first excerpt subjects were shown the excerpt from the second movie.

The written summaries were coded into idea units (Stafford & Daly, 1984). Two raters completed this task with initial agreement exceeding 95%. When there were disagreements, the two raters discussed the issue until agreement was reached.

To test the hypotheses of this study, six coding categories were created and each idea unit was coded for whether it fit each category. The six categories were as follows:

1. Text: Idea units in this category were straightforward reports of what occurred in the excerpt (e.g., "Husband comes out of bathroom when the guests are going to arrive.").
2. Inference: Plausible inferences from the film excerpts making up this category. Included were general impressions, judgments of relationships, and such (e.g., "Perhaps, however, they are both unhappy deep down because it is apparent they both need alcohol to be around each other.").
3. Self-Referents: This category included descriptions of the personal relevance of the excerpts (e.g., "I felt uncomfortable simply because I hate when people use foul language to argue.").
4. Conversation: Idea units in this category were ones that were inferences tied directly to the conversations (e.g., "Their conversation seemed to slip into a form they must have used when they were in love.").
5. Errors: Clear errors in descriptions of what happened in the film excerpts fell into this category.
6. Quotations: Idea units in this category were direct quotations from the film excerpts (e.g., "When the white man asked how lonely, the black fellow said 'No lonelier than you.'").

While an idea unit could be coded only into one of the first two categories it could, plausibly, be placed into more than one of the final four. Two raters completed this coding task. Across categories their level of agreement (adjusted for chance agreements [Krippendorff, 1980] ranged from a low of 79% [for errors] to a high of 100% [for quotes and self-referents]). Because of the potential for differences among subjects in the number of idea units generated, all values used in the analysis were computed as proportions of the total number of idea units generated by a subject for a film excerpt.

Results

Preliminary Analyses. Because two different movie excerpts were used it was critical to determine whether there were differences due to the movie or an interaction between movie and subject condition. A series of seven two-way analysis of variances were calculated where one factor was the level of subject conversational sensitivity (high/low) and the other was the movie excerpt (considered as a repeated factor). There were no statistically significant main effects due to movie excerpt or significant interactions attributable to movie excerpt by subject condition for any of the dependent measures save the proportion of direct quotations. For quotations, there was a significant main effect (p < .003) due to movie excerpt. A significantly larger proportion of quotations was generated when subjects described the movie *In the Heat of the Night* (M = .05) than when they described *Who's Afraid of Virginia Woolf?* (M = .01). This, however, was the only significant effect. There were no meaningful effects for the total number of idea units produced, for the number of inferences, the number of text ideas, the number of errors, the number of self-referents, or the number of conversation inferences. Overall, the conclusion is that the movie excerpt itself had a very limited impact on the inferences made by subjects. Since the differences due to movie were negligible, the responses to the two films were averaged.

Main Analyses. The primary analyses were conducted in a series of steps. The first was a comparison of high and low sensitive individuals on the total number of idea units they produced. The question here was whether there was a difference in the sheer number of idea units produced as a function of sensitivity. A simple t-test between the two subject groups yielded a nonsignificant value ($t(34) = .97$, ns). The average number of idea units produced by subjects was 20.67 (sd = 6.72) with a range from 8 to 34.

The second step was a one-way multivariate analysis of variance with the six proportion scores serving as dependent variables and subject condition (high versus low sensitivity) as the independent variable. The analysis yielded a significant overall effect ($F(6,29) = 2.77$, p < .03). A series of t-tests were then calculated to identify the specific variables affected by subject condition. Since directional predictions were made, one-tailed significance levels were used. Five of the six dependent variables had significant t-values associated with them. Only the proportion of quotes was nonsignificant ($t(34) = -.42$, ns). As anticipated, high sensitive subjects offered proportionally fewer text units and made proportionately fewer errors than low sensitive subjects. On the other hand, highly sensitive subjects made proportionately more inferences, more self-referents, and more conversation inferences than their counterparts, low in sensitivity. Table 15.4 summarizes the relevant numerical information.[4]

People who describe themselves as especially sensitive to conversations focus more on the structure and nature of conversations than do less sensitive individuals. Less sensitive individuals take conversations at face value, reporting mostly on what is actually uttered. Compared to highly sensitive individuals, they apparently fail to integrate deeply what they observe into their memories. Highly sensitive people relate the information in the conversations to themselves and draw more inferences about what, conversationally, is occurring in the interactions than less sensitive individuals. These findings fit well with the sensitivity construct. Conversationally sensitive people should see more alternative meanings in conversations, thus

TABLE 15.4

Summary of Analyses for Sensitivity and Inferences

VARIABLE	LOW	HIGH	t-VALUE	p
Text	.36 (.21)	.22 (.17)	2.23	.02
Inference	.63 (.21)	.75 (.16)	1.80	.04
Error	.03 (.04)	.01 (.02)	2.13	.02
Self	.02 (.04)	.07 (.13)	1.69	.05
Conversation	.13 (.11)	.22 (.12)	2.37	.01

NOTES: Values are means and, in parentheses, standard deviations. Statistical power estimates (Cohen, 1977) for small, medium, and large effects were, respectively, .15, .43, and .76.

drawing more inferences about what occurs. Cognitively, given their interest in conversations, they ought to have better developed representational schema for storing information about the nature of the conversations they observe. And, since social interaction is, theoretically, more central to their lives, they ought to link whatever they see in a conversation to themselves. All of these expectations were confirmed.

STUDY V

The results of Study IV provide initial evidence for the predictive validity of conversational sensitivity. More high-level inferences, an emphasis on conversation characteristics, and a tendency to relate conversations to self mark the recall of highly sensitive individuals. Sensitivity affects what people take away from social interactions. Due to the nature of the data collected, however, it is not possible to determine whether sensitivity affects the ways people perceive social interactions, the ways they recall conversations, or indeed both. An obvious next step is to devise a way to separate these potential outcomes. One way of assessing perceptual differences between high and low sensitive individuals is to conceive of listeners as parsing, or unitizing, incoming stimuli into meaningful chunks of information. Newtson (1976) proposed a procedure for tapping this unitizing process (see Dickman, 1963). Whenever subjects in his experiment felt that a "meaningful event" had occurred in videotapes they were observing, they pressed a button, in essence breaking the observed actions into units. Cohen and Ebbeson (1979), using this procedure, found that when people focus on specific behaviors they use a greater number of units than when they attempt to form general impressions of actors depicted in a videotape. Goodman (1980) noted that the more people focus on a particular aspect of a behavioral enactment, the more units they perceive in that aspect. When told to focus on emotions, subjects parse on the basis of the emotional expressions shown by actors; but when told to focus on meaningful actions, they chunk according to the pattern of instrumental actions by the actors in a videotape. Previous research thus suggests that greater focusing yields more perceived units on those items related to the focus. In the case of conversational sensitivity, highly sensitive individuals should be more focused on social interactions than their less sensitive counterparts. To the degree that this is true, high sensitive people ought to unitize displays that were conversational in nature more finely than low sensitive individuals.

Methods

In total, 37 undergraduate students enrolled in communication courses participated in this project. They were selected from a larger group because their scores on the sensitivity measure were at the extremes of the group (i.e., top and bottom quartiles). There were 19 students in the low sensitive group (M = 109.21, sd = 10.94) and 18 were in the high sensitive group (M = 139.33, sd = 7.10). The difference between the groups in sensitivity scores was significant (t(35) = 9.88, p < .0001).

Subjects came to a room containing small listening booths. After sitting down at booths, subjects listened and watched taped portions of two films that included substantial amounts of social conversation. The two taped excerpts were the same as those used in Study IV. One was from *Who's Afraid of Virginia Woolf?*; the other was from *In the Heat of the Night.* We chose these excerpts for two reasons. First, they are conversationally quite rich. Second, by using the same materials we were able to see if the effects observed in Study IV were a function of the choice of dependent variables. Subjects were told:

> When people observe or even participate in an interaction they often find themselves breaking the exchange into units. That is, they don't always see an exchange as one continuous event but rather as a series of somewhat discrete units. Some people see many different units in a conversation; others see very few. There are no correct answers to this activity. We want you to watch each of the tapes and when you see a new unit happening we want you to tap your finger on the board. By tapping you are indicating that, in your mind, a new unit, however you may define it, has begun.

A two-track tape recorder stored the tapes subjects made along with the conversation they were observing. The order of presentation of the tapes was random.

Results

Preliminary analyses revealed that the sensitivity measure, as a whole, was highly reliable (*alpha* = .94). The coding of the unitizing behaviors was also reliable. When two coders separately coded each tape, their average agreement was greater than 90%.

The unitizing patterns of subjects for each tape were intercorrelated. The correlation was .60 ($p < .001$). While this value was statistically significant, it was not high enough to justify combining the two unitizing activities. Consequently, separate analyses were conducted for each film excerpt. For the *Virginia Woolf* excerpt, the difference between high and low sensitive subjects was not statistically significant, although the means were in the expected direction with high sensitive subjects reporting more units (M = 15.35, sd = 4.37) than low sensitive subjects (M = 13.58, sd = 5.71). For the excerpt from *In the Heat of the Night,* the difference between high (M = 11.65, sd = 5.63) and low (M = 8.63,

sd = 5.83) sensitive subjects approached significance ($t(34) = 1.57, p < .06$). In short, there was a clear trend for highly sensitive subjects to perceive more units than their counterparts low in sensitivity.[5] A separate analysis was done to determine whether there were differences in where high and low sensitive subjects saw breaks. The units were coded into three categories: units set at the start of turns, units set within turns, and units set by major changes in nonverbal patterns. In these analyses the relative proportion of units falling in each category served as the dependent variables. There were no significant effects due to sensitivity.[6]

STUDY VI

Up to this point, conversational sensitivity has been conceptualized as an individual difference: People are assumed to differ reliably in the degree to which they are sensitive and aware of what happens in social interaction. In this vein, a variety of personality and behavioral correlates have been noted. Personality correlates, such as self-monitoring, communication apprehension, and empathy, have been found along with memory and perceptual differences.

An alternative, and equally plausible, perspective views sensitivity as a situational response tied, in part, to the purposes of the interaction and the contextual characteristics of the exchange. Some sorts of interactions may cause people to be far more sensitive to what is happening, conversationally, than others. For instance, discussing a familiar topic in a comfortable setting with little expectancy that the conversation will have any import is likely to arouse far less conversational sensitivity than an exchange with potentially great impact. Quite a bit of research suggests this is a reasonable approach. For instance, the greater one's perceived dependency on another, the more one pays attention to the conversation of the other (Berschied, Graziano, Monson, & Dermer, 1976), the greater one's feeling of being subordinate to another, the more attuned one is to the other's behaviors (Snodgrass, 1985), and the better one's mood, the more one will attend to the positive aspects of conversation (Forgas, Bower, & Krantz, 1984). Moreover, expectations of future interactions (Knight & Valacher, 1981) and one's goals in an interaction (Hamilton, Katz, & Leirer, 1980; Stafford & Daly, 1984) affect how sensitively one approaches the conversation. In short, various situational contingencies surrounding an interaction can make people more or less sensitive to social exchanges. Under what conditions are people especially sensitive to conversations? Study VI probed this question.

Methods

In total, 38 undergraduates received three packets of materials. The first two packets focused on the situational characteristics of conversational sensitivity. In one packet they were asked to remember a recent conversation where they had been particularly sensitive to what occurred. In the other packet they were asked to recollect an exchange where they had been less than entirely sensitive. The order in which subjects completed the two packets was random. At the beginning of each packet subjects read a paragraph describing the situation they were to remember. The paragraph for the high sensitive condition was:

> In this exercise we want you to think of a conversation you recently had when you felt that you were especially perceptive, sensitive, and aware of what was happening in the interaction. We want you to remember a time when you really enjoyed listening to what people were saying, when you were especially attuned to the relationships among people involved in the conversation (e.g., who liked whom, who was in charge), when you were able to "hear" hidden meanings in what people were saying, when you found the conversation memorable, and when you could see, ahead of time, where people were going with what they were saying.

The paragraph for the low sensitive situation was as follows:

> In this exercise we want you to think of a conversation you recently had when you felt you were not particularly concerned or worried about what was happening in the

interaction. We want you to remember a time when you really didn't care, one way or the other, about listening to the conversation, when you weren't concerned with the relationships among the interactants (e.g., who liked whom, who was in charge), when you took what was said at face value (not looking for hidden or deeper meanings), when you found little or nothing memorable in the conversation, and when you didn't spend time thinking of what might be coming up in the conversation.

A questionnaire containing items describing a number of potential characteristics of the situation followed each paragraph. After completing the questionnaire for one of the situations, subjects moved to the second packet, read the paragraph describing the other situation they were to remember, and then again completed the questionnaire. Responses to the two questionnaires served as the dependent variables. Finally, subjects completed the third packet containing the 36-item conversational sensitivity measure.

The questionnaire used with each paragraph contained items tapping various aspects of a situation that might enhance a person's sensitivity to social interaction. Items were based upon available literature (e.g., Cody & McLaughlin, 1985) as well as systematic interviews with people who described what made them more or less sensitive in conversations. After data were collected, items were combined to form clusters tapping different aspects of situations. Those clusters are described below.

Results

In addition to answering the questionnaires, subjects responded, in each condition, to the statement "Thinking of that conversation, how aware, interested, sensitive, and involved were you?" using a nine-step scale bounded by the labels "very much" and "very little." A t-test for correlated samples between the two conditions indicated that in the high sensitive condition (M = 1.61, sd = 1.07) subjects reported they were significantly ($t(35)$ = 21.06, p < .00001) more interested, sensitive, and involved in the conversation than they were in the low sensitive condition (M = 7.25, sd = 1.40).

Twelve clusters were generated from the questionnaire. Clusters were created when more than one item referenced the same dimension of the situation. The statistical results are presented in Table 15.5 where the items composing the clusters, average reliability indices, means, and standard deviations are reported.

Briefly, the results suggest that greater conversational sensitivity, as a response to situational characteristics, happens when conversations focus on personal, nonsuperficial topics ($t(35) = 7.22, p < .0001$), violate expectations ($t(34) = 4.25, p < .0001$), are formal ($t(36) = 2.48, p < .02$), interesting and involving ($t(36) = 14.55, p < .0001$) but unpredictable ($t(36) = 1.76, p < .08$), and involve people one likes ($t(36) = 4.01, p < .0001$). People are more sensitive when they enter conversations in a positive mood ($t(36) = 1.89, p < .06$) with distinct purposes in mind ($t(36) = 6.44, p < .0001$), and are concerned with creating a positive impression of themselves ($t(37) = 5.70, p < .0001$). On the other hand, familiarity with the topic ($t(36) = 1.17$, ns), acquaintanceship with the other interactants ($t(37) = 1.15$, ns), and the amount of tension in the exchange ($t(34) = 1.59$, ns) were unrelated to the degree of sensitivity a person felt. A series of additional analyses were completed in which the 36-item sensitivity measure was used as a covariate. The results described above were not substantially different when conversational sensitivity, as a dispositional characteristic, was controlled.

CONCLUSIONS

The studies described in this article were conducted to discover the nature and correlates of conversational sensitivity. The first study, composed of three separate data collections, suggested that sensitivity includes an ability to detect meanings in what others say, a good memory for conversations, an ability to generate a variety of alternative ways of saying something in a social exchange, an interest in listening to conversations, skill at detecting affinity and power relationships in conversations, and an appreciation for the nuances for what is said in social interaction.

The convergent and discriminant validities of the construct were examined in the second and third investigations. Inverse and significant correlations were found among conversational sensitivity and social anxiety, receiver apprehension, and communication apprehension. Positive and significant associations were found among sensitivity and empathy, private self-consciousness, assertiveness, self-monitoring, and self-esteem. Where significant correlations were found, their magnitude was not sizable, indicating that conversational sensitivity, while conceptually related to a variety of other constructs, is not equivalent to them. The third study addressed the very specific question as to whether or not conversational sensitivity was related to self-reported basic social skills as measured by Riggio's (1986) social skills inventory. Sensitivity was positively and significantly correlated with emotional expressivity, emotional sensitivity, social control, and the composite measure of social skills.

Behavioral correlates of conversational sensitivity were examined in the next two studies. In the fourth investigation, highly sensitive individuals' memories of conversations were hypothesized to differ from those of less sensitive individuals. An analysis of subjects' accounts of their "impressions, memories, and thoughts" concerning two movie excerpts revealed that individuals high in conversational sensitivity made proportionately more inferences, self-referents, and conversation-related inferences than their low sensitive counterparts. Those low in sensitivity, on the other hand, made proportionately more direct references to the text and more errors in those references. In the fifth study, subjects unitized conversations from two film excerpts. Since conversationally sensitive individuals ought to be more highly attuned to what happens during an interaction, we hypothesized that these individuals would unitize the conversation into a greater number (smaller) chunks than would those low in sensitivity. The data supported this notion.

TABLE 15.5

Means, Standard Deviations, and Alpha Levels for Situational Dimensions of Conversational Sensitivity

DIMENSION	alpha	LOW	HIGH
Expectation. ("The conversation was very different from most of the conversations I have." "During the conversation something happened that wasn't expected." "What was said was no different than what is said in most conversations." "The other person(s) said something I didn't expect.")	.65	9.26 (3.29)	12.29 (2.75)
Predictability. ("I knew, before the conversation, what the other(s) believed and felt about the topics we discussed." "Even before the conversation started, I knew what was expected: what I should say and what the other would say." "The course of the conversation [i.e., the way it went] was very predictable.")	.83	7.32 (3.06)	8.68 (3.08)
Mood. ("I felt tired and run-down before the conversation began." "I was feeling 'up' (in a good mood) before the conversation began.")	.50	6.63 (1.85)	7.32 (2.17)
Topic Familiarity. ("The topic we discussed was unfamiliar to me before the conversation." "The topic of the conversation was one I knew little about." "I felt I knew a lot about the topic that was being discussed." "The other people in the conversation knew a lot about what we were talking about.")	.71	14.61 (3.00)	15.39 (3.12)
Acquaintance. ("The people involved in the conversation were people I see and talk with everyday." "I knew the other(s) in the conversation well." "I felt I would never see the people involved in the conversation again.")	.71	5.95 (2.44)	5.29 (2.95)
Tension. ("The conversation was more tense than most." "The conversation was unfriendly." "The conversation was calm." "The conversation was a friendly one." "There was a good deal of conflict in the conversation.")	.85	19.46 (3.47)	17.69 (5.66)
Purpose. ("I entered the conversation with many questions in mind." "In the conversation I had a special purpose or goal that I was trying to accomplish." "I entered the conversation with a purpose in mind." "The outcomes of the conversation were going to affect me directly.")	.69	15.68 (2.64)	11.00 (3.77)
Formality. ("The conversation was a very informal one." "The conversation was more formal than most.")	.42	3.54 (1.41)	4.51 (2.01)
Personal. ("The topic being discussed was a very personal one." "The talk was 'superficial.' " "The conversation was an emotional one.")	.76	10.72 (3.40)	5.44 (2.66)
Affinity. ("I didn't like the other person(s)." "The others involved in the conversation were people I really cared for." "I liked the people in the conversation." "I did not trust the other person." "The other person(s) was very similar to me.")	.78	11.51 (4.06)	9.00 (3.18)
Impression-Leaving. ("I was really trying to make a good impression in this conversation." "I wanted people to think well of me in this exchange." "I wanted the other person(s) to think I cared about what was said." "In the conversation I felt a good deal of pressure to say 'the right thing.' ")	.72	13.63 (3.07)	10.18 (3.26)
Involvement. ("I found the conversation of special interest." "I was very involved in the conversation." "The conversation was boring." "The conversation was dull and boring.")	.68	14.57 (2.87)	5.68 (1.77)

Finally, in the sixth study, conversational sensitivity was reconceptualized as a response to a number of contextual variables. Sensitivity is aroused in situations where conversations focus on personal topics, violate expectations, and are unpredictable, formal, interesting, and involving. In situations where sensitivity is aroused, people are in a positive mood, enter with particular purposes, and are concerned with impression management.

Conceptually, the idea of conversational sensitivity can be considered in terms of the framework presented by Dworkin and Goldfinger (1985) on social affordances. In accordance with Gibson's (1966) notions, they propose that people differ in their processing biases, paying attention to, anticipating, and remembering different affordances of a situation. They demonstrate, for instance, that there may be a general processing bias for social situations and that sociability affects this processing bias. Some people anticipate, focus on, and remember more of the sociability affordances of a situation than others. Individuals high in conversational sensitivity should, likewise, emphasize the affordances tied to social interaction more than others. This greater attention to conversational affordances data may, in the long run, affect the ways highly sensitive individuals organize information about conversation.

In examining the available literature related to conversational sensitivity, it became apparent that the most relevant existing construct in communication research was Cegala's notion of interaction involvement. While sensitivity was conceived independently of Cegala's construct, an examination of the involvement measure raises the concern of duplication. To test whether the same general construct was being tapped, 67 undergraduate students completed the 36-item sensitivity measure and the 18-item interaction involvement instrument (Cegala, 1984). The overall correlation ($r = .28$, $p < .02$), while statistically significant, was not of the magnitude to suggest isomorphism. Among the subscales of the interaction involvement instrument, only the perceptiveness dimension had a significant correlation ($r = .55$, $p < .001$) with sensitivity. The distinction between the perceptiveness dimension of interaction involvement and sensitivity may lie in two areas. First, conversational sensitivity includes dimensions unrelated to the perceptiveness construct (e.g., conversational enjoyment had no correlation with perceptiveness [$r = .00$, ns]). Second, perceptiveness has a subtle emphasis on self-awareness (e.g., "I am keenly aware of how others perceive me during my conversations") that is missing in the sensitivity construct. In short, the two constructs, while related, tap different components of people's beliefs about their interaction behavior.[7]

Another question that arises when considering the construct of conversational sensitivity is whether or not any sex differences are associated with the construct. Previous research with constructs related to sensitivity is mixed on the issue of sex differences. On the one hand, Hall (1978), in a meta-analysis of nonverbal decoding studies, found females more sensitive than males. On the other hand, Bronfenbrenner, Harding, and Gallwey (1958) and Maccoby and Jackin (1974) found little evidence for sex differences (see Hoffman, 1977). In the current studies, where information on respondent's sex was available, there were no differences between males and females on either the overall measure or on the various factors (an exception was that females [M = 15.46, sd = 3.13] were significantly higher [$t(71) = 3.92$, $p < .05$] on listening than males [M = 12.47, sd = 3.27]). One explanation for the very few gender differences may be that sex and status have been confounded in research where sex has been a significant predictor of variables akin to sensitivity (Snodgrass, 1985).

Up to this point some of the components and correlates of self-reported conversational sensitivity have been identified. When sensitivity is considered an individual difference, much remains to be done. A major question left unanswered in the studies described in this article is the veridicality of the self-reports. That is, are people who say they are sensitive actually that way? In some ways, our behavioral studies (Studies IV and V) suggest a match between report and actual behavior. Indeed, it is impressive that a general self-report measure correlates, with some regularity, and in the anticipated directions, with a variety of perceptual and memory indicators. But more needs to be done. There is a long history in psychology of work exploring the accuracy of people's judgment of others (e.g., Bronfenbrenner et al., 1958), which continues today (e.g., Snodgrass, 1985). However, when the focus of attention moves from person perception to conversation or interaction perception, there is far less work. We know relatively little of even the categories people use in organizing their knowledge of conversation (see Forgas, 1979; Forgas & Bond, 1985; Wish, Deutsch, & Kaplan, 1976).

Future research will also have to be concerned with the consequences of conversational sensitivity. Are people who are particularly sensitive to conversational stimuli actually more effective in social interactions? The central emphasis of the sensitivity construct is on people's *receptive* skills, not their *production* skills. There may, however, be some carryover: More sensitive people may also be more effective conversationalists. At the same time, conversational sensitivity may be a double-edged sword. On the one hand, highly sensitive people may leave a conversation with a wealth of information and impressions that others are ignorant about. But, on the other hand, in some situations they may spend far too much time focusing on, interpreting, and remembering the most mundane of conversations. They may, in short, overanalyze what happens. It may well be that in most situations, people who would score high on measures of conversational sensitivity are no more sensitive than anyone else. Instead, they may have the capacity to "turn on" their sensitivity when it is demanded or especially needed and "turn off" their sensitivity at other times. In addition, the studies that have been completed focus solely on passive reception of conversations. In both the fourth and fifth investigations subjects watched conversations. Would there be a different pattern of results were subjects actively participating in an exchange?

Finally, how conversational sensitivity develops represents an interesting avenue for future research. We would anticipate that the more varied communication experiences an individual has, the more conversationally sensitive he or she should be. Participating in a wide variety of social encounters should provide people with experiences that broaden their categories for interaction behavior, making them in turn both more sensitive to interaction and more complex in their construals of social exchanges (Daly, Bell, Glenn, & Lawrence, 1985). In addition, the development of critical skills that emphasize approaches to social interaction from a variety of perspectives should, in all likelihood, enhance sensitivity. Research on the development of role-taking skills is obviously relevant here (Applegate, 1982).

Some comments should be made about approaching conversational sensitivity as a response to aspects of a situation. In the final study this sort of conversational sensitivity was affected, at least in terms of self-reports, by a number of contextual characteristics such as formality, predictability, and topic salience. Future work needs to further examine this conceptualization of sensitivity. First, a good measure of situational sensitivity is required. Obviously, self-report measures can be devised. But are there other, more behavioral, manifestations of sensitivity that serve as indications of people's attentiveness to social interaction? Second, attention should be paid to the components of situations that induce sensitivity. In the study described in this article, situational characteristics were drawn, in an ad hoc fashion, from interviews and previous research. What is required, though, is a systematic analysis of those circumstances that arouse sensitivity. Everyone has experienced, at times, feelings that they should be especially sensitive in a conversation. What happens in interactions to make people feel this way? What keys people to know they should be sensitive? Is it the others involved in the exchange, the potential consequences, something that is said in a certain way? Moreover, do people who vary in dispositional conversational sensitivity react differently when contextual factors hint at the necessity for situational sensitivity? Are highly sensitive people more successful at detecting situational cues prescribing sensitivity than their less sensitive counterparts?

The program of study described in this article started with the observation that people seem to differ in how sensitive they are to what happens in social exchanges. We found that sensitivity has at least eight components, that it correlates in meaningful ways with a number of communication-related personality characteristics, and is related to the ways people process and recall social interactions. Moreover, sensitivity need not be conceived of solely as an individual difference; it can also be viewed as one response people have to certain characteristics of conversational settings.

ENDNOTES

[1] Significant correlations ($p < .05$) were found between the individual factors of the sensitivity measure and a number of the personality measures implemented in this study. Detecting meaning was associated with both the noble self (.21) and the rhetorical sensitivity ($-.16$) dimensions of the rhetorical sensitivity measure; with fantasy ($-.22$) and distress (.13) dimensions of the empathy measure; with the overall PRCA ($-.18$) and its subdimensions of group (.$-.27$), meeting ($-.19$), and conversation ($-.14$) apprehension; with the directiveness (.27), defense of rights (.26), and independence (.24) dimensions of the assertiveness scale; with the overall self-monitoring scale ($-.17$) as well as its subdimensions of extroversion ($-.19$) and acting ($-.27$); and with both public (.12) and private (.26) self-consciousness. Conversational memory was related to all three of the dimensions of rhetorical sensitivity (noble self: .20; rhetorical sensitivity; $-.14$; rhetorical reflector: $-.16$); the empathy ($-.24$) and distress (.12) subscales of the empathy instrument; the overall PRCA ($-.26$) as well as the group ($-.26$), meeting ($-.27$), and conversations ($-.14$) subscales; the directiveness (.17) and independence (.24) scales of the assertiveness measure; all three of the self-monitoring subscales (extroversion: $-.12$; other-directedness: .19; acting: $-.16$); and the public (.11) and private (.14) self-consciousness measures. Conversational alternatives was correlated with the noble self (.16) and rhetorical sensitivity ($-.11$) dimensions of the rhetorical sensitivity measure; the empathy ($-.15$) and distress (.26) dimensions of the empathy measure; the overall PRCA scale ($-.33$) as well as its subdimensions of group ($-.32$), meeting ($-.30$), conversation ($-.24$), and speaking ($-.17$) apprehension; the directiveness (.38), social assertiveness (.31), defense of rights (.28), and independence (.26) subdimensions of the assertiveness scale; the loneliness measure ($-.15$); the self-esteem measure (.25); the overall self-monitoring scale ($-.27$) and its subdimensions of extroversion ($-.34$) and acting ($-.32$); the receiver apprehension scale ($-.26$); and the social anxiety dimension ($-.35$) of the self-consciousness measure. Conversational imagination

was tied to the fantasy dimension ($-.26$) of the empathy scale; the acting dimension ($-.11$) of the self-monitoring measure; and private self-consciousness (.11). Conversation enjoyment was associated with both the noble self (.12) and the rhetorical sensitivity ($-.14$) dimensions of the rhetorical sensitivity measure and the speaking (.15) subdimension of the PRCA. Interpretation was related to the distress (.26) dimension of the empathy measure; the overall PRCA ($-.23$) and its subdimensions of group ($-.17$), meeting ($-.13$), conversation ($-.22$), and speaking ($-.21$) apprehension; the directiveness (.23), social assertiveness (.15), and independence (.22) subdimensions of the assertiveness measure; the self-esteem (.15) scale; the overall self-monitoring measure ($-.14$) as well as its subdimensions of extroversion ($-.14$) and acting ($-.21$); the receiver apprehension scale ($-.28$); and the social anxiety ($-.12$) and private self-consciousness (.13) subdimensions of the self-consciousness measure. Finally, perceiving affinity was correlated with both the noble self (.18) and the rhetorical sensitivity ($-.17$) subdimensions of the rhetorical sensitivity measure; the perspective-taking ($-.13$), the empathy ($-.12$), and the distress (.17) subdimensions of the empathy measure; the overall PRCA ($-.14$) and its subdimensions of group ($-.17$) and conversation ($-.17$) apprehension; the directiveness (.25), social assertiveness (.23), defense of rights (.15), and independence (.20) subdimensions of the assertiveness measure; the loneliness scale ($-.13$); the self-esteem measure (.22); the extroversion ($-.15$) dimension of the self-monitoring measure; the receiver apprehension measure ($-.13$); and the social anxiety ($-.15$) subdimension of the self-consciousness measure.

[2] Hart et al. (1980) suggest that investigators use partial correlations when using their measure. We completed such partials and found no substantial differences from the results described in this study.

[3] The individual factors of the sensitivity measure were significantly ($p < .05$) correlated with a number of the subdimensions of the social skills inventory. Detecting meaning was related to emotional sensitivity (.41), emotional control (.23), and social manipulation (.26). Conversational memory and conversational imagination were not correlated with any of the dimensions. Conversational alternatives was associated with emotional control (.23), social control (.39), social sensitivity ($-.23$), and social manipulation (.25). Conversation enjoyment was related to emotional expressivity (.20), emotional sensitivity (.39), social sensitivity (.37), and emotional control ($-.21$). Interpretation was associated with social sensitivity ($-.31$), emotional control (.24), and social control (.25). Perceiving affinity was tied to emotional expressivity (.24) and emotional sensitivity (.60), and perceiving control was correlated with emotional sensitivity (.38).

[4] The individual factors of the sensitivity measure were significantly ($p < .05$) correlated with a number of the coding categories. The proportion of text-based idea units was correlated with detecting meaning ($-.33$), conversational alternatives ($-.51$), conversational imagination ($-.30$), and perceiving control ($-.28$). The inference proportion was correlated with detecting meaning (.29), conversational alternatives (.46), and perceiving control (.27). The proportion of errors was correlated with conversational memory ($-.31$), conversational alternatives ($-.36$), conversational imagination ($-.60$), and

perceiving control ($-.54$). The proportion of self-referents was uncorrelated with any of the subscales. The conversation inferences proportion was correlated with detecting meaning (.29) and conversational alternatives (.31). The proportion of quotes was related to conversational imagination (.28). It should be remembered, in interpreting these values, that the sample was composed of individuals who scored one standard deviation above or below the mean.

[5] When the two unitizing scores were averaged for subjects, the difference between high ($M = 13.59$, sd $= 4.38$) and low sensitive ($M = 11.0$, sd $= 5.20$) subjects approached significance ($t(34) = 1.54$, $p < .07$).

[6] In a separate analysis, the correlations between each of the subscales of the sensitivity measure and the average unitizing index were computed. Only the memory component was correlated significantly ($r = .28$, $p < .05$) with the overall unitizing pattern of subjects. When we examined the correlations of the sensitivity indices with the unitizing scores for each of the film excerpts separately we found somewhat different patterns. For *Who's Afraid of Virginia Woolf?* the correlation between the number of units and the "make-up" component of the scale was significant ($r = .27$, $p < .06$); for *In the Heat of the Night* the number of units recorded by subjects was significantly correlated with memory ($r = .33$, $p < .03$) and with liking for conversations ($r = .26$, $p < .07$).

[7] It may well be that another component of conversational sensitivity is some degree of self-awareness in social interaction. Sensitivity may include a more refined sense of both how one affects others in conversing and how others respond to the individual's conversation enactments. Additionally, given the significant correlation between the composite sensitivity measure and the perceptiveness dimension of interaction involvement, one might argue that sensitivity represents a refined version of the construct measured by the perceptiveness dimension.

REFERENCES

Applegate, J. L. (1982). The impact of construct system development on communication and impression formation in persuasive contexts. *Communication Monographs, 49,* 277-289.

Archer, D., & Akert, R. M. (1977). Words and everything else: Verbal and nonverbal cues in social interpretation. *Journal of Personality and Social Psychology, 35,* 443-449.

Beatty, M., & Payne, S. (1984). Listening comprehension as a function of cognitive complexity: A research note. *Communication Monographs, 51,* 85-89.

Berschied, E., Graziano, W., Monson, T., & Dermer, M. (1976). Outcome dependency: Attention, attribution, and attraction. *Journal of Personality and Social Psychology, 34,* 978-989.

Bronfenbrenner, U., Harding, J., & Gallwey, M. (1958). The measurement of skill in social perception. In D. C. McClelland, A. L. Baldwin, U. Bronfenbrenner, & F. L. Strodtbeck (Eds.), *Talent and society: New perspectives in the identification of talent* (pp. 29-111). Princeton, NJ: Van Nostrand.

Briggs, S. R., Cheek, J. M., & Buss, A. H. (1980). An analysis of the self-monitoring scale. *Journal of Personality and Social Psychology, 38,* 679-686.

Buck, R. (1976). A test of nonverbal receiving ability: Preliminary studies. *Human Communication Research, 2,* 162-171.

Buck, R. (1983). Nonverbal receiving ability. In J. M. Wiemann

& R. P. Harrison (Eds.), *Nonverbal interaction* (pp. 209-242). Newbury Park, CA: Sage.

Buck, R. (1984). *The communication of emotion.* New York: Guilford.

Cegala, D. J. (1981). Interaction involvement: A cognitive dimension of communication competence. *Communication Education, 30,* 109-121.

Cegala, D. J. (1984). Affective and cognitive manifestations of interaction involvement during unstructured and competitive interactions. *Communication Monographs, 51,* 320-338.

Cegala, D. J., Savage, G. T., Brunner, C. C., & Conrad, A. B. (1982). An elaboration of the meaning of interaction involvement: Toward the development of a theoretical concept. *Communication Monographs, 49,* 229-248.

Cody, M., & McLaughlin, M. (1985). The situation as a construct in interpersonal communication research. In M. L. Knapp & G. R. Miller (Eds.), *Handbook of interpersonal communication* (pp. 263-312). Newbury Park, CA: Sage.

Cohen, J. (1977). *Statistical power analysis for the behavioral sciences.* New York: Academic Press.

Cohen, C. E., & Ebbeson, E. B. (1979). Observational goals and schema activation: A theoretical framework for behavior perception. *Journal of Experimental Social Psychology, 15,* 305-329.

Crowne, D. P., & Marlowe, D. (1964). *The approval motive: Studies in evaluative dependence.* New York: John Wiley.

Daly, J. A., Bell, R., Glenn, P., & Lawrence, S. (1985). Conceptualizing conversational complexity. *Human Communication Research, 12,* 30-53.

Daly, J. A., & McCroskey, J. C. (Eds.). (1984). *Avoiding communication: Shyness, reticence, and communication apprehension.* Newbury Park, CA: Sage.

Davis, M. H. (1983). Measuring individual differences in empathy: Evidence for a multidimensional approach. *Journal of Personality and Social Psychology, 44,* 113-126.

Dickman, H. R. (1963). The perception of behavior units. In R. G. Barker (Ed.), *The stream of behavior.* New York: Appleton-Century-Crofts.

Douglas, W. (1984). Initial interaction scripts: When knowing is believing. *Human Communication Research, 11,* 203-219.

Dworkin, R. H., & Goldfinger, S. H. (1985). Processing bias: Individual differences in the cognition of situations. *Journal of Personality, 53,* 480-501.

Fenigstein, A., Scheier, M., & Buss, A. (1975). Public and private self-consciousness: Assessment and theory. *Journal of Consulting and Clinical Psychology, 43,* 522-527.

Fletcher, G. J. O., Danilovics, P., Fernandez, G., Peterson, D., & Reeder, G. D. (1986). Attributional complexity: An individual differences measure. *Journal of Personality and Social Psychology, 51,* 875-884.

Forgas, J. P. (1979). *Social episodes: The study of interaction routines.* London: Academic Press.

Forgas, J. P., & Bond, M. H. (1985). Cultural influences on the perceptions of interaction episodes. *Personality and Social Psychology Bulletin, 11,* 75-88.

Forgas, J. P., Bower, G. H., & Krantz, S. E. (1984). The influence of mood on perceptions of social interactions. *Journal of Experimental Social Psychology, 20,* 497-513.

Funder, D. C., & Harris, M. J. (1986). On the several facets of personality assessment: The case of social acuity. *Journal of Personality, 54,* 528-550.

Gibson, E. J. (1969). *Principles of perceptual learning and development.* New York: Appleton-Century-Crofts.

Gibson, J. J. (1966). *The senses considered as perceptual systems.* Boston: Houghton Mifflin.

Gibson, J. J. (1979). *The ecological approach to visual perception.* Boston: Houghton Mifflin.

Goffman, E. (1967). *Interaction ritual.* New York: Doubleday.

Goodman, N. R. (1980). *Determinants of the perceptual organization of ongoing action and emotion behavior.* Unpublished doctoral dissertation, University of Connecticut. Summarized in Buck (1984).

Hall, J. A. (1978). Gender effects in decoding nonverbal cues. *Psychological Bulletin, 85,* 845-857.

Hamilton, D., Katz, L., & Leirer, V. (1980). Cognitive representation of personality impressions: Organizational processes in first impression formation. *Journal of Personality and Social Psychology, 39,* 1050-1063.

Hart, R., & Burks, D. (1972). Rhetorical sensitivity and social interaction. *Speech Monographs, 39,* 75-91.

Hart, R., Carlson, R., & Eadie, W. (1980). Attitudes toward communication and the assessment of rhetorical sensitivity. *Communication Monographs, 47,* 1-22.

Hoffman, M. L. (1977). Sex differences in empathy and related behaviors. *Psychological Bulletin, 84,* 712-722.

Isenhart, M. (1980). An investigation of the relationship of sex and sex role to the ability to decode nonverbal cues. *Human Communication Research, 6,* 309-318.

Johnson, J. A., Cheek, J. M., & Smither, R. (1983). The structure of empathy. *Journal of Personality and Social Psychology, 45,* 1299-1312.

Knight, J. A., & Vallacher, R. R. (1981). Interpersonal engagement in social perception: The consequences of getting into the action. *Journal of Personality and Social Psychology, 40,* 990-999.

Krippendorff, K. (1980). *Content analysis.* Newbury Park, CA: Sage.

Lorr, M., & More, W. W. (1980). Four dimensions of assertiveness. *Multivariate Behavioral Research, 15,* 127-138.

Maccoby, E. E., & Jacklin, C. N. (1974). *The psychology of sex differences.* Stanford, CA: Stanford University Press.

McCroskey, J. C., & Beatty, M. J. (1986). Oral communication apprehension. In W. Jones, J. Cheek, & S. Briggs (Eds.), *Shyness: Perspectives on research and treatment* (pp. 279-293). New York: Plenum.

Newtson, D. (1976). Foundations of attribution: The perception of ongoing behavior. In J. H. Harvey, W. J. Ickes, & R. F. Kidd (Eds.), *New directions in attribution research* (Vol. 1, pp. 223-247). Hillsdale, NJ: Lawrence Erlbaum.

Petrie, C. R., & Carrel, S. D. (1976). The relationship of motivation, listening capability, initial information, and verbal organizational ability to lecture comprehension and retention. *Communication Monographs, 43,* 187-194.

Riggio, R. E. (1986). Assessment of basic social skills. *Journal of Personality and Social Psychology, 51,* 649-660.

Rosenberg, M. (1965). *Society and the adolescent self-image.* Princeton, NJ: Princeton University Press.

Rosenthal, R., Hall, J. A., DiMatteo, M. R., Rogers, P. L., & Archer, D. (1979). *Sensitivity to nonverbal communication: The PONS test.* Baltimore: Johns Hopkins.

Russell, D., Peplau, L. A., & Cutrona, C. E. (1980). The revised UCLA loneliness scale: Concurrent and discriminant validity evidence. *Journal of Personality and Social Psychology, 39,* 427-480.

Sabatelli, R. M., Buck, R., & Dreyer, A. (1982). Nonverbal communication accuracy in married couples: Relationships with marital complaints. *Journal of Personality and Social Psychology, 43,* 1088-1097.

Snodgrass, S. E. (1985). Women's intuition: The effect of subordinate role on interpersonal sensitivity. *Journal of Personality and Social Psychology, 49,* 146-155.

Snyder, M. (1974). The self-monitoring of expressive behavior. *Journal of Personality and Social Psychology, 30,* 526-537.

Snyder, M. (1979). Self-monitoring processes. In L. Berkowitz (Ed.), *Advances in experimental social psychology* (Vol. 12, pp. 85-128). New York: Academic Press.

Snyder, M., & Cantor, N. (1980). Thinking about ourselves and others: Self-monitoring and social knowledge. *Journal of Personality and Social Psychology, 39,* 220-234.

Snyder, M., & Gangestad, S. (1986). On the nature of self-monitoring: Matters of assessment, matters of validity. *Journal of Personality and Social Psychology, 51,* 125-139.

Stafford, L., & Daly, J. A. (1984). Conversational memory: The effects of recall mode and memory expectancies on remembrances of natural conversations. *Human Communication Research, 10,* 379-402.

Walker, R. E., & Foley, J. M. (1973). Social intelligence: Its history and measurement. *Psychological Reports, 33,* 839-864.

Wheeless, L. R. (1975). An investigation of receiver apprehension and social context dimensions of communication apprehension. *Speech Teacher, 24,* 261-268.

Wish, M., Deutsch, M., & Kaplan, S. (1976). Perceived dimensions of interpersonal relations. *Journal of Personality and Social Psychology, 33,* 409-440.

16

The Functions of Empathy (Decentering) in Human Relations

MARK V. REDMOND

Empathy, in its broadest usage, is considered a fundamental dimension of interpersonal and communication competence. Empathy enhances a person's understanding of others, and the ability to make predictions about others. Understanding and prediction make empathy a possible tool for persuasion, compliance gaining, relational development, and counseling. Empathy affects decision making about others and attribution. Empathy acts to reflect what has been perceived and creates a supportive/confirming atmosphere. Each function of empathy generally reflects a different conceptualization of empathy. The term "decentering" is offered as the more appropriate alternative term to represent the overall phenomenon with empathy as a subconstruct.

INTRODUCTION

Empathy has been identified as an affective phenomenon by some scholars (Allport, 1961; Mehrabian & Epstein, 1972; Langer, 1967, 1972) and as a cognitive phenomenon by others (Barrett-Lennard, 1981; Borke, 1972; Katz, 1963; Kogler-Hill, 1982). Empathy has been defined as a "vicarious emotional response" (Mehrabian & Epstein, 1972), as "imaginative transporting" (Dymond, 1948), as "role-taking" (Gladstein, 1983), and as "expressing understanding" (Barrett-Lennard, 1981). This variety of conceptualizations attributed to the same concept is problematic for researchers and scholars. Johnson, Powell, and Reynolds (1983) pointed out that each investigator appears to be measuring a different phenomenon but all are labeling it "empathy." The phenomena under study share certain commonalities, which can best be termed "decentering." Decentering includes any phenomenon which concerns itself with how persons react or respond to information they have about another. Empathy can then be thought of as a form of decentering that produces emotional consonance between one person and another.

When the literature on empathy is examined without regard for the variations in conceptualizations, some valuable insights can be obtained about the functions empathy (in all of its manifestations) plays in human relations. An examination of the functions reflected in the literature on empathy circumvents arguing about the conceptual variations by placing the focus on the functional similarities. The purpose of this article is to identify the primary functions of empathy in human relations. The functions will be discussed in terms of how they might serve the receiver of an empathic response, the sender of an empathic response, or both the receiver and the sender. Discrepancies in empathy research and theory can potentially be reduced when the empathic contextuality that is reflected in the various functions is clearly identified.

EMPATHY AND COMMUNICATION COMPETENCE

Empathy functions as a major contributor to communication competence by enhancing understand-

From Redmond, M. V. (1989). The functions of empathy (decentering) in human relations. *Human Relations, 42*(7), 593-605.

ing, prediction, and adaptation. Empathy as an element of communication competence represents the broadest application of empathy to communication. Empathy is repeatedly identified as one of the basic competencies in communication and interpersonal competence theories (Allen & Brown, 1976; Argyris, 1965; Bochner & Kelly, 1974; Larson, Backlund, Redmond, & Barbour, 1978; Wiemann & Backlund, 1980). Conceptual and methodological difficulties with both empathy and communication competence have limited the production of consistent research findings. Redmond (1985) presented evidence that communication competence and perceived empathy are not discrete concepts. Redmond argued that the skills that underlie the production of communication competence are the same skills that underlie the production of an empathic message. By definition, a person cannot produce a message that is empathic that is not also communicatively competent.

Communication competence is considered a necessary human quality (Allen & Brown, 1976; Spitzberg & Cupach, 1984). Since empathy is a component of communication competence, empathy too must be seen as a necessary human quality. Empathy seems to be accepted as an essential communication skill without much question, but is empathy really essential? Is empathy essential to human relations? In reality, most messages do not appear to represent specific adaptation to the other, but rather represent a form of egocentric communication. Messages are understood not because the message represents a specific adaptation to the other, but because most people communicate with people who are very similar to themselves and are thus able to understand the egocentric messages of others (Dickson, 1982; Redmond, 1983; Shantz, 1981). Empathy then becomes desirable but not essential. Persons can communicate competently without having to empathize with their receivers; those persons might not be liked, or might not be as effective as they might be, but they are able to operate at a competent level. (Empathy is being used here and throughout the remainder of this pa-

per as a global term, essentially equated with decentering.)

Empathy provides two functions that contribute to communication competence: (1) the ability to understand another more completely and accurately, and (2) to predict or anticipate another's action or reaction. The ability to competently interact with others should be enhanced by understanding the others. Such understanding increases the likelihood of displaying behaviors appropriate to the situation and person. Understanding through empathy also contributes to communication effectiveness; thus, those who can decenter or empathize are able to present strategically adapted messages. The use of fantasy-based information in decentering allows a person to anticipate situations and predict the reactions of others. That anticipation aids in the assessment and selection of the most effective strategic message. Empathy role in facilitating adaptation to another inextricably links empathy to competence, as it is this ability to adapt that is identified as the most general and basic conceptualization of competence (Spitzberg & Cupach, 1984).

EMPATHY AND PERSUASION/ COMPLIANCE GAINING

The role of empathy in adaptation serves as the foundation for empathy's persuasive function. The success rate for persuasive messages or compliance gaining should increase in proportion to the amount and accuracy of empathy with a given individual. Underlying empathy's role in persuasion is the assumption that a speaker can empathize with another in advance of actually observing the emotional state of another. This proactive, anticipatory quality has been only implied in the literature and not specifically identified because empathy is usually conceptualized as a reactionary process. The ability to predict another's emotional reaction is a cognitive function, though not devoid of some affect. This creates a paradox; the empathizer could experience the emotional state of the other before the other even has received the stimulus that will induce that emotional state. This anticipatory empathy is not confined to the persuasive context, but to any situation where the empathizer has advance knowledge of a situation that will affect another, thus producing statements like "I know how they're going to feel about this when they find out."

This predictive aspect of empathy was incorporated in a theory of compliance gaining advanced by Hunter and Boster (1978). Their model is based on persuaders using empathy to predict whether a given compliance gaining strategy will evoke a positive or negative effective response from the listener. Their resistance to some previously collected data led them to conclude that the empathic persuader would select messages where the message is more positive than the ethical threshold and reject messages more negative or equal to the threshold. The ethical threshold seems to be a tolerance threshold for the affective impact of a message. In other research, empathic understanding was found to be used more frequently in intimate relationships to produce persuasive strategies to overcome high resistance than when there was low resistance (Cody & McLaughlin, 1985). In essence, people in intimate relationships who do not foresee much resistance to a proposal or request do not engage in extensive decentering, probably because their egocentric messages are effective in dealing with low resistance issues.

EMPATHY AND MAKING DECISIONS ABOUT OTHERS

Empathy can have an important impact on decisions which involve people with whom the decision-maker empathizes. The process and outcome of deciding on whether to fire an employee who is not performing very well would be quite different between an empathic manager and a non-empathic manager. Harris (1981) advocated the development of empathy in managers as a means of enhancing the decision-making process. Berlo (1966) called this impact of empathy on decision making "sym-

pathy." Sympathy, rather than being desirable as Harris claimed, is seen as incapacitating the empathizer from taking action which might not be in the best interest of the other. Empathy affects decisions made in anticipation of an interaction and decisions made during an interaction. The feedback received to an adapted/empathic message "may provide us with new insights and information and may alter our prior decision on the best way to attack a problem or implement a decision" (Berlo, 1966, p. 140).

Besides the potential sympathetic response, empathy might cause biased or incomplete information processing. Bock, Guinaud, and Perkins (1984) found that empathy limits the information processed about another and thus cause rating errors when assessing the anxiety of a speaker. Attribution research seems to indicate that there are limitations to what information gets included in the analysis of another, and thus in the decision-making process. Empathic decision makers might produce poorer decisions than non-empathic decision makers because of the restriction on the information used in decision making caused by empathizing, even though empathy/decentering would generate an internal source of information that non-empathic decision makers would lack.

EMPATHY AND ATTRIBUTION/ IMPRESSION FORMATION

Research on attribution theory indicates that "actors tend to attribute the causes of their behavior to stimuli inherent in the situation, while observers tend to attribute behavior to stable dispositions of the actor" (Jones & Nisbett, 1972, p. 93). These findings suggest that people are able to consider how persons might behave because of their personality traits, but that in general people do not consider the interaction of another's personality and the situation. This places a limit on the quality and accuracy of empathy or decentering applied in interactions with others. While most people take into account some of the information they have about others, they seem to ignore situational information which would lead them to different interpretations and consequently different effective responses. Melburg, Rosenfeld, Riess, and Tedeschi (1984) concluded in their study that empathy alone did "not provide observers with the same perspective or cause them to attend to the same aspects of available information as actors" (p. 206). Empathy affects attribution when empathy is cognitively defined. Keefe (1976) purposely defined empathy as a purely emotional response to avoid the attribution biases inherent in empathy as a cognitive process.

When attribution produces the impression of strong similarity between two people, empathy might rely heavily upon projection or use the self as a source of information for decentering. Berlo (1960) described an "influence theory of empathy" wherein a person makes inferences about another on the basis of a person's own prior interpretations of self. While Berlo dismissed some of the premises of the inference theory, he seemed to define empathy in terms of the ability to make predictions and develop expectations about another's internal state, behavior, and responses without concern for the basis of those predictions; thus, those predictions might be based on projection.

The predictive function of empathy affects and is affected by attribution and impression formation. Kerr and Speroff (1954) used a predictive method to assess empathy. They had subjects interact and then predict the other's responses to a number of items. Bender and Hastorf (1953) challenged the use of this predictive method because they found that subjects who viewed the target person as similar or attractive tended to project their own attitudes on the other. Hobart and Fahlberg (1965) developed a methodology for removing projection from the prediction-empathy score by counting only those items where the subjects are able to accurately predict differences between themselves and the target. However, this method includes an unlikeness bias whereby subjects who see the target person as dissimilar to themselves project negative or opposite attitudes upon the target. What all of this confusion over prediction of another's attitudes

or behaviors shows is that empathy is not a pure process and that a number of other processes are occurring, such as projection. Projection is not inherently undesirable, but measures of empathy which fail to identify, assess, and control these other processes are of limited value and utility.

Not only does empathy affect how one attributes, empathy can also affect the attributions and generalizations made about a person who is perceived as empathic during impression formation. As discussed earlier, communication competence is a quality attributed to someone who is perceived as producing empathic messages. In terms of personality, Hogan (1969) found that those who scored high on his empathy instrument were described as likeable, friendly, possessing considerable charm and tact, outgoing, warm, and very much at ease in the interpersonal situation. Grief and Hogan (1973) produced a description based upon personality instruments that correlated with their measure of empathy: "empathic persons are characterized by a patient and forbearing nature, by affiliative but socially ascendant tendencies, and by liberal but humanistic political and religious attitudes" (p. 284).

People operate on the premise that they are treated by others on the basis of how others see them; in other words, people assume adaptation by others to them. People seem to assume that the others' messages should correspond with their own self-concept and to the information they have disclosed about themselves. People's behavior toward us is supposed to reflect their image of us, but if most communication is egocentric, then this is not a very valid premise. When persons respond empathically they are implicitly sending a message about their impression of others, however accurate or inaccurate that impression might be.

EMPATHY AND RELATIONSHIP BUILDING

As trust develops between two people, self-disclosure increases, thus providing more information on which to base empathy (see Dance & Larson, 1976 for a discussion of decentering and trust). Increases in the information can potentially increase the effectiveness of empathy and decentering. But empathy can also have a positive impact on the sharing of information and the growth of a relationship. Empathic responses can advance the relationship by increasing self-disclosure, confirming the value of another, and creating a supportive communication atmosphere.

Empathy is frequently associated with the development of counseling/helping relationships. Scores of articles have been written about the importance of empathy in developing the most effective relationship between the counselor and the counselee (Gladstein, 1983; Kurtz & Grummon, 1972). The actual impact of empathy on therapeutic outcomes is unclear due to the conceptual and methodological ambiguity associated with empathy. Gladstein (1983) examined the impact of two types of empathy on various aspects of counseling; both types were strongly linked to the development of a close emotional relationship between the counselor and counselee.

The theory and research on how people gather and analyze information about another in the development of a relationship can be applied to empathy, even though no consensus exists in that research (Duck, 1985). Empathy could affect the collection and analysis of information about another in two ways: (1) motivate a person to obtain certain pieces of information to facilitate empathizing, and (2) act as the behavioral response to the information that is collected.

Knapp (1984) developed a schema for the "coming together" of a relationship. In the fourth stage of this five-stage model, Knapp observed, "Empathic processes seem to peak so that explanation and prediction of behavior is much easier" (p. 38). This statement has at least two implications for empathy. First, that empathy peaks prior to the relationship reaching the fifth stage, suggesting that empathy is necessary for a relationship to reach the highest level. Second, according to Knapp, empathy's primary role is explanation and prediction of another's behavior. This conceptualization of empathy encompasses only the self-interest and internal processing that occurs in the empathizer without regard for the impact on the recipient of empathic responses. Knapp's application of empathy to the development of a relationship does not reflect the specific effects on the recipient: confirming the recipient, validating the self-concept, demonstrating understanding, and promoting trust and self-disclosure.

EMPATHY AND CONFIRMATION/SUPPORTIVE COMMUNICATION

A case can be made that empathy is a form of confirmation by examining key elements of both concepts. Katz (1963) stated that empathic communication validates or confirms another's sense of self. Confirmation itself is seen as acceptance of the other's sense of self (Cissna & Sieburg, 1981). Acceptance of the other's sense of self would also appear to be essential to effective empathizing. Acceptance then leads to adaptation. Like empathy, confirming responses are responses adapted to the other's message (Dance & Larson, 1972). The three behavioral clusters associated with confirmation (recognition, acknowledgment, and endorsement) identified by Cissna and Sieburg (1981) also serve as viable behavioral descriptions of empathy, further supporting the premise that empathy is a form of confirmation.

Viewing empathy as confirming might explain both the desirability and impact of empathy on relationships. Empathy apparently acts in a confirming way to influence the four self-experience factors constituting confirmation: (1) the other's existence, (2) being in relation to another, (3) significance or worth, and (4) validation of another's self-experience (Cissna & Sieburg, 1981; Sieburg, 1976). In short, empathic responses help the recipients feel good about themselves. Consistent with the confirming impact of empathy, Gibb (1961) identified empathy as producing a supportive atmosphere while "neutrality" produces a defensive atmosphere.

EMPATHY AND COMFORTING/ CARING/ALTRUISM

Research has found that empathy (including affective role-taking) motivates helping behavior (Batson & Coke, 1981; Hoffman, 1981; Krebs & Russell, 1981; Underwood & Moore, 1982). Research has not produced strong evidence to support a relationship between empathy and altruism. Batson and Coke (1981) presented four studies demonstrating that empathy is associated with helping behavior but not altruism. In their review, they note a difference in the motivation and behavior of those who have a response of personal distress vs. empathy. Hoffman (1981) presented the argument that empathy produces an egoistic motivation for helping another. The argument is that a response of empathic distress leads the empathizer to seek to reduce that distress by aiding the victim, thus reducing the empathic distress. The speed of helping increases with the intensity of the empathic affect and the severity of the victim's distress, and helpful acts reduce the empathic affect more quickly than if no aid is given (Hoffman, 1981).

The weak support found in research findings for a relationship between empathy and altruism is congruent with the research findings on the relationship between empathy and comforting. Burleson (1983) found a statistically significant but moderate to weak correlation between emotional empathy and the level of comforting message strategies ($r = .31$). He claimed the reason for this low correlation might have been the methodology employed, which required subjects to remember or imagine distressed others rather than actually observe distressed others. Additionally, his measure of the levels of comforting message strategies appears to have been more an assessment of cognitive complexity.

Beyond comforting is the impact of empathy on the actual perpetration of violence. Empathy might prevent people from committing acts of violence against those with whom they empathize (Clark, 1980; Moses, 1985). The logic behind this claim is that if persons are empathizing with the target of

their potential aggression they would not be able to carry out their aggressions. Various novels, films, and television programs have been based on the conjecture of what happens when two enemies get to know one another personally and empathize with one another. The enemies are usually unable to continue to be aggressive toward each other. There are two shortcomings to this panacean theory for the elimination of violence: (1) empathy can probably be repressed or ignored, and (2) what if the empathizer is masochistic?

The most notable helping application of empathy is to therapeutic/counseling relationships. The exact role that empathy plays in these relationships is not altogether clear as was discussed earlier. The function of empathy in helping relationships is probably a combination of the other empathic functions, i.e., confirming, understanding, predicting, and reflecting.

EMPATHY AND REFLECTING

Benjamin (1969) suggested that empathy serves "as a mirror in which the interviewee can see his feelings and attitudes reflected . . ." (p. 117). In this capacity, empathy allows the target persons to hear their own ideas and feelings fed back to them. This reflective process could be a great benefit to those seeking help from another. Empathy increases the potential for accurate and complete reflection of the target person's condition. However, producing totally accurate empathic messages might not always be desirable. There is merit in inaccurate empathy as well. Inaccurate reflections might help the target persons search for the cause of the discrepancy between how they feel or think and how the empathizer is perceiving the targets' internal states. Inaccurate empathizing might promote further discussion and clarification while accurate empathizing might result in a reduction or termination of communication if mutual understanding was the motive for communicating. A danger exists when an accurate empathic message is presented without the speaker really being empathic. Some of the counseling training methods seem to ignore this danger, choosing instead to focus almost exclusively on trainees learning empathic phraseology. Empathy involves many steps which should not be shortcut. Two steps to being truly empathic which should not be shortcut are reflected in this definition by Isquick (1981): "Empathy is the ability to perceive another person's feelings and then give back in words those feelings and their meanings" (p. 2).

CONCLUSION

Little consensus exists in the conceptualization or operationalization of empathy even within the same functional contexts. Empathy could easily be considered a nonviable or invalid construct since there has been a failure to reach agreement over its very essence after years of investigation. How can empathy be defined exclusively as "affective" by one scholar while another scholar defines it as "cognitive"? The manner by which empathy has been construed parallels the old story of the six blind wise men who bumped into an elephant. Each blind man defined the elephant according to that portion of the elephant he came into contact with, thus for one wise man the elephant was like a rope (the tail), for another like a tree (the leg), for another like a snake (the trunk), etc. Like the elephant, scholars seem to be examining the various appendages of a more global phenomenon without recognizing the underlying commonalities. There has been a failure to generate new terms or use unique terms for the variety of constructs sharing the label of "empathy." The term "decentering" would work better as the global construct under which other concepts such as empathy, perspective taking, and role taking would be subsumed. Decentering does not have the variety of conceptualizations associated with it that plague empathy. Decentering is the elephant, and empathy is one of its appendages. Decentering is the process of taking into account another person's response to a given situation. Empathy would be a form of decentering that produces an affective response that is consonant with the affective state of another.

Beyond the question of terms and conceptual boundaries lie the applications and functions of empathy. Empathy clearly pervades human relations in a number of significant ways. This paper had identified some of the functions that empathy seems to play in human relationships. Empathy, in its broadest sense, is intrinsically tied to interpersonal and communication competence. Empathy's link to competence rests primarily in empathy's contribution to understanding and the making of predictions about others. Being able to understand and predict or anticipate others' reactions makes empathy a valuable skill in persuasion and compliance gaining allowing an individual to plan and adapt the most effective strategies. Empathy contributes both to the decision-making process about others and to the evaluation of that decision making. In terms of the decision-making process, empathy affects the type and scope of information that is used. Once a decision is made, empathy can be used to monitor and alter the decision-making impact. Empathy affects what information is considered about others, and thus affects the attribution process. People who, as a result of empathizing, perceive others as similar might attribute their own beliefs, values, and attitudes to those others.

Empathy is seen as contributing positively to the development of relationships, most notably helping or counseling relationships. The effects of empathy on relationships is drawn primarily from the final three functions. First, empathy produces confirming/supportive communication. Second, empathy produces helping and comforting behaviors. And third, empathy serves as a means of increasing the accuracy of reflective communication. All three of these functions focus on the impact of empathically motivated communication on another. Such communication will generally enhance the relationship and increase the effectiveness of communication.

Many of the functions identified in this paper need considerably more research before decentering's contribution is very well understood. Thus, while it is clear empathy and decentering have a strong impact on human relations, the nature of the impact, the significance of that impact, and the outcome of that impact are far from clear.

Those who seek to better understand empathy should clearly identify the functional application they are interested in and realize that the form and nature of empathy will vary according to empathy's function. Such variations in application necessitate variations in measures and explain the low intercorrelations that have been found in the past among purported measures of empathy. Scholars also need to recognize that they are not looking at many separate beasts, but rather they are looking at various appendages of an elephant named "decentering."

REFERENCES

Allen, R. R., & Brown, K. L. *Developing communication competence in children.* Skokie: National Textbook Company, 1976.

Allport, G. W. *Pattern and growth in personality.* New York: Holt, Rinehart & Winston, 1961.

Argyris, C. Explorations in interpersonal competence-1. *Journal of Applied Behavioral Sciences,* 1965, *1,* 58-83.

Barrett-Lennard, G. T. The empathy cycle: Refinement of a nuclear concept. *Journal of Counseling Psychology,* 1981, *28*(2), 91-100.

Baston, C. D., & Coke, J. S. Empathy: A source of altruistic motivation for helping? In J. P. Rushton and R. M. Sorrentino (Eds.), *Altruism and helping behavior: Social personality, and developmental perspectives.* Hillsdale, NJ: Lawrence Erlbaum, 1981.

Bender, I. E., & Hastorf, A. H. On measuring generalized empathic ability (social sensitivity). *The Journal of Abnormal and Social Psychology,* 1953, *48*(4), 503-506.

Benjamin, A. *The helping interview.* Boston: Houghton Mifflin, 1969.

Berlo, D. K. *The process of communication.* New York: Holt, Rinehart & Winston, 1960.

Berlo, D. K. Empathy and managerial communication. In C. Press and A. Arian (Eds.), *Empathy and ideology: Aspects of administrative innovative.* Chicago: Rand McNally & Co., 1966.

Bochner, A. P., & Kelly, C. W. Interpersonal competence: Rationale, philosophy, and implementation of a conceptual framework. *The Speech Teacher,* 1974, *23*(4), 37-41.

Bock, D. G., Guinaud, D. O., & Perkins, T. M. The effects of rater communication apprehension and empathy on the evaluation of the speaker: A study of cue utilization. Paper presented at the Annual Meeting of the Speech Communication Association, Louisville, Kentucky, 1984.

Borke, H. Chandler and Greenspan's "Eratz egocentrism": A rejoinder. *Developmental Psychology,* 1972, *7*(2), 107-109.

Burleson, B. R. Social cognition, empathic motivation and adult's comforting strategies. *Human Communication Research,* 1983, *10,* 295-304.

Cissna, K. N. L., & Sieburg, E. Patterns of interactional confirmation and disconfirmation. In C. Wilder-Mott and J. H. Weakland (Eds.), *Rigor and imagination: Essays from the legacy of Gregory Batson.* New York: Praeger, 1981, 253-282.

Clark, K. B. Empathy: A neglected topic of psychological research. *American Psychologist,* 1980, *35,* 187-190.

Cody, M. J., & McLaughlin, M. L. The situation as a construct in interpersonal communication research. In M. L. Knapp and G. R. Miller (Eds.), *Handbook of interpersonal communication.* Beverly Hills: Sage Publications, 1985.

Dance, F. E. X., & Larson, C. E. *Speech communication: Concepts and behavior.* New York: Holt, Rinehart & Winston, 1972.

Dance, F. E. X., & Larson, C. E. *The functions of human communication: A theoretical approach.* New York: Holt, Rinehart & Winston, 1976.

Dickson, W. P. Two decades of referential communication research: A review and meta-analysis. In C. J. Brainerd & M. Pressley (Eds.), *Verbal processes in children.* New York: Springer-Verlag, 1982.

Duck, S. Social and personal relationships. In M. L. Knapp and G. R. Miller (Eds), *Handbook of interpersonal communication.* Beverly Hills: Sage Publications, 1985.

Dymond, R. A preliminary investigation of the relationships of insight and empathy. *Journal of Consulting Psychology,* 1948, *XII,* 228-233.

Gibb, J. R. Defensive communication. *Journal of Communication,* 1961, *11*(3), 141-148.

Gladstein, G. A. Understanding empathy: Integrating counseling, developmental, and social psychology perspectives. *Journal of Counseling Psychology,* 1983, *30*(4), 467-482.

Grief, E. B., & Hogan, R. The theory and measurement of empathy. *Journal of Counseling Psychology,* 1973, *20*(3), 280-284.

Harris, T. Empathy—An essential ingredient of communication. *Management World,* January 1981.

Hobart, C. W., & Fahlberg, N. The measurement of empathy. *The American Journal of Sociology,* 1965, *70,* 595-603.

Hoffman, M. L. The development of empathy. In J. P. Rushton and R. M. Sorrentino (Eds.), *Altruism and helping behavior: Social, **personality,** and developmental perspectives.* Hillsdale, NJ: Lawrence Erlbaum, 1981.

Hogan, R. Development of an empathy scale. *Journal of Consulting and Clinical Psychology,* 1969, *33,* 307-318.

Hunter, J. E., & Boster, F. J. An empathy model of compliance gaining message strategy selection. Paper presented at the Annual Meeting of the Speech Communication Association, Minneapolis, Minnesota, 1978.

Isquick, J. F. Training older people empathy: Effects on empathy, attitudes, and self-exploration. *International Journal of Aging and Human Development,* 1981, *1,* 1-14.

Johnson, J. R., Powell, R. G., & Reynolds, E. V. Empathy: An analysis of the lack of intersubjectivity. Paper presented at the Annual Convention of the Speech Communication Association, Washington, D. C., 1983.

Jones, E. E., & Nisbett, R. E. The actor and the observer: Divergent perceptions and the causes of behavior. In E. E. Jones, D. E. Kanouse, H. H. Kelley, R. E. Nisbett, S. Valins, and B. Weiner (Eds.), *Attribution: Perceiving the causes of behavior.* Morristown, NJ: General Learning Press, 1972.

Katz, R. L. *Empathy: Its nature and uses.* London: The Free Press of Glencoe, 1963.

Keefe, T. Empathy: The critical skill. *Social Work,* 1976 *21,* 10-14.

Kerr, W. A., & Speroff, B. J. Validation and evaluation of the empathy test. *The Journal of General Psychology,* 1954, *50,* 269-276.

Knapp, M. L. *Interpersonal communication and human relationship.* Boston: Allyn and Bacon, 1984.

Kogler-Hill, S. E. The multistage process of interpersonal empathy. In S. E. Kogler-Hill (Ed.), *Improving interpersonal competence: A laboratory approach.* Dubuque, IA: Kendall/Hunt, 1982.

Krebs, D., & Russell, C. Role-taking and altruism: When you put yourself in the shoes of another, will they take you to their owner's aid? In J. P. Rushton and R. M. Sorrentino (Eds.), *Altruism and helping behavior: Social, personality, and developmental perspectives.* Hillsdale, NJ: Lawrence Erlbaum, 1981.

Kurtz, R. R., Grummon, D. L. Different approaches to the measurement of therapist empathy and their relationship to therapy outcomes. In I. M. Marks et al. (Eds.), *Psychotherapy and behavior change.* Chicago: Aldine Publishing Co., 1973 (reprinted form) *Journal of Consulting and Clinical Psychology,* 1972, *39,* 106-115.

Langer, S. K. *Mind: An essay on human feeling* (Vol. 1). Baltimore: The Johns Hopkins University Press, 1967.

Langer, S. K. *Mind: An essay on human feeling* (Vol. 2). Baltimore: The Johns Hopkins University Press, 1972.

Larson, C. E., Backlund, P. M., Redmond, M. V., & Barbour, A. *Assessing functional communication.* Urbana, IL: ERIC, 1978.

Mehrabian, A., & Epstein, N. A measure of emotional empathy: *Journal of Personality,* 1972, *40,* 525-543.

Melburg, V., Rosenfeld, P., Riess, M., & Tedeschi, J. T. A reexamination of the empathic observers paradigm for the study of divergent attributions. *The Journal of Social Psychology,* 1984, *124,* 201-208.

Moses, R. Empathy and dis-empathy in political conflict. *Political Psychology,* 1985, *6*(1), 135-139.

Redmond, M. V. Towards resolution of the confusion among the concepts "empathy," "role-taking," "perspective taking," and "decentering." Paper presented at the Annual Convention of the Speech Communication Association, Washington, D. C., 1983.

Redmond, M. V. The relationship between perceived communication competence and perceived empathy. *Communication Monographs,* 1985, *52,* 377-382.

Shantz, C. U. The role of role-taking in children's referential communication. In W. P. Dickson (Ed.), *Children's oral communication skills.* New York: Academic Press, 1981.

Sieburg, E. Confirming and disconfirming organizational communication. In J. Owen, P. Page, and G. Zimmerman (Eds.), *Communication in organizations.* St. Paul: West Publishing, 1976.

Spitzberg, B. H., & Cupach, W. R. *Interpersonal communication competence.* Beverly Hills: Sage Publications, 1984.

Underwood, B., & Moore, B. Perspective-taking and altruism. *Psychological Bulletin,* 1982, *91*(1), 143-173.

Wiemann, J., & Backlund, P. M. Current theory and research in communication competence. *Review of Educational Research,* 1980, *50,* 185-199.

17

Patterns of Interactional Confirmation and Disconfirmation

KENNETH N. LEONE CISSNA | EVELYN SIEBURG

The "interactional view" of human communication can trace its roots at least to the publication of Ruesch and Bateson's *Communication: The Social Matrix of Psychiatry* in 1951. Bateson, Jackson, Haley, and Weakland's (1956) classic article, "Toward a Theory of Schizophrenia," provided impetus to further work utilizing this view. By 1967, the perspective had emerged further; Watzlawick, Beavin, and Jackson published *Pragmatics of Human Communication* and John Weakland edited a special issue of *The American Behavioral Scientist* devoted to the "new communication," a concise summary of the interactional view. In 1969, Evelyn Sieburg initiated speech communication research at the University of Denver to examine "interpersonal confirmation," a relational construct derived from the interactional view and discussed in a general way by Watzlawick et al., (1967). During the decade since Sieburg's initial work, a body of research literature has grown up about the confirmation construct in an attempt to refine it conceptually and study it empirically in a variety of settings. Because current research in human communication reflects an increasing concern with relational communication (Parks, 1977) and the interactional view (Wilder, 1979), the concept of confirmation is receiving renewed attention from scholars in various disciplines. It is the purpose of this article to integrate what is known about confirmation by (a) explicat-

ing its theoretical bases, (b) describing specific observable behaviors associated with confirming/disconfirming response, and (c) reviewing confirmation research and considering implications for future study.

BACKGROUND

Until the last decade the term "confirmation," as it applies to human interaction, was too imprecise to form a basis for empirical study. Nevertheless it has long been regarded by many as a significant feature of human communication and has provided a useful perspective for examining social acts in terms of their impact upon other people.

The term "confirmation" was first used in an interpersonal sense by Martin Buber (1957), who attributed broad existential significance to confirmation, describing it as basic to humanness and as providing the test of the degree of humanity present in any society. Although Buber did not explicitly define confirmation, he consistently stressed its importance to human intercourse:

> The basis of man's life with man is twofold, and it is one—the wish of every man to be *confirmed* as what he is, even as what he can become, by men; and the innate capacity in man to confirm his fellow men in this way. . . . Actual humanity exists only where this capacity unfolds. (p. 102)

From Wilder-Mott, C., & Weakland, J. H. (Eds.) (1981). *Rigor and imagination: Essays from the legacy of Gregory Bateson* (pp. 253-282). New York: Praeger.

R. D. Laing (1961) quoted extensively from Buber in his description of confirmation and disconfirmation as communicated qualities which exist in the relationship between two or more persons. Confirmation is the process through which individuals are "endorsed" by others, which, as Laing described it, implies recognition and acknowledgment of them. Though Laing developed confirmation at a conceptual level more thoroughly than anyone prior to him, his focus remained psychiatric: he was concerned with the effects of pervasive disconfirmation within the families of patients who had come to be diagnosed as schizophrenic. In such families, Laing noted, one child is frequently singled out as the recipient of especially destructive communicative acts by the other members. As Laing explained it, the behavior of the family "does not so much involve a child who has been subjected to outright neglect or even to obvious trauma, but a child who has been subjected to subtle but persistent *disconfirmation,* usually unwittingly" (1961:83). Laing further equated confirmation with a special kind of love, which "lets the other be, but with affection and concern," as contrasted with disconfirmation (or violence), which "attempts to constrain the other's freedom, to force him to act in the way we desire, but with ultimate lack of concern, with indifference to the other's own existence or destiny" (1967:58). This theme of showing concern while relinquishing control is common in psychiatric writing and is an important element in confirmation as we understand it. Although Laing stressed the significance of confirmation, he made no attempt to define it in terms of specific behaviors, noting only its variety of modes:

Modes of confirmation or disconfirmation vary. Confirmation could be through a responsive smile (visual), a handshake (tactile), an expression of sympathy (auditory). A confirmatory response is *relevant* to the evocative action, it accords recognition to the evocatory act, and accepts its significance for the other, if not for the respondent. A confirmatory reaction is a direct response, it is "to the point," "on the same wavelength," as the initiatory or evocatory action. (1961:82)

In 1967, Watzlawick, Beavin, and Jackson located confirmation within a more general framework of human communication and developed it as a necessary element of all human interaction, involving a subtle but powerful validation of the other's self-image. In addition to its content, they said each unit of interaction also contains relational information, offering first, a self-definition by a person (P) and then a response from the other (O) to that self-definition. According to Watzlawick et al., this response may take any of three possible forms: it may confirm, it may reject, or it may disconfirm. The last, disconfirmation, implies the relational message, "You do not exist," and negates the other as a valid message source. Confirmation implies acceptance of the speaker's self-definition. "As far as we can see, this confirmation of P's view of himself by O is probably the greatest single factor ensuring mental development and stability that has so far emerged from our study of communication" (p. 84). The descriptive material provided by Watzlawick et al., to illustrate disconfirmation includes instances of total unawareness of the other person, lack of accurate perception of the other's point of view, and deliberate distortion or denial of the other's self-attributes.

Sieburg (1969) used the structure provided by Watzlawick as well as the concept of confirmation/disconfirmation to begin distinguishing between human communication which is growthful, productive, effective, functional, or "therapeutic," and communication which is not. She developed measurement systems for systematically observing confirming and disconfirming communication (1969, 1972); she devised the first scale which allowed for measurement of an individual's feeling of being confirmed by another person (1973). She has continued to refine the basic theory of confirmation (1975), and has recently used the concepts to describe both organizational (1976) and family (in preparation) communication systems. During this time, a growing body of theoretical development and empirical research has attempted to explore these important concerns (cf. Cissna, 1976a, 1976b).

THEORETICAL FOUNDATIONS OF CONFIRMATION: RELATIONAL COMMUNICATION

Gregory Bateson (Ruesch & Bateson, 1951:179-181) first used the concepts of "report" and "command" to distinguish two different "sorts of meaning" in communication. Watzlawick et al., (1967:51-54) interpreted these dimensions as equivalent in human communication to the "content" and "relationship" "levels of communication." The content is the "information," the "data," the "what is being talked about." The relationship level of communication provides information on what sort of message this is, how this communication is to be taken, which ultimately describes the nature of the relationship between the interactants. Both of these types of "information" are essential parts of human communication—perhaps even more than we need to know "what we're talking about," we need to know "who we're talking to" and "who the other believes us to be." The relationship level of communication involves communication about communication, and functions then as metacommunication. It provides people with information about the way in which messages are to be interpreted, and hence provides information about the current state of their relationship. Thus, the second axiom suggested by Watzlawick et al., provides the beginning point of our analysis: "Every communication has a content and relationship aspect such that the latter classifies the former and is therefore a metacommunication" (p. 54, emphasis omitted), alternately phrased by Watzlawick and Beavin (1967), "there are many levels in every communication, and one always pertains to the *relationship* in which the communication occurs" (p. 5).

At any given point in a communication sequence it is possible to identify the relationship-oriented metacommunication of one communicator as implying "This is how I see myself (in relation to you in this situation)" (Watzlawick et al., 1967:84). Human beings are always and everywhere offering self-definitions to others and responding to the self-definitions of others. These self-definitions which we offer to one another, as noted earlier, may be responded to in any of three different ways: confirmation, rejection, and disconfirmation. Confirmation communicates an acceptance of the other's definition of self. Rejection of the other's definition of self implies at least a limited recognition of the person being rejected. Disconfirmation involves negating the other as a valid source of any message.

The process of offering and responding metacommunicationally to self-definitions is apparently continuous (though there appears to be some disagreement on this issue), and occurs in both "pathological" and "normal" relationships. Perhaps, it is when these self-definitions are *not* accepted that most people become consciously aware of them—a process Carl Larson (Dance & Larson, 1976:78-79) describes as an "orientational shift" away from the content of communication and toward the relationship, especially toward the self-image which has been rejected (the term rejection as used by Larson seems to include both rejection and disconfirmation, as Watzlawick et al., use these terms).

We must recall also that these relationship messages are only very rarely coded in the digital language of communication content. It is the *analogical* or metaphorical use of human language through which the self-definitions are both offered and responded to (Bateson, 1972). Seldom does one person say to another, "I see myself as dependent on you." And seldom, too, do human beings respond to one another by overtly saying "I agree with how you see yourself in relation to me," "I disagree with how you see yourself," or "You are not a valid message source." The behaviors which we have identified as confirming or disconfirming are those that call out in the other person, relational messages which "say" "You exist," "You do not exist," "We are relating," "We are not relating," and so on. These are the covert messages which seem to have implications for how the individual sees him or her self.

BEHAVIORAL INDICATORS OF CONFIRMATION/DISCONFIRMATION

Our work with confirmation was strongly influenced by John Weakland's (1967) discussion of the "new communication." Its chief feature is a concern with the study and understanding of communication as it evolves in naturally occurring human systems, rather than with some ideal of what communication *should* be. Its primary focus is on features that characterize the interaction of pairs or groups of persons, rather than on properties of single messages or single individuals. Further, this view emphasizes that communication is central in influencing individual behavior, that it is ubiquitous, and especially that research should focus on directly observable behavior, with little if any concern about intentionality. It was this view of communication that we followed in systematizing the confirmation concept in subsequent research. The following section will explain how particular behavioral indicators of confirmation and disconfirmation were selected and systematized.

Dimensions of Confirmation

In the few direct allusions in the literature to confirmation and disconfirmation, several different elements are suggested. Confirmation is, of course, tied by definition to self-experience; our first problem, therefore, was to identify the specific aspects of self-experience that could be influenced positively or negatively in interaction with others. Four such elements seemed significant for our purpose:

1. The element of existence (the individual sees self as existing)
2. The element of relating (the individual sees self as a being-in-relation with others)
3. The element of significance, or worth
4. The element of validity of experience

Thus, it was assumed that the behavior of one person toward another is confirming to the extent that it performs the following functions in regard to the other's self-experience:

1. It expresses recognition of the other's existence.
2. It acknowledges a relationship of affiliation with the other.
3. It expresses awareness of the significance or worth of the other.
4. It accepts or "endorses" the other's self-experience (particularly emotional experience).

Each unit of response is assumed to evoke relational metamessages with regard to each of the above functions, which can identify it as either confirming or disconfirming:

Confirming	Disconfirming
"To me, you exist."	"To me, you do not exist."
"We are relating."	"We are not relating."
"To me, you are significant."	"To me, you are not significant."
"Your way of experiencing your world is valid."	"Your way of experiencing your world is invalid."

In attempting to find behavioral correlates of these functions, we acknowledge that it is not possible to point with certainty to particular behaviors that universally perform these confirming functions for all persons, since individuals differ in the way they interpret the same acts; that is, they interpret the stimuli and assign their own meaning to them. Despite this reservation about making firm causal connections between the behavior of one person and the internal experience of another, we have followed the symbolic interactionist view that certain symbolic cues *do* acquire consensual validation and therefore are consistently interpreted by most persons as reflecting certain attitudes toward them on the part of others.[1] Such cues thus have message value and are capable of arousing in the receiver feelings of being recognized or ignored, accepted or rejected, understood or misunderstood, humanized or "thingified," valued or devalued. This assumption was borne out in a very general way by our research to date (Sieburg & Larson, 1971).

Systematization of Behavioral Indicators

Although the psychiatric literature abounds with clinical illustrations of interaction that is damaging to the self-concept (especially as it occurs between parent and child), no systematization of particular forms of response according to their confirming or disconfirming power has heretofore been attempted. The primary question we set out to answer is: What specific, observable, behaviors influence others in such a way that they feel confirmed or disconfirmed? A second question (only partially answered) is: In real interaction, do these behaviors occur in recognizable clusters? A third question, not yet undertaken, must be: (a) Can these clusters be arranged along a continuum (or a hierarchy) from *most* to *least* confirming, or (b) Does confirmation comprise a distinct dichotomy, or (c) Is this construct best defined by the three states described by Watzlawick et al.? The descriptive material used in systematization of confirmation and disconfirmation was derived from many sources, each of which seemed to relate to one or more of the four functional criteria noted earlier.

Although confirmation has long been identified as crucial in forming and maintaining any human relationship, it has received the most attention in clinical or psychotherapeutic settings, particularly family therapy, and such writings provided the bulk of our material. Of particular value were the contributions of the Bateson group in Palo Alto, of Boszormenyi-Nagy and Framo in Philadelphia, of the Wynne group in Bethesda, and of Laing in London. These clinical accounts of disturbed family interaction seemed at least potentially applicable to any human interaction. It was our hope that interpersonal confirmation would prove to be another aspect of human interaction where transfer of knowledge about a disturbed population could ultimately be made to a normal one.

Systematizing Disconfirming Behavior

It should be noted that the categories of "rejection" and "disconfirmation," as used by Watzlawick et al., (1967) have both been included under our heading of "disconfirmation," thus forming a dichotomy of confirming-disconfirming acts. There are other possible "shapes" of confirmation, several of which have been used in empirical studies, as will be discussed more fully later in this article.

A variety of specific acts and omissions have been noted by clinicians and theoreticians as being damaging to some aspect of the receiver's self-view. We have arranged these behaviors into three general groupings, or clusters, each representing a somewhat different style of response:

1. Indifferent response (denying existence or relation)
2. Impervious response (denying self-experience of the other)
3. Disqualifying response (denying the other's significance)

These clusters include verbal/nonverbal and vocal/nonvocal behaviors. Since they encompass both content and process features of interaction, it meant that scorers must be trained to evaluate each scoring unit in terms of its manifest content, its transactional features, and its underlying structure. In either case, no single utterance stands alone since it is always in response to some behavior or another, and is so experienced by the other as having implications about his or her self. A summary outline of the disconfirming behavioral indicators is included in the appendix.

Disconfirmation by Indifference. To deny another's existence is to deny the most fundamental aspect of self-experience. Indifference may be total, as when presence is denied; it may imply rejection of relatedness with the other; or it may only deny the other's attempt to communicate.

1. DENIAL OF PRESENCE

The absence of even a minimal show of recognition has been associated with alienation, self-destructiveness, violence against others, and with psychosis. Laing used the case of "Peter," a psychotic patient of 25 to illustrate the possible long-term effects of chronic indifference toward a child who may, as a consequence, come to believe that he has no presence at all—or to feel guilty that he *does*, feeling that he has no right even to occupy space.

> Peter . . . was a young man who was preoccupied with guilt *because* he occupied a place in the world, even in a physical sense. He could not realize . . . that he had a right to have any presence for others . . . A peculiar aspect of his childhood was that his presence in the world was largely ignored. No weight was given to the fact that he was in the same room while his parents had intercourse. He had been physically cared for in that he had been well fed and kept warm, and underwent no physical separation from his parents during his earlier years. Yet he had been consistently treated as though he did not "really" exist. Perhaps worse than the experience of physical separation was to be in the same room as his parents and ignored, not malevolently, but through sheer indifference. (Laing, 1961:119)

That such extreme indifference is also devastating to an adult is evident in the following excerpt from a marriage counseling session (Sieburg, personal audiotape). It is perhaps significant that throughout his wife's outburst, the husband sat silent and remote:

Therapist: . . . and is it okay to express emotion?

Wife: Not in my house.

Therapist: Has he [the husband] ever *said* it's not okay to talk about feelings?

Wife: But he never *says* anything!

Therapist: But he has ways of sending you messages?

Wife: [loudly] Yes! And the message is *shut out*—no matter what I say, no matter what I do, I get no response—zero—shut out!

Therapist: And does that somehow make you feel you are wrong?

Wife: Oh, of course not wrong—just *nothing!*

Therapist: Then what is it that makes you feel he disapproves of you?

Wife: Because I get nothing! [tears] If I feel discouraged—like looking for a job all day and being turned down—and I cry—zero! No touching, no patting, no "Maybe tomorrow"—just *shut out.* And if I get angry at him, instead of getting angry back, he just walks away—just nothing! All the time I'm feeling shut out and shut off!

Therapist: And what is it you want from him?

Wife: [quietly] Maybe sometimes just a pat on the back would be enough. But, no!—he just shrugs me off. Where am I supposed to go to feel real? [tears]

2. AVOIDING INVOLVEMENT

Extreme instances of indifference like those above are presumed to be rare because even the slightest attention at least confirms one's presence. Lesser shows of indifference, however, still create feelings of alienation, frustration, and lowered self-worth. Although recognition is a necessary first step in confirming another, it is not in itself sufficient unless accompanied by some further indication of a willingness to be involved.

The precise ways in which one person indicates to another that he or she is interested in relating (intimacy) are not fully known, but several clear indications of *unwillingness* to relate or to become more than minimally involved have emerged from research and have been included in our systematization of disconfirming behaviors. Of particular significance are the use of:

- Impersonal language—the avoidance of first person references (I, me, my, mine) in favor of a collective "we" or "one," or the tendency to begin sentences with "there" when making what amounts to a personal statement (as "there seems to be . . .")
- Avoidance of eye contact
- Avoidance of physical contact except in ritualized situations such as hand-shaking
- Other nonverbal "distancing" cues

3. REJECTING COMMUNICATION

A third way of suggesting indifference to another is to respond in a way that is unrelated, or only minimally related, to what he or she has just said, thus creating a break or disjunction in the flow of interaction.

Totally irrelevant response is, of course, much like denial of presence in that the person whose topic is repeatedly ignored may soon come to doubt his or her very existence, and at best will feel that he or she is not heard, attended to, or regarded as significant. Perhaps for this reason Laing called relevance the "crux of confirmation," noting that only by responding relevantly can one lend significance to another's communication and accord recognition (Laing, 1961:87).

The most extreme form of communication rejection is monologue, in which one speaker continues on and on, neither hearing nor acknowledging anything the other says. It reflects unawareness and lack of concern about the other person except as a socially acceptable audience for the speaker's own self-listening. A less severe communication rejection occurs when the responder makes a connection, however slight, with what the other has said, but immediately shifts into something quite different of his or her own choosing.

Disconfirming by Imperviousness. The term "imperviousness" as used here follows Laing's usage and refers to a lack of accurate awareness of another's perceptions (Watzlawick et al., 1967:91). Imperviousness is disconfirming because it denies or distorts another's self-expression and fosters dehumanized relationships in which one person perceives another as a pseudo-image rather than as what that person really is. Behaviorally, the impervious responder engages in various tactics that tend to negate or discredit the other's feeling expression. These may take the form of a flat denial that the other *has* such a feeling ("You don't really mean that"), or it may be handled more indirectly by reinterpreting the feeling in a more acceptable way, ("You're only saying that because . . ."), substituting some experience or feeling of the *listener* ("What you're trying to say is . . ."), challenging the speaker's right to have such a feeling ("How can you *possibly* feel that way after all that's been done for you?"), or some similar device intended to alter the feeling expressed.

Some elements of what we are now calling imperviousness (including Laing's concept of mystification) are difficult to score empirically because they are socially approved behaviors and may be easily missed if one is attending to the content of the interchange rather than to its structure. For example, reassuring another or trying to minimize self-doubts is often thought to be useful, appropriate, and even helpful behavior, without recognizing that the self-experience of the other person is being questioned. Laing noted this problem and provided the following example of a conversation between a mother and her fourteen-year-old daughter:

> Mother: You are evil.
>
> Daughter: No, I'm not.
>
> Mother: Yes, you are.
>
> Daughter: Uncle Jack doesn't think so.
>
> Mother: He doesn't love you as I do. Only a mother really knows the truth about her daughter, and only one who loves you as I do will ever tell you the truth about yourself no matter what it is. If you don't believe me, just look at yourself in the mirror carefully and you will see that I'm telling the truth.

The daughter did, and saw that her mother was right after all, and realized how wrong she had been not to be grateful for having a mother who so loved her that she would tell the truth about herself. Whatever it might be.

This example may appear somewhat disturbing, even sinister. Suppose we changed one word in it: replace "evil" by "pretty."

> Mother: You are pretty.
>
> Daughter: No, I'm not.
>
> Mother: Yes, you are.
>
> Daughter: Uncle Jack doesn't think so.

Mother: He doesn't love you as I do. Only a mother really knows the truth about her daughter, and only the one who loves you as I do will ever tell you the truth about yourself no matter what it is. If you don't believe me, just look at yourself in the mirror carefully, and you will see that I'm telling you the truth.

The *technique* is the same. Whether the attribution is pretty, good, beautiful, ugly, or evil, the *structure* is identical. The structure is *so* common that we hardly notice it unless the attribution jars. We all employ some recognizably similar version of this technique and may be prepared to justify it. I suggest that we reflect upon the *structure* of the *induction* not only the *content* thereof. (Laing, 1969:121-123)

Many of us might identify the former as disconfirming and the latter as helpful, even confirming; however, the *structure* of the interaction process is a disconfirming one regardless of the content.

A slightly different form of imperviousness occurs when a responder creates and bestows on another an inaccurate identity, and then confirms the false identity, although it is not a part of the other's self-experience at all. Laing calls this pseudo-confirmation (1961:83). Thus a mother who insists that her daughter is always obedient and "never any trouble at all" may be able to interpret her daughter's most rebellious aggression in a way that fits the placid image she holds of her daughter, and the parents of even a murderous psychopath may be able to describe their son as a "good boy." Such a false confirmation frequently endorses the fiction of what the other is *wished* to be, without any real recognition of what the other is or how he/she feels. As noted earlier, this form of disconfirmation also appears as simply a well-meaning attempt to reassure another who is distressed, which too is usually motivated by the speaker's need to reduce his or her own discomfort.

"Don't be silly—of course you're not afraid!"

"You may think you feel that way now, but I know better."

"Stop crying—there's nothing the matter with you!"

"How can you possibly worry about a little thing like that?"

"No matter what you say, I know you still love me."

Such responses constitute a rejection of the other person's expression and often identity, raising doubts about the validity of his/her way of experiencing by suggesting, "You don't really feel as you say you do; you are only imagining that you do."

A subtle variation of the same tactic occurs when the speaker responds in a selective way, rewarding the other with attention and relevant response *only* when he or she communicates in an approved fashion, and becoming silent or indifferent if the other's speech or behavior does not meet with the responder's approval. This may mean that the speaker limits response to those topics initiated by self, ignoring any topic initiated by the other person.

Imperviousness is considered disconfirming because it contributes to a feeling of uncertainty about self or uncertainty about the validity of personal experiencing. Imperviousness occurs when a person is told how he or she feels, regardless of how he or she experiences self, when a person's talents and abilities are described without any data to support such a description, when motives are ascribed to another without any reference to the other's own experience, or when one's own efforts at self-expression are ignored or discounted unless they match the false image held by some other person.

The consequences of imperviousness have received considerable attention in the literature under a variety of labels. Laing (1965) described "mystification," meaning the substitution of a speaker's motivation as a way of exploiting the other while expressing only benevolence. Boszormenyi-Nagy (1965) described disturbed family interaction in which the "autonomous otherness" of certain family members is ignored when another member speaks for them, interpreting their motives and describing their feelings. Buber (1957) expressed it somewhat more poetically when he said, "If we overlook the 'otherness' of the other person . . . we shall see him in our own image and not as he really is in his concrete uniqueness."

Disconfirmation by Disqualification. According to Watzlawick (1964) disqualification is a technique which enables one to say something without really saying it, to deny without really saying "no," and to disagree without really disagreeing. Certain messages, verbal and nonverbal, are included in this group because they (a) disqualify the other speaker, (b) disqualify another message, or (c) disqualify themselves.

1. SPEAKER DISQUALIFICATION

This may include such direct disparagement of the other as name-calling, criticism, blame, and hostile attack, but may also take the indirect form of the sigh of martyrdom, the muttered expletive, addressing an adult in a tone of voice usually reserved for a backward child, joking "on the square," sarcasm, or any of the other numerous tactics to make the other appear and feel too incompetent or unreliable for his message to have validity. This creates a particularly unanswerable put-down by evoking strong metamessages of insignificance or worthlessness. The following examples are spouses' responses from conjoint counseling sessions:

- "Can't you ever do anything right?"
- "Here we go again!" [sigh]
- "We heard you the first time—why do you always keep repeating yourself?"
- "It's no wonder the rear axle broke, with you in the back seat!" [laughter]
- "Why do you always have to get your mouth open when you don't know what you're talking about?"

2. MESSAGE DISQUALIFICATION

Without regard to their content, some messages tend to discredit the other person because of their irrelevance—that is, they do not "follow" the other's prior utterance in a transactional sense. (This is also a tactic of indifference and may serve a dual disconfirming purpose.) Such disjunctive responses were studied by Sluzki, Beavin, Tarnopolski, and Veron (1967) who used the term "transactional disqualification" to mean any incongruity in the response of the speaker in relation to the context of the previous message of the other. A relationship between two successive messages exists, they noted, on two possible levels: (a) continuity between the content of the two messages (are both persons talking about the same subject?), and (b) indication of reception of the prior message (what cues does the speaker give of receiving and understanding the previous message?). If a message is disjunctive at either of these levels, transactional disqualification of the prior message is said to have occurred.

A similar form of message disqualification occurs when a speaker reacts selectively to some incidental clue in another's speech, but ignores the primary theme. Thus the responder may acknowledge the other's attempt to communicate, but still appears to miss the point. This "tangential response" was identified and studied by Jurgen Ruesch (1958), who noted that a speaker often picks up on a topic presented, but then continues to spin a yarn in a different direction. The response is not totally irrelevant because it has made some connection, although perhaps slight, with the prior utterance. Because it causes the first speaker to question the value or importance of what he or she was trying to say, the tangential response is reported to affect adversely a speaker's feeling of self-significance, and is therefore included as a form of disconfirmation.

3. MESSAGE DISQUALIFYING ITSELF

A third way in which a speaker can use disqualification to "say something without really saying it" is by sending messages that disqualify themselves. There are many ways in which this may be done, the commonest devices being lack of clarity, ambiguity, and incongruity of mode. These forms of response are grouped together here because they have all been interpreted as devices for avoiding involvement with another by generating the metamessage "I am not communicating," hence "We are not relating."

Systematizing Confirming Behaviors

Responses that confirm are less clearly defined than disconfirming behaviors because there has been less motivation to study them. In fact, identification of specific acts that are generally confirming is difficult unless we simply identify confirmation as the absence of disconfirming behaviors. More research in this area is clearly needed, but, in general, confirming behaviors are those which permit people to experience their own being and significance as well as their interconnectedness with others. Following Laing (1961), these have been arranged into three clusters: recognition, acknowledgment, and endorsement.

The Recognition Cluster. Recognition is expressed by looking at the other, making frequent eye contact, touching, speaking directly to the person, and allowing the other the opportunity to respond without being interrupted or having to force his or her way into an ongoing monologue. In the case of an infant, recognition means holding and cuddling beyond basic survival functions; in the case of an adult, it may still mean physical contact (touching), but it also means psychological contact in the form of personal language, clarity, congruence of mode, and authentic self-expression. In other words, confirmation requires that a person treat the other with respect, acknowledging his or her attempt to relate, and need to have a presence in the world.

The Acknowledgment Cluster. Acknowledgment of another is demonstrated by a relevant and direct response to his or her communication. This does not require praise or even agreement, but simple conjunction. Buber (Friedman, 1960) recognized this aspect when he wrote that mutually confirming partners can still "struggle together in direct opposition," and Laing (1961) made a similar point when he said that even rejection can be confirming if it is direct, not tangential, and if it grants significance and validity to what the other says. To hear, attend, and take note of the other and to acknowledge the other by responding directly is probably the most valued form of confirmation—and possibly the most rare. It means that the other's expression is furthered, facilitated, and encouraged.

The Endorsement Cluster. This cluster includes any responses that express acceptance of the other's feelings as being true, accurate, and "okay." In general, it means simply letting the other *be,* without blame, praise, analysis, justification, modification, or denial.

Confirming response is dialogic in structure; it is a reciprocal activity involving shared talk and sometimes shared silence. It is interactional in the broadest sense of the word. It is not a one-way flow of talk; it is not a trade-off in which each speaker pauses and appears to listen only in order to get a chance to speak again. It is a complex affair in which each participates as both subject and object, cause and effect, of the other's talk. In short, confirming response, like all communication, is not something one does, it is a process in which one shares.

Presented in this way, it seems inescapable that confirmation represents an idealized view of how communication "should be," rather than how it is, thus violating a principle tenet of the interactional view. Perhaps what we are discovering is that most *real* interaction involves one kind of disconfirmation or another (in varying degrees), and that confirming response exists only as an idealized counterpoint to disconfirmation.

IMPLICATIONS OF CONFIRMATION RESEARCH

In the decade since Evelyn Sieburg (1969) conducted the first "confirmation" research, we are aware of twenty empirical studies which have been reported utilizing the confirmation construct. Thirteen of these have appeared since Cissna's (1976b) review of the literature.[2]

This section will consider several aspects of confirmation research: measurement problems and implications, the relationship between agreement/ disagreement and confirmation/disconfirmation, the possible "shapes" of a confirmation model (whether it is more accurately described as a continuum, a dichotomy, a trichotomy, or a hierarchy), and generalizations from the confirmation research.

Implications for Measurement

Two primary approaches to measuring interpersonal confirmation have been used. One approach involves determining the extent to which one individual exhibits confirming/disconfirming behaviors toward another individual; the second approach involves measuring the extent to which one person *feels* confirmed or disconfirmed by another individual. While other approaches have been used on occasion (especially experimental manipulation of confirming/disconfirming responses as an independent variable), we will, in this article, concentrate on the two major strategies. As many have noted, the interactional view contains constructs that are difficult to operationalize and measure (Wilder, 1979), and this has been especially true of confirmation research.

OBSERVATION OF BEHAVIORS

Consistent with Weakland's (1967) explication of the "new communication," confirmation research has frequently focused on observable behaviors in human interaction. The earliest such observational system was developed by Sieburg (1969) and was later refined (1972). This initial effort, called the "Interpersonal Responsiveness Category System," contained five "dysfunctional" categories and two "functional" categories of response. Using expert judges, she was able to achieve a high reliability after two four-hour training sessions (Sieburg, 1969; summarized in Cissna, 1976b). She then had the judges listen to audio recordings of actual group sessions, scoring frequency of occurrence of various response types.

Sundell (1972) employed a category system based on Sieburg and Larson's (1971) response forms using the behaviors that were described as typical of most preferred and least preferred partners (these were later identified as confirming and disconfirming behaviors). More recently, Aveyard (1977) used only the seven "disconfirming" behaviors identified by Sieburg and Larson in an observational coding scheme. Mathews (1977) created and used a confirmation/disconfirmation observational system specific for librarian-patron interaction, and Hull (in progress) used a variation of Mathew's system, based on Sieburg's (1973) clusters.

Several measurement problems have been identified. Some behaviors, although noted frequently in psychiatric writings, simply did not occur often in these normal populations, especially those behaviors having to do with mystification, impersonal response, and self-disqualifying messages. Noting that these categories occurred so infrequently in the populations used, Sieburg (1969) speculated that these response forms may, in fact, be indicative of psychopathology.

Using the interactional view, the minimal unit of analysis is always the interaction—a statement and its response—which is usually operationalized as the relation of a verbalization to the immediately prior utterance. This is a useful restriction for most purposes, especially when the concern is with relevance of one utterance to the one just prior. For research purposes, it produces a simpler scoring system and increases reliability by making the unit of analysis and categories as narrow and specific as possible. However, confirming acts, and especially disconfirming ones, do not always come neatly packaged in such statement-response units. Like double-binds (Sluzki & Ransom, 1976), other kinds of disconfirming acts are not always evident in one sentence, and considerable expertise is required to recognize the often-lengthy patterns that comprise a disconfirming "act." Even if recognized, these patterns are difficult to score because scoring rules and unit of analysis often do not admit them. Further, some of the behaviors we identified above (e.g., messages which disqualify themselves or the speaker, monologue, or reliance on impersonal language, among disconfirming behaviors) do not require an "interact" for their observation at all. These can be and are observed from one person's utterance only. The interactional quality of these "messages" comes from the fact that they are *experienced* interactionally—participants *perceive* these behaviors as being related to their own behaviors and hence experience them as having something to do with their own identity. I perceive the other as responding to *me,* even if my utterances are not required for scoring the act as confirming/disconfirming.

An additional problem occurs because some individuals have difficulty recognizing forms of disconfirmation that are common in their own experience. An instance of this occurred in Sieburg's initial study in which one of her categories, "mystification," had to be dropped from the observational system because a coder could not agree with the others on what mystification was and when it happened. Several years later, Sieburg heard again from that rater, who had undergone a long period of personal psychotherapy. She reported that in the course of the therapy, she had come to realize that the mystifying response which she had been unable to identify earlier was a response form regularly employed in her childhood family—one that she had come to expect and see as "normal" interactional behavior. Similarly, some freshmen students in Jacobs' (1973) study reported being not in the least disturbed when confronted with professors who were role-playing indifferent behavior—commenting that it was about what they had come to expect from teachers!

Two additional issues regarding measurement emerge from the research. One concerns whether *all* communication events contain the power to confirm or disconfirm or whether confirming and disconfirming events occur only occasionally. That is, whether confirmation is continuous or discontinuous. Most studies have followed Sieburg (1969), assuming that all utterances contain a response to the other's definition of self and hence have confirming or disconfirming properties (Aveyard, 1977; Hull, 1979; Mathews, 1977; Sundell, 1972). Waxwood (1976), on the other hand, seems more consistent with Larson (Dance & Larson, 1976) in viewing human communication as opportunities for confirming and disconfirming events to

occur—from time to time. This issue may be more a conceptual and theoretical one that can reasonably be resolved through reference to empirical research.

A second issue is whether the coding—the determination of whether any piece of behavior is confirming or disconfirming—should be done by an outside observer or by the participants themselves. Most of the confirmation research has followed the positivistic assumption of objective and external observers who have received extensive training to perform their rating task reliably. John Stewart[3] has suggested that the participants themselves may be the more appropriate ones to define these behaviors. Waxwood (1976) used simulated recall interviews, asking participants individually to view the videotapes of themselves interacting and to identify confirming and disconfirming behaviors as well as remark on behaviors the investigator suspected might be experienced as confirming or disconfirming. Stewart suggested that the genuinely relational way to proceed with measurement is to ask participants to discuss the interaction sequences together and to agree among themselves regarding which behaviors were confirming and which disconfirming. Cushman[4] distinguished between measurement schemes which ask the participant (as in self-report scales), ones which rely on external observers, and ones which ask the participants to agree relationally on a definition of the phenomenon. While the latter seems consistent with the thrust of the interactional view, it has not yet been employed in confirmation research. It would also seem to raise the problem discussed above of (untrained) participants not recognizing certain forms of disconfirming behavior, which would not seem to lose their relational power merely because they are out of a person's awareness (Watzlawick et al., 1967:37). Each of these types of systems may well rely on different definitions of the basic phenomenon under study, and/or may tap different aspects of it. As such, there is no necessary reason these should produce highly related results. Whether this is the case remains an empirical question, posing many interesting and perplexing problems.

The indicators of both confirming and disconfirming response include vocal and nonvocal as well as verbal and nonverbal behaviors and the research is weakened if observation does not include all modes. Sieburg (1969) as well as Hull (in progress) used audiotape recordings; Sundell (1972) and Mathews (1977) used live observation; and Aveyard (1977), Waxwood (1976), and apparently Litschutz (1979) used videotapes. Live observations allow for scoring both verbal/vocal and nonvocal behaviors, but have the disadvantages of not being available for reanalysis and are generally limited to interpretation and scoring by one observer. Videotape is clearly the method of choice, and as it becomes increasingly available to academic researchers, scoring procedures can be developed to take advantage of the video-plus-audio modes, with the greater reliability of multiple coders. Refinement of the nonverbal/nonvocal aspects of the indicators may be necessary, especially with regard to congruence of modes—as when spoken words do not "fit" with tone of voice or with accompanying body movement or gesture.

While we do have coding systems for observing confirming/disconfirming behaviors, these have for the most part been developed for sample specific purposes and/or have coded only limited aspects of confirming/disconfirming behaviors. Developments regarding the appropriate unit of analysis, the appropriate locus of observation, procedures for training observers all require continued attention. Ideally, a system should allow for systematically observing and coding both confirming and disconfirming behaviors at least in dyads and small groups, from videotapes or live interaction, with appropriate adjustments made when using audiotape or transcripts.

Measuring Feelings of Being Confirmed/Disconfirmed

Scholars interested in measuring the extent to which an individual feels confirmed by another have generally used the Perceived Confirmation Scale (PCS) developed by Sieburg (1973).[5] The PCS is a six-item Likert-type summated scale. Jacobs (1973) assessed construct validity for the PCS through finding high item-total correlations for each of the six items with three target persons, and by finding that subjects *do* distinguish between target persons in their PCS scores. The interesting findings the PCS yielded (Cissna, 1975, 1979; Clarke, 1973; Jacobs, 1973; Keating, 1977; Sutton, 1976) also support its validity. Though the PCS is rather brief, its reliability seems adequate. Clarke (1973) reported test-retest (three-week interval) reliability of $r = .70$ (married couples) and Cissna (1976b) found $r = .74$ and .92 for samples of day and adult evening students describing their parents (four-week interval), though this sample produced lower test-retest reliability coefficients for same-sex friends ($r = .59$ and .50, for day and evening students respectively). The lower values for same-sex friends can be accounted for in large measure because some students simply didn't remember which friend they used a month earlier. In addition, the phenomenon itself may be changed somewhat during this interval, as student friendships can change fairly rapidly. Internal reliability was assessed through the International Communication Association Committee on the Status of Women's 1978–1979 Research Project (see Cissna, 1979). They studied 980 students and non-students from a variety of sites around the country measuring (among other things) their feelings of being confirmed by three specific people in their lives: (a) a past or present work supervisor, (b) a lover or person with whom they were or had been involved in an intimate or dating relationship, and (c) a same-sex friend. The Cronbach alpha statistics were $\alpha = .82$ (supervisors), .78 (lovers), and .75 (friends).

Serious philosophical questions can be raised, however, concerning our ability to measure perceived confirmation. Confirmation, as we have interpreted it, is derived jointly from immediately observable behaviors as well as from the existential and phenomenological reality of one's own experience. While behaviors are readily observable, confirmation as an internal experience is more difficult, deriving its validity from each individual's perceptions. Again, disconfirmation by "mystification" or imperviousness is a case in point. Laing's (1961) notions were derived from his work with the families of schizophrenic patients. He found his patients to be highly mystified (1965) and highly disconfirmed within their families (Laing & Esterson, 1964). However—and this is crucial—the very fact of mystification may cause the recipient's perceptions to become confused. *Because* they are mystified in a false self, they may experience disconfirmation as confirming (Laing, 1967). Since this kind of disconfirmation is schizogenic (Laing, 1961), it might well confound research findings since the observable behavior reported as disconfirming would not be expected to be congruent with the internal experience reported by the "victim." In other words, some forms of disconfirmation may not necessarily be available to phenomenological introspection. Further, if Laing is correct that mystification and alienation pervade our society, then perhaps many people would experience disconfirmation as confirming and would experience confirming behavior as threatening. The research problem is obvious: if disconfirmation is experienced as confirming, then measurement of the person's experience of feeling confirmed may only provide another echo of mystification.

Confirmation and Agreement/Disagreement

The confirmational effects of agreement and disagreement have been another source of confusion for researchers and theorists. Buber (1957) and Laing were clear that agreement was *not* necessary for confirmation. Laing (1969) wrote: "A partially confirmatory response need not be in agreement. . . . Rejection can be confirmatory if it is direct, not tangential, and recognizes the evoking action and grants it significance and validity" (p. 99). Watzlawick and his colleagues (1967) claim that disagreement at the *relationship* level (rather than disagreement about content) is disconfirming. The early research of Sieburg and Larson (1971) found that "agreement about content" was characteristic of their predominantly male subjects' descriptions of

their "most preferred" persons, although "disagreement about content" was not part of the response pattern of "least preferred" targets. Further empirical investigation of agreement and confirmation has been limited and directed strictly to agreement and disagreement about the content of the discussion. Sundell (1972) found agreement about content to be the most frequent response of the more confirming teachers in his sample, and the response which best distinguished the confirming teachers from the disconfirming ones. Sutton (1976) trained interviewers either to agree or to self-disclose in response to students. Contrary to her hypothesis, self-disclosure was not experienced as more confirming by the females than by the males, and agreement was not experienced as more confirming by the males than by the females. Keating (1977; Cissna & Keating, 1979) studied frequency of agreement and disagreement in discussions between married couples and found a significant negative association between frequency of disagreement and his/her spouse's level of perceived confirmation. S. Leth (1977a), although purporting to measure confirmation and disconfirmation, actually appears to have been measuring various forms of agreement and disagreement.[6] We conclude from his findings that both clear direct agreement and clear direct disagreement are both appropriate and useful (perhaps even confirming) responses in same-sex friendships.

It may be that agreement about content is irrelevant to confirmation despite confused findings. Certainly it is pleasant to have another express agreement with our opinions. So, also, is confirmation usually experienced as pleasant. We should take care, however, that these separate findings do not lead us to create a faulty syllogism: Agreement is pleasant; Confirmation is pleasant; therefore Agreement is Confirmation. Until more data are available, we must conclude that agreement/disagreement *about content* is not related to confirmation/disconfirmation. Agreement or disagreement about another's *self-view* is quite another matter, and denial, rejection, or disagreement with regard to another's self-description must always be regarded as disconfirming. "You are wrong in the way you see yourself" is clearly an impervious response.

Implications for the Nature of Interpersonal Confirmation

There are many different views of the appropriate shape of the confirmation construct. Sieburg at one time (1972) described the hierarchy of confirming responses, building on a base of recognition of the other's existence; Cissna (1976b; Cissna & Keating, 1979) explained confirmation as a continuum from highly confirming to highly disconfirming; Larson (Dance & Larson, 1976:73-90) described two states, acceptance and rejection, both of which had implicit as well as explicit forms, and a neutral area in which the orientational shift from content to relationship did not occur; Watzlawick, Beavin, and Jackson (1967) described three distinct response forms: confirmation, rejection, and disconfirmation. All of these views seem to have been offered somewhat prematurely. A confirmation-disconfirmation dichotomy seems now to oversimplify the phenomenon. For example, the troublesome "impervious response" is qualitatively different and is experienced differently from other disconfirming forms. To view confirmation/disconfirmation as a single continuum raises the problem of weights to assign to various forms of disconfirmation—a question that research has not yet even considered. There are, of course, behaviors that we can distinguish as confirming or disconfirming, and the extent to which individuals exposed to these forms actually *feel* confirmed may well range from high to low. The notion of a hierarchy, while reasonable, is still not verified with research data available. The "indifference" cluster of behaviors which totally denies the existence of the other person seems logically to be the most disconfirming; however, *imperviousness* is more frequently associated with severe pathology. Although we elected to use a dichotomous model of confirmation-disconfirmation, it may be that the three response forms described by Watzlawick *et al.,* confirmation, rejection, and

disconfirmation, come as close as any other system to representing the phenomenon as it exists. We still believe that there are distinguishable levels of interpersonal confirmation, but caution that available evidence has not identified them precisely.

Generalizations from Confirmation Research

Confirmation and disconfirmation have been studied in several ways using a variety of different measurement procedures. In spite of a lack of an essential operational definition of confirmation/disconfirmation, the findings are provocative. These findings, from the speech communication discipline concerning "ordinary" interpersonal relationships, should be considered alongside the considerable body of evidence from psychiatric studies of pathological communication processes (summarized by Sieburg, 1969, 1973, 1975).

The degree of presence or absence of confirming behaviors seems to make a difference in various kinds of human relationships—small groups (Sieburg, 1969), supervisor-subordinate (Jablin, 1977), teacher-student (P. Leth, 1977; Sundell, 1972), and friendships (S. Leth, 1977). The degree to which an individual feels confirmed as a person also is related to success in various relationships—marriage (Clarke, 1973; Cissna, 1975), health professions (Dangott, Thornton, & Page, 1979), and teaching (P. Leth, 1977). Confirming communication is experienced as pleasant and is preferred by individuals over disconfirming communication (Sieburg & Larson, 1971). Patterns of confirming and disconfirming communication are reciprocated—individuals seeming to receive what they send (Sundell, 1972). Confirming and disconfirming behaviors are identifiable by interactants (Waxwood, 1976), and experienced differently by them (Jacobs, 1973). Predominantly confirming individuals have different values than individuals who are less confirming (Mathews, 1977). Confirmation/disconfirmation is the only pattern common to participants' perceptions of their own and others' communication in marriage, father-son, supervisor-subordinate, and counselor-juvenile delinquent relationships (Ross, 1973). Confirming communication patterns may be related to development of high self-concepts (Leth, 1977).

While these findings are only exploratory and should be regarded tentatively, initial research seems to affirm the significance early theorists gave to the confirmation construct.

CONCLUSION

This article has examined the theoretical foundations of interpersonal confirmation as an aspect of relational communication. Specific behavioral indicators of confirming and disconfirming communication have been proposed, completed research has been reviewed, and conclusions have been drawn regarding the confirmation construct and the interactional view on which it is based.

It has been said that one's answers are generally limited by the horizon of one's questions. The behaviors and processes with which we have been concerned here are vital ones. Our goal now is to ask even better questions.

APPENDIX
Summary of Disconfirming Behavioral Indicators

I. Disconfirmation by Indifference
  A. Denial of Presence
    1. Silence when reply is expected; refusal to respond
    2. Looks away while other is speaking
    3. Withdraws physically; leaves the scene
    4. Engages in unrelated activities while other is speaking
  B. Denial of Involvement (relation)
    1. Avoids eye contact
    2. Avoids touch; uses nonverbal "distancing" behaviors
    3. Impersonal language; avoids "self" data, feeling statements, or disclosure of any kind
  C. Rejection by Imperviousness
    1. Monologue, repeated interruption, "talking over" other
    2. Interjects irrelevant comments
II. Disconfirmation by Imperviousness
  A. Denial, distortion, reinterpretation of other's self-expression
  B. Pseudo-confirmation
  C. Mystification
  D. Selective response
III. Disconfirmation by Disqualification
  A. Messages that disqualify the other person
    1. Direct disparagement: insult, name-calling
    2. Indirect disparagement: verbal or nonverbal
  B. Messages that disqualify another message
    1. Transactional disqualification
    2. Tangential response

C. Messages that are self-disqualifying
  1. Unclear, incomplete messages
  2. Ambiguous messages
  3. Incongruity of verbal-nonverbal modes

ENDNOTES

[1] We believe that the interactional view addressed and symbolic interactionism are complementary, and both have influenced the development of this writing. Though symbolic interactionism will not be explicitly identified in the remainder of this article, the informed reader will notice its influence at several points. See Sieburg (1973) and Leth (1977).

[2] The first author will provide a current chronological review and summary of this literature to the interested reader.

[3] Stewart made this recommendation in remarks for a "Lunch Panel" on confirmation and disconfirmation at the Asilomar Conference from which this writing originated, February 17, 1979. The authors of this article also participated in this panel, chaired by Phil Salem.

[4] Cushman's comments were made during the ensuing discussion at the Lunch Panel mentioned above.

[5] P. Leth (1977) also seems to us to have assessed perceived confirmation, though in a very different way. She asked students in an introductory speech communication class to react to their instructors' written critiques of their speeches according to five pairs of bipolar adjectives (unclear-clear, irrelevant-relevant, unrealistic-realistic, atypical-typical, and unhelpful-helpful) and one Likert-type question ("In general this critique agrees with my perception of myself as a public speaker") to which they could indicate the extent of their agreement/disagreement. These six items were summed to produce a score on the "Interpersonal Perception Scale." While the PCS asks subjects to indicate the extent to which they feel confirmed by another in general, Leth appears to have asked subjects to indicate the extent to which they feel confirmed by one specific message of the other.

[6] The issue centers around the definition of confirming and rejecting behaviors. S. Leth's (1977) study involved two separate designs, both of which share common definitions of confirmation, rejection, and disconfirmation. In the experimental design one individual is asked to self-disclose regarding a particular attribute of self and the other is taught to respond with clear, relevant agreement (called confirmation), clear, relevant, disagreement (called rejection), or a response which is neither clear, relevant, nor agreeing/disagreeing (called disconfirmation). In the descriptive, field study design, subjects are asked to indicate how they think their friend would respond to a self-disclosure by them regarding various aspects of their self-concepts using the same categories and definitions used in the experimental study. We do not believe the concepts of confirmation and rejection have been defined and operationalized in ways consistent with the definitions given by Watzlawick, Beavin, and Jackson (1967). For Watzlawick et al., as well as ourselves, the self-definitions and subsequent confirming, rejecting, and disconfirming responses are implicit metamessages, rarely explicitly coded in the digital language. In fact, it is precisely their subtle and out-of-awareness nature that gives these messages their power. S. Leth has tried to take responses to the self-concept out of the fuzzy territory of the analogic and into the clear-cut domain of the digital. His subjects have overtly disclosed an aspect of their self-concept which the other has overtly responded to. Rather than measuring confirmation and rejection as he had intended, we believe that agreement and disagreement have been measured (the operationalization of disconfirmation makes more sense to us as it is in the implicit analogic language of metacommunication). That it is the individual's self-concept which is being agreed and disagreed with is interesting and perhaps important but not sufficient to make the study into one of confirmation and rejection. When one reconceptualizes his interpersonal responses as we have done here, and regards both clear, relevant agreement and clear, relevant disagreement as confirming in contrast to the responses which lack these and are classified as disconfirming, we make different predictions than S. Leth on nine of his twenty-six hypotheses. As it turns out, all nine of these are ones in which S. Leth's predictions were not upheld. We have no difficulty whatsoever seeing rejection (as operationalized in this study as disagreement) as a valid and appropriate form of interpersonal response (cf. Leth 1978:26).

UNIT VI

Persuasion and Compliance Gaining in Personal Relationships

The three articles in the previous unit presented skills that could be used in effective relational management. The ability to persuade others or gain their compliance to a request we make is another interpersonal skill that has generated much interest among communication scholars. Unlike the previous research that has been done on persuasion in public or mediated presentations, the two articles in this unit emphasize the impact of the interactive nature of interpersonal communication on persuasion in relationships. Interpersonal communication is not a static event or even a series of static events, but rather a process in which the two participants are engaged in ongoing and mutually influential transactions. This transactional nature of interpersonal communication has a significant impact on the types of strategies available to us in gaining compliance from others.

The speech communication discipline is rooted in a rhetorical past that focused primarily on public discourse and persuasion. Rhetorical principles provided one avenue of investigation and theorizing concerning interpersonal communication, but rhetorical principles have been generated primarily by examining the situation in which one speaker attempts to influence an audience of many. The principles have not been based on a highly transactive communication context.

In article 18 Miller and Boster identify three elements of personal relationships that must be taken into account in applying persuasive principles to interpersonal communication. The three elements they identify reflect a marked difference between the persuasive situation found in a personal relationship and that found in public speaking. Those three elements are relational history, interaction opportunities, and concern for relational outcomes. The knowledge we acquire in our relational history with another can play a significant role in the interpersonal persuasive process. Included in that knowledge is how the other reacted in previous persuasive encounters. Interaction opportunities is a critical factor in interpersonal persuasive situations. The attempt to gain a particular goal from another might (and does) occur over several separate encounters. In each interaction with another we might continually adapt our approach on the basis of the other's reaction. (As teenagers you probably can remember learning the value of buttering up your parents for a few days before hitting them up for money or some other item.) Our attempts to persuade another are not limited to a one-shot presentation. Finally, Miller and Boster discuss the importance of the effect of persuasive attempts upon the relationship itself. We might gain some material objective, but it might be at the detriment of the relationship. Our persuasive attempts obviously are mediated by how important or unimportant the relationship is to us.

Garko's article (19) introduces the notion of compliance gaining. As a term "compliance gaining" can best be thought of as interpersonal persuasion. The use of this term provides a clean slate, separate from the literature on persuasion, specifically geared to the interpersonal setting. Garko, though, makes the same indictment that Miller and Boster make in regard to persuasion: the failure of the theoretical approaches to consider adequately the communicative nature of the process. Garko's primary focus is on the limitations of a variety of theoretical models of compliance gaining to take into account sufficiently the role that communication plays in an individual gaining compliance.

Garko provides a review of a variety of specific conceptual approaches that are all essentially extensions of two models: social exchange theory and power. In the social exchange approach, gaining compliance is seen as the product of a cost and reward analysis: Individuals are thought to make deliberate decisions about their actions on the basis of potential costs and rewards, and interactions are seen as mutual exchanges of costs and rewards. Power generally is viewed in terms of individuals controlling resources or having some status or power difference (derived from controlling resources). Individuals gain compliance in the power model by controlling and manipulating the resources desired by another.

Garko reviews many of the conceptual approaches to compliance gaining and then critiques each. His critiques serve to make his case for the importance of communication to the compliance-gaining process. He sees communication and compliance gaining as isomorphic; that is, they are essentially the same thing. Indeed, it is difficult to identify a form of interpersonal communication that does not have as its goal some kind of compliance gaining. Even saying "hello" as we pass a friend is usually done in order to preserve a relationship and receive confirmation from the other.

Among the approaches used to investigate compliance gaining has been that of identifying specific strategies. In article 26 by Miller and Parks you will find a list of one of the more popular typologies of compliance gaining by Marwell and Schmidt (see Table 26.3). Take a look at those descriptions after you have read Garko's article to get a clearer understanding of compliance-gaining strategies. Garko argues that such typologies oversimplify compliance gaining by classifying a dynamic process into one category when an individual might actually use a number of strategies over time, all aimed at one goal. The research that uses the typology typically asks respondents to indicate which method they would be most likely to use to gain some particular goal. Obviously, such a procedure fails to adequately take into account the transactional nature of interpersonal communication.

QUESTIONS TO CONSIDER
WHILE READING

ARTICLE 18

A. How do the three characteristics of personal relationships identified by the authors interrelate with one another?

B. What other qualities associated with interpersonal communication can you think of that might have an impact on persuasion in personal relationships?

ARTICLE 19

A. What principles or concepts are identified in the various reviews of compliance-gaining conceptualizations that might have merit in developing an overall theory of compliance gaining?

B. What commonalities are there in the weaknesses identified by Garko in his review of the conceptualizations of compliance gaining?

18

Persuasion in Personal Relationships

GERALD R. MILLER | FRANK BOSTER

As one of us has noted elsewhere (Miller, 1987; Miller and Burgoon, 1978), fields such as communication and social psychology have typically been mapped in a piecemeal, operational fashion, not by recourse to some comprehensive conceptual atlas or master plan. Consequently, problem areas have come to be defined inductively, largely in terms of the labels attached to particular research contributions and contributors. Thus, the area of 'persuasion' consists primarily of those literatures generated by persons who call themselves 'persuasion researchers'. The same can be said for the area of 'personal relationships'.

In terms of traditional scientific goals pertaining to parsimony and orderly theoretical integration, this aura of operationalistic nationalism constitutes a sad state of affairs. As it relates to the two major areas of concern in this article, the *communicative function* of persuasion and the *communicative context* of personal relationships, it has produced two massive bodies of literature, which, while clearly of great mutual relevance, have largely passed like ships in the night. Stated less metaphorically, instances of persuasion research conducted in close relational settings are extremely rare, and references to the concept of persuasion in the literature on personal relationships are equally unusual. These mutual oversights continue to exist even though no one would dispute the claim that personal relationships necessitate considerable persuasive discourse—or, to state the claim more symbiotically, that persuasion and personal relationships are inextricably bound together.

Even if we possessed the insight and imagination to accomplish the task, we could not fully integrate these two vast literatures. Our aims are thus much more modest; though if accomplished, we believe they will contribute to linking the two problem areas more closely. Specifically, we focus our major efforts on identifying three characteristics of personal relationships that distinguish them from casual acquaintanceships or transient encounters with strangers, and we consider some of the general ways that these differences affect the processes and the outcomes of persuasive transactions. Having explicated these three important characteristics of this relational context, we comment briefly but explicitly on some promising avenues for future research, comments that underscore some investigational priorities implied in our earlier remarks. Our approach throughout is both selective and critical; our objective is to accomplish a modicum of scholarly integration and to suggest promising routes for future research travels. Those seeking more exhaustive summaries of the persuasion literature may avail themselves of a number of helpful alternatives (e.g., McGuire, 1969, 1985; Miller, Burgoon and Burgoon, 1984).

Before embarking on our primary journey, however, some brief definitional comments regarding our two principal concepts are in order. The term 'persuasion' refers to attempts to modify behavior by symbolic transactions (messages). Those attempts are sometimes, but not always, linked with coercive force (indirectly coercive). Furthermore, they involve appeals to the reason and/or emotions

From Duck, S. W. (Ed.) (1988). *A Handbook of Personal Relationships* (pp. 275-288). New York: Wiley.

of the intended persuadee(s) (Miller, 1987, esp. pp. 451-2). Since the implications of this definition will become apparent as the writing progresses, two comments will suffice for now. First, the definition excludes nonsymbolic, directly coercive acts—for example spouse-beating or child battering—from the domain of persuasion, while at the same time recognizing that in the rough-and-tumble social world, persuasive appeals are often linked with coercive acts—for example *threatening* to beat a spouse or to batter a child. This distinction permits us to retain the exclusively symbolic nature of persuasion while avoiding the kind of overly rational and polite approach that Simons (1974) has critically labeled a 'drawing room controversy' view of persuasion. Second, the thrust of the definition is *relational*, i.e., it implicitly recognizes the centrality of *reciprocal influence*, rather than positing a unidirectional symbolic path from an *actor* to others being *acted upon*. As we emphasize later, this notion of reciprocity is particularly important in personal relationships.

'Personal relationships', as we conceive of the term, places a premium on developmental processes while at the same time granting that the situational context also enters into the definition (Miller, 1978). Such relationships typically involve a relatively small number of participants and are primarily, though not entirely, transacted in face-to-face encounters. Since they are characterized by frequent, extensive contact and by lengthy duration, they allow participants to achieve considerable social penetration (Altman & Taylor, 1973), to mutually 'screen' each other via a series of social filters (Duck, 1973), and eventually to relate to each other as individuals, rather than undifferentiated cultural entities or role occupants (Miller & Steinberg, 1975; Miller & Sunnafrank, 1982). Finally, as the preceding remarks imply, because participants invest considerable physical and psychic energy in personal relationships, they usually value them highly, and as a result, conflict in or dissolution of such relationships is particularly painful.

THREE RELEVANT CHARACTERISTICS OF PERSONAL RELATIONSHIPS

Most persuasion research [relies] on a one-to-many situational context. In the traditional persuasion study, a relatively large aggregate of receiver/persuadees—a classroom of students, the members of a PTA, and so forth—is exposed to a message attributed to an individual or an institutional source. With few exceptions [a] linear, unidirectional view of the 'transaction' is enforced by the fact that the message is not even presented live. Instead, the persuadees read it, or see and/or hear it on video or audiotape, a procedure that prevents any meaningful reciprocal influence by the audience. After message exposure the persuadees respond to some measure of persuasive effect, usually a paper-and-pencil assessment of attitude change. Thus, the entire enterprise closely resembles a public speaking or mass media setting, though even here the fit is far from perfect, since there is little opportunity for the kinds of audience social facilitation effects one would expect in real-life communicative settings. (Miller & Burgoon, 1978, p. 33)

This characterization of the procedures used in most persuasion research is as apt today as it was in 1978. Clearly, the traditionally dominant setting for persuasion studies bears little or no resemblance to the state of affairs in personal relationships. Although numerous differences are apparent, we will focus on three characteristics of personal relationships that are missing from the investigational milieu of prior persuasion research, characteristics that exert potentially strong influences on the persuasive exchanges of relational partners.

Relational History

We view the inevitability of conflict in personal relationships as axiomatic. Furthermore, when conflict arises in a personal relationship, there are likely to be strong pressures to resolve it quickly, since its existence has both emotional and behavioral consequences for the relational partners.

Persuasion is a commonly employed method of conflict resolution, yet most persuasion studies evidence no vestige of a relationship between persuader and persuadee(s). Indeed, in many instances, actual relationships are an impossibility because the persuasive agent is a figment of the researcher's imagination. By contrast, a relational history is both an empirical and a definitional fact of personal relationships, and since social and behavioral sciences rest largely on the assumption that past behavior affects present and future behaviors, the impact of relational history on persuasive transactions emerges as a given. We will consider some of the particulars of this impact, using as a point of contrast two divergent ways to conceive of such human symbolic activities as persuasion.

The prevalent stance taken by communication researchers, and to a lesser extent by social psychologists, views communication as a process involving considerable cognitive activity and awareness—in the more metaphorical terms of Langer (1978; Langer, Blank, & Chanowitz, 1978), as a highly *mindful* activity. Though this commitment is seldom stated in so many words, it is implicit in the kinds of research questions pursued and the practical advice offered. For example, much of the recent work dealing with the use of compliance-gaining message strategies by persuasive communicators (e.g., Miller et al., 1987; Seibold, Cantrill, & Meyers, 1985; Wheeless, Barraclough, & Stewart, 1983) seems to assume considerable awareness regarding the wide range of possible available strategies and a good deal of studied reflection about which ones to employ in specific situations. Indeed, the very term 'strategy' connotes at least some level of conscious awareness and deliberate choice.

Acceptance of this mindful view of persuasion implies that persons involved in personal relationships will be able to bring much more information to bear when selecting persuasive strategies. Because of their extensive relational history, parties to personal relationships are likely to have more idiosyncratic information about their partners, as well as considerable prior experience in exchanging persuasive messages. By contrast, casual acquaintances and strangers must largely 'commence from scratch' in their attempts to identify optimal persuasive strategies. Choosing and rehearsing of strategies re-

lies primarily on recourse to cultural and sociological generalizations (Miller & Steinberg, 1975; Miller & Sunnafrank, 1982), prior experience in similar situations, and seat-of-the-pants intuition. Granted, writers such as Milgram (1977) have noted that individuals in urban settings often fantasize extensively about the peculiar properties of 'familiar strangers'—i.e., people whom they frequently encounter physically but with whom they do not speak. Though such 'relationships' are an intriguing aspect of urban culture, any individual inferences that occur must, of necessity, be based on cultural and sociological conclusions gleaned from observation of the stranger's nonverbal and verbal demeanor when interacting with others or from direct communicative exchanges with the stranger.

At first glance, this added informational grist for the cognitive-processing mill suggests that persuaders in personal relationships should be more effective in achieving desired persuasive outcomes, for their greater knowledge about their partners should enhance their mindful quest for optimal strategies. Upon considering the matter reciprocally, the situation is not this simple because the partners, in turn, possess greater knowledge about the persuaders, thus enhancing the likelihood of successful resistance to persuasion or of effective counter-persuasive measures. Regardless of precisely how the situation is analyzed in terms of persuasive processes and outcomes, the fact remains that personal relationships offer a richer informational fabric to guide strategy selection and use.

An alternative approach to conceptualizing persuasion rests on the assumption that many persuasive exchanges are routinized, relatively *mindless* activities (Berger & Douglas, 1982; Miller, 1977). This alternative implies that parties to personal relationships may fall into habitual patterns of persuasive exchange; rather than devoting considerable conscious efforts to crafting effective messages, they may develop scripts (Abelson, 1981; Schank & Abelson, 1977) that are routinely invoked when persuasive messages are being transacted. When casual acquaintances and strangers communicate persuasively, such habitual message patterns are, of course, absent.

There is reason to believe that much interpersonal persuasion is, indeed, relatively mindless. For example, one consequence of relational conflict is that the conflicting parties are certain to experience heightened arousal. Contemporary theory and research indicates that when arousal increases, behavior becomes increasingly habitual (Bond & Titus, 1983; Zajonc, 1965). Under these conditions the conflicting parties can be expected to exhibit routine, scripted persuasive message behavior. When both parties perform in this relatively mindless way, the interaction may be described as a *scripted performance* (Abelson, 1981). Sometimes, particularly in cases when a cooperative attitude dominates the interaction, these performances contribute to a successful resolution of conflict (e.g., Brechner, 1977); in other instances, when a competitive stance dominates, scripted performances fail abjectly (e.g., Deutsch & Krauss, 1962). It is possible that the presence or absence of opportunities for the parties to save face (Goffman, 1955) is an important predictor of whether a cooperative or competitive position is adopted (e.g., J. Z. Rubin, 1980).

Some recent investigations have reported evidence of habitual, or mindless, compliance-gaining message behavior (Boster & Lofthouse, 1986; Boster & Stiff, 1984; Lofthouse, 1986). In each of these experiments participants were placed in a situation requiring them to seek compliance by another and their persuasive messages were recorded. In every instance the participants exhibited a limited repertoire of compliance-gaining message strategies. Although it is tempting to attribute this finding to the restrictiveness of the persuasive situation—participants were trying to persuade confederates to participate in a survey—alternative explanations abound. For example, most persons may have a relatively small repertoire of compliance-gaining message strategies that are learned and then used habitually. Alternatively, they may have relatively large repertoires, but the anxiety generated by seeking compliance from another may result in the ha-

bitual use of only one or two message strategies. Yet a third possibility is that arousal and the situation interact to affect persuasive message behavior. Specifically, the pairing of high arousal with available situational cues may heighten the salience of certain messages (Kahneman & Tversky, 1973) while reducing the salience of others.

We suspect that something of this nature occurred in the Boster and Lofthouse (1986) experiment. In this study the telephone calls used to solicit survey participation were placed to confederates who provided standard responses to each call. In one condition participants were told that the confederates were poor students badly in need of money. In this condition monetary appeals were used almost exclusively, with all other appeals being used infrequently. Other conditions that did not contain references to the economic need of the confederate produced a more varied set of appeals.

Even though the Boster and Lofthouse study was not conducted using parties involved in personal relationships, it suggests some factors that may be relevant in such situations. In personal relationships, a persuasive communicator might choose to use a limited range of strategies either because the issue of concern mandates certain strategies *or* because the relational partner is known to be particularly vulnerable to these strategies. Conversely, if a relational partner were known to respond moderately positively to a wide variety of strategies, all of these strategies might be utilized in the persuasive fray.

The preceding analysis suggests several important unresolved questions for persuasion researchers. How do relational partners go about gathering information about each other, and how does the relative availability of such information influence selection of persuasive strategies? What range of strategies is actually used by participants in personal relationships, and how does it compare with the range of strategies used in encounters between acquaintances and strangers? Do individual differences exist in range of strategy use, both in personal and impersonal relationships? Are *persuasive scripts* a fact of personal relationships, and if so, to what extent do they contribute to or detract from the effectiveness of persuasive transactions? Given the amount of prior attention devoted to the study of persuasion, it may seem that answers to such questions as these should be readily available. Unfortunately, examination of the current literature indicates that they have yet to be earmarked for systematic empirical study.

Interaction Opportunities

As indicated previously, the lion's share of existing persuasion research focuses on the effect of a single persuasive message transmitted in an interactional vacuum. Nothing could be more diametrically opposed to the way communication functions in personal relationships, where many messages are exchanged over time and the immediate opportunity exists for evaluative feedback, counterpersuasive messages, and compliance-resisting responses. The two situations are so dissimilar that generalization of findings from the first to the second situation is fraught with hazards. Indeed, the circumstances that prevail in personal relationships permit patterns of communicative exchange and incremental communicative strategies that are impossible to achieve in the typically designed persuasion investigation.

Consider the mundane example of a persuasive exchange between spouses regarding the plans for their next vacation. Assume that the last several vacations have been spent in the same locale and that one spouse hungers for a change of scenery. Although the discontented spouse may conceivably blurt out a demand for a new vacation site, she or he will probably seek to achieve the persuasive goal more subtly. The seeds of the idea may be sown by initiating a conversation regarding the 'grand time' some friends had at an alternative vacation spot, by 'reminiscing' about calamities the couple experienced during last year's vacation, by calling attention to an article in the travel section of the *New York Times,* or by a host of other opening communicative gambits. Once the matter has been

broached, the discontented spouse is likely to proceed through a series of messages, with the aim of the entire sequence being to achieve consensus about the desirability of choosing a new spot for the next vacation.

The ease with which such consensus is achieved will largely depend, of course, on the attitudinal posture of the partner. If he or she is quite pleased with the customary site and wishes to continue vacationing there, attempts to gain a recreational change of venue will be met with resistance. This resistance may take such forms as feigning ignorance about the underlying persuasive goal of the discontented spouse, countering negative reminiscences with positive memories, offering specific inducements to tempt the spouse to return to the familiar vacation haunt, or angrily threatening to forego a vacation if it is not spent at the traditional locale—to mention but a few of the many possibilities.

Even though we have explored this example in some detail, we have not begun to capture the richness of the persuasive dialogue associated with it. Nowhere in the current persuasion literature can one find a concerted attempt to come to scientific grips with such exchanges. The closest that scholars have come to studying them is captured by recent research in the uses of sequential strategies. These techniques create the impression that the persuasive communicator has offered a concession, yet they are effective in obtaining the other's compliance. Furthermore, all the persuasive transactants are able to maintain face rather easily.

One such sequential technique is the door-in-the-face or the reject-then-retreat technique (e.g., Cialdini et al., 1975; Even-Chen, Yinon, & Bizman, 1978; Mowen & Cialdini, 1980; Shanab & O'Neill, 1979). The results of studies examining this technique indicate that if persons do not conform with an initial large request, they become more susceptible to subsequent smaller requests. Although there are disagreements concerning the most feasible explanation for this result, the finding is consistently robust (Dillard, Hunter, & Burgoon, 1984).

Recently, Lofthouse (1986) reported an interesting application of the door-in-the-face technique. In her study, students wrote a paper and were then required to discuss its evaluation with their professor. The professor opened all discussions by asking what grade the students felt they deserved. After they had given their responses, the professor replied that she or he had read the paper and believed that it deserved a grade one level below the marks suggested by the students. Several students accepted the grade specified by the professor without argument. Subsequent interviews revealed that in a substantial proportion of these cases, the participants had employed a door-in-the-face strategy. They began with the belief that their paper deserved a 'B', but when asked, they opined that the paper merited a grade of 'A'. When the professor suggested that the paper deserved a 'B' grade, the students created the illusion of making a concession and accepted, thus receiving the grade they felt all along they deserved.

Not only is this sequential strategy effective, it produces little or no negative affect. The other party has apparently been given her or his way, and is thus happy. Moreover, the strategy renders rebuttal almost impossible. Having suggested initially that the paper merited a 'B', it would have been quite difficult for the professor to change that position and to argue for a lower grade. Cialdini likens such processes to jujitsu—a martial art in which one uses an opponent's strength to one's own advantage:

> This last feature of the process gives the profiteers an enormous additional benefit—the ability to manipulate without the appearance of manipulation. Even the victims themselves tend to see their compliance as due to the action of natural forces rather than to the designs of the person who profits from that compliance. (Cialdini, 1985, pp. 11-12)

Clearly, the door-in-the-face is not the only technique that makes rebuttal difficult. Such sequential strategies as the foot-in-the-door (Baron, 1973; Beaman et al., 1974; Foss & Dempsey, 1979; Freedman & Fraser, 1966; Rittle, 1981), in which compliance with an initial small request makes one more susceptible to a subsequent larger request,

low balling (Cialdini et al., 1978), in which the persuader induces persuadees to perform the desired action and then increases the cost of the action, the legitimization of paltry favors (Cialdini & Schroeder, 1976), in which compliance is enhanced by reducing the perceived size of the complying act, and the that's-not-all technique (Burger, 1986), in which compliance is induced by making the complying behavior more lucrative, have all been shown to be effective in increasing compliance above base rates.

Though these studies represent a step forward from the single messages common to most prior studies, they still fall far short of capturing the persuasive give-and-take occurring in personal relationships. Generally, no prior relationship exists between persuaders and persuadees; a typical procedure involves experimental confederates carrying research participants through a series of persuasive requests of ascending or descending magnitude. Such sequential techniques are undoubtedly common to personal relationships, but the interactive details are considerably more intricate.

To rectify this investigational shortcoming, persuasion researchers will need to depart radically from the procedural habits that have guided most of their research to date. Such a departure will not be simple, for it creates numerous practical and ethical problems foreign to prevailing research practices. Though the desirability of observing actual persuasive exchanges in ongoing personal relationships is easily endorsed, the process is not so readily studied in these environs, particularly if the researcher is concerned about realizing a level of control that permits relatively unambiguous isolation of independent variables. 'To seat 50 undergraduate students in a classroom and measure the impact of a written or spoken message is one thing, to "shadow" each student [or any two students in a personal relationship] as persuasive messages are exchanged in dormitory rooms, cafeterias, [and] bars—to mention but a few possible settings for such exchanges—is quite another, both pragmatically and ethically' (Miller, 1987, p. 449). Nevertheless, eventual understanding of the complex message exchanges occurring in personal relationships demands this kind of ingenuity and commitment; appreciation of the role of interaction in shaping persuasive processes and outcomes cannot be achieved by studying persuasion in interaction-free environments. Although the preceding assertion probably strikes readers as banal and commonplace, its implications remain relevant to today's persuasion researchers.

Concern for Relational Outcomes

Although there are substantial individual differences in argumentativeness (Infante & Rancer, 1982), we believe that most people are reluctant persuaders, and that they are especially reluctant to persuade those with whom they have personal relationships. Several social forces exert an influence on this reticence to persuade. For example, when we are successful in persuading others, they may capitalize on the norm of reciprocity (Gouldner, 1960) to enlist our compliance at some later date.

Generally speaking, persuasive transactions may be evaluated in terms of at least two broad outcomes: first, the relative success or failure in achieving the immediate persuasive objective; second, the effect of the transaction itself on the subsequent relationship between the persuader and the persuadee(s). Thus, a persuader may be successful in achieving an immediate persuasive objective but incur definite relational costs in doing so, such as when a parent's threats result in a child cleaning up the garage but also produce considerable hostility towards the parent. In a similar vein, Whyte (1949) discusses the frustration and tension produced when waitresses attempt to persuade countermen to speed orders.

One of our favorite examples is found in the Woody Allen film *Annie Hall*. Despite her reticence to do so, Allen hectors Diane Keaton to return to school. When she at last complies with his wish, she immediately begins to have an affair with one of her professors, at which point Allen launches an intense, humorous campaign to convince her to drop out of school:

A: 'It's only mental masturbation.'

K: 'Now there's a topic you know something about.'

A: 'Don't knock it; at least I'm making it with someone I love.'

This argument escalates quickly, and the relationship is terminated temporarily.

Conversely, a persuader may fail to realize an immediate persuasive objective but contribute to relational solidarity in the process—for example, because a person uses temperate, 'low-pressure' persuasive appeals, a close friend develops a more favorable opinion of the person's tact, sensitivity, and concern for others, even though the friend is not swayed by the persuasive message. When both broad outcomes are considered, messages that accomplish the immediate persuasive objective without polluting the relational waters are maximally effective; messages that fail in their immediate persuasive objective while concomitantly poisoning the relational waters are maximally ineffective.

A dramatic example of the latter situation was pointed out to us recently by Michael Burgoon (1987). An employee of a large chemical firm contracted a fatal, job-related disease. Interviews obtained from the employee and his family revealed three important items of information: first, despite his illness, the employee remained very committed to both his job and the company; second, other members of the employee's family expressed strong negative feelings towards both the job and the company; and third, the employee and his family were not on the best of terms. Taken together, these three items of information may seem odd, but subsequent questioning clarified them by revealing the following segment of relational history.

For years the employee's relatives attempted to persuade him to resign and to find a less hazardous job. Placed in the position of having to defend his daily departure to work, the employee contended that he held an excellent position at the chemical company and that he intended to keep working there. When he became ill, members of the family increased the frequency and intensity of their persuasive attacks. Accustomed to defending the company, the employee increased the intensity of his own messages. It was at this point that the interviewers uncovered the information summarized in the preceding paragraph.

Students of persuasion will recognize immediately that the family had put the employee in a natural counterattitudinal advocacy experiment (Festinger, 1957; Miller, 1973; Miller & Burgoon, 1973). Quite probably the employee was not so positive towards the chemical company initially, but because he was placed in the long-standing role of company advocate, he persuaded himself to adopt more strongly pro-company attitudes. Conversely, the employee's family engaged in a similar self-persuasion exercise and developed more negative attitudes towards the company. Finally, the constant conflict engendered by their persuasive exchanges produced ill-will between the employee and his family.

This anecdote illustrates several of the previously discussed features of persuasion in personal relationships. First, the communicators are concerned with persuading their target(s); second, their persuasive exchanges have consequences for the development of their relationship; and third, each of the communicators must be prepared to respond to messages from their persuasive target(s). Each of these features has important implications for the generation, selection, and production of persuasive messages, and we shall next briefly consider some of these implications.

If persuasive messages affect relational outcomes, it is reasonable to contend that the partners will both experience and develop an awareness of this process. This argument provides the justification for several experiments examining the impact of relational intimacy and the duration of relational consequences on compliance-gaining message choices (e.g., Cody, McLaughlin & Schneider, 1981; Kaminski, McDermott, & Boster, 1977; Lustig & King, 1980; Miller et al., 1977; Roloff & Bar-

nicott, 1978, 1979; Sillars, 1980b). Generally, these studies have reported nonsignificant findings, and when the results have been statistically significant, the effect sizes have been relatively small (Hunter & Boster, 1979; Jackson & Backus, 1982). It should be stressed, however, that all of these studies asked respondents to role-play persuaders in hypothetical situations and to indicate the likelihood that they would use particular strategies. For reasons that we will detail later, we believe that hypotheses about actual use cannot be tested fairly and powerfully using this role-playing procedure.

Not only may relational outcomes be influenced by the kinds of persuasive message strategies that are employed, the escalation and deescalation of personal relationships may themselves emerge as immediate persuasive objectives. Personal relationships grow at least partly because the parties are mutually oriented towards persuading each other to invest more commitment and resources to the relationship. Conversely, a number of researchers (e.g., Baxter, 1979, 1982; Baxter & Philpott, 1982; Cody, 1982; Miller & Parks, 1982; Wilmot, Carbaugh, & Baxter, 1985) have conceived of the dissolution of personal relationships as a persuasive process and have examined the effectiveness of various kinds of persuasive strategies in furthering this process. Seldom are relational outcomes themselves a primary persuasive aim of persuaders in impersonal settings; at most, the persuasive communicators may seek to create the *illusion* of relational escalation or deescalation in order to further other immediate persuasive objectives.

Indeed, in terms of the two broad persuasive outcomes identified above, people will assign differing values to them depending upon the nature of the particular relationship. Though it would be inaccurate to portray casual acquaintances and strangers as totally unconcerned about the relational consequences of their persuasive exchanges, it seems fair to say that such concerns usually are much greater in personal relationships. As noted earlier, personal relationships involve major investments by the participants. From a social exchange perspective (Blau, 1967; Homans, 1961; Thibaut &

Kelley, 1959) these relationships normally yield greater endogenous rewards than impersonal encounters, and relational friction or breakdown can result in substantial endogenous and exogeneous costs—for example, a troubled marriage often exacts its toll both in the increased stress encountered in the relationship itself and the social disapproval communicated by significant others, the latter frequently being sufficiently threatening that the troubled parties strive valiantly to 'keep up a good front' even though they are experiencing great discord.

By contrast, persuasive communicators in casual acquaintanceships and transient encounters with strangers are more likely to perceive that they have little to lose relationally by marshaling all the persuasive weapons at their disposal in order to achieve their immediate persuasive objective. Hence, they will probably be less reluctant to use punishment-oriented strategies (Miller et al., 1977; Miller & Parks, 1982), to communicate deceptively (Miller, Mongeau, & Sleight, 1986), and to use other aversive and unethical strategies. Indeed, in such extreme relational circumstances as blackmail and confidence games, the persuasive means employed to achieve the immediate objective of economic gain manifest utter contempt for the potential relational implications.

While the preceding discussion makes good theoretical and intuitive sense, it is couched in conditional language because of the dearth of empirical evidence bearing on the issues. Most persuasion studies are concerned solely with assessments of relative success in achieving some immediate persuasive objective: attitudinal and/or behavioral conformity with message recommendations is the stock-in-trade dependent measure of persuasion researchers. Given that these studies have been conducted largely in a relational vacuum, this focus is hardly surprising; it makes no sense to be concerned with relational outcomes in the absence of viable relationships. To return to a familiar lament, however, it also seems foolhardy to place much trust in the generalizability of findings obtained in such a setting when seeking to explain and to understand how persuasion functions in personal relationships.

Once the importance of considering relational outcomes has been established, it becomes obvious that credibility may often be an important persuasive *end* in itself, rather than merely a functional *means* to some immediate persuasive objective. Because of the lack of any ongoing relational context, most prior persuasion research has treated credibility as 'an antecedent, independent variable which influences subsequent persuasive outcomes, rather than a *persuasive outcome* worthy of study in its own right' (Miller & Burgoon, 1978, p. 34, their italics). In personal relationships, many transactions aim primarily at enhancing the credibility of the communicators—or, to invoke a conceptual label more common to the study of personal relationships, such exchanges seek to enhance the communicators' *interpersonal attractiveness*. To acknowledge this fact does not deny the frequent instrumental value of being perceived positively in personal relationships. As with their impersonal counterparts, highly credible communicators in personal relationships are likely to be more successful in achieving their persuasive objectives. Nevertheless, in most personal relationships, communicators devote considerable persuasive energy to *selling themselves* (Miller & Burgoon, 1978), and while there have been some useful lines of research dealing with factors influencing credibility formation in impersonal settings (e.g., Baker, 1965; Giles & Powesland, 1975; Giles & Street, 1985; Jones, 1964; Miller & Hewgill, 1964; Norton, 1983a; Sereno & Hawkins, 1967), much work remains to be done on this process of self-advocacy, particularly as it is practiced in personal relationships.

Taken together, the three characteristics of personal relationships discussed above illustrate the need for bold methodological and procedural departures in future persuasion research. If researchers hope to solve the puzzle of persuasion in personal relationships, they must begin to scrutinize actual persuasive exchanges in these relational settings instead of relying on results based on single-message, large-audience settings, or on the use of hypothetical scenarios that ask respondents to *act* as persuasive *role-players* rather than to *behave* as persuasive *communicators*. Though such an investigational change of course will not be accomplished easily, its achievement is of crucial import for students of persuasion in personal relationships.

IMPLICATIONS FOR FUTURE RESEARCH

As we have stressed repeatedly, few studies have probed the processes and outcomes of persuasion in personal relationships. Although studies have examined, albeit usually indirectly, such issues as the persuasiveness of various message characteristics and strategies, the effect of message choices on relational development, and the effect of message strategies on rebuttal, we are not aware of any study that has investigated this entire set of issues. Furthermore, many studies dealing with these issues are designed and executed inadequately. Because of these limitations, we shall sketch some alternative directions for future studies of persuasive exchanges between persons involved with personal relationships.

To begin with, we have already noted that most studies examining the effects of such variables as relational intimacy and duration of relational consequences on selection of message strategies have employed self-report, role-playing measures. Although we believe that such measures often provide useful information, caution must be exercised in this instance. Hunter and Boster (1987) have shown that ratings obtained for the Marwell and Schmitt (1967) strategies, the typology employed most frequently by researchers studying strategy selection, are unidimensional. Several authors have argued that the single dimension tapped by the strategies is verbal aggression (Boster, 1985; Dillard & Burgoon, 1985; Hunter & Boster, 1987). If so, past research may be reinterpreted to suggest that relational intimacy and duration of relational con-

sequences have little impact on people's verbal aggressiveness in persuasive transactions. Notwithstanding this possibility, verbal aggression is only one dimension of persuasive message behavior, and relational intimacy and duration of relational consequences may well exert effects on other relevant dimensions.

A powerful test of this possibility necessitates an experiment that controls for relational intimacy, duration of relational consequences, or both, while observations of persuasive messages are being made. Whether these observations are made in a controlled or a natural setting, they are necessary before it will be possible to make informed statements about the effects of relational intimacy or duration of relational consequences on actual selection and use of persuasive message strategies.

Scudder (1986) offers of a clue regarding how such an experiment might be performed. He varied the power of participants in a car buying/selling simulation, observed the frequency of various types of threats, and arrived at the impact of the various threats on economic outcomes. An extension of this study that controls for relational intimacy and adds a measure of relational affect would provide useful data for examining issues associated with strategy selection. Even if the persuasive situations were simulated, it would be helpful if the participants consisted of partners in personal relationships.

Alternatively, discourse-analytic techniques could be used to examine transcripts of the persuasive exchanges of persons in compatible and incompatible relationships so as to determine what differences, if any, exist in the persuasive appeals and strategies that are employed. This approach has proved useful in uncovering differences between effective and ineffective negotiations (Donohue & Diez, 1985). Of course, such data must be interpreted cautiously, since causal order is always questionable; the question can be raised as to whether persuasive message behavior causes or is caused by relational development.

Third, as the Burgoon example illustrates, traditional persuasive research concerns are not entirely irrelevant to persuasion in personal relationships. Just as Hovland (1959) underscored with regard to experimental and survey studies of attitude change, there are important differences between passive and active communicative contexts, and we have emphasized several of them. One important additional difference is that actual exchanges typically result in much shorter messages than the kinds of message stimuli that have been employed in passive communicative context studies; when interaction is permitted, long messages are apt to be interrupted. This feature of persuasive message-making in personal relationships may lessen, or even negate, the import of message variables such as certain aspects of organization. Nevertheless, numerous other variables, including fear appeals, logical appeals, humor, and message discrepancy, are excellent candidates for investigational scrutiny.

A CONCLUDING DISCLAIMER

As we reflect on the tone of this piece, we realize that some readers may conclude we have a pessimistic view of the current state of persuasion scholarship. Nothing could be further from the truth; indeed, we believe that the knowledge generated by persuasion researchers constitutes one of the more useful bodies of literature in communication and social psychology. Moreover, the early research on persuasion was purposefully designed to be conducted in large audience settings (Miller, 1987); one is hard pressed to criticize researchers for not solving problems they did not set out to solve.

Two issues do, however, give us cause for concern. First, as noted earlier, our scrutiny of persuasion research and research dealing with interpersonal communication reveals little overlap to the present time. It is no exaggeration to suggest that many view these two areas as conceptually distinct, if not as opposite ends of a continuum. If this chapter succeeds in causing readers to modify this viewpoint and to begin investigating persuasive transactions in interpersonal contexts, then it will have served a useful purpose.

Second, we are less than sanguine about the ecological validity of persuasion experiments conducted primarily in passive communicative contexts, at least as the issue of validity relates to personal relationships. The complexities generated by interaction and by the transactants' relationship render suspect the assumption that the findings of prior persuasion studies can be translated directly to face-to-face, intimate settings. While our position on this issue may be a source of gloom for some readers, we assume a more optimistic posture. Persuasion in personal relationships is a topic ripe for study, and one which, in our opinion, seems certain to yield an abundant harvest.

19

Perspectives on and Conceptualizations of Compliance and Compliance-Gaining

MICHAEL G. GARKO

Scholars have offered a number of different conceptualizations of compliance and compliance-gaining which reflect broader competing perspectives. While there have been attempts to synthesize and clarify the empirical literature on compliance-gaining, there has been little attention devoted to reviewing critically perspectives and conceptualizations focusing on persuaders attempting to get persuadees to do what they want. A review of the theoretical literature reveals that scholars have frequently developed their conceptualizations of compliance and compliance-gaining from a social exchange or power perspective. It is shown how these two perspectives are manifested in the empirical research, especially those studies focusing on factors affecting strategy selection. The argument is made that conceptualizations and empirical studies reflecting these perspectives typically push communication into the background and reward/cost and power principles into the foreground of the compliance-gaining process. Studies on teacher power in the classroom are provided as examples of how it is possible to adopt a power perspective and not undercut the role of communication in the gaining of compliance.

Various writers have commented on the scattered and chaotic nature of the social influence literature.[1] Cartwright (1965), for example, argues "that there is no single body of literature on influence but instead a collection of discrete and more or less independent literatures concerned with various aspects of influence, such as leadership, attitude change, conformity, persuasion, communication, social learning, and socialization" (p. 3).

The scholarship on compliance mirrors the overly diversified and disordered landscape of the social influence literature. Theoretical and empirical studies of compliance-gaining, for example, span across a variety of disciplines (e.g., communication, management, psychology, social psychology, and sociology) and contexts (i.e., interpersonal, small group, organizational, and mass communications). At the same time, empirical studies appear under a number of competing conceptual umbrellas such as persuasion, power, and social influence. This conceptual diversity makes the compliance literature theoretically confusing and empirically murky.

Scholars have attempted to synthesize and clarify the empirical literature on compliance-gaining. Recent reviews and commentaries have focused on the following: 1) taxonomic classification of strategies and tactics, 2) source and situational indicants of strategy selection, 3) methodological procedures for studying the strategic choices potential persuaders make when getting others to do what they want, and 4) general state-of-the-art of compliance-gaining research (e.g., see Boster, 1989; Garko, 1988; Kipnis, 1976, 1984; Kipnis & Schmidt, 1983; Podsakoff, 1982; Seibold, Cantrill, & Meyers, 1985; Wheeless, Barraclough, & Stewart, 1983). These efforts to bring coherence to the empirical literature on compliance-gaining have been useful. Yet, little systematic treatment has been devoted to scholars' theoretical views about the process agents engage in when attempting to get targets to do something that they want. This article seeks to overcome this

From Garko, M. G. (1990). Perspectives on and conceptualizations of compliance and compliance-gaining. *Communication Quarterly,* 38(2), 138-157.

gap in the literature by reviewing and analyzing prominent perspectives on and conceptualizations of compliance and compliance-gaining.[2]

Although the primary focus will be on the theoretical literature, brief attention will be devoted to how a social exchange and power perspective are manifested in empirical studies illustrative of the research on factors affecting agents' choices of compliance-gaining strategies (e.g., Boster & Stiff, 1984; Burgoon, Dillard, Doran, & Miller, 1982; Clark, 1979; Dillard & Burgoon, 1985; Williams & Boster, 1981). Consideration will also be given to a series of important studies focusing on the role of teacher power where communication and power are viewed as closely interrelated (see Kearney, Plax, Richmond, & McCroskey, 1984, 1985; McCroskey & Richmond, 1983; McCroskey, Richmond, Plax, & Kearney, 1985; Plax, Kearney, McCroskey, & Richmond, 1986; Richmond & McCroskey, 1984; Richmond, McCroskey, Kearney, & Plax, 1987).

According to Fisher (1978), "knowledge of any reality depends on one's observing/interpreting it" (p. 58). That is, whatever we know or can know of a phenomenon depends on our interpretation of that phenomenon. That interpretation depends, in turn, on the perspective we use to interpret. "And part of our perspective includes the 'set' or conceptualization we have of the event as it occurs" (p. 58). Therefore, the way in which scholars come to understand and conceptualize the process of compliance-gaining is ultimately a function of the perspective adopted to observe the process. In short, since perspectives and conceptualizations are interdependent, a greater sense of coherence and insight can be brought to the theoretical literature by examining conceptualizations of compliance and compliance-gaining within the framework of the perspectives underpinning them.

PERSPECTIVES

Two theoretical perspectives have shaped scholars' conceptualizations of compliance and compliance-gaining: 1) a social exchange perspective based on

an economic model, and 2) a power perspective based on a resource model. There are numerous versions of each perspective. Yet, several broad observations apply to all of them.

I will argue that the social exchange and power approaches to compliance-gaining share some of the same concepts (especially resources and power) and are vulnerable to the same criticisms. However, this should not be construed to mean that the two perspectives do not differ in important ways. On the contrary, the social exchange and power perspectives represent distinguishable influences on how the phenomenon of compliance has been conceptualized. For example, although the social exchange approach accommodates the "power" construct, it makes assumptions and invokes principles that proponents of a pure power perspective tend to ignore. Moreover, the concept of power serves primarily as a variable in the social exchange view whereas with the power perspective this concept functions as an overarching framework for the study of compliance-gaining.

Social Exchange Perspective

Social exchange theory blends concepts from classical economics and behavioristic psychology. Proponents of social exchange have provided psychological interpretations of such marketplace concepts as "commodity," "gain," "cost," "price," and "profit."

Broadly speaking, social exchange theory attempts to explain human interaction in terms of exchanges that may include a variety of resources (commodities). It focuses specifically on the mutual exchange of rewards (gains) and punishments (costs) between interactants. A reward is any preferred resource that meets a person's needs or reduces his/her drives and inspires interaction. Costs are the inverse of rewards; they discourage exchanges. Profit in an interaction is defined as rewards minus costs.

At least three assumptions are made in social exchange theory. First, it is assumed that individuals are motivated by self-interest in their interactions; that is, they seek to maximize their rewards and minimize their punishments. Second, it is assumed that people make choices based on a rational calculation of rewards and costs associated with alternative choices. A third assumption is that choices are constrained by the amount of control (i.e., power) individuals have over the balance of rewards and costs. Kiesler (1978) argues that social exchange theory is not only a theory involving decisions people must make but also a theory about their power, "where power is defined as the ability to control or influence the rewards and costs of oneself and others" (p. 127).

ECONOMIC EXCHANGE MODEL OF COMPLIANCE-GAINING[3]

King (1975) points out that "the economic exchange analogue or explanation for interpersonal influence has been suggested by many theorists" (p. 58) such as Blau (1964), Homans (1961), Nord (1969), and Thibaut and Kelley (1959). Investigators adopting a social exchange perspective to the study of social influence treat compliance as a potentially profitable or costly outcome for either the agent or target. The economic exchange model of compliance-gaining proposes that agents initiate influence attempts and targets comply in order to maximize rewards and minimize costs. The agent is typically characterized as possessing resources (i.e., power bases to effect compliance) that he/she will trade for compliance, while the target is portrayed as trading compliance for need-related resources. Compliance represents the target's primary resource. The "price" is the amount of compliance the agent will accept in trade for his/her resources that are rewarding to the target. The agent's "cost" is the amount of resources utilized to gain compliance, while the target's "cost" is the degree of compliance the target will give up in order to obtain the desired resource(s). The level of "profit" or "loss" for the agent and target is a function of the extent to which each has maximized his/her rewards and minimized his/her losses.

EVALUATION OF SOCIAL EXCHANGE

Bochner (1984) offers a critical treatment of reward/cost explanations within the context of relationship development that is applicable to the study of interpersonal influence. He identifies three flaws.

First, "reward/cost principles are tautological" (Bochner, 1984, p. 578). Normally, reward/cost explanations cannot be falsified. It is too difficult to determine a priori what is a reward. What may be rewarding to one may be punishing to another. Thus, reward/cost principles often result in circular and retrospective explanations that are incapable of falsification.

Second, "reward/cost principles attempt to reduce the irreducible" (Bochner, 1984, p. 579). Social exchange theorists suggest that the outcomes of such irreducible processes as communicating, influencing, and organizing can be adequately explained by principles of individual functioning, that what an individual brings to an interaction or influence relationship (e.g., resources, needs, motives, predispositions) will determine what will occur after the interaction or relationship begins. According to Bochner (1984), "this not only runs counter to principles of systems—the part cannot control the whole—but also establishes a fixed, individualistic perspective as a causal force in the evolution of dynamic, interdependent processes" (p. 579).

Third, "reward/cost principles oversimplify complex developmental processes by implying that the same system of logic—the rational calculation of rewards and costs—operates at all levels (stages) of development" (Bochner, 1984, p. 579). Compliance-gaining is a dialectical process of development that ebbs and flows, cycles and recycles, and generates contradictions and inconsistencies in social influence relationships (see Benson, 1977, and Wozniak, 1975, on the dialectical perspective). Yet, reward/cost principles suggest that influence develops mechanistically, where agents and targets rationally calculate their rewards and costs for the maximization of gains and the minimization of losses.

In sum, while the metaphor of the marketplace may provide insight into why people interact, it is insufficient to explain how the compliance-gaining process works. Reward/cost principles lack the explanatory power to tell an agent how to make a compliance-gaining attempt rewarding, what to do, what to say, or how to say it. How an agent communicates may play a large role in whether an influence effort will be successful (i.e., rewarding) or unsuccessful (i.e., costly). In short, the compliance-gaining process cannot be adequately explained by an individual's needs, motives, predispositions, or resources. The ebb and flow of communication that occurs between participants during an influence transaction must be taken into account.

Power Perspective

The concept of power has been a dominant force in the study of social influence and compliance. Wheeless, Barraclough, and Stewart (1983) typify how scholars perceive the relationship between power and compliance-gaining. They argue that "the securing of adherence, conformity, cooperation, or obedience—compliance—is not only the manifestation of exercised power, it is the very reason for the existence of power" (p. 121).

RESOURCE MODEL OF POWER

Most social influence theorists adopting a power perspective assert that an agent's ability to exercise influence and gain compliance depends on his/her control over resources (Cartwright, 1965). Kipnis (1976) offers one way to classify resources. He broadly distinguishes between *personal resources* (e.g., intelligence, status, physical strength, communication skills, relationships, etc.), which reside in the individual and *institutional resources* (e.g., weapons, legitimacy of role, economic and legal capabilities, etc.), which the powerholder has available to him/her.

An agent's base of power is often referred to in the literature as "all of the resources—opportunities, acts, objects, etc—that he can exploit in order to effect the behavior of another" (Dahl, 1957, p. 203). Thus, an influencer's base of power can be a blend of personal and institutional resources. For example, "some of the possible bases of a President's power over a Senator are his patronage, his constitutional veto, the possibility of calling White House conferences, his influence with the national electorate, his charisma, charm, and the like" (Dahl, 1957, p. 203).

The resource model of power requires that an agent's base of power be exercised through some means of influence (i.e., compliance-gaining strategies and tactics). Therefore, the base of power refers to what (i.e., resources) is used to influence, while the means of influence indicate how power bases are carried out to gain compliance. If a President wished to use the earlier cited power bases over a Senator, then "the means would include the promise of patronage, the threat of veto, the holding of a conference, the threat of appeal to the electorate, the exercise of charm and charisma, etc." (Dahl, 1957, p. 203).

A resource model of power, then, assumes that (a) without resources there is no power, (b) the target is resource-dependent, (c) as the target attributes more value to the resources the target's dependency and the agent's power rise and (d) once the target decides that the agent's resources are no longer valuable, the potency of the agent's power and the ability to influence diminish.

In sum, with a power perspective based on a resource model it becomes axiomatic to view compliance-gaining as coterminous with power (i.e., the control of resources valued by others). In order to induce compliance, the agent must invoke his/her resources (i.e., bases of power), which may be personal and institutional in nature, and transform them into some actual method of influence.

EVALUATION OF THE POWER PERSPECTIVE

A power perspective based on a resource model possesses at least three deficiencies. The first two are similar to criticisms lodged against the social exchange perspective.

First, a power perspective based on a resource model reduces the process of influence (i.e., compliance-gaining) to principles of individual functioning. The model suggests that the resources an agent brings to a compliance-gaining situation, and not the communication between the agent and target, will determine an outcome of compliance or non-compliance. In essence, the power perspective shifts communication into the background and resources into the foreground of the compliance-gaining process.

Second, the resource model of power oversimplifies the compliance-gaining process. It suggests that the way in which individuals go about getting their way is always an intentional, rational, and unidirectional process, where the agent (a) consciously creates a plan to influence the target, (b) surveys and selects the appropriate resource(s) paying particular attention to the target's resource-needs, and (c) gains compliance when the correct resource or the combination of resources is chosen and presented in strategic or tactical form. In compliance-gaining episodes, however, agents do not always have a well-conceived strategic plan either because they have a tendency to act on impulse or because the situation demands a spontaneous effort. Moreover, they may not have an extensive set of resources from which to choose, even if they do, there is no guarantee that they will elicit compliance from the target.

Third, a power perspective relying on the exercise of resources limits our understanding of the relationship between power and influence. It views the relationship between power and influence as one-way, with power as a necessary condition to gain compliance. While power can lead to influence, the exercise of successful influence (i.e., gaining compliance) can also make one powerful. Moscovici (1976) reminds us that "if power presupposes influence, and is in part a result of influence, we cannot possibly consider it as the *cause* of influence. It cannot be both cause and effect" (p. 62).

In extending his argument, Moscovici (1976) has proposed that the study of social influence should be conducted independently of power. I do not agree. Recent reviews (e.g., Berger, 1985; Wheeless et al., 1983) clearly show that power is an important consideration in the study of social influence. However, whether power operates in the way suggested by the resource model is open for debate. For example, there are individuals who are powerful (i.e., control resources) but are unable to elicit compliance, while there are those who are not powerful but are capable of influencing others. The resource model of power is inadequate in explaining such occurrences, because it assumes that compliance is mechanically predetermined by an agent's control over resources. What individuals say to one another and how they say it during the course of an influence attempt may provide further insight into how the compliance-gaining process works.

Summary

At least two perspectives on compliance-gaining emerge from the literature: 1) a social exchange perspective and 2) a power perspective. The social exchange approach emphasizes the mutual exchange of rewards and costs between interactants. Self-interest, rationality, and control are three assumptions of the social exchange perspective.

Scholars adopting a social exchange view of compliance-gaining rely on an economic exchange model of social influence in which compliance is seen in terms of an outcome reflecting a profit or loss. Each participant in the compliance-gaining episode tries to maximize his/her rewards and minimize his/her losses. The agent will trade resources for the target's compliance, while the target will give compliance for desired resources.

Three criticisms surround reward/cost principles. First, they are tautological. Second, they attempt to reduce interpersonal processes to principles of individual functioning. Third, they oversimplify complex developmental processes.

A power perspective also utilizes the concept of resources in the form of the resource model of power. One of the primary assumptions of the model is that an agent's ability to gain compliance is linearly tied to his/her control of personal and/or institutional resources. The resources constitute the agent's bases of power, which are exercised through compliance-gaining strategies. In order to gain compliance, then, the agent must invoke his/her resources. As the target's need for and value of the resources rises so do the chances of the agent getting his/her way.

The power perspective based on a resource model has three deficiencies. First, it reduces the compliance-gaining process to principles of individual functioning. Second, it oversimplifies the compliance-gaining process. Third, it treats the relationship between power and influence in a unidirectional, linear fashion, with power construed as the cause of influence.

CONCEPTUALIZATIONS

All of the conceptualizations presented in this section, to varying degrees, reflect the social exchange and power perspectives presented above. Etzioni (1975) and Wheeless et al. (1983) rely more on the power perspective than Kelman (1974) and Miller and Steinberg (1975), who primarily enlist reward/cost principles. King's (1975) conceptualization is a synthesis of power and reward/cost elements. Those writers utilizing power to shape their conceptualizations emphasize the resource model and view power as a necessary prerequisite to influence.

One of the important differences among these conceptualizations concerns the emphasis given to communication processes. On the one hand, Etzioni (1975) and Kelman (1974) fail to discuss the role of communication explicitly in the compliance-gaining process. On the other hand, King (1975), Miller and Steinberg (1975), and Wheeless et al. (1983) directly consider communication. King and Wheeless et al., nevertheless, ironically push communication into the background of compliance-gaining episodes, in that they see the agent's power as the prime and most fundamental element in getting one's way with another. As it will be seen, these

writers (whether intentionally or not) conceive communication between the agent and target as merely a way to implement power to gain compliance.

In this section five conceptualizations of compliance will be examined that implicitly or explicitly contain a view of what constitutes the process of compliance-gaining. Each conceptualization is followed by a critical evaluation.

Etzioni

Etzioni (1975) casts his theory of compliance within an organizational context. He characterizes organizations (i.e., social units pursuing specialized goals) as compliance structures. According to Etzioni, such organizational features as specificity, size, complexity, and effectiveness underscore the need for compliance.

Etzioni (1975) defines compliance as "a relationship consisting of the *power* employed by superiors to control subordinates and the *orientation* of the subordinates to this power" (p. xv) [emphasis added]. Power is an agent's ability to induce or influence a target to carry out his/her directives or any other supported norms. Orientation refers to the target's degree of commitment or alienation relative to the agent's power. Thus, compliance is the result of the relationship between those who possess power and those over whom it is exercised. A compliance relationship is, according to Etzioni, asymmetric in that the agent always has more power than the target.

What distinguishes an agent's power are the physical, material, and symbolic resources on which it is based. The resources are manipulated in such a way that the target will find compliance rewarding and noncompliance costly. Etzioni (1975) identifies three types of power bases and the means to exercise them:

(1) *coercive power*-compliance achieved through the application or threat of application of physical sanctions such as infliction of pain, deformity or death; restriction

of movement; control of basic needs such as food, sex, comfort, etc.

(2) *remunerative power*-compliance achieved through the allocation of material resources and rewards such as salaries, wages, commissions, and contributions, fringe benefits, services, and commodities.

(3) *normative power*-compliance achieved through the allocation of symbolic rewards and deprivation.

    a. *pure normative power*-compliance achieved through the manipulation of esteem, prestige, ritualistic symbols like a flag or benediction.

    b. *social power*-compliance achieved through the allocation and manipulation of acceptance and positive responses.

Etzioni (1975) contends that pure normative power is most useful because superiors can exercise it directly down the hierarchy.

In review, the concept of power is essential to Etzioni's (1975) approach to compliance, organizations, and the relationship between the two. The organization is a compliance structure based on the control of physical, material, and symbolic resources. These resources make up an agent's base of power, which can be exercised in the form of coercive, remunerative, or normative power, respectively. Compliance is the outcome of the relationship between powerful superiors, who control resources and exercise their power over less powerful subordinates, who respond to superiors' power with more or less alienation or commitment.

EVALUATION

Etzioni's (1975) power approach to compliance suffers from at least three weaknesses. First, it assumes that power is a necessary condition for the exercise of influence and the gaining of compliance, making the relationship between power and influence unidirectional. Second, it views the relationship between an agent and target (i.e., superior and subordinate) as asymmetric with the agent having more power and influence than the target. Thus, the compliance relationship becomes dependent rather than interdependent. Third, it relies on a static model of power and influence where interaction is assumed but not analyzed. In short, Etzioni's conceptualization of compliance features a linear, individualistic perspective to explain the process of compliance-gaining.

Kelman

Kelman's (1974) conceptualization of compliance is better understood and evaluated when examined within the context of his overall theory of social influence. He says that social influence occurs when a target changes his/her behavior due to an agent's exercise of "induction techniques" (i.e., influence strategies). The influence strategies communicate a behavior to be adopted and the probable effects adoption will have on the target's achievement of his/her goals.

Kelman (1974) distinguishes three processes of social influence:

(1) *compliance*-target publicly conforms in order to achieve a favorable reaction from the agent (i.e., gain rewards and avoid punishments).

(2) *identification*-target publicly and privately conforms in order to establish and maintain a desired self-defining relationship with the agent.

(3) *internalization*-target publicly and privately conforms in order to maintain congruence between the induced behavior and values.

Antecedent conditions characterize each process. Compliance occurs when (a) the target focuses on the effect of his/her behavior, (b) the agent's power is based on means-control (i.e., control over psychological and material resources on which the target's goal achievement depends), and (c) the induction strategies limit the target's choices. Identification occurs when (a) the target focuses on the social anchorage of his/her behavior, (b) the agent's power is based on his/her interpersonal attractiveness (i.e., qualities making a relationship with agent desirable), and (c) induction strategies delineate requirements of a role relationship in which the target's self-definition is anchored. Internalization occurs when (a) the target focuses on the value congruence of his/her behavior, (b) the agent's power is based on his/her credibility (i.e., expertness and trustworthiness), and (c) induction strategies reorganize the target's thinking about paths toward maximizing his/her values.

Kelman (1974) argues that the three influence processes link a target to a social system (e.g., an interpersonal relationship). They allow the target to meet the demands of a relationship thereby protecting the target's integration in it. Kelman identifies a specific linking component for each process:

(1) *compliance*-links through system rules specifying behavioral requirements.
(2) *identification*-links through system roles providing self-definition for the target.
(3) *internalization*-links through system values shared by the target.

In sum, Kelman (1974) views social influence as induced behavior change that can occur on a public and private level through three processes. A set of antecedent conditions characterize the processes. All three processes serve to link the target to the social system.

EVALUATION

Kelman (1974) limits the concept of compliance and the process of compliance-gaining. Within his scheme, compliance can only occur when (a) a target publicly conforms in order to maximize rewards and minimize costs, (b) an agent's power is based on means-control, (c) an agent's influence strategies limit the target's behavioral choices, (d) a target is integrated into a social system through rules or norms, and (e) a target conforms to follow system standards.

Compliance-gaining situations, however, are more dynamic. They may involve targets publicly and privately complying to realize rewards, establishing a relationship with an agent (identification), or sustaining axiological balance (internalization). Other bases of power, for example, those associated with identification and internalization, may be just as salient in compliance-gaining episodes as are an agent's means-control. Further, compliance-gaining attempts do not always limit a target's choices. Sometimes they enhance them. In a compliance-gaining situation, a target is integrated into a rela-

tionship through communication, which involves rules, roles, and values. Finally, agents quite often initiate influence and targets conform not to follow standards of a relationship and thereby maintain the status quo, but to change a relationship, even at great risk.

King (1975) develops his conceptualization of social influence and compliance within a communication framework. He vigorously argues that communication and influence are isomorphic processes, sharing the attributes of being (a) transactional, (b) inevitable results of social situations, (c) receiver oriented, and (d) contextual. Moreover, both processes occur simultaneously:

> The concept of social influence includes all instances in which the behavior of one person induces changes in the state of another person. To do so, however, the behavior of the first individual must be attended to and have meaning attached to it by another, which is the minimal condition of communication. Therefore, all social influence involves communication. Similarly, as communication inevitably results in the alteration of the state of the individual perceiver, all communication involves social influence. (King, 1975, p. 15)

King (1975) identifies normative social influence (NSI) as a major form of influence. NSI is divided into the subprocesses of NSI outcome control and NSI cue control.

NSI outcome control is "manipulative" and "instrumental." It is manipulative because an agent is consciously attempting to influence. It is instrumental because a target complies in order to gain rewards and avoid punishments. Thus, NSI outcome control is an agent's ability to affect a target's outcomes, with the target trading compliance for rewards.

NSI cue control, like NSI outcome control, is manipulative and instrumental but in different ways. It is manipulative in that an agent intentionally influences, but compliance is not mediated by the agent's control of resources desired by the target. Instead, the agent provides a cue that elicits a pre-established disposition that is intrinsically self-rewarding to the target. "The person influenced views the influence as instrumental; he complies with the activated disposition in order to be consistent with himself" (King, 1975, p. 84).

King (1975) postulates that power represents the potential for influence, and influence is the outcome of actualized power. Thus, power functions as an antecedent condition to the gaining of compliance, whether the context involves NSI outcome or cue control.

In terms of NSI outcome control, King (1975) contends that power resides implicitly in the target's dependency. Unless the target perceives the agent "as capable of controlling resources he values, influence will not occur" (King, 1975, p. 66). The agent has power in the exercise of NSI cue control when he/she has knowledge of the target's dispositions.

In sum, King (1975) develops his conceptualization of social influence and compliance based on communication, reward/cost, and power principles. He sees communication and influence (i.e., NSI outcome and cue control) as isomorphic and simultaneous processes that "defy linear description." NSI based on outcome control reflects a form of social exchange where compliance is traded for some valued resource. NSI cue control is exercised when the agent provides cues that elicit predetermined responses. Power is a necessary condition in the eliciting of compliance based on outcome and cue control. Compliance in NSI outcome control stems from the agent's control of resources and the target's dependency on those resources. Compliance in NSI cue control stems from the agent's awareness of target predispositions and the target's desire to maintain cognitive balance.

EVALUATION

King (1975) argues that communication and social influence are irreducible, dynamic, nonlinear processes and that communication is essential to influence processes (e.g., NSI outcome and cue control) and gaining compliance. Paradoxically, King's approach to social influence ultimately leads to a reductionistic and linear interpretation of the compliance-gaining process and to de-emphasizing the function of communication in the process. This observation is based on his use of a linear power model and reward/cost principles.

More specifically, King's (1975) approach reduces compliance-gaining to principles of individual functioning. It is what the agent and target bring to the influence setting and not the communication between them that will specify whether there will be an outcome of compliance after the interaction begins. With NSI based on outcome control and NSI based on cue control, the essential component in achieving compliance is the agent's power, which is brought to the interaction in the form of resources (NSI outcome control) or knowledge of the target's predispositions (NSI cue control). Thus, power becomes the part that controls the whole, the whole being the compliance-gaining interaction between the agent and target. King (1975) reveals the extent to which his conceptualization reduces compliance-gaining to the control of power (i.e., resources) when he says that ". . . in order to determine another's outcomes, the person exerting influence must control the other's attainment of valued goals; that is, he must have power" (pp. 52-53). In other words, compliance-gaining is equivalent to the trading of compliance for resources that are rewarding.

King's (1975) characterization of the role of power in influencing others suggests that compliance-gaining is a linear event, where the agent's power is the stimulus and the target's compliance is the response. In other terms, it could be said that the relationship between the agent and target is one of "interpersonal dependence." In explaining what he calls "actual power," King (1975) clearly describes the influence relationship between the agent and target in linear terms. He comments that "one person can control another's attainment of a valued goal or resource, virtually independent of, or in spite of, the other's thought or action. In other words, regardless of what the target feels, thinks, or does, the person controlling the resource can help or hinder in the target person's attainment of goals" (p. 68). Possessing such power, the agent can go on to gain compliance from the target, and "the only question in such cases is the target's evaluation of the costs and rewards involved in the exchange" (p. 68).

In sum, King (1975) unintentionally undermines his own persuasive argument calling for a transactional perspective of social influence by relying on the resource model of power and reward/cost principles. In fact, King himself points to the equivocal and circular nature of reward/cost principles. He states that the hedonistic assumption of people seeking to maximize rewards and minimize costs "can never be put to adequate empirical test and must, therefore, be accepted or rejected on the basis of faith or personal experience" (King, 1975, p. 59). The practice of social science and inquiry in general requires, however, more than faith and personal experience to verify or disconfirm theoretical principles.

Miller and Steinberg

Miller and Steinberg (1975) synthesize their conception of compliance into their control perspective of interpersonal communication. They define communication as an intentional, transactional, symbolic process, where at least one communicant transmits a message with the purpose of modifying another's behavior. In other words, people communicate to influence-to affect with intent. Within Miller and Steinberg's scheme, "intent to communicate and intent to influence are synonymous" (p. 35).

The basic function of communication, according to Miller and Steinberg (1975), is to control (i.e., influence) the environment in order to realize certain preferred physical, economic, or social rewards. The control function involves communicants making predictions about the effects or outcomes of their communicative strategies, and choosing those strategies based on what they know (i.e., data) about how the receiver of the message will respond. A person has successfully controlled the environment when he/she has influenced to the extent that at least some correspondence is achieved between desired and obtained outcomes. In short, people communicate in order to maximize their rewards and minimize their costs.

Since a person's ability to control the environment depends to a great extent on the willingness of others to comply with the person's message strategies, compliance is an important communicative function. Compliance, as a level of environmental control, occurs when there is an exact correspondence between a communicator's desired and obtained outcomes. When there is a compromise of one's original objectives, Miller and Steinberg (1975) call this level of control conflict resolution. The only requirement is that the competing parties reach an equitable solution about the allocation of some physical, economic, or social rewards.

In sum, people communicate to influence-to affect with intent. The basic purpose of communication is to control the environment to achieve rewards. In other words, to control the environment is to influence through communication. People control or influence the environment when they match to some degree what they want with what they get. Compliance results when desired and obtained outcomes correspond exactly. Conflict resolution occurs when the interactants arrive at a solution that is perceived by the competing parties as equitable.

EVALUATION

One of the useful features of Miller and Steinberg's (1975) scheme is their view that communicating and influencing, as well as influencing and controlling, are synonymous processes. Given the inextricable connection Miller and Steinberg draw between communicating and influencing and controlling it can be inferred that compliance-gaining, as a form of communicative control, is a process exercised intentionally, transactionally, and symbolically.

From a communication perspective, this aspect of Miller and Steinberg's (1975) approach is appealing, because it shows the importance of communication in eliciting compliance and makes compliance-gaining a dynamic communication process. However, there are two limitations of Miller and Steinberg's conceptualization. First, compliance occurs by definition only when the agent achieves exactly what he/she desires or needs. Seldom are an individual's desired and obtained outcomes matched. Moreover, the absence of a mirror image between what an agent wants and what he/she gets, does not necessarily imply a conflict. Second, Miller and Steinberg's thinking about communication and compliance are to a great extent based on reward/cost principles and, thus fall prey to the criticisms of the social exchange perspective discussed above.

Wheeless, Barraclough, and Stewart

Wheeless et al. (1983) contend that the most useful way to use the term "compliance" is to have it refer to "the performance by one person, the target, of specific behaviors desired of the target by another person, the agent" (p. 110). The agent decides what target behaviors would be desirable. He/she attempts to persuade the target to perform the sought-after behaviors through compliance-gaining strategies and tactics. Although attitudes may be present as determinants of behavior, compliance is a behavioral and not an attitudinal result of persuasive communication. In short, compliance "refers simply to target performance of agent-desired behavior(s), whether an intervening cognitive (or other) process is present or not" (Wheeless et al., 1983, p. 111).

Wheeless et al. (1983) offer a clear explanation of what they mean by compliance-gaining. "Gaining" means "eliciting" while "compliance" refers to a response that would not have otherwise occurred except for the agent's presentation of a stimulus or stimuli to the target. Specifically, compliance-gaining behavior is the communication behavior (i.e., strategies and tactics) used to elicit agent-selected behavior from the target. In short, compliance-gaining behavior is the inducement for behavioral conformity.

According to Wheeless et al. (1983), the compliance-gaining process is best conceptualized as the implementation of power (i.e., the perceived bases of control the agent has over the target's behavior). While power represents the potential for exercising influence, compliance serves as the manifestation of that potential. Wheeless et al. (1983) liken the relationship between power and compliance to one of a trunk and branch of a tree. Just as a branch cannot exist without a trunk, the gaining of adherence, conformity, cooperation, or obedience (i.e., compliance) does not occur unless the agent has power. In other words, power presupposes influence.

An agent's bases of power (i.e., bases of control) are the reasons or inducements contained within compliance-gaining tactics. A compliance-gaining tactic is "a verbal message unit that explicitly or implicitly proposes a behavior and provides a reason or inducement through using a power basis that has potential control over behavior that would not have otherwise occurred" (Wheeless et al., 1983, p. 114).

Although not directly stated by Wheeless et al. (1983), it can be inferred from their discussion that the reasons or inducements found within compliance-gaining tactics are the resources comprising the agent's power bases. It can be further inferred that the target is induced to comply because he/she values and desires the resources controlled by the agent.

In sum, Wheeless et al. (1983) argue that compliance is an outcome of power and compliance-gaining the exercise of power. It is the agent's power bases embodied in compliance-gaining tactics that motivate the target to comply. The power bases serve as forms of control over the target. In effect, Wheeless et al. view power as a prerequisite to compliance.

EVALUATION

Paradoxically, while they recognize that compliance-gaining tactics operate as verbal message units, Wheeless et al. (1983) ultimately relegate communication to an ancillary role in the compliance-gaining process. They attribute the success or failure of a compliance-gaining attempt to the agent's bases of power. Communication in the form of compliance-gaining strategies and tactics functions to implement power. In other words, Wheeless et al. assume that the power an agent brings to the interaction of a compliance-gaining situation solely determines what will occur after the interaction begins. Thus, their perspective emphasizes power and pushes communication into the background.

Summary

The conceptualizations examined above serve as examples of how investigators have utilized reward/cost and power principles to develop models for research on compliance and compliance-gaining. Generally, writers reflecting a social exchange perspective (i.e., Kelman, 1974; King, 1975; Miller & Steinberg, 1975) view compliance as an outcome that will result in the maximization of rewards and the minimization of losses. The agent is characterized as being in control of resources that he/she will trade for compliance, while the target, who is resource dependent, emerges as a figure trading compliance for valued resources. Thus, the compliance-gaining process essentially represents an exchange of resources that are rewarding to the agent and target.

Resources also play a major role in the power approach. Power, embodied in the agent's resources, is treated in the conceptualizations as an antecedent and necessary condition to elicit compliance. Proponents of the power perspective, therefore, view the process of compliance-gaining as the exercise of power and compliance as an outcome that would not have otherwise occurred if not for the resources constituting the agent's power bases.

DISCUSSION

Fisher (1978) reminds us that "the perspective one uses to view any phenomenon determines to no small extent what aspects of that phenomenon are considered to be significant or relevant and conversely, which aspects are deemed trivial and irrelevant" (p. 60). It is clear that scholars adopting a social exchange or power perspective to develop their conceptualizations of compliance and compliance-gaining do exactly what Fisher suggests. That is, they emphasize certain conceptual elements and ignore others. For example, a considerable amount of attention is devoted to such concepts as costs, rewards, resources, and power, but little focus is given to communication. This is not to suggest that either perspective is devoid of utility in the study of compliance-gaining because it deemphasizes communication and highlights reward/cost or power principles. As Fisher points out, every perspective suffers from being incomplete or distorted in some fashion.

Nevertheless, the position taken in this essay is that the social exchange and power perspectives, while useful, are inadequate. Both perspectives lead to conceptualizations that potentially undercut communication functions in the process of compliance-gaining. They do this essentially by viewing compliance-gaining as a control phenomenon. With both perspectives, the agent's power serves as the instrument to predict and control the target's behavior. If the agent possesses resources desired by the target or has knowledge of the target's predispositions and the target makes the attribution that the agent is powerful, then the odds are good that the agent will succeed in getting the target to do what he/she wants. Thus, the outcome of a compliance-gaining attempt is reduced to the control of resources (i.e., power) and to psychological processes, where the focus is on what is happening inside the agent and target not on the interaction.

The social exchange and power perspectives are not only reflected in conceptualizations of compliance and compliance-gaining; they are also represented in empirical studies on compliance-gaining, especially those studies focusing on source and situational factors affecting choice of influence strategy. In terms of the social exchange perspective, the notion of reward/cost is found in studies exploring the effect of *benefit to self* (e.g., Boster &

Stiff, 1984; Burgoon, Dillard, Doran, & Miller, 1982; Clark, 1979; Dillard & Burgoon, 1985; Williams & Boster, 1981) and *benefit to other* (e.g., Boster & Stiff, 1984; Dillard & Burgoon, 1985; Hunter & Boster, 1979; Marwell & Schmitt, 1967; Williams & Boster, 1981) on the selection of compliance-gaining message strategies. In these studies researchers examine whether an agent's strategy choices are affected by the extent to which the agent perceives that personal benefits (i.e., rewards) can be gained from the target's compliance or by the degree to which the agent perceives that the target's compliance is in the target's best interest.

In terms of the power perspective, a number of studies focus on the effect of an agent's power on his/her selection of compliance-gaining strategies (e.g., Kipnis, 1972, 1976, 1984; Kipnis & Cohn, 1979; Kipnis & Cosentino, 1969; Kipnis & Lane, 1962; Kipnis & Schmidt, 1983). There are also studies examining the effect of a target's power on an agent's choice of strategy to gain compliance (e.g., Erez & Rim, 1982; Kipnis & Schmidt, 1983; Kipnis, Schmidt, & Wilkinson, 1980; Rim & Erez, 1980). When investigators focus on how strategy selection varies as a function of a target's power, the term "power" frequently refers to the target's status. Higher status means more resources which means more power for the target. Whether focusing on the effect of the agent's or the target's power, all of these studies explicitly or implicitly rely upon the resource model of power described earlier.

The cited empirical research employing concepts and principles from either the social exchange or power perspectives has enhanced our understanding of the compliance-gaining process, particularly that part of the process involving strategy selection. Yet, while studies such as these attempt to study compliance-gaining communication as a means of influence, they ironically underplay the role of communication as a dynamic process in the gaining of compliance. Similar to what occurs in conceptualizations stemming from a power or social exchange perspective emphasis is put on psychological principles of individual functioning and on the control of resources (i.e., power), all of

which reinforces a noninteractive and linear approach to and rendering of compliance-gaining.

There have been, however, empirical studies simultaneously adopting a power perspective and attempting to stage communication in the foreground of compliance-gaining situations. For example, there are a series of seven studies focusing on how teachers use power in the classroom to gain compliance from students (see Kearney, Plax, Richmond, & McCroskey, 1984, 1985; McCroskey & Richmond, 1983; McCroskey, Richmond, Plax, & Kearney, 1985; Plax, Kearney, McCroskey, & Richmond, 1986; Richmond & McCroskey, 1984; Richmond, McCroskey, Kearney, & Plax, 1987). The view adopted in these studies is that "in the usual classroom environment communication between teacher and student, both verbal and nonverbal, is a constant, ongoing process" and that "the use of power in the classroom requires communication" (Richmond & McCroskey, 1984, p. 125). In all seven studies power and communication are viewed as inextricably connected to the extent that "in the absence of communication . . . the teacher in the classroom is powerless" (McCroskey & Richmond, 1983, p. 175). It is assumed that teachers must earn their power with students and this can only be achieved through communication. According to McCroskey and Richmond (1983), "the way(s) the teacher communicates with her/his students to a major extent determine the type and extent of the power he/she exerts over those students. Similarly, the type of power exerted will have a major impact on the quality of teacher-student communication" (pp. 175-176). In sum, the "power in the classroom" studies are concerned with the communication of power as well as the power of communication.

In contrast to the other empirical investigations cited above adopting a power perspective, the "power in the classroom" studies treat communication as fundamental to the gaining of compliance. Communication is not just assumed to play a role in compliance-gaining nor is it conceived as being simply a vehicle to present strategically the resources associated with various bases of power.

Instead, communication is viewed as being ultimately responsible for any outcomes stemming from a compliance-gaining attempt because power requires communication. Although a teacher may control certain bases of power (e.g., coercive, reward, legitimate, referent, or expert), student compliance is not automatic. "The impact of teachers' use of power in the classroom on student learning is mediated by the students' perceptions of that power use" (McCroskey & Richmond, 1983, p. 183), and those perceptions are shaped by communication and not the control of resources (i.e., power).

Palazzoli-Selvini, Boscolo, Cecchin, and Prata (1978) have argued that it is epistemologically inaccurate to view the agent's power as controlling (i.e., causing) the behavior of the target. Power is in the rules of the game, which cannot be altered by the participants of the game (Palazzoli-Selvini et al., 1978). Extending this idea, Bochner concludes (1988), "if the rules are changed so are the 'attributions' about who holds power, who is weak or strong, and how a victimizer can also be a victim" (p. 4). As Palazzoli-Selvini et al. (1978) suggest, the agent and target form a relational system in which they function as elements in a circuit of interaction. Being members of that circuit, neither one has unidirectional power over the other, the relationship, or the interaction, that is the whole. Each member in the compliance-gaining circuit simultaneously influences and is influenced by the other. Thus, causality is circular and not linear and power and compliance are a function of the communication and the relationship between the agent and target and not the control of resources.

What is being called for in this paper is movement away from intrapsychic portrayals emphasizing control and de-emphasizing communication. Rather than viewing compliance-gaining as a function of power it can be conceptualized as an outcome of a transaction that is exercised symbolically. Compliance-gaining, as a form of influencing, is isomorphic with and inseparable from communicating (see discussion on King and Miller & Steinberg).

Such a view suggests several ways in which investigators can advance the empirical study of compliance-gaining. The agent and target in a compliance-gaining situation proactively make symbolic choices. While the agent is selecting message strategies to gain compliance, the target is surveying the interaction and invoking strategies either to resist or support the agent's attempt. To date, however, the primary focus has been put on the agent's strategic message choices. The target is rarely studied in terms of making strategic choices resisting the agent's attempt (see McLaughlin, Cody, & Robey, 1980, for an exception) or supporting it.

Relatedly, a small number of studies have reported findings on compliance-gaining strategy mix (e.g., Kipnis & Schmidt, 1983; Perrault & Miles, 1978). Most investigators treat compliance-gaining as a single-strategy undertaking. They ignore the possibility that agents can invoke a range of message strategies and tactics in the process of getting the target to do something they want. Even more ignored is the idea that targets can also use a mix of strategies to resist or support a compliance-gaining attempt.[4] In short, compliance is infrequently achieved by an agent or resisted by a target with an influence message repertoire consisting of one strategy.

Oftentimes it also takes more than one sequence of interaction (i.e., episode) to gain compliance. Because of intense target resistance an agent may not succeed on the first try in getting the target to do what he/she wants. Thus, an effort to gain compliance might require several attempts spanning across several different points in time. Typically, however, compliance-gaining is studied as a one-shot phenomenon rather than as an episodic event.[5] It would be worthwhile to study the extent to which agents and targets vary their strategies across episodes. It might also prove useful to examine the strategic maneuvers and counter-maneuvers of agents and targets within a given sequence of interaction. Yet, most studies isolate one point in the transaction instead of on the entire sequence of interaction constituting a compliance-gaining episode.[6]

An interactional perspective brings attention to the Batesonian postulate that every message has a report and command dimension, where the former conveys information about *what* is communicated, that is the content of the message, and the latter provides information about the *way* the message is communicated. In their efforts to study the compliance-gaining process, investigators have put the emphasis on the what (i.e., content) and not on the how (i.e., style) of compliance-gaining strategies. It is important to have a change in focus because as Norton (1983) observes, "our workaday world so graphically reveals that it is often not what you say but how you say it that makes a difference" (p. 228). Such a principle would certainly apply to agents and targets communicating in compliance-gaining situations. For example, the way an agent communicates his/her influence strategies could make a difference in whether a target complies. At the same time, the way a target communicates could influence an agent's choice of strategies and the way he/she would communicate those strategies, specifically, or communicate, generally. In a recent study of managerial compliance-gaining, Garko (1988) found that the way a target communicates makes a significant difference in the kinds of compliance-gaining strategies managers select.

In sum, it is my view that the interaction between an agent and target is the lowest common denominator in determining compliance. How agents communicate their influence messages and how targets interpret and respond to those messages is at the root of any useful attempt to explain the compliance-gaining process. Focusing on the interaction through transactional and systemic principles can inspire conceptualizations that move communication from the periphery to the center of the compliance-gaining process and can foster studies that not only assume communication but observe or analyze it directly.

ENDNOTES

[1] I would like to express my appreciation to Arthur P. Bochner, Gerald R. Miller, and Kenneth N. Cissna for reading earlier drafts of this paper. I would also like to thank the anonymous reviewers for their useful suggestions.

[2] A distinction is made between the terms "compliance" and "compliance-gaining" because they represent two different concepts in the social influence literature. Generally scholars use the term "compliance" to mean a behavioral outcome and the term "compliance-gaining" to mean the process of eliciting that outcome.

[3] My discussion of an economic exchange model of compliance-gaining is an adaptation of King's (1975) treatment of an economic exchange model of normative social influence-outcome control.

[4] There have been a few compliance-resisting studies (e.g., Cody, O'Hair, & Schneider, 1982; McLaughlin, Cody, & Robey, 1980; McQuillen & Higginbotham, 1986; McQuillen, Higginbotham, & Cummings, 1984). However, "the amount of research reported on compliance-resisting is quite limited" (McQuillen & Higginbotham, 1986, p. 674).

[5] de Turck (1985) has examined agents' choices of influence strategies across compliance-gaining episodes where the target is resistant. However, such studies are scarce.

[6] Efforts have been made to study compliance-gaining message behaviors by observing actual interaction (e.g., Witteman & Fitzpatrick, 1986). Yet, "most prior research on compliance-gaining has relied on the self-reports of individuals" (Witteman & Fitzpatrick, 1986, p. 130).

REFERENCES

Benson, J. K. (1977). Organizations: A dialectical view. *Administrative Science Quarterly, 22*(3), 1-21.

Berger, C. R. (1985). Social power and interpersonal communication. In M. L. Knapp & G. R. Miller (Eds.), *Handbook of interpersonal communication* (pp. 439-499). Beverly Hills, CA: Sage.

Blau, P. M. (1964). *Exchange and power in social life.* New York: John Wiley.

Bochner, A. P. (1984). The functions of human communication in interpersonal bonding. In C. C. Arnold & J. W. Bowers (Eds.), *Handbook of rhetorical and communication theory* (pp. 544-621). Boston: Allyn & Bacon.

Bochner, A. P. (1988). Interpersonal communication. In E. Barnouw (Ed.), *Encyclopedia of communications.* New York: Oxford University Press.

Boster, F. J. (1989). An examination of the state of compliance-gaining message behavior research. Paper presented at the meeting of the International Communication Association, San Francisco.

Boster, F. J., & Stiff, J. B. (1984). Compliance gaining message selection behavior. *Human Communication Research, 10,* 539-556.

Burgoon, M., Dillard, J. P., Doran, N., & Miller, M. D. (1982). Cultural and situational influences on the process of persuasive strategy selection. *International Journal of Intercultural Relations, 6,* 85-100.

Clark, R. A. (1979). The impact of self-interest and desire for liking on the selection of communicative strategies. *Communication Monographs, 46,* 132-148.

Cartwright, D. (1965). Influence, leadership, control. In J. G. March (Ed.), *Handbook of organizations* (pp. 1-47). Chicago: Rand McNally.

Cody, M. J., O'Hair, H. D., & Schneider, M. J. (1982). The impact of intimacy, rights to resist, Machiavellianism and psychological gender on compliance-resisting strategies: How persuasive are response effects in communication surveys? Paper presented at the annual meeting of the Interpersonal Communication Association, Boston.

Dahl, R. A. (1957). The concept of power. *Behavioral Science, 2,* 201-215.

deTurck, M. (1985). A transactional analysis of compliance-gaining behavior: Effects of noncompliance, relational contexts, and actors' gender. *Human Communication Research, 12,* 54-78.

Dillard, J. P., & Burgoon, M. (1985). Situational influences on the selection of compliance-gaining messages: Two tests of the predictive utility of the Cody-McLaughlin typology. *Communication Monographs, 52,* 289-304.

Erez, M., & Rim, Y. (1982). The relationship between goals, influence tactics, and personal and organizational variables. *Human Values, 35*(10), 871-878.

Etzioni, A. (1975). *A comparative analysis of complex organizations: On power, involvement, and their correlates.* New York: The Free Press.

Fisher, B. A. (1978). *Perspective on human communication.* New York: Macmillan.

Garko, M. G. (1988). An investigation into the role of target communicator style in the managerial selection of compliance-gaining strategies and communicator styles. Unpublished doctoral dissertation, Florida State University, Tallahassee.

Garko, M. G. (1989). Factors affecting the managerial selection of compliance-gaining strategies. Paper presented at the joint meeting of the Southern States Communication Association and Central States Speech Association, St. Louis.

Homans, G. C. (1961). *Social behavior: Its elementary forms.* New York: Harcourt, Brace, and World.

Hunter, J. E., & Boster, F. J. (1979). Situational differences in the selection of compliance-gaining messages. Paper presented at the annual meeting of the Speech Communication Association, San Antonio, TX.

Kearney, P., Plax, T. G., Richmond, V. P., & McCroskey, J. C. (1985). Power in the classroom III: Teacher communication techniques and messages. *Communication Education, 34,* 19-28.

Kearney, P., Plax, T. G., Richmond, V. P., & McCroskey, J. C. (1984). Power in the classroom IV: Teacher communication techniques as alternatives to discipline. In R. N. Bostrom (Ed.), *Communication yearbook 8* (pp. 724-746). Beverly Hills, CA: Sage.

Kelman, H. C. (1974). Further thoughts on the processes of compliance, identification, and internalization. In J. T. Tedeschi (Ed.), *Perspectives on social power* (pp. 125-171). Chicago: Aldine.

Kiesler, S. B. (1978). *Interpersonal processes in groups and organizations.* Arlington Heights, IL: AHM Publishing Co.

King, S. W. (1975). *Communication and social influence.* Reading, MA: Addison-Wesley.

Kipnis, D. (1972). Does power corrupt? *Journal of Personality and Social Psychology, 24*(1), 33-41.

Kipnis, D. (1974). The powerholder. In J. T. Tedeschi (Ed.), *Perspectives on social power* (pp. 82-122). Chicago: Aldine.

Kipnis, D. (1976). *The powerholders.* Chicago: University of Chicago Press.

Kipnis, D. (1984). The use of power in organizations and in interpersonal settings. In S. Oskamp (Ed.), *Applied social psychology annual 5* (pp. 179-210). Beverly Hills, CA: Sage.

Kipnis, D., & Cohn, (1979). Power and affection. Paper presented at the meeting of the Eastern Psychological Association, Philadelphia.

Kipnis, D., & Cosentino, J. (1969). Use of leadership powers in industry. *Journal of Applied Psychology, 55*(6), 460-466.

Kipnis, D., & Lane, W. P. (1962). Self-confidence and leadership. *Journal of Applied Psychology, 46*(4), 291-295.

Kipnis, D., & Schmidt, S. M. (1983). An influence perspective on bargaining within organizations. In M. H. Bazerman & R. J. Lewicki (Eds.), *Negotiating in organizations* (pp. 303-319). Beverly Hills, CA: Sage.

Kipnis, D., Schmidt, S. M., & Wilkinson, I. (1980). Intraorganizational influence tactics: Explorations in getting one's way. *Journal of Applied Psychology, 65*(4), 440-452.

Marwell, G., & Schmitt, D. R. (1967). Dimensions of compliance-gaining behavior: An empirical analysis. *Sociometry, 30,* 350-364.

McCroskey, J. C., & Richmond, V. P. (1983). Power in the classroom I: Teacher and student perceptions. *Communication Education, 32,* 175-184.

McCroskey, J. C., & Richmond, V. P., Plax, T. G., & Kearney, P. (1985). Power in the classroom V: Behavior alteration techniques, communication training and learning. *Communication Education, 34,* 214-226.

McLaughlin, M. L., Cody, M. J., & Robey, C. S. (1980). Situational influences on the selection of strategies to resist compliance-gaining attempts. *Human Communication Research, 7,* 14-36.

McQuillen, J. S., & Higginbotham, D. C. (1986). Children's reasoning about compliance-resisting behaviors. In M. L. McLaughin (Ed.), *Communication yearbook 9* (pp. 673-690). Beverly Hills, CA: Sage.

McQuillen, J. S., Higginbotham, D. C., & Cummings, M. C. (1984). Compliance-resisting behaviors: The effects of age, agent, and types of request. In R. N. Bostrom (Ed.), *Communication yearbook 8* (pp. 747-762). Beverly Hills, CA: Sage.

Miller, G. R., & Steinberg, M. (1975). *Between people: A new analysis of interpersonal communication.* Chicago: Science Research Associates, Inc.

Moscovici, S. (1976). *Social influence and social change.* London: Academic Press.

Nord, W. (1969). Social exchange theory: An integrative approach to social conformity. *Psychological Bulletin, 71,* 174-208.

Norton, R. (1983). *Communicator style: Theory, applications, and measures.* Beverly Hills, CA: Sage.

Palazzoli-Selvini, M., Boscolo, L., Cecchin, G. F., & Prata, G. (1978). *Paradox and counterparadox: A new model in the therapy of the family in schizophrenic transaction.* New York: Jason Aronson.

Plax, T. G., Kearney, P., McCroskey, J. C., & Richmond, V. P. (1986). Power in the classroom VI: Verbal control strategies, nonverbal immediacy and affective learning. *Communication Education, 35,* 43-55.

Perreault, W. D., Jr., & Miles, R. H. (1978). Influence strategy mixes in complex organizations. *Behavioral Science, 23,* 86-98.

Podsakoff, P. M. (1982). Determinants of a supervisor's use of rewards and punishments. A literature review and suggestions for further research. *Organizational Behavior and Human Performance, 29,* 58-83.

Richmond, V. P., & McCroskey, J. C. (1984). Power in the classroom II: Power and learning. *Communication Education, 33,* 125-136.

Richmond, V. P., McCroskey, J. C., Kearney, P., & Plax, T. G. (1987). Power in the classroom VII: Linking behavior alteration techniques to cognitive learning. *Communication Education, 36,* 1-12.

Rim, Y., & Erez, M. (1980). A note about tactics used to influence superiors, co-workers, and subordinates. *Journal of Occupational Psychology, 53,* 319-321.

Seibold, D. R., Cantrill, J. G., & Meyers, R. A. (1985). Communication and interpersonal influence. In M. L. Knapp & G. R. Miller (Eds.), *Handbook of interpersonal communication* (pp. 511-611). Beverly Hills, CA: Sage.

Thibaut, J. W., & Kelley, H. H. (1959). *The social psychology of groups.* New York: John Wiley.

Wheeless, L. R., Barraclough, R., & Stewart, R. (1983). Compliance-gaining and power in persuasion. In R. Bostrom (Ed.), *Communication yearbook 7* (pp. 105-145). Beverly Hills, CA: Sage.

Williams, D. L., & Boster, F. J. (1981). The effects of beneficial situational characteristics, negativism, and dogmatism on compliance-gaining message selection. Paper presented at the annual meeting of the International Communication Association, Minneapolis.

Witteman, H. & Fitzpatrick, M. A. (1986). Compliance-gaining in marital interaction: Power bases, processes, and outcomes. *Communication Monographs, 53,* 130-143.

Wozniak, R. H. (1975). A dialectical paradigm for psychological research: Implications drawn from the history of psychology in the Soviet Union. *Human Development, 18,* 18-34.

UNIT VII

Failure Events, Complaints, and Conflicts

Possession of the skills covered in the previous two units is not enough to ensure that our relationships will progress smoothly and without difficulty. The journey through relational development involves having to deal with relational problems and conflicts. How we respond to those difficulties often dictates the ultimate outcome of the relationship. Possession of the skills that have been covered can make the management of relational difficulties easier. The articles in this unit examine some of the elements that cause problems and conflicts as well as ways we might manage interpersonal conflicts. Specifically, the articles deal with three difficulties encountered in relationships: failure events, complaints, and conflicts.

Of the three difficulties, a failure event is probably the most foreign term to you, but the phenomena will be quite familiar. **Failure events** represent those occurrences in which one partner in a given relationship is perceived to have acted in an unexpected or untoward manner, or perceived to have failed to meet a particular obligation or expectation. Failure events include such things as being late for a date, not returning something borrowed, being caught cheating in a relationship that had been defined as exclusive, moving out of an apartment shared with a friend before the lease is up. When a failure event occurs, the person against whom the failure was committed (the reproacher) is faced with a decision as to what action to take. The act of presenting the issue to the perpetrator or actor is called a **reproach**. The response to a reproach by the actor is called an **account**. The options an actor has in responding to the reproach for the failure represent account strategies. The reproacher then makes an evaluation of the adequacy of the account for the failure event by essentially accepting or rejecting the account. Thus the sequence is: a failure event occurs, a reproach is presented, an account is made, and then an evaluation of the account is made. The following illustrates this process.

> Dimitri agreed to meet Rachel at the library at 7:00 P.M., but didn't show up until 8:00 P.M. (**Failure Event**)
>
> Rachel: Well, its about time you showed up. (**Reproach**)
>
> Dimitri: Sorry, I was tied up at a meeting and didn't have any way to call you and tell you I would be late. (**Account**)
>
> Rachel: Well, it's okay. I got a lot done on some other things. Let's get started on our project. (**Acceptance of the account**)

Article 20 focuses on what factors affect how actors manage their failure events. Specifically, McLaughlin, Cody, and O'Hair are interested in what predicts the type of account an individual will provide. Some of the factors examined include how harsh (aggravated) the reproach is, the nature of the relationship, the severity of the failure event, and amount of guilt. The authors review the literature that establishes five specific account types: silence, refusal, justification, excuse, and concession.

An important concept underlying McLaughlin et al.'s discussion of failure events is that of saving

348

face. Face is the image we wish to portray, the impression we want others to have of us, or how we want others to think of us. Some of the initial work on face by Brown and Levinson is discussed in this article. Brown and Levinson discuss **face-threatening acts,** which are acts that cause the face that we present to be challenged or invalidated to some degree. We are motivated to maintain or save face and are threatened by anything that undermines face. For instance, if I think I am a good teacher and I receive end-of-the-course evaluations on which a number of negative remarks about my teaching are written, then my face as a good teacher is threatened. To save face I would probably tell myself something such as "What do students know anyway?" In much the same way McLaughlin, Cody, and O'Hair discuss reproaches and accounts as being threatening to the reproacher and the actor. There are two types of face: positive face and negative face (which are two distinct types, not opposites). **Positive face** is the image we want others to understand, accept, approve, like, and validate. In essence, positive face is our self-concept, our personality, our sense of self. **Negative face** is the desire to be free to do what you want to do, not to have your actions impeded. Negative face is getting what we want, acting the way we want. Threats to negative face occur whenever we have to alter our behavior from how we would like to behave.

In article 20, failure events are examined in terms of the face-threatening implications to the reproacher and the actor. Account strategies, such as refusing to respond to a reproach, threaten the reproacher's face; confessions or apologies threaten the actor's face. If I ask a student where his paper is, and he does not reply, my face as the authority figure (teacher) is threatened. On the other hand, if the student replies he is sorry it's late, it's his fault for not having it in on time and thus it is the student's face as the actor that is threatened. The notions of face and face-threatening acts have a variety of possible applications to interpersonal communication in such situations as conflict management, compliance gaining, and the unilateral termination of a relationship.

McLaughlin et al. present a number of hypotheses they test by having students recall failure events, provide descriptions of the accounts, and rate the situation according to seven scales. The accounts were coded according to the five categories and those were related to the responses to the scales. For each of the five categories they conducted a regression analysis that identified which of the seven variables would best predict the given account strategy implemented. After the statistical analysis given for each hypothesis, the authors provide a summary of which of the seven variables were predictors of the account strategy.

Article 21 by Alberts also looks at failure events, but in a slightly different manner from the previous article. Alberts focuses more on the reproach (complaint) than previous studies have done. Complaint interactions are seen as one type of an account episode. Alberts is concerned also with the presentation of these complaints within close relationships. His study focuses on the actual interactions of married couples.

Alberts indicates that remedial work is important to romantic relationships. By remedial he means that partners in a relationship must go back and do some repair work on their relationship. Complaints are seen as one way in which couples conduct remedial work in a relationship.

Twenty maladjusted and twenty adjusted couples were audiotaped while discussing issues of disagreement. The tapes were transcribed and coded on the basis of the type of complaint, the response, and the complaint effect. Log linear analysis was conducted on the categorical data. Log linear analysis tests for interaction effects among variables and is similar to multiple analysis of variance or regression. Alberts reports those variables that were found to have significant associations. In addition, a number of analyses are presented comparing the adjusted and maladjusted couples, which provides insights into the different ways in which the couples present and respond to complaints.

Differences in the nature and method of dealing with complaints among romantic couples is consistent with the research that has found various differences among couples in their handling of conflict. Article 22, by Cahn, provides a review of research on conflict in intimate relationships. While intimate relationships are not limited to heterosexual romantic relationships, much of the research tends to fall into that classification. As you read the results of various studies, consider how generalizable the results are to other relationships, such as friendships. The article begins with a definition of interpersonal conflict as "an interaction between persons expressing opposing interests, views, or opinions." Interpersonal conflict, by definition, involves interpersonal communication. It is only when we express an opposing view that conflict occurs. Frequently, we might be upset by a friend's behavior but not say anything. This would not be considered a conflict because no interaction about the issue has taken place. The friend's behavior does create an interpersonal problem for us, however, and we are confronted with a decision about how to handle the problem. Reproaches and complaints are examples of deciding to interact with our partner about the problem, thus moving the problem into a conflict. Cahn discusses two major approaches to conflict: disintegrating communication and integrating communication. In addition, article 22 includes a discussion of the levels of conflict, types of communication associated with conflicts, and their interrelationships. Psychological and social factors related to interpersonal conflict are covered also.

Article 23 by Berryman-Fink and Brunner examines the differences in male and female conflict management styles. Conflict management styles are the manner in which we generally react to an interpersonal conflict. A variety of systems offer different categorizations and labels for the styles. In this study conflict style is assessed using the Thomas-Kilmann Conflict Mode Instrument, which assesses the relative strength of two conflict management dimensions: assertiveness (concern for self) and cooperativeness (concern for relationship). Five combinations of these two dimensions are identified and labeled as conflict management

styles. The "avoiding" style is low in both concern for self and the relationship. It is typified by such behaviors as changing the subject and dismissing the issue as unimportant. This style is usually considered a lose-lose situation since neither party in the conflict gets what he or she wants. The "accommodating" style is high on concern for relationship but low on concern for self. In this style individuals are always "giving in" to their partners' claims. The accommodator places the other and the relationship above self-interests. People who adopt this style avoid conflict by letting others have their way. Accommodating tends to be a lose-win situation, though there are times when it is beneficial to accommodate, which might lead to long-term benefits for the accommodator. The third style, "competing," places strong emphasis on self-concerns and little emphasis on relationship. Competitors want to win, and they see conflict as competition; these individuals are asserting their own interests, often at the expense of the other, and thus these tend to be win-lose situations. Competing style is represented by an unwillingness to concede or compromise and can lead to personal attacks against the other in order to secure ultimate victory. The "compromising" style represents those who demonstrate a moderate concern for self and relationship. Neither concern is particularly strong, and therefore individuals are typically willing to settle for less than they initially request. There is also some concern for the relationship and therefore the compromiser does not push self-interests to the point of damaging the relationship. This style represents both a win-win and a lose-lose situation because, while both partners gain something, they also settle for less than what they usually want. The final style, "collaborating," is considered a win-win situation because both partners get what they want. There is a strong concern for self-interest and for the relationship. Conflicts managed in a collaborative fashion involve both partners attempting to maximize the benefits for each. The collaborators want to see that they get what they want, but also that their partners' needs are met. Berryman-Fink and Brunner analyzed the data they received to see how closely the data fit the prediction about where the five types would fall along the two dimensions. Their results differed from the predicted locations, which they illustrate in their article.

Berryman-Fink and Brunner ask three research questions that look for differences in males and females, both in the reported conflict management style and the effect of a male or female as the target of the conflict. In the procedures, the authors asked the students who participated to think of an important relationship and to respond to the questionnaire items with that person in mind. This means that the students' conflict management style was being described within the context of a specific relationship. Participants were to indicate the sex of the individual, and so the authors were able to examine the reported conflict management style for male-male, female-female, and male-female relationships. Each style was examined to see if there was a significant difference between the males and females. What would you expect they found? They also addressed the issue of whether the gender of the target of conflict made a difference in what style was used. Do you use a different style depending on whether you are having a conflict with a man or a woman? Their last question asked whether there was an interaction effect between the gender of the source and that of the target. That is, do men treat men differently, and do women treat women differently in interpersonal conflicts?

QUESTIONS TO CONSIDER WHILE READING

ARTICLE 20

A. What inferences might you make about how an individual regards the failure event if she or he responds to your reproach with (1) a refusal to respond and (2) a concession?

B. As you read through the procedures and analysis, think of how you would have responded to the study. Think of a particular failure event and your account. What was the reproach like, the severity of the failure, the nature of the relationship, etc.?

ARTICLE 21

A. How applicable do you think the studies' findings are to nonromantic relationships? Why?

B. Which of the following statements would seem to be more accurate? A dysfunctional complaining process leads to relational dissatisfaction. Relational dissatisfaction leads to dysfunctional complaining. Why?

ARTICLE 22

A. In which of the various conflict behaviors (e.g., integrative or disintegrative communication or gender-related differences) do you most commonly engage?

B. The list of psychological and social factors contributing to interpersonal conflict presented in the article is not exhaustive. What other factors can you think of that lead to interpersonal conflict or undermine the ability to effectively manage interpersonal conflict?

ARTICLE 23

A. The authors found differences in the placement of the five styles on the two dimensions of concern for self and concern for relationships from what was predicted. Why?

B. What reasons can you think of to explain the differences in males and females in their conflict management styles and in how they are treated as targets of conflict?

20

The Management of Failure Events: Some Contextual Determinants of Accounting Behavior

MARGARET L. McLAUGHLIN   H. DAN O'HAIR
MICHAEL J. CODY

This study sought to examine the impact upon actors' selection of strategies to manage failure events of several contextual factors: characteristics of the reproacher/actor relationship, communicative goal-orientation of the actors, severity of the failure event, character of the reproach for the failure event, and the actors' degree of expressed guilt. Results indicated that actors elected to make no response when they felt less guilt, when there was no overt reproach, when their instrumental goal (securing honoring) was unimportant, and when the failure event was a severe offense. Concessions were used when the reproachers said nothing or projected a concession, when the offense was severe, when the actors' instrumental goal was important, and when they felt guilty. Actors chose to justify their behavior in high intimate situations where their instrumental goal was less important. Refusal to account was most likely to occur when reproachers used an aggravating reproach form, when actors felt unjustly accused, and when reproachers were dominant. Excuses were fairly uniformly distributed across all contexts.

And the Lord God called unto Adam, and said unto him, Where art thou?

And he said, I heard thy voice in the garden, and I was afraid, because I was naked, and I hid myself.

And He said, Who told thee that thou wast naked? Hast thou eaten of the tree, whereof I commanded thee that thou shouldest not eat?

And the man said, The woman who thou givest to be with me, she gave me of the tree, and I did eat.

And the Lord God said unto the woman, What is this that thou hast done?

And the woman said, The serpent beguiled me and I did eat.

Genesis 3: 9-13

Accounts have been around almost as long as sin has been around. Not only did our biblical progenitors resort to an excuse ("Somebody else made me do it") as they attempted, albeit unsuccessfully,

to extricate themselves from a tight spot; but indeed, most current thinking on account behavior suggests that excuses are hardy perennials in the management of failure, along with evasions, concessions, justifications, and outright denials.

In an important early work on the account ("a linguistic device employed whenever an action is subjected to valuative inquiry," Scott & Lyman, 1968, p. 46), the authors make a fundamental distinction between those accounts that are excuses and those that are justifications. Either or both of these are likely responses to an *offense* (Blumstein et al., 1974) or *failure event* (Schonbach, 1980) when an untoward or unexpected act is committed or an anticipated act or obligation is not fulfilled. In offering an excuse, the actor admits the failure event, but denies that s/he is responsible for it, whereas in offering a justification, the actor accepts responsibility for the failure event but maintains

From McLaughlin, M. L., Cody, M. J., & O'Hair, H. D. (1983). The management of failure events: Some contextual determinants of accounting behavior. *Human Communication Research, 9,* 208-224.

that it was not untoward. Scott and Lyman initially distinguished four forms of excuse: appeal to accidents ("I got held up in traffic"), appeal to defeasibility ("I was drunk"), appeal to biological drives ("I can't help it—I'm a man") and scapegoating ("I blame it on the serpent"). Justifications are classified by Harré (1977) as either conventionalizations ("I wasn't staring into space—I was thinking") or normalizations ("Everybody cheats on his income tax"), and by Scott and Lyman as denial of injury ("Nobody got hurt"), denial of the victim ("She was no good"), condemnation of the condemners ("It's no worse than what you did") and appeal to loyalties ("My mom needed an operation").

The most exhaustive taxonomy of accounts, representing a synthesis of earlier work by Scott and Lyman (1968), Sykes and Matza (1957), Harré (1977) and others, has been provided by Schonbach (1980). In the Schonbach scheme, four fundamental modes of response to a failure event and subsequent reproach are identified: *concessions, excuses, justifications*, and *refusals*. Schonbach's work is also based, in part, on an inductively derived set of account strategies, a procedure advocated by communication scholars (Clark, 1979; Cody, McLaughlin, & Jordan, 1980; Wiseman & Schenck-Hamlin, 1981) for studying interpersonal persuasion strategies.

In a concession, the main characteristic is the explicit acknowledgement of the actor's guilt:[1]

My dad, he wanted to know why I came back from college. I had told him that everything was paid for. Everything wasn't paid for, though. So he demanded an account. He said, "What did you do with all the money you made from January through June?" *I admitted I blew it all.*

I had been dating this girl steady for two years my senior year in high school when this other girl kept flirting with me and called and asked me to come over to her sister's house and see her. Well, I went over there and started sneaking around seeing her and we got things goin' pretty good for a few months, then we called it off. About four months later my girlfriend found out about it and I had to explain just what we were doing and why I was with her. My girlfriend said, "You bastard, just what the f—— were you doing with that little slut?" *I told her it was a mistake I shouldn't have made.*

Other distinctive features of concession include apologies and offers of restitution:

I broke a windshield in a car. The car was not mine. I felt the owner needed an explanation or some reason why that morning it was fine and that afternoon the glass was shattered. The owner said, "What happened to my car?" as I stood beside it. "Who did it?" I said, *"I'm sure sorry* for the broken windshield, but *my insurance will pay for it."* I explained it was one of those freak accidents.

Concession is simply one of several alternative strategies for failure management, and as such is not necessarily isomorphic with the actor's true attitudes toward a reproach. Our observation of daily life suggests that, particularly in intimate relationships, concessions may alternate with refusals to be held to account, or even outright threats:

The other day I hit my girlfriend in the face and it broke her jaw. I soon apologized and tried to explain to her why I did it, because I knew I was in the wrong. She said, "You son of a bitch, why did you do that?" *I told her to don't call me a s.o.b. again or I will break her arm. Then I told her I was sorry for hitting her.*

An excuse is a failure management strategy in which the actor admits that the failure event took place, but nonetheless denies that s/he was able to do anything about it. In one common form of excuse, the actor cites some form of impairment or disability as the cause of his/her failure to meet an expectation:

I borrowed my girlfriend's car one night and I didn't return it. She came by the next day while I was sleeping with a hangover. She was pretty steamed. She said, "Where the hell were you with my car?" *I said I got too drunk last night and fell asleep before I could return it.*

Another form of excuse requires that the actor deliver a recital of misfortunes demonstrating that s/he was temporarily overwhelmed by the pressures of current circumstance and thus not responsible for his/her actions:

I was at work. It was lunch time and we were playing dominoes. The dominoes I had been getting were poor to say the least. Finally I lost my temper and drove my fist into the table. The dominoes rolled off the table and everyone looked at me accusingly. I never lose my temper at work. Later I told a friend, "*You know, I broke up with my fiancée and I just had to give my dog away. My dog is the only friend I had left. My car is ruined and I had to buy a new one. I've taken it pretty well, but it all just caught up with me today.*"

Other forms excuse may take include diffusing the responsibility for the failure event, scapegoating, or appealing to one's own effort and concern before or during the failure event itself (Schonbach, 1980).

Justification is a failure management strategy in which the actor admits responsibility for the failure event, but tries to redefine the nature of the event itself. The typical justification strategy involves minimizing the severity of the offense, by redefining the event as nonserious:

> When I was overseas, a group of us got drunk and tore up a recreation room. The SPs were called and everyone ran but me; subsequently I was brought before my commander to explain my actions. I recounted the evening for him: "We started drinking and playing pool, then we tried to juggle some billiard balls; they disappeared into the ceiling (it was tile); from there we just kept tossing the balls around. Windows got broken. *When I pulled the door off the hinge it was unintentional. We did not set out to break anything; we never viewed it as destruction or vandalism; it was simply rough play.*

Another mode of justification invokes the actor's right to self-fulfillment:

> I was asked by my wife why I went to Sound Warehouse and bought records when we need other things more. *I said that I hadn't bought any albums in a long time,* and it was just two albums.

Sometimes actors justify their actions by comparing them to similar misdeeds by the person reproaching them:

> I am always getting upset with my husband for not leaving me a note when he leaves so that I know where he is and when to expect him back. I always tell him, "You always know where I am and I'm always on time." One day I went shopping with my sister-in-law and didn't leave a note. My husband said, "Where have you been? [teasingly] You should leave a note when you leave." I really felt embarrassed. I said, "*You always forget!*"

Other forms of justification include derogation of the victim, appeal to one's positive intentions, and appeal to higher loyalties.

Refusal is a failure management strategy in which the actor denies that s/he is guilty of the failure event, that the failure event has taken place, or that the accuser is entitled to the right to reproach (Schonbach, 1980).

> I was at a movie with a girlfriend when I ran into my ex, or old girlfriend. When she appeared, I felt that I had to account for my girlfriend I had with me, maybe because me and my ex just broke up a week ago that day. My ex, she ask, what you think you doing?!! Well, my response was "*What the hell you talking about?*" in a low voice.

> My husband, coming in from work, saw a co-worker of mine, a man whom I carpool with, in our house. My husband asked, "What is he doing here?" I was very defensive. I did not feel that the situation warranted an interrogation. I explained that the man had come in to use the restroom. "*But so what? What was wrong with him being in here? Couldn't I invite anyone in that I wanted to?*"

To Schonbach's four categories of failure-management strategies, we would add a fifth: *silence.* Under certain circumstances—for example, when the degree of embarrassment associated with the failure event is severe, or when the actor feels that accounting would simply make matters worse—the strategy of choice may be simply to avoid any reference whatsoever to the untoward behavior.

> One Saturday night I was out all night and was feeling kind of good. That night I spent the night with a friend. I didn't call home and tell my parents that I was spending the night with a friend. I knew my parents were going to be mad. I took a shower and got dressed. Then I hopped in my car and started on my way home. When I entered the house there was my mother cooking over the stove with her angry look on her face. She said nothing. *I felt like explaining why I didn't come home but I knew it would only make things worse.*

Failure Management Strategies, Face-Threatening Acts, and the Aggravation-Mitigation Continuum

Brown and Levinson (1978) have provided an elaborate analysis of the performative aspects of *face-threatening acts.* Such acts may be characterized as threats either to *positive face* (that is, the positive image of self claimed by the interactants) or to *negative face* (the basic claim of interactants of the right to autonomy, territory, personal space, privacy, and, in general, freedom of action) (Brown & Levinson, 1978). Face-threatening acts may be further categorized according to whether they constitute a threat to the speaker's or the hearer's face. Under Brown and Levinson's scheme, failure management strategies like excuse and concession primarily constitute threats to the speaker's face, whereas strategies like justification and refusal are heard mainly as threats to the hearer's face. Excuses offend the actor's negative face in that s/he is seen as experiencing a loss of privacy and autonomy, whereas concessions threaten his/her positive face. Justification and refusals constitute threats to the hearer's or reproacher's positive face in that they convey the speaker's assessment that the hearer's position on some issue (namely, the failure event) is wrong headed.

We would argue that in selecting a strategy to manage a failure event actors take into account that hearers will recognize excuses and concessions as more mitigating than justification and refusals, in that they threaten the speaker's but not the hearer's face; consequently, such strategies will be evaluated as more "polite." Brown and Levinson have also proposed that the actor's estimation of the risk of loss of the hearer's face will determine the type of strategy selected to perform a face-threatening act (Brown & Levinson, 1978). When the risk of loss of face is very great, the actor may elect not to perform the act at all (for example, s/he might choose the failure management strategy of silence although this would only be likely in the event that there was no overt reproach). When the risk of loss of face is minimal, the actor will perform the face-threatening act "badly, without redress" (Brown & Levinson, p. 65), for example, by justifying (denying agreement on the definition of the failure event) or by refusing to give an account. At intermediate levels of risk to the hearer's face, the actor may opt for a "positively polite" strategy like excuse, which assumes that both the actor and the reproacher share the same definition and evaluation of the failure event, or the

more mitigating, negatively polite strategy of concession, which offers redress and assures the reproacher of the actor's regard for his/her freedom of action ("I'm sorry I inconvenienced you by being so late").

Labov and Fanshel (1977), in accounting for variation in the performance of indirect requests, which are of course speech acts that potentially threaten the hearer's negative face, have argued that the degree of mitigation or aggravation associated with indirect requests and related acts is a function of the particular precondition the speaker invokes so that the illocutionary intent of the act is recognized. In making a direct request, if the speaker (S) delivers an imperative specifying that the hearer (H) perform some action X at time Y, and the hearer believes that certain preconditions are in effect (S believes that there is a need for action X, S believes that H has the ability to do X, H is obliged to do X, and S has the right to require H to do X), then the hearer will understand that a valid request for action has been made (Labov & Fanshel, p. 78). Indirect requests may be formed out of these preconditions, and the particular form they take may be more or less mitigating. Generally, Labov and Fanshel argue, references to S's need and H's ability are mitigating, whereas references to H's obligation and S's rights are aggravating: "I sure need your help with my homework" or "Can you help me with my homework tonight?" are more mitigating than "You ought [have] to help me with my homework tonight."

In the case of failure management strategies, in which the actor in effect claims that the preconditions for performing some act did not hold, the pattern of mitigation is just the reverse: references to H's lack of need ("I didn't know it was important") and S's lack of ability ("I couldn't help it") will be heard as mitigating, whereas references to S's lack of obligation ("It wasn't my responsibility") or H's lack of right ("You have no right to complain") will be heard as aggravating. Consequently, we should expect that excuses, which turn on the issue of whether the individual was able to avoid giving offense, and justifications, which invoke the lack of consensus on the importance of the failure event (or the need for the omitted act), will be perceived as less aggravating than refusals, which invoke the issues of the rights of the hearer and the obligations of the speaker.

We propose that in the case of failure management strategies that call for the actor to make an overt reference to the failure event, the strategies can be arrayed along a mitigation-aggravation continuum as follows:

1	2	3	4
concession	excuse	justification	refusal

← ← ← ←   →→→→

mitigation
(least threatening
to hearer's face)

aggravation
(most threatening
to hearer's face)

The higher numbered strategies will be selected with concern for the potential risk of the hearer's loss of face and/or of his own loss of positive face. We expect it to be generally the case that the risk of the other's loss of face will be the actor's primary concern in a failure management situation, inasmuch as s/he is in enough trouble already. Undoubtedly, however, there will be those actors for whom an impending threat to own negative face will be of the utmost concern; in these circumstances the lower numbered strategies will be avoided in favor of strategies like justification and refusal, which present a lesser threat to the actor's sense of autonomy. The strategy in which the actor opts to say nothing will be mitigating in those situations in which there is no overt reproach for the failure event; however, silence will be highly aggravating in the presence of an overt approach.

Contextual Determinants of Strategy Selection in the Management of Failure Events

We propose to examine the impact upon failure management strategy selection of several contextual factors: characteristics of the relationship between the actor and the victimized other (the reproacher), the severity of the failure event, the actor's current communicative goals, the character of the reproach, and the actor's attitude toward the failure event.

Characteristics of the Actor-Reproacher Relationship

Blumstein et al. (1974) argue that in determining whether an account of a failure event ought to be honored, the reproacher or victimized other will be strongly influenced by the adequacy of the account to the situation at hand, especially its appropriateness to the relationship of the parties as it stood prior to the failure event. We can anticipate, then, that the actor will make an effort to adopt a strategy appropriate to the nature of his/her relationship with the reproacher.

Two relational factors that have been obtained again and again in studies of the dimensions of interpersonal relationships are *intimacy* and *dominance* (Bochner, Kaminski, & Fitzpatrick, 1977; Cody, 1978; Cody & McLaughlin, 1980; Forgas, 1976; Wish, 1975). Intimacy has been shown to be a major determinant of strategy selection in interpersonal persuasion and conflict. Fitzpatrick and Winke (1979) found that in relationships characterized as casual involvements, conflict tactics of manipulation and nonnegotiation (refusal to compromise) were frequently reported, whereas among married persons emotional appeals and personal rejection were more frequently utilized. Michener and Schwertfeger (1972) found that the agent's desire to be liked by the target of a power tactic tended to lead to the use of conciliatory rather than potentially disruptive tactics. Clark (1979) found that a persuader who desired liking from a target was more likely to report strategies oriented to helping the other than a persuader who did not. Miller, Boster, Roloff, & Seibold (1977) found that positive strategies were preferred in intimate situations, whereas with nonintimates justifying strategies (evoking the outcomes of compliance or noncompliance) were favored. Our general expectation, then, is that increased relational intimacy will enhance the likelihood that the more mitigating strategies will be used to manage failure events, although as Fitzpatrick and Winke (1979) have argued, the very fact of relational commitment may make possible the use of aggravating strategies on an occasional basis, since the parties are less concerned with the threat of termination.

The comparative relational power of the actor and the reproacher, or the reproacher's relative dominance, can be expected to account for variation in failure management strategies. Falbo and Peplau (1980), in a study of power tactics, found that individuals who place great emphasis on an egalitarian relationship between intimates were most likely to report using negatively polite unilateral strategies (laissez faire and withdrawal) to "get their way," whereas persons who felt that equal power between intimates was less important reported a preference for bilateral strategies such as persuasion and bargaining. Kipnis and Cohen (1980) found that in dating couples the individual who typically made decisions regarding both partners was more likely to employ "strong" interpersonal tactics as opposed to "weak" or "rational" tactics. Blumstein et al. (1974) found that accounts were more likely to be honored when the actor was of higher status. Our expectation is that when reproacher dominance is high, actors will select more mitigating failure management strategies; when actor dominance is comparatively high (and there is a potential risk of loss to own face, but not much chance that the account will not be honored), more aggravating strategies, which preserve the actor's negative face, will be preferred.

A third relational factor that ought to affect the actor's choice of strategy is the potential damage to the relationship that could result as a consequence of the way in which the failure event is managed: the *relational consequences* of the actor's strategy selection. Relational consequences, which was introduced as a potential explanatory variable by Miller and Steinberg (1975), was obtained as an important dimension of interpersonal persuasion situations by

Cody and McLaughlin (1980) and by Cody, Woelfel, and Jordan (in press); (also see Lustig & King, 1980). McLaughlin, Cody, and Robey (1980) found that in high-intimacy relationships, the more aggravating nonnegotiation strategies were rated more favorably when relational consequences were short-term as opposed to long-term, whereas the more mitigating negotiation strategies were preferred when the relational consequences were long-term as opposed to short-term. Although relational consequences has not always been found to produce variation in message strategy selection (Miller et al., 1977), that state of affairs in our judgment stems in large part from the failure of previous researchers to validate their experimental treatments of the variable (McLaughlin et al., 1980). It is important that the consequences variable be assessed in terms of how it is perceived by those who are actually generating the message strategies. In any event, it is our expectation that, all other things being equal, more mitigating strategies will be employed when the potential consequences of damage to the relationship are greater, although aggravating strategies may be more likely to be used in situations of long-term consequence if the actor feels unjustly accused.

Severity of the Failure Event as a Determinant of Failure-Management Strategy Selection

Blumstein et al. found (1) that the offensiveness of a failure event was a significant predictor of whether an account would be accepted, so that the more severe the violation, the more likely the actor was to be held responsible and to be regarded as unrepentant; and (2) that failure events were judged "in the moral abstract" even after the actor had provided an account (Blumstein et al., p. 558). These findings suggest that when the failure event constitutes a severe offense the actor will recognize that "mere excuses" may not result in honoring; consequently, we would anticipate that the most mitigating strategy, concession, will be used when the failure event is very serious and that aggravating strategies will be avoided. It is also very likely that in the event there is a severe offense for which no overt reproach is made the actor will simply elect to say nothing.

Communicative Goal Orientation

Clark and Delia (1979) have argued that the selection of message strategies in a persuasive situation will vary as a function of the relative importance of each of three communicative goals: *relational maintenance,* identity or *face management,* and task or *instrumental achievement.* In choosing a strategy for managing a failure event, the actor may be oriented to meeting one goal or any combination of such goals. The primary instrumental goal of a communicator who must account for a violation or offense is to secure honoring (Blumstein et al., 1974), that is, to see to it that the actor's account of the failure event is accepted. The primary identity-management goal of the actor is to neutralize the potential threat of loss of face. The actor may have to choose a balance between the possible loss of positive face associated with an aggravating strategy and the potential threat to negative face represented by a concession or excuse. Finally, the actor must assess to what extent it is important to select a strategy that will maintain the status quo of his/her relationship with the reproacher. (Under some circumstances the sustaining of a positive relationship may be a primary goal, yet the actor may manage the failure event so as to "correct" the relationship or set the other "straight." For example, the tone of the account might be such as to suggest that the actor does not grant the other a generalized right of reproach or that the actor claims the right to self-fulfillment.)

Our general expectation with regard to the impact of communicative goals is the following: when the actor's goal orientation in any of the three areas is high—that is, when the actor wants his/her account to be honored, wants to maintain positive face, and wants to maintain the relationship—s/he will select a strategy of mitigation, such as excuse or concession.

Nature of the Reproach

The extent to which relational characteristics and goal orientation determine an actor's choice of failure management strategy will be limited to a certain extent by the nature of the reproach with which the actor is confronted. One of the constraints imposed by the conversational system, of course, is that contributions be relevant—that sequentially ordered turns be cohesive (Vuchinch, 1977). Further, certain forms of reproach (for example, "Where have you been?") function as the first member of an adjacency pair (Benoit, 1980; Garvey, 1977), establishing a "slot" for a particular type of next turn.

For the purpose of the present investigation we proposed to investigate the impact of six forms of reproach—(1) *silence,* (2) *behavioral cues,* (3) *projected concession,* (4) *projected excuse,* (5) *projected justification,* and (6) *projected refusal*—on actor's selections of failure management strategies. In using silence, the victimized other makes no overt reproach, but the actor nonetheless feels that an account is in order:

I drove across a dead-end median so I wouldn't have to drive around and was waiting for the traffic to pass so I could get on the street. A policeman pulled over so I got out. *He asked for my license and that was all he said.* I began to try to explain that I was lost and pointed out that others had driven across too. He nodded and handed me a ticket. I thought he should know the reason or excuse why I did it.

We expect that in the case of no overt reproach for the failure event, the actor either will make no response or will elect to employ a mitigating strategy out of a feeling of guilt or obligation that led him/her to project a reproach when none was made.

In giving behavioral cues, the victimized other makes no overt verbalization, but the actor takes his/her cues from the nonverbal behavior of the other:

When I went to the gas station to get my car checked out, the attendant kept shaking his head while he looked under the hood of my car. *His negative and disgusted reactions made me flubber and stumble around with why I did not attend to my car regularly.*

We anticipate that the selection of failure management strategies following a nonverbal reproach will be similar to that for no overt reproach: the actor will concede, make an excuse, or maintain silence.

In a projected concession, the victimized other indicates that an apology and/or restitution is expected and that the actor should feel guilty about the failure event:

My grandparents and my younger brother came to campus from Greenwood to bring me items for my room at school, and when they arrived on campus, I wasn't home. When I got back, my grandmother said, *"Well, it sure was nice of you to have us come down so you could be galivanting all over the country!"*

We anticipated that projected concession could work in two ways: first, the actor could respond with a concession as demanded; second, the actor could become angry at being the object of a guilt induction and respond with a more aggravating strategy such as a refusal.

In projected excuse, the reproacher indicates that s/he expects the actor to deny responsibility for the failure event:

My husband said, "Where the hell have you been? *Did you forget to wind your watch again?"*

Since a projected excuse is usually in the form of a question ("Did you get held up in traffic?"), it is most probable that the response will be in the form of a relevant answer. Consequently, we would anticipate that excuse is the most probable response.

In a projected justification, the victimized other indicates that s/he expects the actor to attempt to defend or to minimize the severity of the failure event:

She (my girlfriend) said, *"I suppose you're going to try and tell me it was just a joke. Don't you think I have any feelings?"*

Since a projected justification constitutes a potential attack on the actor's positive face, we expect that this form of reproach will engender a climate of hostility and consequently elicit account forms such as justification and refusal.

Finally, in a projected refusal, the reproacher suggests that the actor will deny guilt, deny the failure event, or deny him/her the right of reproach:

The theater owner called me into his office one night with the manager present, and began degrading me for what he felt were inaccurate doorman reports I was to fill out daily (bathroom cleanliness, theater temperature, etc.). The owner at first was withholding. *"Now why haven't you been filling these out with the truth?"* he said. *"You can't lie to me.* I saw the bathrooms downstairs and they're absolutely filthy."

Again, projected refusal is a highly aggravating form of reproach, which can be expected to elicit a response in kind.

Attitude Toward the Failure Event

A final determinant of the strategy an actor chooses in managing a failure event is the way that the actor feels about the offense itself. Clearly, if an actor feels unjustly accused, s/he will be unlikely to apologize or to offer an excuse. Similarly, the actor who feels guilty about a failure event will not ordinarily hesitate to use a mitigating strategy. We propose that actors will vary in terms of the degree to which they feel guilt or regret for an offense and that such variation will have a direct impact on their accounting behavior. We have identified three distinctive forms of attitude towards the failure event. Sometimes the actor expresses guilt or regret:

I was invited to visit a friend in Florida for the weekend. I had been dating another person irregularly, so I failed to tell the other person that I was visiting someone of the opposite sex. When I got back, *my conscience made me "spill the beans" to my ex-boyfriend.*

In other failure situations, the actor admits the offense but does not report feeling guilty:

I was dating someone for around two months, and neither of us had gone out with anyone else although we never said we couldn't. An old friend came back into town. *This old boyfriend and I went out for dinner one night, and I felt that I owed the other one an explanation.*

Finally, the actor, feeling unfairly accused, may deny the failure event and/or the right of reproach:

I work for a moving company during the summer. One day we had brought in a small baby crib to be shipped out. When I picked the crib up at the shipper's house, I noticed it was broken in a few places and I noted this on the inventory. After bringing the crib back to the warehouse I came extremely close to running over the crib with the fork lift. Later that day, a fellow worker told me that our warehouse man had told our boss that I had run over the crib. *I felt I had to account for myself in self-defense.*

Hypotheses

Whether or not an actor elects to employ one of the five account forms described above in managing a failure event is, in our judgment, a linear logistic function of several contextual variables: the characteristics of his/her relationship with the reproacher, the intensity of his/her communicative goal orientation, the severity of the failure event in abstract moral terms, the character of the reproach, and the actor's degree of felt guilt about the offense. Of course, not all of these variables can be expected to have a bearing on each strategy.

H_1: Actors will elect not to make an overt accounting in failure management situations characterized by low reproacher dominance, low actor goal orientation (relational, face, and instrumental), greater severity of the failure event, reproacher use of silence, reproacher use of behavioral cues, and low expressed guilt.

H_2: Actors will use concessions to manage failure events in situations characterized by high intimacy, high reproacher dominance, high actor relational and instrumental goal orientation, greater severity of the failure event, reproacher use of silence, behavioral cues, or projected concession, and a high level of expressed guilt.

H_3: Actors will use excuses to manage failure events in situations characterized by high intimacy, long-term consequences, high instrumental goal orientation, greater severity of the failure event, reproacher use of projected excuse, and high expressed guilt.

H_4: Actors will use justification to manage failure events in situations characterized by high intimacy, short-term relational consequences, low reproacher use of projected justification, and low expressed guilt.

H_5: Actors will refuse to account for a failure event in situations characterized by low reproacher dominance, long-term relational consequences, low relational and face goal orientation, reproacher use of projected concession, projected justification, or projected refusal, and low expressed guilt.

METHOD
Subjects

Subjects were 278 undergraduates enrolled in introductory courses in interpersonal communication at Texas Tech University and the University of Oklahoma. Administration of the test materials took place during regularly scheduled class periods. Subjects participated in the study in fulfillment of course requirements. Forms were completed anonymously.

Procedures

Subjects were informed that the experimenters were interested in learning what people say when they have to account for themselves: that is, what people say when they feel that, for one reason or another, they have to answer to someone else because of something they did or failed to do. They were given the following examples of account situations:

For example, you might have to account to your boss for why you were late to work; your girl/boyfriend might expect you to account for your failure to call when you were expected to; your professor might expect you to account for your absence from the midterm exam. Sometimes we give accounts even if no one asks for one, because we think that our behavior needs accounting for, or because we think that the other person thinks that our behavior was questionable. For example, when you return your two-month overdue book to the library, the librarian may glance at the due date and say nothing, but you may still feel a need to explain yourself. Or, when you run into an old friend while shopping at the mall, you may feel that you ought to say something right off the bat about why you haven't contacted him lately. On some occasions you may feel you have to account or explain yourself when you've done nothing wrong, from your point of view. For example, you go home for Thanksgiving and your father demands to know why you've grown a mustache.

Subjects were first asked to recall a situation in which they felt that they were expected to give an account because of some real (or apparent) failure event. They were instructed both to describe the circumstances that led them to feel that an account was expected and to be as specific as possible about the nature of the alleged offense. Next, they were asked to recall as best they could the actual words used in the reproach for the failure event. If there had not been a verbalized request for an account, they were asked to indicate that that was the case.

After recalling the nature of the reproach, subjects were asked to recall, in as close to the exact words as possible, what, if anything, their response had been in the situation. Finally, they were asked to rate the recalled situation against a 14-item set of 9-step scales designed to measure (1) *intimacy* of the reproacher and the actor, (2) *relational consequences* of honoring of the account, (3) *dominance* of the reproacher over the actor, (4) importance of *instrumental goals* to the actor, (5) importance of *positive face-management goals* to the actor, (6) importance of *relational maintenance goals* to the actor, and (7) *severity* of the failure event. The items measuring intimacy, relational consequences, and dominance were adapted from scales developed by Cody and McLaughlin (1980). The remaining items were newly developed for the present study. The actual scales employed are presented in Table 20.1.

Coding of Reproach Strategies, Account Strategies, and Expressed Guilt

Subjects' open-ended written responses were coded first for predominant type of reproach (silence, behavioral [nonverbal] cues, projected concession, projected excuse, projected justification, and projected refusal). If more than one type of reproach was present, the first type reported was coded as the predominant one. Indices of category agreement on a reliability sample of 20% ranged from 75% for behavioral cues to 92% for projected excuse. Guetzkow's P was equal to .85, with an upper limit of .92 and a lower limit of .78 (Guetzkow, 1950).

Responses were coded next for the presence or absence of each of five categories of account: silence, concession, excuse, justification and refusal. Indices of category agreement, calculated on a reliability sample of 20%, ranged from 70% for justification to 81% for excuse. Guetzkow's P was .76, with a lower limit of .68 and an upper limit of .84.

Finally, the open-ended descriptions of the circumstances surrounding the felt need to account were coded trichotomously for degree of expressed guilt (expression of guilt or regret over failure event, admission of failure event but failure to express guilt, denial of failure event and/or denial of right to reproach). The index of category agreement was 100% for all three categories. Guetzkow's P was 1.00.

ANALYSIS OF DATA

Obtained alpha reliability estimates for the rating scale data were intimacy (alpha = .81), relational consequences (alpha = .75), dominance of the reproacher (alpha = .61), importance of instrumental goals (alpha = .55), importance of positive face-management goals (alpha = .58), importance of relational maintenance goals (alpha = .72), and severity of the failure event (alpha = .76).

For each of the five types of account a separate stepwise logistic regression analysis was conducted to assess the goodness-of-fit of the predicted models of accounting behavior to the observed data. Rating scale data (intimacy, consequences, etc.) were treated as continuous variables; and the type of account, type of reproach, and expressed guilt were treated as categorical variables. In the linear logistic model, the expected proportion of "successes" (1-valued presence as opposed to 0-valued absence) of the dichotomous dependent variable (say, the presence of justification in a message) in a cell is given by

$$\frac{e^{\alpha+\beta\chi}}{1+e^{\alpha+\beta\chi}}$$

The constant α and regression coefficients B_i are

TABLE 20.1

Rating Scales Used to Measure Intimacy, Dominance, Relational Consequences, and Goal Orientation

VARIABLE	SCALES
Intimacy of the Actor-Reproacher Relationship	"This situation involved an intimate relationship"/"This situation involved a superficial relationship"
	"This situation involved a shallow relationship"/"This situation involved a very deep relationship"
Relational Consequences of the Account	"What I said (or didn't say) in this situation potentially could have had future consequences for the relationship between me and the other person"/"What I said (or didn't say) in this situation could NOT have had potential future consequences for the relationship between me and the other person"
	"The outcome of this situation could have potentially harmed the relationship between me and the other person"/"The outcome of this situation could NOT have potentially harmed the relationship between me and the other person"
Dominance of the Reproacher over the Actor	"I am usually submissive to the other person in this situation"/"I am usually NOT submissive to the other person in this situation"
	"The other person in this situation usually dominated me"/"The other person in this situation usually did NOT dominate me"
Importance of Instrumental Goals	"It was NOT very important to me that the other person in this situation believe me"/"It was very important to me that the other person in this situation believe me"
	"It was very important to me that the other person accept my account of things"/"It was NOT very important to me that the other person accept my account of things"
Importance of Positive Face-Maintenance Goals	"I was very concerned with the image I presented to the other person in this situation"/"I was NOT very concerned with the image I presented to the other person in this situation"
	"It was NOT very important for me to have the person in this situation think favorably of me"/"It was very important for me to have the person in this situation to think favorably of me"
Importance of Relational Maintenance Goals	"I was NOT very concerned with maintaining a good relationship with the person in this situation"/"I was very concerned with maintaining a good relationship with the person in this situation"
	"It was very important to me whether or not I disrupted the normal relations I have with the other person"/"It was NOT very important to me whether or not I disrupted the normal relations I have with the other person"
Severity of the Failure Event	"The behavior I felt obligated to account for was a severe offense"/"The behavior I felt obligated to account for was not an offense at all"
	"The behavior I felt I was expected to account for was very serious"/"The behavior I felt I was expected to account for was not serious at all"

estimated by a maximum likelihood procedure in which the value of

$$\frac{\prod\limits_{1+1}^{\pi} e^{\alpha+\beta\chi}}{\prod\limits_{1+1}^{\pi} (1+e^{\alpha+\beta\chi})}$$

is maximized (Cox, 1970).

Variables are entered into or removed from the regression equation on the basis of their ability to improve the fit of the predicted model to the observed scores. The contribution of a variable to the improvement of fit is measured by a χ^2 of association that is interpreted in the usual way; that is, a variable is entered into the model if the degree of improvement of fit is significantly ($p < .15$) large. Goodness-of-fit is assessed by a likelihood χ^2 statistic that will be nonsignificantly small if the deviations of the observed proportions of success from the fitted proportions are nonsystematic (i.e., chance fluctuations) (Goodman, 1978). Ideally, the confidence level associated with the goodness-of-fit χ^2 should approach 1.00.

Of the 278 subjects, 15 reported that they used silence in a situation in which they felt an account was expected. A summary of the stepwise regression results is given in Table 20.2.

The final equation for predicting that a subject would use silence in a failure management situation was

$$\theta_i = \frac{(\exp^{\alpha+\beta\chi})}{(1+\exp^{\alpha+\beta\chi})}$$

where α was -4.336 and the β_i were 1.082 (silence) $+4.177$ (expressed guilt$_1$) $+3.533$ (expressed guilt$_2$) $-.241$ (dominance of the reproacher) $+.219$ (severity of the failure event) $-.290$ (importance of relational goals).[2] Goodness-of-fit was excellent, with $\chi^2 = 91.887$; $df = 272$; $p = 1.00$. (The reader will note in Table 20.2 that the p value associated with the goodness-of-fit χ^2 is

reduced to 1.00 with the entry of the constant. What this means is that the best "guess" for y is 0, since the overwhelming majority of respondents were "failures" with respect to the variable. Although this may suggest that the significant χ^2 is artifactual, it does in fact represent the inclusion of a genuine probability-of-occurrence estimate in the equation similar to those used in classification functions [Lachenbruch, 1975]).

The percentage of correct classification was highest when the log odds ($\ln[\theta_i/1 - \theta_i]$) cutpoint was set at -3.11: 87 percent of the 1's and 67 percent of the 0's were correctly classified by the linear logistic function. Comparative histograms of the predicted probabilities of success for the 1's and 0's are presented in Figure 20.1 (a) (b). Results of the analysis indicated that the failure to give an account was associated with the reproacher's not saying anything, with a lesser degree of expressed guilt, with less important relational goals, with greater severity of the failure event, and with less dominance by the reproacher. Hypothesis 1 was only partially supported, inasmuch as instrumental and face-managing goals and behavioral cues were not important predictors of silence.

Of the 278 subjects reporting, 83 used a concession strategy in responding to a failure event. A summary of the stepwise regression results is given in Table 20.2. In the final equation for predicting that the actor would concede, α was equal to -3.212, and the β_i to .411 (silence) $+.407$ (projected concession) -1.849 (expressed guilt$_1$) $+.380$ (expressed guilt$_2$) $+.154$ (severity of the failure event) $+.207$ (instrumental goals). Goodness-of-fit was adequate but not outstanding: χ^2 was equal to 291.94; $df = 271$; $p = .182$. The percentage of correct classification was highest when the log odds cutpoint was set at $-.967$: 76% of the 1's and 60% of the 0's were correctly classified by the linear logistic function. Comparative histograms of the predicted probabilities of success for the 1's and 0's are presented in Figure 20.2 (a) (b). Subjects were most likely to report using concessions when they felt guilty, when instrumental goals were important, when the failure event was severe,

TABLE 20.2

Summary of Stepwise Logistic Regression Results for Five Accounting Behaviors

ACCOUNT TYPE	STEP NUMBER	TERM ENTERED/REMOVED*	df	LOG LIKELIHOOD	IMPROVEMENT CHI-SQUARE	p	GOODNESS-OF-FIT CHI-SQUARE	p
Silence	0	Constant		−58.38			116.76	1.000
	1	Silence	1	−54.82	7.12	.008	109.64	1.000
	2	Exp. Guilt	2	−51.46	6.72	.035	102.92	1.000
	3	Relational Goals	1	−49.27	4.39	.036	98.54	1.000
	4	Severity	1	−47.41	3.73	.054	94.81	1.000
	5	Dominance	1	−45.94	2.92	.087	91.89	1.000
Concession	0	Constant		−169.48			338.96	.006
	1	Exp. Guilt	2	−156.11	26.74	.000	312.21	.061
	2	Instr. Goals	1	−151.71	8.80	.003	303.42	.107
	3	Severity	1	−149.82	3.77	.052	299.64	.128
	4	Silence	1	−147.67	4.30	.048	295.35	.158
	5	Proj. Concession	1	−145.97	3.40	.065	291.94	.182
Excuse	0	Constant		−183.26			366.51	.000
	1	Exp. Guilt	2	−172.93	20.68	.000	345.84	.002
	2	Proj. Refusal	1	−167.88	10.10	.001	335.75	.007
	3	Rel. Consequences	1	−166.05	3.64	.056	332.10	.009
	4	Intimacy	1	−164.70	2.71	.100	329.39	.011
	5	Instr. Goals	1	−161.92	5.56	.018	323.84	.017
Justification	0	Constant		−144.99			289.99	.284
	1	Intimacy	1	−140.26	9.47	.002	280.52	.413
	2	Silence	1	−137.83	4.87	.027	275.65	.478
	3	Instr. Goals	1	−136.26	3.14	.076	272.51	.514
Refusal	0	Constant		−107.15			214.30	.998
	1	Exp. Guilt	2	−89.48	35.33	.000	178.96	1.000
	2	Silence	1	−85.86	7.25	.007	171.72	1.000
	3	Proj. Refusal	1	−83.10	5.52	.019	166.20	1.000
	4	Proj. Justifica.	1	−80.77	4.65	.031	161.55	1.000
	5	Proj. Concession	1	−78.46	4.64	.031	156.92	1.000
	6	Silence*	1	−79.46	1.99	.158	158.91	1.000
	7	Dominance	1	−77.38	4.15	.042	154.76	1.000
	8	Rel. Consequences	1	−74.74	5.28	.022	149.48	1.000

FIGURE 20.1

Histograms of Predicted Probabilities of Silence for Group 1 (a) and Group 2 (b)

(a)

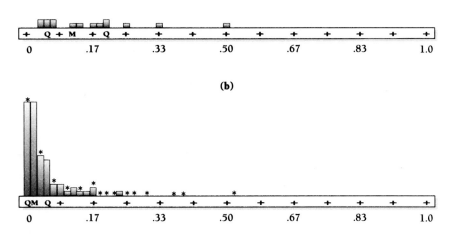

= 3 responses in Figure 20.1 (b)
* = fewer than 3 responses in Figure 20.1 (b)

when the other person made no reproach, or when the reproacher projected that the actor would concede. Hypothesis 2 was partially supported; however, intimacy, reproacher dominance, and relational goal orientation were not important predictors of the use of concession.

Of the 278 subjects, 175 reported using excuse as an accounting strategy. A summary of the stepwise regression results is given in Table 20.2. In the final equation for predicting the use of excuse, α was -5.218, and the β_i were -5.469 (projected refusal) -1.228 (expressed guilt$_1$) $+.543$ (expressed guilt$_2$) $-.137$ (intimacy) $-.129$ (consequences) $+.191$ (instrumental goals). Goodness-of-fit, however, was poor: the final χ^2 was 323.84 ($df = 272$), with a p value of .017. It was apparent that discrepancies between fitted and observed proportions of success were too large to be attributed to chance. Hypothesis 3 was not supported.

Of the 278 subjects, 60 reported using justifi-

cation to manage a failure event. A summary of the stepwise regression results is given in Table 20.2. In the final equation for predicting the use of justification, α was equal to -1.532, and the β_i were $-.330$ (silence) $+.216$ (intimacy) $-.159$ (instrumental goals). Goodness-of-fit was adequate; the final value of χ^2 was 272.514 ($df = 274$), with a p value of .514. The percentage of correct classification was highest when the log odds cutpoint was set at -1.237: 65% of the 1's and 65.14% of the 0's were correctly classified by the linear logistic function. Comparative histograms of the predicted probabilities of success for the 1 group (users of justification) and the 0 group are given in Figure 20.3 (a) (b). The use of justification as an accounting strategy was associated with greater relational intimacy, a lesser rate of silence on the part of the reproacher, and less important instrumental goals. Hypothesis 4 was only partially supported: relational consequences, dominance, projected justification,

FIGURE 20.2

Histograms of Predicted Probabilities of Concession for Group 1 (a) and Group 2 (b)

(a)

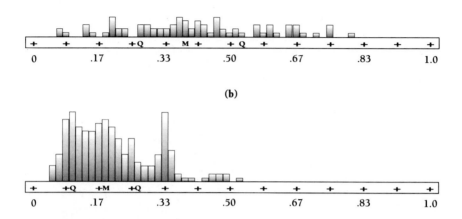

(b)

and expressed guilt were not important predictors of the use of justification.

Finally, 36 of the 278 subjects reporting indicated that they refused to give an account of the failure event. A summary of the stepwise regression results is given in Table 20.2. In the final equation for predicting the likelihood of refusal, α was equal to 3.930 and the β_i were .795 (projected concession) $+5.895$ (projected justification) $+1.667$ (projected refusal) $+2.012$ (expressed guilt$_1$) $-.893$ (expressed guilt$_2$) $+.202$ (consequences) $+.260$ (reproacher dominance). Goodness-of-fit was excellent: χ^2 was equal to 149.48; $df = 271$; $p = 1.00$. The percentage of correct classification of refusals was greatest when the log odds cutpoint was set at -2.287: 80.56% of the 1's and 77.69% of the 0's were correctly classified. Comparative histograms of the predicted probabilities of success for the 1's and 0's are given in Figure 20.4 (a) (b). Refusing to give an account was more likely when the actor denied the failure event; when the reproacher projected a refusal, a concession, or a justification; when reproacher dominance was greater; and when the relational consequences of honoring were less important. Hypothesis 5 was partially supported:

goal orientation was not an important predictor, while the hypothesized sign for reproacher dominance was in the wrong direction.

SUMMARY AND CONCLUSIONS

The purpose of the study was to examine the contexts within which individuals select one of five types of failure management strategy. It was our contention that such strategies can be arrayed along a mitigation/aggravation continuum; further, that contextual factors determine the extent to which the actor elects to be mitigating in dealing with a failure event.

The hypothesized model for predicting the use of excuses did not fit the obtained data. Excuse was by far the most popular mode of failure management and may simply reflect the fact that most people in judging their own behavior attribute failure to the circumstances of the situation rather than to their own bad intentions. This is consistent with the view that actors are more likely to attribute causes of their own behavior to environmental constraints rather than their own predispositions,

Histograms of Predicted Probabilities of Justifying for Group 1 (a) and Group 2 (b)

(a)

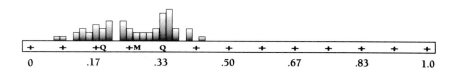

(b)

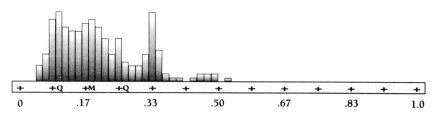

Histograms of Predicted Probabilities of Refusal for Group 1 (a) and Group 2 (b)

(a)

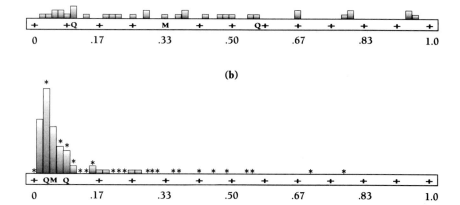

(b)

relative to observers (Jones & Nisbett, 1972). For the other failure management strategies our expectations were generally supported. The character of the reproach was an excellent predictor of the account strategy: mitigating reproaches led to mitigating account behavior, and aggravating reproaches invoked aggravating strategies in response. This finding is consistent with reciprocity or accommodative effects observed for self-disclosure and for noncontent aspects of speech (Cappella & Planalp, 1980; Giles, 1980; Martin, 1978; Rubin, 1975). A second successful predictor was the degree of expressed guilt. Concessions were the strategy of choice when the actor felt guilty; when s/he felt little guilt or felt unjustly accused, the failure-managing strategies employed were refusals and silence. The findings on expressed guilt are consistent with an equity interpretation (Walster, Walster, & Berscheid, 1978). Severity of the offense was shown to be a good predictor for certain of the strategies: when the failure event was serious, subjects reported using mitigating strategies like concession. Severity did not, however, predict the usage of aggravating strategies. Finally, the importance of instrumental goals was useful in predicting whether the actor would elect to say anything at all and in determining whether s/he would choose a concession or a justifying strategy. Low instrumental goal orientation was associated with the use of justification and with the actor's choosing not to give an account.

Several of the contextual factors examined turned out to be poor or inconsistent predictors. For example, the reproacher's use of behavioral (nonverbal) cues was not associated with strategy selection in any systematic way. We can probably attribute this failure of prediction to the general ambiguity most persons feel in attempting to interpret nonverbal cues and to their consequent reluctance to grant a "cold stare" the status of a speech act, that is, to treat it as a reproach of a particular sort.

The actor's orientation to relational maintenance and face-saving goals was not in general predictive of strategy selection, nor were relational intimacy and dominance found to be significant predictors

in more than a few types of account strategies. Perhaps it is fair to say that in most situations in which a failure event must be dealt with, actors will be anxious to avoid opprobrium and to repair the social fabric; and, indeed, we found very little variability and negatively skewed distributions for the two goal orientation variables. As far as the intimacy and dominance variables are concerned, we were simply forced to conclude that the actual nature of the offense itself and the way the two parties, actor and reproacher, appear to feel about it are the prepotent determinants of the way the failure event is managed. That is, within the same relationship, strategies for remedying the effects of untoward acts may vary considerably, depending on the nature of the very specific circumstances surrounding the offense and its evaluation.

We see several promising directions for future research. The most important of these directions would be to use an approach that would be superior to the analysis of "recalled" events—to induce subjects to have "failures" or perceived failures in a laboratory setting and record their accounts to an experimenter or to a confederate. Similarly, accounts can be obtained in naturalistic settings; for example, persons returning defective merchandise to a store or turning over an unwanted pet to the pound are likely candidates for spontaneous account giving.

ENDNOTES

[1] The descriptions of failure events that we use as examples were collected from subjects participating in the research reported here. Emphasis has been added by the authors.

[2] Expressed guilt$_1$ is an orthogonal vector representing the contrast between expressing guilt (-1) and denying the failure event ($+1$). Expressed guilt$_2$ is an orthogonal vector representing the contrast between expressing guilt ($-$) and admitting the failure event but not reporting feeling guilt ($+$).

REFERENCES

Benoit, P. Structural coherence production in the conversations of preschool children. Paper presented to the Speech Communication Association, New York, 1980.

Blumstein, P. W., Carssow, K. G., Hall, J., Hawkins, B., Hoffman, R., Ishem, E., Maurer, C. P., Spens, D., Taylor, J., & Zimmerman, D. L. The honoring of accounts. *American Sociological Review,* 1974, 39, 551-566.

Bochner, A., Kaminski, E., & Fitzpatrick, M. A. The conceptual domain of interpersonal communication. *Human Communication Research,* 1977, *3,* 291-302.

Brown, P., & Levinson, S. Universals in language usage: Politeness phenomena. In E. N. Goody (Ed.), *Questions and politeness: Strategies in social interaction.* Cambridge: Cambridge University Press, 1978.

Cappella, J. N., & Planalp, S. Talk and silence sequences in informal conversations III: Interspeaker influence. *Human Communication Research,* 1981, *7,* 117-132.

Clark, R. A. The impact on selection of persuasive strategies of self-interest and desired liking. *Communication Monographs,* 1979, *46,* 257-273.

Clark, R. A., & Delia, J. Topoi and rhetorical competence. *The Quarterly Journal of Speech,* 1979, *65,* 187-206.

Cody, M. J. A multidimensional scaling of naturalistic persuasion situations. Paper presented to the Speech Communication Association, Minneapolis, 1978.

Cody, M. J., & McLaughlin, M. L. Perceptions of compliance-gaining situations: A dimensional analysis. *Communication Monographs,* 1980, *47,* 132-148.

Cody, M. J., McLaughlin, M. L., & Jordan, W. J. A multidimensional scaling of three sets of compliance-gaining strategies. *Communication Quarterly,* 1980, *28,* 34-46.

Cody, M. J., Woelfel, M. L., & Jordan, W. J. Dimensions of compliance-gaining situations. *Human Communication Research,* in press.

Cox, D. R. *The analysis of binary data.* London: Methuen, 1970.

Dixon, W. J., & Brown, M. B. (Eds.). *BMDP-79: Biomedical computer programs, P-series.* Berkeley: University of California Press, 1979.

Falbo, T., & Peplau, L. A. Power strategies in intimate relationships. *Journal of Personality and Social Psychology,* 1980, *39,* 618-628.

Fitzpatrick, M. A., & Winke, J. You always hurt the one you love: Strategies and tactics in interpersonal conflict. *Communication Quarterly,* 1979, *27,* 3-11.

Forgas, J. The perception of social episodes: Categorical and dimensional representations of two different social milieus. *Journal of Personality and Social Psychology, 34,* 199-209.

Garvey, C. The contingent query: A dependent action in conversation. In M. Lewis and L. A. Rosenblum (Eds.), *Interactions, conversation and the development of language.* New York: Wiley, 1977.

Goodman, L. A. *Analyzing qualitative/categorical data.* Cambridge, MA: Abt Books, 1978.

Giles, H. New directions in accommodation theory. *York Papers in Linguistics,* 1980, *9,* 105-136.

Guetzkow, H. Unitizing and categorizing problems in coding qualitative data. *Journal of Clinical Psychology,* 1950, *6,* 47-58.

Harré, R. The ethogenic approach: Theory and practice. In L. Berkowitz (Ed.), *Advances in experimental social psychology* (Vol. 10). New York: Academic Press, 1977.

Jones, E., & Nisbett, R. The actor and observer: Divergent perceptions of the causes of behavior. In E. Jones, D. Kanouse, H. Kelley, R. Nisbett, S. Valins, and B. Weiner (Eds.), *Attribution: Perceiving the causes of behavior.* Morristown, NJ: General Learning Press, 1972, pp. 1-26.

Kipnis, D., & Cohen, E. S. Power tactics and affection. Paper presented to the Eastern Psychological Association, Philadelphia, 1979.

Labov, W., & Fanshel, D. *Therapeutic discourse: Psychotherapy as conversation.* New York: Academic Press, 1977.

Lachenbruch, P. A. *Discriminant analysis.* Hafner Press, 1975.

Lustig, M. W., & King, S. W. The effect of communication apprehension and situation on communication strategy choices. *Human Communication Research,* 1980, *7,* 74-82.

Martin, T. L. Intimacy and reciprocity of exchange: A comparison of spouses and strangers. *Journal of Personality and Social Psychology,* 1978, *36,* 72-81.

McLaughlin, M. L., Cody, M. J., & Robey, C. S. Situational influences on the selection of strategies to resist compliance-gaining attempts. *Human Communication Research,* 1980, *7,* 14-36.

Michener, H. A., & Schwertfeger, M. Liking as a determinant of power tactic preference. *Sociometry,* 1972, *35,* 190-202.

Miller, G. R., Boster, F., Roloff, M. E., & Seibold, D. Compliance-gaining message strategies: A typology and some findings concerning effects of situational differences. *Communication Monographs,* 1977, *44,* 37-51.

Miller, G. R., & Steinberg, M. *Between people: A new analysis of interpersonal communication.* Chicago: Science Research Associates, 1975.

Rubin, Z. Disclosing oneself to a stranger: Reciprocity and its limits. *Journal of Experimental Social Psychology,* 1975, *11,* 233-260.

Schonbach, P. A category system for account phases. *European Journal of Social Psychology,* 1980, *10,* 195-200.

Scott, M. B., & Lyman, S. Accounts. *American Sociological Review,* 1968, *33,* 46-62.

Sykes, G. M., & Matza, D. Techniques of neutralization. *American Sociological Review,* 1957, *22,* 667-669.

Vucinich, S. Elements of cohesion between turns in ordinary conversation. *Semiotica,* 1977, *20,* 229-257.

Walster, E. M., Walster, G. W., & Berscheid, E. *Equity: Theory and research.* Boston: Allyn & Bacon, 1978.

Wiseman, R. L., & Schenck-Hamlin, W. A multidimensional scaling validation of an inductively derived set of compliance-gaining strategies. Paper presented to the Speech Communication Association, Anaheim, 1981.

Wish, M. Role and personal expectations about interpersonal communication. Paper presented at the United States–Japan Seminar on multidimensional scaling, San Diego, 1975.

21

An Analysis of Couples' Conversational Complaints

J. K. ALBERTS

This study sought to examine the connections between couples' complaint behavior and their feelings about their relationships. Associations among complaint type, complaint response type, complaint affect, and relational adjustment were analyzed. Results indicated that adjusted couples were significantly more likely to manifest behavioral complaints, positive affect, and agreement responses. Maladjusted couples were significantly more likely to engage in personal characteristic complaints, negative affect, and countercomplaint responses. No other associations were found. It was also determined that adjusted and maladjusted couples did not differ significantly with regard to the number of complaints made.

Communication scholars, psychologists, and sociologists, among others, have attempted to determine why some marital relationships are successful while others are not. In attempting to determine this, a number of these scholars have discovered that verbal interaction between husbands and wives can account for much of the variance in marital success or failure (Burgess, 1981; Fitzpatrick, 1983; Gottman, 1979). More specifically, studies by Locke, Sabagh, and Thomas (1957) and Navran (1967) indicate that marital satisfaction and "good" communication are correlated at .80. Consequently, a number of studies have attempted to describe how satisfied and dissatisfied (or adjusted versus maladjusted) couples communicate and manage conflict (Fitzpatrick, 1983; Gottman, 1979; Thomas, 1977) in order to determine more precisely the communication strategies associated with marital adjustment.

Reported here are the results of a study which was conducted in order to extend our knowledge of couples' marital adjustment and their communication behavior. Specifically, this study examined couples' conversational complaint behavior; it sought to determine how variables such as complaint type, complaint affect, and complaint response are associated with couples' subjective feelings about their relationships. Complaint behavior was chosen as the area of examination because complaints are pervasive, problematic and likely to be connected to a couple's relational satisfaction or adjustment.

An analysis of couples' complaint interactions is best conducted in the context of the research on remedial work and account episodes. Remedial work is defined by Goffman (1971, p. 109) as interaction which transforms "what could be seen as offensive into what can be seen as acceptable." Accounting sequences are one conversational strategy used to enact such remedial work. The account sequence consists of four parts: the failure event, reproach, account, and evaluation (of the account) (Schonbach, 1980, p. 195). Failure events are defined by Schonbach (p. 195) as "deviant acts committed or obligations omitted," and the account is the "statement made . . . to explain (the) unanticipated or untoward behavior" (Scott & Lyman, 1968, p. 46).

From Alberts, J. K. (1988). An analysis of couples' conversational complaints. *Communication Monographs, 55,* 184-197.

Complaint episodes, which consist of a complaint and complaint response, are attempts to perform remedial work during conversational interaction. A complaint is defined by the *Oxford English Dictionary* (1971, p. 722) as "an outcry against or because of injury; representation of a wrong suffered; utterance of a grievance." Both Doelger (1984, p. 15) and Paulson (1982, p. 4) define complaints as statements of dissatisfaction with the actions (or lack of action) of another. The essential nature of a complaint is best captured by Edmondson's (1981) corollary "H did P, P bad for S" (where H = hearer and S = speaker). A complaint, then, is a call for remedial work; it functions as a reproach in response to some failure event. In order to enact the necessary remedial work, the complaint recipient must provide some type of explanation of his/her behavior during the complaint response, which functions as an account. Thus, complaint interactions are one type of account episode.

While extensive research has been conducted on account behavior (Blumstein et al., 1974; Cody & McLaughlin, 1985; McLaughlin et al., 1983a, 1983b; Morris, 1985; Remler, 1978; Schonbach, 1980; Scott & Lyman, 1968), most of it has focused predominantly on the account rather than the reproach (McLaughlin et al., 1983b, is one notable exception). Also, relatively little research has concentrated upon complaint interactions as a type of accounting sequence. However, research on both accounts and complaints indicates that remedial work of this nature is important in intimate relationships.

Morris (1985) explains that many accounting episodes occur in response to disagreements about rules and that rules (and discussions of such) become substantive issues when dispreferred outcomes are experienced. He adds that experiencing dispreferred outcomes is most likely when participants' rules are substantially different, the participants are highly interdependent, and the interaction is highly consequential, a set of circumstances likely to occur in romantic relationships. Cody and McLaughlin (1985, p. 50) write that "in long-term interpersonal relationships . . . persons are often re-

proached for behavior which appears to violate the requirements of a role (for example, lover, child, subordinate) vís a vís some focal counter-role (lover, parent, superior)." For these reasons, accounting episodes are likely to occur frequently in intimate relationships such as marriage.

Several studies on complaints reveal that complaining behavior, as well as being pervasive, is problematic for many married couples. On the basis of two studies (Cunningham, Stanbull, & Kelley, 1973; Tiggle, Peters, & Kelley, 1977, cited in Kelley, 1979), Kelley developed a fifteen category typology of problems couples believed that they faced. The first three categories were primarily instances of conflict about conflict behavior. The third of those categories consisted of influence attempts and nagging (or complaining[1]). As early as 1938, a study by Lewis Terman showed that unhappy couples were distinguished from happy ones by the extent to which they reported their partner's being argumentative, critical, nagging, etc. (Kelley, 1979, p. 154). Thus, complaining may be a central and difficult aspect of marital relationships.

Research focusing upon couples' relational satisfaction and/or their complaint interactions indicates that relational satisfaction and complaining behavior are associated. Cousins and Vincent (1983) examined aversive and supportive behavior following spousal complaints involving non-marital issues. They discovered that negative responses tended to inhibit further complaining while, unexpectedly, positive responses had no affect on further complaining. The researchers suggested that a decrease in aversive responses rather than an increase in supportive responses would improve marital complaint interactions. However, this study measured only verbal activity; increased verbal output is not a guarantee of a successful complaint interaction.

Gottman (1979) and Thomas (1977) examined couples and their conflict and complaining behavior. Gottman performed a detailed sequential analysis of the videotaped conversations of twenty-eight couples, half of whom were drawn from a clinical sample and half of whom were not.

Gottman concluded that the most dysfunctional complaint interaction, and the one most frequently enacted by unhappily married couples, was cross-complaining, a complaint-countercomplaint sequence. Gottman also examined audiotapes of a group of distressed couples previously studied by Raush et al. (1974) and determined that a similar pattern was obtained in this study—discordant couples manifested cross-complaining (Gottman, 1970, pp. 129-130).

In a series of studies conducted both in the laboratory and in couples' homes, Thomas analyzed couples' conflict interactions and decision-making. He discovered that the two most frequent complaint sequences for dissatisfied married couples were complaint-countercomplaint and complaint-disagreement.

Other studies have examined complaints as a conversational phenomenon (Coulthard, 1977; Doelger, 1984; Edmondson, 1981; Turner, 1970). These analyses suggested that complaints are likely to engender disagreeing, justification, or apology responses. All of this research tended to focus almost exclusively upon the complaint response; it did not address other aspects of the complaint interaction.

The research on accounts, complaints, and couples' relational satisfaction suggests that remedial work is important to romantic relationships, occurs frequently, and often creates problems. Furthermore, studies such as those by Gottman, Raush and Thomas indicate that relational satisfaction may be connected to a couple's conflict and complaint interactions. What none of these studies explained was what it is people complain about; nor do they provide information about the range of responses complaint recipients use. As well, those studies which focused on marital complaints examined only the behavior of distressed couples; little information was provided about how non-distressed couples interact. Thus, much is still unknown about couples' complaint interactions and their feelings about their relationships.

While a variety of research on accounting episodes has been conducted, little of that research has examined such episodes in the context of close relationships. Much of it has analyzed interactions between strangers (McLaughlin et al., 1983b), examined subjects' perceptions of unknown others' behavior (Blumstein et al., 1974), or was based on recall data of episodes with a variety of intimate and non-intimate partners (McLaughlin et al., 1983a). Research on couples' complaint behavior, therefore, can contribute not only to greater understanding of communication strategies and relational adjustment but also to increased understanding of accounting behavior in close relationships.

Prior research on repair and complaint episodes has focused on the account/response portion of these interactions. As Cody and McLaughlin (1985, p. 52) point out, only recently has the focus shifted to the constraints, both interactional and situational, on the kinds of moves participants are likely to make during accounting behavior. This is even more true of the complaints research. Thus far, studies on complaining have examined the complaint response exclusively. These studies have not considered what contextual factors, aside from relational adjustment, could be influencing the choices that interactants make during a complaint episode.

Cody and McLaughlin (1985, p. 52) propose that in accounting episodes two factors, which they call the aggravation-mitigation continuum (Labov & Fanshel, 1977) and perception of the situation, influence the type of account a participant makes. They suggest that moves which are more "mitigating" tend to elicit like moves while moves which are relatively "aggravating" tend to engender aggravating moves (Cody & McLaughlin, 1985, p. 52). For example, McLaughlin et al. (1983a) found that one of the best predictors of an interactant's choice of remedial strategy was the way in which that person was reproached; they also found that more mitigating accounts tended to lead to more mitigating evaluations of those accounts.

It follows, then, that during complaint interactions, the "aggravation" level of the complaint could also affect the response type selected by the complaint recipient. In fact, I would suggest that during couples' complaint episodes it is the type of complaint and the affect with which that complaint is offered which influence the response a complaint recipient is likely to choose. It is not clear how relational adjustment might interact with these two factors. A couple's relational adjustment could influence the complaint type and/or affect as well as the complaint response, as has been suggested. Or it is possible that it is merely complaint type and/or affect which actually contribute.

However, it has not been established previously what types of complaints are offered nor how these complaints tend to be delivered. Therefore, before a study could be conducted to analyze the relative contribution of these factors, a preliminary study had to be performed in order to develop a typology of complaint types and affect. As well, although a category system of accounts has been established and a number of complaint responses suggested by a variety of sources, no definitive typology of complaint responses had been delineated. Consequently, a preliminary study was performed in order to determine appropriate categories for describing complaint type and response type, as well as affect.

A TAXONOMY OF COUPLES' COMPLAINT BEHAVIOR

In a preliminary study (Alberts, 1987), 52 heterosexual couples were interviewed concerning their complaint interactions with each other. Each member of the couple provided an example of a complaint given to and one received from the relational partner. Additional information concerning intent, location, and timing of the interaction, preceding and succeeding events, and beliefs about desirable complaint behavior was collected (see Appendix A).

The collected data were used to provide a descriptive taxonomy of couples' complaint and response types. Based on a content analysis, it was determined that appropriate categories for couples' complaint types were: behavioral, performance, personal characteristic, personal appearance, and complaining. The complaint responses collected in the study were placed in five categories: agree, justify, denial, countercomplaint and pass. These response categories roughly correspond to the accounts categories delineated in McLaughlin et al. (1983a): concessions, excuses, justifications, refusals, and silence. The complaints taxonomy combined excuses and justifications[2] and added the category of countercomplaints.

A behavioral complaint was a complaint made about actions done or not done. For example, a man complained, "Why haven't I had a cooked meal all week?" A performance complaint, on the other hand, had to do with how an action was performed (not whether or not it was done), such as "You're driving too fast." A personal characteristic complaint concerned the whole person, his/her personality, attitudes, emotional nature or belief system. One man said to his partner, "You're a snob." Personal appearance complaints involved comments about the partner's looks, such as "You have a fat butt and better lose weight." Finally, there were complaints about complaining, for example, "You're always complaining" or "Quit whining."

The complaint responses fell into five categories as well. The largest number of responses were justifications/excuses. For example, when one man received the complaint he did not talk enough, he replied, "The other people talk so much I never had a chance to say a word." Denial responses included statements which refused to acknowledge the legitimacy of the complaints, disagreed with the complainer, or which refused the requested change. A husband who received the complaint he never listened replied, "I do too." Agreement responses were statements which either explicitly agreed that the complaint was legitimate or that change was necessary, or which provided implicit agreement through an apology. Countercomplaints involved responses which answered the complaint with a complaint. One female complained her husband was "too wizzy" and "turned the corner too fast," to which he replied "I'd rather be wizzy than pokey like you." Also included in the response typology was the pass. A pass occurred whenever the recipient ignored the complaint or failed to respond verbally.

The preliminary study indicated that behavioral complaints were by far the most frequently occurring complaint type (accounting for 72% of the complaints); these complaints were met most frequently with justification responses. Personal characteristic complaints tended to occur second most frequently (17%) and were most often answered with denials. The study also revealed that men and women did not differ significantly in their reported complaint types, response types, nor in the responses they gave to particular types of complaints. In addition, the data, unexpectedly, suggested that satisfied and dissatisfied couples did not differ in their reports of their complaint behavior. However, because these results were based on a small subsample (19 of the 52 couples)[3] and couples' *reports* of their behavior, a study of couples' actual conversational behavior needed to be conducted.

METHOD

PARTICIPANTS

Forty heterosexual couples engaged in the taped interactions examined in this study. All of the couples had been either married or living together for a minimum of 6 months; twenty-three (53%) of the couples were married and seventeen (47%) were living together. The individuals ranged from 19 to 71 years old. A diversity of socioeconomic and educational backgrounds was represented. Three of the individuals had only an elementary school education, and 12 held college degrees. Two of the 12 were pursuing graduate degrees, and 1 had attained a master's degree. The sample included a blue collar worker, bank teller, department store clerk, several housewives, a bank president, a religious education director, and a variety of others. The sample was acquired through solicitation of volunteers. Undergraduate students recommended couples (friends, parents, other relatives), and a snowball technique was employed. That is, couples who were initially contacted for participation in the study recommended other couples as potential participants. Though the initial participants were suggested by undergraduate students, no couples composed only of undergraduate students were used, and only four subjects in the pool were undergraduate students.

As the sample was formed, couples were selected whose relational adjustment scores represented a range that could be divided into the subgroups of adjusted and maladjusted. Twenty couples were chosen who fell into each category based on Spanier's Dyadic Adjustment Scale (1976). For this study, because it was designed to study normal couples and not clinical ones, it was decided to place all couples in the category of maladjusted in which one member had a score of 100 or less. The adjusted couples had a mean DAS score of 242.5 while the maladjusted couples had a mean score of 195.5. The obtained alpha reliability estimate for the Dyadic Adjustment Scale was .90. A t-test was conducted on the DAS scores for the two groups; the two groups were significantly different, $t(38) = 7.49$, $p < .001$.

PROCEDURES

Participants were informed that the experimenter was interested in learning how couples discuss issues on which they disagree. First, each member of the couple filled out Spanier's (1976) Dyadic Adjustment Scale privately. Once the DAS was completed, each member was given a modified version of Strodtbeck's Revealed Differences Form (1951). The Revealed Differences Form was modified by updating some of the scenarios and adding a few additional scenes. In addition to the twenty items on the Revealed Differences Form, each member of the couple was asked to write a scene which described a problem area or area of disagreement in their relationship.

After the participants completed the forms, the investigator circled all items on the Revealed Differences Form on which the couple disagreed. The couple was then instructed to discuss these items while a tape recorder recorded the interaction. The couples were encouraged to strive for agreement, but, if that was not possible, they were allowed to "agree to disagree." They also were asked to discuss the item they each had written. The couple was encouraged to talk for between thirty minutes and an hour.

CODING OF COMPLAINT TYPE, COMPLAINT AFFECT, AND RESPONSE TYPE

The 40 tapes yielded 19 hours and 43 minutes of interaction. The length of the tapes ranged from 15 minutes to 1 hour. Of the approximately 20 hours of tape, 47% (9 hours, 16 minutes) was produced by adjusted couples and 53% (10 hours, 27 minutes) was produced by maladjusted couples.

Once the data were collected, each tape was transcribed. These transcriptions were typed in script form and attempted to capture both overlapping speech and laughter as well as the actual words spoken.

After the tapes were transcribed, 25% (10) of the tapes were coded to establish coding reliability. First, three coders listened to each tape as they read through the transcript. Three additional passes were then made through the transcripts while the tapes were playing; at each pass, a different variable was coded: presence of complaints and responses, category of complaints and responses, and complaint affect.

The first task required the coders to read through each of the transcripts while listening to the tapes and to indicate which utterances contained complaints and responses. Once agreement among the three coders was reached as to which utterances were complaints and responses, the coders once again read through the transcripts and listened to the tapes; this time, however, the coders marked each complaint and response with the appropriate category label. Surprisingly, only behavioral and personal characteristic complaints were located on the transcripts; however, responses were located which fell into all of the response categories.

The third pass through the transcripts involved coding the complaints for affect. Complaint affect was coded as positive, neutral, or negative, a standard categorization for affect (Krokoff, Gottman, &

Roy, 1986, p. 12).[4] To aid in coding for affect, the coders used four semantic differential scales which provided an operational definition for positive, negative, and neutral affect. The four scales measured kindness/cruelty, positivity/negativity, softness/hardness, and humor/seriousness.

For the three coding tasks, simple agreement among the coders was 88% for presence of complaints and responses, 93% for category placement, and 83% for affect. Cohen's Kappa reliability index for the three were .69, .71, and .64.[5] Differences were resolved through discussion. The remainder of the data were coded by the researcher.

Finally, the transcripts were placed into the proper category for relationship status, 20 in the adjusted and 20 in the maladjusted, based on the couples' Dyadic Adjustment Scores.

RESULTS

Once the data were coded they were placed into a contingency table for analysis (see Table 21.1). After the data were tabled, the cells were weighted by 0.5 to compensate for the empty cells, and the data were subjected to log linear analysis.[6]

A log linear analysis was conducted on the tabled data in order to establish the relationships among the four variables (A = marital adjustment, B = complaint type, C = complaint affect, D = response type). Initially, the likelihood-ratio chi-square values were generated in order to determine the hierarchy of effects to be entered into the log linear model (see Table 21.2). An examination of the residual and component chi-square comparisons resulted in the selection of Model Seven.

The most parsimonious model, then, included A, B, C, D, and the A X B, A X C, and A X D interactions. In order to test the associations among the four variables, specific-effects parameters were tested with a z statistic. This was a two-tailed test, so a z statistic of 1.96 or greater was needed to achieve significance. However, because of the repeated z tests being conducted on the data and the associated probability of an increase in Type I

TABLE 21.1

Complaint, Type, Affect, and Complaint Response for Adjusted and Maladjusted Couples

MARITAL ADJUSTMENT	COMPLAINT TYPE	AFFECT	RESPONSE TYPE				
			AGREE	DENY	JUSTIFY	COUNTER-COMPLAIN	PASS
Adjusted	Behavioral	Positive	6	5	4	3	3
		Neutral	17	6	24	5	8
		Negative	9	10	6	0	1
	Personal Characteristic	Positive	3	1	1	0	3
		Neutral	3	1	5	0	4
		Negative	1	3	1	0	2
Maladjusted	Behavioral	Positive	4	1	5	1	2
		Neutral	10	16	20	16	12
		Negative	7	15	14	8	8
	Personal Characteristic	Positive	2	1	2	1	4
		Neutral	5	8	7	4	8
		Negative	6	10	5	9	4

TABLE 21.2

Likelihood-Ratio Chi-Square Values

MODEL	MARGINALS	RESIDUAL		COMPONENT		
		L^2	df	L^2	df	p
1	A	219.07	58			
2	A B	169.15	57	49.92	1	0.01
3	A B C	93.71	55	75.98	2	0.01
4	A B C D	80.21	51	13.5	4	0.01
5	AB C D	73.32	50	6.89	1	0.01
6	AB AC D	61.48	48	11.84	2	0.01
7	AB AC AD	45.21	44	16.27	4	0.01
8	AB AC AD BC	40.92	42	4.29	2	0.10
9	AB AC AD BC BD	34.75	38	6.17	4	0.25
10	AB AC AD BC BD CD	22.32	30	12.43	8	0.10
11	ABC AD BD CD	22.28	28	0.04	2	0.50
12	ABC ABD C	19.63	24	2.65	4	0.50
13	ABC ABD ACD	6.88	16	12.75	8	0.10
14	ABC ABD ACD BCD	3.26	8	3.62	8	0.50
15	ABCD	0	0	3.62	8	0.50

L^2 = maximum likelihood-ratio chi-square

error, each z test was performed at an enhanced numerical level of significance. Consequently, an experimentwise z statistic of 2.12 was needed to achieve significance.

Having established there was an association between marital type and complaint type, $z = 2.13$; between marital type and affect, $z = 2.27$; and between marital type and response type, $z = 2.48$, the lambda effects were examined to determine which levels of marital type were associated with which levels of complaint type, affect, and response type (see Tables 21.3, 21.4, and 21.5). The analysis revealed that there was a significant association between relationship type and complaint type, $L^2(1) = 6.89, p < .01$. As Table 21.3 reveals, when compared to satisfied couples, dissatisfied couples' complaint interactions were composed of significantly more personal characteristic complaints. Conversely, the satisfied couples' complaints were composed of significantly more behavioral complaints.

There was also a significant association between marital type and affect, $L^2(2) = 11.84, p < .01$. The data indicate that satisfied couples' complaints did tend to be delivered more frequently with positive affect while dissatisfied couples' complaints were more frequently delivered with negative affect. However, there was no difference between the couples in terms of neutral affect.

The final significant association found was between relationship type and response type, $L^2(4) = 16.27, p < .01$. Prior research had indicated that dissatisfied couples engaged in countercomplaint and disagreement (or denial) responses (Gottman, 1979; Thomas, 1977), but no research had suggested what responses satisfied couples used. As Table 21.5 reveals, the data from the study confirm Gottman and Thomas' contention that dissatisfied couples' complaints tended to be responded to more often with countercomplaints; however, it does not confirm Thomas' claim that dissatisfied couples are more likely to use denial responses. These data also revealed that adjusted couples' complaints were significantly more often answered with agreement responses than were maladjusted couples'.

TABLE 21.3

Specific Effects for Marital Type and Complaint Type

COMPLAINT TYPE	MARITAL TYPE		
	ADJUSTED λ	MALADJUSTED λ	z TEST
Behavioral	.152	−.152	2.133*
Personal Characteristics	−.152	.152	−2.133*

* $p < .05$ (experimentwise)

TABLE 21.4

Specific Effects for Marital Type and Affect

AFFECT	MARITAL TYPE		
	ADJUSTED λ	MALADJUSTED λ	z TEST
Positive	.260	−.260	2.274*
Neutral	−.002	.002	−0.019
Negative	−.258	.258	−2.536*

* $p < .05$ (experimentwise)

TABLE 21.5

Specific Effects for Marital Type and Response Type

RESPONSE TYPE	MARITAL TYPE		
	ADJUSTED λ	MALADJUSTED λ	z TEST
Agree	.325	−.325	2.447*
Deny	−.003	.003	−0.024
Justify	.136	−.136	1.070
Countercomplain	−.406	.406	−2.219
Pass	−.041	.041	−0.289

* $p < .05$ (experimentwise)

No other significant associations were found. The data indicated that neither complaint type and response type, $L^2(4) = 6.17$, $p < .25$, nor affect and response type, $L^2(8) = 12.43$, $p < .10$, nor complaint type and complaint affect, $L^2(4) = 4.29$, $p < .25$, were significantly associated.

Aside from discovering the differences in actual complaint behavior, another question which needed to be answered was whether adjusted and maladjusted couples differed in the number of complaints in which they engaged. It could have been that it was not so much how the couples complained as it was the number of complaints which affected their feelings about their relationship. It was discovered that adjusted couples did engage in fewer complaints than did maladjusted (135 vs. 215), but this difference was not significant, $t(38) = 1.52$, $p < .20$.

DISCUSSION

This study was designed to examine the relationship between couples' complaint behavior and their feelings about their relationships. It had been claimed that distressed and non-distressed couples interacted differently during complaint exchanges. If this were true, what aspects of the complaint interaction differed between the two couple types? Earlier research on complaints had focused almost exclusively upon how relationship type influenced complaint response type. However, research on account episodes suggested that other variables, such as reproach (or complaint) type, could influence accounting behavior. Therefore, the study examined whether interactional variables such as complaint type and complaint affect could be influencing the type of response an interactant chose, apart from his or her feelings about the partner.

It was determined that adjusted and maladjusted couples differed in their complaint behavior. Furthermore, it was found that they differed not only in the type of responses they used during complaint interactions but also in the type of complaints made and the type of affect they used when offering those complaints. It was shown that adjusted couples tended to offer more behavioral complaints, used more positive affect, and responded more often with agreement responses. Maladjusted couples, on the other hand, offered more personal characteristic complaints, used negative affect more often, and more often responded with countercomplaints. These findings suggested a more complex view of what occurred during a complaint interaction.

Because the couples differed along all three dependent variables, it was necessary to discover if those variables were associated with each other as well as with relationship adjustment. McLaughlin and Cody's (1983a) study, for example, indicated that type of reproach was the best predictor of an interactant's choice of remedial account. Thus, it was anticipated that complaint type or complaint affect would play an influencing role in the types of complaint response that interactants chose. However, in the present study this was not the case. It was revealed that it is relationship type which has the strongest influence on the type of response a participant is likely to offer to a given complaint. It could be that in such intimate relationships as romance and marriage one's feelings about one's partner color one's communication behavior more strongly than that partner's immediate behavior.

This further suggests that if a couple wishes to alter their complaint behavior, it will require effort on the part of both participants to make that change. Merely having the complainer make more behavioral complaints will not necessarily result in more positive affect nor in more agreement responses. Instead, each participant would need to make changes in his or her complaint behavior.

The implications of this study seem clear: Couples' feelings about their relationships are connected to their complaint behavior. What is not clear is whether the differences in complaint behavior preceded or followed the couples' feelings about their partners. Other research (Kelley et al., 1985; Markman, 1979; 1981) indicates that negative communication precedes relational dissatisfaction; however, it is quite likely that couples' relational definitions and their communication behavior mutually influence one another. Thus, it is probable that if couples do make changes in their complaint behavior, their feelings about the relationship will be influenced.

The results of this study provide a more comprehensive view of couples' conversational complaint behavior than has previous research. Complaint research to date has focused primarily upon response types without considering other variables that might characterize couples' complaint behavior. As well, prior research focused on distressed couples' behavior without delineating how it is that non-distressed couples perform complaint interactions. It is not enough to know what distressed couples do; if dysfunctional couples wish to change, they need a model of effective complaint behavior.

It is now with somewhat greater confidence that researchers may state that complaint behavior is connected to couples' feelings about their relationships. However, there are several aspects of this research which should be pursued. First, an analysis similar to this one could profitably be conducted on couples who offered a wider range of relationship adjustment, particularly in the lower range. A study with a normal and a "clinical" population might not only be of interest but might offer additional insight into what is "dysfunctional."

As well, in future research on complaints, it would be more productive to use the response categories suggested by the accounts research. In the present study, excuses and justifications were combined into one category on the basis that both were attempts to relieve the complaint recipient of negative typification because of the complainable. (A second motive was to minimize the presence of small cell frequencies.) However, accounts research indicates excuses and justifications can function in different ways and have different consequences. Consequently, it would be advisable in future studies to place excuses and justifications into separate categories. In addition, by using similar categories, the findings from accounts and complaints research can be more fully integrated.

Finally, a most important study to pursue would be one that provides an in-depth analysis of the structure of couples' complaint interactions. This project did not allow such a comprehensive study, yet such an analysis could reveal much about how couples differ in the structure of their interactions as well as what types of complaint structures lead to quick or "successful" resolutions. In addition, this research could reveal more about how complaint behavior is sequenced.

This and other research indicates that a couple's feelings about their relationship are, in fact, related to how they engage in conflict communication. As well, this study reveals it is not the presence or absence of such communication that makes a difference, it is how that communication is enacted. Therefore, through studying *how* it is that satisfied and dissatisfied couples perform complaint and other conflict communication, it is possible to contribute to a developing theory of both marital relationships and conflict communication.

Complaints Interview Schedule

Couple #_____

Hi. I am conducting interviews on complaint behavior between men and women in romance relationships. I would like to interview each of you separately. I appreciate your volunteering to help me out.

All of us give and receive complaints. We can complain about ourselves, complain directly to other people, and complain about events or people who are not present. Little is known about how people make complaints directly to other people nor how people respond to such complaints in romance relationships. I'm trying to learn more about this behavior.

I. First, I'd like to ask you for some demographic information.
 1. Male _____ Female _____
 2. How long have the two of you been romantic partners?
 6 mos.–1 yr. _____ 1–5 yrs. _____ 6–10 yrs. _____ 11–15 yrs. _____
 3. Are you married or living together?
 4. How old are you?

II. Now I'd like to ask you about a complaint you have made.
 1. Please try to recall the exact wording of a complaint you have made to your partner.
 2. How did your partner respond?
 3. Please try to repeat as exactly as possible what your partner said.
 4. When did this complaint occur?
 Where were you?
 What were you doing?
 5. What was said or done just before this complaint was made?
 6. What was said or done after your partner responded to the complaint?
 7. Why did you make the complaint? What did you hope to accomplish?
 Did you? Why/why not?

III. Now I'd like to ask you about a complaint you have received.
 1. Please try to recall the exact wording of a complaint you have received from your partner.
 2. How did you respond?
 3. Please try to repeat as exactly as possible what you said.
 4. When did this complaint occur?
 Where were you?
 What were you doing?
 5. What was said or done just before this complaint was made?
 6. What was said or done after you responded as you did?
 7. Why did you respond as you did? What did you hope to accomplish?
 Did you? Why/why not?

IV. Now I'd like to ask you some general questions about complaints.

1. What do you normally complain about to your partner?
2. What does your partner normally complain about to you?
3. When do complaints between the two of you usually occur?
4. What type of complaints do you find hardest to deal with?
5. Have you ever felt your partner was complaining to you but s/he was not?
   Could you give me an example?
   Why did you think it was a complaint?
6. Have you made a complaint to your partner but s/he did not realize it?
   Could you give me an example?
7. What type of responses do you think are effective? Ineffective?
8. What do you think is the best way to complain? The worst way?
9. Ideally, how would you like for your partner to respond to your complaints?

ENDNOTES

[1] Nagging is defined as finding fault or complaining in a persistent manner (*Random House College Dictionary,* 1972, p. 883).

[2] Justifications and excuses were combined into one category because both response types attempt to maintain the face of the complaint recipient. As well, separating the categories would lead to introducing yet another level into the contingency table and would increase the number of small cell frequencies. Combining the categories minimized the problems associated with the presence of numerous small cell frequencies and the resultant difficulties in attaining sufficient statistical power.

[3] In the preliminary study there were few highly adjusted or maladjusted couples. For the most part, the couples tended to be moderately adjusted; the mean DAS for the couples was 223. Couples who fell one standard deviation above and one standard deviation below the mean were selected to represent adjusted and maladjusted couples. Ten couples had scores one standard deviation above and 9 couples had scores one standard deviation below the mean, so a subsample of 19 was used for this analysis.

[4] Affect was categorized based on a hierarchy of vocal cues. Positive cues included caring, warmth, tenderness, empathy, cheerfulness, affection, happiness, laughter and concern. Negative cues included tension, whining, fury, coldness, impatience, blame, sarcasm, and anger. Neutral affect was assigned when vocal cues carried no discernable affect.

[5] Cohen's Kappa reliability index assesses interobserver agreement beyond that which would be expected by chance alone. It is a conservative index which is usually lower than the standard reliability index of agreements divided by agreements plus disagreements.

[6] The presence of void cells does not preclude log-linear analysis if the cells are a result of sampling artifacts (that is, are sampling zeroes as opposed to structural zeroes, as is true in these data. To proceed mathematically a small numerical quantity, usually .5, is added to each cell count to facilitate the computation of chi-square statistics (Kennedy, 1983, pp. 225-226).

REFERENCES

Alberts, J. (1987, February). *A descriptive taxonomy of couples' conversational complaints.* Paper presented at the annual meeting of the Western Speech Communication Association, Salt Lake City, UT.

Blumstein, P. W., Carson, K. G., Hall, J., Hawkins, B., Hoffman, R., Ishem, E., Maurer, C. P., Spens, D., Taylor, J., & Zimmerman, D. L. (1974). The honoring of accounts. *American Sociological Review, 39,* 551-566.

Burgess, E. W. (1953). *Courtship, engagement and marriage.* Philadelphia: J. B. Lippincott.

Cody, M. J., & McLaughlin, M. L. (1985). Models for the sequential construction of accounting episodes: Situational and interactional constraints on message selection and evaluation. In R. L. Street & J. N. Capella (Eds.), *Sequence and pattern in communicative behaviour* (pp. 50-69). London: Edward Arnold.

Cody, M. J., Woelfel, M. L., & Jordan, W. J. (1983). Dimensions of compliance-gaining situations. *Human Communication Research, 9,* 99-113.

Coulthard, M. (1977). *An introduction to discourse analysis.* New York: Longman.

Cousins, P. C., & Vincent, J. P. (1983). Supportive and aversive behavior following spousal complaints. *Journal of Marriage and the Family, 45,* 678-681.

Doelger, J. (1984). *A descriptive analysis of complaints and their use in conversation.* Unpublished master's thesis. University of Nebraska, Lincoln, NE.

Edmondson, W. J. (1981). On saying you're sorry. In F. Coulmas (Ed.), *Conversational routine: Explorations in standardized communication situations and prepatterned speech* (pp. 273-288). New York: Moulton Publishers.

Fitzpatrick, M. A. (1983). Predicting couples' communication from couples' self-reports. In R. N. Bostrom (Ed.), *Communication Yearbook 7* (pp. 49-82). Beverly Hills: Sage.

Goffman, E. (1971). *Relations in public: Microstudies of the public order.* New York: Basic Books.

Gottman, J. M. (1979). *Marital interaction.* New York: Academic Press.

Kelley, H. H. (1979). *Personal relationships: Their structure and processes.* New York: Wiley & Sons.

Kelly, C., Huston, T. L., & Cate, R. M. (1985). Premarital relationship correlates of the erosion of satisfaction in marriage. *Journal of Marriage and the Family, 47,* 167-178.

Kennedy, J. J. (1983). *Analyzing qualitative data.* New York: Praeger.

Krokoff, L., Gottman, J. M., & Roy, A. K. (1986). *The blue-collar couple: A re-evaluation.* Unpublished manuscript.

Labov, W., & Fanshel, D. (1977). *Therapeutic discourse.* New York: Academic Press.

Locke, H. J., Sabagh, G., & Thomas, M. M. (1967). Interfaith marriages. *Social problems, 4,* 319-333.

Markman, H. L. (1979). Application of a behavioral model of marriage in predicting satisfaction of couples planning marriage. *Journal of Consulting and Clinical Psychology, 47,* 743-749.

Markman, H. L. (1981). Prediction of marital distress: A five-year follow-up. *Journal of Consulting and Clinical Psychology, 49,* 760-762.

McLaughlin, M. L., Cody, M. J., & O'Hair, H. D. (1983a). The management of failure events: Some contextual determinants of accounting behavior. *Human Communication Research, 9,* 208-224.

McLaughlin, M. L., Cody, M. J., & Rosenstein, N. E. (1983b). Account sequences in conversations between strangers. *Communication Monographs, 50,* 102-125.

Morris, G. H. (1985). The remedial episode as a negotiation of rules. In R. L. Street & J. N. Capella (Eds.), *Sequence and pattern in communicative behaviour* (pp. 70-84). London: Edward Arnold.

Navran, L. (1967). Communication and adjustment in marriage. *Family Processes, 6,* 173-184.

Oxford English Dictionary. (1971). New York: Oxford University Press.

Paulson, C. J. (1982). Confirmation and the complaining process. Unpublished doctoral dissertation, University of Denver, Denver, CO.

Random House College Dictionary. (1972). New York: Rand McNally.

Rausch, H. L., Barry, W. A., Hertel, R. K., & Swain, M. A. (1974). *Communication, conflict, and marriage.* San Francisco: Jossey-Bass.

Remler, J. E. (1978). Some repairs on the notion of repairs. *Chicago Linguistic Society, Papers from the Ninth Regional Meeting, 14,* 391-402.

Schonback, P. (1980). A category system for account phases. *European Journal of Social Psychology, 10,* 195-200.

Scott, M. N., & Lyman, S. M. (1968). Accounts. *American Sociology Review, 33,* 46-62.

Spanier, G. B. (19767). Measuring dyadic adjustment: New scales for assessing the quality of marriage and similar dyads. *Journal of Marriage and the Family, 38,* 15-28.

Strodtbeck, F. L. (1951). Husband-wife interaction over revealed differences. *American Sociological Review, 17,* 468-473.

Thomas, E. J. (1977). *Marital communication and decision making: Analysis, assessment, and change.* London: Collier Macmillan.

Turner. R. (1970). Words, utterances, and activities. In J. Douglas (Ed.), *Understanding everyday life* (pp. 169-187). Chicago: Aldine.

22

Intimates in Conflict: A Research Review

DUDLEY D. CAHN

Although a great deal of research has been conducted in each of the subjects of interpersonal communication, intimate relationships, and interpersonal conflict, some researchers have chosen to concentrate on the intersection of these subjects because of its practical importance and common occurrence in everyday life. As much as intimates might like to avoid it, they often experience interpersonal conflict. *Intimacy* is by definition a close personal relationship in which two persons are mutually dependent and engaged in joint actions (Braiker & Kelley, 1979). Research reveals that intimate couples are more likely than acquaintances to experience frequent and intense disagreements.

According to Bell and Blakeney (1977), *interpersonal conflict* may be defined as interaction between persons expressing opposing interests, views, or opinions. This definition identifies interpersonal conflict as a form of human communication.

Interpersonal conflict between intimate partners goes beyond differences regarding a specific problem, issue, or argument because of the emotional nature of their relationship. Couples who experience more frequent and severe interpersonal conflicts tend to be more unhappy and dissatisfied than couples who engage in fewer and less severe conflicts.

Alternatives to constructive conflict management are detrimental for several reasons (Barry, 1970). First, they create stress. Unresolved conflicts leave couples unhappy, doubting, and irritated (Duck, 1988; Lloyd & Cate, 1985). Moreover, according to Rusbult, Johnson, and Morrow (1986),

exiting from the relationship and partner neglect are destructive problem-solving responses and were more powerfully predictive of couple distress than are giving voice to problems and passive loyalty.

Second, alternatives to constructive conflict management make matters worse. For example, conflict is negatively related to feelings of love during relational dissolution (Braiker & Kelley, 1979; Canary & Spitzberg, 1989; Lloyd & Cate, 1985). Moreover, Schafer, Braito, and Bohlen (1976) found that marital conflicts and tensions contribute to a lack of self-concept support and accurate role-taking.

It is also common for negative acts from one partner to be reciprocated by negative acts from the other. In both distressed and nondistressed couples, negative communication behavior is more likely to be reciprocated than positive (Gottman, Markman, & Notarius, 1977; Margolin & Wampold, 1981; Wills, Weiss, & Patterson, 1974). Of course, there is greater negative reciprocity for dissatisfied couples than for happy ones (Gottman, 1982a, 1982b; Margolin & Wampold, 1981; Pike & Sillars, 1985).

Because destructive conflict behavior may harm intimate relationships, it is important to better understand interpersonal conflict. Numerous studies by empirical researchers and counselors appearing in several related disciplines, especially in psychology, communication, and family studies, have attempted to answer the question: What are the bases, processes, and outcomes of interpersonal conflict in intimate relationships? The problem is

From Cahn, D. D. (Ed.) (1990), *Intimates in conflict: A communication perspective* (pp. 1-22). Hillsdale, NJ: Erlbaum.

that these different lines of research lack coordination. Some studies merely duplicate those in other fields. Some are undertaken without awareness that the same questions are being asked in related disciplines and therefore do not benefit from insights and progress being made there. Even in cases where researchers in different disciplines attempt to answer some of the same questions using experimental methodology, each researcher deals with a discipline's unique issues and writes in its jargon.

There is a need for a review that pulls together loose ends as a step toward building a consensus among social scientists. Although reviews exist on each of the subjects of interpersonal communication, intimate relationships, and conflict, there is no comprehensive review of empirical studies on interpersonal conflict in intimate relationships. By examining research on intimates in conflicts, a review may provide an answer to the question "Where do researchers go from here?"

In keeping with this author's purpose to cut across the social sciences in the study of intimates in conflict, this article interrelates the empirical findings of numerous studies in a way that charts progress toward answering the following basic questions: What is unique about conflict in intimate relationships? How might intimate conflicts be classified? What are the bases of destructive conflict between intimates? In the final section, answers to these questions lead to a discussion of the implications of past empirical findings for future research.

WHAT IS UNIQUE ABOUT CONFLICT IN INTIMATE RELATIONSHIPS?

Conflict As a Process

Different theorists argue that interpersonal conflict is a process consisting of three stages. According to Gottman (1982a, 1982b), distressed couples appear to respond verbally with complaints and criticism in the first phase and nonverbally with hostile behaviors in the second phase. In the third phase, distressed couples find it difficult to agree on a solution.

Another three-stage process is proposed by Coombs (1987). First, *potential* interpersonal conflict is experienced within a person when faced with a choice between two or more incompatible options or goals (Type I). Second, the interpersonal conflict becomes an *actuality* when interaction reveals that the partners want different things, but they think that these differences can be resolved (Type II). Third, the conflict becomes *more serious* when the parties perceive that there is no mutually acceptable outcome and unwanted sacrifices must be made for resolving their differences (Type III). At the third level, self-interests usually replace mutual interests; there are winners and losers; and exercises of power likely dominate the process. For intimates, this stage of the conflict process may significantly alter or even destroy the nature of the relationship. Coombs observed that self-interest drives the individual from Type II to Type III levels, whereas common interest drives a couple from Type III level to Type II or I.

Multidimensionality

Research indicates that the conflict process is multidimensional. Argyle and Furnham (1983) reported that conflict between intimates and nonintimates consists of emotional conflict and criticism factors.

Emotional Conflict. This conflict, which is greater in more intimate relationships, consists of competing for attention/affection and control as well as conflict over money/possessions, beliefs/values, independence from each other, emotional help and support, normal daily activity, and being able to understand and empathize with each other.

Criticism. This factor, based primarily on problems with the partner's behaviors, includes a concern that the other is behaving unwisely, conflict over each other's habits and lifestyle, and not being able to discuss personal problems.

According to Argyle and Furnham, these factors are greater in intimate than in nonintimate relationships.

The emotional and critical dimensions of conflict pertain to three different lines of research on intimate partners. Lewis and Spanier (1979) showed that marital happiness and interaction form one dimension of marital quality, whereas a separate dimension included three intimate conflict subgroups—ongoing marital problems, specific disagreements, and marital instability. When studying the dimensions of marital quality, Johnson, White, Edwards, and Booth (1986) discovered three intimate conflict factors: (a) the amount and severity of conflict between the spouses, (b) the extent to which personal traits and behaviors of either spouse has led to problems in the marriage; and (c) the views and behaviors directed toward termination of the marriage. Thus, it appears that interpersonal conflict between intimates is a multidimensional construct consisting of emotional and critical aspects of specific disagreements, ongoing problems, and changing intimate relations.

Levels of Conflict

Interpersonal conflicts also occur at different levels depending on the topic (Braiker & Kelley, 1979).

Behavioral Conflicts (Level 1). These conflicts include conflict over specific behaviors, such as different preferences for popular music, current arts entertainment and dance, discussion topics, recreational activities, and sexual behaviors.

Normative Conflicts (Level 2). Involved here are conflicts over the unique norms and rules of the relationship such as different preferences for household duties, economic-support responsibilities, and authority relations between partners.

Personal Conflicts (Level 3). Level 3 conflicts concern a partner's characteristics, dispositions, and attitudes including life values, selfishness, inconsiderateness, and affectional relations.

Of course not all conflicts are limited to only one level. For example, problems like excessive drinking and sexual promiscuity can relate to all three levels. In addition to these three levels of conflicts, couples describe a fourth (the *conflict process* itself), the necessity of resolving metaconflicts about how to deal with conflicts at lower levels. At this level, arguments are about the partner being argumentative, critical, nagging, complaining, quick-tempered, or oversensitive (Braiker & Kelley, 1979).

These categories of conflict actually represent levels because there is a tendency for individuals to raise conflict to higher levels than seemingly justified. For example, when specific behaviors are actually "the problem," partners tend to describe the problem at a higher level, namely at the normative or personal levels. This escalation to higher levels may have incentive value. Where criticism of specific behaviors may not achieve results, expressed disagreement on relationship rules and personality are more likely to get the partner's attention. Thus, conflict at higher levels may motivate constructive work on the problems that exist at a lower level.

In summary, intimate conflict is an emotional and critical process consisting of specific disagreements, ongoing problems, and/or relationship instability involving different levels. The complex nature of intimate conflict has resulted in three different types of research studies discussed next.

HOW MIGHT INTIMATE CONFLICTS BE CLASSIFIED?

Across a wide diversity of studies, intimate interpersonal conflicts are of three different sorts that may be grouped according to the nature of the type of communication involved.

Specific Disagreements. Some researchers focus on a specific communication act or interaction, namely, an argument over a particular issue. Sometimes this disagreement is referred to as a difference of opinion or view, a complaint, criticism, hostile/

coercive response, defensive behavior, or unpleasant action. In any case, a couple overtly disagrees on some issue.

Problem-Solving Discussion. Other researchers focus on a more encompassing communication situation known as a negotiation or bargaining session or problem solving discussion that may deal with an ongoing problem—consisting of more than one conflicting issue.

Unhappy/Dissolving Relationships. Finally, still other researchers study the general pattern of communication characteristic of dysfunctioning couples, stormy marriages, and couples who report that they are unhappy, dissatisfied, maladjusted, or seeking counseling.

Although research on intimate interpersonal conflict frequently makes clear which of these types of conflicting couples are being studied making classification straightforward, many studies examine different ways these couples respond as alternatives for dealing with conflict. The problem is that, without comparisons across these studies, one is easily confused by the many options available to intimates presented in the literature. It is helpful to know that each type of conflict varies in degree and complexity (Weingarten & Leas, 1987) and that different alternatives exist for different degrees and complexities of conflict.

Specific Disagreements

Couples of the first type of conflict have a specific disagreement. According to Weingarten and Leas (1987), although real differences exist and relational tensions stem from the fact that people perceive their goals, needs, action plans, values, and so on to be conflicting, most conflict of this type does not threaten a relationship. Anger when it is expressed is short-lived. Frequently, these couples are able to work through their differences without the help of a third party.

What specific acts function as alternatives when partners disagree with each other about a particular issue? Obviously, they may ignore one another or resort to physical abuse, but if they choose to argue with one another what are their options? Utilizing Kipnis' (1976) Interpersonal Conflict Scale, Fitzpatrick and Winke (1979) surveyed single and married subjects' uses of communication tactics in their relationships. They found that the more favorable strategy of empathic understanding was not as popular as the alternative negative strategies. In opposite-sex relationships, respondents who showed the most commitment to the relationship (i.e., the married ones) indicated that they were more likely to use the strategies of emotional appeal or personal rejection to gain their own way. Those who indicated the least involvement in the relationship were more likely to use the strategies of manipulation and non-negotiation. In any case, when confronted with conflict, partners were most likely to resort to more negative strategies for dealing with interpersonal conflict. To avoid escalation to more serious conflict stages, couples need to rely more on empathic understanding.

Problem-Solving Discussion

Whereas a single issue is at stake with the first type of conflict, the next type involves several issues, although they may be reduced to a single complex problem. Weingarten and Leas (1987) pointed out that partners may be motivated more by a need for self-protection than they are by a need to solve particular problems. Or, more seriously, they may be motivated by a power motive where "winning" becomes the key dynamic of the conflict. The emotional climate is one of frustration and resentment, and anger erupts easily often over trivial matters and usually dissipates slowly. Although the partners feel ambivalent about the personal compromises they perceive are required, they would like to resolve their differences, but do not know how. For this type, although real differences often exist, an interpersonal communication problem usually exists as well. Improving communication can make it easier to solve the real problems and to negotiate differences. Presumably, for this type, education, training, or counseling are needed to help couples develop constructive communication attitudes and problem-solving skills.

What specific acts function as alternatives when partners experience *problems* of the second type? For this type of conflict, partners may: (a) *compete–force* (argue the strongest), (b) *accommodate–smooth* over (give in), (c) *avoid–withdrawal* (not argue or deal with the issue), (d) *compromise* (wheel-and-deal; give and take), and (e) *collaborate–confront* to reach a mutually satisfying solution (Bell & Blakeney, 1977; Blake & Mouton, 1964; Thomas & Kilmann, 1974).

Fitzpatrick (1988) examined couples' interactions for examples of conflict avoidance, accommodating, collaborating, and competing strategies for managing conflict and found that "traditional couples" were more cooperative and conciliatory and engaged in avoidance more than they claimed, "independent couples" tended to be more confrontative, and "separate couples" were more likely to engage in hostile acts and avoidance. Ideally, these couples should work toward identifying mutually satisfying (i.e., "win–win") as opposed to more frequent individually satisfying (i.e., "win–lose") agreements.

Unhappy (Dissolving) Relationships

Couples experiencing the third type of conflict have had it with one another. Outsiders, friends, or lovers are enlisted, not in support of the relationship, but as an alternative to it. Weingarten and Leas (1987) claimed that these couples are known for their willingness to hurt one another and view defeat of the partner as more important than either winning issues or solving particular problems. They may become physically violent. The emotional climate ranges from one of alienation and antagonism to one charged with volatility, rage, and hopelessness. No reconciliation is possible until the intensity of the conflict is reduced through therapy, or steps toward disengagement are taken.

For the third type of conflict, what general categories of acts function as alternatives when a marriage or serious long-term relationship is in serious trouble? Rusbult and Zembrodt (1983) discussed four characteristic reactions:

Exit, actively ending the relationship, destroying the relationship.
Voice, actively and constructively expressing dissatisfaction, with the intent of improving conditions.
Loyalty, remaining passively loyal to the relationship.
Neglect, ignoring the partner, spending less time together, allowing the relationship to atrophy.

These behaviors vary in destructiveness (Rusbult et al., 1986). Exit and neglect are destructive, whereas voice and loyalty are constructive. In comparison with men, women engage in somewhat higher levels of voice and loyalty and may behave less neglectfully.

Other researchers have found four types of conflicts and outcomes. As part of a study of fertility decision making, Rands, Levinger, and Mellinger (1981) asked 244 California married couples to respond to questions about the kinds of conflicts they encountered, their conflict style, their expected outcome of the conflict, and their marital satisfaction. Four main ways of dealing with interpersonal conflict were found that varied along dimensions of aggressiveness and intimacy. The four patterns were:

1. a nonintimate-aggressive pattern, about 30% of the sample, least satisfying especially when the partner is seen as uncompromising,
2. a nonintimate-nonaggressive one, about 20% of the sample,
3. an intimate-aggressive pattern, about 20% of the total,
4. an intimate-nonaggressive one, about 30% of the sample, which couples found the most satisfying.

In the second subtype, some spouses appeared to tolerate their relationship rather well, even though it was unexciting. For some of the spouses in the third subtype who achieved intimacy after a confrontation, spouses' high intimacy seemed to counteract their attacking behavior. The researchers found that perceptions of conflict outcome varied from one extreme in which there was less intimacy following the conflict and the other in which the spouses felt closer, understood each other better, had fun making up, and tended to compromise. It is useful to note that Rands et al. (1981) observed that 30% of the couples in their study tended to select less intimate and more aggressive ways of dealing with conflict situations that resulted in less satisfaction.

Finally, Cahn (1987) has observed that couples may continue, repair, renegotiate, or disengage from an intimate relationship depending on four factors: relationship (dis)satisfaction, availability of more desirable alternatives, size of investments in the relationship, and social system constraints (family, friends, boss, etc.). Couples may ignore or tolerate problems in their relationship due to investments and social system constraints, engage in outside affairs rather than improve their primary relationships, or disengage without attempting to resolve the problems.

In many cases, partners experiencing the third type of conflict (unhappy relationship) are better off separated at least temporarily while individuals undergo therapy and job training. Helping individuals gain control over their own lives and enlarging their perceived arena of independent choice seems both to lessen the dependency that underlies their tolerance of abuse or dissatisfaction and to diminish their need to oppress others. If partners learn to exist on their own, they may then choose to work on their relationship or end it.

Thus, studies of intimate interpersonal conflict may be classified as dealing with different communication patterns, namely, specific verbal disagreements, problem-solving discussions, or unhappy (dissolving) relationships. Each line of research has its own alternatives, some more destructive than others. Interestingly, research shows that couples are more likely to resort to destructive alternatives than choose constructive ones. The reason for the popularity of more destructive approaches is the subject of the next section.

Interrelationship Among Types of Conflict

Oftentimes, the three types of conflict studies (specific disagreements, problem-solving discussions, and unhappy relationships) are interrelated. Rausch, Barry, Hertel, and Swain (1974) observed husbands in unhappy marriages and determined that they used more coercive strategies and fewer reconciling acts in response to coercive strategies. Unhappy couples were found to be more coercive and less cognitive in their disagreements and conflict discussions (Billings, 1979). Meanwhile, Fitzpatrick (1988) and Pike and Sillars (1985) discovered that more satisfied couples used conflict avoidance to a greater extent than did the dissatisfied couples.

Moreover, dissatisfied couples appear to engage in particular destructive communication behaviors when engaging in specific disagreements. Studying satisfied and dissatisfied couples, Gottman (1979) found that unhappy couples were more likely to engage in cross-complaining sequences and less likely to engage in validation sequences. According to Ting-Toomey (1983), partners may choose among the following alternatives that may be classified as disintegrative or integrative.

Disintegrative communication options are as follows:

Confronting directly attacks, criticizes, or negatively evaluates the other's feelings/ideas, and consists of negative evaluations, loaded questions, and direct rejection.

Complaining discloses discontent and resentment through indirect strategies of blame aimed at the other, a third party, and/or the situation.

Defending persists in clarifying one's own position in spite of other's feelings/ideas and involves justifying one's own actions, those of others, and/or the situation.

Integrative communication options are as follows:

Confirming reveals one's understanding of the situation and openly conveys acknowledgment, empathy and/or acceptance of partner's feelings/ideas.

Socioemotional description refers to descriptive statements made in a leveling manner.

Instrumental questioning consists of task-oriented questions for factual information or further elaboration.

Ideally, intimate partners who value their relationship should argue in a way that contributes to integration of the relationship and avoid statements and nonverbal communications that lead to disintegration, but unfortunately the latter course is the more common. According to Ting-Toomey, marital partners typically begin a conflict in a manner directly attacking one another with criticism and negatively loaded statements, followed by attempts to justify oneself and blame the other.

Although the research just described on destructive communication behavior during specific disagreements has not established a causal link with relationship dissatisfaction, it is known that conflict escalates. Thus, it might be argued that partners may start out with specific disagreements that may lead to problem-solving discussions and may terminate in unhappy relationships. Rands et al. (1981) described a nonintimate-aggressive pattern that escalates to include other issues. Once hostility is expressed by either partner, Gaelick, Bodenhausen, and Wyer (1985) showed that it is likely to escalate in frequency over the course of the interaction. Similarly, Menaghan (1982) linked the level of problems to the choice of coping efforts suggesting a worsening spiral. She concluded that as problems mount, typical coping choices may actually exacerbate distress and relationship problems.

WHAT ARE THE BASES OF DESTRUCTIVE CONFLICT BETWEEN INTIMATES?

Although there may be many more bases for intimate conflict, recent empirical investigation has focused on two types, psychological variables that should be included in research on conflict and social contexts in which conflicts occur. The psychological variables include romantic involvement, relationship dissatisfaction, gender and sex type, and personality. These psychological variables are discussed here.

Psychological Factors

Romantic Involvement. Ironically, one of the bases for destructive conflict styles is the nature of the intimate relationship itself, namely, the romantic, passionate dimension. Fry, Firestone, and Williams (1983) assessed the influence of romantic involvement on the integrative bargaining of dating couples. The bargaining process and outcomes of 74 dating couples was compared with that of 32 mixed-sex stranger pairs. Although the stranger dyads indicated zero romantic involvement, dating couples were distributed over a broad range of degrees of romantic feelings for their partners. Romantic involvement was found to detract from the dyad's ability to discover mutually advantageous outcomes.

Relationship Dissatisfaction. Much of the research on destructive interpersonal conflict uses couples seeking counseling. Such couples are usually functioning at low levels; they are often unhappy, dissatisfied, maladjusted, distressed, or unstable.

Genshaft (1980) found that distressed couples are more defensive than nondistressed. Birchler, Weiss, and Vincent (1975) obtained data that showed that distressed couples engaged in fewer positive and more negatives during casual conversation and problem solving than did nondistressed couples. Gottman et al. (1977) observed that distressed couples were likely to begin a discussion by cross-complaining, followed by negative exchanges without ending with a contract sequence. Rands et al. (1981) discovered a nonintimate-aggressive pattern. Margolin and Wampold (1981) reported less problem solving, and more verbal and nonverbal negative behaviors in distressed couples than in nondistressed, although there were male–female differences in communication conflict patterns (Margolin & Wampold, 1981). According to Ting-Toomey (1983), low marital adjustment interaction was mainly characterized by unique reciprocal patterns of confront → confront, confront → defend, complain → defend, and defend → complain verbal interacts.

Gender and Sex Differences. Barry (1970) investigated the health of spouses' personalities and found that the husband's personality was a greater factor in a happy marriage than the wife's. The "healthier" the husband's personality, the more capable he is of being emotionally supportive of his wife and thus less likely to engage in severe and destructive conflict. Belsky, Lang, and Rovine (1985) observed that the decline of marital quality during the first 6 months is worse for wives than for husbands. Women experience negative relationships between length of marriage, elation, and absence of anxiety (Mathes & Wise, 1983). Negative affect reciprocity upsets husbands more than wives who appear to want a response to the expressions of their negative feelings. As Levenson and Gottman (1985) reported, marital satisfaction declines most when husbands do *not* reciprocate their wives' negative affect, and when wives *do* reciprocate their husbands' negative affect.

Sex differences in perception and interpretation may function as another source of conflict in intimate relationships. Men (and not women) tend to interpret their female partners' lack of love expression as an indication of hostility, whereas women (not men) tend to interpret their male partner's lack of hostility as an indication of love (Gaelick et al., 1985). According to White (1985), wives tend to perceive much more agreement than husbands despite the actual state of affairs.

For males, the most salient aspect of conflict (in terms of relationship quality) is the stability of the conflict issue. Greater perceived stability of conflict issues is related to lower levels of love and commitment to the relationship. The more females bring up the same issue, the more the males want to disengage. For females the number of conflicts is most salient to the relationship quality (Lloyd, 1987).

Demands on women differ from those placed on men in intimate relationships. As a consequence of demands external to their marriage that are different for husbands and wives, men and women follow different paths of personal development that makes intimacy difficult later (Swensen, Eskew, &

Kohlhepp, 1984). For example, according to Berryman-Fink and Brunner (1987), men are more likely than women to compete in conflicts, whereas women are more likely than men to use a compromising style. It should be noted that, conflict or not, sex-typed spouses (traditional man–woman roles) best understand each other, whereas undifferentiated mates least understand their spouses (Indvik & Fitzpatrick, 1982).

Women also differ from men in conflict communication behavior. Women disclose significantly more about their problems and tensions than do men (Burke, Weir, & Harrison, 1976). Gottman (1982a, 1982b) found that men are less responsive to negative affect from their spouses than women are. Levenson and Gottman (1985) found that men are more likely than women to withdraw and avoid conflicts. Moreover, women are more likely than men to offer accounts to their children for seeking divorce (Cushman & Cahn, 1986). Finally, women tend to reciprocate men's negative communication more than vice versa.

According to Hawkins, Weisberg, and Ray (1980), men and women differ in what they prefer from men in conflict communication. Women prefer less control, more openness, and more sharing of deep emotions than men do. Men prefer less conventional style expressions and more speculative and analytic behavior from women than women prefer to engage in. Also, men tend to value the instrumental dimension of a romantic relationship, while women value the affectional dimension (Rettig & Bubolz, 1983).

Personality. Personality variables are linked to the conflict management modes/styles of confronting, smoothing, and forcing.

> *Confronting:* Exploring options, redefining problems, and finding productive solutions.
> *Smoothing:* playing down the conflict or giving into the other to keep everyone happy.
> *Forcing:* employing power; believing that victory goes to the strongest.

Achievement motivation was linked to confronting and aggression to forcing (Bell & Blakeney,

1977). Positive correlations were found between affiliation-smoothing, deference-forcing, succorance-smoothing, nurturing-smoothing, dogmatism-confronting, and Machiavellianism-confronting. Negative correlations were found for affiliation-forcing and Machiavellianism-smoothing (Jones & Melcher, 1982).

Individuals were found to be quite consistent in their conflict management styles or modes both within and across content domains, and the mode of conflict management could be predicted quite well from knowledge of certain intellectual and personality characteristics (Sternberg & Soriano, 1984). Moreover, strong consistencies in conflict management styles were observed by individuals across different situations, and at the same time, widespread differences were observed across individuals (Sternberg & Dobson, 1987). It should be noted, however, that although personality measures continued to correlate with the style/mode of conflict management, little association was found between preference for particular styles/modes and actual observed conflict behavior (Kabanoff, 1987).

If depression is viewed as a personality variable, Kahn, Coyne, and Margolin (1985) found that couples with depressed spouses engaged in more destructive problem-solving behavior than normal couples.

In addition to including psychological variables in studies of conflicts, researchers should also attend to the social contexts in which the conflicts occur. These social contexts are discussed next.

Social Contexts

Marital Stages. Some stages of a couple's marital career also act as an antecedent to conflict by making the relationship temporarily unhappy. Belsky et al. (1985) examined marital quality and found that it declines especially over the first 6 months after the wedding ceremony. Swensen et al. (1984) investigated changes in love and marital problems and found that younger married couples appeared to have more marriage problems than older couples. Also, in comparison to retired and middle-aged couples, younger couples had a comparatively intense engagement style of interaction, characterized by alternation between analytic confrontation and humorous remarks (Zietlow & Sillars, 1988).

Why should younger marriages have more problems than older marriages? In studies conducted by Burr (1972) and Miller (1976), children were shown to interfere with couples' companionship activities and reduce marital satisfaction. This was especially true for two working parents. Others have also reported that the more hours wives worked and the presence of school-age children in the family contributed significantly to marital instability, problems, and disagreements (Johnson et al., 1986; Munro & Adams, 1978; Schumm & Bugaighis, 1985). Researchers reported, however, that the trend toward greater problems and decreasing marital satisfaction reverses itself in later years (Anderson, Russell, & Schumm, 1983).

Exceptions should not go unnoticed. In spite of a large literature that demonstrates correlations between the presence of children, marital problems, and relationship dissatisfaction, White and Booth (1985) found that the transition to parenthood did not seem to affect marital happiness, interaction, disagreements, or number of marital problems. The effects of children and working parents may depend more on the attitudes, needs, and goals of a couple. Some couples may find the presence of children or a working wife an added asset to the couple's relationship satisfaction, whereas others do not.

Low Family Strengths. Due to lack of family strengths, some couples are ill prepared to deal with conflicts (Birchler et al., 1975; MacKinnon, MacKinnon, & Franken, 1984). Compared to a high family strengths group identified by an empirical measure, the low family strengths group reported less satisfaction with the family and with the quality of life, health, home, time, financial well-being, and the overall quality of life. This group was more likely to acquire social support and resort to passive appraisal. It was also found to display lower scores on idealistic distortion, marital satisfaction, personality issues, *communication, conflict resolution,* financial management, leisure activities, sexual relations, children and marriage, family and friends, and religious orientation. Because past negotiations and outcomes provide the context for future renegotiations (Scanzoni & Polonko, 1980), couples may be ill equipped for constructively managing conflicts.

Power Differences. Power differences may precede conflicts and make them harder to resolve. The structure of decision-making power is significantly related to effective marital and family functioning. For example, wife-dominated partners are least satisfied; next is the husband-dominant group (Ting-Toomey, 1984). Men and women who are not equitably treated are less content in their marriages and perceive the marriage as more unstable than men and women in equitable marriages (Utne, Hatfield, Traupmann, & Greenberger, 1984). Relative to androgynous gender couples, couples with undifferentiated or dominant, aggressive partners reported the lowest relationship quality (Kurdek & Schmitt, 1986). However, in contrast to the commonly supported egalitarian finding, Kolb and Straus (1974) found that families above the median in husband-to-wife power tend to be high in marital happiness.

Unequal couples are more likely to want to dissolve than egalitarian partners. Hill, Rubin, and Peplau (1976) found that 54% of the unequal couples broke off their relationships within 2 years, whereas only 23% of the equal couples were disengaged. In another study, 75% of those who under- or over-benefited in their relationship disengaged from it, but only 25% of the equitable couples broke up (Cody, 1982). Again, not all studies support the egalitarian principle, however. According to Chafetz (1980), the more equal partners are to one another, the higher the rate of marital dissolution.

Cultural Difference and Social Changes. According to Cahn (1985), couples who have different cultural perspectives experience more frequent and intense interpersonal conflict than couples from the same culture. Moreover, Swensen and Trahaug (1985) reported that the move from "institutional"

marriages (for convenience of society) to "intrinsic" marriages (based on love; for convenience of individuals) has increased marital satisfaction and decreased marital problems. However, Rausch et al. (1974) argued that this cultural swing has resulted in couples demanding more of their relationship than a comfortable stasis.

Consequently, among the factors researchers have identified as bases of interpersonal conflict are psychological variables of romantic involvement, unhappy or dissolving relationships, gender differences and sex type, personality variables, and social contexts such as some marital stages like younger marriages with children and working parents, lack of family strengths, power differences, cultural differences and social changes.

Implications for Research

According to the Braiker and Kelley's (1979) definition of intimate relationships, intimates may be same- or opposite-sex close friends as well as lovers and mates. A review shows, however, that most of the research has been on married couples. Thus, there is a need for more studies of close friends and lovers as well as mates. Moreover, following Bell and Blakeney (1977), this chapter identifies interpersonal conflict as a form of human communication—that is, interaction between persons expressing opposing interests, views, or opinions.

This article includes studies that extend research on conflict resolution and conflict management processes. The term *conflict resolution* is oriented toward the value of confrontation and bringing it successfully to an end. The term carries with it the idea that sometimes confrontation is desirable. This article suggests that conflict resolution is most useful in cases where relationships have broken down.

Conflict management, however, refers to alternative ways of dealing with conflict, including avoiding it altogether. This article suggests that, in newly formed or growing intimate relationships, the relationship itself may take precedence over resolving the conflict, so managing conflict is key rather than necessarily resolving it. Believing that confrontation is not always necessary, useful, or beneficial, theorists suggest that conflict may be handled through a variety of coping mechanisms that in turn may be further categorized as functional or dysfunctional.

Although the study of interpersonal conflict attempts to better understand an important element in the development of intimate relationships, the uncoordinated research efforts across disciplines has resulted in problems of generalizability and usefulness. One of the main sources of difficulty may be attributed to the different concepts of interpersonal conflict used by different researchers that lead to confusion over the nature of the communication processes involved.

Intimate interpersonal conflict may be fruitfully viewed as a communication process with multiple dimensions and levels. Typically, researchers categorize as conflict a wide range of phenomena that vary in seriousness, dimensionality, and levels. Researchers should determine more precisely the dimension and level in their study, limit their generalizations accordingly, and where possible compare and contrast their findings with other studies. Along these lines, some useful questions might be:

How does a couple keep a conflict from escalating to higher levels or stages?

How can the discovery of the dimensions of conflict (Argyle & Furnham, 1983) benefit research on interpersonal conflict?

How might couples be trained to avoid disintegrative communications and to use integrative communications (Ting-Toomey, 1983)?

How might couples be trained in constructive communication attitudes and skills that underlie successful problem-solving discussions (Weingarten & Leas, 1987)?

Conflicts may be usefully categorized according to one of three types of communication situations: (a) verbal disagreements, (b) problem-solving discussions, and (c) unhappy (dissolving) intimate relationships. Researchers need to clearly identify the type of conflict under examination, restrict their generalizations to that type, and compare/contrast their findings to those of the other types. For ex-

ample, researchers have shown that unhappy relationships of the third type manifest particular patterns of negative communication and negotiation practices of the first and second types (Fitzpatrick, 1988; Gottman, 1979; Pike & Sillars, 1985; Rausch et al., 1974; Ting-Toomey, 1983). Other questions that might be asked are: (a) under what conditions do particular patterns of negative communication of the first type contribute to unhappy relationships of the third type? and (b) How do particular problem-solving approaches of the second type result in unhappy relationships of the third type?

Future research should also give attention to conflict as a symptom of a problem and conflict as a cause of a problem. Interpersonal conflict may reflect factors that underlie dissatisfying relationships. In this case, both the relationship dissatisfaction and the interpersonal conflict are effects of deeper problems in an intimate relationship. For example, a couple may be both unhappy and argue frequently because a partner often wastes money on pornography. Meanwhile, interpersonal conflict may be the cause and differentiate happy from unhappy couples. For example, a couple may be dissatisfied because a partner is argumentative, quick-tempered, or oversensitive. Consequently, the following questions are in need of answers:

Are patterns of conflict as a cause and as an affect both equally destructive in intimate relationships?

Are negative patterns of conflict as a cause and as an effect similar?

There are many bases or antecedents to destructive conflict in intimate relationships, including romantic involvement, relationship (dis)satisfaction, gender differences and sex-type, and personality. Thus, researchers need to include these psychological variables in their experimental designs or restrict their generalizations accordingly. When collecting data from subjects, researchers should ask themselves:

How romantically (Fry et al., 1983) involved are the partners?

How satisfied (i.e., Ting-Toomey, 1983) with their intimate relationship are the partners?

Are the partners male or female? What psychological gender and sex type are they?

Are the partners' personality types identified as affiliation, succorance, and nurturing or are they identified more as deference, dogmatic, and Machiavellian?

What are other personality variables that function as antecedents in intimate conflict?

Research shows that certain social contexts also function as antecedents and influence the nature of conflict, its bases, processes, and outcomes. Therefore, researchers need to compare/contrast subjects from different social contexts or restrict their generalizations accordingly. Some questions to keep in mind when collecting data from subjects include:

At what marital stage (i.e., Zietlow & Sillars, 1988) are the partners?

Are the partners as a unit high or low in family strengths (i.e., MacKinnon et al., 1984).

Are the intimate partners egalitarian in their relationship with each other, or are there significant power differences between them?

Are the partners from the same or different racial or ethnic groups in a country? Are they from the same cultural group as those in studies used for comparison?

Are the partners from the same time period or social era as those in studies used for comparison?

What are other social contexts that function as antecedents in intimate conflict?

REFERENCES

Anderson, S. A., Russell, C. S., & Schumm, W. R. (1983). Perceived marital quality and family life-cycle categories: A further analysis. *Journal of Marriage and the Family, 45,* 127-139.

Argyle, M., & Furnham, A. (1983). Sources of satisfaction and conflict in long-term relationships. *Journal of Marriage and the Family, 45,* 481-93.

Barry, W. A. (1970). Marriage research and conflict: An integrative review. *Psychological Bulletin, 73,* 849-857.

Bell, E. C., & Blakeney, R. N. (1977). Personality correlates of conflict resolution modes. *Human Relations, 30,* 849-857.

Belsky, J., Lang, M. E., & Rovine, M. (1985). Stability and change in marriage across the transition to parenthood: A second study. *Journal of Marriage and the Family, 47,* 855-865.

Berryman-Fink, C., & Brunner, C. (1987), The effects of sex of source and target on interpersonal conflict management styles. *Southern Speech Communication Journal, 53,* 38-48.

Billings, A. (1979). Conflict resolution in distressed and nondistressed married couples. *Journal of Consulting and Clinical Psychology, 47,* 368-376.

Birchler, G. R., Weiss, R. L. & Vincent, J. P. (1975). Multimethod analysis of social reinforcement exchange between maritally distressed and nondistressed spouse and stranger dyads. *Journal of Personality and Social Psychology, 31,* 349-360.

Blake, R. R., & Mouton, J. S. (1964). *The managerial grid.* Houston: Gulf.

Braiker, H. B., & Kelley, H. H. (1979). Conflict in the development of close relationships. In R. L. Burgess & T. L. Huston (Eds.), *Social exchange in developing relationships* (pp. 135-168). New York: Academic Press.

Burke, R. J., Weir, T., & Harrison, D. (1976). Disclosure of problems and tensions experienced by marital partners. *Psychological Reports, 38,* 531-542.

Burr, W. (1972). Satisfaction with various aspects of marriage over the life cycle: A random middle-class sample. *Journal of Marriage and the Family, 32,* 29-37.

Cahn, D. (1985). Communication competence in the resolution of intercultural conflict. *World Communication, 14,* 85-94.

Cahn, D. (1987). *Letting go: A practical theory of relationship disengagement and reengagement.* Albany: SUNY Press.

Canary, D. J., & Spitzberg, B. H. (1989). A model of the perceived competence of conflict strategies. *Human Communication Research, 15,* 630-649.

Chafetz, J. (1980). Conflict resolution in marriage: Toward a theory of spousal strategies and marital dissolution rates. *Journal of Family Issues, 1,* 397-421.

Cody, M. (1982). A typology of disengagement strategies and an examination of role intimacy, reactions to inequity, and relational problems play in strategy selection. *Communication Monographs, 49,* 148-170.

Coombs, C. H. (1987). The structure of conflict. *American Psychologist, 42,* 355-363.

Cushman, D. P., & Cahn, D. D. (1986). A study of communicative realignment between parents and children following the parents' decision to seek a divorce. *Communication Research Reports, 3,* 80-85.

Duck, S. (1988). *Relating to others.* Chicago: Dorsey.

Fitzpatrick, M. A. (1988). *Between husbands and wives: Communication in marriage.* Beverly Hills, CA: Sage.

Fitzpatrick, M. A., & Winke, J. (1979). You always hurt the one you love: Strategies and tactics in interpersonal conflict. *Communication Quarterly, 27,* 3-11.

Fry, W. R., Firestone, I. J., & Williams, D. L. (1983). Negotiation process and outcome of stranger dyads and dating couples: Do lovers lose? *Basic and Applied Social Psychology, 4,* 1-16.

Gaelick, L., Bodenhausen, G. V., & Wyer, R. S. (1985). Emotional communication in close relationships. *Journal of Personality and Social Psychology, 49,* 1246-1265.

Genshaft, J. L. (1980). Perceptual and defensive style variables in marital discord. *Social Behavior and Personality, 8,* 81-84.

Gottman, J. M. (1979). *Marital interaction: Experimental investigations.* New York: Academic Press.

Gottman, J. M. (1982a). Emotional responsiveness in marital conversations. *Journal of Communication, 16,* 108-119.

Gottman, J. M. (1982b). Temporal form: Toward a new language for describing relationships. *Journal of Marriage and the Family, 44,* 943-962.

Gottman, J. M., Markman, H., & Notarius, C. (1977). The topography of marital conflict: A sequential analysis of verbal and nonverbal behavior. *Journal of Marriage and the Family, 39,* 461-477.

Hawkins, J. L., Weisberg, C., & Ray, D. (1980). Spouse differences in communication style: Preference, perception, behavior. *Journal of Marriage and the Family, 42,* 585-593.

Hill, C., Rubin, Z., & Peplau, L. (1976). Breakups before marriage: The end of 103 affairs. *Journal of Social Issues, 32,* 147-68.

Indvik, J., & Fitzpatrick, M. A. (1982). "If you could read my mind, love . . ." Understanding and misunderstanding in the marital dyad. *Family Relations, 31,* 43-51.

Johnson, D. R., White, L. K., Edwards, J. N., & Booth, A. (1986). Dimensions of marital quality. *Journal of Family Issues, 7,* 31-49.

Jones, R., & Melcher, B. (1982). Personality and the preference for modes of conflict resolution. *Human Relations, 35,* 649-658.

Kabanoff, B. (1987). Predictive validity of the MODE conflict instrument. *Journal of Applied Psychology, 72,* 160-163.

Kahn, J., Coyne, J. C., & Margolin, G. (1985). Depression and marital disagreement: The social construction of despair. *Journal of Social and Personal Relationships, 2,* 447-461.

Kipnis, D. (1976). *The power-holders.* New York: Academic Press.

Kolb, T., & Straus, M. (1974). Marital power and marital happiness in relation to problem-solving ability. *Journal of Marriage and the Family, 36,* 756-766.

Kurdek, L. A., & Schmitt, P. (1986). Interaction of sex role self-concept with relationship quality and relationship beliefs in married, heterosexual cohabiting, gay, and lesbian couples. *Journal of Personality and Social Psychology, 51,* 365-370.

Levenson, R. W., & Gottman, J. M. (1985). Physiological and affective predictors of change in relationship satisfaction. *Journal of Personality and Social Psychology, 49,* 85-94.

Lewis, R., & Spanier, G. (1979). Theorizing about the quality and stability of marriages. In W. Burr, R. Hill, F. Nye, & I. Reiss (Eds.), *Contemporary theories about the family* (pp. 268-94). New York: The Free Press.

Lloyd, S. A. (1987). Conflict in premarital relationships: Differential perceptions of males and females. *Family Relations, 36,* 290-294.

Lloyd, S. A., & Cate, R. M. (1985). The developmental course of conflict in dissolution of premarital relationships, *Journal of Social and Personal Relationships, 2,* 179-194.

MacKinnon, R., MacKinnon, C., & Franken, M. (1984). Family strengths in long-term marriages. *Lifestyles: A Journal of Changing Patterns, 7,* 115-126.

Margolin, G., & Wampold, B. (1981). Sequential analysis of conflict and accord in distressed and nondistressed marital patterns. *Journal of Consulting and Clinical Psychology, 49,* 554-567.

Mathes, E. W., & Wise, P. S. (1983). Romantic love and the ravages of time. *Psychological Reports, 52,* 839-846.

Menaghan, E. (1982). Measuring coping effectiveness: A panel analysis of marital problems and coping efforts. *Journal of Health and Social Behavior, 23,* 230-234.

Miller, B. C. (1976). A multivariate developmental model of marital satisfaction. *Journal of Marriage and the Family, 38,* 643-657.

Munro, B., & Adams, G. R. (1978). Love American style: A test of role structure theory on changes in attitudes toward love. *Human Relations, 3,* 215-228.

Pike, G., & Sillars, A. L. (1985). Reciprocity of marital communication. *Journal of Social and Personal Relationships, 2,* 303-324.

Rands, M., Levinger, G., & Mellinger, G. D. (1981). Patterns of conflict resolution and marital satisfaction. *Journal of Family Issues, 2,* 297-321.

Rausch, H., Barry, W. Hertel, R., & Swain, M. (1974). *Communication, conflict and marriage.* San Francisco: Jossey-Bass.

Rettig, K. D., & Bubolz, M. M. (1983). Interpersonal resource exchanges as indicators of quality of marriage. *Journal of Marriage and the Family, 45,* 497-509.

Rusbult, C. E., Johnson, D. J., & Morrow, G. D. (1986). Impact of couple patterns of problem solving on distress and nondistress in dating relationships. *Journal of Personality and Social Psychology, 50,* 744-753.

Rusbult, C. E., & Zembrodt, I. M. (1983). Responses to dissatisfaction in romantic involvements: A multidimensional scaling analysis. *Journal of Experimental Social Psychology, 19,* 274-293.

Scanzoni, J., & Polonko, K. (1980). A conceptual approach to explicit marital negotiation. *Journal of Marriage and the Family, 42,* 31-43.

Schafer, R. Braito, R., & Bohlen, J. M. (1976). Self-concept and the reaction of a significant other: A comparison of husbands and wives. *Sociological Inquiry, 46,* 57-65.

Schumm, W. R., & Bugaighis, M. A. (1985). Marital quality over the marital career: Alternative explanations. *Journal of Marriage and the Family, 48,* 165-168.

Sternberg, R. J., & Dobson, D. M. (1987). Resolving interpersonal conflicts: An analysis of stylistic consistency. *Journal of Personality and Social Psychology, 52,* 794-812.

Sternberg, R. J., & Soriano, L. J. (1984). Styles of conflict resolution. *Journal of Personal and Social Psychology, 47,* 115-126.

Swensen, C. H., Eskew, R. W., & Kohlhepp, K. A. (1984). Five factors in long-term marriages. *Lifestyles, 7,* 94-106.

Swensen, C. H., & Trahaug, G. (1985). Commitment and long-term marriage relationship. *Journal of Marriage and the Family, 47,* 939-945.

Thomas, K. W., & Kilmann, R. H. (1974). *Thomas-Kilmann conflict mode instrument.* Tuxedo, NY: Xicom.

Ting-Toomey, S. (1983). An analysis of verbal communication patterns in high and low marital adjustment groups. *Human Communication Research, 9,* 306-319.

Ting-Toomey, S. (1984). Perceived decision-making power and marital adjustment. *Communication Research Reports, 1,* 15-20.

Utne, M. K., Hatfield, E., Traupmann, J., & Greenberger, D. (1984). Equity, marital satisfaction, and stability. *Journal of Social and Personal Relationships, 1,* 323-332.

Weingarten, H., & Leas, S. (1987). Levels of marital conflict model: A guide to assessment and intervention in troubled marriages. *American Journal of Orthopsychiatry, 57,* 407-417.

White, J. M. (1985). Perceived similarity and understanding in married couples. *Journal of Social and Personal Relationships, 2,* 45-57.

White, L. K., & Booth, A. (1985). The transition to parenthood and marital quality. *Journal of Family Issues, 6,* 435-449.

Wills, T. A., Weiss, R. L., & Patterson, G. R. (1974). A behavioral analysis of the determinants of marital satisfaction. *Journal of Consulting and Clinical Psychology, 42,* 802-811.

Zietlow, P. H., & Sillars, A. L. (1988). Life-stage differences in communication during marital conflicts. *Journal of Social and Personal Relationships, 5,* 223-245.

23

The Effects of Sex of Source and Target on Interpersonal Conflict Management Styles

CYNTHIA BERRYMAN-FINK | CLAIRE C. BRUNNER

This study investigated the effects of subject sex and target sex on reported conflict management styles. Subjects (n = 147) were instructed to think of either a same- or opposite-sex person while completing the Thomas-Kilmann Conflict Mode Instrument. Results indicated that males were more likely than females to report using a competing style, while females were more likely than males to report using a compromising style. Regardless of their own gender, all subjects were more likely to report using an accommodating style if the target was female. Implications of these findings are discussed.

Numerous theoretical orientations can be used to predict sex differences in interpersonal conflict management behavior. Specifically, research on expectancy theory, bargaining, and communicator style leads to the prediction that women will be more cooperative and men more competitive in conflict situations. According to expectancy theory, men are expected to use verbally aggressive persuasive message strategies while women are expected to avoid such strategies.[1] Bargaining theory indicates that men tend to focus on maximizing their own goals while women emphasize equitable relationship outcomes in bargaining situations.[2] Research on communicator style reveals that women tend to use a style which stresses interpersonal relations and is perceived as attentive and open while men tend to use a style considered dominant and challenging of others.[3]

SEX DIFFERENCES IN CONFLICT MANAGEMENT BEHAVIOR

Despite theoretical expectations, results from research on male/female conflict management pref-erences and behaviors are equivocal. A number of studies report significant differences in the conflict behavior of males and females,[4] with males preferring styles characterized as antisocial,[5] dominating,[6] and competitive,[7] and females preferring styles described as prosocial, regressive,[8] compromising,[9] and avoiding.[10] Other studies find no clear-cut sex differences in interpersonal conflict management behavior.[11] Sex, therefore, seems to be an inadequate predictor of one's choice of conflict management behavior. Indeed, a complex array of factors has been found to influence one's behavior in conflict, including the relative power in the relationship,[12] the expected behavior from the partner,[13] the perceived resources of the partner,[14] the degree of liking for the partner,[15] personal needs,[16] and personality factors.[17] In organizational contexts specifically, research has shown one's choice of conflict handling behavior to be mediated by the amount of conflict, the organizational structure, individual personal/culture factors, the relationship between conflicting parties,[18] the topic and source of the disagreement,[19] the relative abilities of the conflicting

From Berryman-Fink, C., & Brunner, C. C. (1987). The effect of sex of source and target on interpersonal conflict management styles. *Southern Speech Communication Journal, 53*, 38–48.

parties, and the reciprocity of cooperative and non-cooperative behaviors.[20]

An additional variable which may influence one's conflict management behavior is sex of conflict partner. Relatively few studies have examined the effect of target sex on males' and females' conflict handling preferences and behavior. Fitzpatrick and Winke[21] found that males reported a tendency to use non-negotiation strategies (dogmatic assertions, repetition of points, resentment toward partner) with same-sex best friends while females reported using strategies of personal rejection, empathic understanding, and emotional appeals in conflicts with same-sex best friends. Research in an organizational setting found that both male and female subordinates were less likely to withdraw from a conflict with a woman supervisor and less likely to use a confronting style in conflicts with male supervisors.[22] Other research reports that sex of the target is not a salient feature in determining appropriate conflict management styles.[23]

Perhaps the inconsistent findings on sex differences in conflict management behavior may be explained by simultaneously examining the effects of sex of source and target on conflict styles. Men and women may not differ in their use of conflict styles, but may report a preference for certain styles based on whether they find themselves in conflict with a same-sex or opposite-sex other.

Purpose

The purpose of this study is to investigate the effects of sex of source and sex of target on interpersonal conflict management styles. There is insufficient evidence to support specific directional hypotheses regarding differences between males and females, differences as a function of target sex, or differences in conflict styles used in same-sex or opposite-sex dyads. Thus, the following research questions are proposed:

RQ1: Do males and females differ in their use of interpersonal conflict management styles?

RQ2: Do individuals differ in their use of interpersonal conflict management styles with male and female targets?

RQ3: Is there an interaction between sex of the source and sex of the target which affects the source's choice of interpersonal conflict management styles?

METHOD

Variable Measurement

A five-category scheme for measuring interpersonal conflict-handling behavior has received wide support in the conflict literature. Introduced by Blake and Mouton,[24] the model identifies two conceptually independent dimensions of interpersonal behavior: (1) assertiveness, defined as behavior intended to satisfy one's own concerns, and (2) cooperativeness, defined as behavior intended to satisfy another's concerns.[25] The dimensions combine to produce five conflict styles. While terminology for the five styles has varied among researchers,[26] the most common labels derived from the Thomas-Kilmann Conflict Mode Instrument[27] are: avoiding (unassertive, uncooperative); competing (assertive, uncooperative); accommodating (unassertive, cooperative); collaborating (assertive, cooperative); and compromising (intermediate in both assertiveness and cooperativeness).

The Thomas-Kilmann Conflict Mode Instrument measures preferences for each of the five conflict styles by structuring 60 questions into 30 forced-choice dichotomies. Each style is paired with the other four styles an equal number of times. Subjects select the statement in each pair corresponding to their preferred behavior in a conflict situation. This forced-choice pairing results in a five-scale ipsative measure. Although nonipsative self-report measures of conflict styles are available,[28] their validity has been questioned because self-reported conflict preferences correlate highly with the perceived social desirability of the conflict style. In contrast, the forced-choice format of the Thomas-Kilmann scale produces a measure which does not correlate significantly with social desirability.[29]

Previously reported test-retest reliabilities for this measure have ranged from .61 to .68. The internal consistencies of items measuring each of the five modes (coefficient alpha) have ranged from .43 to .71.[30] The reliabilities (coefficient alpha) obtained in this study are as follows: competing = .79, collaborating = .50, compromising = .42, avoiding = .51, and accommodating = .60. While these scores are moderate, they are higher than those reported for four alternate conflict style instruments.[31]

Subjects and Procedure

Subjects included 147 students (71 males, 76 females) from the introductory interpersonal communication course at a large midwestern state university. They were instructed to think of an important relationship with either an opposite-sex or same-sex person while completing the Thomas-Kilmann Conflict Mode Instrument. Frequencies in the four cells created by combinations of subject sex and target sex variables were as follows: (1) male subject and male target, n = 36; (2) male subject and female target, n = 35; (3) female subject and male target, n = 40; and (4) female subject and female target, n = 36. Subjects ranged in age from 18 to 24 years old. The questionnaire booklet was completed in class during the first week of the course.

Data Analysis

Due to the ipsative nature of the data obtained from the paired, forced-choice format of the Thomas-Kilmann Conflict Mode Instrument, a multivariate analysis of variance (MANOVA) would have resulted in a singular matrix, rendering multivariate statistics impossible to compute.[32] Therefore, a series of five two-way (sex of subject by sex of target) univariate analyses of variance (one for each of the conflict styles) were computed. This method was chosen so that answers to the three research questions, regarding main effects for sex of subject and sex of target and the possible interaction between these two variables, could be assessed simultaneously.

RESULTS

Some researchers have questioned the five-style approach to conflict management behavior by reporting factor-analytic studies which produce only three interpersonal conflict styles.[33] In these studies, however, the two underlying dimensions of concern for self (assertiveness) and concern for the relationship (cooperativeness) are identifiable. To confirm this two-dimensional structure in the present study, responses to the Thomas-Kilmann Conflict Mode Instrument were submitted to a multidimensional scaling analysis utilizing the ALSCAL procedure.[34] Results indicated strong and clear support for the suggested two-dimensional structure. A plot of the five styles along these two dimensions is presented in Figure 23.1.

Ranges for scores on the five conflict management styles were as follows: competing, 0-12; collaborating, 1-12; compromising, 2-12; avoiding, 1-12; and accommodating, 1-12. Overall means for each of the five conflict style modes reveal the rank order of the most-used to least-used styles as follows: (1) compromising (7.11); (2) avoiding (6.48); (3) collaborating and accommodating (both at 5.93); and (5) competing (4.57).

The first research question sought to explore differences between males and females in their reported use of the five conflict management styles. Means for males and females, along with the corresponding F-ratio from the appropriate univariate ANOVA, are presented in the left-hand portion of Table 23.1.

Inspection of Table 23.1 reveals that main effects for subject sex were found for two of the five styles. For the competing style, the mean for males (5.15) was significantly higher than the mean for females (4.01); a power estimate of .95 was obtained.[35] For the compromising style, the mean for females (7.51) was significantly higher than the mean for males (6.68); power was estimated at .98.

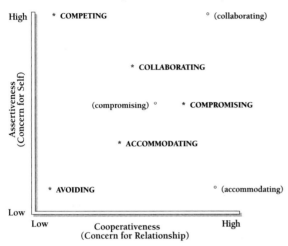

FIGURE 23.1

ALSCAL Analysis of Conflict Styles

* Asterisk indicates findings in the present study. Theoretical predictions, where discrepant from findings, are indicated by a ° and labeled in parentheses.

The second research question inquired about possible differences in subjects' reported use of conflict management styles according to the sex of the target person with whom they were engaged in conflict. Means for male targets and female targets, along with the corresponding F-ratio from the appropriate univariate ANOVA, are presented in the right-hand portion of Table 23.1.

The results displayed in the table indicate that subjects' reported use of conflict management styles differed according to whether they were in conflict with a male target or a female target. For the accommodating style, subjects scored significantly higher if the target person was female (6.38) than if the target person was male (5.50); power was estimated at .95.

The third research question suggested the possibility of an interaction effect between sex of subject and sex of target; however, results of the five univariate ANOVAs indicated no significant interactions for any of the five styles.

DISCUSSION

This study provides empirical support for a two-dimensional model which produces five conflict-management styles. A comparison of the graphic representation of the Thomas-Kilmann Conflict Mode Instrument with the plotting of the multidimensional scaling of this instrument (see Figure 23.1) shows a similar structure. The major discrepancy is that the compromising style was viewed as more cooperative than the collaborating or accommodating styles.

Theoretical Implications

This research finds that males and females differ in two significant ways in their reported use of conflict management styles: (1) Males are more likely than females to report that they compete in conflicts; (2) females are more likely than males to report that they compromise in conflicts. These findings are consistent with a number of studies of gender effects in conflict management behavior.[36] That males in this study reported being more competitive and females more compromising provides empirical support for theoretical predictions which arise from expectancy theory and bargaining theory.[37]

On the question of whether target sex influences one's conflict behavior, individuals in this study reported that they tend to accommodate more to females than to males. Sex-role literature generally and conflict management literature specifically provide no reasonable explanation for this finding. Subsequent researchers might explore possible mediating factors such as the relative power of the conflicting parties, the behavioral attributions toward the target, the history of conflict strategies in the relationship, the salience of the conflict issue, personality factors, and nature and salience of the relationship or conflict issues.

On the question of interaction between sex of actor and sex of target, this study finds no relationship. Perhaps one's own sex, psychological sex-role identity, personal needs, or personality traits are

TABLE 23.1

Means and F-Ratios for Conflict Styles by Subject Sex and Target Sex

	MALE SUBJECTS	FEMALE SUBJECTS	F		MALE TARGETS	FEMALE TARGETS	F
Competing	5.15	4.01	4.97*		4.80	4.31	0.99
Collaborating	5.62	6.21	2.59		5.84	6.01	0.25
Compromising	6.68	7.51	5.77*		7.20	7.01	0.23
Avoiding	6.42	6.53	0.06		6.66	6.28	0.94
Accommodating	6.13	5.74	0.81		5.50	6.38	4.46*

* $p < .05$

stronger determinants of conflict handling behavior than is the gender composition of the relationship. Additional relational factors not explored in the present study, such as dominance, status, and authority, may also have an effect.

Applications

While past research has indicated that the collaborating style is most prevalent,[38] the most-often reported style in the present study was the compromising style. Clearly, both collaborating and compromising are perceived as positive styles because of their moderate to high concern for both self and other. The findings of this study thus have practical application value for training in conflict management techniques, as they support the assumption that most people consider the needs of both parties when managing conflict.

The results of this study provide information on the relationship of gender and conflict management behavior. To fully understand the complex nature of interpersonal behavior in conflicts, researchers must systematically examine personality, relationship, and contextual factors as they affect self-reported and behavioral indices of conflict management styles. Only after we understand what motivates individuals to select certain behaviors in conflicts can we deal with the effectiveness of strategies for managing interpersonal conflicts.

ENDNOTES

[1] Michael Burgoon, James, P. Dillard, and Noel E. Doran, "Friendly or Unfriendly Persuasion: The Effects of Violations of Expectations by Males and Females." *Human Communication Research* 10 (1983): 283-294.

[2] Jeffrey Z. Rubin and B. R. Brown. *The Social Psychology of Bargaining and Negotiation* (New York: Academic Press, 1975).

[3] Barbara M. Montgomery and Robert W. Norton, "Sex Differences and Similarities in Communicator Style," *Communication Monographs* 48 (1981): 121-132; John E. Baird and Patricia Haves Bradley, "Styles of Management and Communication: A Comparative Study of Men and Women," *Communication Monographs* 46 (1979): 101-111.

[4] See, for example, Joyce H. Frost. "The Influence of Female and Male Communication Styles on Conflict Strategies: Problem Areas," paper presented at the International Communication Association Convention. Berlin, West Germany, June 1977; Ralph H. Kilmann and Kenneth W. Thomas, "Developing a Forced-Choice Measure of Conflict-Handling Behavior: The "MODD" Instrument," *Educational and Psychological Measurement* 37 (1977): 309-325; Michael E. Roloff and Bradley S. Greenberg, "Sex Differences in Choice of Modes of Conflict Resolution in Real-Life and Television," *Communication Quarterly* 27 (3) (1979): 3-12; J. R. Imler, "The Effects of Occupational Category, Organizational Level, Organizational Size, Sex, and Conflict Opponent on the Conflict-Handling Styles of Hospital Management Personnel." unpub. MBA thesis. Youngstown State University, 1980; M. Afzalur Rahim, "A Measure of Styles of Handling Interpersonal Conflict." *Academy of Management Journal* 26 (1983): 368-376; Pamela S. Shockley-Zalabak and Donald Dean Morley, "Sex Differences in Conflict Style Preferences." *Communication Research Reports* 1 (1984): 28-32; and William R. Todd-Mancillas and Ana Rossi, "Gender Differences in the Management of Personnel Disputes," *Women's Studies in Communication* 8 (1985): 25-33.

[5] Roloff and Greenberg 3-12.

[6] Kilmann and Thomas 309-325; Imler 1980; Todd-Mancillas and Rossi 25-33.

[7] Frost 28-32.

[8] Roloff and Greenberg 3-12.

9 Rahim 368-376; Shockley-Zalabak and Morley 28-32.

10 Frost: Rahim 368-376.

11 See, for example, Mary Anne Fitzpatrick and Jeff Winke, "You Always Hurt the One You Love: Strategies and Tactics in Interpersonal Conflict," *Communication Quarterly* 27 (1) (1979): 3-11; Patricia Renwick, "The Effects of Sex Differences on the Perception and Management of Superior-Subordinate Conflict: An Exploratory Study," *Organizational Behavior and Human Performance* 19 (1977): 403-415; Leslie A. Baxter and Tara L. Shepherd, "Sex-Role Identity: Sex of Other, and Affective Relationship as Determinants of Interpersonal Conflict-Management Styles," *Sex Roles* 4 (1978): 813-825; Pamela Shockley-Zalabak, "The Effects of Sex Differences on the Preference for Utilization of Conflict Styles of Managers in a Work Setting: An Exploratory Study," *Public Personnel Management Journal* 10 (1981): 289-295; J. L. Howell, "The Identification, Description, and Analysis of Competencies Focused on Conflict Management in a Human Service Organization: An Exploratory Study," diss., U of Massachusetts, 1981; D. C. Bell, J. S. Chafetz, and L. H. Horn, "Marital Conflict Resolution: A Study of Strategies and Outcomes," *Journal of Family Issues* 3 (1982): 111-131; Robert J. Sternberg and Lawrence J. Soriano, "Styles of Conflict Resolution." *Journal of Personality and Social Psychology* 47 (1984): 115-126; and Terrie Temkin and H. Wayland Cummings, "An Exploratory Study of Conflict Management Behaviors in Voluntary Organizations," paper presented at Speech Communication Association Convention, Denver, November, 1985.

12 See, for example, R. L. Kahn, D. M. Wolfe, P. R. Quinn, J. D. Snoek, and R. A. Rosenthal, *Organizational Stress: Studies in Role Conflict and Ambiguity* (New York: Wiley, 1964); Kenneth W. Thomas, *Conflict and Conflict Management;* M. Dunnette, ed., *The Handbook of Industrial and Organizational Psychology* (Chicago: Rand McNally, 1976) 889-935; and R. F. Zammuto, M. London, and K. W. Rowland, "Effects of Sex on Commitment and Conflict Resolution," *Journal of Applied Psychology* 64 (1979): 227-231.

13 See, for example, Kenneth W. Thomas and L. R. Pondy, "Toward an 'Intent' Model of Conflict Management Among Principal Parties," *Human Relations* 30 (1977): 1089-1102; Alan L. Sillars, "Attributions and Communication in Roommate Conflicts," *Communication Monographs* 47 (1980): 180-200; and Alan L. Sillars, "Attributions and Interpersonal Conflict Resolution," J. H. Harvey, W. I. Ickes, and R. F. Kidd, eds., *New Directions in Attribution Research* (Hillsdale, NJ: Lawrence Erlbaum, 1981) 279-305.

14 H. Michener, J. Vaske, S. Schleifer, J. Plazewake, and L. Chapman, "Factors Affecting Concession Rate and Threat Usage in Bilateral Conflict," *Sociometry* 38 (1975): 62-80.

15 Baxter and Shepherd 813-825.

16 See, for example, D. N. Weart, "The Relationship of Teachers' and Principals' Interpersonal Relations Orientations and Preferences for Conflict Management Techniques," diss., U of Rochester, 1972; R. Ross and Sue DeWine, "Interpersonal Needs and Communication in Conflict: Do Soft Words Win Hard Hearts?" paper presented at the SCA Convention, Chicago, November, 1984.

17 See, for example, Charles E. Watkins, "An Analytic Model of Conflict," *Speech Monographs* 41 (1974): 1-5; Kenneth W. Thomas and Ralph H. Kilmann, "Interpersonal Conflict-Handling Behavior as Reflections of Jungian Personality Dimensions," *Psychological Reports* 37 (1975): 971-980; E. C. Bell and R. N. Blakeney, "Personality Correlates of Conflict Resolution Modes," *Human Relations* 30 (1977): 849-856; and R. E. Jones and B. Melcer, "Personality and Preference for Modes of Conflict Resolution," *Human Relations* 35 (1982): 649-658.

18 Linda L. Putnam and Charmaine E. Wilson, "Communicative Strategies in Organizational Conflicts: Reliability and Validity of a Measurement Scale," in M. Burgoon, ed., *Communication Yearbook 6* (Beverly Hills: Sage, 1982): 629-652.

19 See, for example, Patricia A. Renwick, "Impact of Topic and Source of Disagreement on Conflict Management," *Organizational Behavior and Human Performance* 14 (1975): 416-425; Temkin and Cummings, 1985.

20 Richard A. Cosier and Thomas L. Ruble, "Research on Conflict-Handling Behavior: An Experimental Approach," *Academy of Management Journal* 24 (1981): 816-831.

21 Fitzpatrick and Winke 3-11.

22 Zammout et al. 227-231.

23 Baxter and Shepherd 813-825.

24 Robert R. Blake and Jane S. Mouton, *The Managerial Grid* (Houston: Gulf, 1964).

25 For validation that the dimensions of assertiveness and cooperativeness underlie conflict mode choices, see Boris Kabanoff, "Do Feelings of Cooperativeness and Assertiveness Affect the Choice of Conflict Management Mode?" paper presented at the Academy of Management Meeting, San Diego, August, 1985.

26 See, for example, P. R. Lawrence and J. W. Lorsch, *Organization and Environment* (Boston: Graduate School of Business Administration, Harvard University, 1967); Jay Hall, *Conflict Management Survey: A Survey on One's Characteristic Reaction to and Handling of Conflicts Between Himself and Others* (Conroe, TX: Teleometrics International, 1969); and Kenneth W. Thomas and Ralph H. Kilmann, *Thomas-Kilmann Conflict Mode Instrument* (Tuxedo, NY: Xicom, Inc., 1974).

27 Thomas and Kilmann, 1974.

28 See, for example, Blake and Mouton, 1964; Lawrence and Lorsch, 1967; and Hall, 1969.

29 Kenneth W. Thomas and Ralph H. Kilmann, "The Social Desirability Variable in Organizational Research, An Alternative Explanation for Reported Findings," *Academy of Management Journal* 18 (1975): 741-752.

30 Kenneth W. Thomas and Ralph H. Kilmann, "Comparison of Four Instruments Measuring Conflict Behavior," *Psychological Reports* 42 (1978): 1139-1145.

31 Thomas and Kilmann 1139-1145.

32 Fred N. Kerlinger, *Foundations of Behavioral Research* (New York: Holt, Rinehart & Winston, 1973).

33 See, for example, Putnam and Wilson 629-652; Alan L. Silars, Doug Parry, Stephen F. Coletti, and Mark A. Rogers, "Coding Verbal Conflict Tactics: Non-verbal and Perceptual Correlates of the Avoidance-Distributive-Integrative Distinction," *Human Communication Research* 9 (1982): 83-95.

34 This type of analysis was chosen to explore the dimensional structure of the Thomas-Kilmann Conflict Mode Instrument because the ipsative nature of this scale precludes application of factor analytic techniques. The ALSCAL procedure was accessed through *SAS Supplementary Library Users Guide, SAS*

Institute, 1980.

35 Jacob Cohen, *Statistical Power Analysis for the Behavioral Sciences* (New York: Academic Press, 1977).

36 See, for example, Imler, 1980; Kilmann and Thomas, 1977; Rahim, 1983; and Roloff and Greenberg, 1979.

37 See, for example, Burgoon et al., 1984; K. B. Hoyenga and K. T. Hoyenga, *The Question of Sex Differences: Psychological, Cultural, and Biological Differences* (Boston: Little, Brown, 1979); J. K. Kalat, *Biological Psychology* (Belmont, CA: Wadsworth, 1981); Eleanor Maccoby and Carol N. Jacklin, *The Psychology of Sex Differences* (Stanford: Stanford University Press, 1974); and Judy C. Pearson, *Gender and Communication* (Dubuque: Wm. C. Brown, 1985); B. Major and J. Adams, "Role of Gender, Interpersonal Orientation, and Self-Preservation in Distributive-Justice Behavior," *Journal of Personality and Social Psychology* 45 (1983): 598-608; B. Major and Kay Deaux, "Individual Differences in Justice Behavior," J. Greenberg and R. I. Cohen, eds., *Equity and Justice in Social Behavior.* (New York: Academic Press, 1982); and Rubin and Brown, 1975.

38 Thomas and Kilmann 971-980.

UNIT VIII

Relational Disengagement

The articles you have read thus far have progressed from the initiation of interpersonal relationships to the application of interpersonal skills in those relationships to the management of interpersonal difficulties. The final issue to be addressed from this relational perspective concerns the termination of interpersonal relationships. One consequence of the failure events and conflict you read about in the previous unit can be the decision to end a given relationship. The final three articles in this volume deal with the process of ending a relationship. Theory and research on the dissolution of relationships is not abundant. However, scholars of interpersonal communication have been increasing their investigation into this aspect of relationships. While there has been a large body of literature generated on divorce in marital relationships, little has been done to investigate the role of interpersonal communication in that process. In addition, marriage is only one type of relationship and is unique in many ways. The majority of relational disengagement occurs in nonmarital relationships and those have not been examined thoroughly. The three articles in this unit emphasize the role of interpersonal communication in relational disengagement. The articles also expand the focus to a variety of relationships other than marriage.

The four main studies presented in article 24 by Baxter tapped various age groups, including pre-teens, teenagers, college students, and post-college adults in their recollections of break-ups of romantic relationships. The results of those studies as well as the findings from other studies were used to examine communication strategies used to terminate relationships. Baxter found two underlying dimensions to disengagement: directness and other-orientation. Directness represents how forthright an individual is in telling a partner that he or she wants out of the relationship. Strategies vary in how directly or indirectly we communicate our desire to terminate a relationship. Baxter identifies a number of variables that affect the degree of directness in disengaging. Other-orientation represents the degree to which we are concerned with the costs or harm we will cause our partner in breaking up. Strong other-oriented disengagers would seek to help the other maintain "face" while breaking up. Directness was found to be the dominant factor related to disengagement strategies.

This article also refers to the theory by Brown and Levinson on face. Given the previous discussion of face in dealing with failure events, you should be able to understand why a unilateral dissolution (one member wants out and the other does not) would be a face-threatening act to the member wanting to maintain the relationship. Being told your friend does not want to see you anymore might be a reproach for some relational failure event. Failure events, complaints, and interpersonal conflicts all have the potential to precipitate relational disengagement. One of the six factors identified in a flow chart of disengagement by Baxter is whether the process is caused by a gradual onset of problems (incrementalism) or a sudden onset of problems (a critical incident). Duck, in article 25, also discusses the "sudden death" of a relationship caused by some failure event.

Baxter addresses three particular issues dealing with disengagement. The first considers what type of communication strategies are used to disengage. The second examines qualities, such as age and sex, that are associated with disengagement strategies. And third, Baxter looks at relational-level attributes as related to disengagement. Baxter concludes by putting together the sequence of events in the disengagement process in the form of a flow chart.

Duck, in article 25, begins with a general discussion of what he calls "straw models" of relational disengagement, which are logical extensions of why a relationship might end drawn from the attraction and relational initiation theory. He then discusses the weaknesses of such approaches in explaining what really occurs in relationship disengagement, presenting a model of phases he believes individuals experience when dissolving a relationship, based upon several assumptions. One assumption is that individuals continually evaluate the relationships they are in. This process involves some of the principles underlying social exchange theory. Duck believes we periodically consider the costs and rewards associated with a given relationship, which then influences our resolve to remain in or to terminate that relationship. According to Duck, in more stabilized relationships such an assessment occurs only in times of conflict or transition. Another assumption underlying Duck's phases is that we reach thresholds that provide the impetus to move from one phase to another. In essence, we reach a point where we have had enough. Each threshold is preceded by a decision point that an individual faces. The process of relational disengagement begins in Duck's model with some threshold of relational dissatisfaction occurring, a breakdown. After the first threshold is exceeded there are four phases that are passed through in moving to an ultimate break-up. The first, the **intra-psychic phase,** is essentially our private analysis and evaluation of the relationship. We are faced with the question of whether to share our concerns

with our partner. The next, the **dyadic phase,** occurs when we reach the decision to broach the topic of ending the relationship with our partner. This phase is obviously one that is critically linked to interpersonal communication. A couple's discussions about ending the relationship can result in attempts to repair and preserve the relationship, to redefine the relationship (such as "let's just be friends"), or to end the relationship. When both partners accept that the relationship is going to end, there is a discussion of the best way to manage the disengagement, which is the **social phase** of the model. The final phase actually occurs after the relationship has been terminated and involves how we personally choose to remember the relationship and how we present the break-up to others. Duck calls this phase the **grave-dressing phase** because of its similarity to the practice of dressing up new graves at cemeteries by placing flowers and wreaths over the newly dug dirt. For each of his phases Duck identifies a variety of goals, concerns, and possible research issues.

In article 26, Miller and Parks also incorporate the principles of social exchange theory in examining the disengagement process. Unlike Duck's approach, which tends to be centered on the decision process occurring in one individual, Miller and Parks's approach is much more attuned to the transactional nature of interpersonal relationships. Relational dissolution is seen as a joint product of the levels of satisfaction of both partners in a relationship. This approach allows them to explore those situations in which one person wants out of the relationship and the other wants to remain. There are three social exchange elements that constitute the assessment of a given relationship: outcomes, comparison level, and comparison level for alternatives. **Outcomes** represent the relative rewards and costs associated with the particular relationship. **Comparison level** is how the outcomes of the current relationship compare with the outcomes we have experienced in previous relationships or ones we believe we deserve. **Comparison level for alternatives** is how the outcomes of the current relationship compare with our predictions of the potential outcomes in relationships we could pursue or escalate with others. In the figure included in the article, these three factors are ranked relative to the strength of each. Thus the ideal relationship is one in which the outcomes are greater than the comparison level, which is greater than the comparison level of alternatives for both partners.

Before they present this model, Miller and Parks discuss some of the problems that have been inherent in dissolution research. They then provide a list of specific communication markers that might be expected to be associated with disengagement. These "markers" are behaviors exhibited by an individual or a relationship, which indicate that the relationship is de-escalating or dissolving. The markers include such behaviors as decreasing interaction, decreases in touch, and less use of the present tense.

The article finishes by discussing disengagement as a compliance-gaining process; that is, an individual is attempting to get his or her partner to agree to end the relationship. Miller and Parks review the literature on compliance gaining and present a four-part typology for classifying the sixteen strategies of Marwell and Schmitt based upon the continua of reward-punishment orientation and recipient-communicator onus (responsibility). Miller and Parks believe there is value in combining compliance gaining and social exchange theory to examine disengagement. They offer several hypotheses based on this combination, such as first attempts to terminate a relationship will be reward oriented.

While the set of readings on interpersonal communication in this text ends with the termination of relationships, it is hoped that this will not cause you to finish the readings on a "downer." Fortunately, many relationship never experience this last step in relational development. One can adopt the philosophy that no relationship ever comes to an end because we always will be affected by our past relationships, even though we no longer actively interact with our previous partners. Think about significant people from your past with whom you no longer interact. Don't they still have an influence on how you think and behave? The amount of influence might continue to decrease over time, but in a sense no interpersonal relationship is ever terminated.

As you finish this text, pause to reflect on the cumulative impact of these readings on your understanding of interpersonal communication. The readings represent a wide and diverse examination of a phenomenon that has a significant effect on all of us. It is hoped that you gained a stronger appreciation and keener understanding of interpersonal communication as well as personally benefiting through an application of the concepts and research findings to your own interpersonal experiences.

QUESTIONS TO CONSIDER
WHILE READING

ARTICLE 24

A. Under what conditions is directness most likely to be used as the disengagement strategy and by whom?

B. How might disengagement from nonromantic relationships be similar to and different from disengagement from romantic relationships?

ARTICLE 25

A. How might the latent theories of dissolution relate to Duck's model of the disengagement phases?

B. Think of a particular relationship you recently terminated. How did the process you experienced compare with Duck's model? What parts did you not experience? What did you experience that is not reflected in the model?

ARTICLE 26

A. Which markers seem to be the most direct and which the most indirect in conveying desire to end a relationship?

B. Think of some of the ways relationships you have been involved in have ended. Which social exchange alternative best matches your situations? What compliance-gaining strategies have you used or have been used on you to end the relationship? What was the effect?

24

Accomplishing Relationship Disengagement

LESLIE A. BAXTER

Borrowing the words of American poet Emily Dickinson, the dissolution of a relationship ". . . is all we need of hell." Certainly, if the importance of a social phenomenon were gauged by its degree of stress and its frequency, relationship dissolution or disengagement would rank as one of the most significant features of social life. Relationship disengagement threatens both the physical and emotional health of its participants (Bloom et al., 1978; Newcomb & Bentler, 1981). In addition, the disengagement of a relationship exacts emotional costs from family and social network members associated with it, for example, the children of divorcing parents (Greenberg & Nay, 1982; Levitin, 1979; Longfellow, 1979). The significance of dissolution-induced stress is underscored by the pervasiveness of the phenomenon (Hill et al., 1976; La Gaipa, 1981b; Milardo, 1982; US Government, 1981). However, despite the social significance of relationship disengagement, it has received limited attention from researchers. To help to fill this void, in 1978 the author began a series of ten studies into relationship disengagement. This chapter describes the central assumptions and questions, the major findings, and general conclusions of this research program.

CENTRAL ASSUMPTIONS AND QUESTIONS OF THE RESEARCH PROGRAM

The research program has been guided by four core assumptions which are briefly summarized below.

Collectively, these assumptions have focused the program around three research questions, and these are introduced below as well.

A central assumption of the research program is a process conceptualization of disengagement. As others have noted (Duck, 1982a; Hagestad & Smyer, 1982), disengagement research is often framed in a conceptualization of the phenomenon as a single event in time rather than a through-time process. The disengagement-as-event perspective is characterized by two central issues: (1) the antecedents of break-up, and (2) the consequences of break-up. The first leads researchers to seek demographic, psychological and relationship variables which predict and explain the subsequent relationship disengagement event. The second leads researchers to explore the psychological, social and economic effects of the disengagement event. By contrast, a process-oriented perspective is more likely to address the following questions:

1. Are there discernible phases or stages of disengagement through which relationships pass?
2. How do relationship parties go about accomplishing their unbonding?

These questions focus on the internal dynamic of the disengagement rather than the predictors and consequences of the break-up event. Knowledge of the antecedent and consequent conditions of disengagement as an event has theoretical as well as practical significance. Nonetheless, a complementary conceptualization of relationship disengagement as a process is equally necessary for a complete understanding of the phenomenon. Dis-

From Duck, S.W. & Perlman, D. (Eds.) (1985), *Understanding personal relationships: An interdisciplinary approach* (pp. 243–265). Newbury Park, CA: Sage.

solution stress, for example, may be related to the manner in which the parties go about disengaging, regardless of the break-up event per se.

The prevalence of disengagement-as-event research cannot be attributed to the absence of theoretical work on disengagement as a process. A decade ago, Altman & Taylor (1973) posited that relationship break-up was simply the relationship growth process in reverse, a view perpetuated by some (Knapp, 1978; Miller & Parks, 1982) and questioned by others (Duck & Lea, 1983). Other theorists have advanced process views of disengagement which are not bound conceptually by the reversal hypothesis (Bohannan, 1970; Bradford, 1980; Froiland & Hozman, 1977; Kessler, 1975; Salts, 1979). For the most part, these latter perspectives focus on the emotional stages of marital break-up. More recently, Duck (1982a) has advanced a process view of disengagement which encompasses both psychological and social domains and generalizes to marital and non-marital relationships. In the intra-psychic phase of Duck's model, the individual privately contemplates his or her dissatisfactions with the other party. Presuming that relationship costs outweigh rewards, the relationship enters the dyadic phase in which the two parties negotiate their unbonding. The dissolution of the relationship is publicly presented to social network members in the third, or social, phase. The final phase in Duck's model, that of grave-dressing, involves the psychological and social recovery from the break-up. All the studies in this research program have dealt with Duck's dyadic phase, examining how parties accomplish the break-up when at least one of them has reached a decision to terminate the relationship.

The need for study of non-marital relationship disengagement, in addition to the study of marital separation and divorce, comprises the second assumption of the research program. Given that some two million Americans divorce annually (Bloom et al., 1979), marital break-up should be accorded substantial research attention. Nonetheless, many other types of personal relationships experience break-up, with emotional costs comparable to those experienced in divorce. They, too, merit research attention. Further, people no doubt bring to marital break-up the disengagement 'scripts' learned from the many relationship dissolutions experienced in childhood, adolescence and early adulthood. An understanding of such break-up experiences may provide insight into why people react as they do in marital break-ups.

A third basic assumption of the research program flows from the author's grounding in the communication discipline. Interaction is the sine qua non of relationships; it is through communicative action that persons initiate, define, maintain and terminate their social bonds. Communicative exchange constitutes the core of Duck's dyadic phase, which may account for the research program's concentration on this phase of breaking up rather than, for example, the more psychologically based intra-psychic or grave-dressing phases.

The final core assumption of the program is that disengaging relationship parties are proactive, goal-accomplishing agents. This non-mechanistic view of people has become increasingly evident in recent social psychological theory (Harré, 1977; 1980; Harré & Secord, 1972). An important, but often overlooked, tenet of this non-mechanistic view is what Ginsburg (1980) aptly described as 'situated action.' Human action is embedded in social situations; some situations are conducive to active agency whereas others are less so. Familiar, predictable and unproblematic situations are conducive to automatic and 'mindless' behavior, for example, whereas novel, unpredictable, or difficult situations promote attentive monitoring and intentional choice-making by actors (Berger & Douglas, 1982). The physical and emotional difficulties referenced above, and the relationship dissatisfactions which prompt dissolution to begin with, indicate that disengagement is a problematic and difficult social situation for the relationship parties and thus a phenomenon in which actors are likely to function as proactive agents. This assumption reasonably leads to a research focus on the strategies by which agents attempt to accomplish relationship break-up.

Collectively, these four assumptions have crystallized the research program around the following three research questions:

1. What are the communicative strategies by which disengagers accomplish the unbonding of informal personal relationship?
2. Does disengagement strategy choice vary systematically by selected individual and relationship attributes?
3. What sequencing patterns, if any, characterize the process by which parties dissolve their relationships?

Three basic methodologies have been employed in addressing these questions: (1) retrospective recall; (2) hypothetical scenarios; and (3) ongoing diary monitoring of relationships. Both structured and free-response data have been solicited through all three of these methods. The advantage of a multi-method research program is that the limitations of one method are offset by the assets of another. Further, replication of findings across different methods serves to enhance the validity of those conclusions.

With this overview of the research program's central assumptions and research questions, let us turn to the findings which have emerged to date. Results will be organized around the research questions rather than listed in the chronological order in which the studies have been conducted.

MAJOR FINDINGS

What Are the Communication Strategies by Which Disengagers Accomplish the Unbounding of Informal Personal Relationships?

Four studies in the research program have focused on the variety of ways in which parties attempt to dissolve their personal relationships. The program began with an exploratory study in which almost one hundred young adults were asked in questionnaire form to describe the details of how they accomplished the disengagement of recalled personal relationship (Baxter, 1979b, unpub.). Because the vast majority of these relationship dissolutions re-flected a unilateral as opposed to a bilateral desire, the reported strategies were those enacted by the disengager against the broken-up-with party. The thirty-five disengagement strategies derived from these free-response questionnaires provided the basis for two studies (Baxter, 1982), in which over 200 college respondents indicated the likelihood with which the strategies would be used to disengage from hypothetical relationship scenarios; the likelihood-of-use ratings from each study were factor-analyzed in order to reduce the strategy set to a more parsimonious number. The most recent study in the research program sought free-response recollections from approximately one hundred young adults on the sequential episodes or turning points which comprised the dyadic phase of recalled romantic relationship break-ups (Baxter, 1984); accounts included both unilateral and bilateral desires to exit the relationship, with the majority of cases representing unilateral desires.

For parsimony's sake, these four studies will not be summarized individually. Despite differences in method and labeling, however, they point consistently to a basic set of disengagement strategies which appear to vary on two underlying dimensions: directness and other-orientation. Direct strategies explicitly state to the other party one's desire to exit the relationship, whereas indirect strategies try to accomplish the break-up without an explicit statement of the goal. Other-orientation captures the degree to which the disengager attempts to avoid hurting the other party in the break-up. Other-oriented strategies display explicit face-work (Brown & Levinson, 1978; Goffman, 1967) to avoid embarrassment or manipulation of the other party, whereas self-oriented strategies display primarily expedience for self at the other party's cost. These two underlying dimensions appear to capture the findings from other researchers' factor-analytic studies of disengagement strategies, as well (Cody, 1982; Perras & Lustig, 1982, unpub; Tanita, 1980, unpub.). In order to concretize these rather abstract underlying dimensions, prototypical strategies which capture the extremes of each dimension are presented below with account excerpts taken from Baxter (1984).

Directness and indirectness in disengagement strategies can take many forms. Among unilateral desires to exit, indirectness is manifested in three basic prototypical actions: withdrawal, pseudo–de-escalation and cost escalation. Withdrawal involves avoidance-based behaviors in which the disengager reduces the intimacy of contact and/or lessens the frequency of contact with the other party. Withdrawal is illustrated in this excerpt from a respondent account:

I took a stand that related to too much homework for an excuse to avoid her. She then initiated notes to me which contained certain things that both of us didn't like about the relationship. I never answered the notes . . .

Pseudo–de-escalation involves a false declaration to the other party that the disengager desires a transformed relationship of reduced closeness; the action is indirect because the desire to exit totally from the relationship is not made explicit to the other party. The pseudo–de-escalation action is illustrated in this account excerpt:

I arranged to talk with her in a neutral location . . . What I said basically was: 'Let's go back to being just friends' (knowing full well I meant I wanted to salvage my ego, and hers, by saying indirectly, the relationship was totally over).

Cost escalation involves behavior toward the other party which increases his or her relational costs; it is indirect action because the disengager tries to accomplish the dissolution without an explicit statement of the termination goal. Costs can be escalated in many ways, but the following excerpt illustrates the behavioral type:

I thought I would be an 'asshole' for a while to make her like me less . . .

Parties in a bilateral dissolution display basically two types of indirect action in accomplishing their break-up: fading away and pseudo-de-escalation. Fading away is characterized by implicit understanding that the relationship has ended. The following account excerpt captures the flavor of fading away:

My lover was a married man who was visiting overnight on his way through Portland. On the way to the airport the next day, we hardly spoke at all. When we did speak it wasn't concerning our relationships. We both knew that it was over . . .

Pseudo–de-escalation is similar to that discussed above under the unilateral resolution to exit, but the deception is mutual rather than one-sided in this instance. The two relationship parties maintain the pretense of a continuing relationship, meanwhile intending total non-contact with one another. As one respondent wrote:

We communicated the desire to try and continue the relationship ['just friends'], but I said this just to make the parting less painful, and he said it for the same reason.

Directness similarly manifests itself in a variety of forms. Among unilateral disengagers, basically two forms of directness can be noted: fait accompli and state-of-the-relationship talk. Fait accompli actions are characterized by an explicit declaration to the other party that the relationship is over, with no opportunity for discussion or compromise. In contrast, state-of-the-relationship talk is characterized by an explicit statement of dissatisfaction and desire to exit in the context of a bilateral discussion of the relationship's problems. The following two excerpts illustrate the difference in tone which distinguishes these two forms of unilateral directness:

On the 'phone, I told him I was tired of seeing him and that I was bored with him. I said I never wanted to see him again (fait accompli).

He brought up the issue of breaking up by saying that the fights we'd been having lately were due to our different needs . . . We talked about it a long time . . . At the end of the talk, we both agreed that we should break up (state-of-the-relationship talk).

Among two-sided desires to exit a relationship, directness is displayed in two strategy prototypes: attributional conflict and negotiated farewell. Although both parties may wish to exit the relationship, they may have very different views of what went wrong and who is to blame. Attributional conflict captures a conflict, not over whether or not to exit, but on why the exit is necessary. Attributional conflict is clearly evident in this account:

> We had a most awful scene yelling and screaming at each other. . . . We both wanted out, but we were both angry with the other for causing the hurt.

Negotiated farewell involves explicit communication between the parties which formally ends the relationship; however, unlike attributional conflict, this discussion is noticeably free of hostility and argument. The difference in tone is evident in comparing the above account excerpt with the following:

> Our relationship had been having a lot of problems, and we both experienced them. When we'd both had it, we went to dinner and had a good talk about what was going on.

Although the excerpts presented above have been used to illustrate prototypical indirectness and directness, it is apparent that the other-orientation dimension also underlies the strategy types. Cost escalation, fait accompli, withdrawal and attributional conflict appear to display limited other-orientation. Cost escalation clearly manifests little other-orientation in attempts to increase the relational costs for the other party. Attributional conflict also displays limited other-orientation in that the disengagers attempt to disparage one another for causing the break-up. Fait accompli presents the other party with a situation over which he or she has no control, a condition which Brown & Levinson (1978) argue is threatening to self-esteem, or face. Last, withdrawal also limits the other party's control over the situation; it is difficult for the other party to change the disengager's goal or to deal with the relationship's apparent problems when the disengager can't be contacted or refuses to talk beyond the superficial level.

The remaining prototypical strategies illustrated above accomplish at least a modicum of face-work on the other party's behalf, if not on behalf of the disengager, as well. A state-of-the-relationship talk at least gives the appearance of a bilateral discussion about the relationship's problems, thereby allowing the other party the pretense of exerting some control over the situation. Pseudo–de-escalation avoids total rejection of the other party in the pretense of a continuing, if transformed, relationship, thereby lessening the blow to the other's self-esteem. Bilateral pseudo–de-escalation allows both parties to save face in the pretense of a continuing relationship; in claiming that they are 'still friends,' both parties verbalize the other's social worth. Fading away allows the bilateral disengagers to save mutual face by ignoring completely their shared failure (Brown & Levinson, 1978). Last, in a negotiated farewell, the disengagers part after a sense-making session in which neither party individually is blamed by the other for the relationship's demise; in verbalizing self-blame, shared blame, or blame attributable to forces outside the relationship, each disengager absolves the other of individual responsibility for the stigmatized relationship failure.

Does Disengagement Strategy Choice Vary Systematically by Selected Individual and Relationship Attributes?

Individual-Level Attributes: Age. Disengagement strategies were examined as a function of four individual-level variables. The first of these, age, has both practical and theoretical import. At the practical level, relationship dissolution is common not only in adult relationships but in childhood and adolescent relationships, as well (La Gaipa, 1981b; Rubin, 1980); thus, a comprehensive understanding of the disengagement phenomenon necessitates study across age groups. At a theoretical level, studying how children, adolescents and adults accomplish relationship disengagement may contribute to the literature on developmental differences in social cognitions about relationships (La Gaipa, 1981b; Bell, 1981). Age differences have been examined in two studies in the research program. Although results are preliminary, they are nonetheless suggestive of possible developmental differences.

In the context of a broader research goal of comparing relationship initiation and disengagement strategy repertoires, almost 200 ten-year-olds, fifteen-year-olds, twenty-one-year-olds and post-college adults (mean age thirty-one years) provided free-response data on all the possible ways they could think of to accomplish relationship initiation and disengagement goals (Baxter & Philpott, 1982). Because the purpose of this study was to examine the implications of attribution theory for relationship initiation and termination, parallel two-dimensional typologies of strategy types were developed for the two relationship goals using existing attribution-based work, specifically Jones' (1964) ingratiation research and Kelley's (1967) 'attribution cube' work. For parsimony's sake, these typologies will not be discussed in detail. Almost all the variation in the data occurred on the ingratiation/anti-ingratiation dimension. This dimension reflected the directness and other-orientation features identified above, with the strategy counterparts of fait accompli and withdrawal (other negation and exclusion activity, respectively) dominating the termination data.

Age differences were apparent in the number of different strategy types which comprised both the initiation and the disengagement repertoires. Preadolescents had less diversified strategy repertoires than did adolescents and young adults. Pre-adolescents as a group displayed a composite disengagement repertoire consisting of only two strategies—other negation and exclusion. Although these two strategies were most frequent in the composite disengagement repertoires of the other age groups as well, the last three groups also evidenced repertoires which contained other strategy types. Further, the older respondents gained this strategy diversity through the reduced salience of other negation. These findings are partially confirmed in the friendship work of Bigelow & La Gaipa (1980). These researchers found that verbal confrontation and avoidance dominated the termination strategy profiles of their nine- to seventeen-year-old subjects, a finding consistent with the salience of other negation and exclusion in these data. However,

contrary to the dichotomous composite repertoire noted for pre-adolescents, Bigelow & La Gaipa reported the greatest range of termination strategies among their middle childhood age group.

The smaller repertoire size for pre-adolescents is quite reasonable in the light of work in social perspective-taking (Clark & Delia, 1976; 1977; O'Keefe & Delia, 1979; Delia et al., 1979). Pre-adolescents are cognitively less adept at taking the perspective of the other. Yet it is only through such perspective-taking that one is likely to realize the need for a diverse repertoire which maximizes the adaptation to diverse others.

The limited repertoire diversity which characterizes preadolescents as opposed to older persons may also be a reflection of differences in how the friendship relationship is conceived. Use of a disengagement strategy such as exclusion, for example, implies a view of friendship in which frequent contact is a necessary pre-condition. A growing body of literature on developmental differences in friendship cognitions in fact suggests that children have relatively simplistic conceptions of friendship which gain complexity with age (La Gaipa, 1981b; Bell, 1981).

Across age groups, the diversity of the strategy repertoire was greater for the initiation goal than for the disengagement goal. This suggests that as early as ten years of age, people have acquired a more sophisticated social repertoire for accomplishing relationship initiation as opposed to relationship disengagement, a discrepancy which continues into adulthood. On the one hand, this finding may provide a partial reason for why disengagement is a problematic social phenomenon; the parties lack sufficient diversity in their social skills repertoire. On the other hand, it may lend support to the claim by several theorists (cf. Rodin, 1982) that disengagement and initiation are not mirror opposites. This latter issue is developed in detail in response to the third research question below.

A second study has considered possible age differences in the most preferred strategy of disengagement (Baxter & Philpott, 1981b, unpub.). As part of the data collection procedures for the Baxter & Philpott (1982) study, each respondent was asked to select the most preferred strategy from his or her self-generated list and to provide a reason for the selection. Across age groups, the most frequently selected strategies were other negation and exclusion, which capture extremes in directness and indirectness, respectively. In a comparison of the frequencies with which these two strategies were selected as preferences, pre-adolescents tended to display more directness (other negation) than did other respondents. This finding is consistent with that noted by Bigelow & La Gaipa (1980) in their work with middle childhood through late-adolescence age levels. Children may be unaware of the threat posed to the other's esteem in being broken-up-with and thus may opt for greater directness in strategy preference. This may be a function of the child's unsophisticated perspective-taking, as discussed above, or it may reflect a view of friendship in which turnover rather than stability is the expected norm.

Respondent Sex and Sex-Role Orientation. Despite the claim by sociologist Robert Bell (1981, p. 55) that 'there is no social factor more important than that of sex in leading to friendship variations,' biological sex has not emerged as a source of significant variation in disengagement strategy use in two studies in the research program—the exploratory study cited above under question one (Baxter, 1979b, unpub.) and a second study whose details are presented below in response to question three (Baxter, 1979a). Disengagement work by others, however, has noted significant sex differences, although the pattern of these differences is not consistent across studies (Rubin et al., 1981; Wright, 1982).

A more productive approach may rest not with biology but with psychological sex role orientation, that is, whether someone has been socialized to display stereotypical masculine, stereotypical feminine, or a combination of masculine and feminine behaviors (Bem, 1974, 1975). The two studies summarized above with regard to age differences also

assessed respondent sex-role orientation among adolescents and adults using the Bem Sex Role Inventory (Bem, 1974). Results indicated no significant difference among the sex-role orientation groups on the diversity of disengagement strategy repertoires (Baxter & Philpott, 1981a, unpub.). However, sex-role orientation significantly affected disengagement strategy preferences (Baxter & Philpott, 1981b, unpub.). Androgynous persons, that is, those socialized to feel equally comfortable with both masculine and feminine behaviors, were least likely to employ the withdrawal/avoidance strategy of exclusion and most likely to employ direct other negation. It could be that a direct and open verbal declaration to the other party has elements of stereotypical masculinity and elements of stereotypical femininity which would produce ambivalence towards directness for both sex-typed categories of persons, that is, for masculine and feminine sex-role orientations (Bem & Lenney, 1976). The masculine sex-typed person would not be inclined to employ directness because it displays a stereotypical concern with relationships. The feminine sex-typed person would also find directness unappealing because it displays stereotypical masculine assertion.

Communication Apprehension. The final individual-level variable to receive attention in the research program is the disengager's level of communication apprehension (Baxter, 1980, unpub.). Among communication researchers, substantial theoretical and empirical energy has been directed toward understanding the effects of this debilitating dispositional apprehension about interacting with others (McCroskey, 1977; 1982). Individuals high in dispositional communication apprehension typically respond with withdrawal from and avoidance of interaction with others (McCroskey, 1982). It seems reasonable to suspect that the same behavior would occur in disengaging from relationships. However, if the disengagement situation were sufficiently anxiety-arousing, even the normally low communication-apprehensive individual would perhaps be cast in a highly apprehensive state, thereby behaving in a manner not unlike the dispositionally high communication-apprehensive individual. In a comparison of dispositionally low and high communication-apprehensive individuals, those high in communication apprehension employed less directness and more avoidance action in disengaging relationships than those low in dispositional communication apprehension. To a lesser extent, the high communication-apprehensive also employed less other-oriented action than the low communication-apprehensive individual. This makes sense, because several of the other-oriented strategies involve interaction of some sort with the other party. Thus, although relationship disengagement may be anxiety-arousing, it does not heighten the anxiety level of the dispositionally low communication-apprehensive to the point of negating differences with the dispositionally high apprehensive in directness of action.

Relationship-Level Attributes

Prior Relationship Closeness. Relationship closeness was experimentally manipulated in the hypothetical scenarios employed in Baxter's (1982) first study cited above. As anticipated, disengagers employed less indirectness and more other-orientation as the prior closeness of the relationship increased. These findings were confirmed independently of this research program by Cody (1982), who asked his respondents to recollect a disengaged relationship.

The politeness theory posited by Brown & Levinson (1978) provides a useful framework in which to interpret these findings. Prior relationship closeness may motivate the disengager to display concern about the other party's 'face,' avoiding an embarrassing and emotionally painful experience for the other. This motivation to reduce threat to the other's esteem, in turn, may be the product of two factors: the other party's power or betrayal potential, and the perceived obligations which accompany close relationships. As Davis (1973) has noted, the closer the relationship the more the par-

ties have learned about one another's private selves, affording them substantial betrayal potential to publicly expose one another's private selves if so motivated. Being the 'broken-up-with' party might provide the necessary motivation to betray the disengager's confidences; the 'broken-up-with' role, after all, is perceived quite negatively by relationship parties (Hill et al., 1976). Because formerly close relationship partners should have accumulated more private information than parties in relationships of less closeness, the former's betrayal potential is a greater threat to the disengager's own face in closer relationships. The disengager should therefore show more concern about the other's face in formerly close relationships in an attempt to ameliorate the effects of the break-up.

Apart from the other's betrayal potential, the disengager may display concern for the other's face based on expectations of the rights and obligations which accompany close relationships. The disengager is ultimately accountable to his or her social network, and network members may perceive that the disengager 'owes' this concern for the other's face based on prior rewards the person had reaped from the relationship. Failure to meet this obligation on the part of the disengager may be met with threat to his or her own face as network members respond with appropriate sanctions.

The concern-for-the-other's face threat should result in increased use of polite strategies, according to Brown & Levinson's (1978) reasoning. Other-orientation clearly displays such politeness, but directness is the opposite of what Brown & Levinson would regard as polite. Given the above discussion of relationship obligations, disengagement of a close relationship may be a circumstance in which indirectness is the impolite action. In a once-close relationship, the disengager may 'owe' a direct account of why the disengagement is desired. Further, Brown and Levinson (1978) themselves argue that indirectness will be abandoned whenever there is a need for information efficiency. Davis (1973) cogently argues that people in close relationships have succeeded in 'sewing together' every dimension of their separate lives, unlike members of a more superficial relationship in which interdependence is established only in quite restricted domains of the parties' lives. The forms of interdependence are many and varied in the close relationship, requiring open disengagement strategies in order to untie successfully the parties' many connective threads.

Romantic vs. Nonromantic Relationship Types. The romantic vs. nonromantic basis of the relationship prior to its dissolution has also been studied. In the initial exploratory study of the research program (Baxter, 1979b, unpub.), disengagers reported more directness in romantic as opposed to nonromantic relationships. In a study to be discussed in more detail below, in response to the third research questions, Baxter (1983) replicated this finding. The directness associated with romantic relationships may be a simple by-product of relationship closeness on the assumption that romantic relationships are perceived as closer than nonromantic friendships (Knapp et al., 1980).

However, a sex composition factor may be operating, as well. Because cross-sex relationships are typically perceived as romantically based in this culture (Bell, 1981), and because the samples in these studies contained few homosexuals, romantic relationships were overwhelmingly cross-sex, whereas nonromantic relationships were largely same-sex in nature. Males and females are socialized with different sets of communicative behaviors and interpretations for those behaviors (Maltz & Borker, 1982), perhaps explaining the greater directness employed in cross-sex disengagements. Cross-sex partners may not understand one another's subtle and indirect cues of dissolution, necessitating more overt and explicit interaction.

Factors Associated with the Break-Up. The final three relationship-level factors are all associated with the nature of the break-up. The first of these factors, perceived cause of the relationship's demise, was experimentally manipulated in a series of hypothetical scenarios in Baxter's (1982) second study. Results indicated greatest directness with an externally attributed locus of cause; when the at-

tributed cause rested with either or both relationship parties, there was a likelihood across conditions of increased indirectness. External attribution may be less likely to threaten the face of the relationship parties than attributions to one or both of the members. The safety of external causal attributions may be one factor which contributed to the correlation of break-ups with external events, such as vacations, for the pre-marital couples studied by Hill, Rubin, and Peplau (1976).

One might reasonably have anticipated that less other-oriented behavior would accompany a perception that the other party was to blame for the relationship demise; yet, no differences were noted on the other-orientation dimension as a function of causal attribution. Initiating the break-up may itself constitute sufficient retribution against the other for causing the break-up because of the stigma associated with the broken-up-with role (Hill et al., 1976).

The mutuality of the desire to dissolve the relationship has been examined in four studies of the research program, two using the hypothetical scenario method (Baxter, 1979a, 1982) and two using the relationship recollection method (Baxter, 1979b, unpub., 1984). No significant differences have been found in three of the four studies, with the fourth (Baxter, 1984) reporting greater likelihood of initial indirectness among unilateral as opposed to bilateral resolutions to exit. The general pattern of no differences between the unilateral and bilateral conditions may be attributable to possible differences in function which may accompany the disengagement strategies in these two conditions. In the unilateral desire to dissolve the relationship, the disengager's actions perform an informational and/or a persuasive function. In the bilateral condition, however, disengagement action constitutes confirmation of what is already understood by both parties.

The final relationship-level attribute to receive research attention is the anticipated future contact between the two relationship parties. Baxter's (1982) first study reported a tendency toward less indirectness with anticipated future contact, a finding replicated by Perras & Lustig (1982, unpub.). Anticipated future contact maintains interdependence between the parties, perhaps necessitating direct talk to establish the terms of this relationship transformation.

Conclusions

For both individual-level and relationship-level attributes, most of the variation in reported strategy use occurred on the directness dimension of the strategy typology; only occasionally did differences emerge on the other-orientation dimension. This may reflect a social desirability bias in the research methods, with respondents reporting limited variability from the socially desirable other-oriented behavior. Alternatively, the directness dimension may be the single dominant feature of relationship disengagement as perceived and enacted by relationship parties.

This section has summarized research which is somewhat static in nature; the primary goal has been that of determining individual and relationship attributes associated with the disengager's strategy use during the dyadic phase of Duck's (1982a) four-stage model. The next section reviews research from the program which has focused on the dynamic and sequential features of the dyadic phase of the disengagement process.

What Sequencing Patterns, If Any, Characterize the Process by Which Relationship Parties Dissolve Their Relationships?

As discussed above, study of the process of relationship disengagement has often been grounded in the 'reversal hypothesis,' that is, the assumption that disengagement is merely the reverse of the relationship growth process. This is an important assumption, for it allows the researcher to presume an understanding of the break-up process from already accumulated work on relationship growth.

Several studies in the research program have addressed the validity of the reversal hypothesis, in general finding both confirmation and disconfirmation depending on the particular feature of interaction under study. Of course, a rejection of the reversal hypothesis, either in whole or in part, obligates the researcher to understand the sequential patterns of break-up in their own right, and several studies in the research program have been conducted with this goal in mind. These two sets of studies are reviewed below.

Validity of the Reversal Hypothesis

Baxter (1979a) initiated examination of the reversal hypothesis by considering one of the most frequently studied variables in the personal relationships literature, self-disclosure. Over one hundred adults were randomly assigned to hypothetical scenarios which varied relationship status (subject intent to continue/disengage the relationship vs. other's intent to continue/disengage). Respondents indicated the likelihood that they would interact with the hypothetical other on a variety of topics with varied intimacy value. Consistent with the prediction of the reversal hypothesis, respondents with the intent to disengage the relationship displayed significantly less intimacy of disclosure than those with the intent to continue the relationship.

More recently, Baxter (1983) examined a larger number of dimensions upon which reversals could potentially occur: specifically, Knapp's (1978) eight dimensions of relationship communication. It was anticipated that reversal would occur for some of the dimensions but not for others. Central to the argument for differential reversal is the realization that disengaging parties cannot simply forget the social knowledge and predictability of one another accumulated during the relationship's prior history. To the extent that communication behavior is based on the parties' knowledge or predictability of one another, rather than their liking of each other, it should not necessarily display a reversal effect. Reciprocally, to the extent that communication behavior is based on positive affect rather than familiarity and predictability, it should manifest reversal during disengagement.

In asking approximately one hundred young adults to assess the degree of reversal experienced on the dimensions for both a disengaged romantic relationship and a disengaged nonromantic relationship, the argument for differential reversal gained substantial support. As expected, and consistent with the findings of Baxter (1979a), the greatest reversal was noted for the depth of disclosure dimension. Further, disengaging relationship parties did not display a reversal on those communication characteristics related to the parties' social knowledge of one another, for example, familiarity with one another's idiosyncratic behaviors.

Baxter & Wilmot (1982) employed a different methodology to explore further the reversal hypothesis, asking university-level students to keep diaries for a two-week period on the encounters which occurred in two targeted relationships, one opposite-sex and one same-sex. The monitored relationships were divided into those which were rapidly escalating, moderately escalating, stable, and disengaging based on respondents' data across the two-week period. The results suggested that reported satisfaction with the relationship encounters, the perceived importance of the encounters, the perceived personalness or disclosiveness of encounter interaction, and the perceived smoothness of interaction progressively declined from the rapidly escalating to the disengaging relationships. These findings are fully supportive of the reversal hypothesis. However, contrary to reversal predictions, disengaging relationships were not characterized by a reduction in the number of encounters and topic breadth was not reduced.

The fourth and final study to examine assumptions of the reversal hypothesis was discussed above in reference to age differences in initiation and disengagement strategy repertoires (Baxter & Philpott, 1982). For all age groups, the diversity of the relationship growth strategy repertoire was greater than that of the disengagement strategy repertoire, possibly reflecting a qualitative difference in the communicative burden assumed by the actor in

these two social efforts. Relationship initiation may require the agreement of both parties to succeed; in contrast, relationship disengagement, at least in informal relationships, perhaps can be accomplished by a single party. This observation, in turn, is the foundation for the claim that initiation may be a conjunctive communicative task, whereas disengagement may be a disjunctive communicative task. The conjunctive nature of relationship initiation is evident in the fact that the actor must convey both of the following attributions to the other party: 1) that he or she is interested in establishing the relationship, and 2) that he or she is worthy of the other's investment in a relationship. Unless both of these attributions are apparent to the other party, a relationship will not form. By contrast, informal relationship disengagement is a disjunctive task in that only one of the following attributions may suffice to accomplish the dissolution: 1) that he or she is no longer interested in the relationship, or 2) that he or she no longer merits investment by the other party. Although the attributions for disengagement are the direct opposites of those for initiation, the argument is that the two relationship processes are not merely the reverse of one another but qualitatively different phenomena. The distribution of strategy types for both the composite initiation repertoire and the composite disengagement repertoire supported this conjunctive-disjunctive analysis (Baxter & Philpott, 1982).

Collectively, these four studies suggest that relationship disengagement is not captured well in the reversal hypothesis. Reversal effects are consistently apparent in the degree of self-disclosure enacted by disengaging parties. However, as one shifts away from affect-based features of communication to more cognitively based features, the reversal metaphor becomes less useful. The final two studies of the research program examine process issues in the dyadic negotiation of disengagement outside the assumptions of the reversal hypothesis.

Process Features of Disengagement

Baxter & Philpott (1980, unpub.) examined the process dynamics of relationship disengagement by asking respondents to complete a hypothetical scenario which set the scene of an opposite-sex relationship pair in which one party sought to disengage from the relationship. The critical unit of analysis in the study was the 'action round,' defined as an attempted disengagement action on the part of the disengager. When indirectness was named by the respondent as the initial disengagement action in the story completion, the result was a story which portrayed a more protracted disengagement period than was the case when direct actions were imagined to initiate the break-up. This finding is quite consistent with the results of another study in the research program in which the most frequently mentioned regret expressed by disengagers was reliance on indirectness (Baxter, 1979b, unpub.).

More recently, Baxter (1984) asked close to one hundred young adults to record all the important stages, turning points, or periods in the break-up of a romantic relationship, commencing with the initial point at which the relationship began to dissolve. Using the analytic induction method (Bulmer, 1979), a flow chart of the disengagement process was developed. Respondent accounts were then traced through the flow chart on a case-by-case basis in an attempt to discern the most frequent trajectories or paths of disengagement.

The flow chart model of disengaging is reproduced in Figure 24.1. Although it is complex, the model captures the six critical features of the dissolution process by which the recollected relationships varied: 1) the gradual vs. sudden onset of relationship problems; 2) the unilateral vs. bilateral desire to exit; 3) the use of direct vs. indirect actions to accomplish the disengagement; 4) the rapid vs. protracted nature of the disengagement negotiations; 5) the presence vs. absence of relationship repair attempts; and 6) the final outcome of termination or continuation of the relationship. These six features become apparent in progressing

FIGURE 24.1

Flow Chart of Disengagement

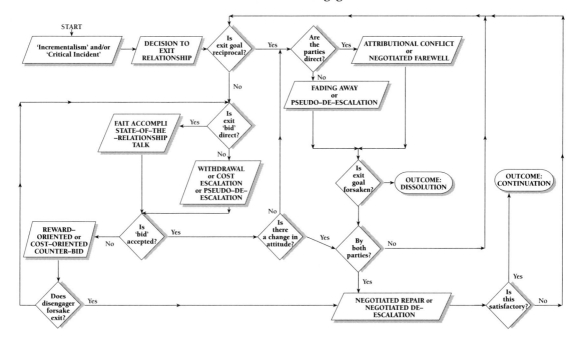

through the flow chart from the point of entry to the point of exit. This progression is shown in the seven steps depicted in Figure 24.1. Overall, 25 percent of the accounts contain a 'critical incident' as their starting point. At Step 2, two-thirds of the disengagements were unilateral in nature. These were typically initiated through indirect action (Step 3). Most partners resisted terminating their relationships (Step 4), with this being especially likely in response to indirect unilateral disengagement bids. In the vast majority of examples, attempted (Step 5) repair efforts proved unsatisfactory and the parties cycled back through the flow chart for additional disengagement work.

The complexity of the flow chart model suggests the large number of paths or trajectories which are possible for any given relationship disengagement once an exit decision has been reached by at least one person. However, variation among disengagements can be summarized in terms of the five distinctive features of the flow chart, exclusive of the gradual vs. sudden onset of the disengagement. If these features were independent of one another and equally likely to occur, the number of possible different trajectories through the flow chart would be 2 to the fifth power. Fortunately, a much smaller number of possibilities captures the major variations in the accounts!

The most frequent disengagement trajectory was unilateral in the desire to exit, with the disengager opting for indirect action which met resistance from the other party. This trajectory is characterized by no repair efforts, ultimately leading to the termination of the relationship. It is labeled *persevering indirectness*, and accounted for 30 percent of the codable disengagements in this data set.

An additional seven trajectories were evident in this data set, but they each accounted for a much smaller proportion of cases (7–17 percent). For parsimony's sake, these additional trajectories will not be itemized in detail. Collectively, however, their presence supports the observation by Kressel et al. (1980) that researchers must begin to give serious attention to the patterned differences in relationship break-ups, rather than operating on the assumption that a single trajectory suffices to capture the process.

CONCLUSIONS

The purpose of this final section is twofold. First, the major findings of the research program will be summarized. Second, recommendations for future research will be introduced.

The ten studies completed to date in the research program have focused on the dyadic phase of Duck's (1982a) four-phase model of dissolution. The primary findings can be captured in four summary observations:

1. Strategies by which relationship parties accomplish the disengagement of their relationship appear to vary on two underlying dimensions: directness and other-orientation.
2. Indirectness is a pervasive feature of disengagement, although variations in strategy use are apparent for several individual-level and relationship-level attributes. In particular, directness is more likely for pre-adolescents and for adults who are androgynous in sex-role orientation or dispositionally low in communication apprehension. Directness also is more likely under these relationship conditions: prior relationship closeness, a romantic as opposed to nonromantic basis for the relationship, an external locus of cause for the relationship's demise, and anticipated future contact between the relationship parties.
3. Relationship disengagement is not merely the reverse of the relationship growth process. Because they have acquired knowledge and predictability about one another, the relationship parties cannot simply return to their former 'stranger-like' state. Further, the communicative task which faces the disengager may be qualitatively different from the communicative task which faces the relationship initiator.
4. Relationship disengagement is multi-faceted and complex, and cannot be captured adequately by a single sequential pattern. The most frequent

disengagement trajectory is characterized by a unilateral desire to exit the relationship, strategy indirectness, protracted 'cycling' through multiple disengagement attempts, and an ultimate outcome of dissolution. However, this trajectory accounts for only one-third of all disengagements; seven additional trajectory patterns are evident.

These findings are preliminary, with much additional work necessary before the disengagement process is fully understood. Four recommendations for future research attention seem especially worthy of note. The first deals with social skills research in accomplishing relationship disengagement. A contributory factor to dissolution stress may be the manner in which the relationship parties accomplish the disengagement. A pervasive strategy is indirect withdrawal and avoidance, yet such a strategy appears to result in an increased negative response from the other party and a protracted period of disengagement action. Additional research needs to address how people acquire their disengagement strategy repertoires and the possibility of skill deficits in this area of relationship conduct.

Second, subsequent work could benefit from dual perspective data, that is, perceptions from both relationship parties. Dual perspective data obviously hold methodological promise in affording a cross-check of each party's separate relationship perceptions. As Duck & Sants (1983) observe, however, dual perspective data hold theoretical promise, as well. Disengagements in which the parties share a similar vision of why and how their relationship dissolves may differ dramatically from disengagements characterized by discrepancies about causes of the break-up or about perceptions of the dissolution process itself.

The third recommendation for future research deals with Brown & Levinson's (1978) theory of face redress or politeness. The underlying strategy dimensions which emerged in these studies bear remarkable resemblance to Brown & Levinson's face-work characteristics. At several junctures throughout this article the Brown & Levinson theory has been used as a framework to assist in the interpretation of study findings. Obviously, this theoretical treatment has been on a post-hoc basis, and future work could usefully undertake direct examination of the role which face threat holds in the disengagement process. Critical to this examination will be the realization that a disengaging pair is embedded in a social and cultural system with its associated norms of appropriate behavior. Although some theoretical work has begun to appear on the broader social norms which constrain the conduct of dissolution (Duck, 1982a; La Gaipa, 1982), research-based work is needed.

The fourth, and final, recommendation is a call for additional work on the process dynamics of disengagement. It is important to capture process features through longitudinal data collection in addition to retrospective recall. The diary record method employed by Baxter & Wilmot (1982, unpub.) merits further use by researchers interested in understanding the disengagement process.

Whether retrospective or longitudinal, process-oriented insights into disengagement must be embedded in the larger process context of the relationship's history. Several studies in the research program have examined covariation between strategy use and relationship history variables, but this research has not considered possible covariation between prior relationship processes and the process trajectories of disengagement. Research needs to determine how relationship initiation and growth processes relate to processes of disengagement.

25

A Topography of Relationship Disengagement and Dissolution

STEVE DUCK

This chapter is about relationship dissolution and yet is not the traditional form of research review that an editor habitually embodies. Since the present writing presumes to take us on a journey to something of a New World rather than on a tour of already very familiar and well-mapped territory, the need is rather for a forward-looking but basic orientation towards key areas of the topic. This would localize and orient us towards those existing careful analyses that seek to provide insights into specific topics and aspects of the ending of relationships (e.g., Albert & Kessler, 1978; Altman & Taylor, 1973; Knapp, 1978; Laner, 1978; Salts, 1979; Scott & Powers, 1978). What is presently lacking, however, is a framework for locating and understanding such mini-maps; for showing whether relationship growth relates to disengagement; indicating where communication processes fit in, how attribution ties in, and so on. . . .

I will begin my task by considering some essential, if familiar, points about the nature and character of relationship dissolution, and by then going on to consider the relevance of present theoretical formulations about interpersonal *attraction* for understanding its opposite, namely, relationship decline. Finally, I will propose a general mapping for the topics in the area. A map is only implicitly a theory and this does not propose an explicit theory of relationship dissolution—but it does, I hope, indicate the potential interest and the range of research challenges that lie in the area of future

workers for a range of academic and applied research disciplines.

In discussing relationship dissolution I will adopt here . . . a consistent terminology. Following Duck (1981), I will use the terms "dissolution" and "termination" to refer to the permanent dismemberment of an existing relationship, as distinct from "breakdown" which refers to such turbulence or disorder in a relationship that may or may not lead to dissolution. I will adopt the term "decline" to refer to reduction of intimacy without actual physical withdrawal from relationship and hence decline encompasses those instances that involve the restructuring or reformulating of a close relationship as a less intimate and more distanced one (e.g., when a couple get divorced but remain friends). I use the term "disengagement" to cover the processes of withdrawing from a relationship that constitute most of the subject matter for the present chapter and others in this volume—such processes as the negotiation of the dissolution of the relationship, reducing commitment, and restructuring social networks. Finally, I will refer to the "Person" as the active dissolver of the relationship and to the "Partner" as the other individual involved.

Throughout any discussion of relationship disengagement and dissolution it must be clearly noted that many different sorts of relationship termination can be identified both at the dyadic and at the network level. Davis (1973) led the way here, drawing useful distinctions between dissolution of

From Duck, S.W. (Ed.) (1982). *Personal relationships, 4: Dissolving relationships* (pp. 1–29). New York: Academic Press.

formalized and of informal relationships; pointing out the psychological and theoretical relevance of the duration of a relationship prior to its dissolution; noting the significance of the type of relationship before disengagement (whether a casual acquaintance, a close friendship or a romantic attachment); finally, and most usefully, drawing attention to the importance of the expectations of the partners concerning the post-dissolution relationship state.

Nevertheless, in my view the most important observation for research is that we must avoid the risk of seeing relationship dissolution as an event. On the contrary, it is a process, and an extended one with many facets: affective, behavioral, cognitive; intra-individual, dyadic and social. Dissolution usually occurs after the relationship breaks down, but breakdown and dissolution are psychologically distinct. Similarly we have learned to distinguish "liking" and "relationship formation": liking for someone is a common basis for making a relationship but is not enough on its own. In the case of "liking" and "relationship" it took some 20 years to clarify the links between the one and the other (Hinde, 1979, 1981). In the case of "breakdown" and "dissolution" the present major research issues concern precisely the mechanisms and the processes through which the one leads into the other and why, sometimes, it does not.

We must also plainly acknowledge that the activity leading to relationship dissolution is not necessarily consciously "driven," even if we can cite instances where "strategic deletion of a relationship" is indeed a person's goal (Baxter, 1980). It is undesirable to assume that disengagement is necessarily orderly, predictable and certain. Most often it is messy, uncontrolled and uncertain (Duck & Miell, 1981). Neither should we assume that relationship dissolution represents a choice completely unlimited by other constraints such as network pressures, peer-group influences, and management of social "face." A strictly intra-psychic or strictly dyadic model of relationship dissolution is an inadequate single explanation of all the observable processes: people do not always in reality have the

freedom of choice that they appear to have in theory. We are all subject to the normative social and cultural constraints that apply to relationship conduct. Finally, we should not assume that all relationship dissolution is necessarily undesired or necessarily a bad thing, meriting management, correction, or therapy. For one thing some relationships stifle the individuals' growth and their dissolution can be a creative act of rejuvenation, full of promise and freedom. For another thing not all relationships "matter" in deep psychological or personal ways such that, for instance, the dissolution of a temporary working partnership is not usually a powerful psychological experience. . . .

INTERPERSONAL ATTRACTION AND RELATIONSHIP DISSOLUTION

Because interpersonal attraction and communication researchers have hitherto been much more attentive to the beginning and successful progression or conduct of relationships, studies of breakdown and ending of relationships are relatively scarce and make reference to growth and development of relationships only as a source of analogy or of inspiration. Altman and Taylor (1973), for instance, proposed that disengagement is a reversal of relationship growth ("like a film shown in reverse" in their elegant analogy). Albert and Kessler (1978), on the other hand, analogize from the ending of social encounters to the ending of relationships, pointing out the commonalities between parting rituals after social encounters and those that inhere in dissolution of relationships. Such analogies are very useful first guides to the understanding of specific components of the whole process. Indeed, their strength lies in their recognition that disengagement and dissolution represent not so much a single act as a process created from sequences of actions. Unfortunately, they are also very limited in scope and lack empirical support or have actually been challenged (Baxter, 1981). Other analyses contend that reversal of relationship growth simply cannot be what occurs in relationship dissolution.

Duck and Lea (1982), for instance, argue that partners' information about one another does not decline as a relationship dies, but is simply gathered in different ways, with different intents, or from different perspectives; intimacy decline carries different meanings from those carried by intimacy growth; liking does not decline in steady linear fashion; self-disclosure changes in form as well as decreasing in scope. In short, a reversal analogy is logically suspect as well as empirically unsupported.

Four Latent Models of Dissolution

Perhaps, then, we have not made the best use of existing work on intimacy growth, preferring to use the study of beginning and development of relationship merely as a steady source of insight and analogy about relationship dissolution without any attempt to integrate it theoretically. It is, indeed, astonishing that theoretical and empirical work on interpersonal attraction and relationship development has not brought its contribution to bear on the questions of relationship dissolution. Yet even at first sight there are many simple research-based observations that seem to apply. For instance, if theorists argue that relationship growth is caused by attitude similarity or personality variables, then one would expect explanations of relational failure and dissolution to be cast in such terms also. There are enough of such explanations available in the interpersonal attraction literation, after all (see, e.g., Duck, 1977, or Berscheid & Walster, 1978, for a hint of the range of factors that could provide possible accounts). I will pick on three that are already latent in such literature ("Pre-existing Doom" ideas; "Mechanical Failure"; "Process Loss") and one which is peculiar to dissolution ("Sudden Death"). My intent is to indicate that they can each shed some light on the parts of the whole process but that some overarching view of the total enterprise is also needed.

Pre-Existing Doom. Several theories of initial attraction and/or relationship growth imply quite un-

ambiguously that certain inherent features of individuals necessarily enhance their chances of a satisfactory relationship. Thus we can readily find the suggestion that physical attractiveness or extraversion promotes liking (e.g., Perrin, 1921; Hendrick & Brown, 1971). More subtly, others have shown that IQ similarity enhances attraction (Austin & Thompson, 1948) or that socioeconomic similarity does so (Byrne et al., 1966). Other even more complex proposals suggest that discovery of attitude similarity (Byrne, 1971) or of different depths and types of personality similarity (Duck, 1977) will emerge to enhance attraction. It ought to follow then, that pairs of individuals lacking such characteristics, or failing to demonstrate them, will be likely to dissolve relationships or will fail to engage. But where are the studies of physical attractiveness and breakdown, of extraversion and disengagement, of IQ and dissolution, of socioeconomic status and dissolution, of attitudes and dissolution, or of personality matching and dissolution? I know of only one single study (i.e., Duck & Allison, 1978) that has so far investigated the personality matching of pairs of friends who formed a relationship which they later dissolved. It was found, as would be predicted, that pairs who had originally selected one another from the available pool were more similar than those who had not; but within this set, those who subsequently fell out were less similar than those who stayed together. The results thus seem to be consistent with present theoretical notions about relationship growth, but this one study really is a rather inadequate basis for firm propositions along those lines. Whilst such studies are of limited value to the overall picture about relationship dissolution, they are of value none the less and merit amplification. This would help us to establish the extent to which failure of relationships can be predicted independently of process within the relationship—by using knowledge of the pre-existing characteristics of the partners that are predictive of their match (un)suitability.

Mechanical Failure. Several recent suggestions about termination of relationships (e.g., Baxter &

Philpott, 1980; Hatfield & Traupmann, 1981) have urged that the poor conduct of the relationship by one or both partners is the ultimate cause of dissolution. Thus iniquitous or inequitable conduct of interactions or failures to communicate with one another satisfactorily may bring the partnership to a tottering collapse. The selfishness and thoughtlessness of a partner are indeed frequently-cited reasons for dissolving personal relationships, as seems intuitively obvious (Levinger, 1979). Such occurrences and such theories presuppose that partners are, in all other respects, suited to each other; yet it seems to the present author at least plausible that *some* "mechanical failures" actually reflect the partners' inherent unsuitability to each other. For instance, partners' pre-existing value structures may make it effectively impossible for a given pair of partners to negotiate satisfactory role-relations between them during the gradual development of the relationship. This would store up trouble for the future and vitiate the prospect that partners could later develop or conduct the partnership in a concerted and mutually satisfactory manner (a possibility derivable from Murstein's, 1977, SVR model, at least). Until such possibilities are studied effectively, we just won't know.

Process Loss. A subtler version of the foregoing point derives from consideration of research on group problem-solving. Steiner (1972) noted that human resources are rarely optimally employed and actual productivity invariably falls short of potential productivity through faulty process ("process loss"). It would be surprising if this general human tendency were not observable in the context of personal relationships. We would expect that some partners would fail to develop a relationship to its theoretically optimal level and so become dissatisfied with it to the extent that they may even wish to terminate the relationship. At present, many theories of interpersonal attraction contain the unstated assumption that if individuals possess or share a given characteristic (e.g., physical attractiveness or attitude similarity) they will be able to "use" it to further their relationships. A slightly dif-

ferent assumption is that all individuals not only possess but can effectively use the skills that are necessary to maximize a relationship's potential. Thus for instance, it might seem plausible to assume that if attitude similarity is attractive it is so because people can detect it in life to the same degree and with the same significance as they do in the laboratory. Yet Duck (1977, pp. 153–156) and Byrne (in Baron et al., 1974, pp. 43–45) have shown why such an assumption is unwarranted. For instance, partners may be unsuccessful in their attempts to reveal such similarity to one another, or the opportunity for doing so may be allowed to slip by, or they may fail to recognize subtle instances of similarity when they arise. In such a case, faulty process would prevent the potential influence of attitude similarity being successfully realized in subjective terms and it cannot therefore be assumed in such cases to have its full effect on attraction levels. Such process loss would predictably lead to the failure to reach a satisfactory level of relationship and hence may create dissatisfaction with the relationship and lead to its ultimate dissolution.

Research on such a possibility is, in my view, an indispensable means of discovering the true life-some significance of the factors unearthed in the past 20 years' research on interpersonal attraction. It is a subtler version of the frequent complaint that factors found to be influential in laboratory study are not necessarily significant to the same extent in real life. However, as readers will readily detect, it places the origin of the difference *in the two interacting partners* rather than in some undefined (as it usually is) metaphysical difference between "laboratory" and "real life" (which is usually left crucially undefined also, Duck, 1980b). At least this version of the point makes it researchable—whilst also relating dissolution and growth of relationships to the same theoretical propositions.

Sudden Death. A relatively obvious proposition in the context of relationship dissolution, yet which has little connection with relationship growth, is that new, surprising, and significant negatively charged information about a partner can hasten the relationship's death. Discovery of a partner's adultery, betrayal of trust, or deception, and instances of personal renunciation or simple ratting on the relationship are obvious examples of such inputs that are likely to bring a sudden end to a relationship. The interpretation and explanation of their effects is, however, problematic for two reasons. In the first place, they do not invariably and inevitably lead to dissolution of the relationship. As Hagestad and Smyer report in detail, some marriages survive repeated discoveries of partner's adultery, betrayal, deceit, brutality, and perversion. So there is no *psychological* necessity that such things do indeed cause the sudden death of the relationship: if they do, then they have to be "allowed" to do so, or "identified" as causes; but they may simply cause the intimacy or relationship level to be "cranked back a notch," as when partners remain friends after divorce. In the second place, many adulterous, deceitful rats would claim that their negatively loaded acts *followed* rather than caused dissolution, and represented not the true ending of the relationship but their redressing of the balance once it had, in effect, already ended for them.

It is with the recognition of such familiar points that we begin to find even more clearly thrust into the foreground the inadequacy of single-focus intra-individual models of relationship dissolution. It is necessary to consider and account for the persuasive influence of such factors as probability of entering a satisfactory alternative relationship, probability of being able to create a publicly acceptable "story" about the break-up, fear of partner (as in, for example, the case of battered wives, who may be afraid to leave a rebarbative spouse), guilt or anxiety about consequences to other parties (e.g., children)—and a host of other psychological influences.

A General Model of Relationship Dissolution

The problem is not that the above models (or "straw models," perhaps!) are incorrect but that they have only local or limited concern with some small part of the jigsaw puzzle. Each of the four proposes something about relationship dissolution that seems to contain an element of truth or an element of observable fit with reality. Each of them describes something that is an intuitively plausible contender for the prize of Dissolution Cause: partners' individual qualities, poor conduct of the relationship, inability to realize relationship potential, or impulsive selfish acts all seem likely to contribute to a relationship's demise. Yet their inadequacy as explanations of relationship disengagement and dissolution is made apparent through their magnification of some single element of a process that, in our more reflective moments, we know just cannot be that simple nor so radically different and disjunctive from normal relationship activity. In the first place, negative information about the partner or the relationship has no simple mechanistic results any more than other information has upon the relationship: instead it has to be processed by the individuals involved, has to be larded with personal significance, and has to lead to a desire to withdraw. It does not invariably do so and, indeed, in the normal course of relationship development some sorts of negative information often have very little effect at all. Yet research has so far failed to clarify the psychological algebra involved in such decisions and why it is that partners often tolerate "objectively" unacceptable partners. The first problem, then, is one for cognitive social psychologists. The second problem is different in scope, however. It is that relationship dissolution not only has to happen but has to be managed and dealt with in a teeming social context. Real friends, real relatives, real social institutions may have to be informed about the dissolution and, if the relationship was a significant one, these social entities will probably have a strong view about the whole thing. Partners who otherwise intend to dissolve their relationship may be cowed into inactivity by anticipations of such reactions from the social network.

One of the theoretical problems that confronts us at this stage, then, is the issue of how such "local" components of the broader canvas should be placed. How does dissolution relate to relationship growth? What similarities and differences are there between the two cases? What is the relationship between partners' individual qualities and relationship conduct in the dissolution equation? At what point(s) in the process are they each considered and balanced out in the partners' minds? When do individuals weigh up their desire to withdraw against their guesses about the likely responses of significant outsiders? In essence these research problems can be represented as hinging on the difficult judgment of the relative weights of cognitive and social elements in relationship dissolution at different points in the process.

This topographical problem actually takes us to the roots and confronts us with the inadequacies of predominant research styles in the general area of interpersonal attraction research. It implicitly points to weaknesses in research styles that require remedy: four examples only will be given here.

First, predominant theoretical models in social psychology at present stress the rational judgments that individuals make and they underplay the social pressures that confront the person intending to consider or execute such decisions. In the present context we can assume that persons are strongly driven by emotions and feelings—or, at the very least, that their decisions create emotion and feelings that have to be dealt with when they arise. My argument in the rest of the chapter will thus be essentially contextualist: that any "rational" judgments must be seen in the context of the social constraints upon executing them; that cognitive activity, on the other hand, represents a context for dealing with social pressures (e.g., when individuals create rational accounts of their relationship dissolution in order to satisfy relatives or to justify themselves publicly).

A second weakness in present research is the assumption that individuals conduct their relationships in each other's presence, and until recently there has been too little account taken of the evaluative, reflective, fantasizing, assessment work that people do in the absence of their partner (Duck, 1980a).

A third dominant impression is that most of our interpersonal attraction or social intercourse is directed towards strangers, but Wheeler and Nezlek (1977) have gathered data to indicate the balance of people's actual social participation, and Duck and Miell (1981, 1982) have used diary records to study the frequency and type of encounter with friends as they develop in natural settings over ten- and twenty-week periods. From this it is clear that individuals, quite unexpectedly, are very tentative and uncertain about even their deep, long-lasting relationships. They are continually reviewing and assessing their friendships—even when these are "objectively" stable and are reported as deep, constant and satisfying. People are still, nonetheless, evidently insecure and vigilant—perpetually re-evaluating both their developing and even their well-established friendships.

Fourthly, and most important, Emler (1981) has questioned the implication in interpersonal attraction research that people sit and discuss their attitudes, personality characteristics, traits, and so on. On the contrary, he finds that in real-life encounters people discuss other people and gossip—particularly about personal events rather than attitudes or states. Clearly a general approach to relationships—and particularly relationship-dissolution processes—will need to be based on a more accurate assessment of what people actually do in dissolving relationships. In preliminary work, Duck and Miell (in preparation) and Duck and Palmer (in preparation) have made a modest start by recording the amounts of time spent in given activities before, during, and after relationship dissolution. The change of activity patterns may itself be one of the first indicators that the relationship is faltering and it seems an intuitively plausible idea that patterns of interaction change in systematic ways as the relationship deteriorates. For instance, Duck and Miell and Duck and Palmer find that persons report a change in the location of meeting with partners in distressed relationships (from private accommodation to public social places) and that the initiator of interactions is more likely to be the other person when things go badly but mutual when they are going well. It is important that other more significant dimensions of social participation rates and characteristics be explored in future research. We need a database and we need to avoid the footsteps of researchers into interpersonal attraction who for too long ignored, or failed to first gather data about, people's actual relationship behavior, and merely isolated particular interaction or encounter "packages" for experimental study.

Such points, then, bring us inexorably to another theoretical issue that also arises here. It has its simplest expression in the form of a query about how relationship growth relates to decline and dissolution—or, more accurately, how *what we know about* relationship growth relates to *what we know about* decline and dissolution of relationships. It is naive to assume a sudden catastrophe-like switch from relationship development to relationship dissolution: real social life just is not like that most of the time. However, neither am I convinced that decline is the reversal of growth, any more than aging is the reversal of child development: indeed, it makes far more sense to see one as a continuation of the processes characterizing the other rather than simply its reverse (Duck, 1981; Duck & Lea, 1982; Duck & Miell, 1982). The contention here is that we must start to regard dissolution as the end point of a series of psychological processes which have some overlap and similarity with those that also produce relationship growth: it is largely the products which differ, not the processes. I will propose here that relationship partners continually review the state of their relationship in an attempt to achieve or negotiate a mutually acceptable form of involvement. They do this when the relationship is developing *and* when it is deteriorating; when it is starting *and* when it is ending. During the early formative stages of a relationship this activity is naturally both necessary and frequent. It can yield crystallization of the relationship, intimacy growth, or containment and decline of involvement depending on partners' intentions. During later stages of a relationship's life it becomes necessary less frequently and resurges only in times of conflict or transition (e.g., relocation, marriage, birth of chil-

dren). Such activity is proposed to be largely conscious, private, evaluative and concerned with consideration of the present form of the relationship apropos of its likely future form (see Figure 25.1).

Importantly, then, a proposal like this does not view decline and growth as the reversal of one another: rather each is the contrary product of the same generative process of evaluation and assessment. *Ultimately* the two diverge but they start from the same place. Clearly evaluations of partner, attribution, communication and consideration of social consequences are not occurring only in dissolution: they run through "relationshipping" as a whole, both when it is going well and when it is not. Accordingly, in Figure 25.1 I present a sketch of some of the processes and decisions taken in the course of formulating and dealing with the problem of creating a satisfactory form for an established close relationship. It can be seen that I emphasize the similarities of process between relationship building and early phases of relationship demolition, merely contending that the intermediate products and the final stages are different in kind.

Whilst previous speculations about relationship ending have contrasted affective processes with the social barriers that contain their effects (e.g., Levinger, 1979), the present proposals will argue that the two are psychologically linked through an intermediate, dyadic, phase. It will be suggested that early points of disengagement are marked by predominantly intra-psychic, individualistic processes; that these merge slowly into dyadic processes, where the two partners begin to face up to, and deal with, the fact that one of them wishes to close the relationship; and that the final phase is a social, or network, phase where the partners together or separately negotiate the "public presentation" of the relationship dissolution. A post-dissolution phase is also proposed: here partners clean up the picture and tidy the last resting place of the memories associated with the relationship (see Figure 25.2).

Such a proposal is based on the belief that there are several non-exclusive ways to depict the process of relationship disengagement. For instance, there is a model implicit in the comments made in the

FIGURE 25.1

Some Steps and Decisions in Relationship Development and Decline

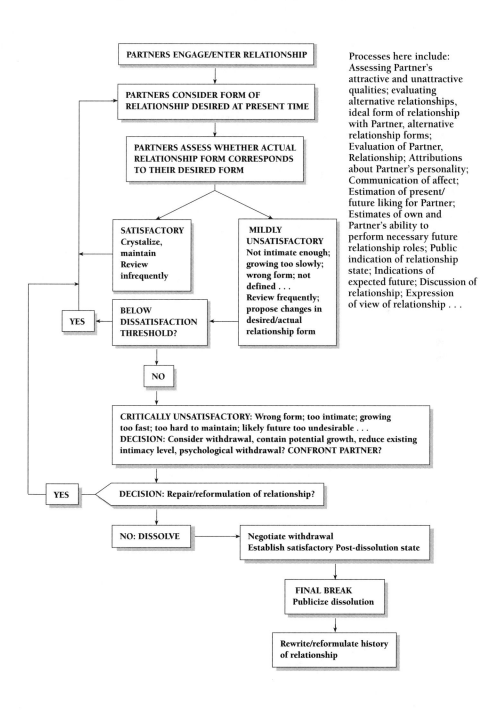

PARTNERS ENGAGE/ENTER RELATIONSHIP

PARTNERS CONSIDER FORM OF RELATIONSHIP DESIRED AT PRESENT TIME

PARTNERS ASSESS WHETHER ACTUAL RELATIONSHIP FORM CORRESPONDS TO THEIR DESIRED FORM

SATISFACTORY Crystalize, maintain Review infrequently

MILDLY UNSATISFACTORY Not intimate enough; growing too slowly; wrong form; not defined . . . Review frequently; propose changes in desired/actual relationship form

BELOW DISSATISFACTION THRESHOLD?

YES

NO

CRITICALLY UNSATISFACTORY: Wrong form; too intimate; growing too fast; too hard to maintain; likely future too undesirable . . . DECISION: Consider withdrawal, contain potential growth, reduce existing intimacy level, psychological withdrawal? CONFRONT PARTNER?

DECISION: Repair/reformulation of relationship?

YES

NO: DISSOLVE

Negotiate withdrawal Establish satisfactory Post-dissolution state

FINAL BREAK Publicize dissolution

Rewrite/reformulate history of relationship

Processes here include: Assessing Partner's attractive and unattractive qualities; evaluating alternative relationships, ideal form of relationship with Partner, alternative relationship forms; Evaluation of Partner, Relationship; Attributions about Partner's personality; Communication of affect; Estimation of present/ future liking for Partner; Estimates of own and Partner's ability to perform necessary future relationship roles; Public indication of relationship state; Indications of expected future; Discussion of relationship; Expression of view of relationship . . .

FIGURE 25.2

A Sketch of the Main Phases of Dissolving Personal Relationships

BREAKDOWN: Dissatisfaction with relationship

↓

| Threshold: I can't stand this any more |

↓

INTRA-PSYCHIC PHASE (See Fig. 25.3)
Personal focus on Partner's behavior
Assess adequacy of Partner's role performance
Depict and evaluate negative aspects of being
   in the relationship
Consider costs of withdrawal
Assess positive aspects of alternative relationships
Face "express/repress dilemma"

↓

| Threshold: I'd be justified in withdrawing |

↓

DYADIC PHASE (see Fig. 25.4)
Face "confrontation/avoidance dilemma"
Confront Partner
Negotiate in "Our Relationship Talks"
Attempt repair and reconciliation?
Assess joint costs of withdrawal or reduced
   intimacy

↓

| Threshold: I mean it |

↓

SOCIAL PHASE (see Fig. 25.5)
Negotiate post-dissolution state with Partner
Initiate gossip/discussion in social network
Create publicly negotiable face-saving/
   blame-placing stories and accounts
Consider and face up to implied social
   network effects, if any
Call in intervention teams?

↓

| Threshold: It's now inevitable |

↓

GRAVE DRESSING PHASE
"Getting over" activity
Retrospection; reformulative postmortem attribution
Public distribution of own version of break-up story

foregoing section: namely, that the partners' characteristic qualities influence their conduct of the relationship in a way that produces process loss until a critical cataclysmic event or discovery finally creates the public grounds on which to terminate the relationship. Alternatively, the structure of chapter organization in the present volume offers another implicit system for conceptualizing the process of relationship dissolution. It can be seen that this stresses the public conduct of the wish to terminate and deals with issues surrounding social management of the dissolution. Such a model emphasizes the expression and conduct of dissolution rather than its inherent causes.

These two ways of conceptualizing relationship dissolution are not necessarily incompatible: they are merely different perspectives. Likewise, the third possibility which I am about to consider in detail simply represents a further different viewpoint over the phenomena. It begins with an emphasis on the private decisions that must be faced by a person wishing to foreclose on a relationship, goes on to discuss communicative and strategic matters within the dyad, focuses on the social negotiations that follow, and finally addresses the issue of publicly accounting for the break. In short it proposes four broad phases to relationship dissolution, each one requiring the person and the partner to focus on different issues, make different decisions, contemplate different sorts of behavioral-strategic questions, and make different social responses from those faced in the other phases. The forces and emotions that press upon the two persons at different points of the process of dissolution must be seen to differ and change as things proceed. They do not remain constant nor of a single type throughout, and at each new point there is a requirement for extended psychological and behavioral energy—one psychologically important reason why fatigue and stress are often reported to attach to persons who attempt to dissolve established close relationships (Bloom et al., 1978).

The relevant forces pressing upon the persons at each point will be proposed here to be problems of the social management of each stage of the process.

Thus once one decides that one's partner is no longer liked, one is faced with the social management problem of telling him or her so; once one wishes to withdraw from the relationship, one is faced with the social management problem of negotiating disengagement; once one has reached a satisfactory stage in the negotiation, one is faced with the social management problem of letting the social network know that one of its constituent pairings is dissolved; once it is dissolved one must face up to explaining what happened. Accordingly the person is faced with a range of at least four strategic problems. *First,* the person who wishes to leave must first find a plausible (private) justification for doing so. I contend that Persons do this by an attempt to assess and evaluate Partner's alleged inadequacies, faults, and incompetences. They thus face the strategic issues of how best to cope with a defaulting Partner, and whether to confront Partner about these negative discoveries or avoid confrontation. *Second,* the two partners who know that at least one of them wants to change the relationship are faced with a range of strategic choices centered on the question "Should we attempt to repair or to dissolve the relationship?" The management and negotiation of the repair or dissolution are complex social processes. *Third,* a final range of behavioral strategic choices faces two partners who have agreed upon, agreed to accept, or are confronted with a unilateral demand for, dissolution. At this stage the choices concern the best or most effective way of managing the impending dissolution and communicating it to the immediate social network—how to arrive at the desired post-dissolution state. *Finally,* and most important, partners must choose how and where to attribute the blame for the dissolution after it has occurred. So the model suggests that the four broad stages, each with its consequent focus of attention for Person and with its accompanying behavioral manifestations, are as follows: first, an intra-psychic stage where Person focuses on Partner and Partner's behavior, the result being a private evaluation of Partner's performance; second, a dyadic phase where the partners jointly focus on the relationship, its merits and provisions,

its chances of repair—the result being discussions about the future of the relationship; third, a social phase focusing on management of the consequences of the desired dissolution; last, gravedressing phase that tidies up the relationship's last resting place and puts up public markers of its ending.

MAPPING RELATIONSHIP DISENGAGEMENT AND DISSOLUTION

Perhaps it reflects well on psychologists that we are too prone to assume that people are nice (cf. Moscovici, 1972) and that their niceness pours over to flood their behavior in relationship disengagement and dissolution. We assume that people will feel guilty about hurting their partner; we assume that they will control outbursts of negative feelings; we assume that they will handle disengagement—at least in the beginning—in a covert, indirect, defused, sanitized and socially packaged way. Thus several workers have noted the tendency, in turbulent relationships, for partners to prefer avoidance styles to confrontational ones (e.g., Kaplan, 1976). Studies of communication in turbulent relationships assume that there will be only "leakage" at the early stages of withdrawal rather than straightforward nastiness (Duck, 1980c); studies of behavioral strategy choice assume initial unwillingness to confront the partner once a negative view of partner is being formed (Baxter, 1980).

Tacitly assumed in all such approaches is the belief that partners wish to avoid, and struggle to prevent, public demonstration of disaffection. Following from that is the assumption that such forms of ambivalence, indecision and oscillation as have been identified are partly due to social pressures and strains coming into sharp conflict with personal, emotional ones. Yet it is surprising that at present there are no explicit studies of argument, insult, recrimination, negative exchange, the whips and scorns of growing hostility and "the spurns that patient merit of the unworthy takes" (Shakespeare, 1599/1951). It is true that there are *subsequent* well-recognized social constraints on the open expression of a desire to withdraw once it is formed, but these are due not so much to inherent niceness as to the partners' realistic recognition of the social sanctioning power of surrounding social networks—indeed persons often adopt indirect means of withdrawal and simultaneously regret doing so (Baxter, 1979b). Also there are general social consequences of "being negative." To say derogatory things about a partner is to open oneself to the charge of being a negative or disloyal person; if the dissolving relationship was a close one, then the public display of strongly negative views of the formerly close partner opens one to a charge of capriciousness or earlier bad judgment. Ambivalence, uncertainty and plain cowardice are hard to distinguish, in this context, from social and cultural pressures to uphold the ideal values of friendship and one's own public "face."

Nevertheless, researchers must recognize that there are several separable forms of decision and indecision that surround the transformation of a private relational disturbance into a publicly acknowledged relational failure—and "niceness" does not create them. For instance, there may be genuine ambivalence or doubt about the Partner as well as unwillingness to accept the implications of a negative view of Partner. Furthermore, ambivalence, inconsistency and oscillation can be due to indecision whether to adopt an expressive or repressive coping style with the growing disaffection with Partner (Kaplan, 1976) or a confrontational or avoidance style once one has accepted one's negative view of Partner (Baxter, 1979b). Finally there is the kind of oscillation noted by Altman and Taylor (1973), where partners have confronted and accepted the issues that are separating them, but oscillate between withdrawal and intense reconciliations. These oscillations continue until the point where the ideal post-dissolution state is achieved, at which point the dissolution is set in social concrete. Equally one must note the different sorts of strategic choice that confront Person at each point, and the several psychological and social thresholds that have to be crossed (see Figure 25.2). It is the

proposal of the present model that several such thresholds are arranged in a sequential manner, beginning with the creation of one's own private justification for wishing to withdraw and ending with the public presentation of a termination agreed or accepted by both partners themselves.

Figure 25.2 gives a schematic depiction of the major concepts at each stage or phase of the dissolution process and each phase is further elaborated in a subsequent figure. It can be seen from Figure 25.2 that the emphasis of the early phases of the model is conceived to be a cognitive one, especially focused on evaluation and decision-making. Later phases are the times where the actions consequent upon such evaluation and decision-making are executed. At these stages the Person is faced with real behavioral, strategic choices about the best ways for socially managing and executing the growing intent to dissolve the relationship.

Perhaps it needs to be reiterated that although the first stress of the present map falls on cognitive activity, this is not primarily a cognitive model. I simply wish to analyze the dissolution process and, by doing so, to illustrate that different research techniques are needed to illuminate the full richness of each phase. Thus self-report techniques would be most suitable at one phase, communication analysis would be better in another, and social process analysis in yet another.

The subsequent discussion deals with the four phases suggested as primary foci for future research. In so doing, the discussion assumes that for at least one partner the threshold of Unbearable Dissatisfaction with the state of the relationship has been crossed, i.e., that the relationship is, for that person, in the process of breakdown or turbulence. This person is supposed in the present scheme to begin to seek and consider active grounds for withdrawing from the relationship as the first step towards dissolution of the relationship in its previous form or its renegotiation into a less intimate form. Accordingly, the first phase of the present model focuses on the intra-psychic activity that the person produces in seeking a justification for withdrawing from the relationship. This is seen as a bridging phase between breakdown and dissolution: Person doesn't yet know which of the two possibilities will actually result.

Intra-Psychic Phase: Focus on Partner

Researchers have been reluctant to study relational turbulence for fear that this may itself generate dissolution of the relationship. Studies, on the whole, are either retrospective in character (e.g., Hill et al., 1976) or tend to deal with hypothetical relationships (e.g., Baxter, 1980) and they look for evidence of a reducing satisfaction with the relationship or an increase in the difficulty of maintaining it. They assume, therefore, that partners have passed a stage where they have begun to reflect on the relationship negatively and that they are concerned to negotiate disengagement. In contrast, I suspect that there are a few psychological stages before partners get to this point. The present model assumes that an early stage towards dissolution involves a strong evaluative focus on the Partner, not on the relationship as such, and that such a focus is used to create a justification for dissatisfied feelings, for psychological withdrawal, or even for leaving—a justification that satisfies oneself privately and will be used as the basis for subsequently confronting the Partner when and if that occurs.

Traditional psychological explanations that might be used to explore the creation of such justifications have been couched in terms of Equity and Exchange, but not explicitly in connection with the formation in one partner's mind of such a justification of withdrawal. My point is that such a consideration of Equity and Exchange is necessary but not by any means sufficient for relationship extinction. In my view it merely sets in train a set of other psychological processes as outlined in the model (see Figure 25.3) and subsequent subsections of this chapter. Equity and Exchange evaluation does not, of itself and without other *social* processes, such as consulting confidants, create more than a ground plan for dissolution.

Furthermore, there are several sides to the evaluation of Equity and Exchange since merely noticing imbalance and actually taking action about it are different psychological activities with different relational consequences. The mere noticing of Inequity is a cause of dissatisfaction personally, but doing something about it makes the problem a dyadic, not an intra-psychic, individual one. I would speculate that once a person has formulated the view that relationship Equity or Exchange is significantly out of kilter, the consequence is *not* immediate confrontation with the Partner but instead, on the individual level, some brooding recriminative response, or a social consultation with a confidant and a general private sense of discomfort. I am claiming, then, that such a process is *essentially* private, or one that is not immediately communicated directly to the offending Partner. Although private in the normal way, such processes are nonetheless accessible to researchers using self-report and interview techniques to study individuals, as well as to Equity researchers studying couples. But we may be unjustified in assuming that proper calculation of actual Exchange is the only way in which such decisions get taken. There is too little research in social psychology, and in this area too, on errors and misjudgments (but cf. Backman & Secord, 1962). Mismatched perceptions, mistakes, and misunderstandings are frequent causes of relational turbulence and these can occur outside or inside the interactions that make up a relationship. Brooding outside an interaction is quite as powerful a cause of relational disaffection as is misconduct within one. Deep, private contemplation about the desired and achieved course of a relationship; perpetual, normal monitoring of relationships; the actual build-up towards dissolution, planning and organizing it are all private events that are not necessarily communicated to the Partner. Much happens *outside* the vital encounters composing relationships, such as fantasy, recapitulation, planning, evaluation and quiet assessment of Partner, Self and the relationship (Duck, 1980a). When one comes to consider the first moves in breakdown or dissolving of personal relationships, then, it is even clearer that such activity must be counted into the

FIGURE 25.3

Intra-Psychic Phase of Relationship Dissolution

Goals
Identifying causes of dissatisfaction with Partner
Identifying problems with present form of relationship
Adjusting Partner's behavior
Increasing satisfaction with Partner
Increasing satisfaction with relationship

Major specific concerns	Researchable manifestations and consequences
To weigh up Partner's behavior	Hostility; vigilance, evaluation, increased personal attribution
To assess internal dynamics of relationship	Equity/Exchange Focus
To express discomfort (but not directly to Partner)	Consultation with confidants; "Leakage"
To question one's relationship judgments	Self-Doubts; Recrimination; Negativity in personal descriptions of Self and Partner and "Life"
To find ways to modify Partner's behavior and to change relationship outcomes	Changes in communication style and communication focus within the relationship
To convince oneself that leaving could be better than staying	Anxiety, stress, guilt, indecision, brooding

Final outcome
The resolve to confront Partner

formulae. Revenge, planning, stressful anxiety and many other such actions and thoughts just might exert a great initial influence on relationship decline and the psychological algebra occurring in it.

In sum, the essential focus of this intra-psychic stage is hypothesized to concern vigilance about Partner's behavior, sifting and assessment of relevant evidence, worries over Equity and Exchange, and the weighing up of the internal dynamics of the relationship. It is essentially cognitive activity, and is essentially private, leaking to Partner undramat-ically and unintentionally. In this respect, then, it is importantly different from what occurs in the next (dyadic) phase. In the intra-psychic phase, choices are hypothesized to be strictly related to these issues above, but will have non-cognitive effects (e.g., "leakage" of disaffection by means of non-verbal behavior; communicative changes and reduced display of intimacy or relatedness). During the process of deciding that one might be justified in withdrawing from the relationship the Person will probably be focusing attention first on means of coping with the Partner and attempting to modify Partner's faulty behavior. One would expect the Person to become hostile to the Partner, to recriminate about the relationship, to feel discomfort and vigilance in interactions and perhaps to undergo some changes in attitudes to self and life—all of which are measurable. Additionally one might expect to find changes in behavior, such as increasing consultation with confidants or other outsiders to unburden and clarify the festering negativity felt about Partner: "My wife doesn't understand me" is a characteristic style of this phase of the enterprise.

The Person may indeed press on no further than minimal psychological withdrawal or resentment, or may go as far as half-hearted involvement in other parallel relationships such as affairs. At this point it seems uncertain that a Person will be convinced that the relationship is over, and hopes of improvement are primary. The choice of strategic action at this phase is presumably centered on the way to cope with one's feelings of negativity towards Partner, but a secondary component concerns choices of method to set Partner aright and an evaluation of whether it is in fact possible ever to do so. If the Person concludes that Partner's faults are inherently unalterable only then is a different coping strategy needed. Such a conclusion by the Person is thus a likely first step on the path to actual withdrawal and turns private dissatisfaction into a more active phase of dissolution with different concerns.

At some point the Person undoubtedly considers the desirability of the relationship in the context of alternatives (Thibaut & Kelley, 1959), as a separate issue that goes beyond mere dissatisfaction with the Partner. Such private calculations need not yet involve the Partner: they are personal judgmental problems requiring decisions whether leaving is better than staying, whether the negative aspects of Partner really do outweigh the positive values of the relationship. Considerations of Comparison Levels for Alternatives (Thibaut & Kelley, 1959) would be likely to arise here, but not for the last time, and evaluation of the costs of leaving have to be pitted against the costs of staying. To have formed the

opinion that one is justified in leaving, the Person must have concluded that enough areas of the relationship are irredeemably dissatisfactory or that the positive aspects of none of them outweigh the disadvantages of the remainder. Researchers should be able to identify and distinguish two sorts of ambivalence or oscillation in the Person at this phase. First, the Person in such straits is likely to be genuinely undecided about the future of the relationship and hence to show the agitation, stress and ambivalence that characterize people making any major decisions. Secondly, the Person is now faced with major social issues: whether or not to confront the Partner with the decision; when and how to do so. Such decisions will have to be based on personal knowledge of the Partner's likely response. The Miller and Parks (Article 26, this volume) compliance-gaining strategy model fits best here (although it is more complex than this): Persons will need to refer to their store of knowledge about their erstwhile Partner in order to know how best to effect their desire to redefine the relationship. At this stage researchers investigating the relationship are likely to detect oscillation between desires to confront Partner and desires to avoid confrontation (Baxter, 1980), but it is psychologically and focally a different sort of oscillation from the agitated indecision about the Partner noted previously.

Once such issues of confrontation and negotiation with Partner begin to appear, and once, effectively, the decision is taken to redefine the relationship, the Person enters a different phase and the focal concerns shift towards dyadic issues; that is, away from personal, private, intra-psychic issues towards those directly involving *both* partners.

Dyadic Phase: Focus on the Relationship

Perhaps, by now, the relationship is so turbulent that both partners start to reassess it. But if not, a unilateral decision to reveal one's dissatisfaction with and to the Partner inevitably confuses things. Persons intending to redefine the relationship will now have their resolve questioned, will have to give reasons, will have to present a case that satisfies other people not just themselves, will be presented with alternative explanations of events that they had regarded as critical to their decision . . . and so on. Alternatively, the announcement of the wish to redefine the relationship might be dismissed by the Partner as a mere power ploy. Or the response of the Partner may be extreme or unpredicted. The costs of going ahead with disengagement may now seem underestimated. The personal costs to Partner may now appear to be much greater than had been initially supposed. In short, an additional series of psychological forces comes into play, not least of which will be negotiation about the Person's reasons for wanting to redefine the relationship, about explanations for conflict, and about attributions.

The present model delineates this phase as beginning with the Person's consideration of the most effective strategy to renegotiate the relationship (see Figure 25.4). Accordingly, it would predict that the Person is essentially aggrieved and hostile, in such a way that attitudes to the Partner are extremely negative. Negativity about Partner and decision-generated stress are demonstrable through the non-verbal and verbal channels of social communication and the reader is referred to the chapter by Miller and Parks (Article 26). My point here is that any such communicative changes reflect private turmoil, and that they reflect oscillations and ambivalence about how to approach the Partner rather than about the relationship and its dissolution management. These latter appear later on in the sequence and are distinct, different sorts of turmoil.

Once discussions begin, however, the Person is going to be confronted with other issues than those which concern his/her own private judgments about Partner's behavior. These are likely to begin with the implications—for the *Partner*—of the Person's negative evaluation of them. Partners themselves, if the Person does not, will be likely to point out their own costs in the relationship in its present form, the consequent costs of discussing redefinition of the relationship, the costs of actually disengaging, and the costs of managing the disengagement in public (that is, for other members of the network).

A Person's resolve can be shaken at this stage by several things. For instance, such stress may be caused to Partner by such discussions that the Person may decide not to go through with it after all. Or Partner's claims to be able and willing to put matters right may effectively block off the Person's intent to redefine or dissolve the relationship.

At this stage, then, an intent to redefine or dissolve the relationship can be (temporarily) abandoned; or processes of repair, focused on amending Partner's behavior and/or the Person's expectations, can be initiated. This merely reflects the beginnings of that sort of oscillation within the relationship noted by Altman and Taylor (1973) where partners do not agree about dissolution and so go through counterpoised phases of intense reconciliation and of withdrawal. Such oscillations are consequently about something psychologically different from those noted earlier and hence must not be confused with them in theory and research.

Even if the partners agree to redefine or dissolve the relationship, their problems are not over. They must turn to discussing, for instance, the distribution of shared goods and face up to the job of "presenting" the disengagement to other people as well as to actually conducting it satisfactorily. Again, the real implications of doing so may strike partners for the first time and cause slowing down of the disengagement or else may promote vigorous attempts at repair of the flagging relationship. If such repair attempts are unrealistic, however, the focus must, at some stage, turn away from individuals' behavior *in* a relationship, and towards the nature of the relationship itself and its theoretical potential *as a working social relationship* if both partners were to act ideally.

Next, then the partners start to explore what the relationship *ought* to be like—its ideal state—rather than focus on how they have actually conducted it. Partners presumably ask themselves a number of crucial questions. Is it realistic to expect the relationship to work? Is it the right sort of relationship? Is it, perhaps, unduly stifling or constraining to the

FIGURE 25.4

Dyadic Phase of Relationship Dissolution

Goals
Confronting Partner
Gaining compliance from Partner
Redefining relationship
Repairing/Dissolving Relationship

Major specific concerns	**Researchable manifestations and consequences**
To confront Partner with Person's dissatisfaction	Hostility; Negative communication style
To present own view of relationship	Guilt; Anxiety
To express discomfort directly to Partner	Stress
To assess costs (to Partner) of own views	Increased private discussion with Partner
To evaluate Partner's view of relationship	Withdrawal from other contacts, temporarily
To cope with Partner's rejoinders	Anger
To weigh up relationship together	Experimental withdrawal/ experimental repair
To consider alternative or ideal forms of the relationship under review	Increased fantasising about future form of the relationship
To choose between Repair and Dissolution	

Final outcome
Resolve to dissolve/repair the relationship

partners, such that they would be better out of it after all? Researchers who discover indecision or oscillation here are picking up fluctuations between experimental withdrawal from the partnership and experimental repair of it. Likely scenarios for disengagement and for a patched-up relationship can be proposed, replayed, considered. The partners' costs if they reveal, manage, or confirm the breakdown of relationship need at this stage to be realistically stressed and evaluated against the alternatives of redress and repair.

At this stage the partners are concerned, then, with the issue of Repair versus Dissolution. Oscillations reflect their attempts to achieve the ideal or desired scenario in the light of discussions in this phase (cf. Altman & Taylor's, 1973, discussion of attempts to achieve the desired post-dissolution state). My point is that at this stage the partners may oscillate both about the ideal post-disengagement state and also about the post-*discussion* state, which may not in fact be dissolution. Some partners may genuinely decide to repair the relationship rather than to dissolve it. However, the ambivalence about dissolution is probably genuine: we need not assume that partners are always crystal clear about their intentions and so they may communicate about them confusingly.

Where repair of the relationship is rejected as a possibility, the final steps in this phase involve preparation for the post-dissolution state: essentially this means starting to create the "public story" about the causes and course of the disengagement. We should note that there are presently no generally developed understandings of the social systems and psychological mechanisms that are used to indicate graduated withdrawals from relationships. However, it is clear that those things that are indicators of disaffection are also the means of registering intent and of conducting disengagement. Thus changes in communicative styles are part of a complex social process for indicating withdrawal from a relationship as well as being ways of "leaking" intent (see Miller & Parks, this volume). However, in momentarily stressing communicative changes that take place we have not attended fully enough to the self-relevant or personal effects that occur within the individual: the need to escape blame or to serve one's own self-interest which may "drive" the processes of negotiation of withdrawal from the relationship and the searching for scapegoats. The present model assumes that such scapegoating becomes a major focus of the next two phases.

Social Phase: Facing the Public Consequences

Assuming that the negotiated push towards dissolution is accepted as a reality by both partners, the final phase represents a working out of the social and public consequences of executing and publicizing the decision (see Figure 25.5). At this stage, for certain, the partners are faced with constraining forces of a social kind—ones that are not strictly affective. Borrowing Lewin's ideas, Levinger (1979) has referred to "Barrier Forces" that help to hold a relationship together or prevent it coming apart—above and beyond its emotional cement. Such things as network pressure, sanctioning powers of social groupings, the implied loss of status consequent on disengagement, the legal powers of social institutions, and so on, are such Barrier Forces that may hold together an emotionally decayed relationship. (La Gaipa [1981a] has given fuller consideration to the power of such factors in the relationship conduct and the disengagement processes, respectively.) Perhaps they should be regarded as forces that prevent *rapid* dissolution rather than as forces that prevent dissolution altogether. However that may be, it is in this phase that a simple individual or dyadic model of relationships is least useful: the social network is the significant base and background for the dissolving relationship in this phase. Accordingly, parts of the negotiation and evaluation processes that occur here will undoubtedly be concerned with what to tell the neighbors and friends, but also with how to handle and cope with partners in the network after disengagement or dissolution, i.e., whether the relationship is merely much reduced in intimacy or actually terminated.

There are thus at least three separate issues for research at this phase:

First, a major problem for the disengaging pair is the personal issue of how to handle their own status change (probably a status loss). In a society where "couplehood" is valued, normative, and expected, the sudden return to singlehood is a major problem for dissolving marital or courtship partners (Bohannon, 1970b). Not only are there unattractive implications of relationship loss, in terms of labels of failure and consequent lowered social values, there are also social problems. Much of our society's life is based on the assumption that people are paired: pairs of people are invited to dinner parties; it is even true that pairs of people are usually the socially negotiable unit that is invited to play tennis and bridge! A single person, one without an appropriate partner, is thus something of a difficulty for *other people* to manage in a vibrant social environment.

FIGURE 25.5

Social Phase of Relationship Dissolution

Goals

To dissolve the relationship
To have the dissolution recognized
  and accredited by the relevant
  social network(s)
To come out of it all socially and
  psychologically intact

Major specific concerns

To create agreed post-dissolution
  state of relationship
To create acceptable post-dissolution
  state for partners
To consider implied status changes
To evaluate consequences of
  dissolution

To place blame
To save face
To create and distribute public
  stories about the relationship
  dissolution

To obtain public sanction for
  the dissolution

Researchable manifestations and consequences

Oscillation between reconciliation
  and withdrawal
Doubts and anxieties about own
  future

Trial repair vs. trial withdrawal
Stress, mourning, fear of "loss"

Gossip
Scapegoating
Attributing blame
Seeking causal explanation for break

Marketing versions and accounts of
  the break

Final outcomes

Publicly acknowledged dissolution
  of the relationship
Move to grave-dressing

Grave-dressing phase

Goal
To get over it all and put it behind one
Concerns
To create an acceptable personal
  story for the course of the
  relationship, its beginning and
  its end
To tidy up the memories associated
  with it
Manifestations and consequences
Reinterpretative attributional work
  concerned with "getting over it"
  (i.e., redressing and reconceptual-
  izing the relationship path and
  significance: distinct from
  attributing blame for the break).

The second issue for research and analysis, currently a focus of sociological and anthropological inquiry, concerns the means by which the network adjusts to the loss of a previously acknowledged constituent pairing. The problem is as much an adjustment problem for the network as it is one for the pair themselves within the network. For instance, difficulties for others in the social network stem from the fact that since both members of the dissolved pair were members of the network also, the network probably continues to see both of them, at least in the beginning. They are thus faced with the awkward problem of taking sides in the dispute, managing the disturbance, and generally facing up to a relationship that now has a spoiled identity. Fears of such social consequences and awareness of such social pressures operate as major restraints on Persons' freedom of action in these circumstances. Both in their own imagination and, perhaps, also through actions by a Partner unwilling to accede to disengagement, Persons can be restrained even at this point from carrying out a wish to withdraw. They may decide to stay physically in a hollow marriage, for instance, and yet withdraw psychologically.

As a third research topic, most in sympathy with present styles in social psychological research, we need to attend carefully to the attribution processes and "ordinary explanation" work that partners undertake in order to prepare their own public story about the relationship dissolution and help themselves to get over the relationship loss. . . .

These three areas constitute separable research issues and present new, different problems. The stresses that they create for partners are also separable from those observable in other phases: by this stage the partners have accepted the break and have to face up to it. Physical and psychological stresses are thus going to be consequent on a sense of loss (Bowlby, 1979), status change (Bloom et al., 1978) and bereavement—i.e., consequent on doubt about their personal future rather than on doubt, ambiguity or ambivalence about the future of the relationship.

Grave-Dressing Phase: Tidying Up the Accounts

Once the main psychological "work" of dissolving a personal relationship is over, the problem remains of what to do with the memories associated with it. The processes here remind me of grave-dressing: the attempt to neaten up the last resting place of the corpse and to erect public statements of its form, contribution, and importance. Much of the activity of getting over a relationship concerns simplification, rationalization and beautification of the course, themes, and outcomes of the relationship when it still flourished. . . .

This neglected aspect of relationship dissolution is an important one, nevertheless, and it is recognized tacitly in the objections that are sometimes raised against retrospective reports of relationship dissolution. It is noted that such accounts may reflect bias, idealization, self-interest, and so on. What is missed is the fact that such processes are not mere accidents or psychological epiphenomena: they are probably psychologically crucial to the persons coming to terms with the relationship dissolution. Noting that they are different from attributions about a relationship that still has a chance of surviving, we should examine them vigorously to explore their underlying dynamics and to find out what they tell us about the serious business of grave-dressing a dead relationship.

CONCLUDING OBSERVATIONS: PRACTICAL CONSEQUENCES

Again let me reiterate the cartographic nature of this model. I have laid things out in relation to one another in a way that seems to suggest that the process is slow and deliberate or that only one person does all the deciding. I do this for analytic convenience only, since we do not yet know for instance, whether it is this slow, nor whether all disengagements begin at Phase 1 so explicitly, nor whether (as seems likely) it is naive to assume it is all one-sided. I have given little emphasis to the mechanisms by which relationship dissolution is avoided, or by which repair is effected. Studies of dissolution of relationships are sorely needed so that we can tell if these are separate issues.

Nonetheless, some general thoughts about this empirically neglected area of dissolving personal relationships arise to summarize the intent. . . . First, the area of interpersonal attraction research has not yet given proper general weight to the deserving problems of relationship termination. Nor do its theoretical emphases adequately address the dissolution of relationships. Secondly, parallels between entry and withdrawal; between growth and dissolution; and between ending of encounters and ending of relationships have not been adequately tested. Thirdly, the phases in the process of dissolution need extended analysis and research attention: disengagement and dissolution are not simple events but complex processes.

The problems of dissolving personal relationships, however, are not simply intellectual, theoretical exercises. There are practical implications of a growing understanding of the process, both in terms of improved ability to recognize relationships that would be best dissolved and also since it would produce a useful input to the *prevention* of dissolution and to the *repair* of relationships where this is desirable. There are two distinct aims and two kinds of product here: first, we should aim to explore and validate techniques to prevent dissolution and to promote repair of relationships where partners wish it; secondly, we should attend to the contrary side that would tell people how to unhitch without nearly dying—namely, we should investigate techniques and constructive advisory programs to facilitate withdrawal and stress-free disengagement where it is desired. In short, it would be an error to assume that our only applications of research in this area would be to give advice to counselors wishing to repair relationships. Repair

of persons can sometimes mean dissolution of destructive relationships, yet persons do not always have an effective set of strategies and skills for so doing. We are, after all, socialized to *preserve* relationships, not to get out of them neatly. . . . My argument is that we can help them to go further.

As part of a move towards fulfilling both of these intentions, we can note that the present model proposes that there are many parallel and sequential processes of decision and strategy choice. The handling of these different "crisis nodes" requires different skills in disengaging partners and techniques in counselors which have yet to be fully depicted. Strategy choice can concern the general nature of behavior in the dyad (openly hostile, subtly manipulative, regretful, accepting, etc.). It can also, on the contrary, concern considerations of complementarity of strategy (tacit acceptance of partner's withdrawal, tacit or open resistance, counterstrategy to withdraw first oneself, etc.). Strategy choice in Phase 1 concerns focus on (re)establishing exchange equality within the relationship or on alternative relationships. In other phases, different sorts of choice have been identified and discussed. Each of these strategic possibilities has different therapeutic implications and requires entirely different sorts of decisions and actions by the Person and his or her Partner. The trick for present research is to explicate the dissolution process in ways that help us maximize input to therapeutic, counseling and guidance programs.

Understanding relationship dissolution is a problem in its own right. Nevertheless, parsimonious explanation of growth and decline in intimacy, starts and endings, development and dissolution of relationships can only be a Good Thing for personal relationships research. It will better equip us to deal with the pressing practical issues such as prevention of dissolution and repair of relationships. If I do not miss my guess, these will be prime issues in society during the coming years.

26

Communication in Dissolving Relationships

GERALD R. MILLER | MALCOLM R. PARKS

Studies of how people actually communicate as their relationships come apart comprise a null set. Only a few studies focus on the dissolution process and most of these rely on *post hoc* analyses of terminated relationships (Duck & Allison, 1978; Levinger, 1976). Participant accounts or retrospective self-reports are the most common form of data (e.g., Burgess & Wallin, 1953; Hill et al., 1976; Weiss, 1975). Although such data are both very useful and readily obtained, they cannot offer an adequate description of the dissolution process itself. Individuals may have difficulty recalling anything beyond the most general emotional outlines of what was said and done during termination (Bradford, 1977). Members of the same relationship often give strikingly different accounts for its demise (Weiss, 1975). Moreover, accounts can change as time passes and prior attachments erode. Accounts and retrospective self-reports probably say as much about people's current circumstances as about their previous actions. Research on dissolution has consequently proceeded with an incomplete description of one of its major phenomena. This chapter seeks to remedy this deficit by first outlining a series of communicative markers for the dissolution process and by then discussing a preliminary typology of communication strategies which can be used to derive hypotheses about how people actually dissolve their relationships.

Although the challenges of conducting and interpreting behavioral research have been widely noted (Duck & Allison, 1978; Keiser & Altman, 1976; Knapp, 1978; Levinger, 1976), few of the ambiguities and controversies currently holding back dissolution research can be resolved without studies of communication behavior. These difficulties include (1) ambiguity in defining what the dissolution process is and specifying where it begins; (2) confusion regarding the role of affective-cognitive variables in describing the dissolution process; (3) controversy concerning the application of relationship growth concepts to the dissolution process; and (4) differences of opinion about whether dissolution processes are general or relationship-specific.

Failure to explicate the exact nature of dissolution has been a persistent source of ambiguity. Several investigators (e.g., Albert & Kessler, 1978; Knapp, 1978; Knapp et al., 1973) view encounter endings as a model for relationship endings. Yet little attention has been devoted to exploring the validity of this common analogy. Previous attempts to identify parts or stages of the dissolution process have usually lacked either firm empirical support (e.g., Knapp, 1978) or generality across relationship types (e.g., Bradford, 1977; Burgess & Wallin, 1953; Weiss, 1975). Most researchers have simply avoided the problem of explicating dissolution by treating it as a more or less discrete act. This tendency is readily apparent in studies that merely compare ongoing and terminated relationships.

The incomplete explication of dissolution also contributes to ambiguity in the distinction between temporary relationship breakdowns and permanent dissolution (cf. Duck, 1981). There have been few empirical attempts to resolve the current debate re-

From Duck, S. W. (Ed.) (1982). *Personal relationships, 4: Dissolving relationships* (pp. 127-154). New York: Academic Press.

garding the relationship between breakdowns and dissolution. When the extended dissolution process has been more fully explicated, researchers will possess better grounds for discriminating between breakdowns which are part of a larger dissolution process and those which are relatively independent markers of passing turbulence. Studies describing the communication behaviors which mark the course of relationships and studies identifying the communication strategies which actively alter that course will inevitably make comparisons between breakdowns and dissolution more explicit by providing data about the contexts that surround them, their consequences, and their accompanying description by the parties involved. By gathering a detailed descriptive base of the relevant temporal sequences of observable behaviors, researchers will help to clarify the nature of relationship dissolution.

The uncertain status of affective–cognitive variables in theories of relationship change is another major source of ambiguity. Although most studies of relationship change have focused on such variables as attraction, similarity, intimacy, and commitment; it is doubtful that these variables alone provide an adequate framework for understanding either the growth or decline of relationships (Duck, 1981; Parks, 1981). For one thing, many relationships dissolve before variables such as intimacy and commitment come into play, and many social "Barrier Forces" can continue to bind a relationship that has affectively dissolved (Levinger, 1976). Furthermore, many other processes take over from the influence of purely affective-cognitive states once the relationship begins to develop, and the social management of the relationship becomes as much a communication issue as does the participants' communication of their own attraction to each other. Finally, since individuals can influence each other only through symbolic exchanges, investigations of communication provide the crucial link between participants and thus the means of transcending a purely individual level of analysis. Therefore, studies of communication are essential even when dissolution is conceptualized in terms of affective–cognitive variables. There is a great deal of research on variables which influence affective–cognitive states such as attraction and similarity, yet there is comparatively little research showing how changes in these states influence actual communication behavior (Siegman, 1979).

A third source of controversy centers on *the relationship between development and dissolution processes*. Altman and Taylor claimed that dissolution was "analogous to a film shown in reverse" (1973, p. 174). The assumption that dissolution is the reverse of development has been widely adopted (Davis, 1973; Knapp, 1978; Schutz, 1958). Obviously, however, there are a number of asymmetries between development and dissolution. For instance, while development can be viewed in terms of progressive information acquisition and uncertainty reduction (Berger & Calabrese, 1975; Berger et al., 1976; Miller & Steinberg, 1975), dissolution need not be characterized by progressive information loss. In fact participants in dissolving relationships often step up the search for new and damaging information. Development and dissolution may bring differing behaviors into play; and even when similar behaviors are present in development and dissolution, their mix and sequence may be quite different (Duck, 1981). Perhaps the most obvious asymmetry is that relationships require joint action to develop, but can be ended by unilateral action (Simmel, 1950).

While these asymmetries should not be ignored, a complete bifurcation in theories of development and dissolution would be premature, since there is little empirical basis for either accepting or rejecting the reversal assumption. The next section of this chapter attempts to stimulate an empirical resolution by defining a set of communicative markers which should describe both the development and the dissolution process if the reversal assumption is valid. After that, we will go on to view communicative attempts to terminate a relationship within the broader framework of compliance-gaining strategies. Gaining compliance is a central activity on both sides of the developmental cycle. Although it is true that relationships develop through joint action, it is also true that the desire to develop is not always shared at a given moment, causing participants to employ communication to nudge each other along. Thus, it is possible to consider both development and dissolution as aspects of the more general social influence process.

Much the same point can be made about the debate regarding *whether dissolution processes are relationship-specific*. Writers frequently accentuate differences between friendship, dating relationships, and marriage (e.g., Duck, 1981; Hill et al., 1976). Research on divorce has often focused on relationship-specific variables. Although differences between relationships certainly exist, most relationships are mixtures of common and unique elements. The relative impact of each type of element must be examined before the question of generality can be resolved. The following sections identify sets of behavioral markers and communication strategies which can be observed across a wide variety of relationships. We believe that they are particularly useful empirical tools for sorting out the common and unique elements of the dissolution process across relationships.

COMMUNICATIVE MARKERS IN DISSOLVING RELATIONSHIPS

There is no shortage of speculation about what happens when relationships disintegrate. Feelings of attraction, warmth, and intimacy diminish; similarity decreases along with the participants' ability to coordinate their interactions; dissolving relationships are ridden with anxiety and conflict; distance, in some metaphoric sense, increases between participants. Unfortunately none of these very general descriptions isolates observable features of the dissolution process. This section attempts to develop a behavioral description by linking specific characteristics of communication with assumptions about reversal and the role of the affective-cognitive variables. Four types of variables, each of which can be observed over time and across a broad variety of relationships, are discussed: (1) global interaction characteristics; (2) communication network char-

acteristics; (3) non-verbal communication characteristics; and (4) verbal communication characteristics. Specific behaviors and their hypothesized relationships to dissolution are summarized in Tables 26.1 and 26.2.

TABLE 26.1

General and Non-Verbal Communication Characteristics of Dissolution

---

Global Interaction Characteristics
1. Decreases in the duration of encounters
2. Increases in the time between encounters

Communication Network Characteristics
1. Decreases in the frequency of mutual interaction with those outside the relationship
2. Decreases in the number of mutual members in participants' communication networks
3. Increases in the frequency of negative comments about the partner and the overall relationship to those outside the relationship

Non-Verbal Communication Characteristics
Proxemic Codes
1. Decreases in physical proximity
2. Decreases in the rate and duration of touch
3. Decreases in the ratio of forward to backward body leans
4. Decreases in the rate and duration of direct body orientation
Kinesic Codes
1. Decreases in the rate of head, hand, and arm movements
2. Increases in the rate of leg, foot, and self-touch movements
3. Decreases in the rate and duration of smiling
4. Decreases in the rate and duration of mutual looks to the face
Paralanguage and the Temporal Features of Speech
1. Decreases in pitch variation
2. Increases in the discrepancy between participants' mean vocal intensities
3. Increases in the frequency and duration of simultaneous speech
4. Increases in the "non-ah" speech disfluency ratio
5. Increases in the discrepancy between participants' mean speech durations
6. Decreases in the rate of speech
7. Increases in the frequency and duration of within-utterance pauses
8. Increases in the duration of switching pauses
Codes Involving the Use of Objects
1. Decreases in the similarity of dress and object preferences
2. Decreases in access to the other person's possessions
3. Decreases in the acquisition of joint possessions
4. Decreases in the frequency of "intimacy trophy" display
5. Increases in the rate of object manipulation during interaction

---

TABLE 26.2
Verbal Communication Characteristics of Dissolution

Word Choice and the Construction of Statements
Spatio-Temporal Designation
1. Decreases in the use of the present tense
2. Decreases in the use of future-tense references to the relationship
3. Increases in the use of adverbial clauses
4. Increases in the use of temporal modifiers
5. Increases in the ratio of non-immediate to immediate demonstrative pronouns
Denotative Specificity
1. Increases in the frequency of over-inclusive statements
2. Increases in the frequency of under-inclusive statements
Agent-Action-Object Relationships
1. Decreases in the ratio of pronouns implying mutuality to pronouns implying individuality
2. Increases in the frequency with which negative superlatives and absolute statements are used to describe the other person
3. Increases in the use of the passive tense
4. Increases in the frequency of qualifying words and phrases
5. Increases in the frequency of explicit causal references to the other person, people outside the relationship, and events or forces outside the relationship

Statement Choice and the Construction of Encounters
1. Decreases in the frequency of evaluative statements
2. Increases in the ratio of reconciling and appealing acts to rejecting and coercive acts
3. Increases in the number of exchanges in conflict encounters
4. Decreases in topic dwell-time

Global Interaction Characteristics

Dissolution is frequently equated with a decrease in the overall amount of communication between participants (e.g., Altman & Taylor, 1973; Davis, 1973; Knapp, 1978). More specifically, we would expect dissolution to be characterized by both a decrease in the duration of encounters and an increase in the time between encounters. However, dissolution does not necessarily imply a total cessation of communication. Former partners may maintain contact as a matter of choice, continuing obligation, or by virtue of their similar location in the physical and social environment. Divorced persons, for example, often maintain contact not only with their former spouse, but also with the former spouse's family

and kin (Spicer & Hampe, 1975; Weiss, 1975). Individuals may maintain indirect contact through third parties even when direct communication ceases.

Communication Network Characteristics

Most research has ignored the dissolving pair's relationship to the larger communication network in which it is embedded. Yet a number of network characteristics ought to change systematically as a given dyad dissolves. Members of a dyad may interact with outsiders less frequently as a couple because of increased uncertainty and difficulty in planning joint activities (Weiss, 1975). Their social circles should contain fewer mutual members as participants pursue increasingly independent goals (Knapp, 1978; Scanzoni, 1968). Also, communication with outsiders may contain more frequent negative statements about the partner and the overall relationship (Waller & Hill, 1951). Finally, in addition to these relatively specific changes in communication, it is possible that the stress accompanying dissolution may fan out to affect a person's general behavior in all of his or her other relationships (Bloom et al., 1978).

Non-Verbal Communication Characteristics

Changes in most non-verbal communication codes accompany the dissolution process. These changes have been grouped around four types of codes: proxemic codes, kinesic codes, codes involving paralanguage and the temporal features of speech, and codes involving the use of objects.

Proxemic Codes. A large number of studies have linked spatial behavior with such affective states as attraction, affiliation, intimacy, and commitment (Argyle, 1975; Davis, 1973; Hall, 1966; Harper et al., 1978; Kendon, 1967; Mehrabian, 1971a, 1972). Although there are some exceptions and qualifications (e.g., Argyle, 1975; Bartels, 1977; Mehrabian, 1972), most studies report positive associations between these affective states and: (1) physical proximity; (2) the rate and duration of touch; (3) the ratio of forward to backward body leans; and (4) the rate and duration of direct body orientation. These patterns should reverse during dissolution if the more general assumptions about reversing affective states are correct.

Kinesic Codes. Assumptions about affective states also form the basis for hypotheses regarding bodily motions in dissolving relationships. The overall rate of head, hand, and arm movements has been positively related to affiliation variables (Argyle, 1975; Bayes, 1972; Mehrabian, 1971b; Mehrabian and Ksionzky, 1972, 1974). However, excessive motor unrest may signal disaffiliation (Wolff, 1945). Specific motions such as leg and foot movements, including walking around and touching one's own body, increase when individuals feel tense (Freedman et al., 1972; Mehrabian, 1971b; Mehrabian & Ksionzky, 1972, 1974). Imminent dissolution would presumably be characterized by decreasing rates of head, hand, and arm movements; and by increasing rates of leg, foot, and self-touch movements.

Facial expressions and gaze behavior have long figured in discussions of development and dissolution. Smiling, as one would expect, is a relatively clear indicator of affiliation (Argyle, 1975; Bayes, 1972; Rosenfeld, 1966). Predictions about gaze are not so simple. The functions of gaze range from expressing liking to monitoring threatening opponents (Kendon, 1967). Researchers have developed a large and frequently confusing set of gaze variables (Cappella, 1981; Cranach, 1971; Harper et al., 1978). Findings consequently do not form a consistent pattern. Comparisons of friend and stranger dyads show few differences in gaze behaviors (Bartels, 1977; Breck, 1978). On the other hand, studies have generally reported positive relationships between the frequency or duration of mutual looks to the face and a series of affective variables (e.g., Argyle, 1975; Exline & Winters, 1965; Harper et al., 1978; Mehrabian, 1971a, 1972; Rubin, 1970). Although support is far from unanimous, most stud-

ies suggest that the frequency and duration of mutual looks increase during development of relationships and decrease during dissolution.

Interactional synchrony and congruent body positioning are widely mentioned indicators of closeness and involvement (Condon, 1975; Davis, 1973; Kendon, 1970; Knapp, 1978; Scheflen, 1964, 1973). Unfortunately, the actual evidence of synchrony in body movements is scant. Cappella (1981) could find only five studies which were directly relevant. Four of the five could offer only anecdotal support and the most thorough investigation (McDowall, 1978) disconfirmed the synchrony hypothesis. Failure to support such a frequently repeated hypothesis testifies to the need for more rigorous behavioral research.

Paralanguage and the Temporal Features of Speech. Most discussions of relationship change have treated paralanguage as a psychological variable. Thus, tonal qualities are often said to become "warm" or "soft" as relationships develop and "cold" as they dissolve (e.g., Argyle, 1975; Davis, 1973; Knapp, 1978). These terms lack physical referents and therefore represent perceiver evaluations rather than behavioral variables. Few studies have examined objective features of the voice in relationship to dissolution and development. Scherer's (1974) tightly controlled experiments using a Moog synthesizer are an exception. He found that lower levels of pitch variation were associated with negative judgments of emotion (e.g., anger, boredom, disgust, fear). Natale (1975) found that the discrepancy between participants' vocal intensities decreased over the course of several meetings. Dissolution should be characterized by decreased levels of pitch variation and increasing discrepancies in vocal intensity (loudness) if assumptions about reversal and the role of affective variables are valid.

Several characteristics of vocalization may be viewed as behavioral referents for more general images of synchrony. For example, conversations in intimate relationships are perceived as smooth, coordinated, and efficient (Knapp et al., 1980).

Altman and Taylor concluded that "the well-developed relationship functions in a meshed fashion without verbal or physical stumbling" (1973, p. 133). Conversely, as relationships dissolve, participants should have greater difficulty managing their interactions. The frequency of simultaneous speech might increase as turn-taking patterns break down. So, too, might the frequency of speech disfluencies. A number of studies (cf. Harper et al., 1978) show that behavioral measures of disfluency, such as Mahl's (1959) "non-ah" ratio, are positively related to anxiety. Moreover, opportunities to participate in conversation may become imbalanced when individuals lack shared expectations about how to structure their encounter. In dyads composed of strangers, for example, the duration of one person's speech is negatively related to the duration of the other person's speech (Kendon, 1967); whereas in more established dyads, durations of speech are positively correlated (Chapple, 1940; Kendon, 1967; Matarazzo et al., 1964).

Several studies imply that the rate of speech and the amount of pausing ought to be related to the process of development and dissolution. Speech rate generally increases when individuals are more affiliated (Mehrabian, 1971b; Mehrabian & Ksionzky, 1972). Higher speech rates are positively related to perceptions of warmth (Bayes, 1972). Although the relationship between speech rate and anxiety is ambiguous (Mehrabian, 1971b; Murray, 1971), the amount of silence is positively related to situational anxiety (Harper et al., 1978). For instance, families with a history of emotional or social problems tend to spend more time in silence than normal families (Ferreira & Winter, 1968). Previous studies (Allen et al., 1965; Siegman, 1979) have also shown that perceptions of warmth are negatively related to pauses within utterances and pauses between speakers' turns (switching pauses). Taken as a group, these studies suggest that dissolution will be accompanied by decreasing speech rate, increasing frequency and duration of within-utterance pauses, and increasing duration of switching pauses.

Codes Involving the Use of Objects. Behavior towards objects can provide powerful clues about the overall nature of a relationship. Knapp (1978), for example, notes that similarities of dress and object preferences often decrease in dissolving relationships. Access to the other person's possessions may decrease as well (Altman & Taylor, 1973). Furthermore, individuals in dissolving relationships will probably acquire fewer joint possessions. Rings, jewelry, photographs, and other "intimacy trophies" which symbolize better days will be displayed less frequently (Knapp, 1978). Finally, the increased discomfort thought to characterize dissolving relationships may be reflected by increased rates of object manipulation during interaction (Mehrabian & Ksionzky, 1972, 1974).

Verbal Communication Characteristics

Few studies actually focus on patterns of verbal communication in dissolving relationships, although verbal code use is widely presumed to change as relationships come apart. Self-disclosure figures prominently in discussions of development (e.g., Altman & Taylor, 1973), but it is beset with a host of measurement problems (Chelune, 1979) and often cannot be clearly applied to the dissolution process. Our discussion deals with the relatively observable features of verbal code use across two admittedly crude categories: (1) word choice and the construction of statements, and (2) statement choice and the construction of encounters. The specific behavioral changes outlined below are summarized in Table 26.2.

Word Choice and the Construction of Statements. Wiener and Mehrabian (1968) have probably contributed the most to our speculation concerning very specific aspects of language change in dissolving relationships. Their exploration into the linguistic correlates of non-immediacy yields a wealth of variables. Some are not relevant to our purposes, while others are modified in order to apply more directly to the dissolution process. None the less, we have followed Wiener and Mehrabian in hypothesizing that dissolution should be accompanied by changes in three aspects of word choice and sentence construction: spatio-temporal designations, denotative specificity, and agent-action-object relationships.

Verb tenses, adverbs, and demonstrative pronouns reflect the spatio-temporal relationships between the speaker, listener, and the topic of conversation. Participants should have little difficulty focusing on the "here and now" in well-developed, smoothly functioning relationships (Wiener & Mehrabian, 1968). As relationships dissolve, however, word choice and statement construction might show progressive spatio-temporal distancing. We could expect a decreased use of the present tense to describe events actually occurring within the current encounter (Mehrabian, 1971a; Wiener & Mehrabian, 1968). Participants ought to make fewer future tense references to their relationship (Knapp, 1978). Spatio-temporal distancing may also be displayed in greater use of clauses beginning with terms like "when," "where," "during," and "while." Temporal modifiers such as "before," "after," "at first," and "later" should be used more frequently in dissolving relationships. Finally, spatial displacements might be reflected by a changing ratio among demonstratives. The frequency of the words "that" and "those" should increase relative to the frequency of the words "this" and "these." Although these are exceedingly specific variables, past research (Wiener & Mehrabian, 1968) has shown that each can distinguish between different levels of affiliation.

Mehrabian (1971a) assumed that ambiguity-producing behaviors were a sign of non-immediacy or disaffiliation. He further asserted that ambiguity resulted from statements which were either too specific or not specific enough. Inappropriate denotative specificity can be indicated by several features of word choice and statement construction (Wiener & Mehrabian, 1968). Statements become over-inclusive when the implied subject or object is placed in a more general class rather than standing alone. Responding to a question regarding how one liked dinner at a particular restaurant by saying, "The whole evening was nice," would count as an instance of over-inclusiveness. Conversely, under-inclusiveness occurs when the subject or object refers to just a part or attribute of an implied whole (e.g., "I liked the salad"). Negations of positive comments when affirmations are possible also reflect under-inclusiveness (e.g., "It wasn't bad"). Each type of inappropriate specificity implies a discrepancy in the way communicators categorize and respond to each other and the content of their discourse. Such discrepancies should become more frequent as relationships dissolve.

Individuals linguistically separate themselves from one another as their relationship dissolves. This process is exemplified by changes in agent-action-object relationships (Wiener & Mehrabian, 1968). Knapp (1978) hypothesized that pronouns which portray the participants as a couple (e.g., "we," "us," "our," "ours") will be used less frequently than pronouns which reinforce the separateness of the individual (e.g., "I," "me," "my," "mine," "you," "your," "yours"). Tangential support for this hypothesis can be gleaned from Premo's (1979) finding that strangers used fewer statements of "joint situation" than married couples. Speakers also distance themselves from the relationship by using negative superlatives and absolutistic statements to describe the other, his or her actions, or the overall relationship (Knapp, 1978). Finally, dissolution should be characterized by changes in the expressed responsibility for actions and evaluations. Individuals who wish to distance themselves from their partners or the overall relationship are more likely to place responsibility for their actions and evaluations in the other person or the external environment. They are correspondingly less likely to express personal or shared responsibility. The redistribution of responsibility in dissolving relationships is indicated by increased use of the passive voice, more frequent qualification (e.g., "perhaps," "maybe," "somehow"), and more frequent explicit causal references to the other person or events and persons outside the relationship (Mehrabian, 1971a; Waller & Hill, 1951; Wiener & Mehrabian, 1968).

Statement Choice and the Construction of Encounters. Researchers are presented with a vast array of theoretical possibilities for describing language use at the level of the overall encounter. Since our concern is limited to variables that have been linked to the dissolution process and whose measurement requires relatively low levels of observer inference, the paragraphs below only hint at the variety of ways in which linguistic changes could be described.

Altman and Taylor (1973) hypothesized that evaluative statements would occur more frequently as relationships developed and less frequently as they dissolved. Although we know of no complete tests of this hypothesis, three studies provide indirect support. Ayres (1981) found that persons make more evaluative comments as their relationship develops. Premo (1979) showed that married couples use more statements of agreement and disagreement than strangers. Ferreira and Winter (1968) reported that families experiencing emotional or social problems used fewer statements of agreement and disagreement than normal families. If our now well-worn assumptions are still valid, dissolution should be characterized by decreases in the overall frequency of explicit agreements and disagreements with the other person's views and actions.

An investigation of communication and marital conflict by Raush et al. (1974) offers a useful framework for exploring changes in the content of verbal communication. Couples enacted roles which either increased closeness or maintained distance. Spouses' communication was then coded into six categories, four of which occurred more often in one role than the other. Acts of emotional reconciliation were almost twice as frequent in closeness roles as distance roles, and acts appealing for the other's support or assistance were over seven times more frequent in closeness roles. Inversely, acts rejecting the other's views or selfhood were over four times more frequent in distance roles, and acts of coercion—e.g., power plays, personal attacks, threats, guilt inductions—were about twice as frequent in distance roles as closeness roles. These findings suggest that a useful measure of relationship change might be the ratio between reconciling and appealing acts on the one side and rejecting and coercive acts on the other. Such a measure reflects larger dialectical perspectives on closeness and distance in interpersonal relationships (Altman, 1975; Goffman, 1961, 1967; Parks, 1981; Schwartz, 1968; Simmel, 1950, 1971).

This closeness/distance ratio also encompasses several other findings and hypotheses about relationship dissolution. Davis (1973) and Knapp (1978), for example, concluded that the number of favors requested and given declines as relationships come apart. The ratio of disagreements to agreements is higher for distressed married couples than for non-distressed couples (Gottman et al., 1977; Riskin & Faunce, 1972). Raush et al. (1974) found that coercive acts were more frequent in "discordant" than in "harmonious" couples. Threats to terminate the relationship are especially coercive and play an important role in the divorce process (Waller & Hill, 1951). The overall implication is that the frequency of reconciling and appealing acts ought to decrease relative to the frequency of rejecting and coercive acts as relationships dissolve.

Conflicts in dissolving relationships are swept along by the growing wave of rejection, coercion, and general emotional disaffiliation. Once a conflict begins, participants may have difficulty controlling it (Altman & Taylor, 1973; Knapp, 1978). Conflict episodes are consequently protracted in dissolving relationships. This view is indirectly supported by Raush and his associates (1974) who found that the number of conflict exchanges was almost twice as great among "discordant" couples as "harmonious" couples.

The amount of time participants devote to a given conversational topic generally increases as their relationship develops (Ayres, 1980, 1981). Conversely, "topic dwell-time" should decrease as the relationship dissolves. People may simply run out of things to say because they are less willing to disclose their personal feelings (Altman & Taylor, 1973; Baxter, 1979a; Davis, 1973; Knapp, 1978). In addition, participants may have greater difficulty holding conversation on a given topic as their ability to coordinate speech sequences decreases.

In this section we have described the communicative bits and pieces of the dissolution process. Our discussion stands in distinct contrast to perspectives which portray dissolution as a unitary act. Yet articulating the elements is only the first step towards constructing a more general description. The elements combine to form complex patterns characterized by compensation and matching, substitution, distinct sequences, and widely varying rates of change (Altman & Taylor, 1973; Cappella, 1981; Keiser & Altman, 1976). Moreover, patterns of verbal and non-verbal codes may reflect the uncertainty and confusion so often experienced as relationships come apart. Although research on patterns of multiple behaviors over time is certainly more difficult than research on single behaviors in single encounters, it is this more demanding research that yields some of the best opportunities to resolve empirically the ambiguities and controversies now hampering descriptions of relationship dissolution.

SELECTION AND USE OF COMMUNICATIVE STRATEGIES IN DISSOLVING RELATIONSHIPS

Having examined some possible behaviors that serve as communicative markers of dissolution, we now present a preliminary conceptualization of the role of communication in dissolving relationships. In developing our perspective, we shall identify specific types of communicative strategies that can be used in relational dissolution. When identifying such strategies, at least two alternative courses of action are possible: first, to explain dissolution as a particularistic behavior; second, to view it as a special instance of a general type of behavior. Some writers (e.g., Baxter, 1979b, 1980) have opted to treat communication during relational disengagement as a relatively particularistic, unique behavioral process. This approach has the advantage of

producing a set of strategies whose labels are clearly linked to the act of disengagement—e.g., *withdrawal* and *avoidance* strategies, *positive tone* strategies, and *open confrontation* strategies—but at the possible expense of sacrificing conceptual and theoretical generality. Stated differently, if one assumes that communicative strategies aimed at accomplishing relational dissolution do not differ in kind from strategies invoked for a variety of other ends, a potentially useful conceptual web can be spun at a higher level of abstraction.

As implied earlier, we have chosen to accept the previous assumption; i.e., the generalist assumption that dissolution is a special instance of a general type of behavior, namely, compliance gaining or social influence. In other words, messages seeking to terminate relationships inevitably embody a *persuasive* intent. As we shall shortly demonstrate, acceptance of the assumption that communicative attempts to end relationships do not differ in kind from attempts to sell automobiles, to elect political candidates, or to marshall support for social policies permits application of a somewhat modified general set of compliance-gaining strategies, initially developed by Marwell and Schmitt (1967), to the process of relational dissolution. This is not to say, of course, that there are no relevant differences between the acts of ending a 20-year marriage or friendship and selling a used Ford, but rather that the same strategic options for achieving compliance apply to both situations.

Any preliminary conceptualization of the role of communication in dissolving relationships must also take into account differences in the relational dynamics of the involved dyad. Parties to a relationship may disagree about the desirability of termination or may differ in the intensity of their motivation to terminate. Since variation in either or both of these factors is likely to influence the particular disengagement strategies employed, the range of strategies used, and the probable response to specific strategies, a useful initial step lies in specifying some of the relevant alternatives available to relational partners. We next provide such a specification, utilizing a social exchange perspective that draws heavily on the seminal work of Thibaut & Kelley (1959; Kelley & Thibaut, 1978).

Some Relational Alternatives Relevant to the Dissolution Process

Figure 26.1 contains examples of six possible dyadic alternatives in ongoing relationships, using two hypothetical participants, *A* and *B*. The six situations are but a small subset of possible alternatives; they have been singled out as useful cases for developing our conceptualization. Furthermore, an understanding of the six illustrative cases should allow the interested reader to extend our reasoning to other relational alternatives.

Three relational variables utilized by Thibaut and Kelley: Outcomes, Comparison Level (CL), and Comparison Level for Alternatives (CLalt) are central to our formulation. In common with most social exchange theories, the magnitude of relational Outcomes is determined by the ratio of perceived rewards to perceived costs (1959, pp. 12–13). Comparison Level is the "standard by which the person evaluates the rewards and costs of a given relationship in terms of what he [she] feels he [she] deserves" (p. 21). In essence, Comparison Level represents a subjective yardstick based on all previous relationships that the individual has experienced. Thus, individuals with histories of highly favorable relational experiences will impose demanding standards on any particular relationship, while persons of more modest relational success will manifest less stringent standards of evaluation. Finally, Comparison Level for Alternatives is defined as "the lowest level of outcomes a [relational] member will accept in the light of available alternative opportunities" (p. 21). Consequently, if someone perceives that a number of attractive alternatives exist, he or she will demand reasonably high outcomes from a given relationship; if available alternatives are relatively unattractive, expectations concerning relational outcomes will be considerably more modest.

Application of these three variables to the situation diagrammed in Figure 26.1a reveals that the relationship is quite attractive for both participants. Both are realizing Outcomes that exceed their Comparison Levels, and the perceived alternatives (CLalt) do not exceed their CLs. No contemplating of dissolution would be expected in this situation save for possible allusions to the ensuing hardship that would result if termination were somehow imposed—e.g., "I'd be lost without you!" or "I don't know what I'd do without you!" Popular literature, cinema, and television typically portray the intense initial stages of a romance in this way.

Perusal of Figure 26.1b reveals a marked change in mutual relational alternatives. Although dissolution is not currently a viable option, relational attractiveness has declined for both participants, with Outcomes falling below CL but remaining above CLalt. The partners are mutually dependent but are relatively unenthusiastic about their relational lots. References to dissolution may be introduced to try to bring the partner's behaviors more into line with desired Outcomes—e.g., "I don't know how much longer I can tolerate your selfishness and lack of concern without splitting." Indeed, continued displays of punishing behaviors coupled with threatening counter-messages could well produce the situation depicted in Figure 26.1c. Here both parties agree that the relationship is beyond redemption and that dissolution is necessary. Unfortunately, their consensus takes the form of the "lesser of evils," since all perceived alternatives fall below CL. Parting is therefore likely to be accompanied by acrimonious, hostile message exchanges—e.g., "This is all your fault!" or "If you weren't so damned stubborn and self-centered, we could have worked things out!"

By contrast, Figure 26.1d captures the conditions for a maximally harmonious, friendly termination. Not only do the participants agree on the necessity of relational dissolution, they also perceive the existence of alternatives whose Outcomes lie above their CLs. These alternatives may include the presence of another attractive relational partner, internalization of the belief that autonomy is highly preferable to psychologically debilitating relational

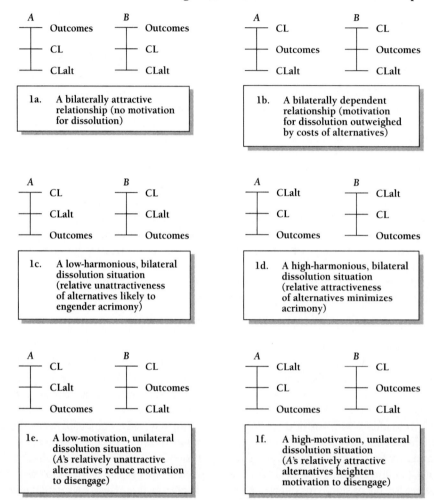

FIGURE 26.1

Some Relevant Social Exchange Alternatives in *A*'s and *B*'s Relationship

1a. A bilaterally attractive relationship (no motivation for dissolution)

1b. A bilaterally dependent relationship (motivation for dissolution outweighed by costs of alternatives)

1c. A low-harmonious, bilateral dissolution situation (relative unattractiveness of alternatives likely to engender acrimony)

1d. A high-harmonious, bilateral dissolution situation (relative attractiveness of alternatives minimizes acrimony)

1e. A low-motivation, unilateral dissolution situation (*A*'s relatively unattractive alternatives reduce motivation to disengage)

1f. A high-motivation, unilateral dissolution situation (*A*'s relatively attractive alternatives heighten motivation to disengage)

dependence, or a variety of other factors. Regardless of the precise nature of the alternatives, they cushion the trauma of termination; and while it would be naive to anticipate absolutely no verbal conflict, the participants should be able to separate with minimal recrimination.

The four preceding situations share the important characteristic of symmetrical perceptions, i.e., both parties define the social exchange dynamics

identically; Figure 26.1e represents the first instance of asymmetry: whereas *A* wishes to dissolve the relationship; *B* wants to maintain it, a circumstance that frequently characterizes troubled relationships (Burgess & Wallin, 1953; Davis, 1973; Hill et al., 1976; Waller & Hill, 1951). This situation, along with the one depicted in Figure 26.1f, most clearly underscores the persuasive nature of the dissolution process. Short of abrupt withdrawal, A can realize the goal of relational termination only by gaining B's compliance, by communicating with B in ways calculated to raise B's CLalt above his or her relational Outcomes. To be sure, A can decide to exit suddenly from the relational field, but this decision may itself pose additional costs for A; especially in highly developed, heavy commitment relationships or in relationships where B has the means for punishing A's withdrawal. Such sudden flight may be branded as socially irresponsible by some of A's significant others; or in certain instances, it may even open the door for legal action against A as when charges of desertion or failure to provide child support are lodged against an errant husband. For that matter, B may simply persist in pursuing A and in hectoring A to resume intensive contact. Thus, notwithstanding the dramatic appeal of instant dissolution and despite the fact that some relationships do end abruptly (Baxter & Philpott, 1980; Burgess & Wallin, 1953; Davis, 1973), A will often follow the more conservative path of using symbolic means in order to manipulate B's assessment of the relationship.

Obviously, A's motivation to disengage will vary, depending upon his or her evaluation of available relational alternatives. In the situation described in Figure 26.1e, motivation to dissolve the relationship is relatively low because A's CLalt, while falling above Outcomes, is below CL. Since A perceives no exceedingly attractive alternatives, he or she is likely to proceed about the task of gaining compliance cautiously. Indeed, A may be unwilling to use certain disengagement strategies because of the potential costs associated with them. Punishment strategies, for example, are likely to result in greater relational stress and conflict, a price A may be reluctant to pay given the relatively low value assigned to CLalt.

On turning to the situation depicted in 1f, circumstances are altered radically. Here A is strongly impelled towards dissolution by the availability of highly attractive alternatives. Compliance gaining can thus be expected to become a no-holds-barred activity, with A using every strategic weapon in his

or her symbolic arsenal, if necessary, to persuade B to accept the desirability, or at least the inevitability, of dissolution. In fact, should all else fail, A may follow the course of unilateral withdrawal regardless of the potential costs associated with this decision.

Where bilateral agreement exists on the desirability of dissolution, as in 26.1c and 26.1d, communication will typically concern *means* rather than *ends;* i.e., compliance-gaining attempts will center on the details of dissolution. If real property or other financial assets are at stake, which is usually true when the parties are living together, considerable negotiation and bartering can be expected. Negotiation is also the rule when custody and/or support for dependent others is involved, as in the case of divorces involving children. Sometimes the demands of one party may so sharply alter the social exchange perspective of the other that agreement about the desirability of dissolution ceases to exist. For example, when faced with the prospect of extremely expensive alimony or child-support payments, a husband's perceived costs may increase sharply, with the result that CLalt falls below Outcomes causing the husband to change his mind about dissolving the marital relationship. Exchanges regarding dissolutional details would typically be more stressful and conflictful under the circumstances described in 26.1c, since both parties' lack of highly attractive alternatives will motivate them to maximize the rewards and minimize the costs of dissolution. When attractive alternatives exist, as in 26.1d, both parties are more likely to compromise or to surrender certain means and objectives to hasten the process of dissolution.

For those cases of unilateral disengagement described above (26.1e and 26.1f), our analysis has centered on the objectives of the relational partner who is motivated to dissolve the relationship. This is clearly an oversimplification, for the Outcomes of the two parties are interdependent. B is likely to resist A's compliance-gaining strategies and to counter with strategies of his or her own. As Davis puts it, B may even "*filibuster* to delay the adjournment of the terminal talk for as long as possible, eventually forcing the other to call for *cloture* and thus twist the sinew-severing knife he [she] wields still deeper" (1973, p. 272, italics in original). A complete conceptualization of the role of communication in dissolving relationships must eventually take account of this transactional nature of the process. Though our preliminary conceptualization falls short of a comprehensive transactional analysis, it permits generation of some hypotheses about message exchanges which are based on a reciprocal view of the dyad.

Thus far, we have alluded to compliance-gaining strategies in generic terms. It remains for us to offer a more specific typology of strategies and to generate some sample hypotheses concerning the selection and the effects of compliance-gaining strategies during the process of dissolving relationships. Hopefully, these two steps will illustrate the heuristic merit of our conceptualization.

A Typology of Compliance-Gaining Strategies Used in Relational Dissolution

An initial attempt to develop a comprehensive taxonomy of compliance-gaining message strategies was made by Marwell and Schmitt (1967). Drawing upon various sources (Etzioni, 1961; French & Raven, 1960; Jones, 1964; Kelman, 1961; Parsons, 1963; Schmitt, 1964; Skinner, 1953; Thibaut & Kelley, 1959), these researchers generated a list of 16 strategies. These strategies are summarized in Table 26.3, using examples related to the process of relational dissolution.

To determine the dimensionality of their strategies, Marwell and Schmitt asked 608 undergraduate students to indicate how likely they would be to use each of the 16 appeals in four different compliance-gaining situations. The resultant factor analysis yielded a five-factor solution, summarized in Table 26.4 along with the labels assigned to each of the factors.

Miller et al. (1977) extended the taxonomical work of Marwell and Schmitt by performing a modified replication of the latter researchers' original study. There was one substantive and two procedural differences in Miller et al.'s approach. Substantively, while Marwell and Schmitt's four situations were devised with no guiding criteria save the desire to devise situations that would encourage use of most strategies, Miller et al., relying on a conceptualization developed by Miller and Steinberg (1975), sought to devise two non-interpersonal and two interpersonal situations. The non-interpersonal situations involved relationships that had developed only to the point where participants were assumed to have based most of their predictions about message outcomes on cultural and sociological information, whereas the interpersonal situations involved more fully developed relationships where participants were assumed to have based at least some of their predictions on psychological information they had gained about the relational partner. Procedurally, Marwell and Schmitt sampled exclusively from a population of college students, while Miller et al. sampled from a broader population; and Marwell and Schmitt employed factor analysis to examine strategy dimensionality, while Miller et al. used a clustering procedure.

Results indicated a great deal of inter-situational variance in the clusters, suggesting that the 16 strategies are highly situation-bound. Only one of the strategies, *liking,* was likely to be used in all four situations, with respondents reporting a high likelihood of use for *altruism* in three of the four situations. Respondents also reported a high likelihood of use for more of the strategies in the non-interpersonal situations, with the interpersonal situations characterized by a tendency to report use of fewer strategies and to avoid the use of Punishing Activity strategies to a greater extent. Generally, then, the findings did not bode well for the possibility of reducing the 16 strategies to a smaller set which would hold together across communicative situations.

Later studies have further underscored the problem of imposing a heuristic, economical factor structure on Marwell and Schmitt's taxonomy. Hunter and Boster (1978) report that the strongest determinant of strategy use lies in whether the

TABLE 26.3

Marwell and Schmitt's Typology of 16 Compliance-Gaining Strategies (from Marwell & Schmitt, 1967, 357–358; reproduced by permission)

1. Promise	(If you comply, I will reward you.) You offer to release community property if your relational partner will agree to dissolution.
2. Threat	(If you do not comply, I will punish you.) You threaten to take all community property if your relational partner will not agree to dissolution.
3. Positive Expertise	(If you comply, you will be rewarded because of "the nature of things.") You tell your relational partner that it will be a lot easier on both of you if he/she agrees to the dissolution.
4. Negative Expertise	(If you do not comply, you will be punished because of "the nature of things.") You tell your relational partner that if he/she does not agree to the dissolution, it will be an extremely difficult emotional experience for both of you.
5. Pre-giving	(Actor rewards target before requesting compliance.) You finance a vacation for your relational partner to visit friends before telling him/her you wish to dissolve the relationship.
6. Aversive Stimulation	(Actor continuously punishes target making cessation contingent on compliance.) You refuse to communicate with your relational partner until he/she agrees to discuss the possibility of dissolution.
7. Debt	(You owe me compliance because of past favors.) You point out to your relational partner that you have sacrificed to put him/her through college and that he/she owes it to you to let you live your life as you desire.
8. Liking	(Actor is friendly and helpful to get target in a "good frame of mind" so that he/she will comply with the request.) You try to be as friendly and pleasant as possible with your relational partner before bringing up the fact that you want to dissolve the relationship.
9. Moral Appeal	(A moral person would comply.) You tell your relational partner that a moral person would let someone out of a relationship in which he/she no longer wished to participate.
10. Positive Self-Feeling	(You will feel better about yourself if you comply.) You tell your relational partner that he/she will feel better about him/herself if he/she lets you go.
11. Negative Self-Feeling	(You will feel worse about yourself if you do not comply.) You tell your relational partner that denying you your freedom will make him/her feel like a terrible person.
12. Positive Altercasting	(A person with "good" qualities would comply.) You tell your relational partner that because he/she is a mature, intelligent person, he/she will want you to do what is best for you.
13. Negative Altercasting	(Only a person with "bad" qualities would not comply.) You tell your relational partner that only someone who is cruel and childish would keep another in a relationship which the other desired to leave.
14. Altruism	(I need your compliance very badly, so do it for me.) You tell your relational partner that he/she must free you from the relationship to preserve your sanity.
15. Positive Esteem	(People you value will think highly of you if you comply.) You tell your relational partner that his/her friends and relatives will think highly of him/her for letting you go.
16. Negative Esteem	(People you value will think worse of you if you do not comply.) You tell your relational partner that his/her friends and relatives will be ashamed of him/her if he/she tries to prevent you from leaving.

TABLE 26.4

Oblique Factor Loadings for the 16 Compliance-Gaining Strategies.**

Technique	Factor I	Factor II	Factor III	Factor IV	Factor V
Promise	0.507*	0.210	0.023	0.035	0.010
Threat	0.056	0.566*	0.034	0.024	0.219
Expertise (positive)	0.010	0.002	0.521	0.259	−0.002
Expertise (negative)	0.101	0.118	0.488*	0.070	0.195
Liking	0.563*	−0.030	0.150	0.142	−0.017
Pre-Giving	0.663*	0.041	0.021	0.111	0.074
Aversive Stimulation	0.126	0.560*	0.062	0.071	0.095
Debt	0.023	0.210	0.070	0.037	0.486*
Moral Appeal	−0.111	0.150	0.103	0.363*	0.286
Self-Feeling (positive)	0.121	0.011	0.047	0.732*	0.042
Self-Feeling (negative)	−0.031	0.149	−0.012	0.556*	0.289
Altercasting (positive)	0.117	0.009	0.175	0.599*	−0.090
Altercasting (negative)	−0.010	0.209	−0.059	0.371*	0.343*
Altruism	0.217	0.013	0.116	−0.018	0.530*
Esteem (positive)	0.135	−0.066	0.118	0.557*	0.182
Esteem (negative)	0.010	0.099	−0.008	0.345*	0.526*

* Items used to define the five factors.
** From Marwell and Schmitt, p. 360 (reproduced by permission). They name the five factors as follows: Factor I, Rewarding Activity; Factor II, Punishing Activity; Factor III, Expertise; Factor IV, Activation of Impersonal Commitments; Factor V, Activation of Personal Commitments.

communicator perceives his or her goal to be self-benefit or benefit of the recipient of the communication. If the communicator believes that the message recommendation primarily benefits the recipient—e.g., "You should refrain from over-eating"—any strategy is fair game, but if the communicator believes that the recommendation involves self-benefit—e.g., "You should wash my car tomorrow"—certain strategies are typically deemed inappropriate. Although provocative, this finding suffers from two limitations when applied to the process of relational dissolution: first, interpretation of self-versus other-versus *joint*-benefit is likely to suffer from distortion and rationalization in highly charged dissolution settings; second, the question

of how to classify the total set of compliance-gaining message strategies remains unanswered.

Most recently, Burgoon et al., (1980) have reported that the Marwell and Schmitt typology fails to yield an interpretable factor solution. They argue that the 16 appeals suffer from a good deal of conceptual redundancy while at the same time failing to constitute an exhaustive inventory of strategies, the latter point having been granted by Marwell and Schmitt in their original study. Burgoon et al. conclude with the pessimistic prognosis that the typology has limited utility and needs revamping.

Several features of the Marwell and Schmitt typology point to the need to approach strategy classification for the relational dissolution process from a somewhat different stance. One of their strategies, *liking,* does not refer to a specific symbolic assertion but rather to a cluster of possible preparatory behaviors calculated to get the relational partner "in a good frame of mind" before presenting the compliance-gaining appeal. Though such an approach may sometimes be used in dissolving relationships—e.g., the party seeking dissolution may treat the reluctant partner in a friendly, empathic way immediately prior to confronting him or her with some specific proposal for termination—it may often be counterproductive because it actually enhances the perceived relational Outcomes for the party who is unwilling to end the relationship. Furthermore, as noted above, *liking* is not, strictly speaking, a specific message strategy, but rather a set of antecedent behaviors used to "prepare" the relational partner for the actual compliance-gaining message. The typology we will propose focuses entirely on specific message strategies.

In addition, preliminary research by the first author using college respondents attests to the complexity and potential redundancy of the 16 strategies proposed by Marwell and Schmitt. Not only do respondents typically require a great deal of time to respond, they frequently have difficulty distinguishing among and identifying the various strategies, even when these strategies are orally explained and written examples are provided. Indeed, when respondents were asked to write specific examples of the various strategies for the particular situations involved, many of their examples did not conform with strategy definitions. Such comprehension problems would undoubtedly be aggravated when studying the general process of relational dissolution, since many relational partners do not have the benefit of a college education.

A beginning step towards a simplified typology of strategies can be found in a list of control strategies posited by Miller and Steinberg (1975). These authors identify three, more metaphorically labeled, types of strategies: Dangling Carrot, Hanging Sword, and Catalyst strategies. The Dangling Carrot and Hanging Sword categories are analogous to Marwell and Schmitt's Rewarding Activity and Punishing Activity factors. The Catalyst strategies are represented by some of the items in both the Activation of Impersonal Commitments and Activation of Personal Commitments factors of the Marwell and Schmitt analysis. Miller and Steinberg characterize catalyst strategies in the following way:

> A communicator tries to elicit a desirable response, but rather than offer a reward or threaten a punishment, he [she] reminds his [her] listener of a course of action that the listener would probably find desirable. This method relies for its effectiveness on getting the individual to behave in a self-reinforcing way without directly rewarding or punishing him [her]. The controller must supply the stimulus message to trigger this process, but the listener is largely acting as his [her] own change agent. (1975, p. 125)

In other words, Catalyst strategies place the onus for action on the recipient, with compliance occurring because the recipient perceives he or she is behaving in a self-reinforcing, ego-enhancing manner and not because of the communicator's active manipulation of rewards and punishments. Examples from the Marwell and Schmitt typology include *moral appeal, altruism,* and *positive/negative self-feeling.*

Obviously, as illustrated by the strategies of *positive/negative self-feeling,* a Catalyst strategy can be either reward- or punishment-oriented. This fact suggests that compliance-gaining message strategies can be classified on at least two general dimensions: a reward/punishment dimension and a communicator-onus/recipient-onus dimension. Such a classification yields the following four types of strategies:

1. *Communicator-onus/Reward-oriented strategies:* the communicator specifies the rewards that will be forthcoming to the recipient if the latter complies with the persuasive request.
2. *Communicator-onus/Punishment-oriented strategies:* the communicator specifies the punishments that will be forthcoming to the recipient if the latter fails to comply with the persuasive request.
3. *Recipient-onus/Reward-oriented strategies:* the communicator specifies the positive self-reinforcing contingencies that will accrue for the recipient if the latter complies with the persuasive request.

4. *Recipient-onus/Punishment-oriented strategies:* the communicator specifies the negative self-reinforcing contingencies that will accrue for the recipient if the latter fails to comply with the persuasive request.

This four-part typology is illustrated more in Figure 26.2, which depicts the scheme as a four-cell grid with a modified list of the Marwell and Schmitt strategies grouped in the appropriate cells. For reasons noted above, the list does not include *liking.* In addition, Marwell and Schmitt's original *moral appeal* has been extended to include both *positive* and *negative moral appeal,* an extension that makes the *moral appeal* strategies consistent with the *self-feeling* and *altercasting* strategies. In any event, the precise strategies are relatively unimportant, since the purpose is not to support the exhaustiveness or the exclusivity of Marwell and Schmitt's strategies but rather to demonstrate that a wide variety of particular compliance-gaining message strategies fit nicely into one of the four more general types of strategy.

We propose that these four general categories of compliance-gaining message strategies, when combined with the social exchange perspective of relational alternatives discussed earlier, can be used to generate numerous hypotheses concerning the role of communication in relational dissolution.

FIGURE 26.2

Four-Category Typology of Compliance-Gaining Message Strategies

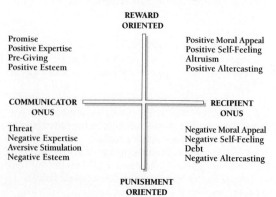

The following section demonstrates the potential utility of our conceptualization by providing a sample of these hypotheses. The offered hypotheses do not exhaust the predictions that could be generated in the six illustrative relational situations, nor do they take into account the many additional dyadic situations that could be diagrammed. Clearly, an extensive programmatic research effort could be undertaken using this conceptualization, a program dealing with the details of relational dissolution as a compliance-gaining phenomenon.

Some Sample Hypotheses Derived from the Conceptualization

The following general hypothesis concerning serial selection of compliance-gaining strategies is expected to hold regardless of the relational exchange alternatives:

Hypothesis: Initial compliance-gaining messages aimed at relational dissolution will rely primarily on Reward-oriented strategies.

This hypothesis rests on the assumption that exchanges employing Punishment-oriented strategies increase relational costs for the communicator because such strategies heighten stress and conflict. Thus, a communicator seeking to achieve the goal of relational dissolution should initially construct messages using Reward-oriented, or pro-social (Roloff, 1976) strategies, a prediction supported by prior research on negotiating strategies (Donohue, 1978). In the event that these Reward-oriented strategies fail, the communicator's decision as to whether to shift to Punishment-oriented strategies will depend upon his or her perceptions of alternatives; specifically:

Hypothesis: Communicators seeking relational dissolution will: (a) employ a wider range of strategies *if necessary,* and (b) use a greater number of Punishment-oriented strategies in high-motivation, unilateral dissolution situations than in low-motivation, unilateral dissolution situations.

The rationale for this hypothesis has been outlined earlier. In low-motivation, unilateral situations, the relative unattractiveness of alternatives may deter the communicator from using strategies that are likely to increase further his or her own relational costs. When alternatives are attractive, however, as is true of high-motivation, unilateral dissolution situations, the communicator will often be willing to pay the relational costs associated with Punishment-oriented strategies, particularly since such strategies may be seen as also markedly increasing the relational costs for the reluctant partner.

Though we have suggested two hypotheses dealing with the selection of particular types of strategies, it should be emphasized that it would also be possible to posit a hierarchy of relational motivations and to link specific strategies with differing motivational goals. For instance, certain strategies—e.g., *debt* or *positive* or *negative moral appeal*—may be particularly effective for restoring or repairing relational Outcomes, while others may work better for such purposes as reformulating the relationship, reducing the level of relational intimacy, or withdrawing psychologically from the relationship. Future theorizing and research should seek to cast light on this possibility.

Predictions can also be generated concerning differences in strategy selection for low-harmonious, versus high-harmonious bilateral dissolution situations. It was suggested above that compliance-gaining exchanges in such situations typically center on the details of dissolution. When alternatives are perceived as relationally unattractive, relational partners are more apt to approach the dissolution process in a hostile frame of mind, a circumstance leading to the following hypothesis:

Hypothesis: Communicators negotiating the dissolution of their relationship will use a greater number of Punishment-oriented strategies in low-harmonious, bilateral dissolution situations than in high-harmonious, bilateral dissolution situations.

The three preceding sample hypotheses are but a subset of those that could be generated regarding strategy selection. At times our discussion of strategy selection and sequencing may have taken on an inexorably deterministic tone not in keeping with our actual view of the process. Strategies are not like missiles which, once fired, cannot be aborted. As a result of the counter-strategies employed by relational partners, the intrusion of changes in relationally extrinsic circumstances, or a variety of other factors, the party initially motivated to seek dissolution may change his or her mind, either in terms of electing to remain in the relationship or selecting a radically different strategy, or strategies, to bring about dissolution. Obviously, the analysis presented here has not taken into account the situational, communicative, and personal factors that may produce marked changes in strategic decision-making, and the issue remains open to future conceptual and empirical spadework.

A number of hypotheses concerning the effectiveness of various strategic alternatives can also be posited. For example, it can be argued that Recipient-onus strategies will generally be perceived more positively by message targets than will Communicator-onus strategies, thereby establishing a more favorable climate for dissolution negotiations. Similarly, some pro-social strategies may actually alter perceptions of relational Outcomes and of CLalt in ways calculated to reduce the probability of assenting to dissolution; as a consequence, these strategies are actually counterproductive *if* the desired goal is to achieve dissolution. All of these areas, as well as others, provide potentially fertile grounds for investigation, and each is suggested by the preliminary conceptualization that we have sketched.

Conclusion

We have identified some of the possible communicative markers of dissolving relationships, developed a preliminary conceptualization of the role of communication in relational dissolution—including a typology of compliance-gaining strategies that can be used to accomplish termination—and provided some research hypotheses derived from the conceptualization. Throughout we have focused on possible message exchanges that occur as relationships are coming apart. As a consequence we have largely ignored the act of physically leaving the relational field, even though we realize that some relationships are dissolved in this way, because we do not view such a course of action as a communicative strategy.

Although we believe that our conceptualization is relevant to relationships at all stages of development, we acknowledge that most of our discussion has centered on highly developed relationships entailing considerable commitment by the participants. Clearly, the calculus of CLalt and relational Outcomes often differs markedly for casual, less developed relationships; indeed, as Hill et al. (1976) have noted, casual college romances sometimes ter-

minate solely because of a separation imposed by the summer vacation—popular song lyrics notwithstanding, many couples do not see each other "in September." Yet even if the primary value of our conceptualization lies in analyzing the dissolution of highly developed relationships—a concession we are not presently prepared to make—it will still be useful, since it is precisely these relationships which assume greatest significance in the lives of most people and, for that matter, in the eyes of many researchers interested in the process of dissolving relationships. Hopefully, future research will produce an empirical yardstick for assessing whether our approach advances understanding of the complex phenomenon of relational dissolution.

COPYRIGHT ACKNOWLEDGMENTS

NAME INDEX

Page numbers followed by "n" refer to notes.

SUBJECT INDEX